Perspectives on Strategic Marketing Management

Perspectives

on Strategic

Marketing

Management

ROGER A. KERIN
Edwin L. Cox School of Business
Southern Methodist University

ROBERT A. PETERSON
Graduate School of Business
The University of Texas, Austin

ALLYN AND BACON, INC.

Boston · London · Sydney · Toronto

Copyright © 1980 by Allyn and Bacon, Inc., 470
Atlantic Avenue, Boston, Massachusetts 02210. No
part of the material protected by this copyright
notice may be reproduced or utilized in any form
or by any means, electronic or mechanical, including
photocopying, recording, or by any information
storage and retrieval system, without written
permission from the copyright owner.

Library of Congress Cataloging in Publication Data

Main entry under title:

Perspectives on strategic marketing management.

  Bibliography: p.
  1. Marketing management—Addresses, essays,
lectures. I. Kerin, Roger A. II. Peterson, Robert A.
HF5415.13.P38   658.8   79-16899
ISBN 0-205-06722-0

Printed in the United States of America.

To Our Families

Contents

Preface

A metamorphosis in the marketing management function is underway. The traditional operating orientation of marketing executives is gradually being overshadowed by strategic planning considerations. And yet, few practicing and prospective marketing executives have been exposed to the content and process of strategic planning, not to mention the implications of strategic planning for marketing management.

This text is designed to acquaint marketing practitioners and students with current perspectives on strategic marketing management. Accordingly, the organization of the text and the collection of readings are a departure from what one would expect to find in a traditional marketing management text.

Five major sections form the structure of the text. Thirty-one articles account for its content. The five sections are titled:

1. Introducing Strategic Marketing Management
2. Corporate Strategic Planning
3. Strategic Marketing Planning
4. Strategic Marketing Management Tasks
5. Strategic Response to Change

Section 1, *Introducing Strategic Marketing Management,* is an introductory statement on the decisions, concepts, and managerial questions applicable to a strategic marketing orientation. A brief overview of the PIMS project findings and Boston Consulting Group perspectives on product portfolio strategies is also included. Section 2, *Corporate Strategic Planning,* contains readings that highlight the context, content, and process of corporate strategic planning. Section 3, *Strategic Marketing Planning*, introduces techniques, concepts, and strategies arising from current practice and research on strategic decision making in marketing. Section 4, *Strategic Marketing Management Tasks,* provides an overview of contemporary thought on market segmentation and targeting analysis, marketing-mix formulation decisions, and marketing control methods. Finally, Section 5, *Strategic Response to Change,* offers a selection of readings describing reformulation and recovery strategies necessary to confront social, political, competitive, and economic threats and opportunities in the marketing environment.

The articles contained in each section represent the current thinking on strategic marketing management practice. Almost half of the articles were published within a year of the preparation of this text. Another third were published within a two-year period preceding the text's preparation. The articles themselves represent the perspectives of forty-six prominent marketing and management academicians and practitioners. We thank these authors for the opportunity to publish their work and the contributions they have made to our understanding of strategic marketing management.

The final selection of articles in the text represents a comprehensive review of numerous contributions made by many marketing and management thinkers. Space limitations preclude inclusion of all that has been written on the topics examined. Therefore, a list of suggested readings is included in each section for those who wish to read further on topics of special interest to them.

We wish to thank the following sources for permission to reprint the articles contained in the text:

American Marketing Association
Business Horizons
BusinessWeek
California Management Review
Harvard Business Review
Indiana University Press
Industrial Marketing Management
Journal of Advertising Research
Journal of Business
Journal of Contemporary Business
Journal of Marketing
Journal of Marketing Research
Management Decisions
MSU Business Topics
Sloan Management Review

We also wish to thank the numerous reviewers who assisted us in formulating an outline for a text of this type and gave their suggestions for "state-of-the-art" articles on the topics included: Richard Cardozo, University of Minnesota; Roger Strang, University of Southern California; Paul Bloom, University of Maryland at College Park; Kenneth Hardy, The University of Western Ontario; William Kehoe, University of Virginia; Barton Weitz, University of California, Los Angeles; Thomas Kinnear, The University of Michigan. Finally, we are grateful to Ms. Mary McKee for her editing assistance and to Ms. Ann Vilches for her typing assistance.

Roger A. Kerin
Robert A. Peterson

Perspectives on Strategic Marketing Management

1

Introducing Strategic Marketing Management

A strategic marketing management orientation will be a prerequisite for marketing practitioners in the 1980s. Adherence to a strategic marketing orientation implies that a marketing manager subscribe to a synoptic view of the total business of an enterprise rather than to individual markets and product-service offerings. In effect, this means that future managers must place strategic considerations on an equal footing with operational activities.

This first section is designed to acquaint the reader with both the *process* and the *analytical framework* of strategic marketing management. The first reading, entitled "The Strategic Marketing Management Process," highlights the types of decisions and concepts applicable to strategic marketing management. In particular, decisions involving the determination of business mission, strategic alternatives, operational task requirements, and reformulation and recovery strategies are discussed and illustrated through examples. Current perspectives on the organizational structure necessary to manage the process are also outlined.

The second reading introduces two of the analytical frameworks currently being used to complement the strategic marketing management process. Both frameworks illustrate the increasing role of financial management perspectives in marketing. The *Profit Impact of Marketing Strategies* (PIMS) project, currently under the sponsorship of the Strategic Planning Institute, is designed to identify profit determinants in marketing and corporate strategy. Major findings from this project, in addition to their strategic implications, are summarized in the reading. The Boston Consulting Group has developed a framework for strategic marketing management based on the experience-curve phenomenon and product portfolio management. Strategic implications of this framework are introduced in this reading and expanded upon throughout the text.

SELECTED ADDITIONAL READINGS

Ansoff, H. Igor, "The State of Practice in Planning Systems," *Sloan Management Review* (Winter 1977), pp. 1–24.

Business Week, "Olin's Shift to Strategy Planning" (March 27, 1978), pp. 102ff.

Buzzell, R. D., B. T. Gale, and R. G. M. Sultan, "Market Share–Key to Profitability," *Harvard Business Review* (January–February 1975), pp. 97–106.

Henley, Barry, "Strategy and the Business Portfolio," *Long Range Planning* (February 1977), pp. 9–15.

Henley, Barry, "A Fundamental Approach to Strategy Development," *Long Range Planning* (December 1976), pp. 2–11.

Levitt, Theodore, "Marketing Myopia," *Harvard Business Review* (September–October 1976), pp. 26–28ff.

Quinn, James B., "Strategic Goals: Process and Politics," *Sloan Management Review* (Fall 1977), pp. 22–37.

Schoeffler, Sidney, Robert D. Buzzell, and Donald F. Heany, "Impact of Strategic Planning on Profit Performance," *Harvard Business Review* (April–May 1974), pp. 137–45.

Stevenson, Howard, "Defining Corporate Strengths and Weaknesses," *Sloan Management Review* (Spring 1976), pp. 51–68.

The Strategic Marketing Management Process

Increasingly, marketing executives are confronted with two parallel and often conflicting decision responsibilities. On the one hand, marketing executives must make *operating decisions* related to the short-term implementation of marketing programs which effectively utilize allocated resources. On the other hand, they are expected to contribute to *strategic decisions* which guide the organization's financial, managerial, and technological resources to effect long-term linkages with its social, technological, and competitive environment in a manner which preserves the vitality—indeed, the survival—of the enterprise.

An inherent time conflict exists between a strategic focus and operational realities. Strategic decisions focus on long-range planning and resource investments to achieve future outcomes. Operation decisions focus on short-term program implementation and resource allocation to achieve immediate outcomes. Overemphasis on either strategic or operating decision making can affect the health of an organization. For example, industry observers noted that Heublein overemphasized strategic long-range planning and did not devote "enough time to running the store" for its Kentucky Fried Chicken subsidiary.[1] Reduced profits and declining store traffic resulted. Alternatively, Anheuser-Busch management failed to properly assess the strategic implications of the emphasis on light beer by Miller Brewing due to overemphasis on short-term financial and labor capabilities. Miller was thus able to move without competitive retaliation by Anheuser-Busch. In the words of August Busch, III, "We created the atmosphere for that [Miller] success."[2]

Strategic management has evolved in response to the potential dangers just cited. According to Ansoff, strategic management "puts the planning and management of the firm's capability on an equal footing and in a similar time frame with the planning of strategy."[3] Because the marketing function is central to the strategic management concept, marketing executives are increasingly being

---

[1] J. J. O'Conner, "Kentucky Fried Chicken Bone in Heublein's Throat," *Advertising Age* (March 7, 1977), p. 3.

[2] Robert J. Flaherty, "We Missed the Boat . . . We Were Unsmarted," *Forbes* (August 7, 1978), p. 37.

[3] H. Igor Ansoff, "The State of Practice in Planning Systems," *Sloan Management Review* (Winter 1977), p. 21.

called upon to expand their strategic management skills.[4] Hence, a perspective on strategic marketing management is called for.

STRATEGIC MARKETING MANAGEMENT DEFINED

Strategic marketing management is the process that blends broadly defined sets of strategic and operating marketing decisions together for the purpose of directing resources toward opportunities consistent with enterprise capabilities to achieve predetermined outcomes. Strategic marketing management addresses not only the question of *where* the organization should be at a particular time but also the question of *how* it will get there.

Four basic decision sets are included in the strategic marketing management process. They relate to business mission, strategic alternatives, operational task requirements, and reformulation and recovery. Exhibit 1 provides an overview of the decision sets, concepts applicable to each, and the management questions raised.

BUSINESS MISSION

The first set of decisions focuses upon the definition and purpose of an organization from the perspective of consumer needs served. This means that a subtle, synoptic question must be answered: What business are we in? Recently, Gillette pondered this question during the fluorocarbon propellant controversy when customers switched to competitive sticks and roll-on deodorants. In the words of one executive:

> We were like the railroads [which] didn't realize they were in the transportation business. We thought we were in the aerosol business because 80% of all users preferred aerosols and we were the leader in that segment. But when the ozone controversy broke, we found out we were really in the underarm business.[5]

Once Gillette defined itself as being in the "underarm business," it made a concerted effort to develop alternative propellants, with a concomitant allocation of resources and redesign of production capabilities.

A second decision posed at this stage in the strategic marketing management process is examined in response to the question "What do we want to be?" The answer to this question is determined through an assessment of operating measures such as market share, profit and sales growth, and return on investment, as well as through qualitative measures expressed in terms of industry

---

[4] *Marketing News*, "Corporate Strategy: New Role for Marketers: Kotler" (June 30, 1978), p. 4.

[5] *BusinessWeek*, "Gillette: After the Diversification That Failed" (February 28, 1977), pp. 58–62.

EXHIBIT 1
Strategic Marketing Management Process Overview

DECISION SET	CONCEPTS	MANAGEMENT QUESTIONS
Business mission	Business definition; Business purpose	What business are we in? What do we want to be?
Strategic alternatives	Opportunity; Distinctive competency; Success requirements	What might we do? What do we do best? What must we do?
Operational task requirements	Market segmentation; Marketing-mix design; Marketing control	What should we focus on? What should we do? What have we done?
Reformulation and recovery	Contingency management	What if . . . ? What then?

recognition, innovativeness, social and environmental concern, and so forth. This latter point is evidenced by the Ford Motor Company's positioning statement: "We want to be your car company."

The difference between what an enterprise wishes to be and what it is represents a *strategic gap* which must be overcome. This "gap" serves as the motivating force behind the development of strategic alternatives to fill it.

STRATEGIC ALTERNATIVES

A second decision set relates to the identification of strategic alternatives that emerge from the matching of environmental opportunities and threats with organizational capabilities, acceptable levels of risk, and resource commitments. Three questions capture the essence of the decisions made at this stage:

- What might we do?
- What do we do best?
- What must we do?

Answers to these questions are broadly illustrated by the new venture or opportunity criteria voiced by a Hanes Corporation executive:

> . . . products that can be sold through food and drugstore outlets, are purchased by women, sell for less than $3, can be easily and distinctly packaged, and comprise at least a $500 million retail market not already dominated by one or two major producers.[6]

---

[6] *BusinessWeek*, "Hanes Expands L'eggs to the Entire Family" (June 14, 1975), pp. 57ff.

When we consider Hanes's impact with the L'eggs line of women's hosiery, it is apparent that whatever Hanes decides to do in the future should be consistent with what Hanes can do best as illustrated by past achievements in markets whose success requirements are similar.

On a more general level, each of these questions highlights a major concept in strategic marketing management. The *What might we do?* question relates to the *environmental opportunity* concept. The *What do we do best?* question addresses the concept of enterprise capabilities or *distinctive competency*. Distinctive competency describes an organization's principal strengths and weaknesses in such areas as technological expertise, market position, financial resources, and so forth. Finally, the *What must we do?* question poses the issue of determining the *success requirements* in an industry or market. Success requirements are the basic tasks that must be performed to compete successfully in a market or industry.

The linkage between opportunity, distinctive competency, and success requirements is central to the decision-making process at this stage. For example, a clearly defined statement of success requirements serves as a device for matching opportunities with distinctive competency: "What might we do? . . . What must we do? . . . What can we do?" If it is apparent that *what must be done* is not consistent with *what can be done* in order to pursue an opportunity, then the "opportunity" must be reevaluated. Similarly, if an enterprise identifies a threat in its environment, the assessment of strategic alternatives follows the same pattern.

OPERATIONAL TASK REQUIREMENTS

The third group of decisions involves the specification of well-articulated action steps to take advantage of opportunities or minimize environmental threats in a manner consistent with enterprise capabilities. The decisions relate to the operational tasks of marketing management, which include market segmentation, the development of integrated marketing-mix strategies focusing on product-service strategies, pricing strategies, channel-distribution strategies, and promotion strategies, as well as control procedures for assessing performance. The principal questions raised at this stage are, "What is our focus?" and "What should we do?" Both questions are intrinsically related to the assessment of strategic alternatives as illustrated by A&P's "WEO" ("Where Economy Originates") program.[7]

In the years before the WEO program, A&P had watched its sales plateau and its profits shrink while competitive grocery chains continued to increase sales volume and profits. Discounting in the grocery industry was recognized as one of the primary reasons for A&P's performance. The WEO program was directed at the price-conscious grocery-shopper segment (target-market segment)

---

[7] A description of A&P's WEO program from which this example is adapted is found in R. Hartley, *Marketing Mistakes* (Columbus, Ohio: Grid, 1976), Chapter 9.

with an emphasis on discount pricing (price strategy) and a heavy advertising expenditure (promotion strategy). This program increased sales volume by $800 million, *but* produced a profit loss of over $50 million. In the words of one industry observer at the time:

> Its competitors are convinced that A&P's assault with WEO was doomed from the start. Too many of its stores are relics of a bygone era. Many are in poor locations [distribution strategy]. . . . They are just not big enough to support the tremendous volume that is necessary to make a discounting operation profitable [organization capability and market success requirements] . . . stores lack shelf space for stocking general merchandise items, such as housewares and children's clothing [product strategy].[8]

This description exemplifies several pertinent considerations in specifying action steps related to the identification of target markets and marketing-mix strategies. First, determination of an appropriate marketing mix is contingent on the success requirements of the market at which it is directed. Second, a marketing mix must fit the organization's capabilities. Finally, the marketing mix itself must satisfy several tests.

First, is the marketing mix *consistent?* Do the individual components fit together to form a whole as opposed to being fragmented pieces? Does the mix fit the organization, the market sought, and the environment into which it will be introduced? Second, are markets more *sensitive* to certain marketing-mix variables? For example, are markets more likely to respond favorably to a decrease in price or an increase in promotion or other combinations? Third, what *type* and *amount* of *resources* are necessary to perform marketing-mix tasks? Do the costs exceed the benefits in terms of buyer response? Can the organization afford the marketing-mix expenditures? Finally, is the marketing mix properly *timed?* Is the entire marketing mix timely with respect to the nature of the markets and environmental forces?

The marketing mix employed by A&P with the WEO program may be questioned in terms of its consistency and its timing, in particular. Just as the program was gaining momentum, wholesale food prices increased, thus illustrating potential disastrous effects of environmental forces.

Establishing a control mechanism to measure critical differences between planned versus actual results of operations is the final marketing-management task. Without a control system for monitoring progress toward expected outcomes as well as procedures for diagnosing unfavorable variances in performance, an enterprise is analogous to a ship without a compass. A well-conceived control mechanism will help determine whether a planning failure or performance failure is occurring: "A poorly *executed* plan can produce undesirable results just as easily as can a poorly *conceived* plan?"[9] Even though the results

---

[8] E. Tracy, "How A&P Got Creamed," *Fortune* (January 1973), p. 104.
[9] R. Paul, N. Donavan, and J. Taylor, "The RealityGap in Strategic Planning," *Harvard Business Review* (May–June 1978), p. 126.

may be identical, the remedial action will differ. Therefore, a control mechanism is necessary for the development of reformulation and recovery strategies for the firm.

REFORMULATION AND RECOVERY STRATEGIES

The last set of decisions in the strategic marketing management process focuses on contingency management. The questions posed at this stage are of the "if . . . , then. . ." variety: for example, "If forecasted economic conditions are not forthcoming, then . . . ," or "If sales and profit expectations are not achieved during the planning time period, then . . . ," and so forth. The uncertainty of future environments necessitates this "if . . . then . . ." perspective. This view is illustrated by the comment of a marketing vice-president in an industrial materials firm:

> Perhaps the worst thing that can be done is to believe that marketing plans will either automatically fulfill themselves, or that they are necessarily the best plans. Continual rethinking and replanning are vital.[10]

The fact noted earlier that an ill-conceived plan can produce poor results (as can an improperly executed plan) is a basic principle in contingency management and the first step in designing reformulation and recovery strategies. Ill-conceived recovery plans arise from a failure to adequately assess strategic alternatives. As Hartley notes: "Where basic weaknesses exist in a company, any strategy not directed to correcting these weaknesses can only be a short-term solution." [11] Therefore, a contingency management perspective should constantly examine an enterprise's "reason(s) for success" in the past and determine if the reason(s) still exist. Careful review of the firm's environment is necessary to do this, as is an objective appraisal of enterprise capabilities. Improperly executed plans are another matter. Poor execution can be overcome through refinement of the marketing mix; the strategic thrust of the enterprise remains unchanged.

MANAGING THE PROCESS

A structural change in organization is required to implement properly the strategic marketing management process. The principal change involves adopting a *strategic business unit* (SBU) organizational structure. Under an SBU management structure, an enterprise organizes its efforts by industry or markets served rather than by products, functions, or production processes. According to Wright, a business unit "is composed of a product or product lines with identifiable independence from other products or product lines in terms of competition, prices,

---

[10] D. S. Hopkins, *The Short-Term Marketing Plan* (New York: The Conference Board, 1972), p. 16.
[11] Hartley, *op. cit.*, p. 108.

substitutability of product, style/quality, and impact of product withdrawal." [12] An SBU may cross traditional division or profit center lines, and thus requires a structural change in the management of a business. An example of this change is illustrated by General Foods' revision of its food divisions—Birds Eye, Post, and Kool-Aid—with respect to beverages. [13] Before it developed an SBU structure, General Foods marketed beverages using a production-process structure. Frozen beverages were marketed by Birds Eye, powdered beverage mixes came from Kool Aid, and breakfast drinks were marketed by the Post division. Using the SBU approach, a Beverage and Breakfast Food Division was established which markets products of all three technologies since they are naturally linked in the context of user markets served. Product planning and merchandising expertise, which once was diffused among three divisions, is now concentrated under the guidance of a single manager who is responsible for both strategic and operating decisions for beverages.

CONCLUSION

This introductory reading forms a basis for understanding much of what is said throughout this text. The readings in Section 2 focus on corporate strategic planning issues and procedures. Section 3 illustrates contemporary approaches to marketing planning and management in the context of the corporate strategic thrust. The readings in Section 4 highlight how strategic planning considerations have affected traditional marketing-management tasks. Finally, Section 5 illustrates reformulation and recovery strategies necessary to develop a strategic response to changes in the corporate environment.

---

[12] R. V. L. Wright, "A System for Managing Diversity," in S. H. Britt and H. Boyd, Jr., eds., *Marketing Management and Administrative Action,* 4th ed. (New York: McGraw-Hill Book Co., 1978), pp. 46–57.

[13] This example is adapted from M. Hanan, "Reorganize Your Company around Its Markets," *Harvard Business Review* (November–December 1974), pp. 63–74.

Analytical Techniques for Strategic Marketing Management: PIMS and the Boston Consulting Group Perspectives

Two analytical frameworks for the development of corporate and marketing strategy have attracted the attention of management in recent years.[1] One framework, based on the *Profit Impact of Marketing Strategies* (PIMS) project, focuses on the identification of profit determinants of individual business units. A complementary framework proposed by the Boston Consulting Group views the total enterprise as a cash system. Individual business units are assessed by their potential to produce cash immediately, or by their potential as cash producers in the future.

The purpose of this reading is to introduce these analytical techniques and highlight the implications of each for strategic marketing management. The readings in Sections 3 and 4 of the text provide an expanded treatment of these approaches and others in addition to discussing their strategic implications.

THE PIMS PROJECT

The PIMS project is an ongoing, empirically based study of some 150 firms currently under the sponsorship of the Strategic Planning Institute. The data base is derived from the operating experience of over 1000 individual business units.

The major focus of the PIMS project is on the determination of which environmental and company variables affect the firm's Return on Investment (ROI)[2]

---

[1] Major portions of this reading are adapted from N. Capon and J. R. Spogli, "Strategic Marketing Planning: A Comparison and Critical Examination of Two Contemporary Approaches," in B. Greenberg and D. Bellanger, eds., *1977 American Marketing Association Conference Proceedings* (Chicago: American Marketing Association, 1977), pp. 220–23.

[2] Return on Investment is determined in the PIMS project by dividing pretax operating profits by the sum of equity and long-term debt.

and cash flow. Based on the analyses conducted to date, thirty-seven variables have been identified which impact a firm's ROI. These variables are grouped into seven categories: (1) competitive position, (2) industry/market environment, (3) budget allocation, (4) capital structure, (5) production processes, (6) company characteristics, and (7) "change action" factors.[3]

Despite the complexity of profit determination suggested by the sheer number of variables (and their interactions) studied, four variables stand out. *Market share, relative market share* (determined by dividing a firm's market share by the sum of the shares of its three largest competitors), and *relative product quality* are positively related to ROI. *Investment intensity* (investment divided by value added) is negatively related to ROI.

The most striking finding arising from the PIMS project is the pervasive impact of a firm's market share on profit performance. Early findings revealed that, on the average, firms with market shares of less than 7 percent had a 9.6 percent ROI. Conversely, firms with market shares exceeding 36 percent had an average ROI of 30.2 percent. This relationship has been expanded to the point where it has been shown that, on the average, "a difference of 10 percentage points in market share is accompanied by a difference of about 5 points in pretax ROI." [4] More dramatically, results from the PIMS project have led to the conclusion that some minimum market share is a prerequisite for enterprise viability. If this minimum does not exist, then a firm should consider either increasing its market share or abandoning its interests in that market.[5] Exceptions to this rule are discussed later.

Using this line of reasoning, automobile industry observers have suggested that American Motors Corporation does not have that minimum market share required for viability, and possibly survival.[6] American Standard, Inc. has abandoned businesses whose annual sales totaled $500 million due to their lack of market share. A firm's market rank is also considered in this decision process. For example, Eaton Corporation has adopted a policy that states that they must be either first or second in the markets they serve or seriously consider whether they should stay in that business.

Selected Findings

Only recently have the findings from the PIMS project found their way into published sources. A summary of major findings are listed below.[7]

---

[3] An expanded discussion of these variables can be found in S. Schoeffler, R. Buzzell, and D. Heany, "Impact of Strategic Planning on Profit Performance," *Harvard Business Review* (March–April 1974), pp. 137–45.

[4] R. Buzzell, B. Gale, and R. Sultan, "Market Share—Key to Profitability," *Harvard Business Review* (January–February 1975), p. 97.

[5] Ibid., p. 103.

[6] The examples described in this paragraph were obtained from R. Winter, "Corporate Strategists Giving New Emphasis to Market Share, Rank," *Wall Street Journal* (February 3, 1978), pp. 1ff.

[7] These findings are drawn from numerous sources. These include B. Gale, "Selected Findings from the PIMS Project: Market Strategy Impacts on Profitability," in R. C. Curhan, ed., *1974 American Marketing Association Conference Proceedings* (Chicago: American

- Market-share percentage, as a determinant of ROI, is more important for infrequently purchased products (e.g., durable goods and capital goods) than for frequently purchased products (e.g., consumer package goods).
- Market-share percentage, as a determinant of ROI, is more important to businesses whose customers are "fragmented" (i.e., no one customer accounts for a large portion of sales volume) than those businesses whose customers are concentrated.
- Businesses that produce superior quality products and services tend to have a higher ROI than those that do not. Superior quality offerings might offset a small share of market percentage.
- On the average, the higher the ratio of a business's total investment to sales, the lower its ROI.
- In instances where research and development expenditures were high, the average ROI was highest when market share was also large. However, ROI declines dramatically when market share is low.
- In general, ROI diminishes with high levels of marketing expenditures. This relationship is particularly evident among businesses with lower-quality products.
- Businesses with strong market-share positions (greater than 26 percent) realize a substantially higher ROI if they are part of a company that is highly diversified.
- Businesses with a low relative market share at early stages of the product life-cycle can expect a low ROI.
- Entry on a large scale (both production and marketing scale) is necessary for eventual success in rapid growth markets. Market entry strategies should be evaluated on the basis of relative market share achieved and capitalized ROI.
- A firm with a high investment intensity is unlikely to abandon an unprofitable business.
- Businesses with a low investment intensity and a high relative market share have a higher cash flow (measured as a percent of investment) than businesses with opposite characteristics, on the average.
- Fixed-capital-intensive businesses in concentrated industries have a higher ROI than their counterparts in unconcentrated industries.

Marketing Association, 1975), pp. 471–75; D. Hopkins, "New Emphases in Product Planning and Strategy Development," *Industrial Marketing Management*, vol. 6 (1977), pp. 410–19; R. Biggadike, *Entering New Markets: Strategies and Performance* (Cambridge, Massachusetts: Marketing Science Institute, 1977); R. Buzzell, B. Gale, and R. Sultan, "Market Share: A Key to Profitability," *Harvard Business Review* (January–February 1975), pp. 97–106; S. Schoeffler, R. Buzzell, and D. Heany, "Impact of Strategic Planning on Profit Performance," *Harvard Business Review* (March–April 1975), pp. 137–45; P. Nowill, *The Impact of Company Characteristics on Business Level Profitability* (Cambridge, Massachusetts: Marketing Science Institute, 1974); M. Porter, "Please Note Location of Nearest Exit: Exit Barriers and Planning," *California Management Review* (Winter 1976), pp. 21–33; S. Schoeffler, "Cross-Sectional Study of Strategy, Structure, and Performance: Aspects of the PIMS Program," in A. Thorelli, ed., *Strategy + Structure = Performance* (Bloomington, Indiana: Indiana University Press, 1977), pp. 108–21.

- Businesses with broader lines of products relative to competitors and a lower investment intensity tend to have a higher cash flow (measured as a percent of investment) than businesses with narrower lines and higher investment intensity.

Further Considerations in Market-Share Strategy

The findings from the PIMS project provide a number of perspectives on the Market Share/Return on Investment relationship useful for strategic marketing management. Nevertheless, additional considerations of market-share strategy deserve comment.

As noted earlier, businesses with small market shares have the strategic choice of building market share or in some way minimizing their interest (typically resource investment) in that business. Readings in Section 3 of this text address these strategic options. "Planning Gains in Market Share," by C. Davis Fogg, examines strategies for building market share; "Harvesting Strategies for Weak Products," by Philip Kotler addresses strategies for reducing a firm's investment in a business while retaining reasonable earnings or cash flow. Yet, questions arise concerning the longitudinal aspects of building market share, what to do and operating implications when a high market share has been achieved, and alternative approaches for operating a profitable business at low levels of market share. These issues are discussed briefly in the following paragraphs and expanded upon in Section 3.

The benefits of a high market share must be tempered by the costs and implications of obtaining it. Fruhan's artful review of several ambitious attempts at building market share led him to conclude that strategists should ponder answers to three questions before embarking on an expansion program.[8] First, does the company have the necessary financial resources to spend on the endeavor? Second, will the firm remain in a viable position even if its market-share goals are not achieved? Third, will regulatory agencies allow the firm to capture the market share it seeks to obtain? The discussion of A&P's WEO campaign in the first reading in this section highlights the importance of the first two questions. Bloom and Kotler address the third question in their article "Strategies for High Market-Share Companies." [9]

According to Bloom and Kotler, gaining market share or being dominant may be more trouble than it is worth due to antitrust implications and attacks by consumer or public-interest groups. Rather, an enterprise should seek an *optimal market share*. This optimal share occurs "when a departure in either direction from the share would alter the company's long-run profitability or risk (or both) in an unsatisfactory way." [10] Bloom and Kotler point out that attempts

---

[8] W. E. Fruhan, Jr., "Pyrrhic Victories in Fights for Market Share," *Harvard Business Review* (September–October 1972), pp. 100–107. See also B. James, "Market-Share Strategy and Corporate Profitability," reprinted in Section 3.

[9] P. Bloom and P. Kotler, "Strategies for High Market-Share Companies," *Harvard Business Review* (November–December 1975), pp. 63–72.

[10] *Ibid.*, p. 65.

to expand market share beyond the optimal level are not documented in the PIMS data in terms of further increases in ROI. In fact, profitability may decline. This possibility is also raised in the article "Market Share Strategy and Corporate Profitability" in this text.

Finally, Hamermash, Anderson, and Harris take issue with the position that firms with low market shares should consider abandoning interests in that market.[11] They show that Burroughs Corporation (mainframe computers), Crown Cork & Seal Company, Inc. (metal cans), and Union Camp Corporation (forest products) have prospered despite low market-share positions. Recognizing the benefits of large share positions, the authors note that firms can remain viable provided that four elements of strategy prevail. First, low market-share firms must carefully segment their markets to bring their distinctive competencies to bear on markets where larger competitors are weak. Second, research and development expenditures and thrust should focus on lowering production-process costs and being innovative. Third, a "think small" orientation is necessary rather than a "growth" mentality inferred from the PIMS project. Finally, the chief executive must be everpresent and involved in virtually every aspect of the business. The authors conclude that low market-share firms should consider the objective of maximizing return on invested capital rather than achieving higher market share.

THE BOSTON CONSULTING GROUP: EXPERIENCE CURVES AND PRODUCT PORTFOLIO MANAGEMENT

The Boston Consulting Group (BCG), an international management consulting firm, offers a complementary framework for the development of corporate and marketing strategy. The BCG approach is based on two concepts: (1) experience curves and (2) product portfolio strategy.

Experience Curves

The BCG and other groups have long recognized that the total unit cost of production and distribution for a product tends to decline by a consistent percent with each two-fold increase in accumulated output. This consistent decline in unit cost, expressed in constant dollars, is normally in the range of 20–30 percent. The relationship is often illustrated by a graphic plot of unit cost (in real terms) against cumulative production volume; hence the term *experience curve*. This decline in unit cost has been attributed to a number of factors—productivity improvements due to technological change, economics of scale and specialization, product modifications to produce lower costs, and displacement of less-efficient production methods (e.g., labor-intensive versus capital-intensive

---

[11] R. Hamermesh, M. Anderson, Jr., and J. Harris, "Strategies for Low Market-Share Businesses," *Harvard Business Review* (May–June 1978), pp. 95–102.

production methods).[12] Examples of experience curves can be found in two articles reprinted in this text. These articles are "A Strategic Perspective on Product Planning" in Section 3 and "Price-Cost Planning" in Section 4.

The mechanics of the experience-curve phenomenon, however, are less important than its strategic implications. The message given by the experience-curve analysis is straightforward:

- The major-volume firm in a business/market has the greatest potential for the lowest unit costs and largest profits due to accumulated experience.
- Lesser-volume firms in a business/market are likely to be unprofitable or less profitable than the major-volume firm due to their lack of accumulated experience.

The experience-related cost declines are most evident when market growth rates are high and the firm increases its accumulated output through participation in this growth. However, if a firm *dominates* a slower growth market, experience-related cost declines also become possible. It quickly becomes apparent that a firm's products or product lines with the largest accumulated volume in a market will have the largest share of market, lowest unit costs, and a high profit level. This relationship has been documented by the PIMS project as noted earlier.

Product Portfolio Strategy [13]

The BCG has taken the experience-curve reasoning a step further and developed a product portfolio strategy around it. A firm's product portfolio is arrayed in a market-share/market-growth matrix. As shown in Exhibit 1, a firm's products are placed into one of four categories and given names descriptive of their share/growth position and cash-flow direction.

- *Stars*—High market growth/high share (requires cash for growth)
- *Problem Child*—High market growth/low share (requires cash for growth)
- *Cash Cow*—Low market growth/high share (excess cash flow)
- *Dog*—Low market growth/low share (negligible or negative cash flow)

One objective of the product portfolio strategy framework is to ensure that some products exist that supply cash to assist the growth of other products. A broader objective is to establish a mix of products that provides a balanced growth pattern subject to a firm's acceptable levels of risk. Appropriate strategies for generating cash flow and satisfying risk requirements are developed in the Day article "A Strategic Perspective on Product Planning" reprinted in Section 3.

---

[12] B. Hedley, "A Fundamental Approach to Strategy Development," *Long Range Planning* (December 1976), pp. 1–11.

[13] This discussion is based on W. Cox Jr., "Product Portfolio Strategy: A Review of the Boston Consulting Group Approach to Marketing Strategy," in R. Curhan, ed., *1974 American Marketing Association Conference Proceedings* (Chicago: American Marketing Association, 1975), pp. 465–70; G. Day, "Diagnosing the Product Portfolio," *Journal of Marketing* (April 1977), pp. 29–38; and W. Cox, Jr., "Product Portfolio Strategy, Market Structure, and Performance," in H. Thorelli, ed., *Strategy + Structure = Performance* (Bloomington, Indiana: Indiana University Press, 1977), pp. 83–102.

EXHIBIT 1
Market-Share/Market-Growth Matrix

An example of a product portfolio for the General Foods Corporation has been prepared by Professor William E. Cox, Jr.[14] Using published sources, he developed the market-share/market-growth matrix shown in Exhibit 2.[15]

Professor Cox notes that General Foods has a balanced product portfolio with entries in all four categories. Moreover, their strategy generally appears consistent with the product portfolio positions. For example, heavy advertising and marketing support has been given to their "Stars," namely instant breakfast drink (Tang), powdered soft drink (Kool-Aid), and semimoist dog food (Gaines-burgers, among others). "Problem Children" are the dry dog food entries with lower market share in high-growth markets. However, attempts have been made to maintain market share and take advantage of absolute market growth. The ready-to-eat (RTE) cereals have been labeled "Dogs," given General Foods' low market share (16.6 percent share) in this low-growth market. However, Cox notes that attempts have been made to reposition product entries, particularly Grape Nuts, in the higher-growth "natural" cereal market. Finally, General Foods' coffee entries in the ground coffee segment (Maxwell House and Yuban), decaffeinated segment (Brim and Sanka), and instant soluble segment (Maxwell House, Yuban, and Maxim) are its "Cash Cows" and thus produce more cash flow than they require to maintain market share. Cox notes that General Foods has adopted a market-share maintenance policy through advertising and periodic introduction of new products. Parenthetically, current estimates indicate that coffee accounts for 40 percent of General Foods' sales and one-third of its

---

[14] W. E. Cox, Jr., "Product Portfolio Strategy, Market Structure, and Performance," in H. Thorelli, ed., *Strategy + Structure = Performance* (Bloomington, Indiana: Indiana University Press, 1977), pp. 83–102.

[15] *Advertising Age*, August 18, 1975, pp. 133–34.

EXHIBIT 2

Growth/Share Matrix: General Foods Corporation

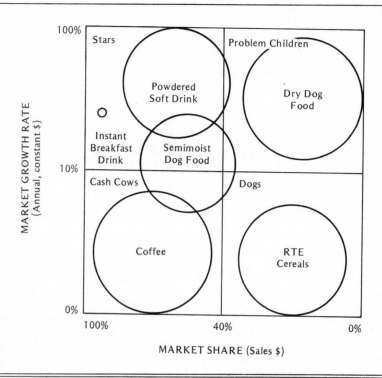

Source: William E. Cox, Jr., "Product Portfolio Strategy, Market Structure, and Performance," in H. Thorelli, ed., *Strategy + Structure = Performance* (Bloomington, Indiana: Indiana University Press, 1977), pp. 83–102.

earnings.[16] Viewed in this light, it is understandable why General Foods has aggressively sought to maintain its share of the coffee market despite recent competitive actions of Proctor & Gamble's Folger's brand in the eastern United States.

CONCLUSION

This reading concludes Section 1. The description of the PIMS project and the Boston Consulting Group perspectives on strategic issues in marketing management form the basis for much of what you will be reading in subsequent sections of the text.

---

[16] H. Menzies, "Why Folger's Is Getting Creamed Back East," *Fortune* (July 17, 1978), pp. 68–76.

2

Corporate Strategic Planning:
An Overview

Charting the course of business organizations in rapidly changing environments has become necesssary for corporate survival and growth in the 1980s. While organizations are growing in size and complexity, they are also experiencing aggressive domestic and foreign competition, slowed economic growth, cost escalation arising from inflation and shortages, increasing government and trade regulations, and unprecedented changes in technology and social values.

Strategic planning and management systems have been designed to cope with and stabilize corporate positions in these turbulent environments. The primary purpose of these formalized systems is to lessen adverse effects of environmental threats and enhance managerial readiness to pursue environmental opportunities through disciplined stewardship of organizational capabilities. No longer can an organization respond only to environmental discontinuities. It must anticipate discontinuities and have comprehensive and integrated action plans which mobilize organizational resources to minimize threats and accentuate opportunities.

In practice, strategic planning involves

> the specification of company objectives and goals and the development of a time-phased plan of action for their attainment. It provides a business with a sense of *direction* for identifying and evaluating new opportunities [or threats], *structure* for mobilizing and allocating resources, and *systems* for monitoring and controlling plans as they are put into effect.[1]

Viewed in this context, strategic planning is an essential element in the strategic marketing management process.

The four articles in this section provide perspectives on the context, content, and process of strategic planning. "Piercing Future Fog in the Executive Suite" provides an overview of the problems with strategic planning in unstable environments and the means used by a variety of companies to cope with these problems.

The second group of articles in this section examine the content and process of strategic planning. Cohen and Cyert provide a step-by-step description of the strategic planning process beginning with the formulation of goals and ending with the measurement, feedback, and control of results. Gerstner illustrates potential applications of strategic planning to marketing in addition to highlighting pitfalls in the strategic planning. Finally, Koontz addresses the issue of why strategic planning efforts sometimes fail and prescribes requisites for effective planning efforts.

---

[1] Robert R. Rothberg, ed., *Corporate Strategy and Product Innovation* (New York: The Free Press, 1976), on p. 8.

SELECTED ADDITIONAL READINGS

Ansoff, H. Igor, "Managing Strategic Surprise by Response to Weak Signals," *California Management Review* (Winter 1975), pp. 21–33.

Emshoff, James R. and Ian I. Mitroff, "Improving the Effectiveness of Corporate Planning," *Business Horizons* (October 1978), pp. 49–60.

Hofer, Charles W., "Toward a Contingency Theory of Business Strategy," *Academy of Management Journal* (December 1975), pp. 784–810.

Paul, Ronald N., Neil B. Donavan, and James W. Taylor, "The Reality Gap in Strategic Planning," *Harvard Business Review* (May–June 1978), pp. 124–30.

Vancil, Richard and Peter Lorange, "Strategic Planning in Diversified Companies," *Harvard Business Review* (January–February 1975), pp. 81–90.

Piercing Future Fog in the Executive Suite

BusinessWeek

For corporate planners and the top executives who rely on their advice, the world has never looked as hostile or as bewildering as it does today. The very uncertainties, from the clouded economic outlook to the energy crisis, that make sophisticated forward planning more vital than ever before, also make accurate planning that much more difficult. "Annual financial plans for a number of companies are going to hell this year," says Jerome Jacobson, senior vice-president of Bendix Corp. "In a rapidly changing economic environment, some plans are out of date in three to six months."

So the very nature of corporate planning is undergoing a dramatic change, and the companies that fare best in coming years may well be the ones that adapt most quickly to the new styles in planning. Today's changes are most clearly visible in two areas:

Flexibility Instead of relying on a single corporate plan with perhaps one or two variations, top management at more and more companies is now getting a whole battery of contingency plans and alternate scenarios. "We shoot for alternative plans that can deal with either/or eventualities," says George J. Prendergast, in charge of planning at chemical giant E. I. Du Pont de Nemours & Co.

Speed Companies are reviewing and revising plans more frequently in line with changing conditions. Instead of the old five-year plan that might have been updated annually, plans are often updated quarterly, monthly, or even weekly. Arizona Public Service Co. last year adopted a "dynamic" budget that looks ahead two years but is rolled over every month. At Ralston Purina Co., a 1 percent change in the price of a prime commodity begins a change in the company's cost models and the whole corporate plan may change accordingly.

This is heady stuff for corporate planners, because it was not so long ago that planning was a marginal blue-sky sort of operation that seldom got more

Reprinted from *BusinessWeek*, April 28, 1975, pp. 46–54.

than a nod from top management. But forward planning became a crucial function and the planner a central figure in the company in the complex, fast-changing business world of the 1960s and 1970s. "Planning has become intimately associated with the whole management process," says George A. Steiner, professor of management at UCLA.

And the role of planning will continue to grow because the outlook is so hazy—not just for business but for all society. What worked before may not work in the future, and a company's very survival may depend on how well it gauges the future. "Many companies feel we are moving into a new era," says Alonzo L. McDonald, managing director of McKinsey & Co. "The 1950–70 assumptions probably will not be good guidelines for the 1970s on."

Indeed, the 1950–70 assumptions simply are not working today and virtually every company has had to rethink not only the content of its plan but also how it makes its plan.

Xerox Corp., for example, started taking a fresh look at its forward plan when "macroeconomics came thundering down at us," says George R. White, vice-president for product planning. The company's re-evaluation not only led to deferring the building of a new corporate headquarters and to the laying off of workers. Xerox also decided to issue, for the first time, a permanent straight debt issue—for $450 million. "It's a straw in the wind," says White, "not as a short-term quick reaction but that the financial basis on which corporations of our size operate is changing."

AN UNCERTAIN FUTURE

For the short term, many companies have simply dusted off their "worst-case" scenarios, a process that C. A. Rundell, Jr., a Tyler Corp. executive vice-president, calls "stray bullet to the heart drills," while still clinging to a basic optimism. For the long term, an assortment of previously unthinkable assumptions, ranging from worldwide political upheaval to an end to economic growth, are all at once on everybody's mind.

Many planners, too, see the world at an economic and cultural watershed. American Standard, Inc., Vice-President Alan C. Root, the company's top planner, argues that while it is difficult to accept the idea of a long-term slowdown, "This is the beginning of a period of great change. It's a transition time for Western economies. What we are concerned with is the period of transition—the next five years."

For corporate planners, and even more for the senior executives who must act on their advice, the problem is not so much that some day they will have to deal with a future that may be cataclysmic, but that they must plan today for a future that has never been more uncertain. Nor are today's often conflicting economic forecasts—even for the immediate months ahead—of much real value to the planner. "Each time you get a forecast," says Glen L. Ryland, Frontier Airlines executive vice-president, "it sets the turnaround date back."

So planners are literally obliged to stress flexibility, which means multiple contingency plans, rather than a single forward plan, and more frequent re-visions. It is not a very satisfactory solution, but as James E. Matheson, director of the Decision Analysis Group at Stanford Research Institute, says, "it is one way of coping with uncertainty." Henry M. Boettinger, corporate planning director at American Telephone & Telegraph Co., calls it "pulsing your way into the future."

In the end, of course, that puts more pressure on top management, which must operate with an eye to numerous plans instead of being able to follow a single scenario. At Exxon Corp., for instance, most-probable-case forecasts have been replaced by less definitive "envelopes" that include a range of possibilities. Says Brice A. Sachs, deputy corporate planning manager: "Today you still have to have a game plan. How do you get to that? Top management judgment and intuition. We don't really pin some things down anymore. There's a lot more thrown at the management."

LEARNING TO REACT QUICKLY

Not only is the decision harder to make, but the stakes at Exxon and elsewhere keep going higher. Until recently, for example, the investment necessary to procure a barrel of oil per day was about $350, says Sachs. Now, for the same amount of oil from the North Sea the investment will be some $9,000. Going to synthetic fuels, the cost could climb to $20,000. The executive must also look further into the future. Adding an additional 300,000 bbl. a day of productive capacity in Saudi Arabia could be carried out in a year or two. To provide for the equivalent capacity through a synthetic plant that converts coal to liquid form will take at least six years. As UCLA's Steiner says: "Time has telescoped. The longevity of a product is much shorter than ever before. But the period of research and development has stretched."

The shocker is the extent to which business did not see all of this coming. "We completely blew interest rates in 1974," admits John B. McKinnon, financial vice-president of Hanes Corp., the hosiery and apparel maker. "We projected a maximum rate of 8% and it was 12%. And we significantly missed our total figures for the fourth quarter. We were forecasting and budgeting for a 10% increase in sales and actually netted out a 7% decrease."

Inland Steel Co.'s director of corporate planning, Philip D. Block III, says his company undershot the mark on last year's sales volume. Both the volume of the steel business and its rate of return in the last two years exceeded the planning estimates. "There was no way we could foresee changes in exchange rates—which made U.S.-made steel more competitive with the foreign product in this country," he says. "Nor were we able to foresee how quickly we would be able to pass along the cost-increase pressures which built up during the period of controls," says Block.

But the downturn, if it threw everyone's primary plans out the window, did prove the value of contingency planning in helping companies turn on a dime, and today that is what planning is all about. "If you can't forecast, all you can do is react quickly," says Gary L. Neale, president of Planmetrics, Inc., a Chicago-based company that currently is helping 76 corporations computerize their planning process to speed up reaction time even more.

Except as theoretical exercises, multiple plans had little use in most companies until recently. Now that it is clear that no planner will ever bat 1.000, they are fast becoming standard operating procedure. "By January," says Hanes' McKinnon, "it appeared that the contingency plans [for recession] that the divisions had drawn up back in November were likely to be the real world." They assumed 15% sales drops and listed specific expense cuts to be made, ranked in six categories of priorities, with dollar figures attached to each. By January some of the divisions had already begun to implement the recession plans. All divisions were ordered to submit new budgets by Apr. 1—three months earlier than usual. The L'eggs division, the company's largest, already is implementing a "Mar. 1 plan" based on forecasts of still lower sales and earnings for the remainder of the year.

This year a lot of "worst case" contingency plans came off the shelf. Mead Corp. has three short-term contingency plans—A, B, and C, standing for aggressive, basic, and conservative. Mead's basic B plan, formulated last October, was scrapped very early. "We even felt our C plan was too optimistic," says Vice-Chairman William W. Wommack, who is in charge of strategy. "We tore everything up and asked for a new ABC, and our current B plan is even lower than our earlier C plan." Mead's new B plan, drawn in January, projects sales of $1.4-billion in 1975, down from the earlier B plan projection of $1.7-billion.

Xerox' White says that the company cannot operate by its originally devised 1975 budget. "We are not distraught at the fact that we have to replan early in the year, but we've never had to do it as broadly as we are having to do it now," he says. Indeed, Xerox now finds itself making and revising plans on almost a nonstop basis.

Similarly, says Bendix' Jacobson, "Our plan requires so many reviews today that it has become a continuous process. It is always being adjusted."

EXPLORING MORE ALTERNATIVES

Perhaps it is merely a reflection of today's pessimism, but most companies in their planning see less risk in cutting back too much than in pruning too little. Frontier Airlines developed a detailed plan for "reasonable size shrink" back in August, when it was in the midst of its best year in history but could see signs of a leveling off and decline in passengers. In mid-November the decision was made to "go down" and the planned shrinkage—a 6% cut in flying hours and a personnel reduction of 142—went into effect in January. A second "shrink" for which planning began in January became effective this month. "We know how to go back up pretty fast," says Ryland. "Our strategy is to anticipate and lead on the downside and wait until we see positive action before we go up."

But contingency plans are flourishing not because business is bad, of course, but because it is so unpredictable. "In this age you can't plan on your plans," says SRI's Matheson. "You should be hedging your bets." Thomas H. Naylor, president of Social Systems, Inc., of Durham, N.C., found in a survey of 346 corporations that 73% were either using or developing a corporate planning model. The chief reason, cited by 78% of all the current users of models, was that they enabled the company to explore more alternatives in its planning.

The real problem arises, as Exxon's Sachs suggests, when it comes to deciding which plan to act upon. Sun Oil Co., which established a corporate planning department five years ago, still was projecting one scenario for the future until last fall. Now it has three. But managers are still asked to develop only one strategy from all those plans. "We form a strategy sensitive to change that can accommodate a wide divergence of economic possibilities," says Rudolph Dutzman, Sun's director of corporate planning.

Daniel T. Carroll, president of Gould, Inc., says that "when your predictions don't work out you don't abort planning, you abort that plan. You also have to have a fire alarm of some sort that says now is the time a contingency has arisen. For example, if incoming orders fall below a certain level for three consecutive months, then implement Plan A. Sometimes we don't even wait for our own incoming orders to drop, but look at the incoming orders of our customers for a signal. That takes artistry."

What really takes artistry, though, is extending scenarios far into the future. It is necessary because today's complex investment and development decisions have longer lead times than ever. Xerox has pushed its long-range planning parameters out to 1990. "We've grown the length of the plan, and we now have five tracks plotted through 1990, where we used to have just one," says Michael A. E. Hughes, vice-president for marketing and technical services.

"The net of all this, when you come to some kind of bottom line, is that we have a company posture that has to be laid against a wider range of scenarios and outcomes than we've used in the past," says White. "This is a substantial change in planning style, because we used to feel comfortable enough about the center line to plan to it and say we'll adjust to discrepancies."

At General Electric Co., which has pioneered in corporate planning, the range of scenarios is also widening. "More than we've ever done before, we are developing this year a look at completely different views of future external environments over a five-year period, in the U.S. and the world," says Reuben Gutoff, senior vice-president for corporate strategic planning. "The point is to stretch our minds and really test."

GE might take a conventional "base" view of the economy that has a one in hundreds of factors; most concentrate their attention on the eight to twelve most crucial to their industry—rate of inflation, consumer spending on nondurables, interest rates, for example. At Tyler, managers have a list of 8 to 10 "key influencing factors" which they suggest their board members keep an eye on all year. The price of ammonium nitrate, an important ingredient for its newly acquired explosives business, currently is at the top of the list.

Even monitoring a dozen variables on a timely basis, though, and evaluating their cumulative effects, can tax a planning department. With a computer, suggests Planmetrics' Neale, not only can long-range and short-range plans be updated continuously, so whenever managers refer to them they are current, but any number of what-if questions can be asked. The probable effect of a change to LIFO from FIFO accounting can be gauged, for example, or the actual effect of a rise in the cost of a critical component can be factored in. At Dow Chemical Co., 140 separate cost inputs—constantly revised—are fed into the corporate model. Such factors as major raw materials costs and prices by country and region are monitored weekly.

Hewlett-Packard Co., using its own H-P 2000 computer, runs as many as 50 different scenarios on four different models—economic statement, intermediate range plan, econometric, and aggregate sales. One major issue last year—whether to sell $100-million of long-term debt—involved some 100 different scenarios on the computer. The models helped the company finally decide to stay with in-house financing.

But planners today are also increasingly concerned about the kind of information that cannot be analyzed by a computer. They worry about the tendency of executives to extrapolate from the statistics of the past. "People tend to project from where they are today," says Mead's Wommack. "The truth of the situation is that the 1973 and 1974 period was an upward blip. On the other hand, 1975 will be way below the trend, and people may project off that."

In addition, the unique event changes everything. "Strategic planning is necessary precisely because we cannot forecast," says management philosopher Peter F. Drucker, noting that a single book, Rachel Carson's *Silent Spring* in the 1950s, changed the attitude of a whole civilization toward the environment. Last year, it was the oil crisis that forced everyone to rethink all their plans.

Chances are slim that planners will foresee world-shaking events sooner than anyone else, but most are trying. American Standard, for example, has factored into its plans the probability of a critical worldwide grain shortage in the late 1970s, in the wake of 5-degree wind changes that will reduce rain in the major producing areas of the world. "We're interested in the price of grains because if grains go up to $6 or $8 a bushel, it's inflationary and we'll have to pay more for money," explains American Standard's Root.

Projecting the effects of external imponderables can be a complex task. Atlantic Richfield Co. has an environmental analysis group that provides an overview, built upon surveys and interviews, of "social factors" such as predicted modes of transportation and consumer preferences. "You can't just extend the graphs on these things, you've got to really understand them," says Robert E. Wycoff, director of corporate planning. "They're not governed by economics."

Similarly, Dow Chemical has a product management team that analyzes new social and political pressures and relates them to its business. The result is what Dow calls its "ESP" (for economic, social, political) report, a formal document that attempts to evaluate risks from all of these factors.

Some imponderables outside the business but directly relating to it can be evaluated in a computer model. SRI and Gulf Oil Corp. recently developed a sophisticated U.S. energy model for an analysis of synthetic fuels strategy. It covers all major energy forms, conversion technologies, transportation modes, and demand. It also projects investment, financing, and resource depletion as-

General Electric's "Stoplight Strategy" for Planning

General Electric Co. thinks it has found at least a partial solution to an age-old corporate planning problem: how to put a value on those critical elements in planning it is impossible to attach a number to. In a decision on whether a product will live or die, for example, the value of a patent or the impact of social change cannot be quantified. By using its Strategic Business Planning Grid, or "stoplight strategy," GE can at least evaluate such factors with something more than just a gut reaction.

"It's the best way we've found to sort disparate businesses," says GE planner Reuben Gutoff. "You eventually have to make a subjective decision, but you put into it all the hard information you can. It's one way to compare apples and oranges."

GE, with 43 distinct businesses, has a lot of apples and oranges. In every annual planning review, each individual business is rated not only on numerical projections of sales, profit, and return on investment, but also on such hard-to-quantify factors as volatility of market share, technology needs, employee loyalty in the industry, competitive stance, and social need. The result is a high, medium, or low rating on both attractiveness of an industry and GE's strengths in the field.

How It Works   If industry attractiveness is seen as medium and GE's strengths as high (Chart A), an "invest and grow"—or green light—decision would result, because the evaluation bars cross in a green square. Both industry attractiveness and business strength are low in Chart B, indicating a red light strategy, or a business which will continue to generate earnings but no longer warrants much additional investment by GE. Chart C represents a business with high industry attractiveness but low GE strength—a "yellow" business that might go either way.

A green business is expected to grow. A red operation's strategy, on the other hand, may involve consolidation of plants, limited technology infusion, reduced investment, and strong cash flow. A yellow business could be borderline, or the business—say, electronic components—could be diverse enough to have both red and green units.

"We don't give definitive weights to the non-numerical factors," says Gutoff, "but they do have weights. At the end of our discussion there is a good consensus on what's green, red, or yellow." The result, he says, is "semiquantitative." After three or four critiques at various levels, the final grids—and decisions—are made by the corporate policy committee—the chairman, three vice-chairmen, five senior vice-presidents, and the vice-president for finance.

The process is not just window dressing. It may prevent costly mistakes. "Interestingly," says one GE planner, "the financial projections are often best on businesses that turn up worst [in the red] on the grid."

pects to the year 2025 and computes price by balancing supply and demand.

Still, the inability of computer model builders to spot unexpected events on the horizon has inevitably provoked widespread disillusionment among planners with econometric models. "Econometric models have gone to pot because of the

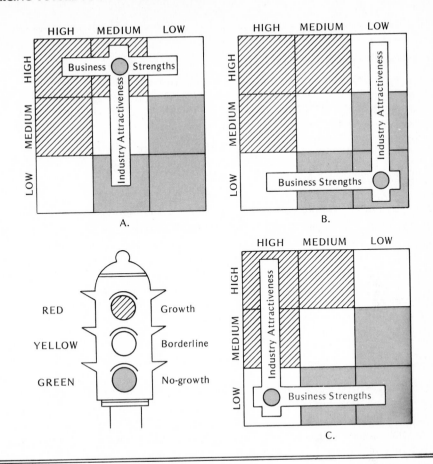

inability to quantify variables going into a model," says A. J. Ashe, vice-president for planning and development at B. F. Goodrich Co. "If you are forecasting the replacement tire market, you have to go back and decide how many miles will be driven, driving patterns, etc. My problem is that relationships never stay the same."

Many large companies scoff at the models but use them anyway. "When you're in an era of profound change you grab at what you can," says Exxon's Sachs. "They're a framework for analysis even if you can't put much faith in them. If anything, we use them more, though we may rely on them less."

More than half of the corporations reporting the use of computer modeling techniques in Social Systems' survey also subscribe to at least one national econometric forecasting service, such as Wharton, Chase, or Data Resources, Inc. (DRI). Many companies subscribe to several. John Doyle, director of corporate development at Hewlett-Packard, says none of the outside econometric models the company uses is particularly helpful by itself, but together they are useful.

But the thrust of planning today is to keep numbers to a minimum, especially when projecting beyond the next 12 months. And the computer is almost always backed by people.

THE DOERS SHOULD BE THE PLANNERS

Xerox' White and Hughes test their plans with word games. "The computers can't possibly handle things that have this many uncertainties," White says, so he assigns key headquarters staff members and a group of outside consultants of various persuasions to critique the plans. Adds Gould's Carroll: "Too often, when you ask for a plan, even a thoughtful guy will make a study in arithmetic. If he isn't forced to say where he wants to end up, he will tend to go along with existing products, and talk competitors rather than competition [for the consumer's disposable income]."

Forcing managers, not just planners, to look at "where they want to end up" is basic to most corporate planning. The idea is that the doers in the company should also be the planners, with the planning department acting as a kind of staff group. The planning itself is not an adjunct to management but an integral part of the business. The prevailing planning style in large corporations is that the goals come from the top of the organization to the bottom, but the plans—even long-term plans—go from the bottom up. And there is nothing in the new sophisticated planning techniques that operator-planners cannot use at any level.

Alternate planning, for example, can be and often should be carried down to the individual business unit, since one part of a company frequently is thriving while another part is dying. At Dow Chemical, says corporate planner J. E. Mitchell, "There is constant contingency planning, product by product. Each major product line has three or four alternate scenarios." In some companies, operating units even make most of their own assumptions about the business environment—usually a function of the planning department. "Our operating officers," says Fluor Corp.'s manager of financial planning, James W. Street, "know as much about the political and economic climate in their areas as anyone in the company. We rely on their judgment in most cases."

With that kind of orientation, planning proves to be a kind of acid test for managers. "If you have a contributory planning process, then the quality of the five-year plan is a direct function of lower-level management. It is as strong or as weak as they are," says Street. Fluor comptroller Ronald G. Cullis says that one unit's five-year plan was "so unsatisfactory that it forced a change in management at the unit." In another instance, two Fluor operating units spent so much time together developing their five-year plans that it prompted a consolidation and a reorganization of the corporate structure. "Corporate planning forces exposure of what really is," sums up Street.

If planning is now working its way up from the bottom in most large companies there is still a focal point of planning at the corporate level that is becoming increasingly significant—resource allocation among the units of a company. Frequently this is the key to the corporation's centralized authority.

At GE, for example, planning is carried out simultaneously but with a different perspective at corporate headquarters and in its 43 strategic business units. "Some type of corporate glue was necessary to tie these pieces together," says GE's Gutoff. "That recognition led to the planning work that pulled to-

gether these decentralized businesses. The business units were charged with doing their own planning, but overlaying that was planning at the corporate level,
where we're going to have to make some tradeoffs, some resource allocations.
It's really the interplay of these two activities that led to the functioning of the
whole GE system."

Corporate planning at RCA Corp. also emphasizes determining which businesses will grow and which will not. "The top-down look on the businesses is as
competitive investments," says George C. Evanoff, vice-president for corporate
development at RCA, which has five major operating groups and 15 primary profit
centers. "We're putting more emphasis on where the resource should be placed
than how it should be applied. For example, do we back domestic satellites?
Our essential plan is an articulation of strategies saying this area should receive
more attention, this one less in terms of resource allocation."

This twin-planning technique—in which diverse business units plan their
own futures but with an override by the corporation—may be the most effective
answer yet to the increasingly knotty control problems facing complex companies spanning several industries. Professor James P. Baughman of Harvard
Business School maintains that as business redefines its post-World War II assumptions, there is a rush away from decentralization to more centralized decision-making. Until recently, decentralization has been gospel and most middle
managers were weaned on the concept. Now with the tightening of control, division managers in many corporations are beginning to complain about loss of
autonomy. "It's cultural shock for a great many divisional executives," who see
their previously delegated power eroding and even their pay threatened, says
Baughman. "But it's also cultural shock for the top managers who aren't familiar
with this sort of decision making."

WHEN PLANS GO OUT THE WINDOW

Wherever the authority lies, there is a perceptible trend toward caution in
corporate planning, not so much for the coming year as for the long term. As
risks mount, companies routinely demand of their businesses a higher return on
investment. Although some executives, such as Rodney S. Gould, senior vice-
president for corporate development at Dravo Corp., still see diversification as a
hedge against uncertainty, much business planning seems more concerned with
how to drop businesses, exit from markets, and retrench than with growing and
expanding.

One way to reduce the danger, even for so strong a company as GE, is to take
risks in bite sizes. "A decade ago our venture activity was pretty well tied up
with major corporate ventures of very large size—nuclear, commercial jet en-
gines, and computers," says Gutoff. "In line with trying to reduce the risk exposure in the company, and at the same time not lose any of the entrepreneur-
ship, we haved moved toward more organically grown, smaller-in-size, larger-
in-number ventures."

Many planners believe that changes facing corporations in the next few years will be fundamental. A whole new political dimension overlays much of their thinking, with a "government interference trend" expected to accelerate in the U.S. as well as elsewhere. Major societal changes such as the low-growth movement are anticipated. Monetary gyrations, rampant inflation, liquidity crises, and inadequate equity markets, while not expected to last indefinitely, are at least viewed as recurring threats to economic stability. Just predicting the future worth of the dollar is a major planning headache. American Standard encourages managers to translate dollars in forward plans to ounces of gold, not only to keep them aware of the continuing erosion of the dollar but to dramatize the need to look at market forecasts in terms of physical units (like thousands of square meters of cast-iron radiators) rather than paper money, which overstates market growth.

The expanding role of government creates new imponderables. Inland Steel has a $1-billion (by 1984) capital expansion program under way, but Block says: "We are wondering just what it is really going to cost us. We are trying to pay for it out of profits, but they depend on adequate selling prices. It is difficult to factor in government interference on pricing and the impact of controls of any kind—including 'jawboning.'" Sun Oil is trying to factor into its planning such possibilities as postponement of certain Environmental Protection Agency regulations, removal of the oil depletion allowance and tax incentives, and imposition of a windfall profits tax.

In addition, some planners see a growing "politicization of capital allocations," as Xerox' White puts it, as the equity market dries up. In other words, government and not the markets would determine where capital should go. "We've seen it already," he says, citing Iran's planned rescue of Pan American World Airways and New York State's aid to the Urban Development Corp.

If political action is an imponderable in the U.S., it is doubly so abroad, and for some of the largest multinational corporations that is currently where most of the action is. Many companies are re-evaluating their prospects as the likelihood grows that foreign sources of raw materials may dry up.

Thus companies are trying to cut their risks in countries considered "difficult" or unstable. These days there are few exceptions. Some companies, for example, now avoid Great Britain, Japan, Italy, and even Australia, as well as the developing countries. "We had been regarding Canada as a jewel, but no more," says Xerox' Hughes.

In the past, executives could at least be reasonably confident about the long-term outlook and plan accordingly. Now many are not so sure. Depression strategies are coming in to fashion at least as alternate scenarios. Hewlett-Packard's Doyle, although he is paying a little more attention to H-P's exposure should things "really go sour" in the near future, says he does not expect a depression "this time around" because government pump-priming should get business moving again. But he thinks none of the underlying problems will have been solved and foresees a depression in 1978 or 1979. Some other planners are just as pessimistic.

In a recent planning conference in San Francisco attended by 65 corporate executives, the basic mood of the audience was one of gloom and the speakers did little to dispel it. As Stanford Business School economist Keith G. Lumsden put it, "there is no cure for the current dilemma." He and other panelists predicted continuing high inflation, only a temporary "whiff of enthusiasm" in the stock market, much lower growth rates in the next four or five years than in the past 15, continuing tight money, and high long-term interest rates. Even the possibility of this kind of long-term scenario complicates corporate planning efforts that in the past have been built on a straight course of optimism.

Risk-taking, then, might be characterized as riskier than ever, and even the most hopeful corporate planners and managers seem to be approaching the future warily. RCA's president, Anthony L. Conrad, has an "innate confidence in the economy, the progress of technology, and the growth of markets," but warns: "The businessman in the current climate has to be very agile. He's confronted with unexpected, unanticipated things. This makes long-range planning more critical, absolutely. As the fellow said, 'it's a very sporty course.'"

Strategy: Formulation, Implementation, and Monitoring

Kalman J. Cohen and Richard M. Cyert

The study of corporate strategy within graduate schools of business has been under way for many years. With the growing complexity of the world and with the increased size of business firms, the need for planning and the development of a corporate strategy has become recognized in the business firm. While many areas of management have been subjected to scientific analysis, the strategy area continues to be characterized by a commonsensical, judgmental approach.

This paper is an attempt to impose structure upon the various problems inherent in the process of formulating, implementing, and monitoring corporate strategy in modern business firms. We begin by identifying the relevant considerations in the strategic planning process and then discussing the manner in which formal models can prove useful to executives in dealing with various subproblems. The paucity of valid, normative propositions in the corporate strategy literature indicates the need for a more scientific approach to this important field.

The nine major steps that constitute the strategic planning process are as follows: (1) formulation of goals; (2) analysis of the environment; (3) assigning quantitative values to the goals; (4) the microprocess of strategy formulation; (5) the gap analysis; (6) strategic search; (7) selecting the portfolio of strategic alternatives; (8) implementation of the strategic program; (9) measurement, feedback, and control.[1] This paper will review these nine steps and present selected ideas that demonstrate how the strategic planning process could

About the Authors: Kalman J. Cohen is a distinguished professor of finance and economics at New York University; Richard M. Cyert is president of Carnegie-Mellon University.

From K. Cohen and R. Cyert, "Strategy: Formulation, Implementation, and Monitoring," *Journal of Business,* vol. 46, no. 3 (Chicago: University of Chicago Press, July 1973), pp. 349–367. Reprinted by permission.

[1] These nine steps into which we have subdivided the strategic planning process are consistent with some viewpoints expressed in the current literature. They are not, however, specifically taken from any single source. They represent our characterization of the problem based upon our knowledge of the literature, discussions with corporate executives, and participation in the process itself. Some other attempts to present a conceptual framework for the strategic planning process are presented in George A. Steiner, *Top Management Planning* (New York: Macmillan Co., 1969), chap. 2.

be improved through use of analytical procedures. The nine steps should not be viewed as a once-and-for-all process of strategic planning, but, rather, as a continuous, ongoing process.[2] The whole procedure is a dynamic feedback process that has neither a beginning nor an end; it is merely for expository convenience that we label the first step as formulating corporate goals.

I. FORMULATION OF GOALS

The first step in the strategic planning process can be viewed as the development of the arguments in the corporate utility function.[3] This specification is made by the coalition responsible for the top-level management of the corporation.[4] Corporate goals must stem from participants within the organization.[5] The goals of a small firm under control of a single entrepreneur are determined solely by him. The goals of a large corporation under control of professional managers are determined by a coalition which typically includes the chairman of the board, the president, and a select group of the more important vice presidents. The group is characterized as a coalition because no one dominates it in the way that a single entrepreneur may dominate his organization.

The final set of arguments in the utility function for the corporation must be accepted by the individuals who are responsible for implementing the policy of the corporation. This acceptance can be induced in a variety of ways that have been characterized by organization theorists as "side payments." [6] At this stage, the goals are specified in qualitative rather than in quantitative terms. Some goals relate to measurable entities such as earnings per share, total sales, share of market, return on investment, rate of growth in sales, rate of profit growth, and so forth. Other goals represent management aspirations which are more dif-

---

[2] This point is aptly illustrated in H. Igor Ansoff, "Toward a Strategic Theory of the Firm," in *Business Strategy*, ed. H. Igor Ansoff (Baltimore: Penguin Books, 1969), esp. fig. 6. That planning should be viewed as a continuous, ongoing process is clearly stated in the following quotation in "Guide to Business Planning," a brochure printed in 1969 (primarily for internal use) at Westinghouse Electric Corporation: "Planning . . . must be a continuous process of evaluations, decisions, and actions. That does not mean that management must continually recycle the whole formal planning process, or that constant revision of data is required. But management must be continually sensitive to changes that can significantly affect previously planned actions. . . . a *continual review* is required to assess the potential impact of current events and current decisions on future performance; but that will not be done if only one short span of time within the year is reserved as 'planning time.' . . . sustained efforts— in reviewing data, reevaluating plans, and assessing performance—are required throughout the year" (p. 7).

[3] A model of discretionary managerial behavior based on the notion of a corporate utility function has been developed in Oliver E. Williamson, *The Economics of Discretionary Behavior: Managerial Objectives in a Theory of the Firm* (Englewood Cliffs, N.J.: Prentice-Hall, Inc., 1964), chap. 4.

[4] See Richard M. Cyert and James G. March, *A Behavioral Theory of the Firm* (Englewood Cliffs, N.J.: Prentice-Hall, Inc., 1963), chap. 3.

[5] This statement does not imply that the goals of the corporation are necessarily identical with the goals of any participants in the organization. See, e.g., H. A. Simon, "On the Concept of Organizational Goal," *Administrative Science Quarterly* 9, no. 1 (June 1964): 1–22.

[6] Cyert and March, pp. 29–32.

ficult to measure: for example, a desire to be the most advanced electronics firm in the United States, a desire to be a leader in community improvements, a desire to be ecologically responsible, and so forth.[7]

In the formulation of corporate goals, the relationships between those goals and the goals of the participants in the organization should be considered by the coalition. If all participants had the same goals and the same perception of the means to achieve them, then there would be no problem in formulating a goal structure for the organization. Similarly, if all participants completely accepted the goals of some single individual (such as the chief executive), the organizational goal structure could be easily understood. However, most organizations consist of individual participants havings sets of personal goals that are different from each other's and from the organization's goals. It is clear from even casual observation that there is no formal weighting process by which the goals of each participant are incorporated into the goal structure in a systematic fashion. Further, it is also clear that each individual does not have an equal vote in determining the goals of an organization. Nevertheless, if the organization is to function effectively, its goals must in some sense be an amalgam of the goals of the participants.

A frequent phenomenon in organizations is the formation of subunits and of subunit goals. These subunits, which are usually work groups, become the object of the participants' identification. Group norms arise and may exert more influence over the individual than the organizational goals. The norms of the group may at some time be in conflict with the organizational goals and the subgroup actions contrary to the interests of the total organization. Still the individual may, in fact, substitute the goals of this subunit for the organizational goals. Hence, in formulating organizational goals, the coalition should consider the effect that they will have on subunit goals and on the potential formation of subunits.[8]

Clearly the corporate goals must be viewed from the standpoint of the social values that are held by members of the coalition. It is necessary to differentiate between the social goals that are proper for the organization to hold and those that are proper for the individual participant to hold. For example, there may be a conflict for some firms between pollution control and profit. This conflict becomes particularly strong when the society has not passed the appropriate laws which embody its social values and the corporation is left with the problem of voluntarily reducing its profit in order to contribute to some social goal. It is not clear whether the organizational coalition can properly take actions that reduce the profit of the organization in order to achieve a set of social goals that the coalition itself holds. Most corporation executives take the position that they do not have the right to impose their own social values on stockholders, but

---

[7] A detailed discussion of the variety of goals pursued by business firms is provided in Steiner (n. 1 above), chaps. 6–7.

[8] See Richard M. Cyert and Kenneth R. MacCrimmon, "Organizations," in *The Handbook of Social Psychology*, ed. Gardner Lindsey and Elliot Aronson, 2d ed. (Reading, Mass.: Addison-Wesley Publishing Co., 1968), 1: 591–93.

they do have a right to fight as individuals for particular kinds of legislation even though the effect of the legislation is to reduce the corporation's profit. There are also an increasing number of attempts to get stockholder approval of particular strategies that will achieve social goals. In the final analysis, however, business firms are profit-seeking organizations, and society depends on them to seek profit as a means of achieving the optimum allocation of resources.[9]

In summary, we have stressed the fact that goal formulation is a process of determining the arguments in the corporate utility function. The particular set of goals that the corporation selects must take into account the personal goals of the members of the organization and the goals of subunits. The coalition must also consider the problem of social goals and the extent to which they are going to be represented in the corporate goal structure. In this first step of the strategic planning process, no attempt is made to assign quantitative values to the set of elements in the goal structure.

II. ENVIRONMENT AND THE FIRM [10]

The organization and the environment are parts of a complex interactive system. The actions taken by the organization can have important effects on the environment, and, conversely, the outcomes of the actions of the organization are partially determined by events in the environment. These outcomes and the events that contribute to them have a major impact on the organization. Even if the organization does not respond to these events, significant changes in the organizational participants' goals and roles can occur.[11]

Most organizations attempt to learn from interaction with the environment and respond to changes caused by the environment. Both the learning and response are easiest when the environment is disjoint. In such cases, the causal links among the sectors of the environment are relatively short and events in one sector are likely to have only minor effects on events in other sectors. The organization can then usefully partition such a disjoint environment and consider the sectors in isolation. For example, a multinational firm selling products under different brand names in each of several countries can change policy in one market and analyze the effects without considering interactions with other markets. The learning and response are more difficult for the organization when the environment is complex and long chains of causal links and events in one sector have profound effects on other sectors. In such an environment, the organization must consider the whole sequence of possible effects of any action it takes. For

---

[9] *Social Responsibilities of Business Corporations* (a statement on national policy by the Research and Policy Committee of the Committee for Economic Development, New York, June, 1971).

[10] Some of the material in this section has been directly taken or paraphrased from Cyert and MacCrimmon, pp. 593–602.

[11] An extended discussion of the manner in which roles and tasks within an organization should be influenced by the environment is presented in Paul R. Lawrence and Jay W. Lorsch, *Organization and Environment: Managing Differentiation and Integration* (Boston: Division of Research, Graduate School of Business Administration, Harvard University, 1967).

example, large steel companies must consider the effects that a price increase will have on various sectors of the environment—on labor unions, competitors, consumers, and government.

The parts of an environment that are relevant differ according to the type of organization. For the business firm, economic conditions are of prime importance. When the economy is in an expansionary period, many possible actions can yield the necessary resources to allow the firm to survive and grow. Conflict with other organizations in the environment will be minimized since all organizations can readily meet their basic resource requirements. Conflict within the organization will also generally be reduced because the preferences of the various coalition members can be more easily satisfied. An expanding economy not only makes it relatively easy for the firm to attain its current goals, but also offers the possibility for the firm to expand its goal set. The degree to which the goal set is expanded depends on the expected duration of the favorable economic conditions. Such a change in goals may lead to some internal conflict as the various coalition members assert their own preferences. However, these internal conflicts will not be seriously disruptive, since the firm's increased resources permit all coalition members to achieve higher levels of utility.

In contrast, when economic conditions are unfavorable, goal attainment becomes more difficult and the firm will devote increasing attention toward its goal set. Continued failure to meet its goals without any apparent possibility of increasing resources generally results in a reduction of goal values. In the face of economic adversity, typical firm responses are to tighten operations by postponing expansion plans, engaging in cost-cutting drives, reducing the number of participants, and so on. The extent of these actions depends on the amount of slack in the organization. At the beginning of unfavorable economic conditions, the organization will usually have considerable slack accumulated during more favorable times. If economic conditions continue at a low level for an extensive period of time, it becomes increasingly difficult to remove slack without reducing services that were previously considered essential. Eventually this set of events will lead to changes in the organizational structure. Some roles may be eliminated completely and other roles may be extensively modified. Serious internal conflict among the individual participants will occur and will result in participants leaving the organization both voluntarily and involuntarily.[12]

---

[12] Examples of the manner in which adverse economic circumstances can lead to extensive organizational changes have been described in Williamson, chap. 6. A more detailed example of the disruptive influences that a sudden adverse economic environment can have on an organization is the impact of the crisis of 1920 on General Motors. This point is dramatically illustrated in the following quotation from Alfred D. Chandler, *Strategy and Structure: Chapters in the History of the American Enterprise* (New York: Doubleday, 1966): ". . . the automobile market had collapsed . . . but, by the end of October [1920], the situation had become so serious that many General Motors managers were having difficulty finding cash to cover such immediate needs as invoices and payrolls. . . . during the crisis, the prices of General Motors stock plummeted. Then came Durant's disastrous attempt to sustain the price by buying General Motors' stock on credit which led to his financial difficulties and his retirement as president on November 20, 1920. Ten days later, Pierre du Pont took over the presidency. . . . once he agreed to serve, Pierre acted quickly and firmly. The day after he took office, he began a systematic review of the corporation's position and problems. And one

The impact of changing economic conditions is reduced if the organization is prepared for them. Thus, organizations attempt to plan ahead; as a basis for planning, forecasts must be made of future changes in economic conditions. These forecasts are, of course, more accurate when the economic environment is relatively stable over time. The organization has more difficulty in learning the structure of the environment and accurately predicting its future states when the environment is highly volatile. Unfortunately, these are the circumstances when forecasts are most essential.

For whatever planning horizon the firm uses, it is necessary to make predictions for the entire planning period. In particular, it is necessary to make predictions of various aggregate economic variables which are relevant for the firm. These aggregates include GNP, price indices, unemployment rates, and similar measures of the state of the economy at benchmark dates during the planning period. It is desirable that these predictions be made at the corporate level and transmitted to the operating units of the firm as a basis for their specific planning. In this way, all planning activity of the firm is conducted under a uniform set of predictions. The predictions will not necessarily be single-valued estimates. The firm may find it useful to develop several plausible alternative economic scenarios and to require its operating units to formulate plans for each alternative.[13]

In addition to aggregate economic predictions, it is necessary for the firm to make predictions about future conditions in the industries and markets in which it operates. An industry forecast is usually made in terms of the total dollar sales expected for the industry. From such forecasts, the firm can predict its future sales over the planning period by making assumptions about the market shares that it will obtain. In making these assumptions the firm must make predictions about the behavior of its present and potential competitors.[14] Estimates must be made of the prices competitors will charge, of their advertising policies, and of the product changes competitors will make. In this regard it is highly useful for firms to maintain an elaborate information system on their competitors. Relevant information on competitors can be obtained from public sources such as financial statements, from information gathered from the firm's salesmen, and from executives who meet rival executives at professional meetings. All of these sources can be utilized to build up a data base on each of the firm's major competitors.

III. ESTABLISHMENT OF QUANTITATIVE TARGETS

After goals have been qualitatively formulated and after the environmental analysis has been completed, the firm's coalition is in a position to establish quan-

---

of his very first acts *was to approve the plan worked out by Alfred Sloan which defined an organizational structure for General Motors*" (p. 157, italics added).

[13] For a survey of various approaches to forecasting the future environment, see Steiner (n. 1 above), chap. 8.

[14] The importance of analyzing competitors is stressed in S. Tilles, "Making Strategy Explicit," in Ansoff (n. 2 above), pp. 186–90.

titative targets.[15] Quantitative targets essentially impute quantitative values to those previously formulated goals that are capable of being stated in quantitative terms. These quantitative targets are often usefully established for planning purposes in terms of rates of growth. Thus one goal may be that the firm's profit should grow at some specific annual rate over the planning horizon. Part of the process of establishing quantitative targets also involves weighting the importance of the various targets. Thus, the firm conceivably might weight achievement of its sales goal more than achievement of its profit goal. This weighting is important when the firm may be in a position to achieve some but not all of its goal set. Given the weighting it is then possible to specify strategies which are appropriate when it is impossible to attain all the various targets. Goals stated in terms of absolute levels rather than rates of change require target dates to be specified. It is generally necessary for a plan to have values for the relevant goals specified for various benchmark dates. This is frequently done, permitting the firm to project *pro forma* balance sheets and profit and loss statements for the individual years within the planning horizon.

One useful heuristic for planning is the process of "backward induction." [16] This approach requires that a specific set of desired values be established for the various goals for the final period of the planning horizon, for example, 5 years from now. The planners specify, for instance, the values the firm should have for sales, profit, capital investment, and so on during the fifth year. On the basis of these specifications, the planners work backward to see where the firm must be in the fourth year if it is to achieve the goals in the fifth year and so on back to the first year of the plan. This process of backward induction is a useful addition to the planning process. It enables the planner to establish a viable plan for the entire planning horizon. Several iterations may be required, and, in this process, goals may be modified.

We have discussed the establishment of quantitative targets from the perspective of the corporation as a whole. Frequently, however, it is also desirable to establish quantitative targets for various collections of operating units within the corporation, for example, groups or divisions, by disaggregating the previously established corporate-wide targets.

This description of the first three planning steps completes the macrophase of the planning process. The next step is to have each operating unit within the firm formulate its own set of plans.

IV. THE MICROPROCESS OF STRATEGY FORMULATION

The fourth major step in the planning process can be referred to as "the micro-aspects of strategy formulation." Each operating unit in the corporation formulates its own strategic plan over the relevant time horizon. The time horizon

---

[15] Cf. Russell L. Ackoff, *A Concept of Corporate Planning* (New York: John Wiley & Sons, 1970), chap. 2.

[16] An explanation of backward induction is presented in Morris H. DeGroot, *Optimal Statistical Decisions* (New York: McGraw-Hill Book Co., 1970), pp. 277–78.

chosen for strategic planning will vary depending upon the nature of the firm, but 5 years is a typical time horizon for strategic planning in business organizations. It often will be desirable for some qualitative aspects of the strategic plan to be formulated over a 10- or 20-year horizon, even though detailed quantitative projections may be made only for an intermediate-term time horizon such as the next 5 years.

Before each operating unit can develop its own strategic plan, it is necessary for the senior executives of the corporation (or their staff members) to provide the managers of the operating unit with some background information.[17] This centrally provided information should consist of at least the following items:

1. Some guidelines concerning the nature of the strategic planning process should be provided. The emphasis should be put on actively involving relevant executives in the planning process in order to focus their attention on strategic considerations. Especially at the level of the operating units, there is a tendency for managers to worry primarily about immediate problems. A formalized planning process is necessary to induce managers to think seriously about long-term strategy for the operating unit.

2. The relevant goals that top management wants the operating unit to be concerned with should be explicitly stated.

3. All operating units should be provided with the results of the broad analysis of the economic environment undertaken in corporate headquarters. To the extent that relevant technological or product-market forecasts were centrally made, these should also be transmitted to appropriate operating units. There may be economies in having some of the technological and product-market forecasts made centrally even though they are relevant only to particular operating units in the corporation.

On the basis of this corporate information, each operating unit should develop its own strategic plan, in both qualitative and quantitative terms. A major activity which each operating unit must undertake in developing its strategic plan is a critical, thorough analysis of the environment for its own particular mix of products and markets. A reasonably broad definition of the operating unit's product-market mission needs to be adopted for this purpose. Given this broad view of its product-market posture, the operating unit must attempt to analyze its external environment to discover significant economic, market, and technological developments. As part of its environmental analysis, the operating unit must identify its major present and potential competitors. In addition, the operating unit should make an internal analysis to uncover those areas in which it has had problems and successes in the past in order to diagnose hitherto unrecognized strategic obstacles and opportunities. In the light of these external and

---

[17] An interesting discussion of one procedure for coordinating the planning done at various levels in a corporation is provided in Ackoff, pp. 133–37.

internal analyses, the operating unit must then determine where its comparative advantage exists.

This analysis should result in a set of recommended strategic programs for each operating unit. Several types of recommendations may be relevant. These might involve pricing strategy, product-line strategy, marketing strategy, programs of cost reduction for existing products and markets, new products to be developed, new markets to be entered, major research and development expenditures, major advertising campaigns, and major physical investments. In proposing the operating unit's diversification into additional products and markets, recommendations should be made as to whether this diversification should be accomplished by means of internal growth or through external acquisition. Enough detailed information should be given in the verbal discussion and the quantitative projections so that executives at higher levels in the corporation can independently determine the impact of undertaking, postponing, or rejecting each element in the recommended strategic plan.

V. THE "GAP ANALYSIS"

The fifth major step consists of aggregating upward the strategic plans formulated by each operating unit to obtain aggregate strategic plans for the corporation as a whole and for any relevant subdivisions. This upward aggregation of the specific quantitative projections made by each operating unit for the next 5 years can readily be done by a process of simple summation. Equally important, however, is the upward aggregation of the qualitative, verbal aspects of each operating unit's strategic plan. The hierarchical pattern utilized in the upward aggregation process should be carefully chosen to make the most logical sense for the particular corporation. It might first involve consolidating the operating units into departments, then consolidating the departments into divisions, then consolidating these divisions into groups, and, finally, consolidating the groups into the corporation. Of course, the number of levels present in this upward aggregation process, and the particular labels attached to each level of consolidation, will differ from firm to firm.

The immediate aim of the aggregation is to enable a "gap analysis" to be

Table 1 An Example of a Perceived-Gap Matrix

Corporate Goals	Time Periods in the Planning Horizon				
	Year 1	Year 2	Year 3	Year 4	Year 5
Total sales revenue (million $)	+ 2.5	− 7.3	−10.9	−18.7	−28.3
Earnings per share ($ per share)	+ 0.05	− 0.11	− 0.31	− 0.80	− 1.35
Index of geographical dispersion (percentage)	−15	−13	− 9	− 7	− 6

performed at higher organizational levels in the firm.[18] This gap analysis might be made only at the corporate-wide level, or, instead, preliminary gap analyses might be made at each of the "collection points" at lower organizational levels (for example, initially at the departmental level, then at the divisional level, and finally at the group level) prior to the corporate-wide gap analysis.

Regardless of the organizational level at which the gap analysis is performed, the procedural aspects of it are much the same. In particular, the projected performance of the corporation as a whole (or for whatever organizational subdivision the gap analysis is being performed) is compared to the quantitative targets which have been established for the corporation (or the appropriate subdivision). Since the corporation generally has multiple goals, the gap analysis should be done for each goal. Thus for each goal of importance to the corporation, the projected figures will be subtracted from the targets established for that goal in order to develop a perceived gap. For any particular goal, for example, earnings per share, this perceived gap can be expressed as a function of time (for example, year-by-year over a 5-year horizon). Thus, the gap analysis process can be usefully viewed as developing a "perceived-gap matrix," as illustrated in Table 1. The rows in this matrix designate the various corporate goals, for example, total sales, earnings per share, some measure of geographical dispersion, and so forth. The columns of this matrix correspond to various points of time within the planning horizon, for example, years one, two, three, four and five. The entries in this matrix are the perceived gaps along each goal for each particular point of time. The manner in which this perceived-gap matrix can be used to initiate strategic search will be discussed in connection with step six below.

VI. STRATEGIC SEARCH

A gap between the goals specified at the corporate level and the predicted achievement developed through the microanalysis stimulates the firm to search for new strategies in order to achieve its goals.[19] The strategic search process generally first focuses on internal activities. For example, the firm may begin its search by reviewing its price strategy to see whether it can achieve its goals by raising prices. More broadly, the firm may review its entire marketing strategy. Another area for search is the cost structure of the firm with a view toward establishing a strategy for cost reduction. Still another area for internal search is research and development. All of these areas, and others which may be undertaken, fall into the category of internal search.

If the measures discovered by internal search do not entirely close the gap, the firm then turns to external search. In this phase the firm begins to examine

---

[18] A different approach to the gap analysis is discussed in H. Igor Ansoff, *Corporate Strategy* (New York: McGraw-Hill Book Co., 1965), chap. 8.

[19] A general discussion of the empirical process of search behavior within an organization is presented in James G. March and Herbert A. Simon, *Organizations* (New York: John Wiley & Sons, 1958), esp. pp. 173–74, 180. A discussion of search behavior which focuses more directly on issues of corporate strategy is contained in Ansoff, ibid.

the environment with a view toward bringing new resources into the firm to enable it to achieve its goals. Frequently this is accomplished through a strategy of acquisition of other firms. In general, the firm searches for acquisitions which would result in economies of scale or positive externalities. An economy of scale would result from an acquisition that would enable the firm to use some of its resources more intensively, for example, by producing or distributing a new product with already existing facilities or manpower. Positive externalities would result from a new (complementary) product whose sale would increase the sales of the firm's present products, from elimination of overlapping facilities (such as branch or headquarter offices), from the acquisition of new technical talent, and so forth. A frequent source of economies resulting from acquisition is the more intensive utilization of capable managers. It is clear that in any economy, including the U.S. economy, there is a significant shortage of good managers.[20] Thus, firms which have capable managerial talent may be able to benefit from acquisitions that do not appear to be a synergistic fit. However, because of the ability of the acquiring firm to supply good management, these acquisitions may prove highly successful.

There is at present in the United States much evidence that legal power will be invoked to restrict the acquisition policy of firms.[21] This development reduces the efficacy of external search and increases the importance of internal search. This change in turn emphasizes the need to develop organizational policies that will permit managers with entrepreneurial ability to advance within the firm. Thus it is important that planning activity not restrict initiative by developing inflexible policies; instead, the planning process should induce division managers to feel responsible for developing new business ideas as part of the strategic plans for their own divisions.[22]

VII. SELECTING THE PORTFOLIO OF STRATEGIC ALTERNATIVES

In the sixth step of the strategic planning process, the perceived-gap matrix was used to trigger several different types of strategic search. The purpose of this

---

[20] Marvin Bower, *The Will to Manage* (New York: McGraw-Hill Book Co., 1966), pp. 92–94.

[21] U.S. Congress, House, Committee on the Judiciary, Antitrust Subcommittee, *Investigation of Conglomerate Corporations*, 92d Cong., 1st sess., June 1, 1971. On p. 5 of this report, the following statements are presented: "This public attention, notoriety and industry demand sparked unprecedented attention at the national level to the problem of corporate mergers. In the first 6 months of 1969, at least 8 major investigations were under way at the national level into Federal questions concerning mergers and acquisitions by conglomerate corporations." On the same page, Chairman Celler is quoted as stating: "It may be that the traditional standards of the antitrust laws against mergers and corporations which 'may be substantially to lessen competition, or tend to create a monopoly' need reevaluation in the light of economic and political effects of conglomerate mergers."

[22] Litton Industries is one corporation which was able to obtain this type of behavior by their division managers under their "opportunity planning" process. This is described in Edmund P. Learned et al., *Business Policy: Text and Cases,* rev. ed. (Homewood, Ill.: Richard D. Irwin, Inc., 1969), pp. 833–39.

search is to develop a strategy set that consists of possible strategic actions. Each of the members of this set is a strategic action that might be undertaken by the corporation as a whole (or by appropriate subdivisions). For example, a strategy set might include proposals for changes in pricing policy, major cost-reduction campaigns, changes in product design, new market introduction plans, diversification into specific new product-market alternatives, major investments in physical facilities, and the acquisition of particular products or of entire firms.

The fact that a set of possible strategic actions has been developed does not imply that each action will be adopted as part of the strategic plan. From the strategy set, management selects a particular portfolio of strategic actions; this portfolio constitutes the corporation's new strategic plan.[23]

The seventh step of the strategic planning process, as we have described it, focuses on the way in which corporations should develop a strategic plan. Because of the rather casual manner in which strategic planning is approached in most corporations, however, little emphasis is placed on the portfolio aspects of the problem. The usual approach is to judge each proposed action as it is uncovered in the search process strictly on its own merits. If the proposed action proves acceptable at this point, then the action is adopted as part of the new strategic plan. When enough proposed actions are adopted in this manner to close the perceived gap (or if the gap is closed by lowering the goal values), strategic search is terminated and the new strategic plan has been formulated. One deficiency in this typical approach is that management fails to evaluate interactions among possible strategic actions. A more complete analysis from a portfolio viewpoint will often lead to a different evaluation of a particular proposed action because of interaction effects. A second deficiency of the usual approach is that strategic search may be prematurely terminated.

The nature of the strategic search process in organizations often prevents an objective evaluation of proposed actions. When a coalition member advocates a potential action he thereby becomes identified with the action. When this identification becomes close, the coalition member may view the ultimate adoption or rejection of the proposed action as a measure of his personal power position within the coalition. The strategic planning process would be far more effective if the proposed actions could be divorced from individual sponsorship. Typically, however, this is difficult to accomplish because proposed strategic actions are brought to the attention of the coalition through a chain of successive sponsorships within the organization. In this chain, each manager in the hierarchy attempts to convince his immediate superior of the merits of the proposed action and sponsorship of the proposal passes upward with acceptance.[24]

The difficulty of the coalition's making an objective evaluation of proposed actions is further complicated by the loss of information as proposals filter up-

---

[23] See E. Eugene Carter and Kalman J. Cohen, "Portfolio Aspects of Strategic Planning," *Journal of Business Policy* 2, no. 4 (Summer 1972): 8–30.

[24] This process has been analyzed in E. Eugene Carter, "A Behavioral Theory Approach to Firm Investment and Acquisition Decisions" (Ph.D. diss., Carnegie-Mellon University, 1969).

ward through the organizational hierarchy. So many details concerning proposals are eliminated in "the selling process" that it becomes virtually impossible for coalition members to analyze interaction effects even if they so desired. Thus, each coalition member sponsoring a proposal becomes an "uncertainty absorber" with respect to the proposed actions that he advocates.[25] This situation effectively forces the coalition into the necessity of making personal judgments concerning the competence of its members in the guise of selecting a strategic plan. In order to minimize personal conflict among coalition members, the coalition frequently adopts rules of thumb to allocate strategic resources among organizational subunits in some objective but nonoptimal manner, for example, budgeting research and development expenditures in proportion to sales and authorizing automatic reinvestment of depreciation charges.

VIII. IMPLEMENTATION OF THE STRATEGIC PROGRAM

Once a portfolio of strategic alternatives has been established for the corporation (as well as for each group, division, department, and operating unit in the corporation), the next step in the strategic planning process is implementation of the program.[26] We will focus on the implementation problem from the standpoint of overall corporate strategy, but analogous considerations also apply at other levels in the organizational hierarchy.

In order to develop an operational procedure for implementing the agreed-upon strategic program, it is necessary to decompose the broadly stated strategy into a time-phased sequence of plans regarding such actions as new product developments, new market introductions, external acquisitions, capital investment projects, management development, manpower recruitment, and so forth.[27] The various activities necessary to implement any particular strategy should be defined in terms of each type of resource required. It is common practice to reduce this specification of resource requirements to monetary terms. Unfortunately, in many firms, the underlying detail is then lost and only the dollar budget for the strategic program remains as a permanent control document. With this loss of detail and transformation into monetary terms, a subtle change in attitudes also occurs. In place of the inspiration and imagination displayed in the development of the plan, management has merely a set of monetary constraints within which it must operate. This primary emphasis on monetary con-

---

[25] Cf. March and Simon (n. 19 above), p. 165: "Uncertainty absorption takes place when inferences are drawn from a body of evidence and the inferences, instead of the evidence itself, are then communicated. . . . through the process of uncertainty absorption, the recipient of a communication is severely limited in his ability to judge correctness."

[26] An overall discussion of some problems involved in implementing strategic plans is contained in Steiner (n. 1 above), chap. 11.

[27] Decomposition of the broadly stated strategy into a time-phased sequence of plans is analogous to some of the steps involved in the planning-programming-budgeting system that was developed during the 1960s in the Department of Defense. See Charles J. Hitch, *Decision-making for Defense* (Berkeley, Calif.: University of California Press, 1967), pp. 21–39.

siderations has the effect of replacing the manager's entrepreneurial spirit with a bureaucratic attitude. The long-term goals of the strategic plan are displaced by the short-term goal of operating within budget.

In arguing that the financial budget should not be the sole form to which the strategic plan is reduced, we nonetheless acknowledge that financial budgets are essential. The various forms of short-term plans and budgets should be consistent with the strategic plan. Such interaction can be accomplished by initially defining the plans and budgets for the coming year as the first-year components in the quantitative projections developed as part of the 5-year strategic plan. If necessary, of course, these initial figures for the coming year can then be further disaggregated in the short-term planning and budgeting process.

It is obvious that any attempt to forecast the future (especially several years ahead) is bound to be subject to errors. Unfortunately, however, many planning and budgeting systems place undue reliance upon the accuracy of the underlying forecasts. More realistically, strategic plans and their accompanying operating budgets should be formulated on a contingency basis. Some type of decision-tree analysis may be a useful planning aid for this purpose.[28] At a minimum, operating budgets for the next year as well as strategic plans for the next 5 years should be in a variable budget format, rather than the more usual fixed budget format. To the extent possible, however, various major contingencies should be envisioned and probabilities of occurrence assigned to each one. Alternative plans of action can then be developed for each contingency having a sufficiently high probability of occurrence. Obviously, in this regard, some type of computerized planning and budgeting model would be extremely helpful in developing suitable contingency plans.

In order to implement any specific strategic program successfully, it is necessary to obtain enthusiastic cooperation from executives at various levels of the corporation. One way of achieving acceptance of the strategic plan by lower-level executives is to have these executives actively participate in the planning process. The approach to strategy formulation that we have described requires such participation in the process of developing the plan (especially in the micro-process of strategy formulation and in strategic search).

It is critical as part of the implementation process to examine the formal organizational structure.[29] Although major changes in structure will occur relatively infrequently, it is nevertheless important to determine whether minor modifications will increase the likelihood of achieving the goals specified by the strategic plan. By organizational structure we mean the particular description of the roles of the organization, the allocation of decision-making power, and the placing of responsibility. There must be a matching of the structure with the requirements

---

[28] For an example of the use of decision-tree analysis, see Harvey M. Wagner, *Principles of Operations Research* (Englewood Cliffs, N.J.: Prentice-Hall, Inc., 1969), pp. 18–20.

[29] An appropriate framework for this purpose is presented in Ackoff (n. 15 above), chap. 5. An interesting analysis of the manner in which a firm's organizational structure should be adapted to match the product-market portfolio defined by its overall strategy is presented in E. Raymond Corey and Steven H. Star, *Organization Strategy: A Marketing Approach* (Boston: Division of Research, Harvard Business School, 1971).

for decision making, coordination, and control emanating from the plan.[30] Generally changes in organizational structure are made along the centralization-decentralization dimension. The strategic plan should be analyzed to determine whether the organizational structure should be shifted in either direction. For example, if the firm acquires a new product that has little relationship to the current product mix, it may be desirable to decentralize decisions relating to the new product. Such decentralization places decision-making power in the roles where appropriate information and knowledge exist.

Speaking more generally, the main factors affecting the degree of decentralization of an organization are its size, the environment (benign or hostile), subunit interdependency, and technology.[31] As an organization grows larger, the cost of maintaining centralized control increases. If the environment is hostile (in the sense that mistakes will be easily exploited by competitors), there will be an increased tendency toward centralization. Similarly, if there is a high degree of interdependency among subunits, more centralization is often necessary. If the technological changes associated with the firm's activities require large investments in order to exploit them, the tendency to centralize is increased. Technological changes that reduce the costs of communications provide an impetus toward decentralization. In order to relate the strategic plan effectively to the organizational structure, management should determine whether there will be any significant changes in size, environment, subunit interdependency, and technology resulting from the plan. If so, modifications of the organizational structure should then be made as part of the implementation process.

IX. MEASUREMENT, FEEDBACK, AND CONTROL

An essential component in the strategic planning process is the development of operational measures of the extent to which the corporation and appropriate subunits thereof are in fact adhering to the agreed-upon plan.[32] Additional information should also be developed to help management determine whether the strategic plan may no longer be appropriate. Corporate targets have already been specified in operationally measurable quantitative terms (see Section III above). It is, therefore, relatively simple to obtain periodic measurements of corporate performance (or subunit performance), and to relate these in a time-phased manner to the targets.

It must be recognized, of course, that any attempt to measure performance and to provide feedback on the degree of goal attainment is an evaluation process which introduces possible pitfalls.[33] Once the "rules of the game" have

---

[30] For a brief discussion of organizational design problems, see Herbert A. Simon, *The New Science of Management Decision* (New York: Harper Bros., 1960), pp. 12–13.

[31] See Cyert and MacCrimmon (n. 8 above), pp. 584–85.

[32] For a discussion of some common approaches to the measurement, feedback, and control aspects of strategic planning, see Kenneth R. Andrews, *The Concept of Corporate Strategy* (Homewood, Ill.: Richard D. Irwin, Inc., 1971), chap. 7.

[33] A discussion of some pitfalls that may arise in the measurement and feedback system associated with long-range planning is provided in E. Kirby Warren, *Long-Range Planning: The Executive Viewpoint* (Englewood Cliffs, N.J.: Prentice-Hall, Inc., 1966), chap. 5.

been laid down, the players can be expected to alter their behavior so as to "look good" according to the "scorecard" which is kept on them. Therefore, it is essential that the summary evaluative measures conform as closely as possible to the important corporate goals. It also is important that the detailed measures used for ex ante decision analyses are exactly the same as (or at least consistent with) the corresponding measures for ex post performance evaluation. Otherwise, one would expect serious biases to be introduced into strategic decision making and implementation in order to make the performance evaluations look good, often at the expense of the desired corporate objectives.

Dangers inherent in the measurement and feedback process are intensified when attention is focused solely on one type of summary figure, for example, ROI (return on investment), defined as the income after taxes allocated to a profit center divided by the total funds (or investment) utilized by that profit center. Most strategic expenditures are of such a nature that they produce net cash outflows in their early years, accompanied (hopefully) by net cash inflows in later years. If the short-term return on investment measure is in jeopardy at a particular profit center for a given year, it would appear easy for the manager of that profit center for a given year, it would appear easy for the manager of that profit center to eliminate or reduce strategic expenditures this year, in order to have a better short-run performance evaluation. The emphasis on short-run performance is aggravated in organizations where the profit center manager can expect to hold that particular organizational role for only a few years.

By having many dimensions of performance on which measurements are made and feedback provided, it is less easy for executives to find ways of arbitrarily "winning the game" at the expense of the long-run corporate objectives. In particular, if the various actions required to implement the profit center's strategic program are clearly spelled out (manpower requirements, research and development projects, physical investments, and so forth), then the profit center manager should be required to explain deviations from the various actions specified in the strategic plan.

SUMMARY

In this paper we have outlined the nine major steps that constitute the strategic planning process. Our discussion of strategy formulation, implementation, and monitoring is primarily intended as a normative, rather than as a descriptive, presentation. We would expect that the actual process in a few firms which have concentrated on strategic planning would be generally similar to the framework that we have sketched. We have not, however, made any conscious attempt to describe the manner in which this process is conducted in any particular firm. Unfortunately, we do not believe that most firms approach strategic planning in the serious, logical manner that we have advocated. Thus, this present paper must be regarded as being normative in nature, rather than an empirical description of the strategic planning process in real organizations.

The nine major steps into which we have divided the strategic planning process can be usefully grouped into three phases: formulation, implementation, and monitoring of strategy. Strategic planning should be viewed as being a repetitive, cyclic process. Any firm should repeat this entire process periodically, for example, annually.

The first seven steps together constitute the formulation phase. A prerequisite to any serious attempt to undertake strategic planning is the specification of the overall goals of the organization. This is normally the responsibility of the coalition comprising the top management of the firm. Although initially the goals are stated in qualitative terms, it is ultimately necessary to formulate goals in quantitative terms, for example, as a sequence of target values over several time periods. Before quantitative targets can be meaningfully assigned to the goals, however, it is necessary to analyze relevant portions of the environment in order to determine the type of performance that may generally be feasible. For a business firm, one of the most significant aspects of the environment is the general condition of the economy. Aggregate economic predictions must also be transformed into more specific predictions concerning the various industries and markets in which the firm operates. After specific quantitative goals have been established at the corporate level, it is then critical for the various operating units independently to establish their own strategic plans. A corporate-wide aggregation of the plans produced by each operating unit then provides a prediction of the total corporate performance that would result if no further changes in direction were provided by central management. This implied corporate performance is then compared to the quantitative corporate goals to indicate what gaps there may be in predicted goal achievement. When there are significant positive gaps, that is, when aspirations exceed expected performance, strategic search is initiated both at the corporate level and in various operating units. The objective of strategic search is to discover possible new strategic actions that will improve the performance of the firm beyond that implied by the aggregation of the previously prepared microplans. The senior executives in the firm are then responsible for selecting a particular portfolio of strategic actions from the set of possible strategic actions uncovered in the strategic search process. This portfolio constitutes the new strategic plan for the corporation, thus ending the strategy formulation phase.

Implementation of the strategic plan constitutes the second major phase of the strategy process. The basic problem of implementation is to put the strategic plan into effective action. One of the critical steps in implementing the strategy is to decompose the broadly stated plan into a time-phased sequence of specific action programs. This basically is a specification of the various types of resources that will be required at particular dates in order to achieve the planned strategy. Another critical aspect of the implementation process involves considering possible changes in the organizational structure of the firm if these will increase the likelihood of achieving the plan.

The final phase in the strategy process involves monitoring the extent to which the plan has been effectively implemented and remains appropriate. This requires that various relevant aspects of performance be measured and compared with corresponding aspects of the plan. The behavioral effects of any measurement, feedback, and control system need to be considered to avoid inducing types of motivation that lead to undesirable forms of behavior.

It is our view that the framework we have suggested for the strategic planning process can lead to formulation of serious research efforts that will develop techniques for improving the effectiveness of strategic planning. Such research efforts can be expected to proceed in at least two different directions. On the one hand, some aspects of the strategic planning process can be formulated in rigorous quantitative terms, and the power of management-science techniques and computer systems can be brought to bear to help improve those aspects of the process where the relevant issues can be sharply and definitively stated. On the other hand, some other aspects of strategic planning, which typically have been viewed in qualitative terms and approached solely on the basis of judgment, wisdom, and experience, can be subjected to a more rigorous scientific analysis by the use of the behavioral sciences. We are not maintaining that strategic planning will ever be reduced to a fully automated process in which executive judgment is unnecessary. We do believe, however, that further research efforts will put into clearer focus those areas where executive judgments are essential, thus enabling executives to perform better those tasks in which they have a comparative advantage. This will be possible only when other aspects of the strategic planning process (the ones in which quantitative models, computer-based information systems, and behavioral science concepts possess some comparative advantage) are more rigorously analyzed and understood. The end result will be an improved process of strategic planning, in which the judgment, wisdom, and experience of executives are combined with the judicious use of quantitative and scientific concepts in a manner which effectively exploits the comparative advantages of each component and participant in the process.

Even without waiting for further research efforts to be successfully completed, however, most firms can greatly improve the effectiveness of their strategic planning process by adopting the framework that we have outlined in this paper. Such a framework does not necessarily involve the use of sophisticated quantitative models and computer techniques. Rather, it requires only that the executives in a business firm devote some serious efforts to the strategic planning process and recognize the critical problems inherent in it. Most executives are fully capable of participating effectively in this process if they only take the time to do so. Preoccupation with short-term operating problems unfortunately reduces the attention that most executives pay to strategic planning. It is clear, however, that for the well-being of particular firms as well as our entire economic system, major attention must be paid to produce more effective strategic planning systems in most American corporations. It is only by having effective strategic planning processes that the American economy will have the ability to provide the innovations and adaptations which are necessary to produce an efficient allocation of economic resources in the dynamic society in which we now live.

Can Strategic Planning Pay Off ?

Louis V. Gerstner, Jr.

One of the most intriguing management phenomena of the late 1960s and 1970s has been the rapid spread of the corporate or strategic planning concept. Except for the so-called computer revolution, few management techniques have swept through corporate and governmental enterprises more rapidly or completely. Writer after writer has hailed this new discipline as the fountainhead of all corporate progress. In 1962, one published report extolled strategic planning as "a systematic means by which a company can become what it wants to be" (Stanford Research Institute). Five years later, it was called "a means to help management gain increasing control over the destiny of a corporation" (R. H. Schaffer). By 1971, praise of strategic planning verged on the poetic; it had become "the manifestation of a company's determination to be the master of its own fate . . . to penetrate the darkness of uncertainty and provide illumination of probability" (S. R. Goodman).

It is not surprising, therefore, that one company after another raced to embrace this new source of managerial salvation, and, as a result, most major companies today can boast a corporate planning officer, often with full attendant staff. It seemed appropriate to ask some CEOs whether strategic planning has lived up to its advanced billings. Three anonymous reactions were as follows:

> Strategic planning is basically just a plaything of staff men.

> It's like a Chinese dinner: I feel full when I get it, but after a while I wonder whether I've eaten at all!

> Strategic planning? A staggering waste of time and money.

Some CEOs, of course, would disagree with these comments, and certainly few, if any, would agree publicly. But the fact remains that in the large majority of companies corporate planning tends to be an academic, ill-defined activity with little or no bottom-line impact. Observations of many companies wrestling

---

About the Author: Louis V. Gerstner, Jr. is a partner in McKinsey & Co., management consultants.

Reprinted from *Business Horizons*, vol. 15 (December, 1972), pp. 5–16. Copyright, 1972, by the Foundation for the School of Business at Indiana University. Reprinted by permission.

with the strategic planning concept strongly suggest that this lack of real pay-off is almost always the result of one fundamental weakness, namely, the failure to bring strategic planning down to current decisions. Before describing this problem and some possible ways to overcome it, I shall briefly define what I mean by the term "strategic planning."

FORECASTS ARE NOT STRATEGIES

Many strategic planning programs begin with the extension of the annual operating budget into a five-year projection. This can be a valuable exercise, particularly for institutions that have operated on a yearly or even monthly planning cycle. Most companies, however, soon discover that five-year operational and financial forecasts, in and of themselves, are ineffective as strategic planning tools for a fundamental reason: they are predicated on the implicit assumption of no significant change in environmental, economic, and competitive conditions.

In other words, they are purely extrapolative projections, and, by practically everyone's standards, fall far short of real strategic planning. They offer no overview, no analyses of external trends, and no perceptive insights into company strengths and weaknesses—elements that both theorists and practitioners would agree are central to real corporate planning.

Forecast planning of the sort I have described can usually be identified by leafing through a company's planning documents. Pages and pages of accounting information, detailing five years of financial forecasts with little or no explanatory material, are one earmark. Graphs of projected future performance also tend to follow a predictable pattern; that is, if recent performance has been good, the forecast calls for more and more of the same—on into eternity.

On the other hand, if performance has been poor, the forecast will allow for a year or two to effect the inevitable turnaround, and then—off to eternity. (The manager doing the forecasting hopes, of course, that he will get promoted before the two-year period is up.) Working with forecasts like this, executives tend to dismiss the second, third, fourth, and fifth years as irrelevant and continue to concentrate solely on the current year, that is, the annual budget. Most companies seem to have passed beyond forecast planning, and its weaknesses are fairly manifest—namely, a preoccupation with accounting data as the principal output of a planning program and the assumption that the future, at least in relation to general economic indexes, will closely resemble the past.

Recognizing these weaknesses, many institutions have introduced a more rigorous planning program aimed at defining or redefining the basic objectives, economics, competitive profile, and outlook of the company. These formal strategic planning processes show a distinct family resemblance. They usually begin with an assessment of environmental trends and an analysis of the company's strengths and weaknesses. A statement of corporate goals is then developed. From these three elements, a juxtaposition between the organization's present position and its desired position is derived; comparison of the two positions de-

FIGURE 1   The Basic Strategic Planning Concept

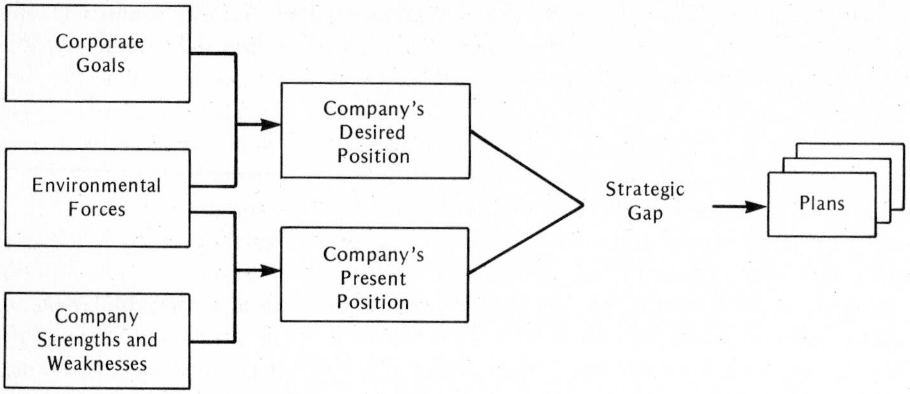

fines the well-known strategic gap. Finally, plans are developed to close the gap and bring the two positions together (Figure 1).

Of course, the steps required to arrive at the statements of present and desired position are quite detailed. For example, one large U.S. company requires each of its more than 50 profit centers to include in the annual strategic plans all the information shown in Figure 2. For each profit center, the initial written output may run to a hundred pages. Such an effort is inevitably painful and time-consuming, but it may be necessary in the first planning cycle. Barring major changes inside or outside the company, subsequent plans can be considerably shorter. Since the specific elements of a good strategic plan have been described in many texts, I shall not dwell on them here. Instead, I shall move on to the central question of why strategic planning so often fails to pay off and what can be done about it.

FIGURE 2   Elements of a Strategic Plan

ENVIRONMENTAL ASSESSMENT	DIVISION'S POSITION
1. Broad economic assumptions	1. Statement of mission
2. Key governmental/regulatory threats	2. Interrelated set of financial and non-financial objectives
3. Major technological forces	3. Statements of strengths and weaknesses
4. Significant marketing opportunities/threats	4. Forecast of operations—profits and cash flow
5. Explicit competitive strategies for each major competitor	5. Major future programs

Strategic options

Alternative strategies (at least two)
Requirements for implementing each strategy
Contingency plans

MAKE DECISIONS—NOT PLANS

As mentioned earlier, the most fundamental weakness of most corporate plans today is that they do not lead to the major decisions that must be made currently to ensure the success of the enterprise in the future. All too often, the end product of present-day strategic planning activities is a strategic plan—period. Nothing really new happens as a result of the plan, except that everyone gets a warm glow of security and satisfaction now that the uncertainty of the future has been contained. Unfortunately, warm feelings do not produce earnings or capture market share. Neither do graphs of five-year earnings projections, gap charts, or complex strategy statements.

What does produce earnings are strategic decisions, and strategic decisions should be the ultimate output of a strategic planning program. That is, the strategic plan should clearly set forth the critical issues currently facing a company or division in terms of alternative courses of current action. If there are more than five or six issues, they are probably the wrong ones. If the decisions do not involve major risks or investments and/or changes in competitive posture, they are the wrong decisions. If the decisions do not have to be made now, they are wrong.

This is the creative leap that too many managements fail to make in strategic planning. They fail to ask, "What do we do now as a result of this plan?" They fail to recognize that the end product of strategic analysis should not be plans but current decisions. Some of the reasons why the leap to decisions is not made are important to understand.

It Is Risky Probably the most significant reason is that stating plans in terms of decisions frequently requires an executive to take a personal stand on an important and controversial issue. In other words, it can often make or break his career. All of us can call to mind men who have staked their careers and reputations on major strategic recommendations, for example, Learson leading IBM into digital computers, and Donaldson opening DLJ to public capital.

But most of us can also call to mind a few corporate casualties of such decisions—men who took a strong position as an adversary on a major strategic move and found themselves on the losing side. So the leap to decisions takes courage, and most executives prefer to play it safe. We can look at the top management teams of too many companies without finding any risk-taking, success-story managers.

It Is Difficult Strategic planning, almost by definition, deals with the most complex questions facing a company. Just assembling the data to measure the variables is a considerable task. Moreover, once the data are in hand, the real job begins—the job of synthesizing critical issues and strategic options to resolve those issues. This is fundamentally a creative process. It cannot be programmed or systematized. To structure meaningful, practical action programs requires insight, wisdom, and perspective. Many executives find it an elusive, uncomfortable task.

It Requires Leadership   Most strategic decisions are controversial. The underlying issue being addressed is rarely new to the corporate executive team; typically, it has been debated within the company for some time. I use the word "debate" advisedly; these discussions tend to be problem-definition, opinion-swapping sessions. Because the issues they address have vital implications for individual careers, they soon become less than objective, and they almost never lead to action. In some companies propositions such as "We ought to liquidate that business" can bounce about in the executive committee for months or even years without any decisions being made. The missing ingredient is the leadership needed to push through tough-minded analysis and action on controversial matters.

I know of one company that has been facing a rather critical strategic problem for fully a year now—namely, survival. The underlying strategic issues were correctly identified and thoroughly analyzed over three years ago. A detailed action program was outlined. It is still valid, still ready for implementation, yet the company is headed for bankruptcy. The reason is simple: the CEO simply cannot bring himself to make some tough decisions. He is waiting and hoping that his key lieutenants will reach a consensus. Given the nature of the decisions, this is impossible. In a situation of this kind only the CEO can exert the needed leadership, and this CEO is not the man to do it.

The Value System Works against It   Too often a company's executive motivation system flies in the face of strategic decision making. This occurs for two reasons. First, good managers tend to be promoted so fast that they never have to live with the medium- to long-run outcome of their plans. Second, incentive compensation is often tied either to short-term earnings performance or to stock-price movements, neither of which has anything to do with strategic success.

DOWN TO THE "BOTTOM LINE"

As we have seen, the leap from plans to decisions is an entrepreneurial step that cannot be reduced to a routine. Making it happen is an educational, attitudinal task, but some concrete steps can be taken to facilitate the process.

Meet External Risks

To begin with, the formal strategic planning program should be thoroughly reviewed to ensure that it requires a decision-oriented approach. Many planning systems simply are not designed to demand decisions as the end product. Instead, they produce forecasts of financial results or statements of objectives, or future action steps. This type of planning, which is basically "momentum" planning as opposed to dynamic planning that is attuned to the realities of external change, often results from excessive internal focus in the planning process. To overcome this problem, heavy emphasis should be given to three critical aspects of strategic analysis that are particularly important in identifying key issues and decisions: evaluating competitive strategies, developing contingency plans, and assessing environmental forces.

Evaluating Competitive Strategies Too many corporate plans fail to give even minimal attention to the present and future action of competitive firms. They set out elaborate strategies without any real consideration of competitive reaction. Two examples of a simple analysis that can be extremely helpful in overcoming this weakness are shown in Figure 3 (note that 3B calls for a review of each major competitor's existing strategy). Figure 4 then attempts to evaluate the strength of the company's own strategy against that of each competitor. In most cases, analysis of this kind leads to the identification of opportunities or threats that call for current management decisions.

Contingency Plans Most companies with active planning programs recognize the value of asking "what if" questions, taking important contingencies into account. Yet few really address this issue in a substantive way. A frequent excuse is that there are so many potential contingencies that it would take years to analyze them all.

The obvious answer to this objection is that one can and should be very selective, and deal only with the one or two possible contingencies that could upset the entire strategy. Here are two examples:

An American packaging company selling a commodity product regularly reviews potential price changes by one of its smaller competitors. This competitor dropped prices sharply several years ago, catching the market leaders by surprise and increasing its own market share significantly.

Last year, in speculating on the major contingencies they might face, the management of the packaging company asked, in effect, "What if they should do it again?" In view of the capacity situation in the industry, it was not an unrealistic question. Accordingly, the company meticulously planned a contingency program to be put into effect if and when its small competitor should move again. Early this year he did. The packaging company was ready and responded immediately and effectively.

An electronic components company depended on a single large customer for 30 percent of its sales. Management simply asked, "What if they should integrate backward?" There was no visible reason to believe that such a move was in the offing, and the question would probably not have surfaced as a serious issue without the forcing device of required contingency planning. But development of the contingency plan led to two real benefits. *First,* it brought out the need for some preventive medicine, and this became a continuing part of the company's relationship with its big customer. *Second,* it led to a detailed economic analysis of the risks and disadvantages to the customer of backward integration. One year later that analysis was instrumental in convincing the customer that a tentative step he had been about to take toward integration would be unwise.

Assessing Environmental Forces We can all think of companies that have failed to anticipate important changes in their external environments. The U.S. automobile industry, with all its vast managerial and financial resources, was simply unprepared for the explosive issues of automotive safety and air pollutants. And during the late 1960s, stockbrokers on Wall Street almost drowned

FIGURE 3   Analysis for Overcoming Competitive Action. A. Example of strategic issues and decisions. B. Assumed strategies of key competitors

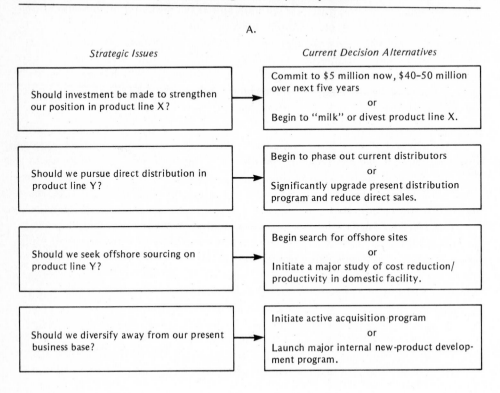

A.

Strategic Issues

| Should investment be made to strengthen our position in product line X? |

→

| Commit to $5 million now, $40–50 million over next five years
or
Begin to "milk" or divest product line X. |

| Should we pursue direct distribution in product line Y? |

→

| Begin to phase out current distributors
or
Significantly upgrade present distribution program and reduce direct sales. |

| Should we seek offshore sourcing on product line Y? |

→

| Begin search for offshore sites
or
Initiate a major study of cost reduction/productivity in domestic facility. |

| Should we diversify away from our present business base? |

→

| Initiate active acquisition program
or
Launch major internal new-product development program. |

Current Decision Alternatives

B.

	Competitors		
	A	B	C
Product line			
Systems primarily		X	
Components primarily	X		
Systems and components			X
Markets			
Domestic	X		
Worldwide		X	X
Domestic with foreign licenses			
Technology			
Leader	X		X
Follower		X	
Customers			
Government		X	X
OEM	X		X
Direct		X	X
Profit economics			
Mass production/high volume			X
Specialized, high price	X	X	

FIGURE 4   Assessing Corporate Plans against Each Competitor's Strategy

	KEY ELEMENTS OF OUR STRATEGIC PROGRAM			
COMPETITOR A's BASIC STRATEGY	BUILD CONTINENTAL PRODUCTION CAPACITY	EXPAND CONTINENTAL SALES FORCE	"UNBUNDLE" SYSTEM PRICING	CONCENTRATE R&D ON APPLICATIONS
Component supplier	Effective	Neutral	Effective	Neutral
Domestic only	Neutral	Strong	Neutral	Neutral
OEM market	Neutral	Neutral	Effective	Effective
Leader in technology	Neutral	Neutral	Neutral	Weak
Specialized/high price	Weak	Neutral	Effective	Weak

in their own success because they had failed to anticipate the volume growth of the industry and its attendant "back-office" requirements.

Despite the difficulties of forecasting sociopolitical or even marketplace trends, the most aggressive companies are energetically taking steps to raise their present level of competence in this arena. These are some of the approaches they have found productive:

Drawing on the work of the so-called futurologists, who seek to identify major developments emerging in the world. Their work is rarely directly applicable to a given industrial situation, but it can serve as a starting point for rigorous internal assessment of issues highly relevant to the corporation's future.

Building on broad economic forecasts. Here again it will be necessary to translate general trends into specific issues, but this simply requires thoughtful attention by corporate management and their advisers. A number of large companies annually prepare a general economic forecast to be used by all their operating units. These forecasts cover such subjects as government spending programs, expected major shifts in international trade and monetary policies, and potential new regulatory programs in ecology, safety, hiring, and so on.

Simply requiring a written assessment of critical environmental trends in every strategic planning document.

The assessment of environmental forces is not easy; nevertheless, the major issues (and therefore the strategic decisions) facing many institutions today are arising more and more in the external sociopolitical milieu. Merely being able to anticipate the issues (even if the "right" response is not clear) is a lot better than being caught completely unaware.

Provide Effective "Top-Down" Leadership

Since the purpose of strategic planning is to make basic decisions on the future course of the company, it is ultimately a responsibility of the CEO and his key lieutenants. In other words, top management cannot confine itself to perusing written plans and giving a perfunctory once-a-year approval. That would be abdication, not responsible delegation. To ensure that the right set of critical issues and decisions is in fact identified, top management must actively involve itself in the planning process. Even before the process of issue identification begins, the CEO should satisfy himself that the company's financial targets are properly integrated.

Most companies today include some statement of financial objectives in their corporate plans. Surprisingly often, however, these objectives fail to take into account the inherent interrelationships among most financial targets. Sales, earnings, and return-on-investment targets, which are of course inextricably interlinked, often are set apart from each other in the manner of a diner ordering a meal at a Chinese restaurant: one from group A, two from group B. Since the objectives chosen are inherently inconsistent and thus worthless if not actually debilitating, the result is frequently a case of strategic indigestion.

More important, too many companies fail to recognize the potential advantages of making trade-offs among various financial objectives. As Figure 5 shows, a company can choose widely different sets of financial and operating objectives and still achieve an identical overall earnings-per-share target. Each set of objectives implies a fundamentally different way of operating the company, and each set is internally consistent.

Again, top management can vitally enhance the effectiveness of the whole strategic planning process by instituting a regular and rigorous process of *strategic review*. Most companies today accept without question the fact that operational planning is inseparable from operating control, that one without the other is meaningless. But too often they ignore the logical corollary in the strategic planning area and omit the vital follow-up linkage between planning and control. To be sure, top management conscientiously reads the strategic plans and sits through strategic planning presentations, but it rarely challenges the validity of the plans or their relevance to current decisions. This situation is dangerous, because a division manager cannot be both advocate and challenger of his strategic plan.

Strategic review should not be a mechanistic process. One of the most successful approaches I have seen is to get a few key members of the top management team out of the office for two or three days of informal but intensive review of the strategic options as set forth in the plan. Superb leadership by the

FIGURE 5   Three Strategies to Achieve 15 Percent EPS

HIGH VOLUME APPROACH		HIGH ASSET UTILIZATION APPROACH		AGGRESSIVE FINANCING APPROACH	
Sales growth	15.0%	Sales growth	7.0%	Sales growth	10.0%
PBIT/sales	4.0	PBIT/sales	4.0	PBIT/sales	4.0
Asset turnover	3.5	Asset turnover	4.0	Asset turnover	3.5
Dividend payout	60.0	Dividend payout	60.0	Dividend payout	40.0
Debt/equity	50.0	Debt/equity	50.0	Debt/equity	60.0

FIGURE 6—Testing Key Strategy Assumptions

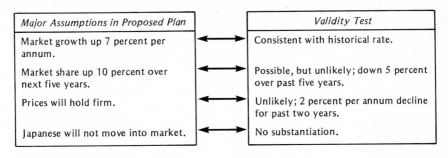

Major Assumptions in Proposed Plan	Validity Test
Market growth up 7 percent per annum.	Consistent with historical rate.
Market share up 10 percent over next five years.	Possible, but unlikely; down 5 percent over past five years.
Prices will hold firm.	Unlikely; 2 percent per annum decline for past two years.
Japanese will not move into market.	No substantiation.

Net assessment:
1. Plan is unrealistically optimistic.
2. Highly unlikely that market share can be increased without substantial price reduction.
3. Competitive threat from Japanese not adequately dealt with.

CEO is required to keep the discussion centered on the critical problems and opportunities, keep it on an objective plane so that no one feels threatened, and come out with a set of actionable decisions as the end product. Given such leadership and adequate advance preparation by the participants, valuable results can be achieved.

Strategy review, of course, is not entirely a free-form creative process; it can be supported by an analytical framework. For example, one CEO has his staff subject the plans submitted by division managers to a set of validity tests designed to identify and evaluate the key assumptions underlying performance forecast in the plan (Figure 6). This top-down testing process ensures that issues and decisions that the division managers have failed to identify will be brought to the surface for top management consideration.

Provide Guidelines for Capital Deployment

As a company diversifies its activities, the task of capital allocation tends to emerge as the central function of the corporate CEO—the heart of strategic decision making in a multibusiness enterprise. Resource allocation or portfolio decisions arise because of the need to maximize overall results by managing a collection of relatively independent operating units or product lines as a single portfolio. This means setting earnings targets and making investment decisions for any one division (or product line) within a framework that encompasses the whole enterprise. Of course, it can be argued that portfolio management is not a required function in a multibusiness company, since the pieces can simply be allowed to operate independently. But by that reasoning, a corporate management team is equally unnecessary, since if all the parts operate independently, there is no "value added" at the corporate or holding company level.

Too often, companies actually undermine their strategic planning programs by approaching major capital deployment decisions purely on a traditional capital budgeting basis. That is, in principle all requests for capital funds are filled no matter what division or product line they come from, provided only that they clear a single financial hurdle such as a pay-back or discounted cash-flow rate of return. Of course, when the requests exceed the available resources, some ranking system is employed, but, in effect, the hurdle is simply raised and a new single-number decision rule is applied uniformly to all requests.

This approach fails to provide any portfolio assessment of the various parts of the enterprise considered as a group. Therefore, capital can flow to a mediocre division or product line at a rate that is the same as—or even faster than—the rate at which it flows to a high-potential division. This simply perpetuates the status quo, frequently negating the value of the strategic planning at the corporate level. In other words, the CEO's all-important decision of allocating capital is blurred and in fact abdicated.

One simple but powerful approach some multibusiness managers are using today is to sort their individual businesses into three broad portfolio categories: sources of growth (future earnings); sources of current and intermediate earnings; and sources of immediate cash flow. One of my colleagues has suggested that these categories relate directly to the so-called product life-cycle curve which can also, for these purposes, be termed a business life-cycle curve. When a company views its operations in this manner, some interesting implications for the capital allocation process may emerge.

Of course, change in capital allocation decisions is only one of the many management implications of multibusiness strategic planning. The impact of this broad perspective can and should carry over to every facet of management responsibility. For example, Figure 7 illustrates its impact on marketing planning and, more important, on decisions relating to the marketing mix.

The need for such top-down guidelines is perhaps most vividly apparent in the "pruning" or divesting activities of a multibusiness company, aimed at milking declining divisions or products for cash, which will then be redeployed in more attractive opportunities. (It is hoped that opportunities exist for redeployment, but this kind of analysis can bring to light imbalances at either end of this spectrum.)

While such a deinvestment program often makes eminent sense from a corporate point of view, it is a rare division or product manager who willingly plans himself out of business. Most managers will argue that the new growth is just around the corner; all they need to get the payoff is a little more investment "up front." For this reason, strategic planning efforts rarely bring deinvestment-redeployment decisions to the surface, unless the CEO has provided explicit guidelines. He must find ways to create an environment in which different planning criteria and different performance criteria are not only acceptable but demanded.

This brings us to the human relations dimension of strategic planning, and the final action step needed to make it effective.

Target Responsibility and Reward Results

No strategic planning program will produce bottom-line results without careful attention to human motivations. This is a highly subjective matter, tied inex-

FIGURE 7 Impact of Multibusiness Strategic Planning on Marketing

MARKETING DECISION AREA	STRATEGY ADOPTED FOR DIVISION OR PRODUCT LINE		
	INVEST FOR FUTURE GROWTH	MANAGE FOR EARNINGS	MANAGE FOR IMMEDIATE CASH
Market share	Aggressively build across all segments.	Target efforts to high-return/high-growth segments. Protect current franchises.	Forego share development for improved profits.
Pricing	Lower to build share.	Stabilize for maximum profit contribution.	Raise, even at expense of volume.
Promotion	Invest heavily to build share.	Invest as market dictates.	Avoid.
Existing product line	Expand volume. Add line extensions to fill out product categories.	Shift mix to higher profit product categories.	Eliminate low-contribution products/varieties.
New products	Expand product line by acquisition, self-manufacture, or joint venture.	Add products selectively and in controlled stages of commitment.	Add only sure winners.

tricably to the leadership style of the CEO, but two general recommendations apply almost universally.

First, involve the decision makers. In a decision-oriented planning environment, developing and implementing strategies can only be the responsibility of line managers. This does not mean that the CEO should do away with his planning staff and planning processes. Rather, it means that the output of such staffs and processes should only be an input to top management. It is top management's responsibility to weigh strategic issues, apply judgment, and make the decisions. Strategic planning may be a staff function, but strategic decision making is the responsibility of the CEO and his top management team. Several companies have underscored this point by requiring division managers to present and defend their strategies and plans in the absence of their staff planners. It seems to work.

Second, reward good strategic decision makers. If all promotions, bonuses, and other rewards go to the executives who meet or exceed short-term budget goals, without regard to the way they position their organizations for future success, then strategies and strategic plans will be no more than a charade. I am not suggesting that short-term performance measures should be eliminated; rather, I am saying that long-term performance milestones must be added and built into the annual performance review, particularly in companies where the best line managers get promoted every eighteen to twenty-four months.

An example of the sort of multidimensional performance appraisal system I

FIGURE 8 Performance Appraisal: Balancing Current and Future Needs

DIVISION MANAGER	CURRENT PERFORMANCE (0–100)			SUCCESS IN IMPLEMENTING LONG-TERM PROGRAM	FUTURE BUILDING PERFORMANCE (0–100)			OVERALL RATING
	PROFITS AS PERCENT OF BUDGET	ROI VERSUS BUDGET	WEIGHTING FACTOR		QUALITY OF STRATEGY	QUALITY OF MANPOWER	WEIGHTING FACTOR	
A	100	100	1	20	20	50	3	310
B	80	100	3	100	80	80	1	530
C	120	90	2	100	90	90	2	585
D	70	70	1	75	80	100	3	475

have in mind is shown in Figure 8. The weighting factors shown are purely illustrative. They should be tailored for each individual operating unit to reflect the importance of short- versus long-term performance. To return to our earlier example, "building" criteria ought to be weighted more heavily in "future growth" units, while short-term goals should have most of the emphasis in "cash" units.

Following the widespread introduction of data processing in the 1950s, many companies sooner or later were obliged to recognize that the promise of this great management tool was stubbornly refusing to materialize. Real, tangible return on investment was low or nonexistent. Today, a great many companies have largely overcome this problem. Not without a struggle, they have substantially brought their computer systems under control, and most of these managements are a good deal wiser for the experience. The most successful among them, I believe, would include at least the following among the lessons they have learned:

- The effort must be integrated directly into the important decision-making activities of the company. Each potential new project must pass the "so what" test.
- The chief executive holds the key to success; his commitment and leadership are absolutely necessary.
- The payoff when it works is substantial, and it can be measured in dollars and cents.

All of these lessons apply to strategic planning. When it is focused on current decisions, under the leadership of a committed CEO, it works. And when it works, we may be sure that the payoff will show on the bottom line.

Making Strategic Planning Work

Harold Koontz

It is widely agreed that the development and communication of strategy is the most important single activity of top managers. Joel Ross and Michael Kami, in their insightful book on the lack of success of many large U.S. companies, said, "Without a strategy the organization is like a ship without a rudder, going around in circles. It's like a tramp; it has no place to go." [1] They conclude from their study that without an appropriate strategy effectively implemented, failure is only a matter of time.

Although strategies are important, their development and implementation have posed many problems. The term *strategy* is often valueless and meaningless, even though it may be mouthed constantly by academics and executives. As one prominent consultant declared with respect to strategic planning, "In the large majority of companies, corporate planning tends to be an academic, ill-defined activity with little or no bottom-line impact." [2]

Many corporate chief executive officers have brushed strategic planning aside with such statements as: "Strategic planning is basically just a plaything of staff men," or "Strategic planning? A staggering waste of time." [3] A number of companies and even some government agencies that have tried strategic planning have been observed wallowing around in generalities, unproductive studies and programs that do not get into practical operation. In one large company, a far too patient president watched a succession of top planning officers and their staffs flounder for twelve years, until his patience was finally exhausted and he insisted on practical action.

The basic cause of disillusionment with strategic planning is the lack of

About the Author: Harold Koontz is Mead Johnson professor of management at the University of California, Los Angeles, and chancellor of the International Academy of Management.

Reprinted from *Business Horizons*, vol. 19 (April, 1976), pp. 37–47. Copyright, 1976, by the Foundation for the School of Business at Indiana University. Reprinted by permission. This article is adapted from a speech presented at the November, 1975 meeting of the International Academy of Management.

[1] Joel E. Ross and Michael J. Kami, *Corporations in Crisis: Why the Mighty Fall* (Englewood Cliffs, N.J.: Prentice-Hall, Inc., 1973), p. 132.

[2] Louis V. Gerstner, "Can Strategic Planning Pay Off?" *Business Horizons* (December 1972), pp. 5–16.

[3] *Ibid.*, p. 5.

knowledge in four areas: (1) what strategies are and why they are important; (2) how strategies fit into the entire planning process; (3) how to develop strategies; and (4) how to implement strategies by bringing them to bear on current decisions.

WHAT STRATEGIES ARE

Strategies are general programs of action with an implied commitment of emphasis and resources to achieve a basic mission. They are patterns of major objectives, and major policies for achieving these objectives, conceived and stated in such a way as to give the organization a unified direction.

For years, strategies were used by the military to mean grand plans made in view of what it was believed an adversary might or might not do. Tactics were regarded as action plans necessary to implement strategies. While the term *strategy* still has a competitive implication, it is increasingly used to denote a general program that indicates a direction to be taken and where emphasis is to be placed. Strategies do not attempt to outline exactly how the enterprise is to accomplish its major objectives; this is the task of a multitude of major and minor supporting programs.

Failure of strategic planning is really one aspect of the difficulties encountered in making all kinds of planning effective. Although the sophistication with which planning is done has risen remarkably in the past three decades, and despite the fact that planning is considered the foundation of management, it is still too often the most poorly performed task of the managerial job. As every executive knows, it is easy to fail in all aspects of effective planning without really trying.

WHY PLANNING FAILS

What are some of the major reasons why effective planning is so difficult to accomplish? By summarizing some of the principal reasons in practice in both business and nonbusiness enterprises, some light may be cast on the reasons for disillusionment and ineffectiveness in many strategic planning programs.

One of the major reasons for failure is managers' lack of commitment to planning. Most people allow today's problems and crises to push aside planning for tomorrow. Instead of planning, most would rather "fight fires" and meet crises, for the simple reason that doing so is more interesting, more fun, and gives a greater feeling of accomplishment. This means, of course, that an environment must be created that forces people to plan.

Another cause of failure is confusing planning studies with plans. Many are the companies and government agencies that have stacks of planning studies. But for a planning study to become a plan, a decision must be made that will commit resources or direction; until then it is only a study.

Problems also arise when major decisions on various matters are made without having a clear strategy, or without making sure that decisions, such as one to develop and market a new product, fit a company's strategy.

Another reason for failure is the lack of clear, actionable, attainable and verifiable objectives or goals. It is impossible to do any effective planning without knowing precisely what end results are sought. Objectives must be verifiable in the sense that, at some target date in the future, a person can know whether they have been accomplished. This can, of course, be done best in quantitative terms, such as dollars of sales or profits. But since many worthwhile objectives cannot be put in numbers, goals can also be verified in qualitative terms, such as a marketing program with specified characteristics to be launched by a certain date.

Perhaps the most important cause of failure in planning is neglecting or underestimating the importance of planning premises or assumptions. These are the expected environment of a decision, the stage on which a certain program will be played. They not only include economic and market forecasts, but also the expectation of important changes in the technological, political, social or ethical environment. They may also include decisions or commitments made, basic policies, and major limitations. One thing is sure: unless people know and follow consistent planning premises, their planning decisions will not be coordinated.

Another problem area is the failure to place strategies within the total scope of plans. Anything that involves selecting a course of action for the future may be thought of as a plan. These include missions or purposes, objectives, strategies, policies, rules, procedures, programs and budgets. Unless strategies are seen as one of the major types of plans, it is easy to regard them as isolated directional decisions unrelated to other kinds of plans.

Ineffective planning may also be the result of failure to develop clear policies. Policies are guides to thinking in decision making. Their essence is defined discretion. They give structure and direction to decisions, mark out an area where discretion can be used, and thereby give guidelines for plans. Without clear policies, plans tend to be random and inconsistent.

Planning often suffers, too, from not keeping in mind the time span which should be involved. Long-range planning is not planning for future decisions, but planning the future impact of present decisions. In other words, planning is planning. Some plans involve commitments that can be fulfilled in short periods, such as a production plan, and others can only be discharged over longer periods, as in the case of a new product development or capital facilities program. Obviously, unless a decision maker does not try to foresee, as best as can be done, the fulfillment of commitments involved in today's decisions, he is not doing the job that good planning requires.

Another danger of planning lies in the tendency of people, especially those with considerable experience, to base their decisions on that experience—on what did or did not work in the past. Since decisions must operate for the future, they should be based on *expectations* for the future, not on experience and facts of the past.

Finally, a major cause of deficient planning is the inability of some people to diagnose a situation in the light of critical or limiting factors. In every problem (opportunity) situation, there are many variables that may affect the outcome of a course of action. But in every problem area there are certain variables that make the most difference. Thus, in a new product development program, the critical factors may be whether a proposed product will fit a company's marketing channels and competence, or whether its efficient production might require capital facilities beyond a company's financial ability. Clearly, the adept decision maker will search for, identify and solve critical factors.

MAJOR TYPES OF STRATEGIES

For a business enterprise at least, the major strategies which give it an overall direction are likely to be in the following seven areas.

1. *New or Changed Products and Services.* A business exists to furnish products or services of an economic nature. In a very real sense, profits are merely a measure—albeit an important one—of how well a company serves its customers.
2. *Marketing.* Marketing strategies are designed to guide planning in getting products or services to reach customers, and getting customers to buy.
3. *Growth.* Growth strategies give direction to such questions as: How much growth and how fast? Where?
4. *Financial.* Every business, and for that matter every nonbusiness, enterprise must have a clear strategy for financing its operations. There are various ways of doing this and usually many serious limitations.
5. *Organizational.* This kind of strategy has to do with the type of organizational pattern an enterprise will follow. It answers such practical questions as how centralized or decentralized decision-making authority should be, what kind of departmental patterns are most suitable, whether to develop integrated profit-responsible divisions, what kind of matrix organization structures are used, and how to design and utilize staffs effectively. Naturally, organization structures furnish the system of roles and role relationships to help people perform in the accomplishment of objectives.
6. *Personnel.* Major strategies in the area of human resources and relationships may be of a wide variety. They deal with union relations, compensation, selection, recruitment, training and appraisal, as well as strategy in such matters as job enrichment.
7. *Public Relations.* Strategies in this area can hardly be independent but must support other major strategies and efforts. They must also be designed in the light of the company's type of business, its closeness to the public, its susceptibility to regulation by government agencies and similar factors.

STRATEGY REQUISITES

For developing major strategies of any kind, there are a number of key requirements. If a company fails to meet them, its strategic planning program is likely to be meaningless or even incorrect.

Corporate Self-Appraisal

This requirement involves asking the questions: What is our business? What kind of business are we in? These simple questions, as many businesses have discovered, are not always easy to answer. The classic case is the railroad industry that too long overlooked the fact that its companies were in the transportation business, and not just the railroad business. Glass bottle manufacturers in the United States almost missed their opportunities by seeing themselves for too long as glass bottle makers rather than liquid container manufacturers, as plastic and metal containers came to be used in many applications in place of glass. Likewise, many believe that the steel companies over the world have stayed too long with the belief that they are steel makers, rather than in the structural materials business, which includes many materials not made of steel.

On answering these questions, a company should be regarded as a total entity, its strengths and weaknesses analyzed in each functional area: marketing, product development, production and other operations areas, finance and public relations. It must focus attention on its customers and what they want and can buy, its technological capabilities and financial resources. In addition, note must be made of the values, aspirations and prejudices of top executives.

In assessing strengths, weaknesses and limitations, an enterprise must, of course, be realistic. In doing so, however, there is a danger in overstressing weaknesses and underestimating strengths. History is replete with examples of companies that have spent so much effort in shoring up weaknesses that they did not capitalize on their strengths. To be sure, weaknesses should be corrected to the extent possible. But taking advantage of identified strengths in formulating strategies offers the most promise.

Assessing the Future Environment

Strategies, like any other type of plan, are intended to operate in the future; thus, the best possible estimate of the future environment in which a company is to operate is necessary. If a company can match its strengths with the environment in which it plans to operate, opportunities can be detected and taken advantage of.

A prerequisite of the assessment of the future environment is forecasting. In general, modern businesses do a fairly good job of forecasting economic developments and markets, although, of course, there can be many errors and uncertainties. Few would have forecast the price impact of the oil-producing nation's cartel and the extent of inflation in recent years. A few companies have found rewarding results in forecasting technological changes and predicting technological developments. Some companies in highly regulated industries have even forecast political environments, particularly governmental actions that would affect their company. But only recently have companies, research institutes and government agencies even started the task of attempting to forecast social attitudes and pressures.

Clearly, the better an enterprise can see its total environment, the better it can establish strategies and support plans to take advantage of its capabilities in preparation for the future. However, experience to date indicates that, except for economic and market forecasts, it is difficult to get the forecast and assessment of other environmental factors into practical use. This can be done through an active and effective program that would use planning premises as the background for decision making, but this is one of the areas of planning that has especially not been performed well.

An important element of the future environment, of course, is the probable actions of competition. Too often, planning is based on what competition has been doing and not on what competitors may be expected to do. No one can plan on the assumption that his competitors are asleep.

Organization Structure Assuring Planning

If strategies are to be developed and implemented, an organizational structure which assures effective planning is needed. Staff assistance is important for forecasting, establishing premises and making analyses. But there is the danger of establishing a planning staff and thinking planning exists when only planning studies exist, rather than decisions based on them.

To avoid ivory-towered and useless staff efforts, several things are needed. A planning staff should be given the tasks of developing major objectives, strategies and planning premises, and submitting them to top management for review and approval. They should also be responsible for disseminating approved premises and strategies, and they should help operating people to understand them. Before major decisions of a long-range or strategic impact are made, the staff group should be given the task of reviewing them and making recommendations. These few tasks can be advantageous in that they force decision makers to consider environmental factors, and also prevent the staff from becoming a detached and impractical group.

Another major organizational device is the regular, formal and rigorous review of planning programs and performance, preferably by an appropriate committee. This has long been done in well-managed divisionalized companies where division general managers are called in before a top executive committee. Perhaps it should be done at lower levels, too. Doing so has the advantage of forcing people to plan, of making sure that strategies are being followed by programs, and where strategies do not exist or are unclear, making this deficiency apparent.

Assuring Consistent Strategies

One of the important requirements of effective strategic planning is to make sure that strategies are consistent, that they "fit" each other. For example, one medium-sized company had a successful sales record as the result of a strategy of putting out quality products at lower prices than its larger competitors, which did their selling through heavy and expensive advertising. Pleased with this success, and after adding to its product line through acquisitions, the company then embarked on an additional strategy of trying to sell through heavy advertising, with disastrous effects on profits.

The Need for Contingency Strategies

Because every strategy must operate in the future, and because the future is always subject to uncertainty, the need for contingency strategies cannot be overlooked. If a regulated telephone company, for example, has had some of its services opened to competition (as has happened recently in the United States when other companies were allowed to furnish facilities that were once the monopoly of the telephone companies), and adopts a strategy of aggressive competition on the assumption that regulatory commissions will allow competitive pricing, the strategy would become inoperative if the commissions do not actually allow such pricing. Or if a company develops a strategy based on a certain state of technology, and a new discovery changes materially the technological environment, it is faced with a major need for a contingency strategy.

Where events occur which make a strategy obsolete (and they often can without warning), it is wise to have developed a contingent strategy based on a different set of premises. These "what if" kinds of strategies can be put into effect quickly to avoid much of the "crisis management" that is seen so often.

PRODUCTS OR SERVICES STRATEGIES

To develop strategies in any area, certain questions must be asked in each major strategy area. Given the right questions, the answers should help any company to formulate its strategies. Some key questions in two strategic areas will be examined: new products and services, and marketing. A little thought can result in devising key questions for other major strategic areas.

One of the most important areas is strategy involving new products or services, since these, more than any other single factor, will determine what a company is or will be. The key questions in this area may be summarized as follows.

• *What Is Our Business?* This classic question might also be phrased in terms of what is *not* our business. It is also necessary to raise the question: What is our industry? Are we a single product or product-line industry, such as shoes or furniture? Or are we a process industry, such as chemicals or electronic components? Or are we an end-use industry, such as transportation or retailing?

• *Who Are Our Customers?* Peter Drucker has long said that the purpose of a business is to "create a customer," although he could hardly have meant to create customers without regard to profits. In answering this question, it is important to avoid too great an attachment to *present* customers and products. The motion picture industry failed to avoid this when home television first appeared on the market and was considered a threat to movie theaters. They fought television for years until they realized that their business was entertainment and their customers wanted both motion pictures in theaters and on television. They then found one of their most lucrative markets in renting old movies to television and in using their studios and other facilities for producing television shows.

• *What Do Our Customers Want?* Do they want price, value, quality, availability, service? The success of the Hughes Tool Company, for example, has been based largely on a shrewd analysis of what oil and gas well drillers wanted, and furnishing them with the exact drill bit, of a high quality, in the place the bit was needed, and with adequate service to support the product. Likewise, IBM's leadership in business computers has been due in large part to its knowledge of what customers wanted and needed; maintaining advancement of product design; having a family of computers; and developing a strong service organization.

• *How Much Will Our Customers Buy and at What Price?* This is a matter that involves what customers think they are buying. What they consider value and what they will pay for it will determine what a business is, what it should produce, and whether it will prosper. The answer to this question will be a key to product or service strategy.

• *Do We Wish to Be a Product Leader?* It may seem that the answer to this question would be obvious, but it is not. Some companies owe their success to being a close second in product leadership. The product leader will often have an advantage in reaching a market first, but such a company may incur heavy costs of developing and attempting to market products which do not become commercial successes, as well as those which do. One of the major airlines, for example, prided itself on being the leader in acquiring and putting into service new aircraft. But after suffering financial losses as a result of their extensive debugging of several new planes, they adopted the strategy of letting someone else be the leader, and becoming a close second.

• *Do We Wish to Develop Our Own New Products?* Here again, a company must decide whether it should develop its own new products, whether it should rely on innovations by competitors to lead the way, or whether it should lean heavily on product development by materials suppliers. In the chemicals field, such innovative raw materials producers as duPont and Dow Chemical discover new chemical compositions and then cast about to ascertain where they can be used in new products. Companies without adequate resources to mount a strong product research program can often find a gold mine of product ideas in the developments of such suppliers.

• *What Advantages Do We Have in Serving Customer Needs?* Most companies like to have a unique product or service that is difficult for a competitor to duplicate. Some larger companies look only for products that require a high

capital investment in tooling and machinery, heavy advertising, strong engineering, expensive service organizations, and similar characteristics that tend to discourage the entry of smaller competitors into a market. Many larger companies
also purposefully keep out of products with small-volume markets—products
that can be manufactured and marketed by small companies—feeling that the
smaller operator can offer a personalized service and incur lower overhead costs
than the larger company.

• *What of Existing and Potential Competition?* In deciding on a product
strategy, it is important to assess realistically the nature and strength of existing
competition. If a competitor in a field has tremendous strength in new products,
marketing and service, as IBM has had in the computer field, a company should
consider carefully its chances to enter the field. Even the large RCA Corporation
found it had to swallow a loss of some $450 million after attempting unsuccess-
fully to compete with IBM with a head-on strategy.

• *How Far Can We Go in Serving Customer Needs?* There are often important limitations. One is, of course, financial: a company must consider
whether it has the financial resources to support necessary product research,
manufacturing facilities, inventory and receivables, advertising and marketing,
and a requisite service competence.

Legal limitations may also be important, as Procter and Gamble found
when it was forced by the antitrust laws to divest itself of the Clorox Company
(household bleach), or as certain pharmaceutical companies have found when
their introduction of new products is held up by the Pure Food and Drug
Administration.

Other important limitations may be found in the availability of suitably competent managers and other personnel. Thus, Ford, a well-managed automobile
company, had difficulties in managing Philco. Litton Industries apparently found
that running its shipbuilding subsidiary was beyond its managerial abilities.

• *What Profit Margins Can We Expect?* A company naturally wants to be
in a business where it can make an attractive profit. One of the keys is the gross
profit margin, that profit above operating expenses which will carry overhead
and administrative expenses and yield a desired profit before taxes.

• *What Basic Form Should Our Strategy Take?* In formulating a product or
service strategy, a company should determine the direction it wishes to go in
terms of intensive or extensive product diversification. If it follows an intensive
strategy, it might move in the direction of market penetration—going further in
present product markets. Or it might decide on one of market development—
going into markets it has not been in before. Thus, Reynolds Aluminum years
ago expanded into such consumer products as aluminum kitchen wrappings.
Or a company might concentrate on developing, improving, or changing products it already has.

If a company follows an extensive product strategy, it can go in three basic
directions. First, it might concentrate on vertical integration. If it is a retailing
company, it might, as Sears Roebuck and Company has done so often, go into

making products it sells. Or if it is a manufacturing company, it might go into retailing, as Sinclair Paints has done. Second, a company might diversify extensively by link diversification, going into products utilizing existing skills, capacities and strengths. Lever Brothers has done this for many years by expanding their operations to a large number of products marketed through grocery stores. A third kind of extensive strategy is conglomerate diversification, going into not necessarily related products with the hope of getting synergistic advantages from combining such skills and strengths as marketing, new product development, management and financial resources. The difficulty with this strategy, as many conglomerates have found, is that too rapid and too varied a program of acquisition can lead to situations that cannot be managed effectively and profitably.

MARKETING STRATEGIES

Marketing strategies are closely connected to product strategies, and must be supportive and interrelated. As a matter of fact, Drucker regards the two basic business functions as innovation and marketing. It is true that a business can hardly survive without these. But while a company can succeed by copying products, it can hardly succeed without effective marketing.

In this area, as in products and services, there are certain questions which can be used as guides for establishing a marketing strategy.

• *Where Are Our Customers and Why Do They Buy?* This question is really asking whether customers are large or small buyers, whether they are end users or manufacturers, where they are geographically, where they are in the production-ultimate user spectrum, and why they buy. Xerox answered some of these questions cleverly and effectively when it saw customers not as copy machine buyers but rather as purchasers of low-cost copies. As a result of their leasing program and charging on a per copy basis, this company has had phenomenal success. Likewise, the Farr Company, one of the nation's most innovative and successful air filter companies, has effectively marketed its engine air filters for locomotives and trucks by the strategy of considering its real customers to be the buyers and users of such transport vehicles rather than the equipment manufacturers. Thus, by getting large railroads and trucking companies to specify Farr filters on new equipment, they in effect forced the use of their filters on equipment manufacturers.

• *How Do Customers Buy?* Some customers buy largely through specialized distributing organizations, as is the case with medical and hospital supplies. Some buy through dealer organizations, as with automobiles. Others are accustomed to buying directly from manufacturers, as in the case of major defense procurement, large equipment buyers and most raw material users in such fields as chemicals, electronic components and steel products; but even in these cases, specialized distributors and processors may be important for certain buyers and at certain times.

• *How Is It Best for Us to Sell?* There are a number of approaches to sell-ing. Some companies rely heavily on preselling through advertising and sales promotion. Procter and Gamble owes much of its success to a strategy of pre-selling customers through heavy advertising and sales promotion expenditures (said to average 20% of every sales dollar). At the same time, a much smaller company in the soap and detergents field, the Purex Corporation, had great suc-cess in selling its liquid and dry detergents through the appeal of lower con-sumer prices and higher margins for retailers. Other companies may find their best strategy is to sell on the basis of technical superiority and direct engineer-ing contacts with customers.

• *Do We Have Something to Offer That Competitors Do Not?* The purpose of product differentiation is, of course, to make buyers believe a company's products are different and better than similar products offered by competitors, whether in fact they are or not. It is often possible to build a marketing strategy on some feature in a product or service that is different, regardless of the sig-nificance of the difference. This may be an attractive innovation in product de-sign or quality, as in the case of Sylvania's push-button television sets. Or it might be an innovation in service, such as American Motors' all-inclusive auto-mobile warranty. Obviously, what every marketer wants is a claim of product or service uniqueness in order to obtain a proprietary position.

• *Do We Wish to Take Steps, Legally, to Discourage Competition?* There are many things a company can do to discourage competition, other than to run afoul of the antitrust or fair trade laws. Mere size and the ability to finance ex-pensive specialized machinery and tools, or a geographically spread sales and service organization, are among these. The success of the Hughes Tool Company in oil drilling bits and that of IBM in the computer field fall into this category. But even medium-sized companies can discourage the very small would-be com-petitors in the same way. Or a company's marketing strategy might be helped by innovative advertising and product image, which will entrench the company in a market and discourage competition.

• *Do We Need, and Can We Supply, Supporting Services?* A company's ef-fectiveness in marketing can be greatly influenced by the degree of need for supporting services such as maintenance, and the ability to supply them. Often, certain foreign-made automobiles were slow in getting a position in the Ameri-can market because of the lack of availability of dealer repair services. Mercedes Benz, for example, had difficulty in making much of a dent in the automobile market until it was able to establish service capabilities in at least the larger cities of the United States. Packard Bell enjoyed a strong position in television in the western states some years ago because of its strong service organization in this area, and for years, because of this, limited sales to that area. The major telephone companies, the Bell System and General Telephone, have recently developed a marketing strategy for their industrial and commercial switchboard systems against the rising competition of special equipment manufacturers by emphasizing their prompt and competent maintenance service capabilities.

• *What Is the Best Pricing Strategy and Policy for Our Operation?* There are many strategies that can be used. Suggested list prices, quantity and other discounts, delivered or F.O.B. seller's place of business prices, firm prices or prices with escalation, and the extent of down payments with orders or prices that vary with labor and material costs are among the wide number of variations. How goods or services are priced may be a matter of custom in a market, a marketing tool of a supplier, a matter of achieving price stability versus price cutting, or may reflect the understandable desire of a producer to guard against losses from uncertainty, as in the case of "time and material" contracts.

IMPLEMENTING STRATEGIES

Thus far, much of the emphasis has been on the development of clear and meaningful strategies. If strategic planning is to be operational, certain steps must be taken to implement it.

Strategies Should Be Communicated to All Key Decision-Making Managers. It naturally does little good to formulate meaningful strategies unless they are communicated to all managers in the position to make decisions on plans designed to implement them. Strategies may be clear to the executive committee and the chief executive who participate in making them, but nothing is communicated unless they are also clear to the receiver. Strategies should be in writing, and meetings of top executives and their subordinates should be held to make sure that strategies are understood by everyone involved.

Planning Premises Must Be Developed and Communicated. The importance of planning premises has been emphasized earlier. Steps must be taken so that those premises critical to plans and decisions are developed and disseminated to all managers in the decision-making chain, with instructions to generate programs and make decisions in line with them. Too few companies and other organizations do this. But if it is not done and if premises do not include key assumptions for the entire spectrum of the environment in which plans will operate, decisions are likely to be based on personal assumptions and predilections. The result is almost certain to be a collection of uncoordinated plans.

Action Plans Must Contribute to and Reflect Major Objectives and Strategies. Action plans are tactical or operational programs and decisions, whether major or minor, that take place in various parts of an organization. If they do not reflect desired objectives and strategies, vacuous hopes or useless statements of strategic intent result. If care is not taken in this area, then certainly strategic planning is not likely to have a bottom-line impact.

There are various ways of ensuring that action plans do contribute to strategies. If every manager understands strategies, he can certainly review the program recommendations of his staff advisers and his line subordinates to see that they contribute and are consistent. It might even be advisable, at least in major decisions, to have them reviewed by an appropriate small committee, such as one including a subordinate's superior, the superior's superior and a staff specialist. This would lend an aura of formality to the program decisions, and important influences on implementation of strategies might become clear. Budgets likewise should be reviewed with objectives and strategies in mind.

Strategies Should Be Reviewed Regularly.   Even carefully developed strategies might cease to be suitable if events change, knowledge becomes more clear, or it appears that the program environment will not be as originally thought. Strategies should be reviewed from time to time, certainly not less than once a year, and perhaps more often.

Consider Developing Contingency Strategies and Programs.   Where considerable change in competitive factors or other elements in the environment might occur and it is impractical to develop strategies that would cover the changes, contingency strategies should be formulated. No one, of course, can wait until the future is certain to make plans. Even where there is considerable uncertainty, there is no choice but to proceed on the most credible set of premises. But this does not mean that a company need find itself totally unprepared if certain possible contingencies do occur.

Make Organization Structure Fit Planning Needs.   The organization structure should be designed to support the accomplishment of goals and the making of decisions to implement strategies. If posssible, it is best to have one position (or person) responsible for the accomplishment of each goal and for implementing strategies in achieving this goal. In other words, end result areas and key tasks should be identified and assigned to a single position as far down the organization structure as is feasible. Since this sometimes cannot be done, there may be no alternative but to utilize a form of grid organization. Where this is done, the responsibilities of the various positions in the grid should be clearly spelled out.

In an organizational structure, the roles of staff analysts and advisers should be defined and used so that staff studies and recommendations enter the decision system at the various points where decisions are actually made. Unless this is done, independent staff work of no value to planning is the result.

Continue to Teach Planning and Strategy Implementation.   Even where a workable system of objectives and strategies and their implementation exists, it is easy for it to fail unless responsible managers continue to teach the nature and importance of planning. This may seem like a tedious process and unnecessary repetition, but learning can be assured in no other way. Teaching does not have to be done at formal meetings or seminars. Rather, much of the instruction can take place in the day-to-day consideration and review of planning proposals and in the review of performance as superiors undertake their normal control functions.

Create a Company Climate That Forces Planning.   As mentioned earlier, people tend to allow today's problems and crises to postpone effective planning for tomorrow. Therefore, the only way to assure that planning of all kinds will be done, and that strategies will be implemented, is to utilize devices and techniques that force planning.

There are many ways that an environment compulsive of planning can be created. Managing by objectives is one way; verifiable and actionable objectives cannot be set without some thought on how they are to be achieved. The rigorous and formal review of objectives, programs and performance will help create a planning environment. Similarly, review of budgets will force people to plan, especially if managers are required to explain their total budget needs and are not permitted to concentrate only on changes from a previous period. As pointed out earlier, a clear results-oriented organization structure and staff assistance in the actual decision process will help force planning. Goals, strategies, policies and premises, if communicated effectively, can also aid the planning process, especially since most people prefer to make decisions that are consistent with them.

Also, since strategies normally involve a fairly long-term commitment, care must be taken to insure that long-range and short-range plans are integrated. There are few day-to-day decisions that do not have an impact on longer-range commitments. In reviewing program proposals, even those that appear to be minor, superiors should make sure that they fit long-range strategies and programs. This is easy to do if managers know what they are and are required to think in these terms.

Strategic planning can be made to have a bottom-line impact. Effective top managers can assure this if they have carefully developed strategies and have taken pains for their implementation. In fact, if a company or any other kind of organization is to be successful over a period of time, it really has no other alternative.

3

Strategic Marketing Planning

The adoption and promise of strategic planning concepts and processes have led marketing executives to give increased attention to the firm's long-term linkages with its environment and resource capabilities. This change in orientation has prompted executives to expand their perspective beyond individual products and markets and consider the nature of a firm's "business."

Not only has the orientation of marketing executives changed due to the strategic planning emphasis, but the analytical framework and measures used to direct marketing efforts have changed as well. Analytical concepts and processes such as market position, product portfolios, PIMS results, marketing audit, and return on investment have become integral parts of marketing management and have influenced the assessment of strategic alternatives in ways not considered in the past.

The readings in this section are grouped under three headings. The readings range from discussing the fundamentals of strategic marketing to implementing strategic marketing options.

A. FUNDAMENTALS OF STRATEGIC MARKETING

The two articles describing the fundamentals of strategic marketing provide an overview of the expanded role of marketing in corporate strategy. The article by Boyd and Larréché is a "state-of-the-art" review of contemporary thought on the design of marketing strategy. A major point made by the authors is that corporate and marketing strategies have blended together due to the complementary perspectives of general managers and marketing executives. "A Strategic Perspective on Product Planning," by Day, describes a systematic procedure for identifying and choosing strategic alternatives using both the PIMS results and the Boston Consulting Group product portfolio perspective.

B. ASSESSMENT OF STRATEGIC MARKETING DIRECTIONS

The two articles on assessing strategic marketing direction address methods for the internal and external appraisal of the firm's marketing posture. "The Marketing Audit Comes of Age," by Kotler, Gregor, and Rodgers, introduces the marketing audit as a mechanism for examining marketing programs against the firm's opportunities, objectives, and resources. The authors' marketing audit outline is particularly noteworthy. "Market Structure Profile Analysis and Strategic Growth Opportunities," by Weber, describes a procedure for assessing growth opportunities for the enterprise and defining growth objectives.

C. STRATEGIC MARKETING OPTIONS

As noted earlier, a firm is typically faced with three strategic marketing options at any time. These options are to increase market share, to maintain market share, or to abandon a business (products) either through gradual disinvestment of resources or through outright elimination of product entries. The four articles reprinted here discuss these three options.

"Market Share Strategy and Corporate Profitability," by James, questions the relationship between market share and profitability. He points out that several latent factors must be considered before adopting a market-share growth strategy. Specifically, he suggests that managers consider market vulnerability, market innovation, market promotion, opportunity costs, and the possibility of regulatory control. Catry and Chevalier caution that the value of market share varies over the product life-cycle, including trends in the market and competitive market structure. The authors illustrate how the expected cash return and cash investment required vary over the product life-cycle and discuss their implications for the selection of market-share investment, maintenance, and disinvestment strategies. "Planning Gains in Market Share," by Fogg, outlines a comprehensive program for building market share. His article examines the means for increasing market share, describes a step-by-step procedure for planning market-share gains, and discusses potential pitfalls that must be considered when embarking on such a program. Finally, Kotler shows how a firm can "harvest" weak products. He defines harvesting as "a strategic management decision to reduce the investment in a business entity in the hope of cutting costs and/or improving cash flow." The article describes how the firm can identify what products can be harvested, how to prepare a harvesting plan, and methods for implementing the harvesting plan.

SELECTED ADDITIONAL READINGS

Bloom, Paul N. and Philip Kotler, "Strategies for High Market-Share Companies," *Harvard Business Review* (November–December 1975), pp. 63–72.

Day, George S., "Diagnosing the Product Portfolio," *Journal of Marketing* (April 1977), pp. 29–38.

Fruhan, William E., Jr., "Pyrrhic Victories in Fights for Market Share," *Harvard Business Review* (September–October 1972), pp. 100–107.

Hamermesh, R. G., M. J. Anderson, Jr., and J. E. Harris, "Strategies for Low Market Share Businesses," *Harvard Business Review* (May–June 1978), pp. 95–101.

Hopkins, David S., *Business Strategies for Problem Products*, New York: The Conference Board, 1977.

Hopkins, David S., "New Emphases in Marketing Strategies," *The Conference Board Record* (August 1976), pp. 35–39.

King, William R. and David I. Cleland, "Environmental Information Systems for Strategic Marketing Planning," *Journal of Marketing* (October 1974), pp. 35–40.

Porter, Michael E., "Please Note Location of Nearest Exit: Exit Barriers and Planning," *California Management Review* (Winter 1976), pp. 21–33.

Winter, R., "Corporate Strategists Giving New Emphasis to Market Share, Rank," *Wall Street Journal* (February 3, 1978), pp. 1ff.

The Foundations of Marketing Strategy

Harper W. Boyd, Jr. and Jean-Claude Larréché

In recent years it has become increasingly commonplace—even fashionable—for both marketing academicians and practitioners to use such military terms as "strategy," "tactics," and "logistics." Though these terms have conveyed the need to think of management as a dynamic undertaking, they are used with less precision than might be desired. The word "strategy" in particular has been used in a variety of ways over the years by marketing people.

In an early paper, Oxenfeldt introduced the concept of market strategy to emphasize the need to define appropriate market targets before determining the composition of the marketing mix.[1] Along this line of thought, marketing strategy also has been viewed as a process which generally consists of analyzing market opportunities, specifying objectives, developing plans, and monitoring performance. The most common usage of the word "strategy" in marketing, however, has been in connection with the various elements contained in the marketing mix; e.g., product strategy, price strategy, communications strategy, and distribution strategy.[2] The term "marketing strategy" also has been associated with the selection of any key options in a marketing situation.[3] More recently, it has been used in conjunction with market share objectives and product/market choices.[4]

About the Authors: Harper W. Boyd, Jr. is Dean and Professor of Marketing, Graduate School of Business Administration, Tulane University; Jean-Claude Larréché is Associate Professor of Marketing, INSEAD, Fontainebleau, France.

Reprinted from G. Zaltman and T. Bonoma, eds., *Review of Marketing: 1978* (Chicago: American Marketing Association, 1978), pp. 41–72, published by the American Marketing Association.

[1] Alfred R. Oxenfeldt, "The Formulation of a Market Strategy," in Eugene J. Kelly and William Lazer, eds., *Managerial Marketing: Perspectives and Viewpoints* (Homewood, Illinois: Richard D. Irwin, Inc., 1962), pp. 34–44.

[2] For example, Robert F. Lusch, John G. Udel, and Gene R. Laczniak, "The Future of Marketing Strategy," *Business Horizons*, Vol. 19, No. 6 (December 1976), pp. 65–74; or J. G. Udell, "Towards a Theory of Marketing Strategy," *British Journal of Marketing*, Vol. 2 (Winter 1968), p. 298.

[3] See for example the 12 marketing "weapons" described by Lee Adler in "A New Orientation for Plotting Marketing Strategy," *Business Horizons* (Winter 1964), pp. 37–50.

[4] Bernard Catry and Michel Chevalier, "Market Share Strategy and the Product Life Cycle," *Journal of Marketing*, Vol. 38, No. 4 (October 1974), pp. 29–34; Paul N. Bloom and

The purpose of this article is to assess the state of the art of marketing strategy and to investigate bases for future research in this field. Marketing strategy first is positioned in relation to corporate strategy and to lower-level strategies within the marketing function. The concept of the product-market domain as an investment unit in marketing strategy then is discussed, and alternative approaches to product-market portfolio analysis are reviewed. Finally, potential future developments in marketing strategy are explored.

ROLE OF MARKETING IN THE FORMULATION AND EXECUTION OF CORPORATE STRATEGY

Though the statement that there are ". . . probably more kinds of strategy and more definitions of it than there are varieties and definitions of economics or politics" [5] seems particularly applicable to marketing strategy, it is also applicable to corporate strategy. Definitions of corporate strategy, however, have tended in recent years to be more complementary than contradictory. Thus, most writers on this subject agree that a firm's strategy is essentially an adaptive search process which is concerned with how a firm deploys its resources over time in response to changes in its environment. Thus, ". . . strategy has to do principally with things external to the company rather than internal to it. It is generally because of the external environment and its ever-changing nature that we are so concerned with strategy formulation." [6]

Ultimately, the firm's strategy is expressed in terms of a set of resource allocation rules which pertain to the relationships between the organization and its environment.[7] These relationships find meaning and specificity in the firm's product-market entries which individually serve as allocation (investment) units. Thus, corporate strategy can be defined in terms of the firm's portfolio of product-market entries. Viewed in this light, corporate strategy clearly provides a way for management to better answer the questions, "What business(es) are we in?" and "What business(es) should we be in?"

Corporate strategy derives from a process—typically referred to as strategic planning—which is essentially *anticipatory* in nature. It consists of: [8]

- Specifying present goals with respect to each of the firm's present product-market entries.

Philip Kotler, "Strategies for High Market Share Companies," *Harvard Business Review,* Vol. 53 (November–December 1975), pp. 63–72; David W. Cravens, "Marketing Strategy Positioning," *Business Horizons,* Vol. 18 (December 1975), pp. 53–61; and Philip Kotler, *Marketing Management: Analysis, Planning and Control,* third edition (Englewood Cliffs, New Jersey: Prentice Hall, Inc., 1976), Chapter 3.

[5] J. C. Wylie, *Military Strategy: A General Theory of Power Control* (New Brunswick, New Jersey: Rutgers University Press, 1967), p. 3.

[6] James R. Collier, *Effective Long-Range Business Planning* (Englewood Cliffs, New Jersey: Prentice Hall, Inc., 1968), pp. 101–102.

[7] H. Igor Ansoff, *Corporate Strategy* (New York: McGraw-Hill, Inc., 1965), p. 103.

[8] See Charles Rossotti, "Two Concepts of Long-Range Planning: An Analysis of Current Practice" (Boston: The Boston Consulting Group, undated).

- Assessing environmental change as it relates to each entry.
- Deciding whether what is anticipated is important enough to warrant changing present entry allocations.

The end goal of this planning system is a future "best-yield" (as determined by some return-on-investment measure) portfolio composed of the firm's product-market entries *given* management's perceptions of the risks associated with alternative investment schedules and the short-term tradeoffs required to satisfy one or more stakeholder groups such as stockholders, labor, consumers, government, and so on. For the ongoing firm, strategy is associated with a *change* (addition and/or deletion) in its product-market entries *and/or* a shift in the importance of an entry. The latter frequently is stated in terms of a change in its market position, i.e., its market share.

Corporate strategy, by definition, constrains all administrative and operational decisions throughout the organization. It serves to integrate the activities of such critical management areas as marketing, finance, and production. Because of the size and complexity of these areas, it is not surprising that each, in turn, seeks to develop its own strategy hierarchy which constrains the actions within its group. Each of these functional area strategies is an extension of corporate strategy and when aggregated they provide substance and meaning to the firm's overall strategy. Each strategy statement in the hierarchy stresses those critical elements which must be emphasized to achieve the firm's overall strategic objective, which is defined as a future best-yield portfolio of product-market entries.

Marketing Strategy

A review of the marketing literature reveals that the word "strategy" has been used in a variety of ways. Its most common usage has been in connection with the *individual* elements contained in the "marketing mix," e.g., product strategy, price strategy, channel strategy, and promotion strategy. Some writers have chosen to define it as the marketing mix itself, given a certain set of market conditions including competitive product positioning and distribution opportunities. In more recent years the literature has indicated use of product-market relationships as the basis for classifying alternative marketing strategies.

It seems clear that a hierarchy of strategies can be defined within the marketing function. Solely for the purpose of this discussion, three levels of strategies are suggested.

1. *Marketing Strategies.* This is the generalized statement which applies to the marketing mix across a set of product-market entries. As such, it is company-specific and stresses the interrelation of those elements related to the product, its price, the distribution system, and the communication function. Thus, it emphasizes the commonality of the various entries with respect to marketing action.[9]

---

[9] See Robert T. Davis, "Marketing Strategy (A)" (Stanford, California: Graduate School of Business, Stanford University, 1975).

An example is the marketing strategy pursued by Cosmetically Yours. Its products were copied from prestige cosmetic firms which had already launched the items successfully through specialty outlets. The firm sold a complete line of products through discount stores using a pilfer-proof package with high visual content to the "young at heart." Price was considerably below that of the prestige brands and communication was entirely through point-of-purchase.[10]

2. *Marketing Element Strategies.* By definition this type and level of strategy is concerned with a specific element and is considerably narrower in scope than a marketing strategy. Within the marketing mix it seeks to generalize across entries and lend substance and meaning to the overall marketing strategy. Thus, there are product strategies such as innovating versus following, price strategies such as skimming versus penetration, channels strategies based on intensity of distribution and channel type, and such alternative promotion strategies as push versus pull.

3. *Product-Market Entry Strategies.* This kind of strategy statement sets forth guidelines pertaining to the management of a specific product-market relationship. It determines what marketing action should be taken as well as the extent of such action and may be said to be essentially goal-oriented. It precedes the formulation of higher-level marketing strategies which summarize and constrain the types of marketing actions which the firm will employ for the individual product-market entry as well as across entries. The more recent marketing management literature has tended to emphasize this particular type of strategy. Given that corporate strategy focuses on product-market relationships, it is not surprising that some writers have used these units as the basis for discussing (classifying) these kinds of strategy. Cravens et al., for example, do so in terms of marketing strategy positions, i.e., those relating to new ventures, growth, market development, market retention, and "balancing." [11] Closely akin to this scheme is a more simplistic one which is concerned with market share objectives (grow, hold, or harvest).[12] Kotler takes a somewhat different tack through his discussion of "analyzing opportunities" which, in turn, classifies different growth possibilities.[13]

Clearly these three levels are hierarchial and interdependent. Each contributes to and, in turn, is constrained by the other. Sequentially, the product-market entry strategies precede the other two types. The three strategy levels can be viewed as part of the firm's allocation rules serving to link marketing to the corporate strategic plan.

To develop a product-market relationship strategy, it is necessary to develop an understanding and definition of products and their related markets because

---

[10] Robert T. Davis, same as reference 9.

[11] David W. Cravens, Gerald E. Hills, and Robert B. Woodruff, *Marketing Decision Making: Concepts and Strategy* (Homewood, Illinois: Richard D. Irwin, Inc., 1976).

[12] Robert D. Buzzell, Bradley T. Gale, and Ralph G. M. Sultan, "Market Share—A Key to Profitability," *Harvard Business Review* (March–April 1972).

[13] Philip Kotler, see reference 4.

these combinations represent the firm's basic investment units. Then an analysis of the relationship between the product and its markets is required. The recommendations on what these relationships should be over time constitute the very essence of corporate strategy. Marketing obviously has considerable responsibility for advising corporate management about these desired relationships, including the costs associated with each. The reliability of these "strategy" recommendations is critical.

PRODUCT-MARKET RELATIONSHIPS

Any attempt to examine product-market relationship strategies must include a definition of a product, a market, and a relationship. In this section these three subjects are explored on an interrelated basis. The term "product-market domain" is used to represent the entries on which marketing strategy and, ultimately, corporate strategy are based.[14] They are, in essence, the firm's *basic investment units* because the firm's income streams derive from the coupling of specific products with specific markets. The yield of the investment made in each is largely a function of the fit between the product and the needs and wants of the target market(s), the size and growth of this market, and the firm's relative competitive market position. Clearly, how these domains are defined and analyzed is critical, not only because of the obvious organizational implications, but because of the potential synergistic effects of an investment made in one domain on the outcome of another. These effects derive not only from costs but also from interactions between buyers in different domains with regard to one or more products sold by the firm.

The Product Hierarchy

At the minimum a product hierarchy must distinguish clearly between different levels of aggregation.[15] At the "top" is the product class which includes all those objects which are close substitutes for the same needs despite differences in shape, size, and technical characteristics. Examples include all automobiles, television sets, refrigerators, margarines, and so on.

Under certain conditions, it can be argued that there is a higher level of aggregation—i.e., one which takes into account the cross-elasticities between product classes which serve basically the same needs. An example would be a combination of such product classes as butter, margarine, and mayonnaise into one superclass called "spreads." Clearly, the interdependency between product classes is an important consideration in strategizing long-term investments in any one class.

A somewhat different higher level of aggregation could emerge from the

---

[14] This term is suggested by Jean-Paul Sallenave in *La Strategie de l'Entreprise Face à la Concurrence* (Paris: Les Editions d'Organisation, 1973), p. 107.

[15] The classification scheme being proposed relies heavily on Rolando Polli and Victor Cook, "Validity of the Product Life Cycle," *Journal of Business* (October 1969), p. 388.

need to take into account the joint costs between product classes manufactured by the same firm, i.e., to determine the firm's overall cost position in relation to competition as well as the relative magnitude of funds available for product and market development. An example would be the aggregation by a firm of various major home appliances (e.g., refrigerators, dryers, washers, and dishwashers) into a single superclass.

Product type is the next level of aggregation. It is a subset of a product class wherein the items differ in size, shape, price, and even form. There may be substantial differences in the production technology used between types. Examples include fresh, frozen, and canned vegetables; electronic, jeweled, and pin-levered watches; and paperback and hard-cover books.

The lowest level in the product hierarchy is the brand, which often is in the form of several stock-keeping units. For food and personal care items these usually consist of different package sizes. For appliances they are items of different colors. For cars the stock-keeping units may be defined in terms of colors and accessories. In some product classes there may be a level between the stock-keeping unit and the product type which could be termed a subtype. An example would be different automobile models (e.g., sports, stationwagon, and four-door sedan) within a type of care such as compact, subcompact, and standard.

There is nothing sacrosanct about the levels of aggregation that a firm should use in defining its product hierarchy or in the terminology used to describe each level. The main considerations are that (1) the more homogeneous the "level," the better the firm can relate its investments to meaningful potential income streams over time, and (2) the level of aggregation selected should provide important insights into the interdependencies among the various levels. The latter point is especially important in providing knowledge about corporate cost position.

Market Hierarchies

The lack of an explicit definition of the market hierarchy to which a given product is linked may hide elements of strategic importance to the firm. The hierarchy is built by using market segments, the most important of which is concerned with how the product is perceived by various groups of potential buyers who have different choice criteria by which they evaluate alternative offerings. These segments are defined largely on the basis of the similarity of choice criteria as well as the ratings accorded alternative brands. They are typically referred to as product segments.[16]

Such a segment approach is the first step in structuring the hierarchy because it links the product to definable groups whose preferences about product class and type attributes are known. Such knowledge points up opportunities for new products as well as product modifications. Further, it provides important

---

[16] See Norman L. Barnett, "Beyond Market Segmentation," *Harvard Business Review* (January–February 1969), pp. 152–165.

guidelines for certain marketing activities such as promotion and pricing. Finally, it is the basis on which brand or product share is determined.

Once the firm's product segments are set, a series of operational segments should be defined. For consumer goods it is necessary first to identify members of the target product segments not only in terms of whether they are heavy or light buyers, but also as to their demographic characteristics and media habits. Then follows the definition of other operational segments which would include, for goods, retail accounts within retail type by geography. If wholesalers were used, such a channel type would be fitted into the hierarchy.

Despite considerable similarity between the hierarchies of segments for consumer and industrial goods firms, the latter type of companies tend to define the buyers of their products and/or services in account terms. One could well argue, however, that there is a more basic segment level by which to cope with the several "buying influentials" within the accounts who have different attitudes toward the product, and who therefore need to be serviced differently.[17]

The more homogeneous the choice criteria of the product segments and the more distinct the segments are, the better the firm can relate its marketing investments to meaningful potential income streams. Though homogeneity typically is defined in terms of response to marketing actions, it should be considered here in connection with such strategic issues as market growth, competitive structures, and servicing costs. Given a brand or product, each operating segment should constitute an investment unit. This investment unit allows the firm to allocate resources among units to influence competitive position and market shares. It should be clear that the market share for a given product derives from the action taken by the firm with respect to each operating segment. The analysis of operating segments in an hierarchical fashion will help in identifying interdependencies with regard to both demand (e.g., image transfers or reinforcement) and the use of common marketing resources (e.g., different levels of distribution channels). Finally, the segment hierarchy is an important integrating scheme because different organizational units within the marketing department serve different segments (e.g., advertising is concerned primarily with groups of household buyers whereas sales is preoccupied with channel segments).

Product-Market Relationships

The relationships can be evaluated best in terms of market share, which serves as a powerful summary measure of the firm's competitive position in a given marketplace. This fact is particularly evident when market share is described in terms of the present value of future profits. The inherent problem with "long-run profit maximization" as the primary economic objective of the firm is that, at best, managers can measure present profitability, and this is not necessarily a good indication of future profits. It can be argued that the single best indicator

---

[17] Yoram Wind and Richard Cardozo, "Industrial Market Segmentation," *Industrial Marketing Management,* Vol. 3 (1974), pp. 153–166.

of the future profitability of any individual product-market entry is the *trend* of the firm's market share. This statement is in keeping with the results of the PIMS (Profit Impact of Marketing Strategies) project which found a significant positive correlation between market share and pretax return on investment.[18] One reason for this outcome is that market share summarizes the *quality* of the relationship between the market and the firm's product in relation to the average performance of competitors. Thus it provides insights into the strength of the product "fit" which over time is the single most important determinant of profitability. Another important advantage of using market share as a surrogate measure of profitability is that it can handle the effect of market growth.[19]

This advantage is calculated by estimating the changing value to the firm of a market share point (for each market segment) in marginal contribution dollars. These amounts are summed at the product level where the joint costs between segments are allocated to get at the product profitability for a specific time horizon. From such data the present value of different levels of share point increases can be estimated. If this can be done across product-market entries—or domains—then the efficiency of the firm's resource allocation process will certainly be enhanced, even though such an approach requires clairvoyance in anticipating competitive actions and reaction. But this problem is inherent to all strategic planning; further, as will be shown, the use of relative market share measures (the firm's share divided by those of leading competitors) helps to mitigate this problem.

Effect of Market Growth on Profitability

Ordinarily, a firm will attempt to exploit an expanding market. It does so by seeking to "buy" market share points in the short term, because over time each share point will increase in value. This approach usually requires the firm to make a long-term investment at the sacrifice of more immediate profits.

The potential effect of a growing market on company profits is easy to understate if the cumulative effect is not taken into account. Consider, for example, the compounding effect of a 10% annual growth rate (in constant dollars) over a five-year period. If annual industry sales are $10 million in the base year, they will rise to $16,105,000 at the end of the fifth year—an increase of more than $6 million. If the firm is assumed to have a share of 30% and to maintain it over the five-year period, then its sales would increase from $3 million in the base year to $4,831,000 in the fifth year.

If one assumes that the firm's *marginal contribution* (net sales less direct costs) *is 50% during the base year, then a 30% share yields a total contribution of $1,500,000 in the base year and $2,415,000 five years later.* Thus, the share point value expressed in marginal contribution dollars increases from $50,000 to $80,500. If the additional marginal contribution obtained through growth is

---

[18] Robert D. Buzzell et al., same as reference 12.

[19] This view is so strongly held that market share is increasingly used by security analysts. See "Rating a Company by Its Market Share," *BusinessWeek*, October 3, 1977, p. 89.

cumulated over the five-year period, the firm receives about $2.6 million additional contribution.

The effect of growth on the value of a share point has been underestimated, however, because its impact on costs has not been taken into account. The Boston Consulting Group (BCG) has presented strong evidence that average industry costs fall as aggregate volume produced increases. They estimate that average costs (expressed in constant dollars) decline by as much as 20 to 30% *on value added* each time the accumulated volume produced is doubled. BCG's evidence is impressive and is drawn from research on both consumer and industrial companies. They label this inverse relationship between accumulated volume and average per unit cost the *experience curve* although the cost reductions eventuate from economies of scale, experience, and the movement of the product through the life cycle. It is important to note that they are referring to all value added costs—not merely production costs.[20]

Because costs drop substantially with accumulated experience, the absolute decrease in costs is tied closely to the rate at which the firm accumulates its experience. If the market is growing rapidly, the company which captures and holds a major share will have a faster decline in its costs than competitors. If growth slows, then a much longer period is required to lower costs by an appreciable amount. To assure the reductions, of course, the firm must make every effort to behave efficiently and to reduce its costs as quickly as possible.

The use of market share measures provides management with insights about the upper limit which should be imposed on the long-term expenditures related to the individual product-market entry.[21] This upper limit must be compared with the projected cost of achieving the share goal. If reasonable estimates of such costs can be made, high-level managers can see more clearly the utility of their various strategy options. Ultimately, market share measures facilitate the forecasting of cash flows and cash availability. They do so by encompassing market growth, the value of this growth in financial terms including the effect of growth on costs, and the need for the firm to gain or hold a given relative share in order to maintain a favorable per unit cost position versus leading competitors. Indeed, by knowing the firm's cumulated relative share, the firm should be able to estimate with some accuracy the per unit costs of major competitors.

Apart from market share and market growth, other "dimensions" are available to help evaluate the attractiveness of various product-market entries or domains as well as to help determine strategy for each. The PIMS project provides a list of such dimensions. From a data base now containing more than

---

[20] See Patrick Conley, "Experience Curves as a Planning Tool: A Special Commentary," *IEEE Spectrum* (June 1970), pp. 63–68; Barry Hedley, "A Fundamental Approach to Strategy Development," *Long Range Planning*, Vol. 9, No. 6 (December 1976), pp. 2–11.

[21] The emphasis placed on market share has been so great that several authors have warned of the dangers inherent in using it as a primary determinant of marketing strategy. See William E. Fruhan, Jr., "Pyrrhic Victories in Fights for Market Share," *Harvard Business Review*, Vol. 50 (September–October 1972), pp. 100–107; Barrie James, "Market Share Strategy and Corporate Profitability," *Management Decision*, Vol. 10 (Winter 1972), pp. 243–252; Paul N. Bloom and Philip Kotler, see reference 4; and Simon Majaro, "Market Share: Deception or Diagnosis," *Marketing* (March 1977), pp. 44–47.

1,000 businesses, several econometric models have been developed to explain financial performance as measured by return on investment (ROI) or cash flow. The basic ROI equation contains more than 60 terms (including interactions) based on 37 quantifiable variables. The key variables in this equation include market share, market growth, investment intensity, industry concentration, marketing expenditures, relative product quality, value added, and capacity utilization.[22]

Other determinants of marketing strategy can be isolated. Some of the more important may be essentially qualitative, as would be the case with those involving legal and social changes, prospects for changing technology, and the unpredictable unavailability of certain raw material sources.

PRODUCT-MARKET PORTFOLIOS [23]

As noted previously, the end product of the strategic planning process is a future best-yield portfolio composed of individual product-market entries, taking into account risk and short-term versus long-term tradeoffs. The decision of which product-market entries to include in the portfolio as well as the extent to which each should be emphasized is a most complex one to make. In an effort to simplify the decision process, several analytical approaches toward the evolution of the "ideal" portfolio have been developed. Though all were designed originally for use at the corporate level with divisions or product groups as entries, it is important to recognize that both conceptually and operationally portfolios can apply to several investment levels within the firm. The construction of a portfolio hierarchy is advisable, commencing with a portfolio of segments related to a given brand managed by a product manager. At the next higher management level, product group managers preside over portfolios composed of products. At the next level, the portfolio consists of product groups, and so on. At each level, the manager attempts to allocate resources, taking into account the interdependencies among the items contained in the portfolio. The use of such a hierarchy provides assurance that interdependencies have been considered. At the very top level, the portfolio decisions center around the resources which need to be diverted from one major corporate undertaking to another.

Three portfolio analysis tools are presented here: the market growth/relative share matrix, the industry attractiveness/company strength matrix, and the di-

---

[22] Robert D. Buzzell et al., same as reference 12; also see Derek F. Abell, "Using PIMS and Portfolio Analysis in Strategic Market Planning," paper presented at the XXIII International Meeting of the Institute of Management Science, Athens, Greece, July 1977; Sidney Schoeffler, Robert D. Buzzell, and Donald F. Heany, "Impact of Strategic Planning on Profit Performance," *Harvard Business Review*, Vol. 52 (March–April 1974), pp. 137–145; Sidney Schoeffler, "Cross-Sectional Study of Strategy, Structure and Performance: Aspects of the PIMS Program," paper presented at the SSP Conference, Indiana University, 1975.

[23] Although the term "product" or "business portfolio" is commonly used, the basic entries in strategic portfolios are investment units which, as noted, should be defined primarily in terms of products *and* markets. Consequently, the expression "product-market portfolio" is used here, which seems more appropriate when discussing marketing strategies.

rectional policy matrix.[24] As a basis for comparing these tools, the portfolio *concept* and its relationship to marketing strategy are discussed first.

The Portfolio Concept

Portfolio management long has been a subject of interest to students and practitioners of finance. In brief, it is the process by which individuals and organizations search out and buy individual securities in light of their future effect on the mix (portfolio) of securities already held. It stresses the interdependency of the individual holdings and that the portfolio is different from the sum of its parts—especially with respect to stability of yield and risk.[25]

A security portfolio is, or should be, dynamic. It is, in the words of Charles D. Ellis, "always in the process of becoming," because the securities composing the fund are continually being changed, the number of shares held in each may change, the stock market is in a continuous process of price adjustment, individual stocks have their own unique periods of instability, and the business of each company may undergo change.[26]

The similarity of the interdependencies among stocks and those among corporate ventures and the emphasis on the dynamics of the environment make it easy to understand why the portfolio concept has found its way into the strategic planning literature. Indeed, as already noted, the end goal of the strategic planning process can be defined in terms of a best-yield portfolio.

Essentially, the concept relates to how a firm develops a strategy for making its investment decisions. It implies that the firm should make its current investments in light of their futurity; i.e., on the basis of their impact on the firm's portfolio whether it is expressed in terms of yield, risk reduction, or the regularity of cash flows. The security portfolio literature contains guidelines for the effective management of a portfolio which with slight modification can easily apply to a firm's product-market entries portfolio.[27]

1. To accumulate "partial positions in stocks slightly held" is a mistake. (Dispersement of resources to such an extent that many of the firm's products hold weak relative share positions is to court disaster.)
2. A portfolio is stronger if its holdings have different life cycles and expected payout periods.
3. It is poor management to have one's largest holdings in securities which

---

[24] For an excellent discussion of the pitfalls in the use of product or business portfolios, see George S. Day, "Diagnosing the Product Portfolio," *Journal of Marketing*, Vol. 41, No. 2 April 1977), pp. 29–38; also Noel Capon and Joan Robertson Spogli, "Strategic Market Planning: A Comparison and Critical Examination of Two Contemporary Approaches," in B. A. Greenberg and O. N. Bellenger, *Contemporary Marketing Thought*, 1977 Educators' Conference, American Marketing Association, 1977, pp. 219–223.

[25] See H. Markowitz, *Portfolio Selection: Efficient Diversification of Investments* (New York: John Wiley & Sons, Inc., 1959).

[26] Charles D. Ellis, "Portfolio Operations," *Financial Analysts Journal* (September–October 1971), p. 36.

[27] Charles D. Ellis, same as reference 26, pp. 37–46.

reflect the past realized profits rather than expected future earnings; investments should take into account the growth in the market.

4. Success and failure should be managed while they are "in motion." (If a firm cannot gain a strong relative market portion before the shakeout period, it should seriously consider "getting out" or "disinvesting.")

The Market Growth/Relative Share Matrix

The best known "tool" for product-market portfolio analysis is the one developed by the Boston Consulting Group (BCG).[28] Product-market domains are represented in a matrix (Exhibit 1) which is structured around market growth (vertical scale) and relative market share (horizontal scale). The relative market

---

EXHIBIT 1

BCG'S Market Growth/Relative Share Matrix. (Size of circle is in proportion to sales in corresponding product-market entry.)

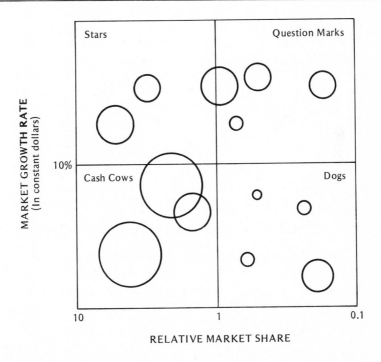

Adapted from Barry Hedley, "Strategy and the Business Portfolio," *Long Range Planning,* Vol. 10 (February 1977).

---

[28] See, for example, Barry Hedley, "Strategy and the Business Portfolio," *Long Range Planning,* Vol. 10 (February 1977), pp. 9–15; George S. Day, see reference 24.

share of a firm in a given product-market domain is computed as its absolute share divided by the share of the leading competitor. The size of a circle in the matrix is in proportion to the firm's sales in the corresponding product-market domain.

This matrix provides a clear representation of the firm's posture in various product-market domains, and shows the evolving cash needs and cash flows among these entries. The upper left quadrant contains the *stars,* market leaders which are still growing fast. Though they typically require substantial investments, they usually show a small positive or a negative cash flow. If a star entry keeps its leadership, it will eventually fall into the bottom left quadrant and become a *cash cow.* It should then become a substantial net cash generator. This cash may be used to reinforce the position of *question marks* in the upper right quadrant which have low market shares in a fast-growing market. The firm should invest heavily in some to increase their relative share, and try to transform them into stars. It should disinvest in others which otherwise will drop to the bottom right quadrant when the market matures and will become *dogs.* These entries have a small relative share in a stagnant market. They are usually barely profitable, have little potential, and are logical candidates for liquidation.

Though the BCG approach relies on a matrix presentation, it in fact integrates the four dimensions of market growth, market position in relation to the leading competitor, size of a product-market entry, and cash flows. It suggests key strategic alternatives in terms of investment and disinvestment and is a conceptually simple and powerful tool. Though the definition of product-market domains and the gathering of underlying data may be laborious, the fact that the matrix requires the use of quantifiable variables enhances its usefulness considerably. In formulating a particular marketing strategy, however, one must be careful to consider other determinants which are not explicit in the BCG matrix. It may be inappropriate to liquidate a dog entry if doing so generates labor unrest and low morale, or to invest in a star if technological changes on the horizon may induce competition from suppliers who integrate forward.

Industry Attractiveness/Company Strength Matrix

Several corporations and consultants have adopted another type of portfolio matrix designed to facilitate the generation of strategies. This matrix, represented in Exhibit 2, has *industry attractiveness* and *company strength* as basic dimensions.[29] These are obviously *composite* dimensions. They are more complete and richer than the market growth and relative market share values used by the BCG, but also more difficult to measure. Each of these dimensions can be defined in terms of a set of subdimensions (obviously including market growth

---

[29] Derek F. Abell, see reference 22; and Derek F. Channon, "Use and Abuse of Analytical Techniques for Strategic Decisions," paper presented at the XXIII International Meeting of the Institute of Management Sciences, Athens, Greece, July 25–29, 1977. Also, see Robert V. L. Wright, "A System for Managing Diversity" (Cambridge, Massachusetts: Arthur D. Little, Inc., December 1974).

EXHIBIT 2

The Industry Attractiveness/Company Strength Matrix

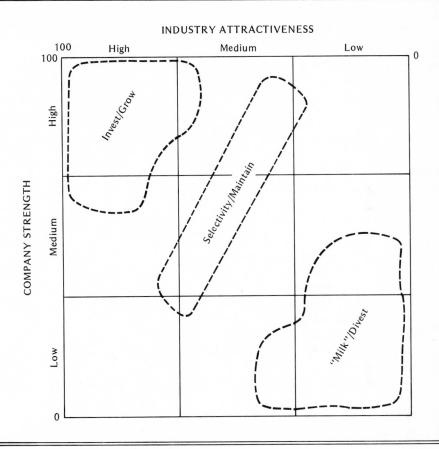

Adapted from Derek F. Channon, "Use and Abuse of Analytical Techniques for Strategic Decisions," paper presented at the XXIII International Meeting of the Institute of Management Sciences, Athens, Greece, July 25–29, 1977.

and market share) according to the more important strategy determinants isolated by the firm. These subdimensions then are used to rate each product-market domain on the industry attractiveness and company strength scales. Finally, the various product-market domains are positioned in this matrix, as in the BCG approach.

In the process of developing the portfolio by using this matrix, the firm considers a large number of variables, both quantitative and qualitative. Consequently, it is more difficult to position a product-market domain in this matrix, and the cash relationships are less apparent. Because the subdimensions used can be tailored to the unique needs of a given firm and its various entries, this matrix has the potential to provide management with a better understanding of the future prospects for a given entry. Its use also reduces the risk of overlooking one or more important factors which bear on the formulation of a marketing strategy.

The Directional Policy Matrix

The Shell Group has developed an even more complete portfolio analysis tool called the Directional Policy Matrix (DPM).[30] The DPM relies on two composite dimensions, *prospects for sector profitability* and *company's competitive capabilities*. The firm's products and competitive products are plotted on a three-by-three matrix such as the one represented in Exhibit 3. For each cell of this matrix

---

EXHIBIT 3
The Directional Policy Matrix

PROSPECTS FOR SECTOR PROFITABILITY

COMPANY'S COMPETITIVE CAPABILITIES		Unattractive	Average	Attractive
	Weak	Disinvest	Phased withdrawal Custodial	Double or quit
	Average	Phased withdrawal	Custodial Growth	Try harder
	Strong	Cash generation	Growth Leader	Leader

Source: "The Directional Policy Matrix: A New Aid to Corporate Planning," Shell Chemicals UK, November 1975.

---

[30] See, for example, Derek F. Channon, reference 29; David B. Montgomery and Charles B. Weinberg, "Implications of Product Portfolio Analysis for Strategic Competitive Intelligence," Graduate School of Business, Stanford University, Research Paper No. 358, February 1977; and "The Directional Policy Matrix: A New Aid to Corporate Planning," Shell Chemicals UK, November 1975.

a strategy type such as "phased withdrawal," "custodial," or "try harder" is suggested.

The use of the DPM involves a hierarchical procedure for rating a product on two composite dimensions. The assessment of prospects for sector profitability is based on the four factors of market growth rate, market quality, industry situation, and environmental aspects. On each of these factors, a product can receive from one to five stars. Such a system is thought to have a greater visual value than numbers. Guidelines are given for the attribution of stars on the basis of subfactors. For example, market quality is determined by use of a list of 10 criteria such as past stability in the sector's profitability, pricing behavior, number of competitors, number of customers, potential new competition, and value added. A global score on prospects for sector profitability is attributed to a given product by converting the star evaluation into a numerical rating (from zero to four) and adding the ratings on all four factors. In the same fashion, the company's competitive capabilities for a given product are evaluated on the basis of three factors (market position, product research and development, and production capability) which are themselves composed of subfactors. After global scores have been obtained on prospects for sector profitability and on the company's competitive capabilities for a specific product, the product is positioned in the directional policy matrix.

The DPM incorporates many more determinants of strategy than does the BCG's product portfolio. It is more similar in this respect to the industry attractiveness/company strength matrix. In addition, it is based on a well-defined hierarchy of these determinants of strategy which facilitates the positioning of a given product. Finally, the consideration of sector profitability rather than the more general industry attractiveness dimension gives a clearer picture of strategic options and their cash flow implications. In this sense, DPM presents an attractive combination of the main features offered by the BCG's product portfolio and the industry attractiveness/company strength matrix. But it is more difficult to operationalize in any quantitative sense than the other two approaches.

Product-Market Portfolios and the Derivation of Market Strategies

The tools described provide powerful support for the formulation of marketing strategies. In particular they can be useful to:

1. *Evaluate the Firm's Current Product-Market Portfolio.* The representation of product-market entries on a matrix reveals the strengths and weaknesses of the firm's overall position by pointing up the interrelationships between the entries—*particularly with respect to cash flows.*

2. *Evaluate the Competitors' Current Product-Market Portfolios.* The product-market portfolios of major competitors can be represented on separate matrices similar to the one used by the firm. These matrices then can be used to analyze the competitors' strengths and weaknesses, to forecast their future strategic moves by individual entry, and to anticipate their reactions to alternative marketing strategies of the firm.

3. *Generate Conditional Projections of the Firm's Future Competitive Situation.* The dynamic nature of the dimensions used in these matrices (e.g., market growth) makes it easier to draft the firm's desired future portfolio. It is possible, indeed desirable, to draw up several future portfolios based on different assumptions about the key strategy determinants.

4. *Guide the Development of a Strategic Intelligence System.* The experience gained in product-market portfolio analysis should pinpoint those areas where additional strategic information is needed as well as specify where continuous information is needed to minimize risk. This information should result in the generation of guidelines for the development of an ongoing strategic intelligence system.[31]

5. *Determining Strategy Options.* This obviously is the goal of the product-market portfolio analysis. These key options can be classified as *corrective, defensive,* or *offensive.* Corrective actions may be called for if the current or the projected future portfolio of the firm is unbalanced. Anticipated moves of competitors may result in the development of a defensive strategy. Finally, opportunities appearing from the firm's and competitors' portfolios may justify the formulation of an offensive strategy. Another way of classifying strategy options is in terms of grow, hold, or harvest market share. These may be part of the corrective, defensive, or offensive options.

The new approaches in product-market portfolio analysis do not provide for the instant formulation of marketing strategies. On the contrary, they involve a long, tedious, and analytical effort in data gathering and analysis. But they do provide a powerful analytical *framework* for the formulation of marketing strategies.

FUTURE DEVELOPMENTS IN MARKETING STRATEGY

The most important recent contributions to marketing strategy have been the explicit formulation of the product-market portfolio concept and the development of ways to analyze the portfolios. Collectively, these contributions have served to integrate numerous marketing concepts and techniques concerned with such subject areas as buyer behavior, product positioning, market segmentation, and product life cycle, as well as those concerned with the marketing mix and individual element strategies.

The availability of the product-market portfolio concept as a building block and the resulting increased interest in marketing strategy should encourage new research undertakings. New developments can be anticipated in the following areas in particular.

1. *Determinants of Marketing Strategy.* In addition to conceptual contributions, the determination of key factors in the formulation of a marketing strategy

---

[31] David B. Montgomery and Charles B. Weinberg, see reference 30.

requires an extensive data base including a large number of product-market ob-servations. The most substantial future developments in this area thus should be expected from major undertakings such as the PIMS project.[32] The continuous extension of the PIMS data base longitudinally and in terms of the number of businesses involved should open new research opportunities, such as the analysis of specific classes of situations or the study of effects over time.

2. *Analytical Approaches to Product-Market Portfolio Analysis.* Variations and extensions of the analytical approaches to product-market portfolio analysis presented here are likely to emerge in the future. More detailed, structured "tools" will be developed which will be linked to current marketing techniques such as market segmentation and product positioning.[33] These tools could be organized around a hierarchy of product-market domains. A related avenue of research is a greater formalization and integration of the entire process of mar-keting strategy formulation based on the product-market portfolio, including data gathering, analysis, generation of alternatives, and choice. Finally, much empirical work is needed to apply and study the relative validity of alternative conceptual tools for product-market portfolio analysis.

3. *Typologies of Marketing Situations and Strategies.* Although the popula-tion of marketing situations and strategic alternatives is literally infinite, classi-fications of major types of situations and strategies have a high potential value for management. They can provide assistance to strategy research projects by helping to formulate hypotheses, develop experimental design, and structure data. Some typologies of marketing situations and strategies already have been proposed, but more complete and systematic ones are needed.[34] They can emerge from studies done on the product-market portfolios, from analyses of determinants of marketing strategy, or from exploratory field work.

4. *Normative Strategic Marketing Propositions.* A normative strategic mar-keting proposition is a rule of thumb for strategic action applicable under cer-tain conditions. It usually takes the form of an "if . . . then . . ." sentence. These propositions obviously have an immediate managerial value when they have been validated, and also can provide hypotheses for research. Recently there has been a research emphasis on the generation of such strategic propositions.[35]

---

[32] Although the main publications on PIMS are now more than three years old, additional research work has been performed in the context of this project. See for instance Robert D. Buzzell and Paul W. Farris, "Industrial Marketing Costs: An Analysis of Variations in Manu-facturers' Marketing Expenditures," Report No. 76-118 (Cambridge, Massachusetts: Marketing Science Institute, December 1976).

[33] See an effort in this direction in Yoram Wind and Henry J. Claycamp, "Planning Product Line Strategy: A Matrix Approach," *Journal of Marketing*, Vol. 40 (January 1976), pp. 2–9.

[34] See, for example, Samuel C. Johnson and Conrad Jones, "How to Organize for New Products," *Harvard Business Review*, Vol. 35 (May–June 1957), pp. 49–62; Lee Adler, same as reference 3; David W. Cravens, see reference 4.

[35] See, for example, William E. Fruhan, Jr., reference 21; Michel Chevalier, "The Strat-egy Spectre Behind Your Market Share," *European Business*, No. 34 (1972), pp. 63–72; Robert D. Buzzell et al., same as reference 12.

Hofer has proposed an approach to generate these propositions in a systematic fashion to develop what he calls a "contingency theory of business strategy." [36] There are obvious problems in the building of such a contingency theory because of the sheer number of possible situations, and the lack of empirical evidence of the validity of the propositions. The development of typologies of marketing situations and additional field research, however, should make this approach more feasible in the future.

5. *Strategic Intelligence Systems.* The design of any information system requires a framework within which information needs can be appraised systematically. The contributions of management science to the analysis of marketing decisions have enabled marketing information systems to evolve from the level of describing operations to that of tactical decision making.[37] Few studies have been reported, however, on the development of information systems for strategic decisions which require more emphasis on environmental and competitive factors.[38] The formalization of product-market portfolio analysis provides a structure which should guide the development of such strategic intelligence systems in the future, as illustrated by the work of Montgomery and Weinberg.[39]

6. *Computerized Models for Marketing Strategy Formulation.* Several marketing models are now available to assist managerial decision making in such areas as advertising, pricing, distribution, brand management, and new product introduction. More recently, joint-space representations of products and segments have provided a basis for formulating marketing strategies taking into account the interactions within a set of product-market entries.[40] Additional computerized tools to assist in the formulation of marketing strategy can be expected in the future, as the approaches to product-market portfolio analysis discussed here lend themselves to quantification.

CONCLUSIONS

During the fifties and early sixties, the formulation of the marketing concept, the marketing mix, and the market strategy brought forth a new, managerial orien-

---

[36] Charles W. Hofer, "Toward a Contingency Theory of Business Strategy," *Academy of Management Journal*, Vol. 18, No. 4 (December 1975), pp. 784–810.

[37] See, for instance, David B. Montgomery and Glen L. Urban, "Marketing Decision-Information Systems: An Emerging View," *Journal of Marketing Research*, Vol. 7, No. 5 (May 1970), pp. 226–234.

[38] Notable exceptions are William R. King and David I. Clelland, "Environmental Information Systems for Strategic Marketing Planning," *Journal of Marketing*, Vol. 38 (October 1974), pp. 35–40; Ralph H. Kilmann and Kyung-Il Ghymn, "The MAPS Design Technology: Designing Strategic Intelligence Systems for MNC's," *Columbia Journal of World Business* (Summer 1976), pp. 35–47.

[39] David B. Montgomery and Charles B. Weinberg, see reference 30.

[40] See, for instance, the STRATOP model in Edgar A. Pessemier, *Product Management: Strategy and Organization* (New York: John Wiley, 1977), Chapter 5; the MARKSTRAT simulation game provides joint-space representations for the formulation of a marketing strategy for a product-market portfolio: Jean-Claude Larréché and Hubert Gatignon, *MARKSTRAT: Design and Implementation of Marketing Strategies in a Competitive Environment* (Palo Alto, California: The Scientific Press, 1977).

tation of marketing.[41] This orientation has stimulated much research in consumer behavior, in market segmentation, in specific problems related to the elements of the marketing mix, and in marketing modeling. This stream of research has undeniably increased the understanding of marketing problems and will continue to do so in the future. Simultaneously, marketing has become established as an important management discipline.

During the sixties, little attention was paid to the formulation of marketing strategies and the tasks facing top marketing executives in terms of allocating major resources among products and markets. This area of marketing decision making was rightly perceived as complex, ill-defined, and difficult to study. Research priorities and opportunities were numerous and more attractive elsewhere. Finally, tactical decisions and product management drew most of the attention in a growth economy. At the same time, corporate strategy was only beginning to be established as a key function of corporate management.

Since the beginning of the seventies, a stream of publications have appeared on the subject of marketing strategy.[42] In parallel, a number of new developments have occurred in corporate strategy, the more important ones of which are concerned with the portfolio concept and the related analytical approaches. Now marketing strategy and corporate strategy begin to meld because of common needs and interests.

Progress in marketing strategy requires a definition of the discipline and a framework to guide future research. The authors have attempted to describe the state of the art on both counts and to suggest ways by which the subject area can be better conceptualized as well as made more operationally viable. Inevitably, because of the subject's complexity as well as its infancy, much that has been done to date can be described best as "tentative" in its findings and conclusions.

---

[41] The following three works were most influential in the development of the managerial orientation of marketing: Theodore Levitt, "Marketing Myopia," *Harvard Business Review,* Vol. 38 (July–August 1960), pp. 24–47; Neil U. Borden, "The Concept of the Marketing Mix," *Journal of Advertising Research* (June 1964), pp. 2–7 (in fact Neil Borden introduced the concept of the marketing mix in his presidential address to the American Marketing Association in 1953); and Alfred R. Oxenfeldt, same as reference 1.

[42] The economic, legal, governmental, and consumerist pressures stemming from the environment are certainly not foreign to this trend as evidenced, for instance, by the emphasis placed on the "pruning" of product lines. See David S. Hopkins, "New Emphases in Marketing Strategies," *The Conference Board Record* (August 1976), pp. 35–39.

A Strategic Perspective on Product Planning

George S. Day

INTRODUCTION

The past decade has seen growing recognition that the product planning function within diversified companies of all sizes involves tradeoffs among competing opportunities and strategies. During this period the combination of more complex markets, shorter product life cycles and social, legal and governmental trends put a premium on minimizing the degree of risk in the product mix. More recently, managers have had to cope with severe resource constraints, stemming partly from weaknesses in the capital markets and a general cash shortage, and the triple traumas of the energy crisis, materials shortages and inflation.

Some of the manifestations of the new climate for product planning are skepticism toward the value of full product lines, unwillingness to accept the risks of completely new products, an emphasis on profit growth rather than volume growth and active product elimination and divestment programs.[1] Yet managements cannot afford to turn their backs on all opportunities for change and attempt to survive simply by doing a better job with the established products and services. Eventually all product categories become saturated or threatened by substitutes and diversification becomes essential to survival. Consumer goods companies are especially feeling this pressure as the productivity of line extensions or product adaptations directed at narrow market segments declines. Also the likelihood of regulatory actions directed at products, such as aerosols

About the Author: At the time of writing, George S. Day was Professor of Marketing, Faculty of Management Studies, University of Toronto.

Reprinted from *Journal of Contemporary Business*, Spring 1975, pp. 1–34, with permission of the *Journal of Contemporary Business*, copyright 1975.

[1] "The Squeeze on Product Mix," *BusinessWeek* (5 January 1974), pp. 50–55; "Toward Higher Margins and Less Variety," *BusinessWeek* (14 September 1974), pp. 98–99; E. B. Weiss, "We'll See Fewer New Products in 1975—Culprit Is Shortage of Capital, Resources," *Advertising Age* (2 December 1974); "Corrective Surgery," *Newsweek* (27 January 1975), p. 50; and Jack Springer, "1975: Bad Year for New Products; Good Year for Segmentation," *Advertising Age* (10 February 1975), pp. 30–39.

and cyclamates, points up the risks of having a closely grouped product line.[2] More than ever, long-run corporate health is going to depend on the ability of product planners to juggle those conflicting pressures of diversification and consolidation.

The pervasive nature of the resource allocation problem in product planning is the focus of this article. The emphasis is on the basic issues of the role of new and established products and markets and the choice of areas of new product development to pursue. The first issue is addressed in the context of the product portfolio, which describes the mixture of products that generate cash and in which the company can invest cash. A detailed examination of the product portfolio begins with its component parts, the product life cycle and the notion of market dominance, and then turns to the implications for strategic planning and resource allocation.

Once the role of new products has been established, the issue of where to look is addressed with an explicit statement of a search strategy. This statement defines the characteristics of desirable opportunities in terms that are meaningful to product planners.

STRATEGIC PLANNING AND PRODUCT PLANNING

There are as many concepts of strategy as writers on the subject.[3] Several of the more useful definitions for our immediate purposes are:

- Decisions today which affect the future (not future decisions)
- Major questions of resource allocation that determine a company's long-run results.
- The calculated means by which the firm deploys its resources—i.e., personnel, machines and money—to accomplish its purpose under the most advantageous circumstances
- A competitive edge that allows a company to serve the customers better than its competitors
- The broad principles by which a company hopes to secure an advantage over competitors, an attractiveness to buyers and a full exploitation of company resources

Following these definitions, the desired output of the strategic planning process is a long-run plan "that will produce an attractive growth rate and a high rate of return on investment by achieving a market position so advantageous that competitors can retaliate only over an extended period at a prohibitive cost."[4]

---

[2] Barry R. Linsky, "Which Way to Move with New Products," *Advertising Age* (22 July 1974), pp. 45–46.

[3] George A. Steiner, *Top Management Planning* (London: Macmillan, 1969); H. Igor Ansoff, *Corporate Strategy* (New York: McGraw-Hill, 1965).

[4] David T. Kollat, Roger D. Blackwell and James F. Robeson, *Strategic Marketing* (New York: Holt, Rinehart and Winston, 1972), p. 12.

Most strategic planning processes and the resulting plans show a distinct family resemblance, although the specifics obviously vary greatly. These specifics usually include [5]: (1) a statement of the mission of the strategic business unit (SBU),[6] (2) the desired future position the SBU and the corporation wants to attain, comprising measurable profitability, sales, market share, efficiency and flexibility objectives, (3) the key environmental assumptions and the opportunities and threats, (4) a statement of the strengths, weaknesses and problems of the SBU and its major competitors, (5) the strategic gap between the desired and forecasted position of the SBU, (6) actions to be taken to close the gap— the strategy and (7) the required resources and where they can be obtained, including financial resources such as net cash flow, the equity base and debt capacity and management capabilities. These are the main elements of the planning process that are relevant to product planning, leaving aside the issues of detailed implementation plans, contingency plans, which state in advance what modifications will be made if key environmental or competitor assumptions turn out to be false, and the monitoring procedures.

What is lacking in the planning process just described is a systematic procedure for generating and choosing strategic alternatives. One of the greatest weaknesses of current strategic plans is the lack of viable strategy alternatives which present very different approaches and outcomes. Too frequently top management sees only one strategy which the SBU has decided is best in terms of its own and the managers' personal needs and objectives. This ignores the interdependency among products (the portfolio aspect)[7] and the possibility that what is best for each SBU is not necessarily best for the entire company.[8] In recognition of this problem, the planning process shown in Figure 1 incorporates an analysis of the product portfolio. The remainder of this paper is devoted to the uses and limitations of the product portfolio and the implications for developing strategy alternates that optimize the long-run position of the firm.

THE COMPONENTS OF THE PRODUCT PORTFOLIO

Market share and stage in the product life cycle have long been regarded as important determinants of profitability. The contribution of the product portfolio

---

[5] This description of the planning process has been adapted from Kollat, et al., *Strategic Marketing;* Louis V. Gerstner, "The Practice of Business: Can Strategic Planning Pay Off?" *Business Horizons* (December 1972); Herschner Cross, "New Directions in Corporate Planning," An address to Operations Research Society of America (Milwaukee, Wisconsin: 10 May 1973).

[6] The identification of "strategic business units" is a critical first step in any analysis of corporate strategy. Various definitions have been used. Their flavor is captured by the following guidelines for defining a business: (1) no more than 60 percent of the expenses should represent arbitrary allocations of joint costs, (2) no more than 60 percent of the sales should be made to a vertically integrated (downstream) subsidiary and (3) the served market should be homogeneous; i.e., segments are treated as distinct if they represent markedly different shares, competitors and growth rates.

[7] E. Eugene Carter and Kalman J. Cohen, "Portfolio Aspects of Strategic Planning," *Journal of Business Policy*, 2 (1972), pp. 8–30.

[8] C. H. Springer, "Strategic Management in General Electric," *Operations Research* (November–December 1973), pp. 1177–1182.

FIGURE 1   Highlighting Product Planning Activities in the Strategic Planning Process

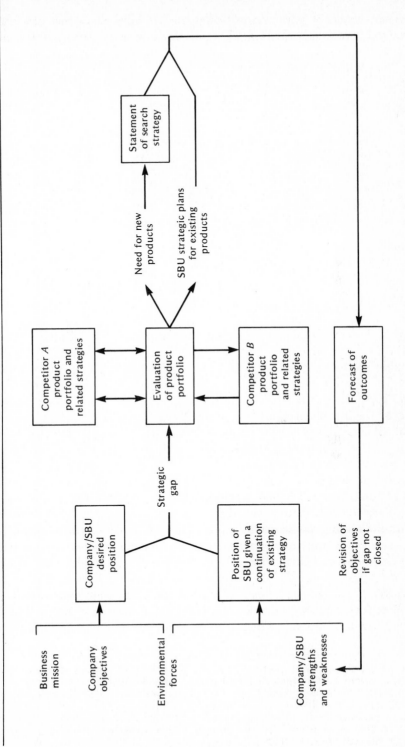

concept is that it permits the planner to consider these two measures simultaneously in evaluating the products of an entire company or a division or SBU.

The Value of Market Share Dominance

The belief in the benefits of a dominant market share is rooted deeply in the experience of executives. It is reinforced by the facts of life in most markets:

- The market leader is usually the most profitable.
- During economic downturns, customers are likely to concentrate their purchases in suppliers with large shares, and distributors and retailers will try to cut inventories by eliminating the marginal supplier.
- During periods of economic growth, there is often a bandwagon effect with a large share presenting a positive image to customers and retailers.[9]

Of course, market domination has its own pitfalls, beyond antitrust problems: ". . . monopolists flounder on their own complacency rather than on public opposition. Market domination produces tremendous internal resistance against any innovation and makes adaptation to change dangerously difficult. Also, it usually means that the enterprise has too many of its eggs in one basket and is too vulnerable to economic fluctuations."[10] The leader is also highly vulnerable to competitive actions, especially in the pricing area, since the leader establishes the basic industry price from which smaller competitors can discount.

The clearest evidence of the value of market share comes from a study of The Profit Impact of Market Strategies (PIMS) of 620 separate businesses by the Marketing Science Institute which, in turn, draws on earlier work by General Electric. Early results indicated that market share, investment intensity (ratio of total investment to sales) and product quality were the most important determinants of pretax return on investment, among a total of 37 distinct factors incorporated into the profit model.[11] On average it was found that a difference of 10 points in market share was accompanied by a difference of about 5 points in pretax ROI. As share declined from more than 40 percent to less than 10 percent, the average pretax ROI dropped from 30 percent to 9.1 percent.

The PIMS study also provided some interesting insights into the reasons for the link between market share and profitability.[12] The results point to economies of scale and, especially, the opportunities for vertical integration as the most important explanations. Thus high-share businesses (more than 40 percent) tend to have low ratios of purchases to sales because they make rather than buy and own their distribution facilities. The ratio of purchases to sales increases from 33

---

[9] Bernard Catry and Michel Chevalier, "Market Share Strategy and the Product Life Cycle," *Journal of Marketing*, 38 (October 1974), pp. 29–34.

[10] Peter F. Drucker, *Management: Tasks, Responsibilities, Practices* (New York: Harper and Row, 1973), p. 106.

[11] Sidney Schoeffler, Robert D. Buzzell and Donald F. Heany, "Impact of Strategic Planning on Profit Performance," *Harvard Business Review* (March–April 1974), pp. 137–145.

[12] Robert D. Buzzell, Bradley T. Gale and Ralph G. M. Sultan, "Market Share, Profitability and Business Strategy," unpublished working paper (Marketing Science Institute, August 1974).

percent for high-share businesses to 45 percent for low-share (less than 10 percent) businesses. But because of economies of scale in manufacturing and purchasing there is no significant relationship between manufacturing expenses or the ratio of sales to investment and the market share. To some degree these results also support the market power argument of economists; market leaders evidently are able to bargain more effectively (either through the exercise of reciprocity or greater technical marketing skills) and obtain higher prices than their competition (but largely because they produce and sell higher-quality goods and services). The fact that market leaders spend a significantly higher percentage of their sales on R and D suggests that they pursue a conscious strategy of product leadership.

Experience Curve Analysis   The importance of economies of scale in the relationship of market share and profitability is verified by the experience curve concept. Research, largely reported by the Boston Consulting Group, has found that in a wide range of businesses (including plastics, semiconductors, gas ranges and life insurance policies), the total unit costs, in constant dollars, decline by a constant percentage (usually 20 to 30 percent) with each doubling of accumulated units of output or experience.[13] Since the experience effect applies to all value added, it subsumes economies of scale and specialization effects along with the well-known learning curve which applies only to direct labor costs.

An experience curve, when plotted on a log-log scale as in Figure 2, ap-

FIGURE 2   Cost Experience Curve Showing Relative Profit Levels of Competitors

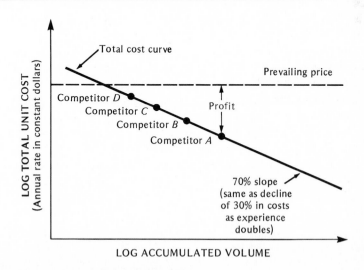

[13] For more extended treatments and a variety of examples, see Patrick Conley, "Experience Curves as a Planning Tool," *IEEE Transactions* (June 1970); *Perspectives on Experience* (Boston: Boston Consulting Group, 1970); and "Selling Business a Theory of Economics," *Business Week* (8 September 1974).

pears as a straight line. The locations of the competitors on this curve are determined approximately by their respective accumulated experience, for which relative market share is a good surrogate (this may not be true if some competitors recently have entered the market by buying experience through licenses or acquisitions). Then it follows that the competitor with the greatest accumulated experience will have the lowest relative costs and, if prices are similar between competitors, also will have the greatest profits. Of course, companies that fail to reduce costs along the product category experience curve and who are not dominant will be at an even greater competitive disadvantage.

Figure 2 shows a price prevailing at one point in time. Over the long run, prices also will decline at roughly the same rate as costs decline. The major exception to this rule occurs during the introduction and growth state of the life cycle, when the innovator and/or dominant competitor is tempted to maintain prices at a high level to recoup the development costs. The high price umbrella usually achieves this immediate end because unit profits are high. The drawback is the incentive to higher-cost competitors to enter the market and attempt to increase their market shares. In effect, the dominant competitor is trading future market share for current profits. This may be sensible if the early leader: (1) has a number of attractive new product opportunities requiring cash, (2) there are potential competitors whose basic business position will enable them eventually to enter the product category regardless of the pricing strategy [14] or (3) significant barriers to entry can be erected.

Product Life Cycle

That products pass through various stages between life and death (introduction → growth → maturity → decline) is hard to deny. Equally accepted is the notion that a company should have a mix of products with representation in each of these stages.

Thus the concept of a product life cycle would appear to be an essential tool for understanding product strategies.[15] Indeed this is true, but only *if* the position of the product and the duration of the cycle can be determined. This caveat should be kept in mind when considering the following summary of the important aspects of the product life cycle:

· Volume and profit growth attract competition during the early *growth* (or takeoff) stage of the life cycle. The product market is even more attractive if the innovator lacks the capacity to satisfy demand. However,

---

[14] "An example of this situation was DuPont's production of cyclohexane. DuPont was the first producer of the product but the manufacture of cyclohexane is so integrated with the operations of an oil refinery that oil refiners have an inherent cost advantage over companies, such as DuPont, without an oil refinery." Robert B. Stobaugh and Philip L. Townsend, "Price Forecasting and Strategic Planning: The Case of Petrochemicals," *Journal of Marketing Research*, 12 (February 1975), pp. 19–29.

[15] Theodore Levitt, "Exploit the Product Life Cycle," *Harvard Business Review* (November–December 1965), pp. 81–94.

these competitors may contribute to the growth of sales by their market development expenditures and product improvements.

- Purchase patterns and distribution channels are still fluid during the rapid *growth* stage. For this reason, market shares can be increased at relatively low cost over short periods of time by capturing a disproportionate share of incremental sales (especially where these sales come from new users rather than heavier usage by existing users).
- As a product reaches *maturity* there is evidence of saturation, finer distinctions in benefits surrounding the product and appeals to special segments.
- There is often an industry shake-out to signal the *end* of the rapid growth stage. The trigger might be an excessive number of competitors who have to resort to price cutting to survive; a dominant producer who seeks to regain share; or a large competitor buying into the market (and all these effects will be accentuated by an economic slowdown). The result is a period of consolidation during which marginal competitors either drop out, merge with other small competitors or sell out to larger competitors.
- During the *maturity* stage, market-share relationships tend to stabilize; distribution patterns have been established and are difficult to change. This, in turn, contributes to inertia in purchasing relationships and selling oriented toward maintaining relationships. Any substantial increase in share of market will require a reduction in a competitor's capacity utilization which will be resisted vigorously. As a result, gains in share are both time-consuming and costly. This is not necessarily the case if the attempt to gain shares is spearheaded by a significant improvement in product value or performance which the competitor cannot easily match. A case in point is the growth in private labels, or distributor-controlled labels, in both food and general merchandising categories.
- As substitutes appear and/or sales begin to decline, the core product behaves like a commodity and is subject to intense and continuing price pressure. The result is further competitors dropping out of the market, since only those with extensive accumulated experience and cost-cutting capability are able to generate reasonable profits and ROI's.
- The *decline* stage can be forestalled by vigorous promotion (plus, a new creative platform) and product improvement designed to generate more frequent usage or new users and applications.[16] Of course, if these extensions are sufficiently different, a new product life cycle is launched.

Measurement and Interpretation Problems

The concepts underlying the product portfolio are much easier to articulate than to implement.

---

16 Harry W. McMahan, "Like Sinatra, Old Products Can, Too, Get a New Lease on Life," *Advertising Age* (25 November 1974), p. 32.

What is the Product-Market? The crux of the problem is well stated by Moran:

> In our complex service society there are no more product classes—not in any meaningful sense, only as a figment of file clerk imagination. There are only use classes—users which are more central to some products and peripheral to others—on a vast overlapping continuum. To some degree, in some circumstances almost anything can be a partial substitute for almost anything else. An eight-cent stamp substitutes to some extent for an airline ticket.[17]

Where does this leave the manager who relies on share of some (possibly ill-defined) market as a guide to performance evaluation and resource allocation? First he or she must recognize that most markets do not have neat boundaries. For example, patterns of substitution in industrial markets often look like continua, i.e., zinc, brass, aluminum and engineered plastics such as nylon and polycarbonates can be arrayed rather uniformly along dimensions of price and performance. A related complication, more pertinent to consumer product markets, is the possibility of segment differences in perceptions of product substitutability. For example, there is a timid, risk-averse segment that uses a different product for each kind of surface cleaning (i.e., surface detergents, scouring powders, floor cleaners, bleaches, lavatory cleaners and general-purpose wall cleaners). At the other extreme is the segment that uses detergent for every cleaning problem. Thirdly, product-markets may have to be defined in terms of distribution patterns. Thus, tire companies treat the OEM and replacement tire markets as separate and distinct, even though the products going through these two channels are perfect substitutes so far as the end customer is concerned.

Perhaps the most important consideration is the time frame. A long-run view, reflecting strategic planning concerns, invariably will reveal a larger product-market to account for: (1) changes in technology, price relationships and availability which may remove or reduce cost and performance limitations, e.g., the boundaries between minicomputers, programmable computers and time-sharing systems in many use situations are becoming very fuzzy; (2) the time required by present and prospective buyers to react to these changes, which includes modifying behavior patterns, production systems, etc. and (3) considerable switching among products over long periods of time to satisfy desires for variety and change, as is encountered in consumer goods with snacks, for example.

Despite these complexities, the boundaries of product markets usually are established by four-digit Standard Industrial Classification (SIC) categories and/or expert judgment. The limitations of the SIC are well known [18] but often do not outweigh the benefits of data availability in a convenient form that can be broken down further to geographic markets. In short, the measure is attrac-

---

[17] Harry T. Moran, "Why New Products Fail," *Journal of Advertising Research* (April 1973).

[18] See Douglas Needham, *Economic Analysis and Industrial Structure* (New York: Holt, Rinehart and Winston); Stanford Rose, "Bigness Is a Numbers Game," *Fortune* (November 1969).

tive on tactical grounds (for sales force, promotional budget, etc., allocation) but potentially misleading for strategic planning purposes.

What Is Market Dominance? A measure of market share, per se, is not a good indicator of the extent to which a firm dominates a market. The value of a 30 percent share is very different in a market where the next largest competitor has 40 percent than in one where the next largest has only 20 percent. Two alternative measures which incorporate information on the structure of the competition are:

- Company share ÷ share of largest competitor
- Company share ÷ share of three largest competitors

The former measure is more consistent with the implications of the experience curve, while the latter is perhaps better suited to highly concentrated markets (where the four-firm concentration ratio is greater than 80 percent, for example). Regardless of which measure is used it is often the case that the dominant firm has to be at least 1.5 times as large as the next biggest competitor in order to ensure profitability. When there are two large firms of roughly equal shares, especially in a growth business such as nuclear power generators, the competition is likely to be severe. In this instance, both General Electric and Westinghouse have about 40 percent shares and don't expect to be profitable on new installations until after 1977. Conversely, when the two largest firms have small shares, say less than 5 percent, neither measure of market dominance is meaningful.

Evidence of market share dominance, no matter how it is measured, will not be equally meaningful in all product markets. Results from the PIMS study [19] suggest that importance of market share is influenced most strongly by the frequency of purchases.

Return on Investment

Share Market	Infrequently Purchased (<once/mon)	Frequently Purchased (>once/mon)
Under 10%	6.9%	12.4%
10–19	14.4	13.7
20–29	17.8	17.4
30–39	24.3	23.1
Over 40	34.6	22.9

Though the full reasons for this difference in profitability are obscure they probably relate to differences in unit costs and prior buyer experience with the

---

[19] Buzzell, Gale and Sultan, "Market Share, Profitability."

available alternatives which, in turn, determine willingness to reduce risk by buying the market leader and/or paying a premium price. Also, the frequently purchased category is dominated by consumer goods where there is considerable proliferation of brand names through spinoffs, flankers, fighting brands, etc., in highly segmented markets. Each of these brands, no matter how small, shares production facilities and will have low production and distribution costs, although they may be treated as separate businesses.[20] It is hardly surprising that the experience curve concept is difficult to apply to consumer goods. Most of the successful applications have been with infrequently purchased industrial products; relatively undifferentiated, with high value added compared to raw material costs and fairly stable rates of capacity utilization.

A further caveat regarding the experience curve concerns the extent to which costs ultimately can be reduced. The experience curve clearly does not happen according to some immutable law; it requires careful management and some degree of long-run product stability (and, ideally, standardization). These conditions cannot be taken for granted and will be threatened directly by the customer demand for product change and competitive efforts to segment the market. In effect, product innovation and cost efficiency are not compatible in the long run.[21]

A related question concerns the relevance of the experience curve to a new competitor in an established market. It is doubtful that a new entrant with reasonable access to the relevant technology would incur the same level of initial costs as the developers of the market.

What Is the Stage in the Product Life Cycle?   It is not sufficient to simply know the current rate of growth of the product category. The strategic implications of the product life cycle often hinge on forecasting changes in the growth rate and, in particular, on establishing the end of the growth and maturity stages.

The first step in utilizing the life cycle is to ensure that the product class is identified properly. This may require a distinction between a broad product type (cigarettes) and a more specific product form (plain filter cigarettes). Secondly, the graph of product (type or form) sales needs to be adjusted for factors that might obscure the underlying life cycle, i.e., price changes, economic fluctuations and population changes. The third and most difficult step is to forecast when the product will move from one stage to another. The specific problems are beyond the scope of this article. However, the range of possibilities is illustrated by these various leading indicators of the "top-out" point.[22]

- Evidence of saturation; declining proportion of new trier versus replacement sales

---

[20] An extreme example is Unilever in the UK with 20 detergent brands all sharing joint costs to some degree.

[21] William J. Abernathy and Kenneth Wayne, "Limit of the Learning Curve," *Harvard Business Review*, 52 (September–October 1974), pp. 109–119.

[22] Aubrey Wilson, "Industrial Marketing Research in Britain," *Journal of Marketing Research*, 6 (February 1969), pp. 15–28.

- Declining prices and profits
- Increased product life
- Industry over capacity
- Appearance of new replacement product or technology
- Changes in export/import ratio
- Decline in elasticity of advertising and promotion, coupled with increasing price elasticity
- Changes in consumer preferences

These measures generally will indicate only the *timing* of the top-out point, and each is sufficiently imprecise that it is strongly advisable to use as many as possible in combination. Forecasts of the product sales *level* to be achieved at the top-out point may be obtained by astute incorporation of the leading indicators into: (1) technological forecasts, (2) similar product analysis (where sales patterns of products with analogous characteristics are used to estimate the sales pattern of the new product) or (3) epidemiological models whose parameters include initial sales rates and market saturation levels estimated with marketing research methods.[23]

ANALYZING THE PRODUCT PORTFOLIO

The product life cycle highlights the desirability of a variety of products/services with different present and prospective growth rates. However, this is not a sufficient condition for a well-balanced portfolio of products that will ensure profitable long-run growth. Two other factors are market share position and the need to balance cash flows within the corporation. Some products should *generate* cash (and provide acceptable reported profits) and others should *use* cash to support growth; otherwise, the company will build up unproductive cash reserves or go bankrupt.[24] These issues are clarified by jointly considering share position and market growth rate, as in the matrix of Figure 3. The conceptualization used here is largely attributable to the Boston Consulting Group.[25]

It must be stressed that the growth-share matrix discussed here is simply one way of conceptualizing the product portfolio. It has been useful as a device for synthesizing the analyses and judgments of the earlier steps in the planning

[23] John C. Chambers, Satinder K. Mullick and Donald D. Smith, *An Executives' Guide to Forecasting* (New York: John Wiley and Sons, 1974); Frank M. Bass, "A New Product Growth Model for Consumer Durables," *Management Science*, 15 (January 1969), pp. 215–227.

[24] Of course the cash flow pattern also may be altered by changing debt and/or dividend policies. (For most companies, the likelihood of new equity funding is limited.) Limits on growth are imposed when the additional business ventures to be supported have too high a business risk for the potential reward and/or the increase in debt has too high a (financial) risk for the potential rewards.

[25] Among the publications of the Boston Consulting Group that describe the portfolio are: Perspectives on Experience (1970) and the following pamphlets authored by Bruce D. Henderson in the general perspectives series: "The Product Portfolio" (1970); "The Experience Curve Reviewed: The Growth Share Matrix or the Product Portfolio" (1973); and "Cash Traps" (1972).

FIGURE 3   Describing the Product Portfolio in the Market Share Growth Matrix. (Arrows indicate principal cash flows.)

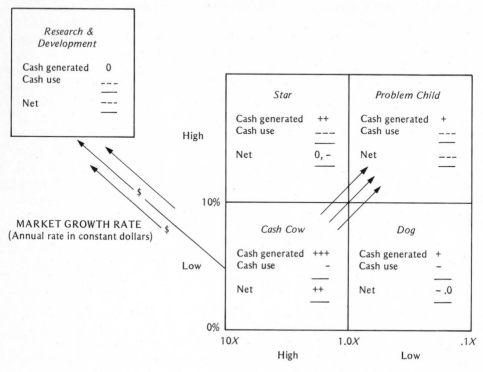

MARKET DOMINANCE
(Ratio of company share to share of next largest competitor)

process, especially in facilitating an approach to strategic decision making that considers the firm to be a whole that is more than the sum of its separate parts. For these purposes, the arbitrary classifications of products in the growth-share matrix are adequate to differentiate the strategy possibilities.[26]

Product Portfolio Strategies

Each of the four basic categories in the growth-share matrix implies a set of strategy alternatives that generally are applicable to the portfolio entries in that category.[27]

---

[26] A similar matrix reportedly is used by the Mead Corporation; see John Thackray, "The Mod Matrix of Mead," *Management Today* (January 1972), pp. 50–53, 112. This application has been criticized on the grounds of oversimplification, narrow applicability and the unwarranted emphasis on investment versus new investment. Indeed the growth-share matrix is regarded by Thackray as primarily a device for achieving social control.

[27] William E. Cox, Jr., "Product Portfolio Strategy: An Analysis of the Boston Consulting Group Approach to Marketing Strategies," *Proceedings of the American Marketing Association,* 1974.

Stars Products that are market leaders, but also growing fast, will have substantial reported profits but need a lot of cash to finance the rate of growth. The appropriate strategies are designed primarily to protect the existing share level by reinvesting earnings in the form of price reductions, product improvement, better market coverage, production efficiency increases, etc. Particular attention must be given to obtaining a large share of the new users or new applications that are the source of growth in the market. Management may elect, instead, to maximize short-run profits and cash flow at the expense of long-run market share. This is highly risky because it usually is predicated on a continuing stream of product innovations and deprives the company of a cash cow which may be needed in the future.

Cash Cows The combination of a slow market growth and market dominance usually spells substantial net cash flows. The amount of cash generated is far in excess of the amount required to maintain share. All strategies should be directed toward maintaining market dominance—including investments in technological leadership. Pricing decisions should be made cautiously with an eye to maintaining price leadership. Pressure to overinvest through product proliferation and market expansion should be resisted unless prospects for expanding primary demand are unusually attractive. Instead, excess cash should be used to support research activities and growth areas elsewhere in the company.

Dogs Since there usually can be only one market leader and because most markets are mature, the greatest number of products fall in this category.[28] Such products are usually at a cost disadvantage and have few opportunities for growth at a reasonable cost. Their markets are not growing, so there is little new business to compete for, and market share gains will be resisted strenuously by the dominant competition.

The product remains in the portfolio because it shows (or promises) a modest book profit. This accounting result is misleading because most of the cash flow must be reinvested to maintain competitive position and finance inflation.[29] Another characteristic of a dog is that individual investment projects (especially those designed to reduce production costs) show a high ROI. However, the competitive situation is such that these returns cannot be realized in surplus cash flow that can be used to fund more promising projects. In addition there are the potential hidden costs of unproductive demands on management time (and consequent missed opportunities) and low personnel morale because of a lack of achievement.

---

[28] It is also typical that the weighted ratio of average market share versus the largest competitor is greater than 1.0. This reflects the contribution of the cash cows to both sales and profits. It also accounts for the familiar pattern whereby 20 percent of the products account for 80 percent of the dollar margin (a phenomenon generally described as Pareto's law).

[29] The Boston Consulting Group defines such products as cash traps when the required reinvestment, including increased working capital, exceeds reported profit plus increase in permanent debt capacity: Bruce D. Henderson, "Cash Traps," *Perspectives*, Number 102 (Boston Consulting Group, 1972).

The pejorative label of "dog" becomes increasingly appropriate the closer the product is to the lower-right corner of the growth-share matrix.[30] The need for positive action becomes correspondingly urgent. The search for action alternatives should begin with attempts to alleviate the problem without divesting. If these possibilities are unproductive, attention then can shift to finding ways of making the product to be divested as attractive as possible; then to liquidation and, finally if need be, to abandonment:

- *Corrective Action.* Naturally all reasonable cost-cutting possibilities should be examined, but, as noted above, these are not likely to be productive in the long run. A related alternative is to find a market segment that can be dominated. The attractiveness of this alternative will depend on the extent to which the segment can be protected from competition—perhaps because of technology or distribution requirements.[31] What must be avoided is the natural tendency of operating managers to arbitrarily redefine their markets in order to improve their share position and thus change the classification of the product when, in fact, the economics of the business are unchanged. This is highly probable when the product-market boundaries are ambiguous.

- *Harvest.* This is a conscious cutback of all support costs to the minimum level to maximize the product's profitability over a foreseeable lifetime, which is usually short. This cutback could include reducing advertising and sales effort, increasing delivery time, increasing the acceptable order size and eliminating all staff support activities such as marketing research.

- *Value Added.* Opportunities may exist for reparceling a product or business that is to be divested; this may involve dividing the assets into smaller units or participating in forming a "kennel of dogs" in which the weak products of several companies are combined into a healthy package. This latter alternative is especially attractive when the market is very fractionated.

- *Liquidation.* This is the most prevalent solution usually involving a sale as a going concern but, perhaps, including a licensing agreement. If the business/product is to be sold as a unit, the problem is to maximize the selling price—a joint function of the prospective buyers need for the acquisition (which will depend on search strategy) and their overhead rate. For example, a small company may find the product attractive and be able to make money because of low overhead.

- *Abandonment.* The possibilities here include giveaways and bankruptcy.

---

[30] The label may be meaningless if the product is part of a product line, an integral component of a system or where most of the sales are internal.

[31] It should be noted that full line/full service competitors may be vulnerable to this strategy if there are customer segments which do not need all the services, etc. Thus, Digital Equipment Corp. has prospered in competition with IBM by simply selling basic hardware and depending on others to do the applications programming. By contrast, IBM provides, for a price, a great deal of service backup and software for customers who are not self-sufficient. "A Minicomputer Tempest," *BusinessWeek* (27 January 1975), pp. 79–80.

FIGURE 4   A Balanced Product Portfolio

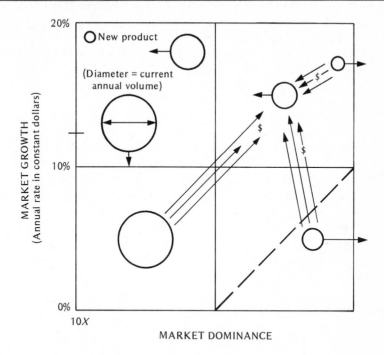

Problem Children   The combination of rapid growth rate and poor profit margins creates an enormous demand for cash. If the cash is not forthcoming, the product will become a dog as growth inevitably slows. The basic strategy options are fairly clear cut: either invest heavily to get a disproportionate share of the new sales or buy existing shares by acquiring competitors and thus move the product toward the star category or get out of the business using some of the methods just described.

Consideration also should be given to a market segmentation strategy, but only if a defensible niche can be identified and resources are available to gain dominance. This strategy is even more attractive if the segment can provide an entree and experience base from which to push for dominance of the whole market.

Further Strategic Implications

While the product portfolio is helpful in suggesting strategies for specific products, it is equally useful for portraying the overall health of a multiproduct company. The issue is the extent to which the portfolio departs from the balanced display of Figure 4, both for the present and in 3 to 5 years.

Among the indicators of overall health are size and vulnerability of the cash cows (and the prospects for the stars, if any) and the number of problem children and dogs. Particular attention must be paid to those products with large cash appetites. Unless the company has abundant cash flow, it cannot afford to sponsor many such products at one time. If resources (including debt capacity) are spread too thin, the company simply will wind up with too many marginal products and suffer a reduced capacity to finance promising new product entries or acquisitions in the future. Some indication of this type of resource misallocation can be obtained from a comparison of the growth rates of the product class and the company's entrant (as illustrated in Figure 5). Ideally, nothing should be in the upper sector where market growth exceeds company growth—unless the product is being harvested.

Competitive Analysis Product portfolios should be constructed for each of the major competitors. Assuming competitive management follows the logic just described, they eventually will realize that they can't do everything. The key question is which problem children will be supported aggressively and which will be eliminated. The answer obviously will be difficult to obtain, but has an important bearing on the approach the company takes to its own problem children.

Of course, a competitive position analysis has many additional dimensions which must be explored in depth before specific competitive actions and reactions within each product category can be forecast.[32] This analysis, coupled with an understanding of competitive portfolios, becomes the basis for any fundamental strategy employing the military concept of concentration which essentially means to concentrate strength against weakness.[33]

FIGURE 5 Market Industry versus Company Growth Rates. (Illustrative diversified company—diameters are proportional to current annual sales volume.)

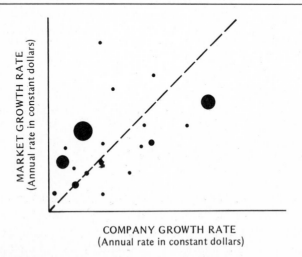

MARKET GROWTH RATE
(Annual rate in constant dollars)

COMPANY GROWTH RATE
(Annual rate in constant dollars)

[32] Dimensions such as product and pricing policy, geographic and distributor strength, delivery patterns, penetration by account size and probable reaction to our company initiatives need to be considered. See C. Davis Fogg, "Planning Gains in Market Share," *Journal of Marketing*, 38 (July 1974), pp. 30–38.

[33] This concept is developed by Harper Boyd, "Strategy Concepts," unpublished manuscript, 1974, and is based on B. H. Liddel Hart, *Strategy: The Indirect Approach* (London: Faber and Faber, 1951).

Dangers in the Pursuit of Market Share   Tilles has suggested a number of criteria for evaluating strategy alternatives.[34] The product portfolio is a useful concept for addressing the first three: (1) environmental consistency, (2) internal consistency and (3) adequacy of resources. A fourth criterion considers whether the degree of risk is acceptable, given the overall level of risk in the portfolio.

The experience of a number of companies, such as GE and RCA, in the main-frame computer business, points to the particular risks inherent in the pursuit of market share. An analysis of these "pyrrhic victories" [35] suggests that the greatest risks can be avoided if the following questions can be answered affirmatively: (1) Are company financial resources adequate? (2) If the fight is stopped short for some reason, will the corporation's position be competitively viable? and (3) Will government regulations permit the corporation to follow the strategy it has chosen? The last question includes antitrust policies which now virtually preclude acquisitions made by large companies in related fields [36] and regulatory policies designed to proliferate competition, as in the airline industry.

Organizational Implications   Although this discussion has focused on the financial and market position aspects of the product portfolio, the implications encompass the deployment of all corporate resources—tangible assets as well as crucial intangibles of management skills and time.

One policy that clearly must be avoided is to apply uniform performance objectives to all products, or SBU's, as is frequently attempted in highly decentralized profit-center management approaches. The use of flexible standards, tailored to the realities of the business, logically should lead to the recognition that different kinds of businesses require very different management styles. For example, stars and problem children demand an entrepreneurial orientation, while cash cows emphasize skills in fine tuning marketing tactics and ensuring effective allocation of resources. The nature of specialist support also will differ; e.g., R and D support being important for growth products and financial personnel becoming increasingly important as growth slows.[37] Finally, since good managers, regardless of their styles, are always in short supply, the portfolio notion suggests that they not be expended in potentially futile efforts to turn dogs into profitable performers. Instead they should be deployed into situations where the likelihood of achievement and, hence, of reinforcement, is high.

Other Methods of Portraying the Portfolio   The growth-share matrix is far from a complete synthesis of the underlying analyses and judgments as to the

---

[34] Seymour Tilles, "How to Evaluate Corporate Strategy," *Harvard Business Review*, 41 (July–August 1963).

[35] William E. Fruhan, "Pyrrhic Victories in Fights for Market Share," *Harvard Business Review*, 50 (September–October 1972).

[36] "Is John Sherman's Antitrust Obsolete?" *BusinessWeek* (23 March 1974).

[37] Stephen Dietz, "Get More out of Your Brand Management," *Harvard Business Review* (July–August 1973).

Table 1 Factors Determining Market and Industry Attractiveness

Market	• Size (present and potential)
	• Growth/stage in life cycle
	• Diversity of user segments
	• Foreign opportunities
	• Cyclicality
Competition	• Concentration ratio
	• Capacity utilization
	• Structural changes (e.g., entries and exits)
	• Position changes
	• Vertical threats/opportunities
	• Sensitivity of shares and market size to price, service, etc.
	• Extent of "captive" business
Profitability	• Level and trend of leaders
	• Contribution rates
	• Changes/threats on key leverage factors (e.g., scale economies and pricing)
	• Barriers to entry
Technology	• Maturity/volatility
	• Complexity
	• Patent protection
	• Product/process opportunities
Other	• Social/environmental
	• Government/political
	• Unions
	• Human factors

position of the firm in each of its product-markets. The main problem of the matrix concerns the growth rate dimension. While this is an extremely useful measure in that it can have direct implications for cash flows, it is only one of many possible determinants of the attractiveness of the market. A list of other possible factor is summarized in Table 1. (Not all these factors will be relevant to all markets.) The importance of each factor depends on the company's capabilities, but careful consideration will help to identify unusual threats, such as impending government regulations, that might significantly reduce future attractiveness. Similarly, market share may not provide a comprehensive indication of the company's position in each market, as in the case of a leader in a market that is rapidly fragmenting.

The qualitative aspects of overall attractiveness and position also can be incorporated into a matrix which portrays the product portfolio (see figure on p. 123). This matrix does not have the immediate cash flow implication of the growth-share matrix; thus, it should be used as a complementary, rather than a replacement, approach.

Industry or market attractiveness. (Arrow represents forecast of change in position. Diameter [of circles] is proportional to share of company sales contributed by product.)

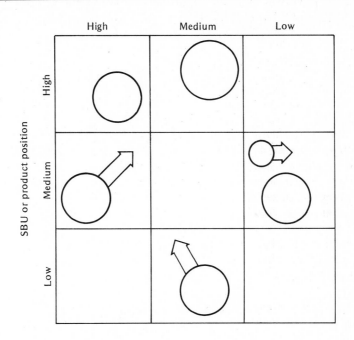

NEW PRODUCT PLANNING

A product portfolio analysis identifies the need for new products or new markets and the probable level of available resources but does not indicate where to look. This presents management with a number of difficult questions:

- What degree of relationship to the present business is necessary and desirable?
- What are the possibilities for internal development versus acquisition?
- When is an innovation preferred to an imitation and vice versa?
- What are the characteristics of desirable new products?

These and innumerable other questions have to be answered before personnel in the product planning, corporate development or other responsible functions can pursue their tasks efficiently. In short, top management must decide how much growth is desired and feasible, the contribution of new versus established products and the broad direction as to how the growth will be achieved.

What is needed is a strategy statement that specifies those areas where development is to proceed and identifies (perhaps by exclusion) those areas that are off-limits. As Crawford notes, "the idea of putting definitive restrictions on new product activity is not novel, but use of it, especially sophisticated use, is still not widespread." [38] The major criticisms of a comprehensive statement of new product development strategy are that it will inhibit or restrict creativity and that ideas with great potential will be rejected. Experience suggests that clear guidance improves creativity by focusing energy on those areas where the payoff is likely to be greatest. Also, experience shows that significant break-throughs outside the bounds of the product development strategy statement can be accommodated readily in an on-going project evaluation and screening process.

The New Product Development Strategy Statement

The essential elements of this statement are the specification of the product-market scope, the basic strategies to be used for growing within that scope and the characteristics of desirable alternatives. These elements guide the search for new product ideas, acquisitions, licenses, etc., and form the basis for a formal screening procedure.

Product-Market Scope   This is an attempt to answer the basic question, "What business(es) do we want to be in?" and is a specific manifestation of the mission of the SBU or company. There is no ready-made formula for develop-ing the definition of the future business. One approach is to learn from defini-tions that have been useful in guiding successful strategies. For example, the General Electric Housewares SBU defines their present (circa 1973) business as "providing consumers with functional aids to increase the enjoyment or psychic fulfillment of selected lifestyles"—specifically those dealing with prepara-tion of food, care of the person, care of personal surroundings and planning assistance. In the future their business will expand to include recreation, en-hancement of security and convenient care of the home.

This statement of the future business satisfied one important criteria: that it be linked to the present product-market scope by a clearly definable common thread. In the case of GE Housewares, the common thread is with generic needs being satisfied (or problems being solved, as the case may be). Ansoff argues that the linkage also can be with product characteristics, distribution capability or underlying technology—as long as the firm has distinctive com-petency in these areas. [39]

Other criteria for appraising the usefulness of a description of the future business opportunities are: (1) specificity—if the definition of product-market scope is too general, it won't have an impact on the organization (e.g., consider the vagueness of being in the business of supplying products with a plug on the end), (2) flexibility—the definition should be adapted constantly to recognize changing environmental conditions (e.g., Gerber no longer can say that babies

[38] C. Merle Crawford, "Strategies for New Product Development: Guidelines for a Criti-cal Company Problem," *Business Horizons* (December 1972), pp. 49–58.
[39] H. Igor Ansoff, *Corporate Strategy*.

are their only business), (3) attainability—can be undertaken within the firm's resources and competencies and (4) competitive advantage—it always is preferable to protect and build on these strengths and competencies that are not possessed as fully by the competition.[40]

Basic Strategies for Growth At the broad level of a new product development strategy, the basic issues are the *growth vector,* or the direction the firm is moving within the chosen product-market scope, and the emphasis on *innovation* versus *imitation.*

There are almost an infinite number of possibilities for growth vectors. The basic alternatives are summarized in Figure 6.[41] There is no intention here to suggest that these strategies are mutually exclusive; indeed, various combinations can be pursued simultaneously in order to close the strategic gaps identified in the overall planning process. Furthermore, most of the strategies can be pursued either by internal development or acquisition and coupled with vertical diversification (either forward toward a business that is a customer or backward toward a business that is a supplier).

The choice of growth vector will be influenced by all the factors discussed

FIGURE 6   Growth Vector Alternatives

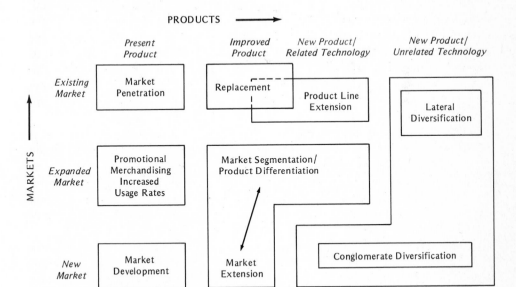

[40] Kenneth Simmonds, "Removing the Chains from Product Policy," *Journal of Management Studies* (February 1968).

[41] This strategy matrix was influenced strongly by the work of David T. Kollat, Roger D. Blackwell and James F. Robeson, *Strategic Marketing* (New York: Holt, Rinehart and Winston, 1972), pp. 21–23 which, in turn, was adapted from Samuel C. Johnson and Conrad Jones, "How to Organize for New Products," *Harvard Business Review,* 35 (May–June 1957), pp. 49–62.

earlier as part of the overall corporate planning process. Underlying any choice is, by necessity, an appraisal of the risks compared with the payoffs. The essence of past experience is that growth vectors within the existing market (or, at least, closely related markets) are much more likely to be successful than ventures into new markets.[42] Therefore, diversification is the riskiest vector to follow—especially if it is attempted by means of internal development. The attractiveness of acquisitions for diversification is the chance to reduce the risks of failure by buying a known entity with (reasonably) predictable performance.

An equally crucial basic strategy choice is the degree of emphasis on innovation versus imitation. The risks of being an innovator are well known so few, if any, diversified corporations can afford to be innovators in each product-market. There are compelling advantages to being first in the market if barriers to entry (because of patent protections, capital requirements, control over distribution, etc.) can be erected, the product is difficult to copy or improve on and the introductory period is short. The imitator, by contrast, is always put at a cost disadvantage by a successful innovator and must be prepared to invest heavily to build a strong market position. While profits over the life of the product may be lower for an imitator, the risks are much lower because the innovator has provided a full-scale market test which can be monitored to determine the probable growth in future sales. Also, the innovator may provide significant opportunities by not serving all segments or, more likely, by not implementing the introduction properly.

The conscious decision to lead or follow pervades all aspects of the firm. Some of the important differences that result can be seen from the various strategic orientations to high technology markets discussed by Ansoff and Steward:

- First to market . . . based on strong R and D, technical leadership and risk taking

- Follow the leader . . . based on strong development resources and the ability to act quickly as the market starts its growth phase

- Applications engineering . . . based on product modifications to fit the needs of particular customers in mature markets

- Me-too . . . based on superior manufacturing efficiency and cost control.[43]

---

[42] According to the experience of A. T. Kearney, Inc., the chances of success are a direct function of how far from home the new venture is aimed. Specifically, the likelihood of success for an improved product into the present market is assessed as 0.75, declines to 0.50 for a new product with unrelated technology into the present market and to 0.25 for an existing product into a new market. The odds of success for external diversification are as low as 0.05. These numbers are mainly provocative because of the difficulties of defining what constitutes a failure (is it a product that failed in test or after national introduction, for example). See "Analyzing New Product Risk," *Marketing for Sales Executives* (The Research Institute of America, January 1974).

[43] H. Igor Ansoff and John Steward, "Strategies for a Technology-Based Business," *Harvard Business Review*, 45 (November–December 1967), pp. 71–83.

Characteristics of Desirable Alternatives Three fundamental questions have to be asked of each new product or service being sought or considered: (1) How will a strong competitive advantage be obtained? The possibilities range from superiority in underlying technology or product quality, to patent protection, to marketing requirements. Another dimension of this question is the specification of markets or competitors to be avoided on the grounds that these situations would blunt the pursuit of a competitive advantage. (2) What is the potential for synergy? This asks about joint effects, or "the mutually reinforcing impact a product-market entry has on a firm's efficiency and effectiveness." [44] Synergy can be sought for defensive reasons, in order to supply a competence that the firm lacks or to spread the risks of a highly cyclical industry, as has motivated a number of mergers in the machine tool industry. Alternatively, synergy can utilize an existing competence such as a distribution system (notable examples here are Gillette and Coca Cola), a production capability, promotional skills, etc. In addition, "financial reinforcement may occur either because of the relative pattern of funds generation and demand . . . or because the combination is more attractive to the financial community than the pieces would be separately." [45] (3) What specific operating results are required? The possibilities here usually are expressed in terms of threshold or minimum desirable levels:

- Rate of market growth
- Payback period (despite its deficiencies it is a reflection of the risk level)
- Minimum sales level. (This is a function of fixed costs and scale of operations; the danger is that a product with good long-run potential will be rejected because of modest short-run sales possibilities.)
- Profit levels, cash flow and return on assets. (Each of these financial requirements must be developed in light of the firm's product portfolio.)

SUMMARY

Too often product planning is conducted as though each established product or service and new product opportunity being sought or evaluated, were independent of the other products of the firm. The implication is that corporate performance is the sum of the contributions of individual profit centers or product strategies. [46]

This article emphasizes the need to consider the interdependencies of products as parts of a portfolio described by market share dominance and market growth rate before overall corporate performance can be optimized. Only then can decisions as to resource allocation, growth and financial objectives and

---

[44] Kollat, Blackwell and Robeson, *Strategic Marketing*, p. 24.

[45] Seymour Tilles, "Making Strategy Explicit," in H. Igor Ansoff (ed.) *Business Strategy* (London: Penguin Books, 1969), p. 203.

[46] Bruce D. Henderson, "Intuitive Strategy," *Perspectives*, No. 96 (The Boston Consulting Group, 1972).

specific strategies be developed for established products and the need for new products identified.

There is little doubt that the future will see increasing acceptance of a broad systems approach to overall corporate strategy, in general, and to product planning, in particular. There are already a number of successful practitioners (who have gained a competitive edge that cannot be ignored) to emulate.[47] More importantly, as the business environment becomes increasingly resource-con-strained there may be no other choice for most firms.

---

[47] See "Selling Business a Theory of Economics," *BusinessWeek* (8 September 1973); "G.E.'s New Strategy for Faster Growth," *BusinessWeek* (8 July 1972); "First Quarter and Stockholders Meeting Report" (Texas Instruments, Inc., 8 April 1973); "The Winning Strategy at Sperry Rand," *BusinessWeek* (24 February 1973); "How American Standard Cured Its Conglomeritis," *BusinessWeek* (28 September 1974); "G.E. Revamps Strategy: Growth through Efficiency," *Advertising Age* (3 June 1974).

The Marketing Audit
Comes of Age

Philip Kotler, William Gregor, and William Rogers

Comparing the marketing strategies and tactics of business units today versus ten years ago, the most striking impression is one of marketing strategy obsolescence. Ten years ago U.S. automobile companies were gearing up for their second postwar race to produce the largest car with the highest horsepower. Today companies are selling increasing numbers of small and medium-sized cars and fuel economy is a major selling point. Ten years ago computer companies were introducing ever-more powerful hardware for more sophisticated uses. Today they emphasize mini- and micro-computers and software.

It is not even necessary to take a ten-year period to show the rapid obsolescence of marketing strategies. The growth economy of 1950–1970 has been superseded by a volatile economy which produces new strategic surprises almost monthly. Competitors launch new products, customers switch their business, distributors lose their effectiveness, advertising costs skyrocket, government regulations are announced, and consumer groups attack. These changes represent both opportunities and problems and may demand periodic reorientations of the company's marketing operations.

Many companies feel that their marketing operations need regular reviews and overhauls but do not know how to proceed. Some companies simply make many small changes that are economically and politically feasible, but fail to get to the heart of the matter. True, the company develops an annual marketing plan but management normally does not take a deep and objective look at the marketing strategies, policies, organizations, and operations on a recurrent basis. At the other extreme, companies install aggressive new top marketing management hoping to shake down the marketing cobwebs. In between there must be more orderly ways to reorient marketing operations to changed environments and opportunities.

From *Sloan Management Review*, vol. 18, no. 1 (Winter 1977), pp. 25–43. Reprinted by permission.

ENTER THE MARKETING AUDIT

One hears more talk today about the *marketing audit* as being the answer to evaluating marketing practice just as the public accounting audit is the tool for evaluating company accounting practice. This might lead one to conclude that the marketing audit is a new idea and also a very distinct methodology. Neither of these conclusions is true.

The marketing audit as an idea dates back to the early fifties. Rudolph Dallmeyer, a former executive in Booz-Allen-Hamilton, remembers conducting marketing audits as early as 1952. Robert J. Lavidge, President of Elrick and Lavidge, dates his firm's performance of marketing audits to over two decades ago. In 1959, the American Management Association published an excellent set of papers on the marketing audit under the title *Analyzing and Improving Marketing Performance,* Report No. 32, 1959. During the 1960s, the marketing audit received increasing mention in the lists of marketing services of management consulting firms. It was not until the turbulent seventies, however, that it began to penetrate management awareness as a possible answer to its needs.

As for whether the marketing audit has reached a high degree of methodological sophistication, the answer is generally no. Whereas two certified public accountants will handle an audit assignment using approximately the same methodology, two marketing auditors are likely to bring different conceptions of the auditing process to their task. However, a growing consensus on the major characteristics of a marketing audit is emerging and we can expect considerable progress to occur in the next few years.

In its fullest form and concept, a marketing audit has four basic characteristics. The first and most important is that it is *broad* rather than narrow in focus. The term "marketing audit" should be reserved for a *horizontal (or comprehensive) audit* covering the company's marketing environment, objectives, strategies, organization, and systems. In contrast, a *vertical (or in-depth) audit* occurs when management decides to take a deep look into some key marketing function, such as sales force management. A vertical audit should properly be called by the function that is being audited, such as a sales force audit, an advertising audit, or a pricing audit.

A second characteristic feature of a marketing audit is that it is conducted by someone who is *independent* of the operation that is being evaluated. There is some loose talk about self-audits, where a manager follows a checklist of questions concerning his own operation to make sure that he is touching all the bases.[1] Most experts would agree, however, that the self-audit, while it is always a useful step that a manager should take, does not constitute a *bona fide* audit because it lacks objectivity and independence. Independence can be achieved in two ways. The audit could be an *inside audit* conducted by a person or group inside the company but outside of the operation being evaluated.

---

[1] Many useful checklist questions for marketers are found in C. Eldridge, *The Management of the Marketing Function* (New York: Association of National Advertisers, 1967).

Or it could be an *outside audit* conducted by a management consulting firm or practitioner.

The third characteristic of a marketing audit is that it is *systematic*. The marketing auditor who decides to interview people inside and outside the firm at random, asking questions as they occur to him, is a "visceral" auditor without a method. This does not mean that he will not come up with very useful findings and recommendations; he may be very insightful. However, the effectiveness of the marketing audit will normally increase to the extent that it incorporates an orderly sequence of diagnostic steps, such as there are in the conduct of a public accounting audit.

A final characteristic that is less intrinsic to a marketing audit but nevertheless desirable is that it be conducted *periodically*. Typically, evaluations of company marketing effort are commissioned when sales have turned down sharply, sales force morale has fallen, or other problems have occurred at the company. The fact is, however, that companies are thrown into a crisis partly because they have failed to review their assumptions and to change them during good times. A marketing audit conducted when things are going well can often help make a good situation even better and also indicate changes needed to prevent things from turning sour.

The above ideas on a marketing audit can be brought together into a single definition:

A marketing audit is a *comprehensive, systematic, independent,* and *periodic* examination of a company's—or business unit's—marketing environment, objectives, strategies, and activities with a view of determining problem areas and opportunities and recommending a plan of action to improve the company's marketing performance.

WHAT IS THE MARKETING AUDIT PROCESS?

How is a marketing audit performed? Marketing auditing follows the simple three-step procedure shown in Figure 1.

Setting the Objectives and Scope

The first step calls for a meeting between the company officer(s) and a potential auditor to explore the nature of the marketing operations and the poten-

FIGURE 1   Steps in a Marketing Audit

Agreement on Objectives, Scope, and Approach → Data Collection → Report Preparation and Presentation

tial value of a marketing audit. If the company officer is convinced of the potential benefits of a marketing audit, he and the auditor have to work out an agreement on the objectives, coverage, depth, data sources, report format, and the time period for the audit.

Consider the following actual case. A plumbing and heating supplies wholesaler with three branches invited a marketing consultant to prepare an audit of its overall marketing policies and operations. Four major objectives were set for the audit:

- Determine how the market views the company and its competitors.
- Recommend a pricing policy.
- Develop a product evaluation system.
- Determine how to improve the sales activity in terms of the deployment of the sales force, the level and type of compensation, the measurement of performance, and the addition of new salesmen.

Furthermore, the audit would cover the marketing operations of the company as a whole and the operations of each of the three branches, with particular attention to one of the branches. The audit would focus on the marketing operations but also include a review of the purchasing and inventory systems since they intimately affect marketing performance.

The company would furnish the auditor with published and private data on the industry. In addition, the auditor would contact suppliers of manufactured plumbing supplies for additional market data and contact wholesalers outside the company's market area to gain further information on wholesale plumbing and heating operations. The auditor would interview all the key corporate and branch management, sales and purchasing personnel, and would ride with several of those salesmen on their calls. Finally, the auditor would interview a sample of the major plumbing and heating contractor customers in the market areas of the two largest branches.

It was decided that the report format would consist of a draft report of conclusions and recommendations to be reviewed by the president and vice-president of marketing, and then delivered to the executive committee which included the three branch managers. Finally, it was decided that the audit findings would be ready to present within six to eight weeks.

Gathering the Data

The bulk of an auditor's time is spent in gathering data. Although we talk of a single auditor, an audit team is usually involved when the project is large. A detailed plan as to who is to be interviewed by whom, the questions to be asked, the time and place of contact, and so on, has to be carefully prepared so that auditing time and cost are kept to a minimum. Daily reports of the interviews are to be written up and reviewed so that the individual or team can spot new areas requiring exploration while data are still being gathered.

The cardinal rule in data collection is not to rely solely for data and opinion

FIGURE 2   Factors in the Selection of a Manufacturer

FACTOR	ALL USERS RANK	COMPANY SALESMEN RANK	COMPANY NON-SALES PERSONNEL RANK
Reputation	5	①	4
Extension of Credit	9	11	9
Sales Representatives	8	5	7
Technical Support Services	①	△3	6
Literature and Manuals	11	10	11
Prompt Delivery	☐2	4	5
Quick Response to Customer Needs	△3	☐2	△3
Product Price	6	6	①
Personal Relationships	10	7	8
Complete Product Line	7	9	10
Product Quality	4	8	☐2

Source: Marketing and Distribution Audit, A Service of Decision Sciences Corporation, p. 32. Used with permission of the Decision Sciences Corporation.

on those being audited. Customers often turn out to be the key group to interview. Many companies do not really understand how their customers see them and their competitors, nor do they fully understand customer needs. This is vividly demonstrated in Figure 2 which shows the results of asking end users, company salesmen, and company marketing personnel for their views of the importance of different factors affecting the user's selection of a manufacturer. According to the figure, customers look first and foremost at the quality of technical support services, followed by prompt delivery, followed by quick response to customer needs. Company salesmen think that company reputation, however, is the most important factor in customer choice, followed by quick response to customer needs and technical support services. Those who plan marketing strategy have a different opinion. They see company price and product quality as the two major factors in buyer choice, followed by quick response to customer needs. Clearly, there is lack of consonance between what buyers say they want, what company salesmen are responding to, and what company marketing planners are emphasizing. One of the major contributions of marketing auditors is to expose these discrepancies and suggest ways to improve marketing consensus.

Preparing and Presenting the Report

The marketing auditor will be developing tentative conclusions as the data comes in. It is a sound procedure for him to meet once or twice with the company officer before the data collection ends to outline some initial findings to see what reactions and suggestions they produce.

When the data gathering phase is over, the marketing auditor prepares notes for a visual and verbal presentation to the company officer or small group who hired him. The presentation consists of restating the objectives, showing the main findings, and presenting the major recommendations. Then, the auditor is ready to write the final report, which is largely a matter of putting the visual and verbal material into a good written communication. The company officer(s) will usually ask the auditor to present the report to other groups in the company. If the report calls for deep debate and action, the various groups hearing the report should organize into subcommittees to do follow-up work with another meeting to take place some weeks later. The most valuable part of the marketing audit often lies not so much in the auditor's specific recommendations but in the process that the managers of the company begin to go through to assimilate, debate, and develop their own concept of the needed marketing action.

MARKETING AUDIT PROCEDURES FOR AN INSIDE AUDIT

Companies that conduct internal marketing audits show interesting variations from the procedures just outlined. International Telephone and Telegraph, for example, has a history of forming corporate teams and sending them into weak divisions to do a complete business audit, with a heavy emphasis on the marketing component. Some teams stay on the job, often taking over the management.

General Electric's corporate consulting division offers help to various divisions on their marketing problems. One of its services is a marketing audit in the sense of a broad, independent, systematic look at the marketing picture in a division. However, the corporate consulting division gets few requests for a marketing audit as such. Most of the requests are for specific marketing studies or problem-solving assistance.

The 3M Company uses a very interesting and unusual internal marketing plan audit procedure. A marketing plan audit office with a small staff is located at corporate headquarters. The main purpose of the 3M marketing plan audit is to help the divisional marketing manager improve the marketing planning function, as well as come up with better strategies and tactics. A divisional marketing manager phones the marketing plan audit office and invites an audit. There is an agreement that only he will see the results and it is up to him whether he wants wider distribution.

The audit centers around a marketing plan for a product or product line that the marketing manager is preparing for the coming year. This plan is reviewed at a personal presentation by a special team of six company marketing executives invited by the marketing plan audit office. A new team is formed for each new audit. An effort is made to seek out those persons within 3M (but not in the audited division) who can bring the best experience to bear on the particular plan's problems and opportunities. A team typically consists of a marketing manager from another division, a national sales manager, a marketing executive with a technical background, a few others close to the type of problems found in the audited plan, and another person who is totally unfamiliar with the market, the product, or the major marketing techniques being used in the plan. This person usually raises some important points others forget to raise, or do not ask because "everyone probably knows about that anyway."

The six auditors are supplied with a summary of the marketing manager's plan about ten days before an official meeting is held to review the plan. On the audit day, the six auditors, the head of the audit office, and the divisional marketing manager gather at 8:30 A.M. The marketing manager makes a presentation for about an hour describing the division's competitive situation, the long-run strategy, and the planned tactics. The auditors proceed to ask hard questions and debate certain points with the marketing manager and each other. Before the meeting ends that day, the auditors are each asked to fill out a marketing plan evaluation form consisting of questions that are accompanied by numerical rating scales and room for comments.

These evaluations are analyzed and summarized after the meeting. Then the head of the audit office arranges a meeting with the divisional marketing manager and presents the highlights of the auditor's findings and recommendations. It is then up to the marketing manager to take the next steps.

COMPONENTS OF THE MARKETING AUDIT

A major principle in marketing audits is to start with the marketplace first and explore the changes that are taking place and what they imply in the way of problems and opportunities. Then the auditor moves to examine the company's marketing objectives and strategies, organization, and systems. Finally he may move to examine one or two key functions in more detail that are central to the marketing performance of that company. However, some companies ask for less than the full range of auditing steps in order to obtain initial results before commissioning further work. The company may ask for a marketing environment audit, and if satisfied, then ask for a marketing strategy audit. Or it might ask for a marketing organization audit first, and later ask for a marketing environment audit.

We view a full marketing audit as having six major components, each having a semiautonomous status if a company wants less than a full marketing audit. The six components and their logical diagnostic sequence are discussed below. The major auditing questions connected with these components are gathered together in Appendix A at the end of this article.

Marketing Environment Audit

By marketing environment, we mean both the *macro-environment* surrounding the industry and the *task environment* in which the organization intimately operates. The macro-environment consists of the large-scale forces and factors influencing the company's future over which the company has very little control. These forces are normally divided into economic-demographic factors, technological factors, political-legal factors, and social-cultural factors. The marketing auditor's task is to assess the key trends and their implications for company marketing action. However, if the company has a good long-range forecasting department, then there is less of a need for a macro-environment audit.

The marketing auditor may play a more critical role in auditing the company's task environment. The task environment consists of markets, customers, competitors, distributors and dealers, suppliers, and marketing facilitators. The marketing auditor can make a contribution by going out into the field and interviewing various parties to assess their current thinking and attitudes and bringing them to the attention of management.

Marketing Strategy Audit

The marketing auditor then proceeds to consider whether the company's marketing strategy is well-postured in the light of the opportunities and problems facing the company. The starting point for the marketing strategy audit is the corporate goals and objectives followed by the marketing objectives. The auditor may find the objectives to be poorly stated, or he may find them to be well-stated but inappropriate given the company's resources and opportunities. For example, a chemical company had set a sales growth objective for a particular product line at 15 percent. However, the total market showed no growth and competition was fierce. Here the auditor questioned the basic sales growth objective for that product line. He proposed that the product line be reconsidered for a maintenance or harvest objective at best and that the company should look for growth elsewhere.

Even when a growth objective is warranted, the auditor will want to consider whether management has chosen the best strategy to achieve that growth.

Marketing Organization Audit

A complete marketing audit would have to cover the question of the effectiveness of the marketing and sales organization, as well as the quality of interaction between marketing and other key management functions such as manufacturing, finance, purchasing, and research and development.

At critical times, a company's marketing organization must be revised to achieve greater effectiveness within the company and in the marketplace. Companies without product management systems will want to consider introducing them, companies with these systems may want to consider dropping them, or trying product teams instead. Companies may want to redefine the role concept of a product manager from being a promotional manager (concerned primarily with volume) to a business manager (concerned primarily with profit). There is the issue of whether decision-making responsibility should be moved up from the brand level to the product level. There is the perennial question of how to make the organization more market-responsive including the possibility of replacing product divisions with market-centered divisions. Finally, sales organizations often do not fully understand marketing. In the words of one vice-president of marketing: "It takes about five years for us to train sales managers to think marketing."

Marketing Systems Audit

A full marketing audit then turns to examine the various systems being used by marketing management to gather information, plan, and control the marketing operation. The issue is not the company's marketing strategy or organization per se but rather the procedures used in some or all of the following systems: sales forecasting, sales goal and quota setting, marketing planning, marketing control, inventory control, order processing, physical distribution, new products development, and product pruning.

The marketing audit may reveal that marketing is being carried on without adequate systems of planning, implementation, and control. An audit of a consumer products division of a large company revealed that decisions about which products to carry and which to eliminate were made by the head of the division on the basis of his intuitive feeling with little information or analysis to guide the decisions. The auditor recommended the introduction of a new product screening system for new products and an improved sales control system for existing products. He also observed that the division prepared budgets but did not carry out formal marketing planning and hardly any research into the market. He recommended that the division establish a formal marketing planning system as soon as possible.

Marketing Productivity Audit

A full marketing audit also includes an effort to examine key accounting data to determine where the company is making its real profits and what, if any, marketing costs could be trimmed. Decision Sciences Corporation, for example, starts its marketing audit by looking at the accounting figures on sales and associated costs of sales. Using marketing cost accounting principles,[2] it seeks to measure the marginal profit contribution of different products, end user segments, marketing channels, and sales territories.

We might argue that the firm's own controller or accountant should do the job of providing management with the results of marketing cost analysis. A handful of firms have created the job position of marketing controllers who report to financial controllers and spend their time looking at the productivity and validity of various marketing costs. Where an organization is doing a good job

---

[2] See P. Kotler, *Marketing Management Analysis, Planning and Control* (Englewood Cliffs, N.J.: Prentice-Hall, Inc., 1976), pp. 457–462.

of marketing cost analysis, it does not need a marketing auditor to study the same. But most companies do not do careful marketing cost analysis. Here a marketing auditor can pay his way by simply exposing certain economic and cost relations which indicate waste or conceal unexploited marketing opportunities.

Zero-based budgeting [3] is another tool for investigating and improving marketing productivity. In normal budgeting, top management allots to each business unit a percentage increase (or decrease) of what it got last time. The question is not raised whether that basic budget level still makes sense. The manager of an operation should be asked what he would basically need if he started his operation from scratch and what it would cost. What would he need next and what would it cost? In this way, a budget is built from the ground up reflecting the true needs of the operation. When this was applied to a technical sales group within a large industrial goods company, it became clear that the company had three or four extra technical salesmen on its payroll. The manager admitted to the redundancy but argued that if a business upturn came, these men would be needed to tap the potential. In the meantime, they were carried on the payroll for two years in the expectation of a business upturn.

Marketing Function Audit

The work done to this point might begin to point to certain key marketing functions which are performing poorly. The auditor might spot, for example, sales force problems that go very deep. Or he might observe that advertising budgets are prepared in an arbitrary fashion and such things as advertising themes, media, and timing are not evaluated for their effectiveness. In these and other cases, the issue becomes one of notifying management of the desirability of one or more marketing function audits if management agrees.

WHICH COMPANIES CAN BENEFIT MOST FROM A MARKETING AUDIT?

All companies can benefit from a competent audit of their marketing operations. However, a marketing audit is likely to yield the highest payoff in the following companies and situations:

• *Production-Oriented and Technical-Oriented Companies.* Many manufacturing companies have their start in a love affair with a certain product. Further products are added that appeal to the technical interests of management, usually with insufficient attention paid to their market potential. The feeling in these companies is that marketing is paid to sell what the company decides to make.

---

[3] See P. J. Stonich, "Zero-Base Planning—A Management Tool," *Managerial Planning,* July–August 1976, pp. 1–4.

After some failures with its "better mousetraps," management starts getting interested in shifting to a market orientation. But this calls for more than a simple declaration by top management to study and serve the customer's needs. It calls for a great number of organizational and attitudinal changes that must be introduced carefully and convincingly. An auditor can perform an important service in recognizing that a company's problem lies in its production orientation, and in guiding management toward a market orientation.

• *Troubled Divisions.* Multidivision companies usually have some troubled divisions. Top management may decide to use an auditor to assess the situation in a troubled division rather than rely solely on the division management's interpretation of the problem.

• *High Performing Divisions.* Multidivision companies might want an audit of their top dollar divisions to make sure that they are reaching their highest potential, and are not on the verge of a sudden reversal. Such an audit may also yield insights into how to improve marketing in other divisions.

• *Young Companies.* Marketing audits of emerging small companies or young divisions of large companies can help to lay down a solid marketing approach at a time when management faces a great degree of market inexperience.

• *Nonprofit Organizations.* Administrators of colleges, museums, hospitals, social agencies, and churches are beginning to think in marketing terms, and the marketing audit can serve a useful educational as well as diagnostic purpose.

WHAT ARE THE PROBLEMS AND PITFALLS OF MARKETING AUDITS?

While the foregoing has stressed the positive aspects of marketing audits and their utility in a variety of situations, it is important to note some of the problems and pitfalls of the marketing audit process. Problems can occur in the objective-setting step, the data collection step, or the report presentation step.

Setting Objectives

When the marketing audit effort is being designed by the auditor and the company officer who commissioned the audit, several problems will be encountered. For one thing, the objectives set for the audit are based upon the company officer's and auditor's best *a priori* notions of what the key problem areas are for the audit to highlight. However, new problem areas may emerge once the auditor begins to learn more about the company. The original set of objectives should not constrain the auditor from shifting his priorities of investigation.

Similarly, it may be necessary for the auditor to use different sources of information than envisioned at the start of the audit. In some cases this may be because some information sources he had counted on became unavailable. In one marketing audit, the auditor had planned to speak to a sample of customers for the company's electro-mechanical devices, but the company officer who hired him would not permit him to do so. In other cases, a valuable new source of information may arise that was not recognized at the start of the audit. For example, the auditor for an air brake system manufacturer found as a valuable source of market intelligence a long-established manufacturers' representatives firm that approached the company after the audit had begun.

Another consideration at the objective-setting stage of the audit is that the management most affected by the audit must have full knowledge of the purposes and scope of the audit. Audits go much more smoothly when the executive who calls in the auditor either brings the affected management into the design stage, or at least has a general introductory meeting where the auditor explains his procedures and answers questions from the people in the affected business.

Data Collection

Despite reassurances by the auditor and the executive who brought him in, there will still be some managers in the affected business who will feel threatened by the auditor. The auditor must expect this, and realize that an individual's fears and biases may color his statements in an interview.

From the onset of the audit, the auditor must guarantee and maintain confidentiality of each individual's comments. In many audits, personnel in the company will see the audit as a vehicle for unloading their negative feelings about the company or other individuals. The auditor can learn a lot from these comments, but he must protect the individuals who make them. The auditor must question interviewees in a highly professional manner to build their confidence in him, or else they will not be entirely honest in their statements.

Another area of concern during the information collection step is the degree to which the company executive who brought in the auditor will try to guide the audit. It will be necessary for this officer and the auditor to strike a balance in which the executive provides some direction, but not too much. While overcontrol is the more likely excess of the executive, it is possible to undercontrol. When the auditor and the company executive do not have open and frequent lines of communication during the audit, it is possible that the auditor may place more emphasis on some areas and less on others than the executive might have desired. Therefore, it is the responsibility of both the auditor and the executive who brought him in to communicate frequently during the audit.

Report Presentation

One of the biggest problems in marketing auditing is that the executive who brings in the auditor, or the people in the business being audited, may have higher expectations about what the audit will do for the company than the actual report seems to offer. In only the most extreme circumstances will the auditor develop surprising panaceas or propose startling new opportunities for the company. More likely, the main value of his report will be that it places priorities on ideas and directions for the company, many of which have already been considered by some people within the audited organization. In most successful audits, the auditor, in his recommendations, makes a skillful combination of his general and technical marketing background (e.g., designs of salesman's compensation systems, his ability to measure the size and potential of markets) with some opportunistic ideas that people in the audited organization have already considered, but do not know how much importance to place upon them. However, it is only in the company's implementation of the recommendations that the payoff to the company will come.

Another problem at the conclusion of the audit stems from the fact that most audits seem to result in organizational changes. Organizational changes are a common outcome because the audit usually identifies new tasks to be accomplished and new tasks demand people to do them. One thing the auditor and the executive who brought him in must recognize, however, is that organizational promotions and demotions are exclusively the executive's decision. It is the executive who has to live with the changes once the auditor has gone, not the auditor. Therefore, the executive should not be lulled into thinking that organizational moves are any easier because the auditor may have recommended them.

The final problem, and this is one facing the auditor, is that important parts of an audit may be implemented incorrectly, or not implemented at all, by the executive who commissioned the audit. Non-implementation of key parts of the audit undermines the whole effectiveness of the audit.

SUMMARY

The marketing audit is one important answer to the problem of evaluating the marketing performance of a company or one of its business units. Marketing audits are distinguished from other marketing exercises in being *comprehensive, independent, systematic,* and *periodic.* A full marketing audit would cover the company's (or division's) external environment, objectives, strategies, organization, systems, and functions. If the audit covers only one function, such as sales management or advertising, it is best described as a marketing function audit rather than a marketing audit. If the exercise is to solve a current problem, such as entering a market, setting a price, or developing a package, then it is not an audit at all.

The marketing audit is carried out in three steps: developing an agreement as to objectives and scope; collecting the data; and presenting the report. The audit can be performed by a competent outside consultant or by a company auditing office at headquarters.

The possible findings of an audit include detecting unclear or inappropriate marketing objectives, inappropriate strategies, inappropriate levels of marketing expenditures, needed improvements in organization, and needed improvements in systems for marketing information, planning, and control. Companies that are most likely to benefit from a marketing audit include production-oriented companies, companies with troubled or highly vulnerable divisions, young companies, and nonprofit organizations.

Many companies today are finding that their premises for marketing strategy are growing obsolete in the face of a rapidly changing environment. This is happening to company giants such as General Motors and Sears as well as smaller firms that have not provided a mechanism for recycling their marketing strategy. The marketing audit is not the full answer to marketing strategy recycling but does offer one major mechanism for pursuing this desirable and necessary task.

APPENDIX A—COMPONENTS OF A MARKETING AUDIT

THE MARKETING ENVIRONMENT AUDIT

I. Macro-Environment

Economic-Demographic
1. What does the company expect in the way of inflation, material shortages, unemployment, and credit availability in the short run, intermediate run, and long run?
2. What effect will forecasted trends in the size, age distribution, and regional distribution of population have on the business?

Technology
1. What major changes are occurring in product technology? In process technology?
2. What are the major generic substitutes that might replace this product?

Political-Legal
1. What laws are being proposed that may affect marketing strategy and tactics?
2. What federal, state, and local agency actions should be watched? What is happening in the areas of pollution control, equal employment opportunity, product safety, advertising, price control, etc., that is relevant to marketing planning?

Social-Cultural
1. What attitudes is the public taking toward business and toward products such as those produced by the company?
2. What changes are occurring in consumer life styles and values that have a bearing on the company's target markets and marketing methods?

II. Task Environment

Markets
1. What is happening to market size, growth, geographical distribution, and profits?
2. What are the major market segments? What are their expected rates of growth? Which are high opportunity and low opportunity segments?

Customers
1. How do current customers and prospects rate the company and its competitors, particularly with respect to reputation, product quality, service, sales force, and price?
2. How do different classes of customers make their buying decisions?
3. What are the evolving needs and satisfactions being sought by the buyers in this market?

Competitors
1. Who are the major competitors? What are the objectives and strategy of each major competitor? What are their strengths and weaknesses? What are the sizes and trends in market shares?
2. What trends can be foreseen in future competition and substitutes for this product?

Distribution and Dealers
1. What are the main trade channels bringing products to customers?
2. What are the efficiency levels and growth potentials of the different trade channels?

Suppliers
1. What is the outlook for the availability of different key resources used in production?
2. What trends are occurring among suppliers in their pattern of selling?

Facilitators
1. What is the outlook for the cost and availability of transportation services?
2. What is the outlook for the cost and availability of warehousing facilities?
3. What is the outlook for the cost and availability of financial resources?
4. How effectively is the advertising agency performing? What trends are occurring in advertising agency services?

MARKETING STRATEGY AUDIT

Marketing Objectives
1. Are the corporate objectives clearly stated and do they lead logically to the marketing objectives?
2. Are the marketing objectives stated in a clear form to guide marketing planning and subsequent performance measurement?
3. Are the marketing objectives appropriate, given the company's competitive position, resources, and opportunities? Is the appropriate strategic objective to build, hold, harvest, or terminate this business?

Strategy
1. What is the core marketing strategy for achieving the objectives? Is it a sound marketing strategy?
2. Are enough resources (or too much resources) budgeted to accomplish the marketing objectives?
3. Are the marketing resources allocated optimally to prime market segments, territories, and products of the organization?
4. Are the marketing resources allocated optimally to the major elements of the marketing mix, i.e., product quality, service, sales force, advertising, promotion, and distribution?

MARKETING ORGANIZATION AUDIT

Formal Structure
1. Is there a high-level marketing officer with adequate authority and responsibility over those company activities that affect the customer's satisfaction?
2. Are the marketing responsibilities optimally structured along functional product, end user, and territorial lines?

Functional Efficiency
1. Are there good communication and working relations between marketing and sales?
2. Is the product management system working effectively? Are the product managers able to plan profits or only sales volume?
3. Are there any groups in marketing that need more training, motivation, supervision, or evaluation?

Interface Efficiency
1. Are there any problems between marketing and manufacturing that need attention?
2. What about marketing and R&D?
3. What about marketing and financial management?
4. What about marketing and purchasing?

MARKETING SYSTEMS AUDIT

Marketing Information System
1. Is the marketing intelligence system producing accurate, sufficient, and timely information about developments in the marketplace?
2. Is marketing research being adequately used by company decision makers?

Marketing Planning System
1. Is the marketing planning system well-conceived and effective?
2. Is sales forecasting and market potential measurement soundly carried out?
3. Are sales quotas set on a proper basis?

Marketing Control System
1. Are the control procedures (monthly, quarterly, etc.) adequate to insure that the annual plan objectives are being achieved?
2. Is provision made to analyze periodically the profitability of different products, markets, territories, and channels of distribution?
3. Is provision made to examine and validate periodically various marketing costs?

New Product Development System
1. Is the company well-organized to gather, generate, and screen new product ideas?

2. Does the company do adequate concept research and business analysis before investing heavily in a new idea?
3. Does the company carry out adequate product and market testing before launching a new product?

MARKETING PRODUCTIVITY AUDIT

Profitability Analysis
1. What is the profitability of the company's different products, served markets, territories, and channels of distribution?
2. Should the company enter, expand, contract, or withdraw from any business segments and what would be the short- and long-run profit consequences?

Cost-Effectiveness Analysis
1. Do any marketing activities seem to have excessive costs? Are these costs valid? Can cost-reducing steps be taken?

MARKETING FUNCTION AUDIT

Products
1. What are the product line objectives? Are these objectives sound? Is the current product line meeting these objectives?
2. Are there particular products that should be phased out?
3. Are there new products that are worth adding?
4. Are any products able to benefit from quality, feature, or style improvements?

Price
1. What are the pricing objectives, policies, strategies, and procedures? To what extent are prices set on sound cost, demand, and competitive criteria?
2. Do the customers see the company's prices as being in line or out of line with the perceived value of its offer?
3. Does the company use price promotions effectively?

Distribution
1. What are the distribution objectives and strategies?
2. Is there adequate market coverage and service?
3. Should the company consider changing its degree of reliance on distributors, sales reps, and direct selling?

Sales Force
1. What are the organization's sales force objectives?
2. Is the sales force large enough to accomplish the company's objectives?

3. Is the sales force organized along the proper principle(s) of specialization (territory, market, product)?
4. Does the sales force show high morale, ability, and effort? Are they sufficiently trained and incentivized?
5. Are the procedures adequate for setting quotas and evaluating performances?
6. How is the company's sales force perceived in relation to competitors' sales forces?

Advertising, Promotion, and Publicity
1. What are the organization's advertising objectives? Are they sound?
2. Is the right amount being spent on advertising? How is the budget determined?
3. Are the ad themes and copy effective? What do customers and the public think about the advertising?
4. Are the advertising media well chosen?
5. Is sales promotion used effectively?
6. Is there a well-conceived publicity program?

Market Structure Profile Analysis and Strategic Growth Opportunities

John A. Weber

In utilizing market structure profile (MSP) analysis, the firm develops a pragmatically oriented market structure profile for each relevant product line it markets. These profiles themselves are policy-oriented in that each profile suggests an appropriate mix of different growth strategies.[1]

The planner begins by estimating industrial market potential (IMP) for the product line of concern. In MSP analysis, the words "industry" and "product line" are synonymous and are defined quite narrowly. An industry or product line is comprised of any and all products which do or can perform the same basic function. Industry market potential is defined in terms of unit sales potential (versus dollar potential) and IMP equals the number of relevant consumers times the number of use occasions which arise per relevant consumer per operating period (usually one year).

Why Firm Sales Fall Short of Industry Market Potential

Once having estimated IMP, the task is to explain in terms of market gaps and marketing gaps exactly why the firm's own sales in that product line fall short of the IMP. Possible reasons include the following:

About the Author: John A. Weber is Associate Professor of Marketing and International Business at the University of Notre Dame. He also has been active as a growth planning consultant to several major corporations. His articles have appeared in various professional journals.

From John A. Weber, "Market Structure Profile Analysis and Strategic Growth Opportunities," *California Management Review*, vol. 20, no. 1 (Fall 1977), pp. 34–46. Reprinted by permission of the Regents of the University of California.

[1] See Robert S. Weinberg, "Top Management Planning and the Computer," Chemical Marketing Research Association, Meeting, Cleveland (December 1965). For an in-depth consideration of the development and many uses of market structure profiles, see John A. Weber, *Growth Opportunity Analysis* (Reston, 1976), 300 pp. This article presents a summary of some of the material in that book.

- *Lack of a full product line* within the relevant market.
- *Absence of or inadequate distribution* to or within the relevant market.
- *Less than full usage* within the relevant market.
- *Sales of directly competitive brands* within the relevant market.

For each market of concern, the planner attempts to quantify these various reasons and presents them in the form of a market structure profile such as the one in Figure 1.

Strategies to Close Market Structure Profile Gaps

Inferences for corporate marketing strategies result from each market structure profile. A different type of corporate marketing strategy is appropriate for clos-

FIGURE 1   Market Structure Profile Example (would be expressed in units—on an annual basis)

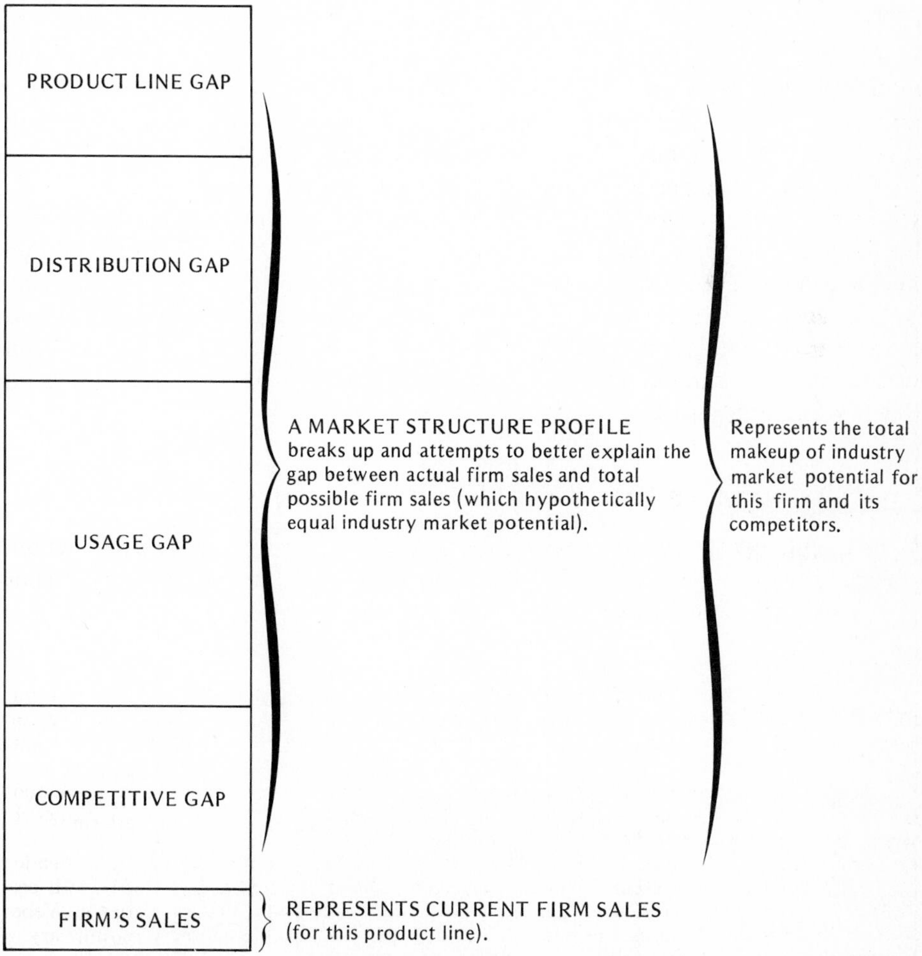

PRODUCT LINE GAP

DISTRIBUTION GAP

USAGE GAP

COMPETITIVE GAP

FIRM'S SALES

A MARKET STRUCTURE PROFILE breaks up and attempts to better explain the gap between actual firm sales and total possible firm sales (which hypothetically equal industry market potential).

Represents the total makeup of industry market potential for this firm and its competitors.

REPRESENTS CURRENT FIRM SALES (for this product line).

ing each gap appearing in the market structure profile. Figure 2 shows some possible strategies and shows which gap each attempts to close.

As implied in Figure 2, market structure profiles can by themselves suggest what corporate marketing strategies are most appropriate in individual markets (for each separate profile). As a general rule, strategies designed to close the largest market profile gaps will be the most marginally productive. That is, more sales per dollar of input are likely to result from strategies designed to close the larger market profile gaps. This is certainly not true in every case but is logical and valid in most instances.

FIGURE 2   Interrelationships between Market Profile Gaps and Corporate Marketing Strategies

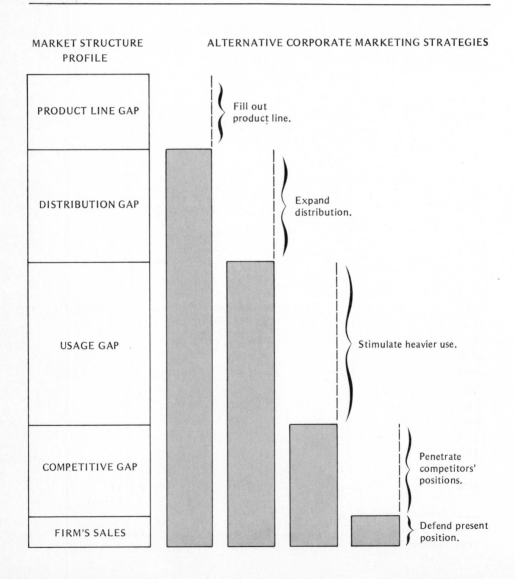

Alternative corporate marketing strategies in turn convert quite directly into the design of advertising themes and marketing programs in general.

DEVELOPING ACCURATE MARKET STRUCTURE PROFILES

Five basic steps are involved in building market structure profiles:

- Estimating *industry market potential (IMP)*
- Estimating the *product line gap*
- Estimating the *distribution gaps*
- Estimating the *usage gaps*
- Estimating the *competitive gaps*

Estimating Industry Market Potential

The first task involved in building a market structure profile is to estimate the industry market potential (IMP) for the firm's relevant product line. In initially making IMP estimates, four precautions should be kept in mind:

1. Define each product line narrowly;
2. Make estimates in terms of unit sales rather than dollar sales;
3. Develop initial estimates for one operating period (usually one year); and
4. Limit the IMP estimates to consideration of the U.S. market only (temporarily ignore the potentials in the international market).

A clarification of each of these precautions is necessary.

1. A broad or generic definition of "industry" is appropriate when a firm is concerned with defining its new product horizons.[2] When defining IMP, however, the terms "industry" and "product line" are synonymous and both terms are defined quite narrowly. In MSP analysis, products included in one industry are all products (of this firm and of competitors) which do or can perform essentially the same function. Products that do not meet this criterion are not in that industry or product line for the purpose of MSP analysis. For example, a firm may describe particular divisions as a baby products division, a food division, a household durables division, an office products division, or an industrial division. All of these industry or product line definitions are much too broad for MSP analysis.

To estimate IMP for such divisions using the principles of MSP analysis, these divisions must be broken down further into groups of products which

---

[2] For a discussion of this point, see T. Levitt, "Marketing Myopia," *Harvard Business Review*, September 1975, pp. 29ff.

perform the same function. For example, cotton swabs, baby shampoo, dispos-able diapers, baby powder, and baby oil are all baby products—but they all fall into separate product lines because they are not functional substitutes for one another.

In line with this, it is important to note that a single product can fall into as many different industries as there are different uses for the product. For example, one can speak of cereal as a breakfast food (one industry) or as a snack (another industry).

2. MSP analysis is concerned primarily with designing and selecting strat-egies to increase unit sales rather than dollar sales per se. Price-change strat-egies are deemphasized so as to focus upon the firm's other growth strategy al-ternatives. Industry market potentials are defined, therefore, in terms of unit sales rather than dollar sales.

3. When estimating IMP for a product line, consider the potential for one operating period (usually one year) only. This becomes a particular point to keep in mind when estimating IMP for products with expected useful lives of greater than one year.

4. MSP analysis is equally applicable in the U.S. alone or on a worldwide basis. Given the great diversity in various international markets, however, and inadequate consumer data in most of these markets, this introduction to MSP analysis focuses upon IMP estimates and MSP analysis for the U.S. market only.

A separate IMP should be determined for each use of the product. Three assumptions are made concerning usage of the product in order to derive IMP: (1) *everyone* who could reasonably be expected to use the product is using it; (2) *everyone who is using it, is using it* on every use occasion; and (3) *every time* the product is used, it is used to the *fullest extent possible*—within reason (in a full dosage, a full serving, and so on).

As suggested previously, it is highly unlikely that these assumptions will hold for any product line. That these assumptions do not hold is the very es-sence of and purpose of using IMP as the starting point for developing a market structure profile. The assorted reasons as to exactly why one firm's sales (FS) fall short of IMP provide the logic and basis for deriving the various subgaps in the market structure profile for each product line of the firm.

Many other methodologies are available to the firm for estimating market potentials.[3] One shortcoming that most other methods have in common, how-

---

[3] For examples of other methodologies for estimating market potentials for consumer markets, see: Wolfe, H. D. and Twedt, D. W., "Establishing Market Potentials," Chapter Six of *Planning and Managing the Promotional Mix*; Kotler, P., "Market Measurement and Fore-casting," Chapter Seven of *Marketing Management*, Prentice-Hall, 1972, pp. 192–225; and Brion, John J., *Corporate Marketing Planning*, Wiley, 1967, pp. 355–363. For methodologies estimating market potentials in industrial markets, see: Appraising the Market for New Indus-trial Products, NICB-SBP No. 123 (espec. pp. 65–98); Stern, Mark E., "Assessing Market Opportunities," in *Market Planning*, McGraw-Hill, 1967; Kotler, P., op. cit., Chapter 7; Wolfe, H. D. and Twedt, D. W., op. cit., Chapter 6; Brion, J. M., op. cit., pp. 364–374; and *Sales Analysis*, NICB-SBP, No. 113, pp. 18, 25, 34.

ever, is that they tend to consider current demand or current industry sales as upper limits to market potential for an individual firm. Such bases severely underestimate the industry market potential—particularly for product lines and products which are in early stages of their life cycles. The method of deriving IMP in MSP analysis overcomes this problem by considering market potential quite apart from actual sales at a given point of time. Only later, when usage gaps are incorporated, do actual sales come into the picture. Industry market potentials therefore tend to be higher when using this approach to estimate market potentials than when using most other approaches.

IMP-Related Growth Opportunities

The firm has four growth opportunities related directly to IMP. These are:

- Natural changes in the size of IMP.
- Discovery of new uses or new user segments for existing products which can provide new IMPs for the firm's present products.
- Innovative product differentiations which can expand existing IMPs.
- Introduction of new product lines which provide new IMPs for the firm.

Estimating the Product Line Gap

A firm faces a potential product line gap for each IMP that is relevant for the firm. A product line gap is expressed as a proportion of IMP. The derivation of the product line gap constitutes the second step in building a market structure profile.

The firm begins deriving a product line gap by specifying the alternative elements which it recognizes in the product line. For a particular product line, elements of the product line can be defined along any of a number of different possible dimensions. Size, options, style, color, flavor, form, quality or distributor brand-related product line gaps may exist for each IMP a firm recognizes.

In enumerating the possible elements of a product line, a firm that is currently adding the relevant product line (Firm A) should focus on one or two basic dimensions—whichever ones are most meaningful for the particular product. Flavor, for example, might be the most important dimension for a firm adding cereal as a new product line.

A firm that has been selling cereal for some time (Firm B), however, should include more dimensions in its enumeration of possible elements of the product line. Relevant dimensions for this firm for the cereal market might include flavor, box size, product composition, and others.

Frequently firm sales breakdowns or industry-wide sales breakdowns along the product line dimension desired by the firm may simply not be available or may be too expensive to generate or acquire. In such cases, *data availability may become the key criterion for selecting the relevant dimension(s)* for differentiation among product line elements.

In most instances, the proportion of current industry sales accounted for by each element gives an appropriate estimation of the proportion of IMP to assign to each product line element. In cases where an innovation or significant product differentiation has recently entered the market as a new product line element, the proportions of current industry sales achieved by each product line element may overestimate its proportions of industry market potential—and appropriate adjustments should be made.

♦ *Product Line Gap-Related Growth Opportunities.* The firm has two growth opportunities related directly to closing product line gaps.

• Filling out existing product lines
• Creating new product line elements through innovation or significant product differentiation

Estimating Distribution Gaps

The product line gap provides one reason why a firm's actual sales in a given product line fall short of the firm's potential sales in that product line. A firm cannot sell a product that it does not offer in its product line. Distribution gaps of various types provide additional explanations for the overall gap between actual firm sales and potential firm sales. Very simply put, a firm cannot sell a product where it does not distribute that product.

Sales of an individual product line of a firm can be adversely affected by any or all of three different types of distribution gaps: coverage gaps, intensity gaps, and exposure gaps. A *distribution coverage gap* exists when a firm does not distribute the relevant product line or any individual element thereof in all geographic regions desired. A *distribution intensity gap* exists when a firm's entire product line or individual elements thereof are distributed in an inadequate number of outlets—within a geographic region where the firm does not have distribution coverage. A *distribution exposure gap* exists when a firm's entire product line or individual elements thereof have poor or inadequate shelf space, location, displays, and so forth—within outlets where the firm does have distribution for the product.

The firm's own definition of complete distribution coverage, intensity, and exposure is essential if the sizes of the various distribution gaps are to be estimated. Complete distribution for a particular product line is defined as a function of three factors: (1) the firm's geographic market horizons; (2) the relevant customer's willingness to shop for the product; and (3) the relevant customer's brand recognition, image of the brand, and brand preference.

As a simple and direct example of the *quantification of a distribution coverage gap,* assume that the firm's geographic market horizon includes the entire U.S., that the firm has a full product line, and that the firm's product line is available in all areas except the Southwest, Greater Los Angeles, and the remaining Pacific regions which account for 9.7 percent, 5.5 percent, and 10.6 percent of IMP, respectively. In this case, therefore, the firm's distribution coverage gap equals:

Area	% of IMP for Firm's Product Line Element
Southwest	9.7
Greater Los Angeles	5.5
Remaining Pacific	10.6
Distribution coverage gap	25.8%

If this firm had a real product line gap of 20 percent of IMP and the different possible elements of the product line were spread evenly from a geographic point of view, then the firm's distribution coverage gap would equal 25.8 percent × 80 percent = 20.7 percent of IMP.

The firm experiences a *distribution intensity gap* only in those geographic regions where it does distribute the product, that is, where it has distribution coverage. Distribution intensity is defined as a proportion of the sales volume of outlets through which the firm is distributing the product line versus the total sales volume of all the outlets through which the firm would like to be distributing its product. The firm's ideal number and mix of outlets are defined directly as a function of the firm's own definition of "complete distribution."

Assume that a firm has a 20 percent product line gap (therefore, 80 percent of IMP product line coverage), that the firm has no distribution coverage in the Southwest (9.7 percent of IMP), Greater Los Angeles (5.5 percent of IMP), or the remaining Pacific (10.6 percent of IMP), and has distribution intensity gaps in each of the other regions of the country, as indicated in column 6 of Table 1. In that case, the firm's total distribution intensity gap equals 8.3 percent of IMP. That is the total of the distribution intensity gaps of the other seven regions times the percent of IMP in each region times the product line coverage in each region. Table 1 shows these calculations.

The firm can experience a *distribution exposure gap* only in those outlets where its relevant product line is sold. For consumer goods, distribution exposure refers to the shelf space, facings, location, displays (size and frequency), other store-related promotions (such as special prices or local advertising) and inventory per store for the firm's relevant product line.

Carrying on with the example above, assume that the firm has distribution exposure (in each relevant geographic area) indicated in column 6 of Table 2. In that case, the firm's total distribution exposure gap equals 11.1 percent of IMP. Table 2 shows these calculations.

In the example being used, therefore, the firm's total distribution gap equals: 20.7 percent of IMP (coverage gap) plus 8.3 percent of IMP (intensity gap) plus 11.1 percent (exposure gap) = 40.1 percent of IMP.

◆ *Distribution Gap-Related Growth Opportunities.* The three types of distribution gaps provide three growth opportunities or strategies for the firm. These are opportunities to grow through:

Table 1 Finding the Distribution Intensity Gap

1	2	3	4	5	6	7
Area	% of IMP	Product Line Coverage	Distribution Coverage	Distribution Coverage Gap as % of IMP	Distribution Intensity Gap	Distribution Intensity Gap as % of IMP
Southwest	9.7 ×	80%	=	7.8		
Greater L.A.	5.5 ×	80%	=	4.4		
Remaining Pacific	10.6 ×	80%	=	8.5		
New England	6.0 ×	80%	×	1	× 10%	= 0.48
Met. N.Y.	7.6 ×	80%	×	1	× 10%	= 0.61
Mid-Atlantic	11.8 ×	80%	×	1	× 10%	= 0.94
East Central	17.0 ×	80%	×	1	× 20%	= 2.72
Met. Chicago	4.0 ×	80%	×	1	× 10%	= 0.32
West Central	12.7 ×	80%	×	1	× 20%	= 2.04
		Product line gap = 20% of IMP		Total distribution coverage gap = 20.7% of IMP		Total distribution intensity gap = 8.3% of IMP

Table 2 Finding the Distribution Exposure Gap

1	2	3	4	5	6	7	8
Area	% of IMP	Product Line Coverage	Distribution Intensity	Distribution Intensity as a % of IMP	Distribution Exposure as a % of Ideal Distribution Exposure	Distribution Exposure as a % of IMP	Distribution Exposure Gap as % of IMP
New England	6.0	80% ×	90% =	4.32	75 =	3.24 from 4.32	= 1.08
Met. New York	7.6	80% ×	90% =	5.49	75 =	4.10 from 5.47	= 1.37
Mid-Atlantic	11.8	80% ×	90% =	8.50	75 =	6.38 from 8.50	= 2.12
East Central	17.0	80% ×	80% =	10.88	90 =	9.79 from 10.88	= 1.09
Met. Chicago	4.0	80% ×	90% =	2.88	90 =	2.59 from 2.88	= 0.29
West Central	12.7	80% ×	80% =	8.13	90 =	7.32 from 8.13	= 0.81
Southeast	15.1	80% ×	90% =	10.87	60 =	6.52 from 10.87	= 4.35

(Assume no coverage in Southwest, Greater L.A., Pacific)

Total distribution exposure gap = 11.1% of IMP

- Expanding geographic distribution coverage.
- Expanding distribution intensity (the number of outlets for the relevant product in each geographic area where the firm now distributes the product).
- Expanding distribution exposure (i.e., to improve the exposure of the firm's relevant product line within individual outlets).

Estimating Usage Gaps

In originally estimating industry market potential, as discussed above, three assumptions were made concerning the usage of the product or service. The three assumptions concerning each use or user segment for the product or service were: (1) everyone who can reasonably be expected to use the product or serve is using it; (2) everyone who is using it, is using it on every "use occasion"; (3) every use is a "full use" (full serving).

These usage assumptions hold in very few market situations. Usually many potential users are not using a product. Many of those who do use the product do not use it on every "use occasion." And, finally, many uses of most products are not "full uses." For each assumption which does not hold for a firm in a given market situation, that firm faces a usage gap.

Reflecting the three complete usage assumptions made in estimating IMP, the firm can face three separate but interrelated usage gaps for each IMP which the firm recognizes. The three usage gaps are referred to as: the nonuser gap, the light-user gap, and the light-usage gap. These usage gaps provide yet three more reasons or explanations why the firm's sales in these product lines fall so short of IMP.

A *nonuser gap* refers to the proportion of IMP accounted for by customers who could potentially use the product but are not using it. A *light-user gap* refers to the proportion of IMP accounted for by those who do use the product but do not use it on every occasion. A *light-usage gap* refers to the proportion of IMP accounted for by use occasions met with a use of the relevant product— but less than a full use.

♦ *Usage Gap-Related Growth Strategies.* Each usage gap represents a separate and distinct growth opportunity for the firm. The three growth opportunities are to:

- Stimulate nonusers to use the product.
- Stimulate light users to use the product on more use occasions.
- Increase the amount of the product used on each use occasion when the product is used.

Estimating Competitive Gaps

The overall competitive gap is a residual—in that it equals what is left over from IMP after the product line gap, the total distribution gap, the total usage gap, and the firm's own sales have been subtracted from IMP.

Since the measurements of the product line gap, the total distribution gap, and the total usage gap have already been covered, the major task remaining in order to come up with the size of the competitive gap is to measure the relevant firm's sales for this product line. For a product line with only one use and for which only one IMP and one market structure profile have been developed, this is rather straightforward—the firm simply determines its unit volume sales for the product line over the past operating period. This figure is subtracted from IMP along with the gaps mentioned above and the residual equals the competitive gap.

For example, assume that IMP equals 80 billion units; the product line gap equals 20 percent of IMP; the total distribution gap equals 40 percent of IMP; the usage gap equals 30 percent of IMP; and firm sales for this product line in the last operation period equaled 3.2 billion units (4 percent of IMP). In this case, the *competitive gap* equals 6 percent of IMP.

In considering product line gaps, it was mentioned that the proportions of current industry sales accounted for by each element of a product line sometimes should not be used as the main determinant of the size of the firm's product line gap. This is true when one of the product line elements is relatively new to the market and represents an innovation or significant product differentiation. A similar adjustment may be called for if a firm feels that product line elements which it does market can penetrate the sales position of product line elements which it does not market—even when its own product line elements represent no innovation or significant new product differentiation.

In either case above, the firm adjusts the product line gap to make it smaller. In one case, the adjustment reflects the firm's attitude regarding possibility of using product line element(s) which it does sell to penetrate the position(s) of one or more elements which the firm does not sell.

In terms of the market structure profile, the firm desiring to "penetrate the substitute's position" adjusts its product line gap downward. The growth opportunity of penetrating the substitute's position(s) does not show up in the market structure profile as part of the product line gap. Rather, this growth opportunity (of penetrating the substitute's position) is added to and shows up as part of the overall competitive gap.

♦ *Competitive Gap-Related Growth Opportunities.* Growth opportunities related to the competitive gap and present firm sales are:

- Penetrating the substitute's position(s).
- Penetrating direct competitor's position(s).
- Defending the firm's present position (present firm sales).

COMPARING STRATEGIC GROWTH OPPORTUNITIES WITH THE AID OF MSP ANALYSIS

The comparison of strategic growth alternatives begins with an estimation of the likely incremental benefits (in terms of new firm sales and profits) to be derived from various alternatives. In some situations, firms rely strictly on judgment and past experience in making such estimates. At other times, firms may acquire secondary data or generate primary data to help make such estimates.

One of the functions of market structure profile analysis is to facilitate the estimation of the likely results (in terms of incremental firm sales and profits) of implementing alternative growth strategies. The profile does not give management a definitive estimate of the likely result of the strategy—but it certainly can aid the manager in estimating a range of possible outcomes and in assigning explicit (if formal decision theory is used) or implicit probabilities to various possible outcomes or payoffs (incremental sales and profits) associated with each strategic alternative.

General Relationships: Market Structure Profiles, Growth Opportunities, and New Firm Sales

A market structure profile serves as a focal point for showing the interrelationships among and between the fifteen growth opportunities enumerated above. Figure 3 summarizes these interrelationships.

- Market structure profiles provide the firm with significant insights concerning the incremental sales which each growth strategy is likely to yield. Review for a moment how each of the fifteen growth opportunities leads to incremental firm sales as expressed in the form of market structure profiles:
- Growth opportunities 1 to 4 can represent totally new markets for the firm's present product line(s). The new market structure profile(s) incorporating these new markets represent the size of the new sales growth opportunity. As new IMPs are recognized and focused upon by the firm, new firm sales result.
- Growth opportunities 5 and 6 represent new product line elements for the firm within existing lines and, as such, mean new firm sales.
- Growth opportunities 7 to 9 represent expanded/improved distribution and availability of the firm's relevant product line. This means new firm sales.
- Growth opportunities 10 to 12 represent expanded usage of the product by relevant potential users. This means new firm sales.
- Growth opportunities 13 to 15 represent improved market share. This usually means new firm sales.

Using Market Structure Profiles to Help Estimate the Incremental Sales Likely to Result from Implementing Alternative Growth Strategies

The preceding paragraph reviews in a very general way how incremental sales resulting from various growth strategies can be expressed in terms of market structure profiles.

Exact estimates of the incremental firm sales likely to result from taking advantage of each growth opportunity cannot be made—even using market structure profiles. The framework provided by MSP analysis does, however, provide a

FIGURE 3   Summary of Growth Opportunities Expressed in Terms of Market Structure Profiles

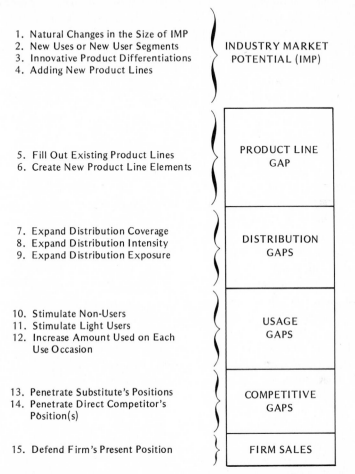

1. Natural Changes in the Size of IMP
2. New Uses or New User Segments
3. Innovative Product Differentiations
4. Adding New Product Lines

INDUSTRY MARKET POTENTIAL (IMP)

5. Fill Out Existing Product Lines
6. Create New Product Line Elements

PRODUCT LINE GAP

7. Expand Distribution Coverage
8. Expand Distribution Intensity
9. Expand Distribution Exposure

DISTRIBUTION GAPS

10. Stimulate Non-Users
11. Stimulate Light Users
12. Increase Amount Used on Each Use Occasion

USAGE GAPS

13. Penetrate Substitute's Positions
14. Penetrate Direct Competitor's Position(s)

COMPETITIVE GAPS

15. Defend Firm's Present Position

FIRM SALES

number of guideposts to help the executive structure his analysis and come up with more accurate estimates of incremental firm sales likely to result from each growth opportunity.

Three market structure profile measures provide particularly helpful insights for making such estimates. These three measures are *industry market potential* (IMP), *relevant industry sales* (RIS), and *real market share* (RMS). Industry market potential has already been discussed in some detail. Relevant industry sales equal firm sales plus the competitive gap(s). Real market share equals

$$\frac{\text{Firm Sales}}{\text{Firm Sales plus the Competitive Gap(s)}}$$

or

$$\frac{\text{Firm Sales}}{\text{Relevant Industry Sales}}$$

These three measures—IMP, RIS, and RMS—become important bases for estimating the incremental sales to be achieved through the various possible alternative growth opportunities. As viewed in terms of market structure profiles, the firm can realize incremental firm sales as a result of: (1) increasing the firm's total IMP; (2) increasing RIS (firm sales plus the competitive gap) while maintaining its present real market share; and (3) improving its real market share.

Overlooking alternative (3) above for the moment, consider how the firm can increase IMP and RIS, while at the same time maintaining its current RMS. Each of the fifteen growth opportunities implies an increase in either or both IMP or RIS.

How Much Will IMP and Relevant Industry Sales (RIS)Increase? The first step toward estimating incremental firm sales is to determine how much IMP and relevant industry sales (RIS) will increase for each growth opportunity. As summarized in Table 3, estimating incremental IMP and RIS is quite straightforward for nine of the growth opportunities (1, 4, 5, and 7–12) but can involve additional research and considerable judgment for the remaining six opportunities (2, 3, 6, and 12–15).

In interpreting Table 3, keep in mind that over time as the firm fills out a product line, as the firm expands its distribution, and as the relevant product line life cycles mature (usage gaps close quite naturally), the key proportion referred to in the exhibit, RIS $\div$ IMP, increases. Except where mentioned otherwise in the exhibit, comments therein refer to the effects of each growth opportunity upon RIS at a given point in time—rather than over the long term.

What Will Happen to the Firm's Real Market Share? The second step toward estimating incremental firm sales is to determine the likely effect of each of the fifteen alternative growth opportunities upon the relevant firm's real market share (RMS). Note, while each growth opportunity certainly can result in increased firm sales, an increase in firm sales does not always imply an increase in real market share.

In considering the concept of real market share, keep in mind that competitive sales of product line elements which the relevant firm does not sell are not included in the competitive gap. Also, competitive sales of product line elements which the firm does produce are included in the competitive gap only to the extent of the relevant firm's own distribution coverage, intensity, and exposure. Because the product line gap element and the distribution gap element are omitted from overall competitive sales, the firm's resulting RMS is larger than traditional market share measures would show.

Table 4 specifically examines the likely effects of each of the fifteen alternative growth opportunities upon the firm's real market share. Estimating the exact real market share resulting from taking advantage of each growth opportunity is subject to the judgmental factors discussed in Table 4. The firm's primary concern should be to estimate whether, in light of factors such as those

Table 3 Estimating the IMP and RIS Likely to Result from Each Growth Opportunity (assuming firm's real market share remains the same)

Growth Opportunity	Estimating Incremental IMP and RIS
1 Natural growth of IMP	Accurate estimate of increased size of IMP is usually possible using secondary data and projections. Proportion RIS ÷ IMP is likely to be the same before and after IMP grows.
2 New uses or new user segments	Accurate estimates of new IMP(s) are possible by using secondary data or generating primary data. Proportion of RIS ÷ IMP is likely to be substantially smaller for the new IMP(s) than for the old IMP(s) (at least at first) because of larger usage gaps or larger distribution gaps.
3 Innovation or significant new product differentiation	Estimating whether and how much IMP will increase as a result of the significant improvement in price/preference of the relevant new product innovation (or differentiation) versus previously existing elements is dependent upon executive judgment and the interpretation of any primary or secondary data which might be used to help make such an estimate. (The proportion RIS ÷ IMP is also likely to increase as a result of the innovation if the relevant firm has been the innovator. See opportunity 6 below.)
4 Adding new product line(s)	Accurately estimating IMP for new product line in straightforward RIS ÷ IMP proportion depends upon firm's own intention as to extent of product line and completeness of distribution and upon size of current usage gaps.
5 Filling out existing product line(s)	The proportion RIS ÷ (IMP — product line gap) remains the same after adding a new product line element as before. Since proportion of IMP assigned to each product line element was determined in developing the original market structure profile, making incremental RIS estimate is straightforward (RIS increases.)
6 Innovation or significant new product differentiation	This is similar to growth opportunity 3 in that it represents the addition of an innovative new element to an existing product line. This contrasts with growth opportunity 3, however, in that no new IMP is projected to result from the new innovation or differentiation. The task herein, therefore, is to estimate to what extent the sales of existing elements will be penetrated by the new element. If the firm in question is offering the new element, this firm's RIS ÷ (IMP — product line gap) projection will increase. Judgment and interpretation of relevant secondary and/or primary data are used to estimate just how much this proportion will increase.
7–9 Closing distribution gaps	The proportion RIS ÷ (IMP — product line gap — distribution gaps) remains the same after closing distribution gaps as before. Since the proportion of IMP assigned to each geographic region, and for varying extents of distribution intensity and exposure, were determined in developing the original market structure profile, making incremental RIS estimates is straightforward. (RIS increases.)

Table 3 (cont.)

Growth Opportunity	Estimating Incremental IMP and RIS
10–12 Closing usage gaps	Incremental RIS equals whatever the closed part of the usage gap equals as a proportion of IMP. Since the definition of full usage was determined in developing the original IMP estimate (and market structure profile itself), making the incremental RIS estimates is quite straightforward over the longer run. Over the short run, however, an adjustment in the incremental RIS estimates may be necessary for the following reason. As new users are converted, over the short run at least, their usage rate (on what proportion of the use occasions the new users will use the product and what volume of the product they will use each time those new users do use the product) may be less than the usage rate for the current average user. This means that over the short run, the total usage gap will not close in direct proportion to the proportion of nonusers being converted into users. Over the longer run, however, the average usage rate for the converted nonusers is more likely to approach the average usage rate for current users.
13 Penetrating substitute's position(s)	RIS increases by the amount of the full substitute's position recognized times the distribution and usage factors.
14 Penetrating direct competitive position(s)	Both IMP and RIS can be affected by this strategy—but quite indirectly—see comments later in this article.
15 Defending present position	Neither IMP nor RIS are directly affected. Strategy is, however, related indirectly to improvements in IMP and RIS—see comments later in the article.

Table 4 Estimating the Likely Effect of Each Alternative Growth Opportunity upon the Firm's Real Market Share

Growth Opportunity	Likely Effects upon Real Market Share
1 Natural growth of IMP	The relevant firm can expect the same real market share as before unless a competitor focuses specifically upon the growth segment of IMP (in which case the relevant firm's RMS might decline). Relevant firm might increase its own RMS by focusing upon growth segment of IMP.

Table 4 (cont.)

Growth Opportunity	Likely Effects upon Real Market Share
2 New uses or new user segments	If the relevant firm is the leader in promoting the new use or to a new user segment, the firm can expect at least as large a real market share (and usually a larger share) in the new profile(s) as in the existing one(s) for this product line. If a competitor firm takes the lead, the relevant firm can expect a smaller RMS in the new profile(s) than in its existing one(s) for this product line.
3 Innovation or significant product differentiation	If the relevant firm is the one which has introduced the innovation, this firm can expect a larger RMS than it has at present as long as the firm can protect its innovation—such as, with a patent—or in some other way maintain superiority in the price/performance of its new element versus other firms' competitive entries. The likely increase in RIS further enhances this firm's situation. If the relevant firm is a follower with the innovation or does not come out with this entry at all (even after competitors have successfully introduced the new element), the relevant firm's RMS may stay the same but RIS and, therefore, firm sales as well, will be declining.
4 Adding new product line(s)	Since the firm has no sales at all in this product line at present, an increase or decrease in RMS is not possible. Given a particular competitive situation in the market, the firm should eventually be able to build for itself an RMS equivalent to the share it holds today in markets where the competitive situation is similar.
5 Filling out existing product line(s)	In most instances, it is realistic for the firm to assume that its RMS will remain the same as the firm fills out the relevant product line. At least two forces, however, may be at work to cause a change in the firm's RMS as the firm fills out its product lines and should be considered (researched) closely by the firm before filling out a product line. Cannibalism can be one problem—sales of the new product line element may eat into the same firm's sales of another product line element. In such an instance, while RIS increases, firm sales might not increase proportionally as much —resulting in a declining RMS for the firm. On the other hand, if the various product line elements complement each other (in terms of color or style, for example), firm sales may increase more than RIS on a proportional basis as the firm fills out its product line—thus resulting in an increased RMS. (NOTE: No distribution or usage assumptions need be made concerning the new product line element(s)— since whatever distribution and usage exists for these elements will be reflected naturally in the RIS.)

Table 4 (cont.)

Growth Opportunity	Likely Effects upon Real Market Share
6 Innovation or significant new product differentiation	Same as for growth opportunity 3.
7–9 Closing distribution gaps	As a firm expands its distribution coverage, over the short run its RMS will usually decline. Over the longer run the firm can expect its overall RMS to either increase, decrease, or remain the same—depending upon the competitive conditions in the new geographic areas covered and upon the resources the firm allocates to penetrating competitors' positions in the new market. Expanding distribution intensity and/or exposure will usually result in a larger RMS (despite the larger RIS) for a firm which starts with very low intensity and exposure (low in terms of the firm's own definition of complete distribution). For a firm already close to having "complete distribution intensity and exposure," however, a further expansion of distribution intensity and/or exposure will lead to an increase in firm sales less than proportional to the increase in RIS—therefore resulting in a declining RMS.
10–12 Closing usage gaps	The firm(s) leading the way with strategies oriented to close usage gaps will be expanding RIS for all firms in the relevant industry. This firm will also usually expand its own RMS. Often, however, especially at later stages of a product line life cycle, the incremental benefits for the leading firm(s) (in terms of increased RIS and RMS) will be outweighed by the incremental cost (such as in promotion dollars) required to bring about those benefits. In earlier stages of a life cycle, such an investment may be very worthwhile—especially for the larger and more dominant firms in the relevant industry.
13–14 Closing competitive gaps	These opportunities/strategies are oriented directly toward improving the firm's RMS—by bringing about an increase in firm sales whether or not RIS is increasing (RIS may indeed increase at the same time because of the simultaneous closure of other gaps in the Market Structure Profile).
15 Defending present market share	As the name of the opportunity implies, the goal here is to maintain present RMS. This is an important strategy for larger, more dominant firms in an industry—regardless of the stage of life cycle for the relevant industry. Strategy is also important for any firm for which RIS is increasing—for whatever reason.

Table 5 Likely Effects of Each Growth Opportunity upon IMP, RIS, and RMS

Growth Opportunity	For Existing Profile(s)				For New Profile(s) Created — Compared with Existing Profile		
	IMP	RIS	RIS/IMP	RMS	IMP	RIS/IMP	RMS
1	↑	↑	Same	Same	None		
2	Same	Same	Same	Same	Yes	Smaller	Larger (if leader)
3	↑	↑ (if leader) ↓ (if follower)	↑ (if leader) ↓ (if follower)	↑	None		
4	Same	Same	Same	Same	Yes	Depends (See Table 3.)	Depends (See Table 4.)
5	Same	↑ (if leader) ↓ (if follower)	↑	Same	None		
6	Can↑	↑ (if leader) ↓ (if follower)	↑ (if leader) ↓ (if follower)	↑	None		
7–9	Same	↑	↑	Depends (See number 6.)	None		
10–12	Same	↑	↑	↑ (if leader) ↓ (if follower)	None		
13	Same	↑	↑	Same	None		
14	Same	Same	Same	↑	None		
15	Same	Same	Same	Same	None		

mentioned in the exhibit, its real market share is likely to increase, remain about the same, or decrease.

The changes in industry market potential, relevant industry sales, and real market share for the relevant firm ultimately determine the incremental sales likely to result from each growth opportunity/strategy. The more IMP, RIS, and RMS increase, the more new firm sales are likely. Table 5 summarizes the changes in IMP, RIS, and RMS discussed in Tables 3 and 4 for each of the fifteen growth opportunities.

Once the firm has estimated the specific effects of each growth opportunity upon IMP, RIS, and RMS, the firm is in a much better position than before (without using market structure profile analysis) to estimate incremental firm sales within a fairly small range.

SUMMARY AND CONCLUSIONS

Market structure profiles provide a focal point for showing the interrelationships among fifteen growth opportunities and can provide the firm with significant insights concerning the incremental sales which each growth strategy is likely to yield.

Three market structure profile measures provide particularly helpful insights for making such estimates. These three measures are *industry market potential* (IMP), *relevant industry sales* (RIS), and *real market share* (RMS). Once the firm has estimated the specific effects of each growth opportunity upon IMP, RIS, and RMS, the firm is in a much better position than before (without using market structure profile analysis) to estimate incremental firm sales within a fairly small range. A firm can use the principles of market structure profile analysis to estimate potential incremental firm sales related to each alternative growth opportunity. The resulting estimates, having been derived through systematic thinking and analysis, provide the relevant firm with very meaningful input for making its growth planning decisions.

Market Share Strategy and Corporate Profitability

Barrie James

The accepted primary objective of most companies, which is reflected in their marketing strategy, is to maximise profitability.

To fulfill the profitability criteria new products are launched into markets with the aim of achieving the highest possible market share and to become the market leader within the shortest possible time span.

This strategy implies that market dominance is essential to enable the company to reap the rewards of the economies of scale and to maximise profitability through maximised sales revenue income and minimised costs since it is presumed that profitability follows the market share. Judging from papers published in the marketing and business press and in case histories it appears that there is a widespread assumption that "Biggest is best"—the greater your market share the greater the profitability.

There are several distinct indicators that a market dominance strategy is not necessarily the most profitable for the company to adopt and that increases in profitability do not automatically follow increases in the market share.

The following paper attempts to identify the latent factors in the areas of market vulnerability, innovation and promotion and the opportunity/cost factors which must be evaluated when planning product/marketing strategies and the individual effect which these hidden factors can have on the brand leaders' profitability. The paper also provides some insight into the problems of correlating brand profitability with market share, as a tool for product/market strategy planning, on three levels—intra-brand, inter-brand and inter-company.

MARKET VULNERABILITY

The increasing level of competition, in all market segments and spiralling marketing, sales and promotional costs, makes it both difficult and expensive to

From Barrie James, "Market Share Strategy and Corporate Profitability," *Management Decisions* (Winter 1972). © Barrie G. James, Zurich, Switzerland, August 1972. Reprinted by permission.

FIGURE 1   Static Market or Low Incidence of Growth

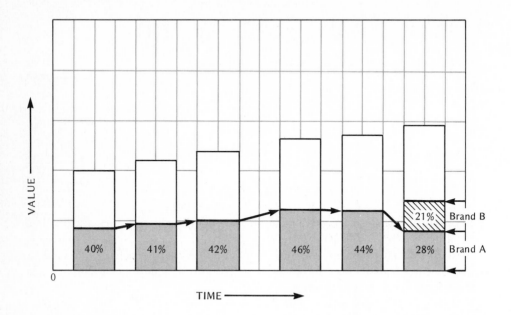

reach the leading market position and still more problematic and costly to maintain this position.

To illustrate the gravity of this situation, a recent survey (1) showed that between 1965 and 1971 some 61% of the brand leaders in 47 product classes in the U.K. grocery market lost share or forfeited the leading position.

Unless a competitive new product successfully introduced into a market expands the total market size appreciably, it will tend to cannibalise market share of existing products.

In a static market, or in a market with a low incidence of growth (see Figure 1), a successful new product entry into the market—brand B—will tend to have the effect of cannibalising the dominant brand A's market share. This contrasts with a market situation (see Figure 2), where the new market entry—brand B[1]—increases the total market size considerably, and the dominant brand—A[1]—whilst losing some market share, does in fact increase sales revenue.

It would appear that the greater the market share of the leading brand and the greater the differential between the leader and other brands in the market place, the greater is the proportionate risk of the leading brand sacrificing part of its share to successful new market entrants—unless the total market expands and the leader can maintain share and increase sales to contain the sales generated by the new entry.

To maintain the market share of the brand leader in a market which is expanding due to both a successful new product entry and increases in consumer demand can be quite a feat. The following example illustrates the position where the brand leader with a 45% market share has to contain both a success-

FIGURE 2   Considerable Expansion in Market Size Created by New Product

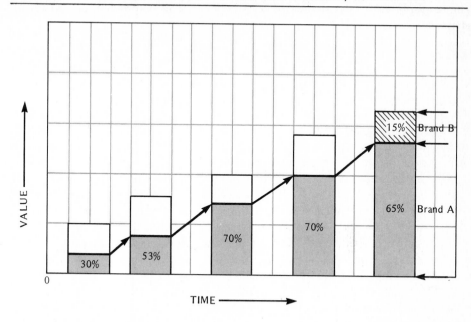

ful new product entry which increases the market by 15% and an increase in the market size of 10% caused by increased consumer demand. To maintain his 45% market share held in 1972, the brand leader must therefore increase his total sales value by 25% during 1973 otherwise he will lose brand share.

	(a) 1972 Base Market Value	(b) Normal Increase on Base Market Value	(c) Increase in Sales generated by New Entry on Base Market Value	1973 Market Value (a + b + c)	Variance 1973 on 1972
Percentage	100%	+10%	+15%	125%	+25%
Percentage value	100	+10	+15	125	—
Brand leader					
Market share	45%	—	—	45%	—
Sales value	45	—	—	56 · 25	+25%

The level of competition naturally varies from market to market thus the degree of vulnerability will also tend to fluctuate in line with competitive intensity. However, the spectre exists that in many markets the brand leader today has a disproportionate chance of maintaining or of improving his dominant share.

MARKET INNOVATION

To minimise the effect of successful competitive new product introductions in the market place, the brand leader tends to be forced into a defensive strategy to protect his share rather than an aggressive offensive strategy designed to both consolidate and increase his share.

Initial defensive tactics under the misnomer "innovation" take the form of launching extenders to the basic product line in an attempt to increase sales overall and thus market share by reaching the smaller sub-market segments and new consumers which have previously been avoided due either to their low volume or price conditions. These tactics may well increase sales and overall market share; however, low volume and price restrictive sub-markets are not indicative of high profitability.

"True" innovation where the brand leader assumes the rôle of the major innovative force in the market necessitates forecasting and/or creating new market trends and attendant consumer demand. The company must then enter the field of researching, creating and marketing new and additional packs, presentations, sizes, flavours, colours, etc. True innovation is both time-consuming and a high risk venture and the areas of consumer and product research and development are costly.

Unless innovations are highly successful they invariably do not generate sufficient extra revenue to cover the innovative expenditure. Constant innovation will also tend to reduce brand profitability and tax resources.

MARKET PROMOTION

There is a definite correlation between the weight of promotional expenditure and the market share obtained.

It is a fairly well accepted maxim in the fast moving consumer products' markets that the market leader must increase his share of promotional support faster than the growth of promotional support of the total market, otherwise he stands a less than even chance of maintaining his leadership. From this it would seem that apart from promotional quality and effect, the greater the weight of promotional support, the more likely is the tendency to maintain and expand the market share.

Unless prices in this situation can be increased and/or the sales revenue increases substantially, continual increases (natural and otherwise), in the overheads and other costs directly attributable to the product such as raw materials, manufacturing, packaging, etc., together with the high level of promotional support costs, will tend to reduce unit and, therefore, total brand profitability.

It may also not be economically feasible to expand a dominant market share beyond a certain point since the extra costs involved, particularly promotional, may in fact produce a disproportionate return on the additional sales and share obtained.

Faced with a strong competitive challenge to a dominant market share the brand leader frequently opts for a price decrease as a promotional tool to fight the challenge. Unfortunately, this seldom works to the advantage of the market leader. Price decreases usually take place some time after the competitive new product introduction, after the weight of the challenge has been assessed. Late retaliatory price reductions do not radically affect the new product's progress if the new product has had sufficient time to develop a demand and a clientèle and thus get entrenched in the market place. Price decreases are also not the most effective way to preserve profitability. For example, a 10% price decrease on a product with a 30% margin requires an increase of 50% in unit volume to give the same net sales income (2).

Price reductions are only effective promotional counters if taken before a strong competitive launch is made, that is, at a time when it is threatened, thus destroying the potential profit opportunities for the new competitive product and deterring its entry.

REGULATORY CONTROL

There is a pronounced trend towards greater interest into and control of all facets of business operations by governmental regulatory agencies in many countries.

An increasing amount of legislation has been enacted or threatened against mergers and acquisitions of directly competitive companies or even of companies within the same industry—generally to forestall moves which are assumed will narrow the competitive market base.

More ominous is the increasing governmental attitude both nationally, and, with the enlarged European Economic Community, multi-nationally, towards the relative market strength of companies. In the United States, for example, the earlier legal decisions stressed that size and the possession of unexercised power was not economically undesirable. The recent decisions indicate that interpretations have changed and that companies must now avoid attempting to deliberately destroy their competitors and to avoid obtaining market control by accretions of power.

It appears that both nationally and internationally governments are coming to the conclusion that all competition is healthy but some competition (dominant) is less healthy than others.

A market dominance strategy may therefore be an unwise policy to adopt in the near future since it may invite government attention which could result in very arbitrary action, as some recent cases have demonstrated.

OPPORTUNITY COST FACTOR

Given the opportunity, it may be more desirable to aim for a smaller share of a larger market rather than a dominating share of a smaller market.

For example: to launch a product with a reasonable chance of obtaining, say, a 15% share of a U.S. $30 million market rather than a product which is capable of reaching 50% of a U.S. $9 million market. Both market entries would give the same sales revenue income; however, the smaller share of the larger market may tend to be the most profitable to the company.

There are several factors which support this theory:

1. Larger markets often attract heavier competition due to the greater size of the rewards available. Heavy competitive activity frequently results in a large number of companies trying to enter the market with new products to gain part of the rewards. A market which has many and frequent new product introductions often tends to become susceptible to absorbing new products, giving the new brand a higher rate of probability of successful entry.

2. In smaller markets where the brand leader is well established with a commanding market share which is increasing, there may well be little opportunity to gain a profitable market share or even a viable market entry. Successful entry in this situation requires a heavy promotional outlay which increases the product pay-out period.

3. By adopting a low-profile market share strategy in a large market which does not attract heavy competitive retaliation from existing products at the time of entry and from future new market entries, there is a possibility of maximising brand profitability created mainly by the lower marketing costs.

4. From an established smaller market share within a large market one can frequently expand market share upwards by skillful marketing rather than by steamroller promotional techniques which are both expensive and often wasteful.

5. With a smaller market share one also has the opportunity of launching a further product into the market to obtain greater overall company market penetration, with a more than proportionate risk of not cannibalising sales and market share of the existing company market entry.

6. By adopting a "wait-and-see" stance the brand with a smaller market share can wait for the brand leader to innovate and educate the market, and if the innovation is successful and meets with consumer acceptance, follow suit. Although the smaller brand will not obtain the majority of sales by not being in the market place first with the new innovation, provided that he enters shortly after, he will gain some part of the innovative sales without the at-

tendant consumer/market development costs, thus obtaining a higher return on his innovational investment cost than the brand leader.

QUANTITATIVE ASSESSMENTS OF MARKET DOMINANCE STRATEGY ON CORPORATE PROFITABILITY

The degree of market vulnerability, the level of innovation, the interaction between quantity, quality and effect of promotional expenditure, the effects of possible adverse legal decisions and the relative opportunity/cost of a product in a market dominance position are often intangible and frequently latent since they cannot be clearly identified and therefore their effects on corporate profitability cannot be quantified.

Therefore, at present, any such assessments must be purely qualitative—based on subjective evaluations.

There is also the possibility that a synergistic effect could take place between the individual influences of these factors which could potentiate the total effect. Conversely, the positive influences of some of the factors may have an antagonistic influence on other, more negative factors which would reduce the total effect of the factors on corporate profitability. For example, a lack of product innovation and its attendant costs for the brand leader in the table salt market could partially compensate for the costs of a heavy promotional campaign to maintain brand share in the face of a strong competitive challenge.

If a formula existed for quantifying the effect of these factors, it would be subject to so many qualifications due to the widely varying conditions existing in each product/market situation that it may well not be universally applicable.

Since the strategist cannot quantify the effects of a market dominance position on profitability he is left with the possibility of correlating the market share with profitability.

To correlate the market share with profitability it may be more desirable to assess both market share in value and unit volume together with net unit profitability which can be quantified, rather than on subjective assessments which are only qualitative.

A method to obtain a correlation of market share with profitability could be stated as:

$$M/PF = \frac{MSVa \times UP}{MSVo}$$

where:

M/PF = Market profitability factor
$MSVa$ = Market share value
$MSVo$ = Market share volume
UP = Unit profitability $\dfrac{(\text{unit volume} \times \text{sales revenue per unit})}{\text{Total costs}}$

FIGURE 3   Operation of Market/Profitability Factor

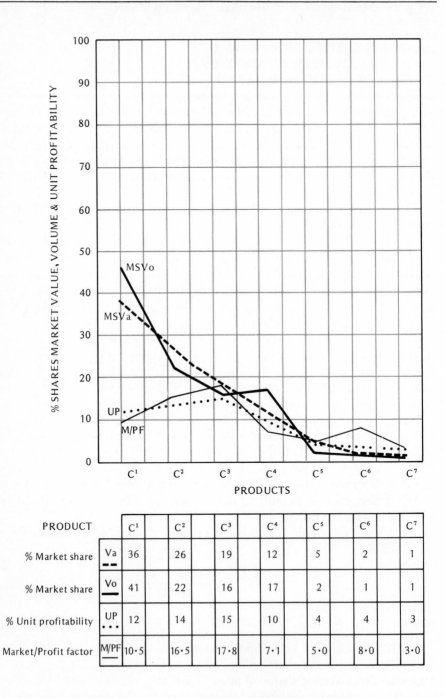

PRODUCT		C¹		C²		C³		C⁴		C⁵		C⁶		C⁷
% Market share	Va	36		26		19		12		5		2		1
% Market share	Vo	41		22		16		17		2		1		1
% Unit profitability	UP	12		14		15		10		4		4		3
Market/Profit factor	M/PF	10·5		16·5		17·8		7·1		5·0		8·0		3·0

An example of the operation of this market/profitability factor based on the interrelationship of value, volume and unit profitability in a hypothetical market situation with seven brand entries is illustrated in Figure 3. (For the purposes of the illustration the unit profitability by brand are assumed or known to be reasonably accurate.)

From the example it can be seen that although product C^1 has the dominating value and volume shares in the market place, the lower unit profitability in part produced by the lower consumer price of the product makes brand C^1 less profitable overall than either brand C^3 or C^2.

The most profitable position in the market would therefore seem to lie where the market profitability factor is the highest in the market place.

CORRELATING BRAND PROFITABILITY WITH MARKET SHARE

(a) Intra Brand Correlation

It is relatively simple, though not always easy, to calculate your own brand's profitability since one has access to and can quantify direct and indirect costs and can compute the assets involved in development and production of the product to obtain the ROI factor.

For many markets statistical data exists on the total market structure and on the sales value and volume of competitive products so that a comparison can be made between your own brand's market performance and its profitability and those of other company brands.

(b) Inter Brand Correlation

The logical step from an *intra* brand comparison is to compare the brand's profit and market share with other, directly competitive brands in the market (3).

This is far more difficult since most companies regard data on profitability as sacrosanct and are reluctant to release cost and profit information. Therefore, inter-brand studies on a costing and profitability basis are extremely rare.

There is also the problem that companies may adopt different costing techniques and/or apply them in varying intensity. Therefore, costs and resultant profitability may not be calculated on the same basis for all products in the market which could result in fluctuations in unit profitability and that, in turn, would make an effective correlation between brands on a market share/profitability comparison invalid.

(c) Inter Company Correlation

It has been suggested that comparisons of companies' profitability, for companies in the same market, with their respective market share can provide a basis for correlation.

Ruling out *monopoly* and *monopsony* market situations, unless all products in a market are produced by one company/product operations—a fairly unusual situation—a company's overall profit cannot be correlated with market share and compared with other products in the same market. Companies diversify not only into other market segments within their industry (i.e., Ford Motor Company in the automotive industry into the passenger car, trucks, buses, agricultural, public service and military vehicle markets and with Fomoco into the accessory and spare parts market) but also enter completely new industries (i.e., Ford's Philco division into the consumer and industrial electronics and aerospace markets). Therefore it would be impossible to correlate Ford's market share in the U.S. passenger car market or in the total U.S. automotive market with Ford's overall profitability since revenue is obtained from many markets in which costs and Ford's market share and profitability can fluctuate widely.

Since many companies now obtain substantial revenue from overseas operations and also from investments, royalties, licensing and patents, profitability in some situations may not be directly attributable to income derived from marketing products per se.

It may be argued that where companies are engaged solely in the marketing of fairly staple or similar items that such a comparison can be made with some accuracy. However, on closer analysis few products can be considered staple or even similar today. Coal, cement, bricks, coffee, tea, bread, butter and even metals are usually available in various grades or qualities for different consumers. Even a fairly standard product like beer is a case in point. For example: a brewer may offer three basic brews—lager, light and dark ales in both standard and premium qualities. In addition he may offer each of these products in the form of canned, bottled and bulk presentations. Thus his beer market is not one but 18 sub-market segments within the total beer market. Since promotional costs will vary not only with competitive intensity but also with the target audience and the costs of manufacture, packaging and distribution may fluctuate widely from one sub-market segment to another, the brewer's total profitability would not be truly representative of his share of the total beer market.

Correlations between a brand's market share and its profitability can only be of value to strategic marketing planning if comparisons are made with other brands in the market. Information is virtually impossible to obtain for other brands to make a meaningful comparison. Comparisons between the total profit of companies and their brand shares cannot produce accurate correlations.

CONCLUSIONS

The majority of product marketing strategies do not take into consideration the possible adverse effects of a market dominance position on corporate profitability.

The main reasons for this situation are twofold:

1. The results of the adverse effects cannot be quantified and are thus regarded as minor factors.
2. The more common situation is that companies are frequently not aware of the effects of a market dominance strategy on corporate profitability.

There is a fair body of evidence to suggest that depending upon a product's category, the market size and structure and conditions in terms of entry, pricing, promotion and competition, market leadership may in fact produce a lower unit profitability than for brands with a smaller market share. Market dominance may also produce decreasing unit profitability after a certain level of market share has been attained as the brand leader fights to stop competitive products eroding its market share. (This second situation bears some similarity with the established economic theories of *division of labour* and *economies of scale*—both of which show decreasing returns after a certain point has been reached.)

With the high rate of new product mortality—variously assessed at anything from 80% to 98%—and the accelerating erosion of the product life cycle in many markets due to the rapidity of commercialisation of technological innovations, companies are being forced to maximise product profitability in the short term period which increases their need for accurate strategic marketing planning.

Unfortunately, strategic long range marketing planning decisions can only, at present, be made on an unsound mixture of past solid marketing research data and on subjective opinions of future trends rather than on formula based decisions. Until companies begin to look more closely at, and analyse the effect of, their marketing strategy decisions on corporate profitability rather than be mesmerised by the mythology surrounding the brand leader, strategic marketing planning will remain in the area of "hunches" and "guesstimates."

REFERENCES

1. The Struggle for Brand Leadership," *Nielsen Researcher* (Oxford), July–August 1972.
2. Goodman, S. R., *Techniques of Profitability Analysis*, Wiley Interscience, 1970.
3. Chevalier, M., "The Strategy Spectre Behind Your Market Share," *European Business and Society*, No. 34, Summer 1972, pp. 63–72.

Market Share Strategy and the Product Life Cycle

Bernard Catry and Michel Chevalier

Possession of 1% market share in the light-duty liquid detergent market is not necessarily a promising competitive posture. In such a mature and highly competitive market, it is questionable that such a small market share can ever yield a satisfactory profit. The attractiveness of a market share position varies according to the structure of the market and the nature of competition. Sometimes a decision to "invest in market share," that is, to increase market share, may be extremely valuable in the long run. In other cases, the most sensible solution may well be to disinvest, that is, to reduce market share with the short-term goal of increasing unit profit enough to offset the unit volume decrease. Market share investment or disinvestment decisions can be based on an analysis of the meaning of a market share position in a given market.

WHAT IS MARKET SHARE?

The definition and computation of a market share figure raises three major operational problems: What measure of sales is to be used? What market are we in? Against which brands is our product competing?

A company's sales may be understood as the sales of groups of product lines, of a specific brand, or even of a given size. Sales may be measured in units or dollars to incorporate size and price discrepancies among rival products. The figures may be based on orders, invoices, consumer purchases, or even consumer

About the Authors: Bernard Catry is a doctoral candidate at the Harvard Business School and a research associate at the Marketing Science Institute, Cambridge, Massachusetts; Michel Chevalier is assistant professor at INSEAD (The European Institute of Business Administration) in Fontainebleau, France.
Reprinted from *Journal of Marketing*, vol. 38 (October, 1974), pp. 29–34, published by the American Marketing Association.

use. Each level has a different meaning but also corresponds to the different degrees of difficulty encountered in obtaining the relevant information. In some cases, consideration should be given to deals, discounts, and concessions. These may be included in promotional expenses, but if they are offered on a continuing basis over an extended period of time they should be deducted from the sales figure. Finally, the handling of intracompany transfers of products and services must be decided in advance.

The market may include all suppliers selling products with the same physical features or products that are bought for the same use by customers. This characterizes the familiar dilemma of defining a market in terms of technical characteristics as opposed to substitutability at the consumer level.[1] General Electric, for instance, views all personal appliances as constituting a single entity; it includes in the corresponding market all competing suppliers of these products, because under many conditions they are substitutable from the customer's view.

Even when the same products are used in the same manner by the same end customers, it may be advisable sometimes to distinguish two or more markets on the basis of the distribution method used. For example, tire companies define different markets and consequently may have different market shares for original equipment and for replacement products, even though these products are technically identical and perfectly substitutable for the end customer. This same point was recently emphasized by Richard L. Johnson, general manager of the Foodservice Marketing Department of H. J. Heinz Company: "There is quite a difference between selling ketchup to a retail grocery organization, which makes a profit on bottled ketchup, and to a restaurant chain, which gives the ketchup away."[2]

Conversely, as Bic's entry into the disposable lighters market tends to indicate, some physically different products may be seen as competitors at the newsstand level in their fight for counter space. The geographical, socio-demographic, or even behavioral scope of the market also must be defined. Strong in the East, the General Foods Maxwell House coffee market position is much weaker in the western part of the United States. Budweiser has the highest share in the national beer market, but in a number of local markets its achievements are less impressive because of the fierce competition of local brands. Finally, the time span of market share evaluation must be specified before any measurement is made if the index is to be used as a control device and a major component of a firm's strategy. In fact, market share is a very convenient and easy-to-understand indicator of the company's activities. But the comparison of its value across segments, the analysis of its changes over time and, therefore, its integration as a major element of the marketing strategy, should only be undertaken with full consideration given to the assumptions underlying its assessment.

---

[1] Jack Z. Sissors, "What Is a Market?" *Journal of Marketing,* Vol. 30 (July 1966), pp. 17–21.

[2] "The Brand Manager, No Longer the King," *BusinessWeek,* June 9, 1973, p. 61.

MARKET SHARE IN MARKETING STRATEGY

Once defined, market share becomes a very convenient tool to assess marketing objectives. Share figures eliminate most of the influence of forces over which marketers have little or no control—such as the amount of disposable income, which influences sales, and the cost structure, which influences profits.

Market share goals are preferred to return-on-investment targets in certain circumstances. Taking General Electric as an example, one may postulate that companies under pressure from the government and antitrust legislation may be willing to limit themselves to a certain percentage of the market they serve.[3] Share figures are also simple and easy to understand; to some business executives, they represent the percentage of the market to which the company is entitled because of its reputation and are a measure of the company's image in the marketplace.

In addition, there is a strong belief among executives that high market share leads or will lead to high profit. This belief derives from the concept of break-even: the higher the sales, the higher the profit. It also comes from the notion of bandwagon effect: a high share offers a positive image to the customer and retailer; it is the best way to keep and gain customers and, therefore, high sales and profit levels. This practitioner's view has been subject to tentative validations both within and across industries. The automobile industry is typical. General Motors, with the highest market share, enjoyed the highest return in the decade of the 1960s, as illustrated in Table 1.

The Boston Consulting Group has stated that its analysis of business dynamics led to the concept of the "experience curve"; that is, the total unit cost of a product declines by a fixed percentage each time the cumulative number of units produced is doubled.[4] Although similar relationships for production

Table 1 Market Share and Profit Level in the Automobile Industry

| Company | Market Share Rank | Return on Equity | | | | | |
		1970	1968	1966	1964	1962	1960
G. M.	1	6.1%	18.2%	21.2%	23.5%	21.3%	16.9%
Ford	2	9.4	13.0	13.3	12.9	14.6	15.6
Chrysler	3	−0.3	14.1	11.4	20.4	8.8	4.6

Source: Value Line Investment Surveys, Vols. 16 to 26, Arnold Bernhard and Company, Inc., New York.

---

[3] Robert F. Lanzilloti, "Pricing Objectives in Large Companies," *American Economic Review*, Vol. 48 (December 1958), pp. 923–960.

[4] The Boston Consulting Group, *Perspectives on Experience* (Boston: The Boston Consulting Group, 1968).

functions had been proposed for many years by some economists,[5] the Boston Consulting Group generalized the concept and developed the strategic implications of these findings. For the purpose of this discussion, experience can be equated with market share and, over a period of time when market positions are relatively stable, market share and profitability are closely related. This approach was tested on many products, including silicon transistors, integrated circuits, and polyvinyl chloride.

Expanding on General Electric's experience, the Marketing Science Institute is presently undertaking a cross-sectional survey to assess the determinants of profitability for several hundred businesses in different industrial sectors. The first results provide evidence that, across business, market share is positively related to profitability, and that this is most often the case in a growing industry.[6]

All of these findings indicate a clear relationship between size and power in a market, the economies of scale obtained, and the profitability of the firm in a given sector; they implicitly or explicitly confirm the importance of market position in a given business. It should, nevertheless, be kept in mind that if high market share results in high profitability, gaining market share may have the reverse effect because it often requires heavy commercial investments. Gaining market share should be considered a long-term investment that will require time and money and that might provide negative results in the short run.[7]

A&P's efforts to increase its market position and switch from supermarkets to discount stores through the W.E.O. campaign would indicate that the chain's managers have clearly in mind some market share objectives. The underlying assumption is that the increased sales volume will eventually bring higher returns on investment. Yet, since launching the operation in the spring of 1972, A&P has not recovered its profit level of the late sixties. This example indicates that even when market share does bring profitability, an increase in market share, although attainable, may be a very costly objective.

MARKET SHARE STRATEGIES

One thing should be clear: the best strategy is not always to increase market share. Although in many cases market share increase may indeed be the best

---

[5] Jesse Markham, *Competition in the Rayon Industry* (Cambridge, Mass.: Harvard University Press, 1952); Frank J. Andress, "The Learning Curve as a Production Tool," *Harvard Business Review*, Vol. 32 (January–February 1954), pp. 87–97; and Winfred B. Hirschmann, "Profit from the Learning Curve," *Harvard Business Review*, Vol. 42 (January–February 1964), pp. 125–139.

[6] Ralph Sultan and Sidney Schoeffler, "Profit Impact of Market Strategy," in *Advertising Research Foundation Proceedings*, 18th Conference (New York: Advertising Research Foundation, 1972); and Sidney Schoeffler, Robert D. Buzzell, and Donald F. Heany, "Impact of Strategic Planning on Profit Performance," *Harvard Business Review*, Vol. 52 (March–April 1974), pp. 137–145.

[7] This was masterfully indicated by William Fruhan, Jr., "Pyrrhic Victories in Fights for Market Share," *Harvard Business Review*, Vol. 50 (September–October 1972), pp. 100–107.

way to obtain long-term profitability, it does not seem that a forceful increase in market share in the buggy whip market could lead anywhere. The selection of market areas or product groups where a long-term shift in market share may be judicious is one of the most difficult trade-offs a marketing manager is faced with. To help in the analysis, it is possible to develop a framework for classifying the different market situations and strategic alternatives.

Two market criteria deserve primary consideration. First, the stage in the product life cycle is a good indication of the trend in primary demand as well as the basic competitive patterns. The number of competitors in a given product group varies over time—from one single firm innovating on the market to a pattern of close competition, sometimes with brand proliferation, at the mature stage. To simplify the presentation, only three phases of the product life cycle are examined here: introduction, maturity, and decline.

The second market criterion that will be used here is the position of a given firm in the market; a firm with a small market share is in a very different strategic position than a firm with a dominant market share. Three classes are, therefore, used here: small market share, average position, and dominant position. Of course, this measure is not made in the abstract and refers in fact to the market share distribution of the firms in a given market. Several means can be used to assess this dimension. It can be done by reference to the largest market-share holder in the product group or, as it is generally done, by reference to the three or four largest firms in the market.

A third dimension necessary to make a complete diagnosis of the marketing position for a given brand refers to the firm's three strategic alternatives in terms of market share. First, a firm can decide to increase its position and, therefore, invest in market share. Second, it can decide to maintain its competitive position by keeping its market share at a constant level. Finally, it can decide to reduce its market position slowly by reducing its market share. This practice is often referred to as a disinvestment. When a market share reduction is carefully planned and implemented, it often provides a good opportunity for cash inflow and profit.

The distinction between the three strategic alternatives should only be made as a result of an explicit decision from the marketing department. Of course, in a purely mathematical sense, the decision of a competitor to increase or decrease its share also modifies the firm's competitive position: when a leader decides to disinvest and slowly gets out of a market, its competitors may see their market share significantly increased. In Table 2, the only dimension taken into account is a voluntary and well-planned decision to modify the brand share; market share rifts are studied only as the result of a strategic decision, and not as the result of unexpected competitive moves.

The three criteria mentioned above—stage in the product life cycle, market share position, and strategic alternatives—provide a good frame of reference with which to analyze the strengths and weaknesses of different firms on the market and assess the shift in emphasis the firm should initiate to take advantage of its position along the different phases of development in a given market.

Table 2 Market Share Diagnosis

Product Life Cycle: Market Share Position of the Firm

Strategic Alternatives	Introduction			Maturity			Decline		
	Small	Average	Dominant	Small	Average	Dominant	Small	Average	Dominant
Increased investment	I++ / E+++ 1	I++ / E++ 0	I+++ / E++ (1)	I++ / E+ (1)	I++++ / E+ (2)	I+++++ / E+ (3)	I+ / E−− (3)	I++ / E−−− (5)	I++ / E−−−−− (6)
Maintaining position	I / E 0	I+ / E+ 0	I++ / E++ 0	I / E 0	I / E+++ 3	I / E+++++ 4	I+ / E− (2)	I / E+ 1	I− / E++ 3
Disinvestment	I / E 0	I− / E 1	I− / E 0	I− / E+ 2	I−−− / E+++ 6	I−−−−− / E+++++ 8	I− / E 1	I−−− / E++ 4	I−−−− / E++ 5

I = Amount of investment required.
E = Expected cash return.
Numbers indicate the overall financial value for the cell ($E - I$).

MARKET SHARE DIAGNOSIS

Table 2 illustrates the frame of reference described above and indicates the different alternative positions that exist over time in a product group. This table provides a complete listing of all available strategic alternatives. Each cell corresponds to a different investment or a different expected gain. The term *investment* in this case has a specific meaning. For example, a firm deciding to increase its position at the introductory stage must make production and marketing investments that will enable it to increase both its brand awareness in its market coverage and its production facilities. Maintaining a position in a mature market does not seem to require such important investments. However, to keep a market position in a fast-growing market it is necessary to tool up and make investments in production facilities to serve an increasing primary demand. Each cell of the table corresponds, therefore, to a different level of investment requirement.

It seems that for a given stage in the product life cycle, and for a specific market position, it is possible to assess a profitability pattern for the whole column. If it is true that market share is related to profitability, then the relationship applies here, and the best position in some cases will be to have a dominant market share. Strategic alternatives, and particularly market share investment, provide the opportunity to reach such a goal.

To assess the value of a given strategy, it is necessary to indicate for each cell the approximate level of investment that will be needed to implement the given strategy, as well as the expected cash return that it may bring in the short run.

This analysis was done in Table 2. The amount of investment necessary is suggested by the number of pluses and minuses following the letter I, while the amount of expected cash return is indicated by pluses and minuses following the letter E. For example, in a mature market, market share increases (or investments) are difficult to obtain. This is why, in general, I is estimated high. It is also considered higher for the dominant brand ($I++++$) than for the weak brand ($I++$). On the contrary, in a mature stage, disinvestments can bring immediate cash inflows ($I----$ for the dominant firm) and provide a considerable expected cash return ($E++++$).

The advantage of this approach is that it is possible to assess for each cell of the table an overall value indicated by the arithmetic sum of cash investments and expected cash returns in the short run.

Adapting Market Share Strategy to Changes in the Market

By referring only to the absolute numbers in the table, it is possible to plot the most adequate marketing strategy. For example, in the introduction stage of the product life cycle the best short-term strategy for a weak brand is to invest in market share. For the dominant firm, the best strategy would be to harvest, although harvesting at this stage would prevent the firm from harvesting at the mature stage, where the arithmetic cash expectation is considerably higher.

Table 3 Market Share Strategies

Strategic Alternatives	PRODUCT LIFE CYCLE: Market Share Position of the Firm								
	Introduction			Maturity			Decline		
	Small	Average	Dominant	Small	Average	Dominant	Small	Average	Dominant
Increased investment	1	0	(1)	(1)	(2)	(3)	(3)	(5)	(6)
Maintaining position	0	0	0	0	3	4	(2)	1	3
Disinvestment	0	1	0	2	6	8	1	4	5

///// Indicate cells providing a good cash return.

▮▮▮▮ Indicate cells with very poor profit level.

Numbers indicate the overall financial value for the cell.

◄— Arrows indicate the best marketing strategies as a function of the product life cycle.

What is important, nevertheless, is not only the short-term value of a given case but the different positions the firm may expect at a later stage of market development. Table 3 gives two examples of this phenomenon. The weak brand investing in market share at the introduction stage may not be very successful and still be in a weak position at the maturity stage. It may also be successful and reach an average or a dominant position when product life maturity occurs. In this case, by maintaining its market position the brand may enter a cell with relatively high short-term advantage. A firm maintaining its position at the mature stage can also end up in many other cells at a later stage of the product life cycle.

It is important to note that some cells correspond to a very poor profit level with little opportunity for shifts to a more satisfactory cell (they are indicated here by ▮▮▮). On the contrary, other cells produce a good cash return (they are indicated here by ▨▨).

The best product strategy seems to be to invest in the early stages of development of the product cycle, then to attain a dominant position at the maturity level, and to stay there long enough and disinvest before the overall market enters its decline stage. This path is indicated in Table 3 by a curved arrow with a dominant position at the maturity stage that provides a profitable disinvestment strategy.

Some cells correspond to poor strategies and should never be implemented in practice. It is, nevertheless, quite common to see some firms with a small market position still investing in market share at a very late phase of development of the market. The value of the table is precisely to warn marketing managers against such ill-considered marketing moves.

Nine Flags, a product launched by Gillette in the men's cologne market, is a good example of a short and not very impressive move on the table. It was launched with market share investment objectives against Aqua Velva at a time when men's attitudes toward cosmetics changed radically. The product was, therefore, launched in a declining market and disappeared rapidly.

A more recent example belongs to a very mature market, bananas. By systematically pursuing a market share objective, Dole was able to challenge the leader, Chiquita, and become a dominant competitor in the banana market. It is clear that the maturity stage for this product will last long enough for Dole to recover its present marketing expenses. United Brands' premium product, Chiquita, seems to have lost its market leadership because management did not want to make aggressive moves. They prefer "to bring better quality products to the market"[8] than to fight for market share. This is not necessarily the best way to take advantage of strategic opportunities in the long run.

Table 3 is also useful in assessing the long-term viability of a firm's product line. A firm that has most of its products in the bottom left of the table is in a poor competitive position. There is, therefore, a constant need for new product development to insure that the firm can always follow successfully the most profitable market share strategic pattern.

CONCLUSIONS

There seems to be a definite pattern of profitability and opportunity for different market share positions over time. It is the marketing manager's responsibility to see that the company's products take full advantage of differences in profitability at different stages of market development.

How can this be done? It seems relatively easy to decrease market share over time and disinvest in a product. Actually, even this may be difficult if one tries to do it at a profit. Disinvesting means gradually decreasing marketing expenses and increasing price, and continuing this strategy as long as the market responds favorably. Here again, timing is quite important. On the one hand, market share disinvestment is usually a long and controlled process; it may last more than a couple of years and bring an extremely high contribution to profit. On the other hand, an untimely move with the wrong changes in marketing emphasis can sometimes lead to a drastic and immediate drop in market share. It seems easier to disinvest then than to disinvest at a profit.

An increase in market share is not much easier to obtain. There are market conditions and times when such an increase is not feasible. The relative strength of the firms on the market and their product positioning may actually create a systematic barrier to profitable market share gains: a firm should be able to recognize such situations where it is easy to increase advertising expenses and cut profit without increasing market share.

Where a market share increase appears feasible, an investment can be realized. But an investment in what? A decrease in price is sometimes considered an effective means of improving one's competitive position in a given market. But if this method is often effective, it is frequently risky. This is particularly true where undifferentiated products are concerned, because it may trigger

---

[8] *BusinessWeek*, June 16, 1973, pp. 54–56.

several price cuts from competitors, thereby immediately canceling the impact of such a move. An increase in advertising expenses is sometimes a better way to operate. However, each case is different and once a market share increase objective is set and considered feasible, then the proper method to reach such an objective should be planned carefully over time.

Marketing strategies must be, in large part, adapted to market share considerations and must take into account the major trends in the market and the competitive structure of that market. If it is true that market share brings profitability, then a close look at the most useful measure of the firm's position vis-à-vis its competitors and the best way to practically modify this position over time may increase its market and profit position.

Planning Gains in Market Share

C. Davis Fogg

Gaining market share is a key factor in reaching a leadership or number one position in any industry. It is particularly important to the achievement of a high volume of profits that can be used to expand a firm's business and pay dividends to stockholders, and to the attainment of leadership profit performance as measured by return on sales and return on investment. It is well documented that the higher a firm's market share the larger its cumulative production of a product, the lower its costs, and the higher its profitability.[1]

However, gaining significant share requires careful planning, thoughtful, well-executed market strategies, and specific account-by-account tactical plans. It requires a comprehensive, well-thought-out, and well-planned program. The purpose of this article is to present such a comprehensive program for gaining market share: to examine ways of increasing share, the key steps in planning market share gains, and the pitfalls that must be anticipated in implementing such a program.

When to Plan Market Share Gains

Typical situations where a business manager should seriously consider a plan to gain market share include: *poor market position*—share must be gained to increase profitability and profit volume; *new products* are being launched head-on against competition; significant *losses in share* have been suffered at the hands of competitors; a *new acquisition* is justified only if sales, profits, and market share can be significantly increased; *competition becomes vulnerable* by

About the Author: C. Davis Fogg is manager of Market Planning for the Electronic Products Division of the Corning Glass Works.

Reprinted from *Journal of Marketing*, vol. 38 (July, 1974), pp. 30–38, published by the American Marketing Association.

[1] See the Boston Consulting Group, *Perspectives on Experience* (Boston, Mass.: The Boston Consulting Group, 1968). Additional unpublished works by The Boston Consulting Group concerning the automotive, brewing, aluminum, cosmetics, and mobile home industries, and using public data, conclude that the higher a firm's market share, the higher its profitability, and that the leader in market share in an industry is usually the most profitable.

virtue of a strike, poor customer service, product shortage, financial difficulties, and the like.

When Share Gains Are Difficult

It should be noted, based on the author's experience, that gains in market share are particularly difficult under several key circumstances. One such situation would be when a firm has low share, is coming from behind, and is attempting to take share away from the leaders. It's easier to grow with the market than take share away from someone who "owns" it. Secondly, it's more difficult to gain share in a commodity market where there is little or no opportunity for a unique product and significant product differentiation. Finally and obviously, share gains are tougher when there is significant competition—competition with an adequate product offering and good distribution channels and methods.

Means of Increasing Market Share

The author has found the following five key strategies to be most important for gaining market share in an industrial market.

1. *Price*. Lower prices below competitive levels to take business away from competition among price-conscious customers.
2. *New Products*. Introduce product modifications or significant innovations that meet customer needs better and displace existing products or expand the total market by meeting and stimulating new needs.
3. *Service*. Offer more rapid delivery than competition to service-conscious customers; improve the type and timeliness of information that customers need from the service organization, information such as items in stock, delivery promise dates, invoice and shipment data, and the like.
4. *Strength and Quality of Marketing*. Field a larger, better-trained, higher-quality sales force targeted at customers who are not getting adequate quality or quantity of attention from competition; build a larger or more effective distribution network.
5. *Advertising and Sales Promotion*. Increase advertising and sales promotion of superior product, service, or price benefits to underpenetrated or untapped customers; advertise new or improved benefits to all customers.

Competitive price, new products, and service are all tangible benefits that are needed by, and can be evaluated by, customers. The marketing organization is a means of both communicating benefits and facilitating service. Advertising and sales promotions are means of communicating benefits to customers and increasing their awareness of a particular manufacturer's product line.

In addition to the five key strategies for gaining share, there are a number of lesser strategies that may be important in select markets and can be considered. These strategies include improving product quality, expanding engineering assistance offered customers, offering special product testing facilities, broadening the product line to offer a more complete range of products, improving the general corporate image, offering the facilities to build special designs quickly, and establishing inventories dedicated to serving one customer.

There are several key considerations that should be taken into account in using these methods to gain market share. First, one or more of these methods should be used only when significant (to the customer) distinct product, price, or service advantages over specific competitors can be found. The advantage must be sustainable for a sufficient period of time to gain targeted share and significant enough to cause target customers to shift their business from a competitor to the firm attempting the market share gain. If a distinct sustainable advantage cannot be found or if competition is extremely competent, aggressive, and expected to counter any attempt to gain share, then the cost of gaining share may far exceed the benefits. Under these circumstances, a firm should look for another business or product line in which to invest for share gain. Second, gains in market share will not only increase sales and profit volume, but will incur significant costs—the "cost" of decreased gross margins as prices are lowered, the cost of developing new products, the cost of new plant capacity to permit decreased delivery time, and the like.

Finally, the time that it takes to implement each method varies from strategy to strategy. Pricing changes can be quickly implemented. Improving delivery may take six to eighteen months if new plant capacity must be added. Strengthening, upgrading, and training of the sales force may take six to twelve months, and developing and launching a new product may take one or more years depending upon the extent and difficulty of technical innovation required. A plan to gain share may, therefore, involve a number of different moves over a relatively long period of time.

Table 1 summarizes the circumstances under which each strategy can be used, how the strategy is applied in the marketplace, and the detailed cost implications of each strategy.

THE PROCESS OF PLANNING SHARE INCREASES

There are eight key steps in the process of planning share increases. They are:

1. *Information Collection.* Collect critical market and competitive information necessary to establish market share goals and strategies for reaching them.
2. *Competitive Analysis.* Define which competitors are vulnerable to specific strategies, why, and what their likely reaction will be to attempts to gain share by different methods.
3. *Product Line Segmentation.* Divide current (or proposed) product lines into groups where there is room for: (a) no gain in share; (b) share gain using nonproduct strategies—such as price, service, or strengthened marketing; and (c) new product and product innovations to gain share.

4. *Establish Overall Share-Gain Goals and Strategies* for each product line marketed.
5. *Key Account Analysis.* Identify where competition is particularly vulnerable at specific key accounts; establish key account goals and share-gain policies, particularly if they deviate from general policies applied nationally throughout the market.
6. *Cost/Benefit Analysis.* Calculate the expected share and profit gains, the costs of achieving these gains; judge whether or not the cost/benefit ratio is satisfactory; repeat steps 1 through 6 until the cost/benefit ratio is acceptable.
7. *Execute the Plan.*
8. *Monitor Results* and modify goals and action, if necessary, to combat competitive reaction or to react effectively to changes in the marketplace.

Figure 1 graphically depicts the planning process. The remainder of the article is devoted to methods of obtaining and analyzing information necessary to implement the process of planning share gains.

Information Collection

The two types of information required to properly plan share gains are: "bottom-up" information typically obtained from salesmen, sales representatives, and industrial distributors; and "top-down" information typically obtained by market research and competitive intelligence activities.

Bottom-up research will accomplish three objectives. First, it will establish overall national competitive practices and patterns, including competitive pricing policies, product line strengths and weaknesses, sales force type, strength and quality, strength of distribution, market penetration, and the like. Second, it will define how vulnerable each key competitor is to moves against him and the extent to which share can be taken away for each distinct product line. Third, it will identify key large volume accounts where business is held by competition, and estimate how much business can be taken away from competition by what means.

In a bottom-up survey, salesmen basically are asked what they feel is needed in price, service, nonproduct benefits, or new products to gain and maintain share in their district or territory. This information can be effectively obtained— either by drawing on the salesman's prior knowledge of, or having him conduct a direct field survey of, a specified sample of accounts. The survey sample normally will include all key large accounts and distributors and a random sample of moderate to small accounts. Salesmen are then asked to identify what each competitor's share is, at which key accounts, what strategies can be effective in taking share away and keeping it for each product line, and how much (for example, in price) is necessary to effect a change in share. They are also asked, based on previous experience or speculation, to predict what each competitor's probable reaction will be to specified moves such as price cuts,

Table 1 Strategies for Gaining Market Share

Strategy	When Use	How Apply in Marketplace	Cost Implications
1. Price	To gain share in a product line (a) where there is room for growth; (b) in launching a new product, preferably in a growth market	A. Set general market price level below average ("catch share generally" strategy) B. Lower prices at specific target customer accounts where reduced prices will capture high volume accounts and where competition is vulnerable on a price basis; lower prices enough to keep the business C. Lower prices against specific competitors who will not or cannot react effectively	• Will lower gross margin by decreasing spread between cost and price for a period of time • Will lower cost as cumulative volume increases and costs move down the experience curve
2. New product	When a new product need (cost or performance) can be uncovered and a new product will (a) displace existing products on a cost or performance basis, or (b) expand the market for a class of product by tapping previously unsatisfied demand	A. Develop and launch the new product, generally B. Target specific customers and market segments where the need for the product is strongest and competition most vulnerable, and immediate large gains in share can be obtained	• Cost of R&D necessary to develop product • Capital expenditures on plant to manufacture the product • Start-up operating losses • Promotion costs of launching the new product
3. Service	To gain share for specific product lines when competitive service levels do not meet customer requirements	A. Improve service generally beyond competitive levels by increasing capacity for specified product lines B. Target specific accounts where improved service will gain share and the need for superior service is high C. Offer additional services required in general or at specific customers—information, engineering advice, etc. D. Expand distribution system by adding more distribution points	• Cost of adding capacity and/or bolstering service systems • Cost of expanding the distribution system, including additional inventories required

4. Quality/strength of marketing	When a market segment or specific customers are getting inadequate sales force coverage (too few calls/month) or inferior quality of coverage (poor salesmen or insufficient information conveyed by salesmen)	A. Add salesmen or sales representatives to improve call frequency above competitive levels in target territories or at target accounts B. Sales training programs to improve existing sales skills, product knowledge, and territorial and customer management abilities C. Sales incentive program with rewards based on share increases at target customers or in target markets or products	• Salary and overhead cost of additional salesmen or representatives • Cost of training or retraining • Cost of incentive program
5. Advertising and sales promotion	(a) When a market segment or specific customers are getting inadequate exposure to product, service, or price benefits compared to competition (b) A change in the benefits offered is made and needs to be communicated	A. Select appropriate media to reach target customer groups B. Set level and frequency of exposure of target customers high enough to create adequate awareness of benefits and counter level of competitive efforts	• Cost of creative work to create campaign • Production and media costs

FIGURE 1 Schematic Diagram of the Process of Planning Market Share Gains

(1) INFORMATION COLLECTION	(2) COMPETITIVE ANALYSIS	(3) PRODUCT LINE SEGMENTATION	(4) ESTABLISH OVERALL OBJECTIVES AND STRATEGIES	(5) SET SPECIFIC ACCOUNT TARGETS	(6) CALCULATE COST/BENEFIT	(7) IMPLEMENT
BOTTOM-UP Information from sales force survey	• Define competitive price, service, selling effort and advertising level for each line • Establish where key competitors are vulnerable • Define what share gain strategies may work against each competitor	LINES TO MILK (Dominant position or no gain possible) Act to keep share, manage for cash Probable cost of gaining share greater than benefit gained	Define, maintain competitive price, service, product innovation	Normal sales budgeting		Continue to manage business normally
		LINES SUBJECT TO SHARE GAIN (Low share, preferably growing market, don't have dominant position, competition considered vulnerable)	• Establish overall share gain goals for product lines, distribution channels, etc. • Set key overall strategies including: • Price decrease and differential to be maintained for specified period of time • Service improvement • Increased selling effort • Increased advertising and promotion effort necessary to gain share • Key accounts to take away from competition	Establish sales territory and specific account targets where competition vulnerable to lower price, improved service or selling effort beyond overall policies	Establish cost/benefits of gaining additional share over "do nothing" or "maintain competitive standards" policy	Execute program for product lines where gains satisfactorily outweigh cost Reiterate process if proposed results unsatisfactory Establish strategy for lines where cost of gains outweigh benefits and lines not subject to share gain
TOP-DOWN Information from market research and competitive intelligence		LINES SUBJECT TO PRODUCT INNOVATION (Unfilled customer need, subsequent new product opportunity or need for substantial improvement of existing products)	Define and develop needed innovation Establish introductory price service, and distribution policies	Define normal new product launch strategy including: • Establishing specific accounts where competition specifically vulnerable to new products or where lower pricing, improved service or selling effort beyond overall policies will gain share	Cost/benefit analysis	Execute program if justified

196

new products, increased field sales coverage, and the like. Such surveys require excellent sample design, a good information-processing system, and careful design of questionnaires to be administered to salesmen in the field and to be administered by salesmen to sample accounts. The number of accounts to be sampled and the amount of information requested must be kept small to avoid overburdening the sales force with information collection.

Top-down research is also important. Professionally conducted surveys of select customers, distributors, and key salesmen can both identify key new product concepts that can be developed and used against competition and confirm or expand on findings from the bottom-up survey. Normal competitive intelligence activities can monitor a competitor's financial condition and ability to respond to an attack on his market, his probable new product policy, and his probable reaction, based on historical information, to each type of share-gain move being contemplated.

Competitive Analysis

An in-depth analysis of competition based on survey results is required to identify those product lines where share gain is thought possible and pinpoint where and how much each competitor is vulnerable to specific share-gain strategies. Table 2 provides a simplified example of such an analysis and the key conclusions derived from the data.

Product Line Segmentation

Management judgment based on the competitive analysis should tentatively divide product lines into three basic categories—product lines where there is:

- No room for share gain
- Room for product innovation and subsequent share gain
- No room for product innovation but room for share gain with existing products

In general, there is *little room for share gain* when competition is highly competent—is equal or superior in strength and ability to penetrate the market, and has significant or dominant market share. There is often little room for gain when a firm has achieved dominant stable market share (usually 35% to 70% of the market) or the market for a product line is stable or declining. In each of these circumstances, the cost of gaining market share will probably outweigh the additional benefits provided by a gain in share. The principal strategy under these circumstances is to manage the product line to produce cash: price only to maintain market share and make only the minimum required investments in product changes, plant and equipment, and marketing. If there is some doubt that a product line falls into this category it should be treated as a product where share gain is possible, and a detailed plan and calculations should be prepared to substantiate whether or not share gains are worth the cost.

There is room to gain share by *product innovation* where significant unfilled

Table 2 Simplified Competitive Analysis

Competitive Dimensions			Us	Competitors			Comments on Data
				A	B	C	
1. Product Position	Market Size	Growth per Year		Market Share			1. Not subject to share gain, manage for cash.
Line 1	$15MM	0%	65%	20%	10%	5%	2. Subject to share gain, A most vulnerable, B, C less so.
2	$30MM	10%	25%	40%	15%	20%	3. Subject to share gain, A, B, C equally vulnerable. Substantial unfilled need for a new product.
3	$20MM	15%	10%	25%	30%	35%	
2. Pricing Strategy							B and C will be easiest to take share away from on price and it will be least expensive to maintain share taken away. A is more competitive, will require larger price differentials to gain and maintain share, and it is therefore more costly to take share away.
H = Price for margin	Line 1		C	C	C	H	
C = Price with market	2		C	L	C	C	
L = Price leader or very aggressive	3		C	L	C	C	
3. New Product Policy							Expect new products first from A, monitor market carefully to identify what they're working on—expect A to imitate earliest any new products introduced.
L = Leader	Line 1		L	L	F	F	
F = Follower	2		F	L	F	F	
	3		L	L	L	F	
4. Overall Marketing Strength							A strongest and equal to us. B and C vulnerable to more intensive selling effort offered by us.
No. Representatives	Line 1		5	10	15	15	
No. Distributors	2		40	35	30	30	
No. Salesmen	3		25	20	10	7	
5. Geographic Strength							We may be weak in district W and should consider adding salesmen, otherwise are equal or superior to competition.
No. Salesmen and Reps							
Territory E			9	7	7	6	
F			7	7	6	6	
G			5	8	7	6	
H			9	8	6	4	
6. Distributor Strength							A approximately equal in strength. B and C weaker and definitely vulnerable.
No. Distributors							
Territory E			12	10	8	7	
F			10	9	7	8	
G			10	9	7	7	
H			8	7	6	6	

7. Delivery Norm (weeks)

Product				
1	6	6	4	7
2	6	3	4	4
3	6	6	7	9

Delivery improvements necessary in 1, 2 to be competitive. Improvement beyond competitive levels will not gain share. Improvement in line 3 will gain advantage against A, B and C according to sales force survey.

8. Penetration by Account Size (%)

$ Market—all products

40 Large	40%	30%	15%	15%
15 Medium	15%	30%	25%	30%
10 Small	10%	30%	20%	40%
$65MM				

We're weak in medium and small accounts, need program to improve penetration and coverage there.

9. Probable Reaction to:

• Lower price
A—Immediate retaliation, continued price reduction to gain share back.
B, C—Weaker response. Will try to hold large accounts.

Cost in taking share away from A on price will be high. B and C more vulnerable.

• New product
A—Will immediately match new product offering.
C—May match immediately.
B—Eventually match.

B and to some extent C vulnerable to new product offering.

• Increased sales coverage
A—Will match.
B, C—Some increase.

B and C vulnerable in some measure to sales coverage, particularly if a new product is launched.

KEY STRATEGIC CONCLUSIONS

1. *Product Policy:* Focus on lines 2 and 3 where gain is possible by increased penetration and growth with the market and product modification for product 3.
2. *Competitive Strategy:* Focus on taking share away from B and C, who are vulnerable to lower pricing and a new product innovation requested by salesmen. Selectively take business away from competitor A—only up to the point where expensive price retaliation is expected.
3. *Marketing Strategy:* Add three salesmen to territory G and one to F to build strength against key targets—B and C. Shift call pattern and develop mktg. programs for medium to small accounts where penetration is poor. Develop distributor promotion program to capitalize on advantage over B and C.
4. *Service:* Invest in capacity to lower delivery time in product 2 to level competitive with B and C. Maintain competitive standards in other lines.

needs can be identified in the market, where it is technically feasible to develop a product to meet those needs, and where the product advantage in the market is sufficient to gain substantial share. In this case, the strategy is to undertake prototype product development and prove that the product is technically feasible before developing a plan to launch the product and gain share.

Finally, there is generally *room for a share gain* when a firm has less than dominant share and survey information indicates that a competitive advantage can be obtained in price, service, or selling and distribution methods and systems. This is particularly true where the product market is rapidly growing and competition is weak, fragmented, or known to be sluggish in reaction to agressive moves by competitors. In this instance, a detailed plan for gaining share is called for as outlined below.

Establishing Share-Gain Goals and Strategies

The competitive analysis will permit establishment of overall share-gain goals and the strategies to be implemented in general in the marketplace and against each key competitor.

After preliminary overall strategies have been established, the two most difficult subsequent tasks are to establish how much change must be made (in price and service, for example) to gain share and approximately how much share gain a given change will produce. Estimates of the sensitivity of market share to proposed changes can be obtained in several ways. First, historical records document share changes based on previous moves by or against competition. Second, and perhaps best, salesmen can estimate the sensitivity of share in their territories and indicate the amount of change necessary to take business away at specified key accounts. Finally, knowledge of competitors, judgment of their probable reactions, and the percentage of share they will permit to be taken away before retaliation should put a limit on expected share gains.

How much share a competitor will allow to be taken away is a function of several factors. The first is his financial condition and ability to retaliate by building additional capacity or investing cash in other means of gaining back share. Second is his business philosophy concerning the product lines in question: does he want profits and incoming cash now, or is he willing to defer current financial return for future, larger returns resulting from maintained or increased share? Finally, the importance of the product line under attack to the firm's total business will influence a competitor's reaction. If the product is of minor importance in the competitor's business, attempts to maintain share are less likely than if the product line constitutes a major portion of his business.

It is important, in addition, to realize that all of the share initially gained during an assault on competition probably cannot be maintained indefinitely, and a portion of the share may have to be "given back" to stabilize the market.

Table 3 is a typical objective and strategy matrix showing overall share-gain goals by product line and detailed strategies by type of product for products sold direct to original equipment manufacturers. Each cell in a strategy matrix will normally include:

Table 3 Competitive Matrix for Products Sold Direct to Original Equipment Manufacturers [1]

Product	Competitor A	B	C	Overall Goals
1	No change	No change	No change	Maintain 65% share, competitive pricing. Manage for cash. Improve service to competitive levels.
2	—Take away 3%. —Focus on accounts X, Y, and Z with below average pricing.	—Take away 6%. —Focus on accounts L, M, and N—below average pricing.	—Take away 6%. —Focus on accounts Q, R, and S.	Increase share from 25%–40% by: • Establishing competitive service and capacity. • Price 3%–7% lower than market.
3	—Take away 5%. —Focus on accounts X and Y where need for product modification great.	—Take away 10%. —Focus on accounts L, M, N, and X with lowered pricing on conventional product.	—Take away 10%. —Focus on accounts Q, R, S, and M—mix of modified product and low price on conventional product.	Increase share from 10%–35% by: • Product modification. • Cutting price on established product 3%–7%. • New plant with superior service.

Overall Strategies for All Products

1. Add salesmen to territories F and G where weak.
2. Shift call patterns to call on more medium to small size accounts.
3. Increase overall advertising level 25% during share-gain period.
4. Maintain competitive service in all lines.

[1] The same type of matrix could also be used for products sold through different distribution channels.

- Share (or sales) to be taken away from competition
- Specific accounts where share is to be gained
- Key strategies—price, product, promotions, change in call patterns, and the like

The simple product line vs. competition matrix in Table 3 assumes that strategy will vary only by competitor and product line. A more complex analysis will be necessary when share-gain strategy is expected to vary along other dimensions such as size of customer, customer's end market (industrial, consumer, computer, etc.), different distribution channels, and the like.

Territory Goals Specific goals are then set for each territory and for key accounts that salesmen have targeted for share gain. The potential share gains are totaled and discounted to factor in probability of success to see if reasonable account and territory goals add up to the overall share-gain goals established in the previous step. These goals become territory and account action steps if the share-gain program is accepted.

Cost Evaluation and Analysis Once program goals are established, the costs and benefits of the proposed plan must be carefully evaluated. Figure 2 is a simplified flow diagram for calculating the incremental costs, benefits, cash flow, and return on investment (ROI) for a firm intending to gain share by a combination of lowered prices on existing products, introduction of a new product, additional field sales coverage, and improved service. The chart lists most of the key items that will have a positive or negative effect on cash flow. The analysis isolates both the gain in profits from newly acquired share and the change in profitability of the base business—that business that would have been obtained without a share-gain plan—as a result of decreased prices and lowered costs as production costs move down the experience curve with increased cumulative volume. This type of analysis is easily adapted for computer calculation.

Assessing Risk A "source of sales analysis" is useful in assessing the risk and realism of a share-gain plan. In general, the higher the portion of a firm's five- to ten-year cumulative sales expected to come from disruptive moves against competition—lowered price, improved service, and new products—the higher the risk of the plan and the greater the advantage over competitors necessary to succeed.

Monitoring and Follow-up An intricate share-gain plan requires careful monitoring and control if it is to be effective. It is particularly important to insure that key account sales targets are being met, and that cost goals are on target and new product introductions are on schedule. Timing is also important. Once implementation begins, competitors will be aware of the threat to their their market share; rapid, timely implementation of share-gain plans can catch competitors unaware, and share gain can take place before competitive retaliation.

FIGURE 2 Schematic Flow of Calculation to Compute ROI and Cash Flow of a Share-Gain Plan

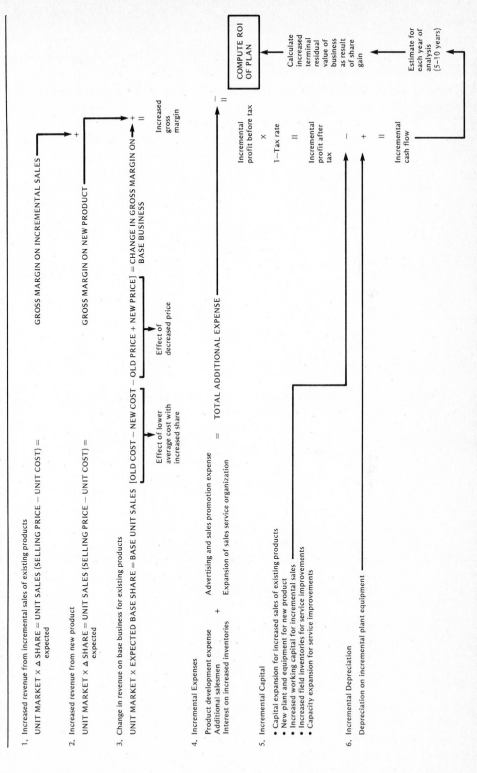

Note: See the Boston Consulting Group, *Perspectives on Experience* (Boston: The Boston Consulting Group, 1968) for a method of calculating the present value of market share gains accounting for the effects of decreasing prices, decreasing unit costs, and increasing unit volume.

203

It is also important to monitor competitive reaction to moves to gain share. Competitive moves should have been anticipated in the plan, figured into the market share targets, and calculations and plans prepared to defend held or gained share with continued price and cost reductions and product innovation.

Finally, it is important to recognize when attempts to stabilize competitive market shares should take place. When it is apparent that goals have been met, and/or the costs of gaining additional share obviously outweigh the benefits, it is important to attempt to stabilize shares by reverting to competitive—not aggressive—price, product, and service policies.

PITFALLS

There are five key pitfalls in implementing a plan to gain share. They are:

1. *Moving Too Slowly* and giving competition time to regroup and retaliate. Pricing, product, and service moves must be made quickly.
2. *Not Doing Enough* and being timid and conservative in moves against competition. Price cuts must be more than adequate, product advantage great and clear, and so on. It does not pay to do "just a little bit" to see if it works.
3. *No Follow Through.* Neglecting the tools necessary to sustain share once gained, such as sustained cost reduction and ability to lower price or sustain excellent service or develop new products. One must be willing to stick with the battle to gain share over a long period of time.
4. *Underestimating Competition* and their ability to react, resulting in higher than forecast costs of gaining share; forgetting to figure the costs of combating competitive reaction in the share-gain financial plan.
5. *Don't Know When to Quit.* Sometimes competitive reaction will be too strong; it is too costly to gain share, and giving up and concentrating on another business is the best policy.

LEGAL IMPLICATIONS OF MARKET SHARE

Finally, before planning significant market share gain and seeking a dominant industry position, plans should be reviewed with legal counsel to insure that planned action is within established antitrust laws and government guidelines. In general, the government will not challenge high market share if it is attained by internal growth and legal competitive activity in the marketplace. The government may challenge market dominance if it is thought to significantly lessen competition in the industry in question or if significant share gains are obtained by acquisition rather than by internal growth.

If one attains a dominant position in a given market, the strategies appropriate to maintain or augment that position must be carefully scrutinized from the legal point of view. Aggressive, competitive action permissible for a firm seeking to improve its position in a fragmented market may be viewed quite differently by the Justice Department if undertaken by a dominant firm seeking to augment or merely defend its position in a concentrated market. A firm that dominates must guard against the possibility that in defending its dominant position, it is accused of predatory conduct that constitutes an abuse of an alleged monopoly position.

SUMMARY

Gaining and keeping significant market share is considered by many to be the single most important key to high, long-term profitability and substantial profit volume. Market share gains must be carefully planned. The vulnerability of competition to changes in price, product, service, marketing and distribution methods, and advertising must be assessed. Potential advantages vis-à-vis competition must be identified and the costs and potential benefits of a plan to gain share carefully evaluated. Overall share-gain goals and strategies must then be translated into sales territory and individual sales account goals for implementation. Although the process of planning share gains is time-consuming and costly, the profit rewards can be substantial.

Harvesting Strategies for Weak Products

Philip Kotler

A division manager in the XYZ Company broke the news to Jim Smith that the company had decided to "harvest" his business unit. Smith had been running his business in the "maintenance mode" for years. Now he was told that his budget for the next year would be cut 20 percent, yet he should not let sales revenue slip by more than 10 percent.

Smith was shaken by the company's decision, especially since he saw some new opportunities on the horizon. He outlined them to the division manager, but in the end the "harvest" decision stuck. Top management was set on reallocating resources from his business to other businesses with a brighter future in the company. Smith's mandate was to maximize the short-term cash flow from his business. Smith thought over his options: raising prices, cutting promotional expenses, reducing product quality, or reducing technical service. He decided in favor of a personal option: He quit.

The decision to harvest a business entity—whether a division, product line, specific product, or brand—is clearly a controversial step. After all, management has three other options for handling a weak business entity. It can pour money into this unit to make it stronger (building strategy), it can budget enough money to maintain sales and profits at the present level (maintenance strategy), or it can abandon the business (divestment strategy). Harvesting the business is a fourth choice by which the company decides to reduce its investment in a business while hoping to "harvest" reasonable earnings or cash flow.

Although much has been written about building, maintaining, and divesting strategies, little has been written on the theory and practice of harvesting. This neglect is surprising in view of the growing application of this strategy and the

About the Author: Philip Kotler teaches marketing at the Graduate School of Management, Northwestern University.

Reprinted from *Business Horizons*, vol. 21 (August, 1978), pp. 15–22. Copyright, 1978, by the Foundation of the School of Business at Indiana University. Reprinted by permission.

NOTE: The author wishes to thank the following persons for their helpful comments during the preparation of this article: Paul N. Fruitt, Sam R. Goodman, Elmer P. Lotshaw, F. Kent Mitchell, and James R. Tindall.

many subtle issues that it raises. General Electric was one of the first companies to assign harvesting missions on a planned basis to its weaker business entities.[1] The Boston Consulting Group popularized harvesting in application to what it called "weak cash cows."[2] H. J. Heinz Company uses the term "milkers" for those businesses that it wants to manage for cash flow. General Foods uses "harvest business" as one of its category management concepts. One business executive told me:

> Many businesses are attempting to make deliberate decisions using these four strategies, but this is all rather new and I'm not sure how well it has been thought out. Of the four, harvesting is most difficult because of the delicate balance required and also because it implies ultimate decline and liquidation. The decision to liquidate is much easier—get out of a bad situation and go on to something better.

Companies applying harvesting strategies have not always been happy with the results. Some business entities should not, in retrospect, have been harvested because total demand later turned around. Other businesses that were put into a harvesting pattern promptly nose-dived into oblivion and destroyed the cash flow expectation. Harvesting is not a strategy to be undertaken lightly. Let us consider the following questions:

- How does harvesting differ from maintaining a business on the one hand and abandoning a business on the other?
- What kinds of products and businesses should be harvested?
- What strategies are effective for harvesting a business?
- What is the best way to implement and control a harvesting program?

THE NATURE OF HARVESTING

Harvesting is not a newly discovered business strategy. The vice president of marketing for a major food company told me that his company has been harvesting products for years without ever calling it that. Unfortunately, the company seemed to have a knack for assigning entrepreneurial managers to manage harvested businesses and maintenance managers to manage growth businesses.

One of the first things to recognize about harvesting is that it is a fuzzy term. "Harvesting" conjures up the image of gathering up the crops after a long season of growth—which suggests, in the business context, that the product has matured and the company is now going to extract the remaining value from the business. Thus harvesting implies the sunset or twilight stage of a product or business in its life cycle. Milking—a term used interchangeably with harvesting—

---

[1] See "Strategic Planning: Three New Slants," *General Electric Monogram,* November–December 1973: 2–6.

[2] The Boston Consulting Group, *The Product Portfolio,* No. 66, 1970.

suggests drawing the "milk," or value, from an asset—the opposite of investing or feeding the asset. These two terms are semantically colorful but functionally fuzzy for business decision purposes.

For our purposes, I will define harvesting as *a strategic management decision to reduce the investment in a business entity in the hope of cutting costs and/or improving cash flow.* The company anticipates sales volume and/or market share declines but hopes that the lost revenue will be more than offset by the lowered costs. Management sees sales falling eventually to a core level of demand. The business entity will be divested if money cannot be made at this core level of demand or if the company's resources can produce a higher yield by being shifted elsewhere.

Harvesting steers a middle course between a maintenance and an abandonment objective. Maintenance of a business entity requires an adequate level of reinvestment to keep up product quality, plant size and efficiency, and customer services. A maintenance objective is appropriate for business units enjoying a stable market, a good market share, and an important position in the company's lineup. "Strong cash cows" are not harvested—they are maintained.

Harvesting differs from abandonment in that the latter decision calls for finding a buyer or arranging for asset liquidation. The company will normally prefer abandonment to harvesting for business units that are losing money. If the company cannot find a buyer, it may sometimes harvest the business temporarily.

The main reason for harvesting a business entity is to pull out cash that can be put to better uses in the company. Too many of yesterday's breadwinners absorb company resources at the expense of keeping the organization from focusing on high opportunity areas. As Peter Drucker has suggested, "When an organization focuses on opportunity, also-rans have to make with what they have or with less." Harvesting amounts to placing a tax on products that are going nowhere to support the creation of tomorrow's breadwinners.

It should be noted that harvesting can be implemented at different rates. Slow harvesting means very gradually reducing the budget support for the business unit so that it almost appears to be a maintenance strategy. Fast harvesting means substantially reducing the budget support for the business unit so that it almost appears to be an abandonment strategy. This distinction is reflected in Union Carbide's description of its Category 4 and 5 products.[3]

> *Category 4:* Strategic planning units (SPUs) are assigned to this category when the primary objective, and the criterion on which performance is evaluated, is maximization of cash flow. These SPUs will receive limited resource support.
>
> *Category 5:* SPUs in this category are candidates for withdrawal either because of competitive weaknesses, incongruence with corporate objectives, or projections of unsatisfactory financial performance. These SPUs will receive limited resource support for a defined period of time.

---

[3] David S. Hopkins, *Business Strategies for Problem Products* (New York: The Conference Board, 1977): 8.

Thus one of the major decisions in a harvesting strategy is the rate at which investment in the business entity should be reduced.

IDENTIFYING WHAT'S HARVESTABLE

Management gets interested in harvesting a business under three different circumstances. In the first instance, the business may be one that is losing money in spite of a heavy budget and which has little prospect for a turnaround. Harvesting seems to be a way to lower the costs and cut losses. However, it can be argued that termination may make more sense in this case than harvesting. In one executive's words, "It is hard to milk a dog. The best thing is to get rid of the dog."

In the second instance, the business may be making money but not going anywhere, and the company may see better opportunities elsewhere. So instead of maintaining the cash cow indefinitely, the management decides to milk the cow for needed funds to invest in more promising areas.

In the third instance, the business entity may be a product that is about to become obsolete. Management will soon have a replacement product ready and therefore decides to harvest the existing product. A divisional manager at General Electric told me:

> If a dominant product of ours is facing sharp price cutting by competitors, we won't necessarily lower our price to save our market share. If we have a new and better product in the works, we will lose market share knowing this is only temporary. We will harvest the old product until the new one comes along.

Thus, a harvesting strategy may be resorted to in quite different business situations. There is no single indicator that reliably points to candidates for harvesting. Any identification scheme must rest on a multiple set of indicators. The following seven indicators are the most important:

1. The business entity is in a stable or declining market.
2. The business entity has a small market share, and building it up would be too costly; or it has a respectable market share that is becoming increasingly costly to defend or maintain.
3. The business entity is not producing especially good profits or may even be producing losses.
4. Sales would not decline too rapidly as a result of reduced investment.
5. The company has better uses for the freed-up resources.
6. The business entity is not a major component of the company's business portfolio.
7. The business entity does not contribute other desired features to the business portfolio such as sales stability or prestige.

If all seven conditions are present, the business entity appears ideal for harvesting. If fewer conditions are met, the harvesting decision becomes more debatable.

Indicator 3 warrants a comment. The actual impact of a harvesting decision on profits should be evaluated on both an incremental and fully-allocated basis. If, by reducing sales volume, allocated corporate expense carried by that business is reduced and the noncancellable portion is spread to other growing parts of the corporation, there could be an attractive paper profit improvement but not a penny more in the bank.

Indicator 4 is perhaps the hardest to evaluate. What will happen to sales volume and revenue if the harvesting decision is implemented? Much depends on the specific harvesting strategy chosen and on the speed and vigor of competitive reaction. Ideally, sales should not fall far below their current level, at least in the short run. If they are expected to fall precipitously, the company should consider instead a "maintain or abandon" decision.

One clue as to where sales will settle can be found by looking at the number of entering and exiting customers from period to period. Suppose 15 percent of the customers in a typical period are new. When the budget is cut, the percentage of new customers will fall since the company will probably reduce its spending to attract new customers. Suppose, also, that old customers fall away at the rate of 5 percent each period. This customer loss rate will continue after harvesting is introduced, and may accelerate if price is pushed up or product quality and service are noticeably reduced. By estimating the likely impact of the particular harvesting strategy on the customer attraction and holding rates, respectively, management can develop a "guesstimate" of the expected sales decline.

Some harvested products have displayed a remarkable staying power long after their marketing support levels have been reduced or removed. Consider the following:

- Bristol-Myers sold the venerable Ipana toothpaste brand rights to two entrepreneurs who continued to produce it and to stock distributors while stopping all advertising. The brand's sales continued for years at a "hard core" level, making good profits for the two entrepreneurs.[4]
- General Foods produced La France (a bluing agent) and Satina (a starch) long after they were superseded by more effective aerosol products, and they continued to sell—at somewhat reduced levels—with virtually no marketing support.
- Lifebuoy, a successful soap in the 1940s, fell into disfavor later because of its strong medicinal smell. Yet Lever Brothers continues to distribute Lifebuoy with virtually no advertising or promotional support. Because the product is priced higher on a per-ounce basis than many leading soaps, it produces enough profit for the company to justify its continuation.
- General Electric decided several years ago to harvest its artillery manufacturing division located in Vermont. Although the division was profitable, GE did not want to risk bad public relations by getting deeper into

---

[4] "Abandoned Trademark Turns a Tidy Profit for Two Minnesotans," *Wall Street Journal,* October 27, 1969: 1.

the arms business. In spite of reducing its investment over a number of years, letting the plant run down, doing little research and development, and raising prices, GE found the demand for these products persisting at a high level. Ironically, the decision to harvest produced a substantial increase in profits.

Thus, the sales of a product can decline to a level of "petrified demand," the term suggested by one marketing investigator as a contingent stage in the product life cycle following a sales decline.[5]

PREPARING A HARVESTING PLAN

The marketing plan for harvesting a product should contain the same elements that are found in any marketing plan. The manager decides, or is told, to sell a certain volume or produce a certain revenue with a stated budget. If objectives are set for both volume and revenue, the setting of a certain price in the harvesting strategy is implied. If only a revenue goal is set, the harvesting manager is free to set the price-volume objectives on the basis of his or her understanding of the demand curve.

The harvesting manager faces a number of options in formulating a plan to achieve the given sales and profit objectives. Every line item in the budget is potentially reducible. One useful way of classifying the available actions is by their degree of competitive visibility. Ideally, the harvested business does not want to alert competitors to its intention. Reducing the plant and equipment expenditures and reducing research and development expenditures are two actions that have minimal competitive visibility. These actions are normally not detectable by the competition. A more visible action would be to reduce certain marketing expenses such as sales force effort or advertising effort. If these expenses are reduced in select cities where there is lower profitability to begin with, they would not necessarily alert competitors to a harvesting intention. Still another action is to raise the product's price. The most visible indications of a harvesting intention are actions taken to trim the quality of the product, reduce the number of items in the line, or cut certain services. If, furthermore, price is raised along with service and marketing cuts, this could clearly indicate a harvesting strategy.

Although a harvesting decision calls for reduced levels of marketing support, the marketing tools at the given resource levels must be handled creatively in order to keep sales as high as possible. It is a good idea, for example, for management to occasionally "splash" some advertising. Sporadic spurts of advertising will recapture consumer and dealer attention and indicate an intention to continue the product in the line. In the same vein, the company should extend occasional deals to the trade to maintain its interest in stocking the product. It is

---

[5] George C. Michael, "Product Petrification: A New Stage in the Life Cycle Theory," *California Management Review*, Fall 1971: 88–91.

even conceivable that packaging might be freshened or the advertising message altered in order to maintain as much interest in the brand as possible.

If the harvest manager decides on a fast harvest, the best move is to cut all plant, equipment, and research and development expenditures; reduce the marketing budget; reduce product quality and service; and raise prices sharply. This will produce a large cash flow increase, albeit for only a short time. If the harvest manager decides on a slow harvest, the first stage calls for expenditure reductions in plant, equipment, and research and development. Later, marketing expenditures can be reduced and prices slightly raised. Still later, product quality and service can be trimmed. This approach produces a smaller increased cash flow but one lasting over a longer period.

Formulating the optimal harvesting plan is not easy. Considerations will differ according to whether the business entity is a division, product line, product, or item. If the business entity is a single product, the management may be able to test alternative harvesting strategies by trying them out in different cities to gauge their impact on sales and profits. If the business entity is a division, the decision has more finality, involves more cost and more people, and must include a larger set of considerations than does the decision to harvest a single product.

IMPLEMENTING THE HARVESTING PLAN

Company management can proceed to implement a harvesting decision in one of three ways. The first way is for management to gradually reduce the budget of the business entity's manager without claiming to harvest the business. As George C. Michael has written, "It is the policy of several corporate managements not to disclose to operating-level management a formal decision to harvest or withdraw support from a product line in order to avoid friction or loss of morale at that level." It can use all kinds of excuses, such as tight money, the need to finance other parts of the company, or the amount of current uncertainty surrounding the business. The manager will be upset about the budget crunch, but not as demoralized as he would be if informed of the harvesting decision. The cost of doing things this way, however, is to cause erratic planning from year to year and a loss of the unit manager's confidence in corporate management.

The second way to implement a harvesting decision is to appoint a new manager to head the business unit, one who is an experienced harvester. Just as some executives are good at producing growth and others at maintaining sales, still others are good harvesters. The problem with this solution is that these harvesting managers become well known inside and outside of the company and signal the company's decision to harvest the business. The harvesting executive's appearance, like that of the Grim Reaper, has serious repercussions for morale and productivity. It might be better to use him as a backdoor consultant than to give him operating responsibilities.

The third way calls for top management to inform the business unit manager of the harvesting decision. Top management will present the reasoning in the light of all the indicators of a harvesting situation. The unit manager will normally ask for a chance to argue against this decision and should be given this opportunity. If the unit manager can convince company management that the business has more potential than they recognize, they may be willing to change their mind and provide adequate funds on a trial basis.

When the unit manager and company management agree on a harvest decision, the decision should be implemented as inconspicuously as possible. The unit manager may share the decision with one or two close associates, but it is not advisable to spread the word broadly. Employee morale is likely to deteriorate in a business unit that is programmed for harvesting. More able employees may leave for other jobs, while others may slacken their productivity.

However, if the company is large and can reassign employees to other jobs, the demoralization impact will be lessened. The unit manager will be judged on the ability to meet the revenue and cash flow objectives set for the harvested business. The manager's reward is based on success in accomplishing the planned objectives. At General Electric, the harvest manager receives a bonus based on meeting the harvesting objectives, with 72 percent of the weight based on current financial results, 16 percent on future benefit performance, and 12 percent on other factors.[6] If the business is harvested successfully, the manager's career opportunities will be as good as those facing other managers in the company.

Competitors must be prevented, as long as possible, from learning of the harvesting decision. Competitors will normally increase their attack on a business that has been put into a harvesting mode. They will increase their marketing expenditures and lower their prices, forcing the harvested unit to "put up or shut down." The harvest manager will need reinforcements to fight back or will have to consider product abandonment. Therefore, competitors must be kept guessing about management's real intention.

Is it possible to hide the harvesting decision from the competitors for very long? This varies in different industries. A consumer packaged goods executive said that his company always made an effort to minimize the visibility of the harvest decision but went on to say:

> I also believe that the decision to harvest or not to harvest must assume that competition will learn of the decision instantaneously. If the success of our harvesting strategy depends on competition not learning of our decision for some period of time, divestiture is a more appropriate course of action.

The company will also want to keep customers in the dark about the harvesting as long as possible. Customers will lose their confidence in a company that has decided to let its plant run down, stop its search for product improvements, reduce its sales force and service, and in general, take steps that reduce the value of the offer. To the extent that customers learn of the harvesting deci-

---

[6] Michael G. Allen, "Diagramming G.E.'s Planning for What's Watt," *Planning Review*, September 1977: 8.

sion, their rate of switching to competitors will accelerate and bring about a faster sales deterioration than anticipated.

MONITORING THE DECISION

A harvesting decision must not be undertaken lightly. It should be based on convincing indicators that the business should be harvested. Once decided, the company should stick to this decision unless there is overwhelming new evidence that the decision should be reviewed. A company that vacillates between a harvesting and a maintenance decision—and even a growth decision—is responding too much to current events. It finds itself building up market share at a great cost after giving it up so easily.

At the same time, the company has to be alert to signs that the harvesting decision may have been a mistake and that profits can be made by reversing the decision. This can happen under two different circumstances. First, management may discover that its decision was based on erroneous information about the current situation. The present sales potential may have been underestimated, or the costs of doing business may have been overestimated. Or management may have thought that a competitor was coming into the market or that a new technology was going to make the business obsolete.

Second, management may have made the correct decision at the time, but new factors caused the marketing environment to change drastically. The sudden onset of inflation and recession in the early 1970s led a lot of consumers to rediscover less expensive products whose sales had been slipping in the affluent 1960s, products like oatmeal, Kool-Aid, and home permanents. Price-conscious consumers migrated to products and brands which in many cases had been put into a harvesting mode. Increased publicity about public health problems was another fact leading consumers to shift to neglected products such as filter-tipped cigarettes and decaffeinated coffee. One frequent argument for harvesting instead of terminating a product is that sudden macroenvironmental changes may bring the product back into favor. At the same time, this argument is used too often by management as an excuse for not vigorously pursuing new opportunities.

SUMMARY

Harvesting is not so much a new strategy as a fuzzy strategy. Companies have been using it for years without having a systematic grasp of its principles and procedures. The Boston Consulting Group, General Electric, and other companies have recently called attention to this strategy. However, very little is known about what, when, and how to harvest.

Most companies today manage a line of products in different stages of their life cycle. They deserve differential resource support depending on their profit outlook and their importance in the company's product portfolio. Between the decision to maintain a product and to phase out a product is the decision to phase it down. Reducing the support given to a product, if the reduction is going to kill the product overnight, does not make sense. However, reducing the support makes sense if the cost can be brought down without sales falling by as much. This is the harvesting solution. It calls for the effective identification of those products that warrant harvesting, the development of an optimal harvesting plan, and the implementation of a harvesting action program that does not alert competitors or alarm employees or customers. As companies gain more experience with harvesting, they will place more of their products in this decision mode and presumably enjoy comparable increases in economic efficiency.

4

Strategic Marketing Management Tasks

Three multifaceted operational tasks are performed by a marketing manager. These tasks include the identification of marketing opportunities, the design and implementation of marketing-mix strategies, and the control and evaluation of marketing programs. Identification of opportunities necessitates procedures for the profitable segmentation of markets and subsequent targeting of marketing efforts. Marketing-mix strategy design and implementation involves decisions focusing on product strategy, pricing strategy, channel strategy, and promotion strategy. Marketing control and evaluation incorporates techniques useful for determining the effectiveness of marketing strategies. The selection of readings in this section represent contemporary perspectives on each of these strategic marketing management tasks.

A. MARKET SEGMENTATION AND TARGETING STRATEGY

In the first article in this section, "Issues and Advances in Segmentation Research," Wind reviews the current status and contemporary approaches to market segmentation. His review is organized according to the major phases of market-segmentation research effort: problem definition, research design, data collection, data analysis, and data interpretation and implementation. Kotler and Zaltman examine the market targeting decision in their article. They trace the origins of new-product diffusion research and propose a theoretical model which is conceptually useful in assessing the "value" of an early adopter of a new product. Their model posits that a buyer's value is affected by (1) his or her propensity to purchase a new product, (2) his or her propensity to become a heavy user of the product, (3) his or her propensity to influence other prospective buyers, and (4) the cost of communicating an effective message to him or her.

B. MARKETING-MIX STRATEGY

Market growth, a firm's market share, and various indices of product performance (return on investment, profit, cash flow) recently have been given increased attention in the realm of product strategy. Two articles in this section illustrate how these factors affect product strategy. In the first article, Hopkins provides an overview of strategic planning concepts applied to product planning and strategy development. Wind and Claycamp describe procedures applicable for the design of strategies for a firm's entire product line.

Two articles in this section highlight both the art and the science of developing a realistic price strategy. Dean's article, "Pricing Policies for New Products," is regarded as a classic statement on pricing strategies for new products. The *skimming* and the *penetration* price strategies outlined in his article in addition to the criteria for their selection are timeless guides for the prospective manager. Dean's retrospective commentary emphasizes the role of cost structure, which Fogg and Kohnken expand upon in the second article in this section. "Price-Cost Planning" establishes a systematic plan for balancing manufacturing cost and price to achieve market share, unit cost, and profit goals. This article complements the first article because it assumes that a product line is already established in the marketplace.

The two articles on distribution strategy focus on the performance dimension of distribution-channel participants. Mallen's article introduces the concept of *functional spin-off* as a rationale for changes in distribution structure as regards the number of middlemen in a channel, the length of a distribution channel, and the number of channels. McCammon and Bates rely upon case studies in their presentation. Rather than focus on manufacturer strategies, however, they examine reseller strategies and the financial implications of strategic planning. Most noteworthy in their article is the description of high-performance strategies for retailers and wholesalers.

Two articles in this section relate to advertising and personal selling, elements of promotion strategy which dominate the decisions made *and* the funds appropriated. "An Attitudinal Framework for Advertising Strategy," by Boyd, Ray, and Strong, offers a framework for advertising strategy design which relates communication messages, product and brand perceptions, and consumer preferences in a systematic fashion to the predisposition of buyers. In the second article, entitled "Manage Your Sales Force as a System," Henry addresses the issue of how to effectively manage the personal sales effort. Using principles adapted from systems engineering, he presents a program useful in gauging the impact of sales activities and addressing salesperson productivity from a strategic management perspective.

C. MARKETING CONTROL

The last two selections in this section examine approaches for the appraisal and control of marketing strategy performance. In "A Strategic Framework for Marketing Control," Hulbert and Toy present a procedure that brings together price, market-share, and market-size variables for the purpose of developing a marketing control system. The system relies heavily upon approaches to variable variance decomposition in addition to managerial opinion and judgment. In the second article, Dunne and Wolk describe a product-channel-market control system. Their technique draws upon basic accounting principles with particular reference to cost allocation and controllability.

SELECTED ADDITIONAL READINGS

Market Segmentation and Targeting Strategy

Dhalla, Nariman K. and Winston H. Mahatoo, "Expanding the Scope of Segmentation Research," *Journal of Marketing* (April, 1977), pp. 34–41.

Green, Paul E., "A New Approach to Market Segmentation," *Business Horizons* (February 1977), pp. 61–73.

Marketing-Mix Strategy

Chevalier, Michel and Daniel Zumino, "Product Line Strategy," *Management Decisions*, vol. 12 (1974), pp. 127–38.

Heskett, James L., "Sweeping Changes in Distribution," *Harvard Business Review* (March–April 1973), pp. 123–32.

Kerin, Roger A., Michael G. Harvey, and James T. Rothe," Cannibalism in New Product Development," *Business Horizons* (October 1978), pp. 25–31.

Lilien, Gary L., Alvin J. Silk, Jean-Marie Choffray, and Murlidhar Rao, "Industrial Advertising Effects and Budgeting Practices," *Journal of Marketing* (January 1976), pp. 16–24.

Monroe, Kent B. and Albert J. Della Bitta, "Models for Pricing Decisions," *Journal of Marketing Research* (August 1978), pp. 413–28.

Shapiro, Bensen, "Manage the Customer, Not Just the Sales Force," *Harvard Business Review* (September–October 1974), pp. 127–36.

Stobaugh, Robert B. and Philip L. Townsend," Price Forecasting and Strategic Planning: The Case of Petrochemicals," *Journal of Marketing Research* (February 1975), pp. 19–29.

Weigand, Robert E., "Fit Products and Channels to Your Markets," *Harvard Business Review* (January–February 1977), pp. 95–105.

Marketing Control

Beik, Leland L. and Stephen L. Buzby, "Profitability Analysis by Market Segments," *Journal of Marketing* (July 1973), pp. 48–53.

Crissy, W. J. E. and Frank H. Mossman, "Matrix Models for Marketing Planning: An Update and Expansion," *MSU Business Topics* (Autumn 1977), pp. 17–26.

Issues and Advances in Segmentation Research

Yoram Wind

Market segmentation long has been considered one of the most fundamental concepts of modern marketing. In the 20 years since the pioneering article by Wendell Smith [97], segmentation has become a dominant concept in marketing literature and practice. Besides being one of the major ways of operationalizing the marketing concept, segmentation provides guidelines for a firm's marketing strategy and resource allocation among markets and products. Faced with heterogeneous markets, a firm following a market segmentation strategy usually can increase the expected profitability (as suggested by the classic price discrimination model, which provides a major theoretical rationale for the segmentation concept [35]).

Realizing the potential benefits of market segmentation requires both management acceptance of the concept and an empirical segmentation study before implementation can begin. The practical importance of segmentation research is reflected in the marketing literature [1] and the actual practice of firms which often undertake segmentation studies and rely, at least to some extent, on the findings in their development and evaluation of marketing strategies.

Examining the current state of the art of segmentation research reveals some discrepancy between academic developments and real-world practice. Academic segmentation research has been one of the most advanced areas of research in marketing. Many of the new analytical techniques proposed in marketing have been applied to and tested in the segmentation area. Real-world segmentation

About the Author: Yoram Wind is Professor of Marketing, The Wharton School, University of Pennsylvania.

Reprinted from *Journal of Marketing*, vol. 15 (August, 1978), pp. 317–37, published by the American Marketing Association.

NOTE: The author acknowledges the helpful comments of Neil Beckwith, Ronald Frank, Paul Green, Robert Peterson, Subrata Sen, and Larry Gibson.

[1] See, for example, the selected bibliography on market segmentation recently published by the American Marketing Association [74].

studies, in contrast, have followed one of two prototypical research patterns [2] with little creativity in design or analysis:

1. *An a Priori Segmentation Design* in which management decides on a basis for segmentation such as product purchase, loyalty, customer type, or other factor. The survey results show the segments' estimated size and their demographic, socioeconomic, psychographic, and other relevant characteristics.

2. *A Clustering-Based Segmentation Design* in which segments are determined on the basis of a clustering of respondents on a set of "relevant" variables. Benefit, need, and attitude segmentation are examples of this type of approach. As in *a priori* segmentation studies, the size and other characteristics (demographic, socioeconomic, purchase, and the like) of the segments are estimated.

Though segmentation studies have been dominated by these two prototypical designs, several major conceptual and methodological developments have been proposed in the academic literature. The advancement of market segmentation research requires, therefore, narrowing the gap between the academically oriented research on segmentation and the real-world application of segmentation research. Segmentation studies should be reevaluated and new designs and analytical approaches considered. Also, the academic work on segmentation should be examined to reflect management's information needs, and to incorporate better the various separate developments in marketing theory (such as the change in the focus of analysis from a single product to an assortment of products [110]) and research (such as the development in overlapping clusters [19] or new measures of attribute importance [48]).

Achievement of these objectives requires a critical examination of the current state of the art in segmentation research, assessment of the major issues involved in the design and implementation of segmentation studies, and a perspective on the direction of future work. The purpose of this article is to provide such a review, for both consumer and industrial markets.[3]

Most segmentation studies have been conducted for consumer goods. Yet the concept of segmentation and most of the segmentation research approaches are equally applicable to industrial market situations [80, 106]. Hence, the intention of this review is to discuss the problems and perspectives of segmentation research in *both* consumer and industrial markets. The review, as summarized in Table 1, is organized on the basis of the five major phases of segmentation research—problem definition, research design considerations, data collection approaches, data analysis procedures, and data interpretation and implementation.

---

[2] The classification of segmentation studies into two categories, the *a priori* and *post hoc*, was suggested by Green [40].

[3] The term "industrial market" refers to all organizational markets [106].

Table 1 Some Major Considerations Involved in Segmentation Research Studies

I. *Problem Definition*
    A. Managerial requirements
    B. A baseline vs. ongoing segmentation
    C. The segmentation model
        1. Selecting the variables for the model
        2. Traditional *a-priori* and clustering-based designs vs. the newer flexible and componential segmentation designs

II. *Research Design*
    A. The unit of analysis
    B. Operational definitions
    C. Sample design
    D. Data reliability
    E. Segment stability
    F. Segment homogeneity
    G. Segmentability of the market
    H. Validation
    I. Cost considerations

III. *Data Collection*
    A. Primary vs. secondary sources
    B. Conventional vs. newer procedures

IV. *Data Analysis*
    A. For determining the segments: classification
    B. For establishing the segments' profiles: discrimination
    C. For simultaneous classification and discrimination

V. *Data Interpretation and Implementation of Results*
    A. Determining the number of segments and selection of target segments
    B. Translating segmentation findings into strategy

PROBLEM DEFINITION

The problem definition stage of segmentation research involves three major considerations: (1) managerial requirements versus the requirements proposed by the normative theory of segmentation, (2) the considerations of conducting a large-scale baseline segmentation study versus a continued series of ongoing segmentation studies, and (3) the specification of the desired segmentation model.

Managerial Requirements

Management acceptance of the market segmentation concept has resulted in the use of segmentation research to answer a wide range of marketing questions about the response of market segments to the firm's marketing strategies (price changes, new product offerings, product changes, advertising themes, promotional efforts, and the like) as well as the selection of target market segments for each of the firm's planned marketing offerings. The typical management questions which trigger and guide many market segmentation studies can be illustrated by the following objectives of several recently conducted concept-testing studies:

- Which new product concepts evoke the highest respondent interest, and how do the evaluations of these concepts differ by respondent groups—heavy versus light product users, and users versus nonusers of the company's brand?
- In terms of target markets for a new product concept, how do interested and disinterested respondents differ by demographic and socioeconomic characteristics, attitudes, and product usage characteristics?
- Can the market for new product concepts be segmented in terms of the respondents' price sensitivity (or other benefits sought), and what are the concept evaluations, attitudes, product usage, demographic, and other background characteristics of the various price-sensitive segments?

These and similar questions, which have guided most of the real-world market segmentation studies, have little to do with the type of questions suggested by the normative theory of market segmentation. Normative theory focuses on how information about customer characteristics and their relation to marketing strategy variables *should* be used in the development and evaluation of a marketing strategy. Several models for the allocation of promotional resources to segments in the presence of uncertainty (both about the response to promotion by customers with given characteristics and about the degree to which each advertising medium reaches these customers) have been proposed [35, pp. 186–241] and conceptually can be extended to other marketing strategy variables. Yet the normative segmentation models have rarely, if ever, been implemented. This discrepancy between the prescriptions of the normative theory and the practice of segmentation research can be attributed, at least in part, to the difficulties in operationalizing the segmentation theory. It is this difficulty in determining the needed data on both the response elasticities *and* reachability by media and distribution outlets that calls not only for undertaking the recommendations for further work suggested by Frank et al. [35, p. 249], but also for a critical reexamination of the nature and value of normative segmentation theory. Understanding management's use of and difficulties in operationalizing segmentation [381], in both profit and nonprofit organizations, is thus a necessary first step toward the reevaluation of the normative theory of market segmentation. The recent work by Tollefson and Lessig [102] and Mahajan and Jain [70], and the new componential segmentation conceptualization suggested by Green and his colleagues [47] therefore represent promising first steps in this direction.

Baseline versus Ongoing Segmentation Studies

Many segmentation studies have been designed as large, single effort, and expensive "baseline" studies. Such studies are justified in a variety of situations in which management would like to understand the basic structure of the market. Yet this type of study rarely has had subsequent effect on the other studies and strategies of a firm. Not uncommonly, after conducting a baseline study, firms continue to undertake other marketing studies such as concept and product test-nig with no regard for the concept of segmentation or the findings of the earlier study. This peculiar situation is partly due to habit—the continuation of past practices of analyzing most marketing research studies at the total sample level and not the segment level—and partly due to management disappointment with the relevance and operationalization of the guidelines provided by many seg-mentation studies.

To benefit fully from segmentation, whether or not baseline studies are con-ducted, management must employ the concept of segmentation in *all* studies, i.e., analyze the data of *all* studies at the segment level. Furthermore, any monitoring of the firm's product performance (on profitability, market share, or growth, for example) should be undertaken not only at the total market level but at the seg-ment level as well [115].

The Segmentation Model

The segmentation model requires the selection of a *basis for segmentation* (the dependent variable) as well as *descriptors* (the independent variables) of the various segments. The variables used as bases for and descriptors of segments have included *all* variables suggested in the consumer behavior literature. These variables can be divided into two types—*general customer characteristics,* in-cluding demographic and socioeconomic characteristics, personality and life style characteristics, and attitudes and behavior toward mass media and distribution outlets, and *situation-specific customer characteristics* such as product usage and purchase patterns, attitudes toward the product and its consumption, benefits sought in a product category, and any responses to specific marketing variables such as new product concepts, advertisements, and the like.

In building an organizational segmentation model, the variables to be in-cluded should be not only the characteristics of the relevant organizational deci-sion-making units (DMUs) but also organizational characteristics such as size and SIC. Both sets of variables include "general" *and* "situation-specific" char-acteristics.[4]

Selection of Variables for the Model   In the selection of variables for the segmentation model, the major considerations are (1) management's specific needs and (2) the current state of marketing and consumer behavior knowledge about the relevance of various variables as bases for, and descriptors of, market segments.

Management needs are an obvious but somewhat neglected consideration. Conceptually, the bases for segmentation could vary depending on the specific

---

[4] For a review of the specific variables that have been used in consumer and organiza-tional segmentation studies, see [35].

decisions facing management. If, for example, management is concerned with the likely impact of a price increase on its customers, the appropriate basis might be the current customers' price sensitivity. If, however, management is concerned with the loss of customers, the basis for segmentation could be actual or likely switching behavior, which in turn could be coupled with a secondary basis such as the reasons for switching. In contrast to the theory of segmentation that implies that there is a *single best* way of segmenting a market, the range and variety of marketing decisions suggest that any attempt to use a single basis for segmentation (such as psychographic, brand preference, or product usage) for *all* marketing decisions may result in incorrect marketing decisions as well as a waste of resources.

Over the years almost all variables have been used as bases for market segmentation. Although no systematic and exhaustive evaluation of this experience has been undertaken, a consensus seems to have emerged that some variables are "better" than others as a basis for segmentation. Some of the author's "preferred" bases for segmentation for consumer and organizational marketing decisions follow.

For general understanding of a market:
  —Benefits sought (in industrial markets, the criterion used is purchase decision)
  —Product purchase and usage patterns
  —Needs
  —Brand loyalty and switching pattern
  —A hybrid of the variables above
For positioning studies:
  —Product usage
  —Product preference
  —Benefits sought
  —A hybrid of the variables above
For new product concepts (and new product introduction):
  —Reaction to new concepts (intention to buy, preference over current brand, etc.)
  —Benefits sought
For pricing decisions:
  —Price sensitivity
  —Deal proneness
  —Price sensitivity by purchase/usage patterns
For advertising decisions:
  —Benefits sought
  —Media usage
  —Psychographic/life style
  —A hybrid (of the variables above and/or purchase/usage patterns)
For distribution decisions:
  —Store loyalty and patronage
  —Benefits sought in store selection

Common to these variables (and in line with the theory of segmentation which centers on differing elasticities to marketing variables) is the focus on various consumers' (and organizational buyers') responses to marketing stimuli. This emphasis on "situation-specific variables" is consistent with the needs of most marketing managers and current findings [35, pp. 66–89; 53, 73]. The heavy reliance on benefits sought [56] (and, in organizational segmentation studies, on criteria used in the purchase decision) and the product or service purchase pattern reflects not only the author's personal bias but also the emphasis of a considerable amount of current segmentation research.

Surprisingly, despite the attention given over the years to *hierarchy of effects* models and more recently to consumers' *information processing* [7, 104], few of the nonpurchase variables, with the exception of benefit, need, and attitude segmentation, have served as a basis for segmentation. Similarly, despite the recent interest in the *entire consumption process* (including usage, maintenance, and disposal [79]), few of the *consumption* (as opposed to *purchase*) variables have been used as a basis for segmentation. Yet, for certain purposes, and especially for public policy decisions, one may want to consider some of these neglected aspects of the consumer decision-making *process* as the dependent variables in a segmentation model [81].

Whereas the selection of a *basis* for segmentation drawn from management needs is straightforward, the selection of variables as *descriptors* of the segments is more complex. This complexity stems from three factors:

1. The enormous number of possible variables. Most of the variables covered in the consumer behavior literature can and have at some time been considered as segment descriptors.
2. The often questionable link between the selected basis for segmentation and the segment descriptors. Segments with varying elasticities to marketing variables may not be identifiable in terms of demographic and other segment descriptors. Conversely, segments defined in terms of demographic and other general customer characteristics tend to be identifiable but may not have varying elasticities to marketing variables. The latter situation restricts management's ability to pursue a segmentation strategy aimed at the given segments (and calls for examination of other possible bases for segmentation). The former situation allows management to follow at least a "self-selection" strategy [35, p. 176].
3. The question of actionability, which relates to management's ability to use information (on the discriminating descriptors) as inputs to the design of the firm's marketing strategy (e.g., product design, copy execution, media scheduling, distribution coverage, etc.).

The second guide to the selection of descriptor variables for the segmentation model is current understanding of the link between the considered variables and actual consumer responses to marketing actions. Surprisingly, despite thousands of academic and commercial studies by marketing and consumer researchers, one can draw very few generalizations as to which variables would have what effect under what conditions. This frustrating state of affairs is primarily due to four factors.

1. Lack of a systematic effort (by both academicians and practitioners) to build a *cumulative* body of substantive findings about consumer behavior.
2. Lack of specific models which link behavior (and other bases for segmentation) to descriptor variables and thus *predict* which descriptor variables should be used.[5]
3. The nonrepresentative nature of most of the academic studies with respect to sample design (e.g., small, convenient samples), type of respondents (e.g., students), and tasks (e.g., non-marketing-related tasks). Even many of the real-world segmentation studies are based on relatively small and nonrepresentative samples.
4. Lack of comparable conceptual and operational definitions of variables across studies.

Because of these limitations all that can be expected from the behavioral sciences and the consumer and organizational buying behavior theories and findings is an initial set of hyoptheses on the likely relationship between consumer (and organizational) concepts (variables) and some specific marketing response. Following this approach, one could establish a set of hypotheses such as:

Consumer likelihood to buy new products increases:
 —the higher the education, income, and occupational status [90].
 —the higher the respondent scores on venturesomeness, cosmopolitanism, social integration, and general self-confidence [82].
 —the lower the perceived risk [90].
Consumer likelihood to switch brands increases:
 —the larger the number of stores shopped.
 —the less the perceived quality differentiation among the brands.
Consumer likelihood to choose a low priced brand increases:
 —the lower the confidence in price as an indication of quality.
 —the lower the perceived social significance of the brand choice.
Consumer likelihood to buy private label brands increases:
 —the higher the education and income of the respondent.
The likelihood of an organization to buy new products (and have a fast rate of adoption) increases: [6]
 —the greater the prestige of the organization.
 —the larger the organization.
 —the more specialized the organization.

---

[5] For a notable exception, see Blattberg et al. [10], who built a model of the ideal prone household, linked the parameters of the model to household demographic variables, and thus predicted which variables should be used as descriptors.

[6] These hypotheses are based on the Rogers and Shoemaker review of the diffusion of innovation literature [92].

—the more financially stable the organization.
—the more cosmopolitan the decision makers' orientation.
—the greater the risk-taking propensity and the lower the perceived risk.
—the younger the decision makers.
—the higher the entrepreneurial orientation of the decision makers.
—the greater the exposure to supportive mass media communications.
—the less formalized the decision process.

These and similar hypotheses can be derived from the current literature on consumer and organizational buying behavior. Such hypotheses can serve as guidelines for the selection of variables in the segmentation model. Subsequent segmentation studies could provide the vehicle for testing these hypotheses.

A relatively neglected area of study has been the examination of the specification of the segmentation models. A notable exception has been regression segmentation models. Examination has suggested that if these models are misspecified by omitted variables or functional forms different from the "true" process, they may be useful descriptors of the true purchase rate (or the group means for similar individuals), although the estimated model coefficient will be biased, except in special circumstances [5]. Beckwith and Sasieni [5] developed misspecification tests for the regression segmentation models. It is desirable to use such tests whenever appropriate and to develop similar ones for other (non-regression) segmentation models.

Traditional a Priori and Clustering-Based Designs versus Newer Flexible and Componential Segmentation Models   Four major types of models can be used in an effort to segment a market. They include the traditional *a priori* and *clustering-based* segmentation models, and the new models of flexible [91] and componential segmentation [47], which are based on different sets of assumptions. The selection of a model depends on management's objectives in undertaking a segmentation study.

A priori segmentation models have had as the dependent variable (the basis for segmentation) either product-specific variables (e.g., product usage, loyalty) or general customer characteristics (e.g., demographic factors). The typical research design for an *a priori* segmentation model involves seven stages.

1. Selection of the (*a priori*) basis for segmentation.
2. Selection of a set of segment descriptors (including hypotheses on the possible link between these descriptors and the basis for segmentation).
3. Sample design—mostly stratified and occasionally a quota sample according to the various classes of the dependent variable.
4. Data collection.
5. Formation of the segments based on a sorting of respondents into categories.
6. Establishment of the (conditional) profile of the segments using multiple discriminant analysis, multiple regression analysis, AID, or some other appropriate analytical procedure.

7. Translation of the findings about the segments' estimated size and profile into specific marketing strategies, including the selection of tarket segments and the design or modification of specific marketing strategy.

Clustering-based segmentation models differ from *a priori* models only with respect to the way the basis for segmentation is selected, i.e., instead of an *a priori* selection of a dependent variable, in the clustering-based approach the number and type of segments are not known in advance and are determined from the clustering of respondents on their similarities on some selected set of variables. Most commonly the variables used in the clustering-based models are needs, attitudes, life style and other psychographic characteristics, or benefits sought. Frequently the clustering procedure is preceded by a factor analysis designed to reduce the original set of variables. Other than the fifth step in the prototypical *a priori* model—the formation of segments—and occasionally the specific sample design, the rest of the steps in the segmentation research design are the same.

Clustering-based segmentation models occasionally are combined with some *a priori* bases. For example, the sample first can be divided into brand users and nonusers (or heavy and light users, and the like) and then the respondents in each *a priori* segment can be clustered according to some other basis for segmentation such as needs, benefits, or the like. This and similar hybrid approaches such as Peterson's *sequential clustering* [86] (i.e., clustering on demographic characteristics followed by attitudinal clustering within each demographic segment), or Blattberg and Sen's multidimensional approach [11, 12] address the problem of intrasegment heterogeneity. Hybrid approaches are particularly useful in organizational segmentation problems in which the first level of segmentation is based on organizational demographic characteristics (e.g., SIC, size) followed by product usage or criteria used in the purchase decision [114]. Despite their conceptual attractiveness, hybrid approaches do require relatively large sample sizes.

In both the hybrid and "pure" clustering models the researcher is confronted with a series of decisions about the selection of a clustering algorithm and the determination of the number of segments. Some of the major considerations in this area are discussed in a subsequent section.

Flexible segmentation. In contrast to *a priori* segmentation in which the segments are determined at the outset of the study, and clustering-based segmentation in which the selected segments are based on the results of the clustering analysis, the flexible segmentation model offers a dynamic approach to the segmentation problem. By this approach one can develop and examine a large number of alternative segments, each composed of those consumers or organizations exhibiting a similar pattern of responses to new "test" products (defined as a specific product feature configuration). The flexible segmentation approach is based on the integration of the results of a conjoint analysis study [52, 120] and a computer simulation of consumer choice behavior [84, 117]. Conjoint analysis studies usually consist of three major parts: (1) preference ranking or rating of a set of hypothetical products, each described as different levels on two factors at a time [63, 64] or as different levels on the full set of factors [46, 53] (the data from this task constitute the input to one of the nonmetric or metric conjoint analysis algorithms [16, 50, 67, 68, 95, 100] which produce a vector of utilities—for the various factors and levels—for each respondent); (2) perceptual ranking or rating of the current brands on the same set of attributes used in the preference task; and (3) a set of demographic and other background characteristics.

The simulation uses these three data bases as inputs and requires the active participation of management in designing a set of "new product offerings" (each defined as a unique combination of product features—specific levels on each of the factors included in the conjoint analysis study). Management participation can be on a real time basis in which managers interact directly with the computer simulation. Alternatively, management can specify in advance a number of plausible new product concepts, or react to a number of "best" product combinations.

The consumer choice simulator is based on the assumption that consumers choose the offering (new product or existing brand) with the highest utility.[7] The simulator is designed to establish (1) the consumer's share of choices among the existing brands, which can be validated against current market share data if available, and (2) the consumer's likely switching behavior upon the introduction of any new product. This phase provides a series of brand-switching matrices. Within each matrix management can select any cell or combination of cells as a possible market segment (e.g., those consumers remaining with brand i versus those who switched to new brand j, etc.). Once the desired segments (cell or cell combination) have been selected, the demographic, life style, and other relevant segment characteristics can be determined by a series of multiple discriminant analyses which can be incorporated in the simulation.

The flexible segmentation approach departs from the traditional *a priori* and clustering-based approaches by offering management the flexibility of "building up" segments (cell or cell combination within any specific brand-switching matrix) based on the consumers' response to alternative product offerings (under various competitive and environmental conditions). In addition, having selected a segment, management has easy (interactive mode) information on the estimated size of the segment and its discriminating characteristics.

Componential segmentation. The componential segmentation model proposed by Green et al. [47] shifts the emphasis of the segmentation model from the partitioning of a market to a *prediction* of which person type (described by a particular set of demographic and other psychographic attribute levels) will be

---

[7] Simulators have been developed not only on the basis of such 0,1 choice rules but also on the basis of a probability of choice; i.e., the utility for a given item is calculated as a percentage of the total utility for the brands the respondent considers in his or her feasible set. More sophisticated choice simulators also have been developed and are suggested elsewhere [50]. Experience to date (with five simulators) suggests that the simple simulator described above can reproduce accurately the market share of an existing set of brands. Yet further experimental work is called for to refine the computer simulations to take into account new features such as consumers' "learning" of factors over time and as a function of the marketing efforts of the firm and its competitors, the description of new item profiles not in terms of deterministic levels for each factor but as a probability distribution over factor levels, etc.

most responsive to what type of product feature. The componential segmentation model is an ingenious extension of conjoint analysis and orthogonal arrays
to cover not only product features but also person features. In componential segmentation the researcher is interested in developing, in addition to parameter
values for the product stimuli, parameter values for various respondent characteristics (demographic, product usage, etc.).

In a typical conjoint analysis approach to market segmentation, a matrix of
subjects by utilities is developed. This matrix can serve as the input to the determination of the profile of some *a priori* segments (e.g., product users versus nonusers) or alternatively as the input to a clustering program which would result
in a number of benefit segments [54]. In componential segmentation, the same
design principles which guide the selection of (product) stimuli are applied also
to the selection of respondents. For example, in a study for a new health insurance product, four sets of respondent characteristics were identified on the basis
of previous experience and management judgment: age (under 50, 50–65, and
over 65), sex (male, female), marital status (married, single), and current insurance status (have some health insurance with the given company, have health
insurance with another company, and do not have any supplementary health insurance). Given these factors and levels, if a full factorial design were used one
would have 36 possible customer profiles ($3 \times 2 \times 2 \times 3$). Employing an orthogonal array design, one can use only nine combinations. Such a design requires
the screening of respondents to select those who meet the nine profile requirements.[8] Each respondent is then interviewed and administered the conjoint
analysis task for the evaluation of a set of hypothetical health insurance products
(also selected following an orthogonal array design of 18 combinations of five
product features each at three levels). Having completed the data collection
phase, the researcher would have a 9×18 matrix of averaged profile evaluations
of the 18 stimuli by the nine groups of respondents. This data matrix then is
submitted to the COSEG (*co*mponential *seg*mentation) model [38] which de-
composes the matrix into separate parameter values (utilities) for each of the
levels of the product feature factors (comprising the stimulus cards) and separate parameter values (saliences) for each of the levels of the four customer profile characteristics (describing the respondents) which indicate how much each
profile characteristic contributes to variation in the evaluation responses.

Given these two sets of parameters, the researcher can make predictions
about the relative evaluation of any of the 243 possible product features (3^5) by
any of the 36 respondent types. The five product feature utilities and four respondent saliences and the standard deviation of the predictor errors (as estimated for the 9×18 matrix) are used with a Monté Carlo simulator to estimate
(1) for each respondent segment the frequency of first choices for each of the
considered new product combinations and (2) for each new product combination the frequency of first choices across segments.

---

[8] Care should be given in the survey stage to count carefully the incidence of each profile
in the population. This step is essential if one wants to use the componential segmentation
model not only for the identification of segments but also for the estimation of the size of each
segment.

The COSEG model offers a new conceptualization for market segmentation because it focuses on the building blocks of segments and offers simultaneously an analysis of the market segment for a given product offering and an evaluation of the most desirable product offering (or positioning). The concept and algorithm of componential segmentation can be extended to cover not only two data sets (product feature and respondent characteristics) but three or more data sets by adding, for example, the components of usage situations.

The model and measurement of componential segmentation apply to both consumer and industrial market situations. In fact, the first commercial application of componential segmentation was conducted by Green and his colleagues for a firm engaged in the marketing of credit cards. This study was concerned with the design of a new credit card and the respondents were retail establishments selected on the basis of four sets of establishment characteristics (type of establishment, size of establishment, the establishment's current favorite card, and the number of credit cards honored by the establishment) [40].

RESEARCH DESIGN

Research designs for a segmentation study depend primarily on the segmentation model used and the researcher's creativity and skills. Each of the four segmentation models (*a priori*, clustering-based, flexible, and componential segmentation) requires a unique research design. Because the specific research designs for the four approaches are discussed elsewhere,[9] this section covers some of the more general considerations involved in the design of any segmentation research project (and which to some extent are also relevant for the design of other marketing studies). These considerations include nine major questions.

1. What is the most appropriate unit of analysis (e.g., an individual, a household, a buying center)?
2. How should the variables be defined operationally, and what is the most appropriate stimulus execution?
3. What is the most appropriate sample design?
4. How reliable are the data and how should one treat unreliable data?
5. How stable are the segments over time?
6. How homogeneous are the segments?
7. How segmentable is the market?
8. How can the results of a segmentation study be validated?
9. What are the cost considerations in the design of a segmentation study?

The Unit of Analysis

The marketing literature recognizes that most purchase and consumption behavior involves more than a single individual (the social context of, and influ-

---

[9] Research designs for *a priori* and clustering-based segmentation are presented in [35], whereas the research designs for flexible segmentation and componential segmentation are described in [91] and [47], respectively.

ence on, purchase and consumption behavior). Yet most of the empirical market segmentation (as well as consumer behavior and marketing) studies ignore this premise and, with few exceptions, center on the individual as the sole unit of analysis.

This discrepancy between the "desired" and actual unit of analysis can be attributed primarily to the conceptual and methodological problems involved in moving from the individual to the multiperson situation. Such a move would require:

1. *Identification of the Relevant Respondents.* Those who should be included in the unit of analysis. In a consumer segmentation study one should determine whether the unit of analysis includes the husband and wife, the mother and children, the husband, the wife, the entire family including both parents and children, etc. Similarly, in an organizational segmentation study one should determine which organizational members should be interviewed—the purchasing agent, the purchasing agent and intended product user, the controller, etc. [113]. The determination of the relevant respondents can either be made in advance or established empirically in the course of the data collection phase by snowball sampling procedures.

2. *Determination of a Multiperson Dependent Variable.* One of the major problems in the analysis of multiperson data is the development of a dependent variable which reflects the decisions of two or more individuals. In this context two cases are trivial: whenever a single measure reflects the results of the preference and decision processes of two or more individuals (as in the case of the actual purchase of a single brand, excluding the case of multibrand purchases, by a household), and whenever the two or more individuals involved are congruent in their preference and choice behavior. There are no statistics on the actual incidence of these two cases. One can safely assume, however, that in many cases there is some degree of incongruency among the members of the buying center.

Analysis of this incongruency can follow two major approaches which differ in the level of analysis. The *aggregate approach* is based on analyzing separately the responses of the husbands and those of the wives and reporting any differences between the two groups (at the total sample or the segment level). This approach can be extended to cover children or any other members of the buying center. Although the easiest for analysis, this approach is conceptually undesirable because it does not solve the problem of intrahousehold (or intraorganizational) incongruency and its effect on the household (or oganization) decision process and behavior.

The second approach is based on *individual household analysis.* In this case each *household* serves as the unit of analysis. For the simple husband-wife case, each household is described in terms of two vectors, one for the husband and one for the wife, and households are clustered on the basis of their similarities on the two sets of vectors. This approach was used in two recent studies. In one study among 120 couples in six metropolitan areas, life style attitudinal data were collected from both husbands and wives, and the 120 households were divided into six segments each representing a unique life style-attitudinal profile *and* different pattern of agreement between husband and wife with respect to the given attitudes. The small sample size does not justify delving into the substantive findings, but they suggest that the proposed approach is feasible. The second study on interest areas did not lead, however, to clearcut interpretable results.

The analysis of husband-wife pairs is relatively simple. Applying the same clustering approach to buying centers composed of three or more individuals is somewhat more complex, especially in the case of the household because households differ with respect to the number of children and adults present and the specific individuals involved in any given decision. In these cases a series of cluster analyses can be conducted. The total sample is divided into subsamples, each homogeneous with respect to the number of relevant decision makers (for example, a subsample of husbands and wives with no children, and another subsample of couples with one child, etc.). The data for each subsample are submitted to a separate cluster analysis to obtain a number of segments for each subsample. The resulting clusters are in turn clustered (with respect to some relevant criterion such as amount and type of household purchases) to obtain a set of higher order clusters which comprise segments from various subsamples.

Similar approaches also can be used in considering a segmentation of organizations. In these cases the first subsamples can be determined on the basis of the composition of the buying center, e.g., only purchasing agents, purchasing agent and user, etc.

3. *Accounting for Multiperson Independent Variables.* Whether the dependent variable is a single or multiple measure, reflecting individual or multiperson choice behavior, one can elect to use as explanatory variables the characteristics of a single individual, the characteristics of two or more individuals, or the characteristics of the household (or organization). Whenever the (demographic, psychographic, and other) characteristics of a single individual are included in the analysis, several multivariate statistical techniques (such as multiple regression analysis or AID) can be used to establish the nature and magnitude of the statistical association between the independent variables and the dependent variable.

If more than the characteristics of a single individual are included, one could treat these as another set of independent variables. Following this approach one could, for example, use the same analytical techniques as those used in the single respondent case (e.g., the brand choice of a household will be explained by using the husband's psychographic characteristics *and* his wife's psychographic characteristics). An alternative approach would be to rely on canonical correlation between the husband's and wife's response sets to reveal those items that are most contributory to husband-wife association. (Null cases could be set up by making random pairings of men and women.)

The third case involves the development of "group type" characteristics (such as group cohesiveness, autonomy, intimacy, polarization, stability, flexibility, etc.). This is the least developed area in both household and organizational studies despite some intriguing early developments in the measurement of group dimensions by social psychologists [60]. Once group type characteristics are developed, their analysis is straightforward and similar to the case in which one uses a single set of individual characteristics as the explanatory variable.

Operational Definitions

Having "passed" the managerial relevance and reasonableness considerations, the segmentation researcher should address the question of how to define operationally the dependent and independent variables. Developing operational definitions for selected variables is not a trivial task. Consider, for example, the situation of a clothing manufacturer who plans the introduction of a line with designs portraying musical instruments, notes, and personalities. A suggested basis for market segmentation is "music lovers." But how could the variable be defined? Should it include persons who respond favorably to the statement, "I love music"? Those who go to classical concerts? Or perhaps those who go to rock concerts? Those who play a musical instrument? Or those who listen to an FM classical music station? Furthermore, how should these variables be measured? Should they be rated on some 2, 3, 4, 5, 6, 7, 8, 9, 10, or 11 point scale? Should they be ranked, assigned a constant sum value, or based on some free response data? Or should they be based on recall or on some diary-keeping procedure? It is evident that any of these or other possible definitions might result in different segment sizes and compositions. Such decisions also have a major impact on the nature of the required analytical procedures.

The importance of a careful operational definition of the dependent and independent variables of the segmentation model can hardly be debated. Yet in many segmentation studies little attention is given to an explicit evaluation of alternative operational definitions. Appropriate definitions and the testing of alternative operational definitions are especially crucial in psychographic research [107, 116] and in conjoint-analysis-based segmentation studies. The results of conjoint analysis are limited to the factors and levels included in the design. Omission of an important factor, exaggeration of the levels of any factor, or alternatively too small a difference among the levels of a given factor might lead to erroneous results.

Having defined the variables of interest and the respondent task, the researcher is still confronted with the question of stimuli execution. In benefit segmentation studies, for example, one can consider presenting the benefits (product features) as verbal descriptions, artist's conceptions, color photographs of hypothetical products, or advertisements (or commercials) for the various benefits. A few studies have been conducted in this area, but little is known about the effect of alternative executions on consumer response and more work is needed.

Sample Design

The objective of any segmentation research study is not merely to explain differences among the specific respondents or to segment the sample, but rather to project the results of the study to the relevant universe. The projectability of results requires the use of an appropriate probability sample. Yet the great majority of segmentation studies rely on a quota sample. If quota samples or strict screening for specific respondent profiles (as required by the componential segmentation model) are used, the researcher must select the respondents for the screening interview on the basis of strict probability procedures and must keep accurate records of the screening data.

Another important consideration is the examination of any systematic differences between respondents and nonrespondents. Whereas nonresponse bias is widely recognized, most segmentation (and marketing) studies tend to ignore it. A growing body of evidence suggests that in many situations nonrespondents differ significantly from respondents. For example, a recent segmentation study for a bread product showed that the respondents to a personal interview had considerably higher bread consumption than those respondents who could not be reached in the first attempt and required 4–6 callbacks to recruit.

Because of the increasing cost of data collection ($30–60 per interview is not uncommon for an hour-long personal interview), the need for projectability, and the relatively small universe of many organizational buying firms, greater reliance should be placed, in both consumer and organizational buying segmentation studies, on rigorous telephone screening (which is less expensive) followed by interviews with a relatively small but select sample of respondents, and a small subsample of nonrespondents.

Data Reliability

Despite the importance of assuring that segmentation analysis is conducted on reliable data, little attention is paid to this issue in most segmentation (and marketing) studies, and the data analyzed are assumed to be reliable. Some variables (e.g., demographic characteristics) are more reliable than others (e.g., attitudes and psychographic characteristics). Whenever there is reason to suspect the reliability of some variables, certain safeguards such as test-retest reliability measures should be considered. With respect to attitude data, if test-retest data are collected, the degree of reliability can be considered explicitly in the factoring procedure.

Green [40] proposes a data collection and analysis procedure in which individual item reliability is used in the factoring process itself. Each attitude item is replicated across a group of respondents and the product moment correlation between the test and retest scores constitutes the measure of each item's reliability. The factoring procedure is a modified principal components method in which the entries of the correlation matrix (the usual starting point of the factor analysis) are modified to give greater weight to the more reliable items. In this way the first principal components—those that are usually retained in subsequent rotation—are the most errorfree, and the discarded components tend to be those that are more errorful. This approach leads to a more meaningful factor structure because the more reliable items have a greater influence in the delineation of that structure.

This and other procedures to handle unreliable data should be considered in the design of segmentation studies because the implicitly assumed reliability may not in fact exist. Of special interest in this context are the developments in the study of *generalizability* [24]. Traditional reliability measures assume that the design of a measuring procedure has been fixed with the possible exception of the number of items, and that one wants a numerical index of the precision of the device (i.e., reliability coefficient). A generalizability study, in contrast, covers (by appropriate analysis of variance design) all possible causes of discrepancies among observations. To date, the generalizability test has not been applied in segmentation (or other marketing) studies. The concept is intriguing and should be explored in the instrument-development stage of segmentation studies.

Segment Stability

An often neglected aspect of segmentation research is the question of segment stability over situations and time; i.e., given the assignment of individual i to segment j, how likely is it that the individual will remain in the same segment over time and different situations? The answer to this question depends on three sets of factors.

1. The basis for segmentation. In general one might hypothesize that the more specific the basis for segmentation (e.g., price sensitivity for or purchase of a given brand) the less stable the segment. Similarly, the more general the basis for segmentation (benefits sought from the product category or needs) the more stable the segment.
2. The volatility of the marketplace. Changes in the competitive activities and other environmental (political, legal, cultural, economic, etc.) conditions are likely to disturb the stability of the segments, and increase the likelihood of switching among segments.
3. Consumer characteristics. All consumers go through basic life cycle changes; even in the short term (within a life cycle stage), consumers may differ with respect to their likelihood to change and the nature of the change.

The specific variables which operate in each of these three sets of conditions must be identified, and the nature and magnitude of their impact on changes in the stability of various segments (e.g., buyers versus nonbuyers, different benefit segments, etc.) should be assessed.

Most of the current segmentation research efforts are based on cross-sectional data. In these cases the stability question is critical in determining the "aging" of the data, i.e., the length of time—two years? one year? six months?—during which the findings of a segmentation study are likely to hold. To date there are only a few unpublished industry cases in which the same market was segmented two or more times during a period of a few years. In these cases (ranging from frequently purchased food products to insurance policies), surprisingly few changes have been observed in the estimated size and composition of various segments over a relatively short period of time (1–3 years).[10]

Longitudinal data are applicable to an analysis of the stability of market segments at the individual level. Yet most of the segmentation researchers using such data have tended to ignore the stability question and instead have tried to develop measures such as brand loyalty, deal proneness, and the like, which reflect the *dynamics* of consumer behavior over a period of time. Whereas the value of such efforts can hardly be debated, it is desirable to use the available longitudinal data to address also the question of segment stability over time and situations. In the few cases in which segment stability was examined (such as [11, 12]), segments based on behavior over time did in fact show stability over three or four years—the length of time for which data were available. Some stability of benefit segments over a two-year period has been found [14]. Similar stability of psychographic segments from two independent samples over a two-year period also was found in an unpublished study by Wells.

Segment Homogeneity

Segmentation studies commonly involve the determination of the segments (based on either *a priori* judgment or a clustering-based approach) followed by the identification of the segment profile on the respondents' other characteristics. The latter stage is usually undertaken by examining the possibility of significant differences between segment means on a set of background variables.

Finding that two or more segments *are* different in terms of their mean profiles does not provide any indication about the possible segments *within* each segment. Members of a "buyer" segment, for example, may buy a given brand for different reasons. They may be very heterogeneous in their needs, demographic characteristics, and information requirements. In principle, almost every segment may, in turn, be decomposable into subsegments. Hence, to achieve intrasegment homogeneity, a very specific multidimensional definition of the basis for segmentation is required.

To fully understand the structure of selected market segments, one must understand the degree of homogeneity of each segment [43] and, in particular, be able to identify the number of subsegments, their relative size, and composition. The most common approach to the identification of subsegments is a hybrid segmentation approach in which the researcher searches for further subsegments among the *a priori* segments by clustering the members of each segment, or alternatively by applying an *a priori* segmentation scheme to each of the segments established by a clustering of respondents. Similarly one can use the sequential segmentation approach suggested by Peterson [86].

More recently, Green and his colleagues [44] suggested the application of

---

[10] This stability has been observed at the aggregate and *not* individual level. It might, therefore, be similar to the case observed by Bass [3] of stable market shares despite considerable brand switching activities within the market.

Lazarsfeld's latent class analysis [69] and orthogonal array designs to the problem of segment partitioning. Latent structure analysis is concerned with the discovery and measurement of the underlying structure of phenomena (e.g., attitudes), when these underlying variables (attitudes) are only probabilistically related to the responses. In the segmentation context one can envision an aggregate multiway contingency table which displays association among two or more categorical variables (such as high and low product usage and high and low brand loyalty) which is decomposed into two or more subtables (based on some descriptor variables such as age, education, etc.)—the latent classes. The entries of the new substables do not show association across the original qualitative variables; yet when the cell entries of the subtables are added, the original association reappears.

The operationalization problems associated with latent structure analysis [78] are solved by use of Carroll's CANDECOMP (*can*onical *decomp*osition) model and algorithm [18] to find the size of each latent class and the estimated probabilities of occurrence for each level of each variable for multiway tables involving up to seven variables. The CANDECOMP model and algorithm were applied to a large study on the characteristics of adopters of a new telecommunications service and revealed managerially meaningful subsegments of adopters [44].

The Segmentability of the Market

Segmentation studies are based on the premise that the given market is heterogeneous and can be segmented. Most empirical segmentation studies support this premise. It is not uncommon, however, to find markets in which no significant differences are found among various segments with respect to their demographic or other relevant consumer characteristics such as response elasticities to marketing variables.[11] In these cases it might be of value to be able to assess the degree of segmentability of a market.

A measure of the segmentability of a market recently was proposed in the context of the componential segmentation model [40]. Before application of the COSEG model the researcher can take the respondents' ratings of the set of product stimuli and submit them to a conventional two-way ANOVA. Using Hays' omega square measure [59], the researcher can obtain an index of the importance of the respondents, the stimuli, and the interaction between stimuli and respondents. If the ω^2 for the subjects and the interaction effects (between stimuli and subjects) are small and the ω^2 for stimuli are large, the market does not seem to be amenable to segmentation given the specific set of respondent characteristics and stimuli (product features).

---

[11] It is important to note, however, that if segments do not have different characteristics (such as demographic features) but do show differing elasticities to marketing variables, management still can use a self-selection strategy [35].

Validation

One of the major discrepancies between the academic and commercial studies of segmentation is with respect to the question of validity. Whereas many academic studies of segmentation do employ some form of validation (primarily cross-validation on a holdout sample), most of the commercially based segmentation studies ignore the question of validity.

The validity of segmentation research is by far the most crucial question facing management. Do the segments discovered in a segmentation study exist in the population? Is the estimated segment size accurate? And how accurate are the estimated segment responses to the firm's marketing actions? Despite the centrality of such questions, only a few validation reports have been published [33, 72] and relatively few firms have made any effort to validate the results of their segmentation studies. Most notable among these efforts is the AT&T validation study of the segments within the residential long distance market. In this and several other unpublished AT&T studies the segmentation results were found to be very predictable of actual market behavior.

In the absence of such external validation, certain validation procedures could be used. The procedure chosen would depend on the specific segmentation model employed. In *a priori* and clustering-based segmentation studies, validation can be undertaken by splitting the sample and predicting segment membership of a holdout sample. In flexible and componential segmentation designs, one can check both the internal validity (e.g., prediction of the evaluation of control stimuli which were ranked or rated by the respondents but were not used in the parameter estimation procedure) and external validity (by comparing the survey's share of choices with the actual share data for each market segment). External validation requires purchase data (e.g., market share) by segment, which are not always available. Similarly, data availability is a problem when one wishes to validate the nonpurchase characteristics of the segments identified in segmentation studies. It is essential, however, for any firm using segmentation research to design and implement follow-up research—either in a test market or the national market—to validate the findings of the segmentation study and the subsequent segmentation strategy.

Cost Considerations

The selection of a segmentation design cannot be done in isolation from cost considerations. Lip service often is given to the concept of cost and value of information. Yet most industry-based segmentation studies are launched with no explicit effort at determining the cost and value of the expected information. Regardless of the politics of setting marketing research budgets, the researcher has a major role in the cost decision because most of the research design considerations and the data collection and analysis procedures have cost implications. One can, for example, assure a higher reliability but it may involve somewhat higher costs. Explicit cost tradeoffs therefore should be made which lead to a selection of research designs based on the intended purpose, the expected information, and the costs involved.

Many design and analysis considerations have only minimal cost implications. In fact, whenever a researcher gives cost considerations as the reason for not using multivariate statistical procedures or for not undertaking some simple cross-validation procedure, one should be suspicious because many of these procedures do not involve higher costs. Furthermore, if a researcher is familiar with and has working knowledge of multivariate statistical techniques, their use in segmentation research can be considerably less expensive both in terms of computer costs and analysts' time.

In most segmentation studies the cost of research design and analysis varies within very narrow ranges. The major variable cost component is data collection. Therefore, major cost savings can be expected from the data collection stage and not from cutting corners at the design and analysis stages.

Compared with the benefits believed to be associated with a segmentation strategy, the cost of segmentation research is often considered trivial. But few efforts have been directed at the assessment of (1) the expected value, in terms of alternative marketing segmentation strategies (versus the base case of no explicit segmentation effort) or (2) the expected cost of implementing different segmentation strategies. More work in this area is required.

DATA COLLECTION

The design and evaluation of alternative data collection procedures have received little attention in academically oriented market segmentation literature. Commercial researchers, however, have made significant contributions in this area, although relatively few innovative data collection approaches have been used in segmentation studies.

Primary versus Secondary Data

Most of the commercially based segmentation studies have used a primary data collection effort and, in particular, cross-sectional surveys. In contrast, the technique-oriented academic segmentation studies tend to use available secondary sources and, in particular, panel data such as the Chicago Tribune and MRCA.

The development and offering of a psychographic data base for the MRCA panel has increased the commercial use of secondary sources in segmentation analysis. Increased usage of this and other secondary data sources (such as TGI or BRI) in segmentation analysis, and their integration with survey data, is desirable because it provides the longitudinal data required for dynamic segmentation analysis.

Other advantages of the greater reliance on secondary data sources are the better samples offered by most national panels, the greater attention (in comparison with the "typical" survey) to quality control of the data collection procedure, and the economic advantages of secondary sources (especially in light of the recent increases in the cost of survey data collection). Of particular interest is the greater accuracy of panel purchase and usage data [118].

Another type of secondary data source of great potential value in segmentation analysis, for many products and services, includes all those data bases which are in some aggregate form rather than based on the individual (or household). For example, census demographic zip code data can offer a rich data base for segmentation analysis of zip codes. They are especially valuable for firms in the direct mail business. Two types of zip code segmentation efforts have been conducted on the basis of selected variables from the REZIDE tapes of the 35,592 U.S. zip codes [22].

1. "Tailor-made" segmentation efforts, on selected variables hypothesized to be related to the response to the specific firm's offering, have been conducted by several firms, resulting in the selection of target zip code areas. Marketing efforts aimed at these segments have led to considerable improvement in response rates.
2. General segmentation of the U.S. based on 71 demographic and socio-economic census variables was conducted by Computer Cartography, Inc. [23] and offered commercially. These data were factor analyzed and then clustered, resulting in 41 clusters which, in turn, were grouped in 12 major zip clusters. Each residential zip is within one of the 41 clusters (such as "upper class mobile professionals and college students in new towns") and also in one of the 12 major clusters (such as "educated elite suburban white family areas" or "lower-middle to middle blue collar nonmetro areas").

Similarly, the more recent developments of UPC data based on automated checkout data could offer a rich data base for "store area" segmentation analysis, especially when linked to electronic fund transfer payment data.

Conventional and Newer Procedures

Most segmentation studies are based on data collected in personal interviews or mail questionnaires. More recently, with the development of computer-based telephone interviewing, the telephone has become a feasible instrument for segmentation-type data collection. Such telephone interviewing can be very efficient because of response-dependent sequencing of questions, ease of reaching the sample units, and the ability to analyze the results as they come in.

In selecting a data collection method, therefore, one should consider a combination of approaches. The Human Population Laboratory [61] undertook a comparison of three data collection strategies containing personal interviews, telephone interviews, and mail questionnaires in different combinations (order of usage). Rate of return and rate of completeness were high in all three strategies. Similarly, substantive findings were virtually interchangeable and there was little difference in validity. The only difference was the cost per interview, which varied considerably by strategy. Accepting these findings suggests that substantial cost saving could be achieved in segmentation studies without sacrificing quality by designing a cost effective and task efficient mix of data collection procedures. However, other studies have shown differences in the response to, and validity of, various data collection procedures [15, 30, 31]. These differences can be accounted for by several factors. Self-administered questionnaires, for example, were found to be better when the information was available in records or possessed by other members of the respondent family. They were also better with highly educated and high income respondents [104].

The major new developments in data collection procedures include computer-terminal-based data collection procedures, two-way cable TV, and home computers. In addition to computer-based telephone interviews, computer terminals have been used for self-administered personal interviews in central interviewing facilities [80, 119] (such as shopping malls). With the advent of portable terminals, such interviews can be conducted at consumers' homes or industrial buyers' offices. Two-way cable TV has been presented for at least a decade as the panacea for data collection problems. Yet its development and dissemination are still more of a promise than a reality. Home computers are a newer development. The current pricing of microcomputers at less than $600 could have a major impact on their distribution and should not be ignored in development of new data collection procedures.

Other less frequently used data collection procedures for segmentation are (1) self-recorded protocol data (which, when content analyzed, can be used to identify the respondent's decision process and serve as a basis for segmentation), (2) unobtrusive measures of respondents' shopping, purchase, and usage behavior [105], and (3) projective techniques and other open-ended interviews. The major problem with using these data bases has been the difficulty in the content analysis of the protocols, open-ended responses, and some of the unobtrusive measures. If content analysis is required, care must be given to the development of a dictionary and other procedures commonly used in content analysis [37] and especially the development of interjudge reliability measures [66].

In selecting data collection procedures(s), one should give attention to the respondents' ability to perform the task reliably, the cost in terms of money and time, and the scale properties required for the intended data analysis.

DATA ANALYSIS

The market segmentation field has been one of the primary and most prolific testing grounds for data analysis techniques. The diffusion of new data analysis techniques often has started with the publication of an academic article on the applicability of some analytical model and algorithm (usually borrowed from mathematical statistics or mathematical psychology, and less frequently from mathematical economics and sociology). The procedure then is applied to a number of academically oriented marketing studies and finally is picked up by some of the more innovative marketing research firms. The diffusion of MDS and conjoint analysis provides good examples of this pattern.

To know the current state of applications of various data analysis techniques to market segmentation studies, therefore, one must continuously keep up to date with three areas.

1. The analytical techniques currently used in segmentation analysis (with a focus on possible problems associated with their use).
2. The analytical developments suggested in the recent marketing literature.
3. Analytical procedures which have not yet been introduced to the marketing literature and which offer some potential in the segmentation area.

The brief review of these areas is organized according to the three major types of analytical techniques used in segmentation research, namely, techniques for (1) classification of respondents into segments, (2) discrimination among the segments, i.e., the determination of segment profiles, and (3) simultaneous classification and discrimination.

Classification Procedures

Classification procedures for determining membership in market segments vary markedly according to the specific segmentation model used. The procedures most commonly employed in *a priori* approaches are sorting and cross-tabulation. Recently, Blattberg and Sen developed a Bayesian classification procedure [13] which they used successfully. When clustering-based segmentation is used, the most common procedures are clustering, MDS, and AID. Componential and flexible segmentation involve primarily conjoint analysis and computer simulation.

These and similar analytical techniques used for the assignment of consumers to segments are widely used and need no further explanation.[12] The focus of this section, therefore, is on some of the possible pitfalls and unanswered questions involved in the use of these techniques, and some of the recent advances in classification procedures.

Sorting and Cross-Tabulation   The dividing line among *a priori* segments generally is arbitrary. Consider, for example, the commonly used segments of heavy and light brand users. How should the sample be divided? Should it be based on the top and bottom 50% of users or only the top 33% and the bottom 33%? Furthermore, should it be based on a number of items bought, frequency of purchase, total dollar purchased, proportion of purchases devoted to the given brand, etc.? In many segmentation studies, too little attention is given to the conceptual implications of the various operational definitions and the sensitivity of the resulting segments to the definitions used.

A priori sorting of respondents can provide insight as demonstrated in the purchase segments of Blattberg and Sen [12]. It is judgmental and requires careful operational definitions of segment boundaries and the use of interjudge reliability measures among the judges who assign subjects to segments. Another

---

[12] For a basic review of these data analytical techniques, see [51].

neglected sorting procedure is the complete enumeration of all possible segments by following a set of assignment criteria. This procedure has been used in two cases.

1. The assignment of consumers to *product assortment* segments based on whether each of a set of products was used or not; i.e., if a product category has, for example, eight products, consumers are assigned to one of 256 (2^8) segments. In most product categories in which the product assortment patterns were analyzed, about 5% of the patterns accounted for 90% or so of the total purchases.
2. Benefit segmentation involving a relatively small number of benefits. If there are, for example, only five benefits and each individual can have either a high or low score on each benefit, there are 32 possible segments. Again, in the few cases in which such procedures have been used, a relatively small number of segments accounted for most of the respondents.

Of special interest in this context are the newer procedures for discrete multivariate analysis [8] which are mostly based on n-way cross-classification analysis. These procedures allow for nonlinearities and in many cases can be superior to the more conventional multivariate statistical techniques.

Clustering A large number of clustering models and algorithms are currently available for the grouping of subjects. These techniques (including Q-type factor analysis and its modifications such as the linear typal analysis [26, 83]) differ in their objectives, type of clustering used, and the specific operationalization of the clustering procedures. The objective of clustering techniques as applied to market segmentation should not be limited to finding a typology of the market under study; one can use clustering also for data exploration, data reduction, and hypothesis generation.[13]

Clustering techniques can and have been categorized in a variety of ways. Hartigan [58], for example, suggested a classification based on mode of search into sorting, switching, joining, splitting, adding, and searching.[14] For market segmentation purposes it might be useful to distinguish between two major types of clustering techniques—those which build up clusters (a bottom-up approach) and those which break down a market into clusters (a top-down approach). The *building up* clustering techniques include several of the commonly used joining algorithms, such as the Johnson hierarchical clustering [65], Sneath single linkage algorithm [58], and various tree structures. *Breaking down* clustering procedures begin by partitioning subjects into two or more clusters, followed by subsequent partitioning of each of these clusters into subclusters. These techniques include a variety of splitting algorithms which, after an initial partitioning, obtain a new partition by switching objects from one cluster to another. The *K*

---

[13] Ball [1] has suggested three additional objectives—model fitting, prediction, and hypothesis testing. These objectives have rarely been used in a segmentation context.

[14] For other classification systems, see for example [29].

means and Howard Harris algorithms are examples of this type of breaking down clustering procedure.

In view of the large number of available clustering [58] and pattern recognition [21] techniques, the critical question facing the researcher is which algorithm (and measures of similarity or distance) and type of measures (standardized, weighted, etc.) are most appropriate under what conditions and for what purposes. The current clustering literature does not provide satisfactory answers to these questions, and researchers tend to select an algorithm on the basis of such considerations as familiarity, availability, and cost of operations rather than appropriateness for a specific set of objectives and constraints.

Of special interest in this area are some of the recent developments in *overlapping clustering*. Clustering procedures used in traditional market segmentation studies were based on the premise of exclusivity; i.e., each individual could have been classified in one and only one cluster (segment). Conceptually, there are a number of situations in which a consumer can belong to more than a single segment (especially if one considers multiple brand usage, different usage occasions, multiple benefits sought, etc.). Several models and algorithms are now available for overlapping clustering [19] and can be used whenever it is conceptually desirable.

Multidimensional Scaling Most multidimensional scaling applications in marketing have been for product positioning [112]. Yet several MDS models and algorithms are suitable for the classification of respondents. Most notable among them is INDSCAL [17, 20] which develops for each respondent a weight on each of the relevant group dimensions. Respondents with similar salience on the perceptual dimensions can thus constitute a segment.

Segments also can be identified on the basis of the commonality of preferences either in a common (total market) perceptual (brand or product feature) space or in spaces unique to each perceptual segment. This grouping of respondents can be undertaken with several alternative models such as MDPREF or PREFMAP [41, 50].

AID and Stepwise Regression Although both of these techniques commonly are used to establish the profile of a segment (given some dependent variable such as purchase), occasionally the resulting segment descriptors (selected tree structures in AID, or the significant variables in the regression) can be used as a way of classifying the respondents into segments which, in turn, can serve as the basis for segmentation in subsequent analysis. Of particular value in this context is AID [98] which has been used successfully in a large number of commercial segmentation studies.

Newer Approaches More recently, multidimensional contingency table analysis [39] has been used to segment a market on the basis of the *probability* of being a "loyal" customer. This approach is utilized by Ogilvy and Mather under the name of logistic response analysis [25].

Discrimination Procedures

The analytical techniques used to profile the segments (which were selected *a priori* or identified in the classification stage) do not vary by type of segmentation model employed. To establish the segments' profiles, market segmentation studies still occasionally include cross-tabulations and some univariate statistical technique. More commonly, however, the procedures applied are multiple regression, multiple discriminant analysis, AID, MCA (multiple classification analysis), or some combination of these techniques.

More recently new procedures have been suggested and applied to the problem of identifying segments' profiles. Among these procedures are latent class analysis, logit and multinomial logit, multivariate probit, and nonparametric techniques.

Latent class analysis (as discussed in the section on segment homogeneity) utilizes the CANDECOMP model and algorithm. This approach was applied to the segmentation of the market for a new telecommunication service [44].

The *multinomial logit model* [42] has been applied to the same segmentation problem. It was preceded by an AID analysis (to determine which predictors, categories within predictors, and interactions should be considered). The logit model was applied to obtain parameter estimates for each predictor (or predictor combination) to test alternative models, and to develop probability estimates for the dichotomous criterion variable [42]. The AID/logit approach to segmentation can be extended to cover polytomous variables (and not only dichotomous data) by applying instead of AID the THAID algorithm [75] followed by a multinomial generalization of the logit model.

The *multivariate probit model* has been used recently in a pilot application to the segmentation area using the probability response coefficients (to each of a set of product features) as a basis for segmentation [88].

These and the more conventional discrimination procedures, and in particular AID, THAID, and the AID-like algorithms such as SIMS (*survey implemented market segmentation*), which is based on a simple cost-profit formulation [71], require relatively large data bases. Whereas this requirement does not create any special difficulty for most consumer market segmentation studies, it does present a major stumbling block for most of the efforts to segment industrial markets. Many industrial market situations involve a relatively small number of customers and require nonparametric statistical procedures and greater reliance on efficient experimental designs. More work on both areas is crucial to progress in industrial market segmentation.

An interesting omission from the segmentation literature is the use of structural equation models (or path analysis) [9, 27]. Conceptually, at least, segmentation models can be constructed as causal diagrams or equivalent sets of linear equations that represent the assumed set of direct and indirect influences among a set of variables. The values of the unknown path coefficients can be estimated to indicate the relative strength of the determinants of the specified dependent variables (in effect a sequence of dependent variables is the recursive model). An excellent example of a segmentation-related problem in which this approach was used is a sociological study on the socioeconomic characteristics of occupational achievement [28].

Simultaneous Classification and Discrimination

Whereas most segmentation studies follow a two-step procedure of first classifying respondents into segments and then establishing their key discriminating characteristics, attempts have been made to develop and apply analytical techniques for the *simultaneous* analysis of classification and discrimination. Canonical correlation analysis has been applied in this context, and more recently the flexible and componential segmentation models.

Canonical correlation has been suggested as a method for segmentation by Frank and Strain [36] who grouped respondents with regard to their cross-classified score categories on each significant canonical variate in the predictor set. However, because canonical correlation measures the shared variation between two sets of variables (by transforming both configurations to some best compromise position), it can be used for segmentation as long as one does not want to relate the predictor set *to* the criterion set. An alternative procedure therefore can be the transformation of the space of predictor variables to best agree with a fixed position occupied by the points in the space of the criterion variables. It can be undertaken by using any number of oblique or orthogonal Procrustes transformations [6, 94].

If the researcher is not concerned with maintaining the distinction of a criterion variable set, canonical correlation or redundancy analysis [103] (a component method which maximizes Stewart and Love's redundancy index [100]) can be considered as a procedure for simultaneously classifying the respondents and determining the key discriminating profiles of the various segments.

Selection of a Plan of Analysis

The choice of data analysis techniques reflects the researcher's familiarity with, and preference for, various techniques. Several questions should be addressed in selection of a specific analytical plan. They are not unlike the ones facing researchers using any multivariate data analysis technique and include: How should one measure the relative importance of the variables—is R^2, for example, an appropriate measure [48, 76, 108]? Should discrimination among segments be based on individual or group level analysis [2, 4]? How should one identify and measure the effect of any response errors [34]?

Unique to segmentation studies is the need to apply a variety of analytical procedures in tandem. Most segmentation studies involve "complex" designs [35] revolving around several hybrid bases for segmentation [57, 101]. However, because one cannot know in advance which basis for segmentation will lead to the identification of meaningful segments, segmentation studies should be *flexible*, allowing diverse analyses aimed at the identification of relevant segments. This need creates special demands for researchers with knowledge of a large number of analytical procedures, good conceptual understanding of alternative segmentation models, and a high level of research creativity.

DATA INTERPRETATION AND
IMPLEMENTATION OF RESULTS

Regardless of how sophisticated the segmentation study, the key to a successful project is the researcher's and user's (management) ability to interpret the results and use them as guidelines for the design, execution, and evaluation of appropriate marketing strategy. The data interpretation stage should be performed *jointly* by the researcher and user, reflecting the researcher's statistical judgment (which differences among segments are statistically significant, etc.) and the manager's product/market knowledge. In this context, two major issues are (1) how to determine the number of segments and select the target segment(s) and (2) how to translate the segmentation findings into marketing strategy.

Determining the Number of Segments
and Selection of Target Segments

One of the most complex questions facing researchers who use a cluster-based approach to segmentation is the determination of the number of segments. The two relevant criteria are the statistical measure of cluster (segment) stability and homogeneity, and the managerial consideration of cost of segmentation. The question of segment stability can be assessed by comparing the results of alternative clustering procedures and computing measures of similarities between the different cluster solutions. Estimating the cost of segmentation involves management's subjective judgment.

Whatever segmentation approach is used, it is management that selects the desired *target segments*. The selection of target segments is a complex "art" type of process which should take into account such factors as the segments' expected response to marketing variables, the segments' reachability, the nature of competitive activity within the segment, and management's resources and ability to implement a segmented strategy for the selected segments.

The cost of segmentation, the problems inherent in any effort to reach effectively a large number of segments, and the complexity of managing a large number of segments all encourage the selection of relatively few segments. However, greater segment homogeneity requires a larger number of segments [32]. To balance these two forces, more rigorous analytical models should be developed. Furthermore, the segment selection decision should not be limited to a single product but should encompass the more realistic and complex case of a product line.

A more fundamental question in the selection of target segments faces public policy decision makers. Whereas a profit-oriented firm can decide to concentrate its efforts on a specific target segment(s), the public policy tradition has been to develop a single policy aimed at *all* consumers. As public policy decision makers move toward greater reliance on consumer (and marketing) research as input to their decisions, they face an increasing conflict between the empirical findings (on the heterogeneous nature of the market) and the traditional concept of the "average" or "typical" consumers. If policy formulators could imple-

ment a segmented strategy, undertaking public-policy-oriented segmentation research projects would present no difficulty. If public policy decision makers were
to insist on a single strategy aimed at an "average" consumer, the concept of segmentation might have to be modified.

Translating Segmentation Findings into Strategy

The most difficult aspect of any segmentation project is the translation of the
study results into marketing strategy. No rules can be offered to assure a successful translation and, in fact, little is known (in the published literature) on how
this translation occurs.

Informal discussions with and observation of "successful" and "unsuccessful"
translations suggest a few generalizable conclusions aside from the obvious ones
such as:

1. Involving all the relevant users (e.g., product managers, new product developers, advertising agency personnel, etc.) in the problem definition,
   research design, and data interpretation stages.
2. Viewing segmentation data as one input to a total marketing information
   system and combining them with sales and other relevant data.
3. Using the segmentation data on a continuous basis. The reported study results should be viewed only as the *beginning* of a utilization program.

Difficulties with, and the nature of, the "translation" of segmentation findings
into strategy depend on whether the segmentation study is used as input to:

1. Idea and strategy generation or strategy evaluation.
2. Product related decisions (i.e., product positioning, design, and price) or
   communication and distribution decisions.
3. Decisions about existing products (i.e., no change, product modification,
   repositioning, or deletion decisions) or new products.

The translation of segmentation findings into new ideas (and strategies) is
usually limited only by the creativity of the users. Most segmentation studies,
and especially those based on consumers' needs, benefits, life styles, or other psychographic characteristics, offer a rich profile of potential target segments which,
in turn, can lead to the generation of a large number of diverse ideas and strategies. Furthermore, if one is concerned, for example, with design of a product or
a communication campaign, each idea can be executed in a variety of ways, the
success of which depends more on the creativity of the designer than on the segmentation findings.

The translation of segmentation findings is more complex when they are used
to *evaluate* (rather than generate) some marketing strategy. In this context, two
situations are distinct—consumer reactions to a new strategy (e.g., new concept
or new commercial) and consumer satisfaction with the firm's current products
and services. In both cases a meaningful evaluation should be done at the market

segment level, and in both cases there is a strong tendency to define segments in terms favorable to the corporate decision makers' objectives.

A major difficulty in the translation of segmentation findings into actionable strategy is management's perceived *ability* to implement the strategy. In industrial marketing, one often hears the argument that salesmen cannot handle simultaneously a number of strategies aimed at a number of segments. Furthermore, organizations, whether in consumer or industrial markets, are on the average reluctant to undertake high-risk strategies. Strategies which depart from current strategy or which require new ways of reaching target segments (e.g., direct mail vs. TV, new distribution outlets, etc.) are viewed as high risks. In providing rigorous input to decisions perceived as involving high risks, segmentation findings can have a major impact.

CONCLUDING REMARKS

Market segmentation has served as the focal point for many of the major marketing research developments and the marketing activities of most firms. Yet too many segmentation researchers have settled on a fixed way of conducting segmentation studies. This tendency for standardization of procedures is premature and undesirable. Innovative approaches to segmentation have been offered in the past few years, and further work on the new conceptual and methodological aspects of segmentation should be undertaken.

Of particular importance seems to be research on the following areas:

1. New conceptualization of the segmentation problem.
2. Reevaluation and operationalization of the normative theory of segmentation, with emphasis on the question of how to allocate resources among markets and products over *time*.
3. The discovery and implementation of *new variables* for use as bases for segmentation (i.e., new attitudinal and behavioral constructs such as consumption-based personality inventories and variables which focus on *likely change* in attitude and behavioral responses to the marketing variables) of the markets for products, services, and concepts.
4. The development of new research designs and parallel data collection and analysis techniques which place fewer demands on the respondents (i.e., data collection which is simpler for the respondent and data analysis procedures capable of handling missing data and incomplete block designs).
5. The development of simple and flexible analytical approaches to data analysis capable of handling discrete and continuous variables, and selected interaction at a point in time and over time.
6. Evaluation of the conditions under which various data analytical techniques are most appropriate.
7. The accumulation of knowledge on successful bases for segmentation across studies (products, situations, and markets).

8. Undertaking external validation studies to determine the performance of segmentation strategies which were based on findings of segmentation studies.
9. Designing and implementing multitrait, multimethod approaches to segmentation research aimed at both the generation of more generalizable (reliable) and valid data.
10. Integration of segmentation research with the marketing information system of the firm.
11. Exploring alternative approaches to the translation of segmentation findings into marketing strategies.
12. Studies of the organization design of firms which were successful and unsuccessful in implementing segmentation strategies.

Review of some of the issues and current advances in segmentation research indicates that, despite the great advances in the management of and research practice of segmentation, numerous frontiers still require creative and systematic study. This review and the other articles in this special issue of *JMR* are presented with the hope of stimulating further advances in this important and challenging area.

REFERENCES

1. Ball, G. H. *Classification Analysis.* Stanford, California: SRI, 1971.
2. Bass, Frank M. "Unexplained Variance in Studies of Consumer Behavior," *in* John U. Farley and John A. Howard, eds., *Control of "Error" in Market Research Data.* Lexington, Massachusetts: Lexington Books, 1975, 11–36.
3. ———. "Analytical Approaches in the Study of Purchase Behavior and Brand Choice," *in* Robert Ferber, ed., *Selected Aspects of Consumer Behavior.* Washington, D.C.: National Science Foundation, 1977, 491–514.
4. ———, Douglas J. Tigert, and Ronald T. Lonsdale. "Market Segmentation: Group versus Individual Behavior," *Journal of Marketing Research,* 5 (August 1968), 264–70.
5. Beckwith, Neil E. and Maurice W. Sasieni. "Criteria for Marketing Segmentation Studies," *Management Science,* 22 (April 1976), 892–908.
6. Berge, J. and M. F. Ten. "Orthogonal Procrustes Rotation for Two or More Matrices," *Psychometrika,* 42 (June 1977).
7. Bettman, James R. *An Information Processing Theory of Consumer Choice.* Reading, Massachusetts: Addison-Wesley, in press.
8. Bishop, Yvonne, Stephen Feinberg, and Paul Holland. *Discrete Multivariate Analysis.* Cambridge, Massachusetts: The MIT Press, 1975.
9. Blalock, H. M., Jr., ed. *Causal Models in the Social Sciences.* Chicago: Aldine-Atherton, 1971.
10. Blattberg, Robert C., Thomas Buesing, Peter Peacock, and Subrata K. Sen. "Identifying the Deal Prone Segment," *Journal of Marketing Research,* 15 (August 1978).
11. ——— and Subrata K. Sen. "Market Segmentation Using Models of Multidimensional Purchasing Behavior," *Journal of Marketing,* 38 (October 1974), 17–28.

12. ——— and ———. "Market Segments and Stochastic Brand Choice Models," *Journal of Marketing Research*, 13 (February 1976), 34–45.
13. ——— and ———. "A Bayesian Technique to Discriminate between Stochastic Models of Brand Choice," *Management Science*, 21 (February 1975), 682–96.
14. Calantone, Roger J. and Alan Sawyer. "The Stability of Benefit Segments," *Journal of Marketing Research*, 15 (August 1978).
15. Cannell, Charles F. and Floyd J. Fowler, "Comparison of Self-Enumerative Procedure and a Personal Interview: A Validity Study," *Public Opinion Quarterly*, 27 (1963), 250–64.
16. Carroll, J. Douglas. "Categorical Conjoint Measurement," presented at Mathematical Psychology Meeting, Ann Arbor, Michigan, 1969. (Discussed in [49, pp. 339–48].)
17. ———. "Individual Differences and Multidimensional Scaling," *in* R. N. Shepard, ed., *Multidimensional Scaling: Theory and Applications in Behavioral Sciences*, Vol. I. New York: Seminar Press, 1972.
18. ———. "Application of CANDECOMP to Solving for Parameters of Lazarsfeld's Latent Class Model," presented at the Society of Multivariate Experimental Psychology Meeting, Gleneden Beach, Oregon, November 1975.
19. ———. "Spatial, Nonspatial, and Hybrid Models for Scaling," *Psychometrika*, 41 (December 1976), 439–63.
20. ——— and Jih-Jie Chang. "Analysis of Individual Differences in Multidimensional Scaling via an N-Way Generalization of Eckart-Young Decomposition," *Psychometrika*, 35 (September 1970), 61–68.
21. Casey, Richard G. and George Nagy. "Advances in Pattern Recognition," *Scientific American*, 224 (1971), 56–71.
22. Claritas Corporation. *REZIDE: The National Zip Code Encyclopedia*. Washington, D.C.: Claritas Corporaion.
23. Computer Cartography, Inc. *Customer Clusters: Development of a Meaningful Socioeconomic Classification System*. Washington, D.C.: Computer Cartography, Inc.
24. Cronback, Lee J. et al. *The Dependability of Behavioral Measurements: Theory of Generalizability for Scores and Profiles*. New York: John Wiley & Sons, Inc., 1972.
25. Cuba, Fred. "Logistic Response Analysis: A Better Way to Slice the Pie," *in* Y. Wind and M. Greenberg, eds., *Moving A Head With Attitude Research*. Chicago: AMA, 1977, 66–69.
26. Darden, William R. and William D. Perreault, Jr. "Classification for Market Segmentation: An Improved Linear Model for Solving Problems of Arbitrary Origin," *Management Science*, 24 (November 1977), 255–71.
27. Duncan, Otis Dudley. *Introduction to Structural Equation Models*. New York: Academic Press, 1975.
28. ———, D. L. Featherman, and B. Duncan. *Socioeconomic Background and Achievement*. Washington, D.C.: U.S. Office of Education, Bureau of Research, 1968.
29. Everitt, Brian. *Cluster Analysis*. London: Heinemann Educational Books, 1974.
30. Ferber, Robert. "Does a Panel Operation Increase the Reliability of Survey Data: The Case of Consumer Savings," *Journal of the American Statistical Association*, 50 (1955), 210–16.
31. ———. "On the Reliability of Responses Secured in Sample Surveys," *Journal of the American Statistical Association*, 50 (1955), 788–810.
32. Fisher, W. D. "On Grouping for Maximum Homogeneity," *Journal of the American Statistical Association*, 53 (1958), 789–98.

33. Frank, Ronald. "Predicting New Product Segments," *Journal of Advertising Research,* 12 (June 1972), 9–13.

34. ────── and William Massy. "Noise Reduction in Segmentation Research," *in* John U. Farley and John A. Howard, eds., *Control of "Error" in Market Research Data.* Lexington, Massachusetts: Lexington Books, 1975, 145–205.

35. ──────, ──────, and Yoram Wind. *Market Segmentation.* Englewood Cliffs, New Jersey: Prentice-Hall, Inc., 1972.

36. ────── and Charles Strain. "A Segmentation Research Design Using Consumer Panel Data," *Journal of Marketing Research,* 9 (November 1972), 385–90.

37. Gerbner, George et al. *The Analysis of Communication Content.* New York: John Wiley & Sons, Inc., 1969.

38. Gibson, Lawrence D. "Beyond Segmentation or Something Is Rotten in Market Segmentation," paper delivered at the Midwest Conference of the AMA, March 1971.

39. Goodman, Leo A. "The Analysis of Multidimensional Contingency Tables: Stepwise Procedures and Direct Estimation Methods for Building Models for Multiple Classifications," *Technometrics,* 13 (1971), 31–62.

40. Green, Paul E. "A New Approach to Market Segmentation," *Business Horizons,* 20 (February 1977), 61–73.

41. ────── and Frank J. Carmone. *Multidimensional Scaling and Related Techniques in Marketing Analysis.* Boston: Allyn and Bacon, 1970.

42. ────── and ──────. "An AID/Logit Approach for Analyzing Large Multiway Contingency Tables," *Journal of Marketing Research,* 15 (February 1978), 132–36.

43. ────── and ──────. "Segment Congruence Analysis: A Method for Analyzing Association among Alternative Bases for Market Segmentation," *Journal of Consumer Research,* 3 (March 1977), 217–22.

44. ──────, ──────, and David P. Wachspress. "Consumer Segmentation via Latent Class Analysis," *Journal of Consumer Research,* 3 (December 1976), 170–74.

45. ──────, ──────, and ──────. "On the Analysis of Qualitative Data in Marketing Research," *Journal of Marketing Research,* 14 (February 1977), 52–59.

46. ──────, J. Douglas Carroll, and Frank J. Carmone. "Some New Types of Fractional Factorial Designs for Marketing Experiments," *in* J. N. Sheth, ed., *Research in Marketing,* Vol. I. Greenwich, Connecticut: JAI Press, 1977.

47. ──────, ──────, and ──────. "Design Considerations in Attitude Measurement," *in* Y. Wind and M. Greenberg, eds., *Moving A Head With Attitude Research.* Chicago: AMA, 1977, 9–18.

48. ──────, ──────, and Wayne S. DeSarbo, "A New Measure of Predictor Variable Importance in Multiple Regression," *Journal of Marketing Research,* 15 (August 1978).

49. ────── and Vithala Rao. *Applied Multidimensional Scaling: A Comparison of Approaches and Algorithms.* New York: Holt, Rinehart and Winston, 1972.

50. ────── and V. Srinivasan. "Conjoint Analysis in Consumer Behavior: Status and Outlook," University of Pennsylvania working paper, 1977.

51. ────── and Donald Tull. *Research for Marketing Decisions,* 3rd edition. Englewood Cliffs, New Jersey: Prentice-Hall, Inc., 1975.

52. ────── and Yoram Wind. *Multiattribute Decisions in Marketing: A Measurement Approach.* Hinsdale, Illinois: Dryden Press, 1973.

53. ────── and ──────. "New Way to Measure Consumers' Judgments," *Harvard Business Review,* 53 (1975), 107–17.

54. ——, ——, and Arun K. Jain. "Benefit Bundle Analysis," *Journal of Advertising Research,* 12 (1972), 31–36.

55. ——, ——, and ——. "Analyzing Free Response Data in Marketing Research," *Journal of Marketing Research,* 10 (February 1973), 45.

56. Haley, R. I. "Benefit Segmentation: A Decision-Oriented Research Tool," *Journal of Marketing,* 32 (July 1968).

57. Hanan, M. "Market Segmentation," *American Management Association Bulletin,* 109 (1968).

58. Hartigan, John A. *Clustering Algorithms.* New York: John Wiley & Sons, Inc., 1975.

59. Hays, William L. *Statistics for the Social Sciences,* 2nd edition. New York: Holt, Rinehart and Winston, 1973.

60. Hemphill, John K. and Charles M. Westie. "The Measurement of Group Dimensions," *Journal of Psychology,* 29 (1950), 325–41.

61. Hochstin, Joseph R. "A Critical Comparison of Three Strategies of Collecting Data from Households," *Journal of the American Statistical Association* (September 1967), 976–89.

62. Hulbert, James and Donald R. Lehman. "Assessing the Importance of the Sources of Error in Structured Survey Data, *in* John U. Farley and John A. Howard, eds., *Control of "Error" in Market Research Data.* Lexington, Massachusetts: Lexington Books, 1975, 81–107.

63. Johnson, Richard M. "Trade Off Analysis of Consumer Values," *Journal of Marketing Research,* 11 (May 1974), 121–27.

64. ——. "Beyond Conjoint Measurement: A Method of Pairwise Tradeoff Analysis," *in* B. B. Anderson, ed., *Advances in Consumer Research,* Vol. III. Proceedings of Association for Consumer Research Sixth Annual Conference (1975), 353–58.

65. Johnson, S. C. "Hierarchical Clustering Schemes," *Pychometrika,* 32 (1967), 241–54.

66. Krippendorff, Klaus. "A Coefficient of Agreement for Situations in Which Qualitative Data Are Categorized by Many Judges," University of Pennsylvania, Annenberg School of Communication, 1966, mimeo.

67. Kruskal, Joseph B. "Analysis of Factorial Experiments by Estimating Monotone Transformations of the Data," *Journal of the Royal Statistical Society,* Series B, 27 (1967), 251–63.

68. —— and Frank J. Carmone. "MONANOVA: A FORTRAN IV Program for Monotone Analysis of Variance," *Behavioral Science,* 14 (1969), 165–66.

69. Lazarsfeld, Paul F. and Neil W. Henry. *Latent Structure Analysis.* Boston: Houghton-Mifflin Co., 1968.

70. Mahajan, Vijay and Arun K. Jain. "An Approach to Normative Segmentation," *Journal of Marketing Research,* 15 (August 1978).

71. Martin, Claude R. and Roger L. Wright. "Profit Oriented Data Analysis for Market Segmentation: An Alternative to AID," *Journal of Marketing Research,* 11 (August 1974), 237–42.

72. Massy, William F., Ronald E. Frank, and Thomas Lodahl. *Purchasing Behavior and Personal Attributes.* Philadelphia: University of Pennsylvania Press, 1968.

73. McCann, John M. "Market Segment Response to the Marketing Decision Variables," *Journal of Marketing Research,* 11 (November 1974), 399–412.

74. Michman, Ronald D., Myron Gable, and Walter Gross. *Market Segmentation: A Selected and Annotated Bibliography.* Chicago: AMA, 1977.

75. Morgan, James N. and Robert C. Messenger. *THAID: A Sequential Analysis Pro-*

gram for the Analysis of Nominal Scale Dependent Variables. Ann Arbor, Michigan: Survey Research Center, 1973.

76. Morrison, Donald G. "Evaluating Market Segmentation Studies: The Properties of R^2," *Management Science,* 19 (July 1973), 1213–21.

77. Myers, John G. "An Interactive Computer Approach to Product Positioning," *in* Y. Wind and M. Greenberg, eds., *Moving A Head with Attitude Research.* Chicago: AMA, 1977, 157–64.

78. —— and Francesco M. Nicosia. "On the Dimensionality Question in Latent Structure Analysis," *in* Reed Moyer, ed., *Changing Marketing Systems: Consumer, Corporate and Government Inter-Faces.* Chicago: AMA, 1969.

79. Nicosia, Francesco et al. *Technology and Consumers: Individual and Social Choices.* Berkeley: University of California Report, 1974.

80. —— and Yoram Wind. "Behavioral Models of Organizational Buying Processes," *in* F. Nicosia and Y. Wind, eds., *Behavioral Models of Market Analysis: Foundations for Marketing Action.* Hinsdale, Illinois: The Dryden Press, 1977, 96–120.

81. —— and ——. "Sociology of Consumption and Trade-Off Models in Consumer Public Policy," *in* Lunn, ed., *Consumer Research for Public Policy,* in press.

82. Ostland, Lyman E. "Perceived Innovation Attributes as Predictors of Innovation," *Journal of Consumer Research,* 1 (September 1974).

83. Overall, J. E. and C. J. Klett. *Applied Multivariate Analysis.* New York: McGraw-Hill Book Company, 1972, 180–239.

84. Parker, Barnett R. and V. Srinivasan. "A Consumer Preference Approach to the Planning of Rural Primary Health Care Facilities," *Operations Research,* 24 (1976), 991–1025.

85. Pekelman, Dov and Subrata Sen. "Utility Function Estimation in Conjoint Measurement," paper presented at the Fall 1974 Conference of the American Marketing Association, Portland, Oregon.

86. Peterson, Robert A. "Market Structuring by Sequential Cluster Analysis," *Journal of Business Research,* 2 (July 1974), 249–64.

87. ——. "Concept Testing: Some Experimental Evidence," *Mississippi Valley Journal of Business and Economics,* 7 (Spring 1972), 84–88.

88. Rao, Vithala and Frederick W. Winter. "An Application of the Multivariate Probit Model to Market Segmentation and Product Design," *Journal of Marketing Research,* 15 (August 1978).

89. Reynolds, W. H. "More Sense About Market Segmentation," *Harvard Business Review,* 43 (September–October 1965), 107–14.

90. Robertson, Thomas S. *Innovative Behavior and Communication.* New York: Holt, Rinehart and Winston, 1971.

91. Robinson, Patrick J. and Yoram Wind. "Multinational Trade-Off Segmentation," *in* Y. Wind and M. Greenberg, eds., *Moving A Head with Attitude Research.* Chicago: AMA, 1977, 50–57.

92. Rogers, Everett M. and F. Floyd Shoemaker. *Communication of Innovations.* New York: Free Press, 1971.

93. Samejima, Fumiko. "A General Model for Response Data," *Psychometrika Monograph Supplement,* Monograph 18, Vol. 37 (March 1972).

94. Schönemann, Peter H. "A Generalized Solution of the Orthogonal Procrustes Problem," *Psychometrika,* 31 (March 1966), 1–10.

95. Shocker, Allan and V. Srinivasan. "LINMAP II: Linear Programming Techniques for Multidimensional Analysis of Preferences with Applications to Conjoint Analysis," *Journal of Marketing Research,* 14 (1977), 101–3.

96. Shugan, Steven M. and John R. Hauser. "P.A.R.I.S.: An Interactive Market Research Information System," Northeastern University, Graduate School of Management working paper 602–002, 1977.

97. Smith, Wendell. "Product Differentiation and Market Segmentation as Alternative Marketing Strategies," *Journal of Marketing*, 21 (July 1956), 3–8.

98. Sonquist, John A. *Multivariate Model Building*. Ann Arbor, Michigan: Survey Research Center, 1970.

99. Srinivasan, V. and Allan D. Shocker. "Estimating the Weights for Multiple Attributes in a Composite Criterion Using Pairwise Judgments," *Psychometrika*, 38 (1973), 473–93.

100. Stewart, Douglas and William Love. "A General Canonical Correlation Index," *Psychological Bulletin*, 70 (September 1968), 160–63.

101. Stout, Roy G. et al. "Usage Incidence as a Basis for Segmentation," *in* Y. Wind and M. Greenberg, eds., *Moving A Head with Attitude Research*. Chicago: AMA, 1977, 45–49.

102. Tollefson, John O. and Parker Lessig. "Aggregation Criteria in Normative Market Segmentation Theory," *Journal of Marketing Research*, 15 (August 1978).

103. Van Den Wollenberg, Arnold. "Redundancy Analysis: An Alternative for Canonical Correlation Analysis," *Psychometrika*, 42 (June 1977).

104. Wallace, D. "A Case for—and against—Mail Questionnaires," *Public Opinion Quarterly*, 18 (1954), 40–52.

105. Webb, Eugene J. et al. *Unobtrusive Measures: Nonreactive Research in the Social Sciences*. Chicago: Rand McNally, 1966.

106. Webster, Frederick, Jr., and Yoram Wind. *Organizational Buying Behavior*. Englewood Cliffs, New Jersey: Prentice-Hall, Inc., 1972.

107. Wells, William D. "Psychographics: A Critical Review," *Journal of Marketing Research*, 12 (May 1975), 196–211.

108. Wildt, Albert R. "On Evaluating Market Segmentation Studies and the Properties of R^2," *Management Science*, 22 (April 1976), 904–8.

109. Wilkie, William L. *How Consumers Use Product Information*. Washington, D.C.: U.S. Government Printing Office, 1976.

110. Wind, Yoram. "Toward a Change in the Focus of Marketing Analysis: From a Single Brand to an Assortment," *Journal of Marketing*, 41 (October 1977), 12.

111. ——."A New Procedure for Concept Evaluation," *Journal of Marketing*, 37 (October 1973), 2–11.

112. ——. "The Perception of the Firm's Competitive Position," *in* F. Nicosia and Y. Wind, eds., *Behavioral Models of Market Analysis: Foundations for Marketing Action*. Hinsdale, Illinois: The Dryden Press, 1977, 163–81.

113. ——. "Organizational Buying Center: A Research Agenda," *in* Gerald Zaltman and Thomas V. Bonoma, eds., *Organizational Buying Behavior*. Chicago, AMA, in press.

114. —— and Richard N. Cardozo. "Industrial Marketing Segmentation," *Industrial Marketing Management*, 3 (March 1974), 153–65.

115. —— and Henry J. Claycamp. "Planning Product Line Strategy: A Matrix Approach," *Journal of Marketing*, 40 (January 1976), 2–9.

116. —— and Paul E. Green. "Some Conceptual Measurement and Analytical Problems in Life Style Research," *in* William Wells, ed., *Life Style and Psychographics*. Chicago: AMA, 1974, 97–126.

117. ——, Stuart Jolly, and Arthur O'Connor. "Concept Testing as Input to Strategic

Marketing Simultations," *in* E. Mazze, ed., *Proceedings of the 58th International AMA Conference*, April 1975, 120–24.

118. —— and David Learner. "A Note on the Measurement of Purchase Data: Surveys vs. Purchase Diaries," Wharton School working paper, 1977.

119. —— and John G. Myers. "A Note on the Selection of Attributes for Conjoint Analysis," Wharton School working paper, January 1977.

120. —— and Lawrence K. Spitz. "Analytical Approach to Marketing Decisions in Health Care Organizations," *Operations Research*, 24 (September–October 1976), 973–90.

Targeting Prospects for a New Product

Philip Kotler and Gerald Zaltman

How can a company identify the best early-adopter prospects for a new product it is about to launch? Suppose its management has already:

1. Found a product idea that appeared to be compatible with the company's objectives and resources;
2. Developed alternative product concepts for the product idea, tested these concepts with a group of potential buyers, chose the best one, and was satisfied that this product concept had good sales and profit potential;
3. Created a prototype that was faithful to the concept as well as packaging that reinforced the product concept;
4. Given the prototype to a sample of potential consumers, who reported strong satisfaction but suggested further improvements;
5. Test marketed the product in a well-selected set of cities with strong results, giving the company the confidence to launch the product regionally;
6. Selected a region with many ultimate customers and few competitors.

Having come this far, the company would like to launch the product so as to gain high early sales. The company attaches great importance to maximizing the speed of adoption of this new product because:

1. Some competitors might be shortly coming into the same market and the company would like to be deeply entrenched at the time of competitive entry;
2. The company would like to verify as soon as possible that market interest is truly strong for this product—it wants evidence of this before laying plans for expansion into the next set of regions;
3. The company's rate of return on its investment will be higher the faster its product penetrates the market for a given marketing budget.

The company would like to avoid certain techniques for stimulating rapid adoption and diffusion of a new product because they are costly and would not represent the marketing mix that it would normally use to enter each market— for example, (1) charging a lower-than-planned price to stimulate earlier trial and repurchase of the product; (2) distributing free samples of the product to acquaint the market as rapidly as possible with the product's existence and virtues; (3) offering price-off coupons or premiums to stimulate early trial; (4) using higher-than-planned levels of advertising expenditures to increase the rate at which consumers learn about the new product.

It is often the case that special incentives may simply precipitate early purchase among those who would ordinarily adopt the product anyway but at a later time. If the product is not a frequently purchased item, the company may gain little and, in fact, may lose money by offering special deals. However, there is a possibility, particularly where a product is radically different, that persons who have a propensity for early adoption in the product area or category may need an added incentive to activate it. Late adopters will be especially likely to adopt or reject the new product more on the basis of information obtained from early adopters than on the basis of special deals. Thus, the firm may wish to target incentives or deals in a special case only to early adopters. This increases the importance of studying early adopters from the special viewpoint to be advocated later. The issue here is whether early adopters (whose behavior is likely to be imitated by late adopters) need special stimulation or whether their natural propensity to adopt will be sufficiently active to make special deals, unusually high advertising, and so forth, unnecessary. At present, existing knowledge about this issue is insufficient to derive meaningful answers; the issue must be addressed on a case-by-case basis.

EARLY-ADOPTER THEORY

There is a body of theory known as early-adopter theory that seems to provide the company with an answer to its problems. We shall state the antecedants of this theory, the theory as it stands today, and, finally, several of its weaknesses. Later, we shall prepare an alternative view of how to identify and reach the best potential early adopters for a specific new product.

Predecessors of Early-Adopter Theory

The mass-market approach, the earliest launching approach used by new-product marketers, consisted of distributing the product widely and informing everyone about it who might be a potential purchaser. For example, a manufacturer of a new cake mix might determine that women constitute the major market for cake mixes and would formulate a launching program to reach and inform as many women as possible. Most women, of course, would not buy the new cake mix; but it was hoped that enough women would buy it to return a satisfactory profit to the firm.

The mass-market approach, however, had at least two drawbacks: (1) it required a heavy marketing expenditure; and (2) it involved a substantial number of wasted exposures to nonpotential buyers. Its high cost led to a new stage of thinking about new-product introduction, that of heavy-user target marketing. Marketers became acutely aware that a small percentage of the users of a product typically accounted for a substantial share of all purchasing (Twedt, 1964). It followed that the marketer should attempt to identify the characteristics of the heavy users of the product class and then cast a narrow net designed to capture their specific interest in the new product. In the case of the new cake mix, the target would no longer be all women but rather women who were heavy users of cake mixes. An attempt would be made to identify their characteristics in terms of their distribution over social classes, family sizes, educational levels, media vehicles, and so on. Using volume segmentation, the marketer would rank different potential adopter classes. Thus it might be found that the heaviest users of cake mixes are housewives under 40 with families of three or more children and low income. It might be found that the next heaviest group of users are housewives under 40 with families of three or more children and medium income. The company would build its marketing plan to reach the first or first two target groups early and later plan to extend the message to the lighter-using groups.

Enter Early-Adopter Theory

But, it was noticed, even within the group of heavy users of a product class, there would be a great difference in (1) how much interest individuals would show in new products and (2) the speed at which individuals would try them. For any new product, a handful of individuals (innovators) would be the first to notice and try the new product; they would be followed by a larger group (early adopters) who would try the product relatively early; others (early majority) would adopt the product after they had seen its growing use; still others (late majority) would come into the market relatively late; and, finally, a few remaining nontriers (laggards) would ultimately come into the market.

Observations in a wide range of contexts led to the hypothesis of a bell-shaped distribution of adoption times. It was further suggested that the first 2.5 per cent of the adopters of a new product be called the innovators; the next 13.5 per cent be called the early adopters; the next 34 per cent be called the early majority; the next 34 per cent be called the late majority; and the last 16 per cent be called the laggards (Rogers and Shoemaker, 1971).

The import of this finding was that the new-product marketer ought to direct his communications not equally to everyone who might be an eventual adopter or a heavy user but rather to those persons who are most likely to adopt the product early. A theory, called the early-adopter theory, grew up around this view, whose premises might be stated as follows:

1. Persons within a well-defined target market will differ in the amount of time that passes between their exposure to a new product and their trial

of the new product. Those who adopt the product early upon exposure may be called the early adopters.

2. Early adopters are likely to share some traits in common, which differentiate them from late adopters. That is, early adoption is not a fortuitous characteristic but rather associated with some common demographic, psychological, or situational factors. Early adopters are people who tend to be first in trying various new products in general or in particular product classes.

3. There exist efficient media for reaching early-adopter types.

4. Early-adopter types are likely to be high on opinion leadership and, therefore, helpful in "advertising" the new product to other potential buyers.

STATUS OF EARLY-ADOPTER THEORY

The premises of early-adopter theory have benefited from a considerable amount of research over the years. The two focal points of research have been premises 2 and 4. Accordingly, it will be useful here to review critically the literature related to these two premises.

There are several flaws with early-adopter research, two of which require special mention. One flaw arises from the way early adopters are most frequently identified. The method consists of introducing the new product in a test market or region and then obtaining the names of the first persons to buy the product. A sample of these people are interviewed and their common characteristics are noted. It might be found, for example, that they have a higher-than-average education. Then the marketing company assumes that early-adopter types have a higher-than-average education and undertakes to aim more of its communications at the higher-than-average educated group.

This information-collection design contains a major fallacy. It rates people on their time of adoption from the time of the product introduction, not their time of adoption from the time of their exposure. What the company really needs to identify is the group of people who responded early after exposure, not the group that responded in the early period. Virtually all research has been based on early adopters relative to the time the product or innovation is introduced rather than the time of first awareness. This distinction is of crucial importance in media planning. There should be more homogeneity between those who adopted early after exposure, and it is their common traits that should be identified. This means that greater attention must also be given to learning which media deliver messages more quickly to people. Media may differ in terms of whom they reach first. Also overlooked is why people rely on particular media and why this differs, if it does, between early and late adopters.

The second major problem concerns the magnitude and persistence of adoption. Almost totally absent in existing research is any consideration of the degree of commitment involved in adoption (as opposed to trial and evaluation) (Kiesler, 1971). Consumers, when trying to satisfy some need or desire, may vary from infrequently using a particular product brand, to using it often, to using it all the time. Media factors may be important here (Maloney and Schonfeld, 1973).

Other problems include:

1. A lack of attention given to interpersonal relations between early adopters and others (there is a need for more "relational analysis" where relationships, not individuals, are the unit of analysis) (Rogers, 1969 and 1973; Burnkrant and Cousineau, 1974);

2. An underemphasis on resistance or nonadoption and discontinuance relative to full adoption and the role of various channels of communication in creating resistance;

3. Limited research on how the perception of different adopter categories differ (a) for perceived innovations versus noninnovations and (b) across different categories of innovations;

4. Limited attention paid to the communications mix implications of feedback loops in adopter and resistor decision making;

5. Limited research on whether particular media have differential effectiveness for innovations as compared to noninnovations and whether this varies by (a) stages of the adoption process, (b) adopter category, (c) product class, and (d) salient attributes of the product or service;

6. A lack of knowledge about the interaction effects between personal and mass-media channels of communication.

Research on the character and behavior of adopter categories has been extensive and is contradictory, probably due in part of the wrong use of exposure measures. Some of the contradictions will be pointed out here. Rogers and Shoemaker (1971), in their study of early adopters, observe that early adopters are no different in age than late adopters, although Arndt (1968) suggests that they may be younger and Bell (1964) suggests that they may be older. Early adopters have frequently been found to have more formal education than others, although there is evidence contradicting this too (Fliegel, 1965). Related to this is the finding that early adopters have higher social status (Zaltman, 1974). Cancian (1967), however, questions the validity of this finding. Many studies indicate that early adopters have larger businesses (Loomis, 1967) while other studies indicate that this is not necessarily true (Czepiel, 1972). Early adopters have been found to hold more positive attitudes toward the use of credit or other forms of borrowing (Dasgupta, 1966), but not in all circumstances (Havens, 1965).

Research is still scanty concerning the psychological states of early adopters, and the research reported is conflicting. Kivlin (1968), Zaltman (1971; and, with Pinson, 1974(a)), and others indicate that early adopters may possess greater empathetic ability, although this observation has not been confirmed in all studies (Rogers and de Ramos, 1965). There is considerable conflict among researchers as to whether early adopters are more (or less) dogmatic than late adopters. Jacoby (1971(a)) and Blake, Perloff, and Heslin (1970) suggest they are, while others (Robertson, 1967) argue the opposite position. The ability to think abstractly is believed to be associated with the early adoption of new products (Smith, 1968), and related to this is the observation in a few studies that early adopters may be more intelligent than late adopters. The propensity to take risk is generally believed to be a trait of early adopters (Boone, 1974; Robertson and Rossiter, 1968), although, again, not in all instances (Taylor, 1974) and not always in a positive way (Schiffman, 1972).

Many other traits have been studied in addition to those mentioned above, and in all cases there is debate as to what the set of conditions are that make a trait operative or inoperative as a causal factor in new-product adopters. Very briefly, these other traits are (1) attitudes toward science; (2) achievement motivation; (3) participation in social affairs; (4) orientations outside the immediate setting; (5) frequency of contact with salesmen; (6) mass-media exposure; (7) exposure to interpersonal communication; (8) information seeking; (9) knowledge of new products; and (10) the likelihood of early adopters being opinion leaders (Cohen and Golden, 1972; Robertson, 1971).

Much research needs to be done to clarify, explain, and, ultimately, help predict and control the functioning of the various social and psychological variables uniquely associated with early adopters. The following is a sample of research questions aimed at increasing our understanding of the role of early adopters in new-product marketing. After each question a reference is cited which either itself raises the research question or is its basis.

1. How do early adopters differ from late adopters in terms of the frequency of engaging in word-of-mouth behavior and in terms of the content of information exchanged (Belk and Rose, 1971; Uhl, Andrus, and Poulsen, 1970)?

2. To what extent are early adopters active-versus-passive opinion leaders in the communication process (Engel, Blackwell, and Kegerreis, 1969)?

3. How do early adopters use information in formulating buying strategy and in deciding to seek or not seek additional information (Engel, Blackwell, and Kegerreis, 1969; Kohn and Jacoby, 1974)?

4. Is there a uniqueness motivation—i.e., a tendency to seek out the novel—that differentiates early adopters from late adopters in terms of their selection, processing, and retention of information (Fromkin, 1971; Lambert, 1972)?

5. How do personality variables for early adopters interact with attributes of new products, and how is this mediated by various communication channels (Goldberg, 1971; Zaltman and Pinson, 1974(b); Donnelly and Etzel, 1973)?

6. How valid are personality studies of early adopters (Myers and Robertson, 1974; Pizam, 1972; Reynolds and Darden, 1972)?

7. Do early adopters differ from late adopters in their perceptions of the

new product because of greater experience with the new product (when other variables are held constant) (Zaltman and Pinson, 1974(b))?

8. When directing advertising to early adopters, should product attributes or should early-adopter ego and social factors be stressed (Jacoby, 1971(b))?

9. Can early adopters be "created" by altering communication strategies in the marketing plan (Mancuso, 1969)?

10. To what extent and by means of what variables can early buyers be identified (Darden and Reynolds, 1974; Ostlund, 1972)?

11. What are the sources of resistance among early rejectors (Zaltman and Dubois, 1971)? Do the same variables that cause rejection by some persons cause early adoption by others (Zaltman, Duncan, and Holbek, 1973)?

12. Are early adopters of optional new products (where not everyone in the home need use them) different from early adopters of mandatory new products (where everyone must use them) (Zaltman, Duncan, and Holbek, 1973; Rogers and Shoemaker, 1971)?

13. What are the differences between early adopters in consumer-goods settings and early adopters in industrial-goods settings (Schiffman and Gaccione, 1974)?

A careful analysis of the literature on early adopters, some of which has been mentioned above, and an examination of the assumptions and implications of the research questions cited leads to several important observations about the current state of early-adopter theory:

1. It is clear that early adopters, in some contexts at least, do differ from late adopters.

2. The underlying variables that account for a given difference between early and late adopters to display itself in one context and not in another still need to be identified.

3. The circumstances in which one particular early adopter trait rather than another becomes important still need to be identified.

4. Little explanation exists concerning the dynamic and causal impact that various sociological and psychological traits have on the "adopt now" or "adopt later" decision.

5. As a consequence of observations 1 to 4 above, the existing inventory of early-adopter knowledge and analytic techniques traditionally used for studying early adopters is inadequate for segmenting and predicting early adopters for given products or product categories.

6. However, a blending of the soundest early-adopter research findings with a bold new perspective and approach can overcome the inadequacies of the present way of segmenting and predicting the relevant early adopters.

7. The new approach we propose is highly promising in terms of aiding new-product management in developing strategies that will enhance its ability to shape or guide new-product adoption and diffusion.

THEORY OF THE BEST PROSPECT CHOICE

Early-adopter theory, particularly the perspective we feel necessary, holds that certain people characteristically are the first to adopt a new product upon exposure and that they should be identified and then exposed to the first communications about the product. But even allowing for the existence of early-adopter types, it would be wrong to equate this group with the best early prospects for a new product. Early-adopter types may not be the best prospects to target for a number of reasons. The trait of early-adoption propensity alone is neither necessary nor sufficient for warranting early targeting.

This can be shown through a simple theoretical model which combines all the criteria that relate to the value of a prospect. The model is offered as an aid to clear thinking about the variables that define the best target individuals for a new-product campaign. While it does not automatically translate into a practical model for media selection, for instance, it does clarify the considerations that should guide early-target selection.

The task is to define, at the time of launching, the value of different prospects for a new product. Let us assume that we could advertise a new product through a direct-mail campaign, that thousands of names of potential users of the product are available to us, but that we cannot advertise to all of them. The mailing-list supplier is able to answer up to four questions about the names on the mailing list. The four questions a marketer would want to ask should be:

1. What is the probability that the prospect would be an early purchaser of the product upon exposure? (Call this probability A = early-adoption propensity.)
2. How much is the prospect likely to buy per year if he tries the new product? (Call this amount Q = heavy-volume propensity.)
3. How much additional purchasing per year is this prospect likely to stimulate in others through interpersonal influence? (Call this amount I = influence propensity.)
4. What is the cost of an effective communication exposure to this person? (Call this cost C = cost of an effective communication exposure.)

We can combine the four factors into the following formula to find the value (V) of a prospect:

(1)
$$V = A(Q + I) - C$$

To illustrate this formula, let us assume that the first prospect on the list has a likehood of only .05 of being an early buyer of this product upon exposure; if he buys, he will probably like it and buy $5.00 worth a year; he is likely to stimulate another $6.00 worth of purchases a year in others; and it will cost $0.20 to communicate an effective message to him. According to the formula, this prospect would be worth:

$$V = .05(\$5.00 + \$6.00) - \$0.20$$
$$= \$0.35$$

Now consider a second prospect for whom the likelihood is .10 of being an early buyer of this product upon exposure; if he buys, he will probably like it and buy \$3.00 worth a year; he is likely to stimulate \$1.00 worth of purchases a year in others; and it will cost \$0.20 to communicate an effective message to him. According to the formula, this prospect would be worth:

$$V = .10(\$3.00 + \$1.00) - \$0.20$$
$$= \$0.20$$

Here we see that although the second prospect is twice as likely as the first to be an early adopter of the new product, he is a less valuable prospect because he will personally consume less and influence less than the first prospect. This is why we said earlier that being an early-adopter type is not automatically equivalent to being the best early prospect.

The reason that the two statuses have been confused is because it is commonly thought that early-adoption propensity (A) is positively correlated with heavy-volume propensity (Q) and heavy-influence propensity (I). To the extent that this is true in a particular product class, new-product marketers are correct in simply targeting their communications to early-adopter types. To the extent that the three variables A, Q, and I are uncorrelated or even negatively correlated, it does not make sense to look only at early-adoption propensity. Suppose it could be shown, for example, that early-adopter types buy less volume of a given new brand than late-adopter types because they are always trying out new brands and dropping the ones they just started using—that is, they are low loyals because of their need for variety. In this case, it can be questioned whether early-adopter types are the best target for new-product launchings.

Or suppose that the early adopters in a particular product class have average or weak social networks and another group of potential adopters, who would normally adopt later, have very strong social networks. Under these circumstances the marketer may prefer to first expose the new product to the slower adopter group along with incentives to encourage earlier-than-normal adopting behavior.

Or suppose the cost of reaching different prospects varies. Suppose it is costlier to communicate to early-adopter types—for example, they may be exposed to fewer or more expensive media. This would further vitiate the theory that early-adoption propensity is alone sufficient for determining whom to target for early communications.

Given that the value of a prospect is defined by the factors in formula (1), what subfactors underlie each of the major factors?

Early-Adoption Propensity

Early-adoption propensity is defined as the probability that a person would be an early purchaser of the product upon an effective communication exposure. Early-adoption propensity is a function of the following subfactors:

1. The extent to which the product has strong need-fulfillment potential for the person (call this F = need-fulfillment potential);
2. The extent to which the person has a new-product orientation (call this N = innovative disposition);
3. The extent to which the product is highly accessible to the individual (call this D = accessibility);
4. The extent to which the individual's income makes the price less important (call this Y = income sufficiency).

Each of these subfactors is important in assessing whether or not a person will have a high propensity toward adopting a particular new product. Let us assume that each factor can be scaled from zero to one. We would propose that these factors would combine in a multiplicative way to affect the early-adoption propensity:

$$(2) \qquad A = F \times N \times D \times Y$$

For example, the highest early-adoption propensity would be found in a person who has a strong need for the new product, tends to search out new products, can easily acquire it without much effort, and can afford the price. The formula is multiplicative because if any factor is weak, the early adoption propensity drops considerably. It is not the case that the propensity would be high simply because two or three factors are very high.

Heavy-Volume Propensity

Heavy-volume propensity is the amount of the new product that the person is likely to buy per period if he tries it. This propensity depends on the following subfactors:

1. The probability that this type of person will be sufficiently satisfied with the new product upon trial to buy it again (call this T = trial-satisfaction probability);
2. The number of times per year that the person makes a purchase in this product class (call this R = product-class re-purchase frequency);
3. The average amount purchased by this person per purchase occasion (call this K = average amount purchased per purchase occasion);
4. The likely share that the new product will enjoy of this person's purchases within the product class (call this S = new product's share of total purchases in the product class).

We would propose that these subfactors would combine in a multiplicative way to determine the person's heavy-volume propensity:

$$(3) \qquad Q = T(R \times K \times S)$$

For example, suppose the person buys into this product class three times a year; he buys $2.00 each time; and he buys the new brand half of the time. This would yield a new-product purchase volume per year of:

$$R \times K \times S = 3 \times \$2.00 \times .50$$
$$= \$3.00$$

But will the individual be sufficiently satisfied as a result of trial to adopt the new product? Let us assume that this probability is .75. Then:

$$Q = .75(\$3.00)$$
$$= \$2.25$$

That is, the probability of sufficient trial satisfaction is used to scale down the value of his purchases if satisfied.

Influence Propensity

Influence propensity is the amount of additional purchasing per year that the prospect is likely to stimulate in others through interpersonal influence. This propensity depends on the following factors:

1. The number of persons the individual interacts with on a conversational basis (call this M = the number of acquaintances);
2. The percentage of persons he influences during the year to try the product who would have not tried it otherwise (call this L = influence ratio);
3. The average volume an influenced person buys per year of the new brand (call this W = the influenced person's volume).

We would suggest that these subfactors also work in a multiplicative way:

(4) $$I = M \times L \times W$$

The prospect's influence potential depends on the number of people he knows, the proportion of them he influences, and the average volume an influenced person buys. We will ignore the fact that the influenced person will, in turn, influence other persons to try the product during the year.

As a further refinement, the proportion of persons that the prospect influences (L) depends on three factors:

1. The person's new-product conversational propensity;
2. The percentage of his acquaintances who are potential purchasers of this product;
3. The degree to which other persons look upon this person as a new-product legitimator.

The prospect will show a higher influence propensity the more he tends to talk about new products he has tried, the more he talks to others who are interested in the product class, and the more he is seen as a legitimator of new-product ideas.

Prospect Communication Cost

Prospect communication cost is the cost of delivering an effective message with a given media vehicle to a given prospect. We can define this cost as some function of the following subfactors:

E_1 = the probability that the individual will be exposed to the message with the media;

E_2 = the probability that the individual will see the message;

E_3 = the probability that the individual will comprehend the message;

E_4 = the probability that the individual will be favorably impressed by the message;

0 = the actual cost of getting the given message exposed to the given individual with the given message.

The function will not be specified except to note that the real cost of communication (C) is higher than the actual cost (0) to the extent that the message-media combination is less than perfectly effective in exposing, informing, and motivating the prospect.

METHODOLOGICAL STEPS IN IDENTIFYING EARLY ADOPTERS

We now turn to the pragmatic problem facing a company that is readying the introduction of a new product and seeking to target its communications and distribution of the new product to the "best prospects." We will assume that the marketer has defined the characteristics of the ultimate target market and that his interest is to reach the best early prospects among them since he cannot make the product and communications instantly available to everyone in the ultimate market.

The perfect solution to this problem would exist if the marketer could turn to a comprehensive and unambiguous body of knowledge about the characteristics of early adopters, heavy adopters, and influential adopters without having to undertake additional research. This body of knowledge would define the demographics, sociographics, psychographics, and media habits of these groups and permit the determination of the best early prospects.

Of course, such a body of knowledge does not exist. As we saw earlier, there are too few solid findings available to the new-product marketer that reliably suggest the characteristics of early adopters, especially for a particular product class. Information on the characteristics of heavy adopters is usually better. Information on the characteristics of influential adopters is not very good. The new-product marketer has to rely mainly on a fresh investigation of the characteristics of these groups for each product class.

There are several stages in the product-development process where organized attention to the question of the characteristics of early adopters could yield useful information. We shall comment on two of these stages: the concept-testing stage and test-marketing stage.

Concept-Testing Stage

The concept-testing stage is undertaken to test the appeal of a new product concept to a potential target user group. Various potential users are asked, among other things, to play back their understanding of the product concept, to express the degree of their interest in the concept, and to express the degree of their buying intent toward the product (Tauber, 1973). Usually missing are questions of the following nature:

1. If you intend to buy the product, how soon after its appearance are you likely to buy it?
   (a) _____ immediately
   (b) _____ within a week
   (c) _____ within a month
   (d) _____ within a year

2. How do you see yourself with regard to buying new products?
   (a) _____ as one of the first persons to buy new products
   (b) _____ as an early adopter of new products after a few others have tried them
   (c) _____ as a late adopter of new products after a lot of people have bought them

3. If you liked the product, would you probably be:
   (a) _____ a heavy buyer
       (more than _____ units per year)
   (b) _____ a medium buyer
       (between _____ and _____ units per year)
   (c) _____ a light buyer
       (less than _____ units per year)

4. If you liked the product, would you probably:
   (a) _____ tell several other persons
   (b) _____ tell a few other persons
   (c) _____ not discuss

5. In what media or media vehicle do you think you would be likely to first learn about this product? _____

The first two questions would reveal those in the sample who are early-adopter types; the third question would reveal those who are heavy-buyer types; the fourth question would reveal those who are influential-adopter types; and the fifth question would reveal the media expectations of potential buyers. The questions will have to be refined through testing because they may either be insufficiently clear or be answered unreliably. Their basic intent is to reveal (1) the kinds of people making up each group and (2) the correlations that might exist among the various traits that are important in indentifying the best prospects. This information would be verified as the product moves through subsequent stages of development. For example, the same or similar questions can be asked again of people who are exposed to the actual physical product in the product-testing stage.

Test-Marketing Stage

If the company decides to place the new product in test markets before making the final launching decision, it can use the test-marketing stage to improve its knowledge of the characteristics of the best early prospects.

This is accomplished by having the marketer vary the channels of distribution, the media, and the messages to determine the level of sales associated with these variations. For example, he might advertise the new product to matched market areas using different media or he might use a succession of media vehicles in each of several weeks in the same market areas. He would then interview early buyers to learn how and when they were exposed to the new product, and would analyze those buyers who bought very soon after information exposure to see if some common characteristics could be identified. Such a set of common characteristics would provide the information he needs to direct his marketing efforts, including advertising copy design and media, to the best prospects for his product in the general population.

If the company skips the test-marketing stage and goes directly into a regional or national launch of the product, the same arguments apply as in the test-marketing stage—that is, as the product is launched in each new market, the marketer must attempt to observe those who buy the product first. He must also determine what factors under his control account for late exposure among other persons, particularly those who are good early-adopter candidates. By conducting marketing research into the characteristics of early adopters, he can keep current and improve the precision of his subsequent marketing efforts.

MEDIA IMPLICATIONS

A basic theme here is that many persons who have high early-adoption potential may be misclassified as late adopters or overlooked as potential early adopters because they adopt late relative to the time the new product was introduced. In fact, they may adopt quite soon after their initial exposure. That they do not become aware of the new product until well after it is introduced suggests that they may have communication patterns that differ from those of persons learning of a new product very soon upon its introduction. This has a very important implication in terms of media selection. Different media may have to be used to reach early those persons who are usually late knowers but otherwise early adopters. To the extent that different media may be necessary and that media and messages interact, it may also be necessary to use different message strategies. This is a second important implication. Unfortunately, information concerning both implications is scarce, and substantial research into this matter is necessary.

Another important media problem, one in which much more research is re-required, concerns the media behavior of early adopters beyond the considerations of identifying what their media exposure is. We need to study further the particular functions various media perform or services they provide for early adopters. Are some media perceived as "legitimators" of new products? Are some media perceived as "introducers"—that is, sources of initial but perhaps unreliable information?

Do some media affect volume of product usage more than other media? Are some media more effective in creating opinion leadership among early adopters? Many more such questions can be generated whose answers have important bearings on overall media strategy for introducing new products.

SUMMARY

We have concentrated on a key question that must be faced at the new-product launching stage but for which data must be collected in earlier stages: How can the company identify and effectively reach the best potential early adopters for a specific new product that is ready to be launched? Company marketers are no longer satisfied with launching a new product to the mass market or to the heavy users only. They want to identify the traits of those who would have a high natural propensity to adopt the new product early upon exposure.

We reviewed the literature on early adopters to discover that it has too few solid findings to guide the marketing planner. Contradictory findings exist about whether early adopters tend to be younger or older, more educated or less educated, of higher or lower social status, etc., than later adopters.

This literature will have to move into the next stage where the conditions under which various traits are associated with early adoption are thrown into better relief.

We also proposed that the most natural early adopters are not necessarily the best early prospects to target for a new product. The marketer, in choosing prospects early in the campaign, should consider four factors: (1) the prospect's early-adoption propensity; (2) the prospect's heavy-volume propensity; (3) the prospect's influence propensity; and (4) the cost of effectively reaching the particular prospect group. Early-adoption theory implicitly assumed that early adopters were also heavy users and high opinion leaders without confirming whether these relations were, in fact, true. A model of the sub-factors underlying each of these major factors was developed.

Ultimately, the determination of the best prospects for a new product has to be researched as the product progresses through the various stages of new-product development. For example, questions asked during the concept-testing stage will indicate the types of people who think that they would buy the product early, buy in substantial volume, and influence others. An analysis of the first persons to buy the product upon exposure during its test marketing will reveal further information about the characteristics of best early prospects for the product. By organized probing during the preliminary stages of product development, the marketer should have a good idea of his best early prospects when he is ready to launch the product.

REFERENCES

1. Arndt, Johan. Profiling Consumer Innovators. In Johan Arndt (Ed.). *Insights into Consumer Behavior*. Boston: Allyn & Bacon, 1968.
2. Belk, Russell, and Ivan Rose. An Investigation of the Nature of Word-of-Mouth Communication across Adoption Categories for a Food Innovation. In David Gardner (Ed.). *Proceedings of the Second Annual Conference, Association for Consumer Research*, 1971.
3. Bell, William E. Consumer Innovators: A Unique Market for Newness. In S. A. Greyser (Ed.). *Toward Scientific Marketing: Proceedings of the 1963 Winter Conference of the American Marketing Association*. Chicago: American Marketing Association, 1964.
4. Blake, Brian, Robert Perloff, and Richard Heslin. Dogmatism and Acceptance of New Products. *Journal of Marketing Research*, Vol. 7, November 1970, pp. 483–86.
5. Boone, L. E. Personality and Innovative Buying Behavior. *Journal of Psychology*, Vol. 86, 1974, pp. 197–202.
6. Burnkrant, R. E., and A. Cousineau. Informational and Normative Social Influence in Buyer Behavior. Paper, School of Business Administration, University of California at Berkeley, 1974.
7. Cancian, Frank. Stratification and Risk-Taking: A Theory Tested on Agricultural Innovation. *American Sociological Review*, Vol. 32, 1967.
8. Cohen, J. B., and E. Golden. Informational Social Influence and Product Evaluation. *Journal of Applied Psychology*, Vol. 56, 1972, pp. 54–59.
9. Czepiel, John. The Diffusion of Major Technological Innovation in a Complex Industrial Community: An Analysis of the Social Processes in the American Steel Industry. Ph.D. Diss., Graduate School of Management, Northwestern University, June 1972.
10. Darden, William, and Fred Reynolds. Backward Profiling of Male Innovators. *Journal of Marketing Research*, Vol. 11, February 1974, pp. 79–85.
11. Dasgupta, Satadal. Village (or Community) Factors Related to the Level of Agricultural Practice. Paper presented at the Southern Sociological Society, New Orleans, 1966, p. 23.
12. Donnelly, James, and Michael Etzel. Degrees of Product Newness and Early Trial. *Journal of Marketing Research*, Vol. 5, August 1973, pp. 295–300.
13. Engel, James, Roger Blackwell, and Robert J. Kegerreis. How Information Is Used to Adopt an Innovation. *Journal of Advertising Research*, Vol. 9, No. 4, pp. 3–8.

14. Fliegel, Frederick C. Differences in Prestige Standards and Orientation to Change in a Traditional Agricultural Setting. *Rural Sociology,* Vol. 30, 1965, p. 288.

15. Fromkin, Howard. A Social Psychological Analysis of the Adoption and Diffusion of New Products and Practices from a Uniqueness Motivation Perspective. *Proceedings of the Second Annual Conference, Association for Consumer Research,* 1971.

16. Goldberg, Marvin. A Cognitive Model of Innovative Behavior: The Interaction of Product and Self-Attitudes. In David Gardner (Ed.). *Proceedings of the Second Annual Conference, Association for Consumer Research,* 1971.

17. Havens, A. Eugene. Increasing the Effectiveness of Predicting Innovativeness. *Rural Sociology,* Vol. 30, 1965, p. 158.

18. Jacoby, Jacob. Multiple-Indicant Approach for Studying New Product Adopters. *Journal of Applied Psychology,* Vol. 55, No. 4, 1971(a), pp. 384–88.

19. Jacoby, Jacob. Personality and Innovation Proneness. *Journal of Marketing Research,* Vol. 8, May 1971(b), pp. 244–47.

20. Kiesler, Charles A. *The Psychology of Commitment.* New York: Academic Press, 1971.

21. Kivlin, Joseph E. *Correlates of Family Planning in Eight Indian Villages.* East Lansing: Michigan State University Diffusion of Innovations Research Dept., 1968, p. 38.

22. Kohn, Carol A., and Jacob Jacoby. Patterns of Information Acquisition in New Product Purchases. *Journal of Consumer Research,* Vol. 1, No. 2, 1974, pp. 18–22.

23. Lambert, Zarrel. Perceptual Patterns, Information Handling, and Innovativeness. *Journal of Marketing Research,* Vol. 9, November 1972, pp. 427–31.

24. Loomis, Charles P. In Praise of Conflict and Its Resolution. *American Sociological Review,* Vol. 32, 1967, p. 25.

25. Maloney, John C., and Eugene P. Schonfeld. Social Change and Attitude Change. In G. Zaltman (Ed.). *Processes and Phenomena of Social Change.* New York: Wiley-Interscience, 1973.

26. Mancuso, Joseph. Why Not Create Opinion Leaders for New Product Introductions? *Journal of Marketing,* Vol. 33, July 1969, pp. 20–25.

27. Myers, James, and Thomas S. Robertson. Stability of Self-Designated Opinion Leadership. In S. Ward and P. Wright (Eds.). *Advances in Consumer Research.* Chicago: Association for Consumer Research, 1974.

28. Ostlund, Lyman. Identifying Early Buyers. *Journal of Advertising Research,* Vol. 12, No. 2, pp. 25–30.

29. Pizam, Abraham. Psychological Characteristics of Innovators. *European Journal of Marketing,* Vol. 6, No. 3, 1972, pp. 203–10.

30. Reynolds, Fred, and William Darden. Predicting Opinion Leadership for Women's Clothing Fashions. *Combined Proceedings: Marketing Education and the Real World and Dynamic Marketing in a Changing World.* Chicago: American Marketing Association, 1972.

31. Robertson, Thomas S. Determinants of Innovative Behavior. Paper presented at the American Marketing Association, Washington, D.C., 1967.

32. Robertson, Thomas S. *Innovative Behavior and Communication.* New York: Holt, Rinehart & Winston, 1971, p. 100.

33. Robertson, Thomas S., and John R. Rossiter. Fashion Diffusion: The Interplay of Innovator and Opinion Leader Roles in College Social Systems. Unpublished paper, Graduate School of Business Administration, University of California, 1968.

34. Rogers, Everett M. *Family Planning Communication Strategies.* New York: Free Press, 1973.

35. Rogers, Everett M. *Modernization among Peasants*. New York: Holt, Rinehart & Winston, 1969.
36. Rogers, Everett M., and E. B. de Ramos. Prediction on the Adoption of Innovations: A Progress Report. Paper presented at the Rural Sociological Society, Chicago, 1965, p. 7.
37. Rogers, Everett M., and Floyd Shoemaker. *Communication of Innovations*. New York: Free Press, 1971.
38. Schiffman, Leon. Perceived Risk in New Product Trial by Elderly Consumers. *Journal of Marketing Research*, Vol. 9, February 1972, pp. 106–8.
39. Schiffman, Leon, and Vincent Gaccione. Opinion Leaders in Institutional Markets. *Journal of Marketing*, Vol. 38, No. 2, April 1974, pp. 43–53.
40. Smith, Donald R. A Theoretical and Empirical Analysis of the Adoption-Diffusion of Social Change. Ph.D. Diss., Baton Rouge, Louisiana State University, 1968.
41. Tauber, Edward M. Reduce New Product Failures: Measure Needs as Well as Purchase Interest. *Journal of Marketing*, July 1973, pp. 61–70.
42. Taylor, James. The Role of Risk in Consumer Behavior. *Journal of Marketing*. Vol. 38, No. 2, April 1974.
43. Twedt, Dik Warren. How Important to Marketing Strategy Is the "Heavy User"? *Journal of Marketing Research*, January 1964, pp. 71–72.
44. Uhl, Kenneth, Roman Andrus, and Lance Poulsen. How Are Laggards Different?: An Empirical Inquiry. *Journal of Marketing Research*, Vol. 7, February 1970.
45. Zaltman, Gerald. Introduction. In B. Sternthal and G. Zaltman (Eds.). *Broadening the Concept of Consumer Behavior*. Chicago: Association for Consumer Research, 1976.
46. Zaltman, Gerald. New Perspectives on Diffusion Research. In David Gardner (Ed.). *Proceedings of the Journal of Advertising Research Second Annual Conference, Association for Consumer Research*, 1971.
47. Zaltman, Gerald, and Bernard Dubois. New Conceptual Approaches in the Study of Innovation. In David Gardner (Ed.). *Proceedings of the Second Annual Conference, Innovations and Organizations*. New York: Wiley-Interscience, 1973.
48. Zaltman, Gerald, and Bernard Dubois. New Conceptual Approaches in the Study of Innovation. In David Gardner (Ed.). *Innovations and Organizations*. New York: Wiley-Interscience, 1973.
49. Zaltman, Gerald, and Christian Pinson. Empathetic Ability and Adoption Research. Paper, Northwestern University, 1974(a).
50. Zaltman, Gerald. Perception of New Product Attributes. Paper, Northwestern University, 1974(b).

New Emphases in
Product Planning and
Strategy Development

David S. Hopkins

Experience in identifying, diagnosing and treating problem products and services leads managements naturally to the notion that prevention would be better than cure. A bank vice president speaks for many when he says: "Constructive action tends to be delayed until signs of trouble become so obvious they *demand* attention. We would benefit by a planned approach to the prevention of crises, rather than developing concerted programs to resolve them."

With heightened awareness that problem prevention is the better course, a number of companies have adopted "keep fit" programs for their product lines. Such programs often make provision for improved possibilities for product planning, control, repositioning and stretchout, as well as for augmenting other functional contributions to product management. And, for some, the discipline of strategic planning has offered an invaluable means for reviewing and restructuring the foundations supporting their product lines.

IMPROVEMENTS IN
PRODUCT PLANNING AND CONTROL

The routinization of product audits during company planning cycles has paid off handsomely. Not only do managers get earlier indications of trouble, but the

About the Author: David S. Hopkins is a Senior Research Associate, Marketing Management Research at The Conference Board—a leading nonprofit business research organization. He is the author of "The Short-Term Marketing Plan," "Options in New-Product Organization," and other marketing-oriented studies published by the Board. His previous positions have been in marketing management and research in both the United States and Australia. He holds an M.A. degree from Oxford University, England.

This article is excerpted from: Business Strategies for Problem Products, The Conference Board, Report No. 714. Copyright, 1977, The Conference Board, Inc.

From David S. Hopkins, "New Emphases in Product Planning and Strategy Development," *Industrial Marketing Management Journal*, vol. 6 (1977), pp. 410–419. © 1977 by Elsevier North-Holland, Inc. Reprinted by permission.

planning procedure itself can be bent to bring to notice early those product/market situations that could prove worrisome later on.

Every company needs to plan precisely because it cannot forecast the future with assurance. Some managements acknowledge they have learned this the hard way. Recognition is widespread that, in the past, too many product plans were assembled with insufficient substance and imagination to withstand the unexpected. Numerous plans, for example, have been driven off course in the wake of inflationary turbulence or recession.

With such lessons freshly in mind, many marketers say they are not giving added emphasis to defensive features in their planning. The first line of such defense, as a rule, is a set of early-warning signals to flag significant variances from planned goals. It has become common practice to integrate monitoring procedures within the follow-up stages of short-term marketing planning in such a way that performance can be measured at regular intervals throughout the year.

A number of companies now also seek added flexibility through probabilistic forecasts and through contingency planning against events that are not necessarily expected, but that—if they were to occur—could have a substantial impact on the fate of their wares in the market (i.e., events such as the introduction of a new product by a competitor, a "price war," or a serious sales reversal at an economic turning point).[1] A large engineering company, for one, directs that each of its operating divisions must prepare a sensitivity analysis to allow for variances in budgeted sales and revenues that might be caused by uncontrollable factors. And, as part of its contingency planning, a food processor asks each of its profit centers to allow for the possibilities of higher fuel costs and reimposition of price controls.

To one degree or another, of course, astute marketers have always given thought to tactical shifts in course that might be appropriate under certain circumstances. But, during recent seasons, a number of companies have wired "trigger points" directly to major decisions on strategy. A critical "go/no go" decision, such as that to eliminate a product or to halt a plant expansion, can result.

New flexibility has often come, too, as the result of what one textile company spokesman describes as "improved feedback techniques and a continual monitoring of product and market fit creating a sharper awareness of marketplace dynamics." A large bank now benefits from computer-aided research studies of its markets which reportedly leave management much better placed to judge trends in consumer behavior and to gauge future market opportunities.

A common aim is that of a housewares producer: "To plan and establish strategies that will preclude problem products in the future." Consequently, the first question management in that company is routinely asking of any product at any stage is: "Does it really fulfill a need and enhance our current and future

---

[1] As an alternative to the "most likely" outcome, some also prepare a "worst case" scenario. Others cover a broader range of possibilities, as in the case of the company preparing three contingency plans labeled "A" for Aggressive, "B" for Basic, and "C" for Conservative.

marketing and product strategies?" Other questions that follow are concerned with:

- The adequacy of profit margins, including examination of the price elasticity of demand in the light of rising costs;
- The sufficiency of arrangements for sales, distribution and after-sales servicing;
- The nature and size of promotional expenditures necessary to sustain the product in the marketplace;
- The realistic evaluation of such factors as the stage of the product's life cycle, the extent of market saturation for the product category, and the outlook for competitive moves and counter-moves.

In their planning and reviews of recent years, many companies have devoted especially close attention to the control or suppression of rising costs. In order to distinguish the varying effects of inflation on each cost element, both plans and monitoring devices sometimes incorporate breakdowns of product costs in as fine detail as possible.

Among those going beyond this is a chemical manufacturer, which has become so concerned that the true picture may be distorted and obscured by inflation that it tries to measure "valued-added in real terms." By means of quarterly analyses of the productivity of labor, materials, energy and capital, it tries to gauge its activities with more accuracy.

PRODUCT REPOSITIONING AND STRETCHOUT

Naturally, not all planning measures intended to forestall product problems from arising are defensive in character. Among the positive steps being taken by some firms are planned efforts to give products a more secure life, sometimes by repositioning them.

Thus, to remind its planners of segmentation influences at work, a capital equipment manufacturer includes among its planning forms one that calls for specification of each product line by "the smallest significant division" of its markets—for example, by industry class, type and size of customer, and geographical area. The reported payoff has come in greater precision in pinpointing the best market opportunities, and in devising strategies and tactics for successful breakthrough, perhaps on a narrow front.

In this same company and others, a market segment is defined as an identifiable group of customers with requirements in common that are, or may become, significant in determining a separate product strategy. The nature of these shared requirements varies, of course, from market to market. It is reported for SCM Corporation, for example, that "because of its technical ability centered around the electric portable [it] has been able to carve out a piece of the office typewriter business without a head-on confrontation with the industry leader." According to SCM, it has "less than a 10% share of total office typewriter sales but profits are good" [1].

**One Company's Checklist of
Desirable Attributes for a Product**

"We find that the best strategy is to concentrate the company's resources on winners, and major problems, rather than on mediocre products. Isolation of the problem components is critical. Before launching a new product, or extending the life of a marginal product, we ask ourselves if the following are favorable:

1. Do we have marketing skills and know-how in the product's marketplace?
2. Do we have patent and/or license protection?
3. Do we have good manufacturing technology and the ability to produce economically a *quality* product at competitive cost?
4. Do we have a good raw material base?
5. Is the potential market size large enough for us to devote sufficient marketing, manufacturing and R&D resources to exceed the "critical mass"? That is, the product must be able to support enough good people and plant and lab facilities to exert an aggressive marketing effort.

"Being an innovator is generally a desirable attribute. 'Johnny-come-lately's in most circumstances have a difficult time meeting the above criteria. We must be selective, carefully husbanding resources to expand on products and services where we have strong capabilities."

*Vice president—marketing,
a chemicals company*

For those managements who find that their products are governed by a demonstrable life cycle, it is often possible to sustain them by means of a "stretchout." This may take the form of trying to prolong any favorable phase of the life cycle, or to revive a product—at least temporarily—that has reached the inflection point where there is risk of maturity turning to decline.

AUGMENTING OTHER FUNCTIONAL
CONTRIBUTIONS TO MARKETING

The "marketing concept"—the notion that all company activities should be directed toward satisfying customers at a profit—has by now won ecumenical affirmation within key nonmarketing functions of many companies. And many marketers, for their part, have come to appreciate that marketing plans alone do not always provide a sufficiently broad base for the effective formulation of *business* strategies. One consequence of these trends has often been a commingling of contributions to product strategies from functions other than marketing.

In particular, today's marketers are finding that strategies designed to forestall product problems often require financial considerations to be held at the forefront of their thinking and planning. Awareness that lack of profitability is so often the surest pointer to a problem means, for them, that costs, price and profits are key elements in any product situation analysis (see box below). A few firms have established a position of marketing auditor or marketing controller who, among other duties, audits marketing costs, prices and profitability. In some other cases, firms are testing the introduction of a product-manager mutation, by making such managers *accountable* for profit to a degree somewhat beyond the looser sense of responsibility for success of the product that has traditionally been theirs. Moreover, the tendency for marketing executives to become more financially oriented is being mirrored by the rising frequency with which financial executives are finding themselves much more intimately concerned with questions of product policies and strategies than in the past [2].

Closer working relationships between managers in the marketing function and their counterparts in R&D, engineering and other technical areas are also reported. In some firms, better synchronization of technological development

---

New Financial Emphasis in Product Management

A senior marketing executive in a packaged foods company is one who sees promising changes developing in the marketing function, which should help to keep the health of product lines within acceptable bounds.

In the past, he says, the company's product managers have focused on raising the volume and market share for their assigned products by "fine-tuning" sales promotion, trade deals, advertising, packaging and other elements in the marketing mix. While the product managers had been generally aware of shifts in the profit contribution of their brands, this knowledge had served mainly as a lever for subsequent price changes, and as justification for altering the level of promotional expenditures for a brand. It was rare for any product manager to discuss either the current or prospective profitability of his products with members of the company's financial management group. (Moreover, says this company spokesman, a product manager working for some other companies would actively be discouraged from doing so.)

But, as repeated by a number of other marketers, changes in the marketing climate have stimulated growing attention to cash flow and to return on assets employed. A consequence has been the encouragement of product managers to work hand-in-glove with their counterparts in the financial function. Within the company, there is a belief that this rapprochement—besides being educational for both parties, and encouraging product managers to apply financial criteria in their decision making—will lead to product strategies that are more realistic in the use of corporate resources. Already, for example, the firm's product managers are said to be showing greater alertness to scheduling price changes to allow for fluctuation in the cost of key ingredients for packaged foods.

with marketing development is expected to benefit product-line performances over the long haul. An example is the equipment producer whose work sheets for the annual plan force a separate categorization of proposed engineering expenditures on behalf of a product line, with distinctions made between planned spending on "maintenance" (that is, efforts to improve existing products), on "new products," and on "advanced programs" that are not yet translatable into identifiable products.

Further evidence of better teamwork turns up where the efforts of marketing researchers and of management scientists are being directed more usefully than before to the solution of practical problems in marketing. A number of consumer product marketers express the belief that mathematical models of one kind or another are likely to play a much larger role in future formulations of product strategy.

THE IMPACT OF STRATEGIC PLANNING

Perhaps often of greater significance than the ideas and tools borrowed from other traditional activities in the company has been the adaptation of strategic planning concepts to the management of individual products and product lines. This development appears to be widespread, and no longer confined to the companies most often found among what might be termed the pioneers and "trend setters."

Formal strategic planning has been defined as "the process of sensitizing a business to the opportunities and threats in the external environment, of determining what objectives are desirable and possible, and of deploying resources to match these objectives" [3]. Evangelists for strategic planning have been general management executives at the corporate and divisional levels—and senior members of supporting planning staffs—who are forced to take a synoptic view of their companies' long-term future. Usually a prime concern has been to map the future course for operating divisions or other major business units, within the setting of a "grand strategy" for the corporation as a whole. Yet, for a growing number of firms, some of the same tools are being applied in the planning and evaluation of individual products or product lines.

From the perspective of marketing management, the mix and interdependence of products comprising a line or the multiple lines of a marketing unit is a critically important element of planning. It has been traditional practice to consolidate all the plans for individual products and to relate them somehow to the overall needs, resources and capabilities of the unit (or company) that makes and sells them. If anything seems seriously out of line, it then becomes a matter of "cut and fit," with support for certain products possibly reduced, new high-priority projects started, or other actions taken.

One effect of the diffusion of strategic planning has been to accentuate the already common inclinations to look beyond the immediate planning context. Increasingly, marketing strategies for individual products are no longer determined in isolation, and "consolidation effectiveness" has become an important goal.

Rising Aspirations

If a product stands out as having a low market share or poor growth prospects, it is natural to regard this as a disturbing sign of weakness. Largely under the influence of those philosophies stressed in strategic planning, a number of managements nowadays prefer to limit their companies' product and service offerings to areas in which they are reasonably assured of either high market share or exceptional growth potential.

A few have set ambitious targets for growth, such as the producer of speciality chemicals now requiring that sales of any product retained in its line must advance at an annual rate of 20 to 25% or better. Numerous other firms have set growth targets of a minimum of 10 to 15% a year on the average. (There are many others, of course, that must be content with lesser gains.)

The PIMS Program

The aim of initiators of the PIMS (Profit Impact of Market Strategies) program was to provide information to management on the profit performance of different kinds of businesses under various competitive conditions.[2] It was hoped to "uncover the laws of the marketplace" through a cross-sectional model of major factors influencing ROI. Some findings from a PIMS study during 1970–1972 of 57 corporations, with 620 separate businesses, have been made public. In brief, profit performance was found to be related to at least 37 factors. But a conclusion given prominence was that market share is "one of the main determinants of business profitability." Return on investment (including long-term debt with equity) was found to increase with growth in market share, on average, as follows:

Relationship of Market Share to Profitability

Market Share	ROI
Under 7%	9.6%
7–14	12.0
14–22	13.5
22–36	17.9
Over 36	30.2

The PIMS research team reportedly was also "convinced that in most markets there is a minimum share that is required for viability. . . . If the market

---

[2] The PIMS program, first located at the Harvard Business School, in 1975 became an independent nonprofit organization called the Strategic Planning Institute. The data base is under the custody of the University of Massachusetts at Amherst.

share of a business falls below this minimum, its strategic choices usually boil down to two: increase share or withdraw" [4].

Other key factors said to be influencing profitability among the participating firms, besides market shares, are:

- The quality of the products or services offered. (Those deemed to have superior quality tended to have higher ROI, even to the point that good quality perhaps would partly offset small market share.)
- Investment intensity. (On average, the higher the ratio of total investment to sales, the lower ROI tended to be.)
- The level of marketing expenditures. (While, in general, ROI was found to be diminished by a high level of marketing expenditures, this applied with special force to businesses with products of lower quality.)
- The level of R&D expenditures. (When R&D spending was high, average ROI hit a peak when market share was also high; but ROI plummeted when market share was low.)
- Corporate size and diversity. (*Very* large companies—those with over $1.5 billion in sales—were found to benefit most in profitability from strong market positions, and also from having a diversity of businesses; but results for "low" and "average" size companies were mixed.)

These and other interacting factors in a profit-level equation were reported to have explained close to 80% of the variations in profitability among businesses in the PIMS data base.[3]

The reasons for coveting a position among the market leaders are plain enough. Most important is the belief that a high-share product is likely to have a lower-than-average burden of costs and a higher-than-average potential for profits. The assumed association of high market share with profitability has been endorsed in broad terms by findings of the PIMS program (see box pp. 284–85). The producer of a high-share item may also be assumed to have other advantages, including potential clout to act first in raising (or lowering) product quality standards or prices.

A few firms in a position to consider the possibility now seriously seek not just a high-share portion of the market for their key products, but actual market dominance. Moreover, for a firm to be dominant in a market, they believe it should have a *substantially* larger share of market than that of the next largest competitor. One large manufacturer of industrial products, for instance, aims for a market share equal to at least one and one quarter times that of the nearest competitor within any product/market category. Its management acts on the assumption that problems are likely to gather, and even divestment should be con-

---

[3] This claim, it has been pointed out, is subject to the limitation that the PIMS sample is a self-selected one. Accordingly, the conclusions apply principally to the kinds of consumer and industrial products typically engaged in by large diversified manufacturing companies.

sidered, in any situation where its share is only in the region of a quarter to a half that of the industry leader.

There are numerous companies, of course, for whom such heady possibilities must remain quite remote. Even some managers who are strongly convinced of the advantages of gaining relative market dominance, and whose own products have some chance of attaining it, admit that the costs and the risks in trying to reach and hold the summit are sometimes too high. It is conceded, too, that a product's contribution to profits may be maximized at a level of market share somewhat below the highest attainable peak.

"Portfolio Management"

Questions of appropriate actions relating to industry growth, market share and product mix merge in the concept of "portfolio management." Although intended generally for application to large business units within a corporation, portfolio management has been shown to have applications also in the strategic decision making carried out on behalf of products and product lines.

It is a commonplace of security analysis that, when reviewing a portfolio of stocks and bonds, the analyst is likely to take at least these three steps:

- Determine the objectives of the holder of the portfolio—e.g., as regards yield, growth potential and degree of risk acceptance.
- Categorize each item in the portfolio in terms similar to the objectives.
- Recommend from time to time that certain holdings be reduced or increased in order to give the portfolio balance and conformity with the objectives.

A number of corporations with diversified operations have found a similar approach valuable in appraising their "portfolio" of businesses and products. In particular, some have followed the advice of consultant firms on standard methods of categorization for appraisal purposes. The outcome has been to formalize —and to popularize—the long familiar mode of operation whereby management attaches different objectives, strategies, priorities or action programs to certain units or products of the company than to others.

As part of such exercises, it is sometimes the practice to prepare a matrix where one axis represents market share, or some broader characteristic of the business or product, while the other axis represents the industry/market situation. Table 1 shows the illustrative possibilities.[4]

In the Boston Consulting Group's approach, for instance, the axes used represent market share and market growth, each divided between high and low. Put very simply, the idea is to balance a company's portfolio between three of the four cells in this matrix:

---

[4] These approaches have been described in publications by the firms themselves, and also independently [5]. For some discussion of the first two approaches, see also Ref. [6].

Table 1

Business/Product Axis	Industry/Market Axis	Developed by
Market share	Market growth	The Boston Consulting Group, Inc.
Strategic competitive position	Industry maturity	Arthur D. Little, Inc.
Business strengths	Industry attractiveness	General Electric Corporation

- "Star" businesses, whose high market share and high market growth make for substantial earnings;
- Developing businesses having as yet unrealized potential for future earnings, although located in a high-growth market; and
- Businesses holding a leadership position within a relatively mature market, and thus able to yield a current surplus of cash flow.

Any business falling within the fourth cell—where the axis of low market share crosses the axis of low market growth—is categorized as a "dog." As such, it is seen as having no permanent place in the portfolio and becomes a possible candidate for elimination.

The other approaches cited take a somewhat different tack. Rather than employ a measure of market share itself, they favor broader concepts of "strategic" competitive position," or "business strength," which take into account not only share of market but also the breadth of the product line, the profit margin, the technology involved, special market relationships and other qualitative factors.

The multicell matrix of Arthur D. Little's "strategy centers" concept employs as a market measurement the degree of "maturity" of the industry, e.g., whether it is embryonic, growing, mature or aging. This firm's approach leans toward a practical application of notions about life cycles of businesses or products.

The second axis of the matrix approach favored by General Electric locates an item with respect to relative "industry attractiveness." This, too, is a multi-factor assessment, including many more elements than market growth alone (see Figure 1).

It is not to be supposed, though, that all managements look with favor on any of the variants of the portfolio management approach. One reporting executive, for example, expresses some doubts about the use of what he terms "mechanistic criteria" for classifying products. Another points to the potential error of assuming that a product once labeled as a "dog" will never have any chance of recovery: Witness the case of a diversified corporation whose paper business, which had been hovering on the breakeven point for several years, unexpectedly —and, apparently, permanently—changed for the better at a time of rising demand and prices. And a food company's vice president has declared that his "hesitation to totally embrace this concept as the ultimate answer to brand resource allocation and control is that it may be too superficial—replacing the proper analy-

Strategic Business Planning at General Electric

A GE executive explains that the words "strategic business planning" have been carefully chosen. "To distinguish what was new and different from existing planning activities," he says, "emphasis was placed on the new dimensions of stronger competition and scarce resources. Strategic business planning was designed to add competitive focus, greater alertness to the changing environment, and stronger attention to allocation of scarce resources, thus providing the 'edge' we were looking for." [5]

GE's strategic planning at the corporate level is concerned with, among many other matters, the setting of corporate objectives and goals, and the conducting of "validity reviews" of plans prepared by the line managers for each of some 40 strategic business units into which the company's operations have been divided. A strategic business unit (SBU) is defined as "a unit whose manager has complete responsibility for integrating all functions into a strategy against an identifiable external competitor." Accordingly, the SBU's are of various sizes and fall at various organizational levels.

GE's portfolio strategy is designed to seek to ensure that earnings are sustained in the near term, while investment resources are guided to the better growth opportunities. Rather than merely applying financial measures, such as discounted cash flow/return on investment, management puts emphasis on examining the conditions under which a business can be successful and profitable. An important tool for this purpose is GE's "business screen"—a matrix for which the two dimensions are "business strengths" and "industry attractiveness." Businesses enjoying a medium-to-strong position in a attractive industry fall within the "Invest/Grow" category (light tinted area on Figure 1). Those engaged in industries that are least attractive, or those whose position in their industry is weak, fall within the "Harvest/Divest" category (the dark tinted area shown in Figure 1). And businesses on the hatched diagonal, ranging from either a weak position in an attractive industry to a strong position in a less attractive industry, are in the in-between category dubbed "Selectivity/Earnings."

As listed in the figure, there are about a dozen factors used to help judge the relative strengths of each business and the relative attractiveness of the industry in which it participates. These multiple judgments—made each year, or more often if there has been change in a critical parameter—play a leading role in projecting business performance and in setting priorities for corporate investment. And they are carried through also to GE's management development program, that is, efforts are made (as the executive previously quoted puts it) to "align the entrepreneurial manager with the growth businesses; the more sophisticated, critical manager with businesses where great selectivity is needed; and the more solid, experienced managers for the tough cost control and investment reduction tasks in the weaker businesses."

All line managers are encouraged, when preparing their SBU plans, to search

---

[5] Michael G. Allen, Vice President Corporate Strategy & Systems, General Electric Company, in an internal GE publication, "Organizing and Managing the Planning Function." The bulk of the above material is drawn, with permission, from this publication, and from a second with the title, "Maintaining Strategies for the Future through Current Crises."

for *the critical issue* that will lead their units to future performance gains, and then to develop specific strategies to bring this about. If they wish, they may pose "what if" questions to a variety of strategic planning models, including GE's profit optimizing model nicknamed PROM.[6]

For corporate management, the validity review consists of a line-by-line appraisal of the substance and quality of each SBU plan. Issues that need to be resolved are singled out at this point, such as: "Should the business go for maximum price increase and fixed cost cuts, even if it dictates foregoing volume and market share?" Thus, the GE business screen is just that—a screen to help assess the relative attractiveness of the company's business units for resource allocation purposes. In the process of so doing, key issues, problems and opportunities are highlighted.

Within the SBU's, strategic planning for individual products or product lines is conducted with similar kinds of searching analysis. Each is treated as though it were part of an investment portfolio. It is an approach that, according to report, may sometimes provide early warning of a latent problem.

FIGURE 1   General Electric's Business Screen and Multifactor Assessment

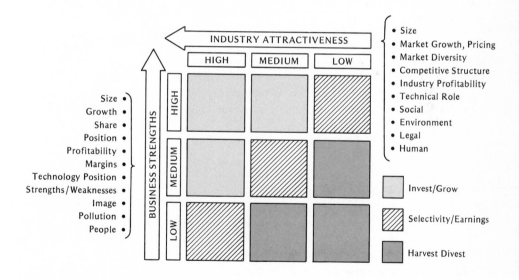

sis of complex business problems with a comparatively easy 'quick fix.'" He believes that "each business profit problem is a unique set of conditions and requires a prognosis and solution to optimize the long-term profitability for that business."[7]

---

[6] The PIMS program (see box pp. 284–85) may be regarded as an offspring of the PROM model first developed internally at General Electric.

[7] William P. Stiritz, Vice President, Grocery Products Division Ralston Purina Company, at The Conference Board's 24th Annual Marketing Conference.

Moreover, users of any kind of a "portfolio package" tend themselves to stress the point that the act of slotting a product into a matrix cell is, necessarily, only a start in planning. It is said to represent no more than a "first cut" at strategy that may be helpful in pointing planners in the right direction, and in ensuring that a uniform method for product evaluation is followed from the outset. The fundamental value of a system of product classification, say its adherents, is not in the matrix notion itself, but rather in the encouragement given managers at all levels to start thinking more about *strategies* relating to their businesses, and less about *numbers* to be entered on planning forms.

Doing What One Does Best

Managements, nowadays, are more likely than in the past to adopt a very tough-minded attitude toward products in an established line. There are general tendencies, too, for managers to be more conscious of the interdependence of all the products or services in a company's portfolio; to be more discriminating and insightful in choosing marketing strategies; and to be more aware that searching only for market opportunities, without also being sensitized to external risks and threats, may represent a new form of marketing myopia. A strong lesson of recent years has been that resources should be directed mainly to those products with the highest return and the best potential, even when this means "red-lining" the others.

Although "Should we be in this business?" is a question still often posed, it may be accompanied nowadays by others—even more probing and specific:

- "What are the company's *core* products and businesses?"
- "How can we win and hold a position of leadership in *each* of these areas?"
- "What *new* businesses should we be entering?"

The search is increasingly for uniqueness, some winning advantage that competitors cannot readily match. Another key question, is: "Where is the leverage?" Someone once said: "If what you have is an abundance of lemons, make lemonade." But the leverage, the unmatched advantage, need not be in a company's physical resources. It may be in low production costs, in technology, in distribution, in marketing expertise, or elsewhere.

"The function of strategy is the function of management," declares the marketing vice president of a forest products company. In his firm, as in others, the imperatives of strategic planning are now being "imprinted" on management behavior, overlaying the imprint of the customer-oriented marketing concept that was so widely felt in earlier years. Whereas product plans and strategies prepared at the operating level were formerly likely to follow a marketing mandate, it is now becoming common practice for them to internalize the needs and resources of the corporation as a whole. A planner in another company speaks of his role as that of a catalyst, "to persuade line managers not to think in terms of product for product's sake, but rather in terms of product for the sake of the

Table 2   Impact of Multibusiness Strategic Planning on Marketing [1]

Marketing Decision Area	Strategy Adopted for Division or Product Line		
	Invest for Future Growth	*Manage for Earnings*	*Manage for Immediate Cash*
Market share	Aggressively build across all segments	Target efforts to high-return/ high-growth segments; Protect current franchises	Forego share development for improved profits
Pricing	Lower to build share	Stabilize for maximum profit contribution	Raise, even at expense of volume
Promotion	Invest heavily to build share	Invest as market dictates	Avoid
Existing product line	Expand volume Add line extensions to fill out product categories	Shift mix to higher profit product categories	Eliminate low-contribution products/varieties
New products	Expand product line by acquisition, self-manufacture or joint venture	Add products selectively and in controlled stages of commitment	Add only sure winners

[1] From Louis V. Gerstner, "Can Strategic Planning Pay Off?", *Business Horizons* (December 1972). Copyright, 1972, by the Foundation for the School of Business at Indiana University. Reprinted by permission.

business," and also "to shift from examining the components of a product's position to examining its dynamics." An illustration of the impact of this kind of thinking on marketing is shown in Table 2.

Perhaps because strategic planning came of age during the economic turbulence of the first half of the 1970s, a number of firms first began to apply its precepts for spotting threats and overcoming weaknesses. Since then, there has been a subtle shift of emphasis in some companies from concern over downside risks to more frequent exploring of upside opportunities.

"We are concerting our efforts where they will do the most good," declares one marketing vice president. "There is much opportunity for expansion and improvement. All we need are people, time and money, and it has become critical to spend these assets wisely."

In seeking answers to probing questions of strategy, it is widely agreed, lies a company's best hope of avoiding problem products in the future.

REFERENCES

1. *The SCM Corporation: A Profile,* published by SCM.
2. Gerstner, Louis V., and Anderson, M. Helen, The Chief Financial Officer as Activist, *Harvard Bus. Rev.* (September–October 1976).
3. Cross, Hershner, Senior Vice President, General Electric Company, in an address on "New Directions in Corporate Planning" to the Operations Research Society of America, Milwaukee (May 10, 1973).
4. Schoeffler, Sidney, Buzzell, Robert D., and Heany, Donald F., Impact of Strategic Planning on Profit Performance, *Harvard Bus. Rev.* (March–April 1974); Buzzell, Robert D., Gale, Bradley T., and Sultan, Ralph G. M., Market Share—A Key to Profitability, *Harvard Bus. Rev.* (January–February 1975).
5. *BusinessWeek* (April 28, 1975).
6. Brown, James K., and O'Connor, Rochelle, *Planning and the Corporate Planning Director,* The Conference Board, Report No. 627 (1974).

Planning Product Line Strategy: A Matrix Approach

Yoram Wind and Henry J. Claycamp

Development of a strategic plan for the existing product line is the most critical element of a company's marketing planning activity. In designing such plans, management needs accurate information on the current and anticipated performance of its products. This information should encompass both (1) consumer evaluation of the company's products, particularly their strengths and weaknesses vis à vis competition (i.e., product positioning by market segment information); and (2) "objective" information on actual and anticipated product performance on relevant criteria such as sales, profits, and market share.

Whereas much has been written in recent years about the use of product positioning in strategic marketing planning,[1] little new information has been published about formal methods of using the product's actual and anticipated performance characteristics in terms of sales, profits, and market share as inputs to the design of a strategic marketing plan for the firm's existing product line. Several attempts have been made to use product sales (or, more explicitly, stage in the product life cycle) as a guideline for marketing strategy, including specific recommendations on items such as the type and level of advertising, pricing, and distribution.[2] Yet these recommendations have usually been vague, nonoperational, not empirically supported, and conceptually questionable, since

About the Authors: Yoram Wind is professor of marketing in the Wharton School, University of Pennsylvania, Philadelphia; Henry J. Claycamp is vice president of marketing, International Harvester Company, Chicago.

Reprinted from *Journal of Marketing*, vol. 40 (January 1976), pp. 2–9, published by the American Marketing Association.

[1] Yoram Wind, "The Perception of a Firm's Competitive Position," in *Behavioral Models of Market Analysis: Foundations of Marketing Action,* Francesco M. Nicosia and Yoram Wind, eds. (Hinsdale, Ill.: Dryden Press, in press).

[2] See, for example: Gosta Mickwitz, *Marketing and Competition* (Helsingfors, Finland: Centraltrykeriet, 1959); Jay W. Forrester, "Advertising: A Problem in Industrial Dynamics," *Harvard Business Review,* Vol. 37 (March–April 1959), p. 100; Eberhard E. Schewing, *New Product Management* (Hinsdale, Ill.: Dryden Press, 1974); and Robert D. Buzzell et al., *Marketing: A Contemporary Analysis,* 2nd. ed. (New York: McGraw-Hill Book Co., 1972).

they imply that strategies can be developed with little concern for the product's profitability and market share position.[3]

In the 1970s, some attention has been given to various aspects of sales, market share, and profitability as guidelines for marketing planning. Most notable of these efforts are the Marketing Science Institute's PIMS (Profit Impact of Market Strategy) project, which examines the determinants of profitability in the modern corporation,[4] and the Boston Consulting Group's product portfolio analysis.[5] These approaches do not, however, provide a comprehensive approach for product line planning based on all three measures—sales, market share, and profitability—which are integrally tied to positioning the product by market segment. The objective of this article is to outline such an approach, based on the development of a product evaluation matrix.

THE PROPOSED APPROACH

The proposed approach to strategic product line planning has two definitional phases followed by five analytical stages. The definitional phases relate to the determination of the strategic product/market area under consideration and the relevant measurement instruments. The analytical phases include: (1) determination of current and past trends for the product line in terms of industry sales, company sales, market share, and profit; (2) integration of these four scales into a single analytical framework, the *product evaluation matrix;* (3) projection of future performance given (a) *no* changes in marketing strategy or competitive or environmental conditions, and (b) a variety of alternative marketing strategies; (4) performance of additional diagnostic analyses to provide further guidelines for the firm's marketing strategies; and (5) incorporation of possible competitive actions and changes in environmental conditions into projection analysis.

The Definitional Phases

Phase A Define the relevant universe in terms of the relevant strategic product/market area. This requires determination of:

1. *The Product* of concern. The product definitions should be clear and unambiguous, and in all cases they should include the relevant subcategories of the product class at both the company and industry levels.

---

[3] For an evaluation of the product life cycle literature, see: Rolando Polli and Victor J. Cook, "Product Life Cycle Models: A Review Paper" (Working paper, Marketing Science Institute, Cambridge, Mass., 1967); Rolando Polli and Victor J. Cook, "Validity of the Product Life Cycle," *The Journal of Business,* Vol. 42 (October 1969), pp. 385–400; and William E. Cox, "Product Life Cycles as Marketing Models," *The Journal of Business,* Vol. 40 (October 1967), pp. 375–384.

[4] Sidney Schoeffler, Robert Buzzell, and Donald Heany, "PIMS: A Breakthrough in Strategic Planning" (Working paper, Marketing Science Institute, Cambridge, Mass., 1974); and Bernard Catry and Michel Chevalier, "Market Share Strategy and the Product Life Cycle," *Journal of Marketing,* Vol. 38 (October 1974), pp. 29–34.

[5] The Boston Consulting Group, *Product Portfolio,* undated brochure.

2. *The Strategic Market* for the given product and the key segments within it. Again, the more specific the definition is, the more operational the resulting analysis will be. For example, separating the domestic from the international market for automobiles (excluding trucks) can be the first step toward establishing the strategic market for automobiles. Within this broad strategic area, further segmentation can be undertaken, for example, by separating the commercial market from the private market. This can provide sharper focus and meaning to the analysis of the product life cycle of subcompact, compact, intermediate, standard, sport, and luxury automobiles.

Phase B Establish the relevant measurement instruments in terms of units (e.g., dollar sales or unit sales), necessary adjustments (e.g., sales per capita), and time (e.g., quarterly or annually).

The Analytical Phases

Phase A Determine and examine the current and past trends in product sales, market share, and profit position in each relevant strategic product/market area. Specifically, it is necessary to establish the following:

1. *Sales Position* for the given product in the strategic market area. Two simple plots of industry and company sales against time are required, followed by the identification of the stage of the product in the classical product life cycle. Each product can be assigned to one of at least three product trend stages: decline, stable (which can in turn be separated into decaying and sustained maturity), and growth. The assignment of a product to one of these three or four categories can be based on the rule established by Polli and Cook [6] or on any other explicit criterion. A sample alternative criterion is:

If the annual sales trend over the past N years is:

- Negative, assign to the *Decline* category.
- 0%–10% increase, assign to the *Stable* category.
- Over 10% increase, assign to the *Growth* category.

The determination of the specific criterion and number of categories is, of course, the responsibility of management, and it is likely to differ across industries and companies.

2. *Market Share Position.* The market share of the company's given product in the strategic product/market area should also be determined. As with the

---

[6] The Polli and Cook approach is based on the percentage change in a product's real sales from one year to the next. Plotting these changes as a normal distribution with mean zero, they determined that if a product has a percentage change less than $.5\sigma$, it is to be classified as in the decline stage. Products with a percentage change greater than $.5\sigma$ were classified as being in the growth stage, and products in the range $\pm.5\sigma$ were considered to be stable. For the application of this approach, see Rolando Polli and Victor J. Cook, "Validity of the Product Life Cycle," *The Journal of Business,* Vol. 42 (October 1969).

number of sales trend categories and the criterion for category assignment, it is also the responsibility of management to determine the number of market share categories and the assignment criterion. For illustrative purposes, three categories and their corresponding assignment rules are as follows:

- If market share is less than 10%, assign to the *Marginal* category.
- If market share is 10%–24%, assign to the *Average* category.
- If market share is over 25%, assign to the *Leading* category.

The market share figures that establish the three categories may, of course, vary from one strategic product/market area to another.

This stage assumes the availability of market share data. In many product areas, such data are available through services such as Nielsen or the Market Research Corporation of America (MRCA). In other areas, a firm may have to rely on expert estimates or relevant secondary sources.[7]

3. *Profit Position.* The firm's profit position in the given strategic product/market area must be specified. Again, it is management's responsibility to establish explicit profit categories. These categories—whether based on return on sales, investment, or equity—should be stated explicitly, and at least three levels should be established to distinguish between *below target, target,* and *above target* profit performance.

The three separate analyses of sales, market share, and profitability result in the assignment of each product, in each of the market segments of any given strategic product/market area, into one category in each of the three areas. This is illustrated in Figure 1, which also includes the plotting of the past trends in company and industry sales, market share, and profitability.

Phase B Once the unidimensional analysis suggested in Phase A is completed, it is necessary to combine the four unidimensional scales—for industry sales, company sales, market share, and profit—into a comprehensive scheme. The integration of the four dimensions into a single analytical framework constitutes the *product evaluation matrix,* which is presented in Figure 2. Positioning all products within this matrix, based on hard data on sales, market share, and profitability, is an essential input to all marketing decisions.

A more advanced approach might be one in which each of the four dimensions is presented as a continuous variable and not as a categorical one that is based on some arbitrary decision rule. Yet, even the simple positioning of a product within this matrix provides clear understanding of the current position of the product on those dimensions that are most relevant for managerial control. Conducting such an analysis for all relevant segments of a product/market strategic area provides management with a summary auditing form that highlights the strengths and weaknesses of the firm's product line in all of its market segments.

This picture of product performance (based on current hard data) can be

[7] Louis W. Stern, "Market Share Determination: A Low Cost Approach," *Journal of Marketing Research,* Vol. 1 (August 1964), pp. 40–45.

FIGURE 1 Establishing a Product's Sales, Market Share, and Profit Position (Current and Past Trends)

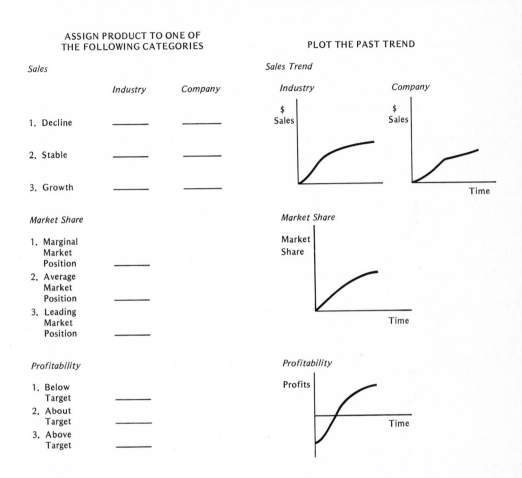

supplemented by a historical trend analysis of the changes in the product's performance over time. Figure 2 also shows a hypothetical path for two products over a three-year period. Product A has been in a growth industry for these three years. In 1973, its company sales were at a stable level, but they did increase to the growth level in 1974 and 1975. Its market share position improved considerably from a marginal share in 1973 to an average share in 1974 and 1975. The major improvement, however, occurred with respect to its profit performance, moving from below target in 1973 to target in 1974 and above target in 1975.

Examination of the performance of hypothetical product B, however, reveals a bleak situation. The product is in a declining industry; its company sales decreased from 1973 to 1974; and while it maintained an "average market share" in 1973 and 1974, its share weakened to marginal in 1975. The only positive sign is that during these three years profits did not decline.

FIGURE 2 The Product Evaluation Matrix: A Hypothetical Example Tracing Two Products over Three Years

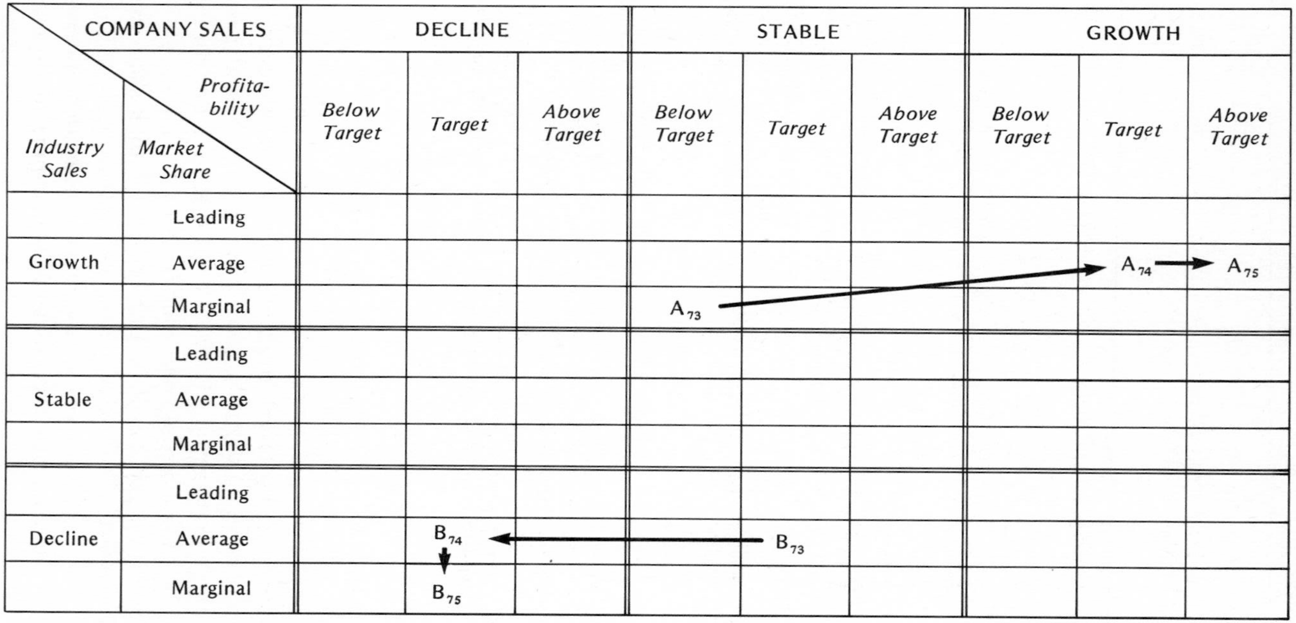

COMPANY SALES		DECLINE			STABLE			GROWTH		
Industry Sales / Profita-bility / Market Share		Below Target	Target	Above Target	Below Target	Target	Above Target	Below Target	Target	Above Target
Growth	Leading									
	Average				A_{73}				A_{74} → A_{75}	
	Marginal									
Stable	Leading									
	Average									
	Marginal									
Decline	Leading									
	Average		B_{74}			B_{73}				
	Marginal		B_{75}							

298

Phase C Although the product evaluation matrix provides a useful tool for controlling the performance of the firm's product line and answering the question "where are we?" it alone cannot serve as a guide for future market actions. To provide such a guide, the analysis must incorporate an orientation to the future and the anticipated impact of alternative corporate marketing strategies. This is achieved by the following two steps:

1. Project the trend in sales, market share, and profitability assuming *no changes* in the firm's marketing strategies and no major changes in competitive actions and environmental conditions. This projection can be based on simple extrapolation of time series data or on any other forecasting procedure used by the firm. It should be done for each product in the strategic product/market area and should provide a range of possible results between the most pessimistic and most optimistic forecasts.

A simplified example of the current and projected positions of two hypothetical products is presented in the first eight columns in the upper panel of Figure 3. These data can then be transferred to the product evaluation matrix (the bottom part of Figure 3) to provide a clear picture of the anticipated trend in the position of each product. At this stage (even without engaging in conditional forecasting), the product evaluation matrix can start providing some useful guidance for the firm's product/marketing strategy for each of its products in the given strategic product/market area.

Product 1 is clearly a poor performer. It is in a declining industry, with declining sales, average market share, and below-target profitability, and if nothing is to change it is likely to stay in this situation (comparison of 1_C with 1_P). Product 2, on the other hand, is in a stable industry and is expected to increase its sales (moving from a "decline" to a "stable" level in this category), while its market share position and profitability do not change (a move from 2_C to 2_P).

2. Since the future performance of a product depends to a large extent on the firm's marketing efforts, a *conditional forecast* should be undertaken in which the sales, market share, and profit of each product are forecast under a variety of marketing strategies. Given a number of alternative marketing strategies, a separate forecasting analysis should be conducted for each and the results of the "best" strategy (according to the four dimensions) incorporated into the product evaluation matrix. If no dominant solution (i.e., "best" on all four dimensions) is revealed, all "best" strategies are to be incorporated into the matrix, as illustrated in Figure 3.

Product 1 has two alternative conditional forecasts. Forecast $1'_{CF}$ suggests no change in the sales position (it remains in a declining industry with decreasing company sales), worsening of market share (from average to marginal), but an improvement in profits from below target to target. A second marketing strategy, however, may result in position $1''_{CF}$, which enables the company to maintain an average market share, increase its sales (from "decline" to "stable" stage), but produces no improvement in its profit position, which remains below target. As-

FIGURE 3 Incorporating Sales, Market Share, and Profit Forecasts into the Product Evaluation Matrix: A Hypothetical Example

Product	CURRENT POSITION (C)				UNCONDITIONAL PROJECTION (P)				CONDITIONAL FORECAST (CF)			
	Industry Sales	Company Sales	Market Share	Profitability	Industry Sales	Company Sales	Market Share	Profitability	Industry Sales	Company Sales	Market Share	Profitability
1	Decline	Decline	Av.	Below Target	Decline	Decline	Av.	Below Target	Decline	Decline	Marg.	Target
2	Stable	Decline	Av.	Target	Stable	Stable	Av.	Above Target	Stable	Stable	Dom.	Target

COMPANY SALES	DECLINE			STABLE			GROWTH		
Profitability / Market Share / Industry Sales	Below Target	Target	Above Target	Below Target	Target	Above Target	Below Target	Target	Above Target
Growth — Dominant									
Growth — Average									
Growth — Marginal									
Stable — Dominant									
Stable — Average				$1''_{CF}$	2_P / 2_{CF}				
Stable — Marginal									
Decline — Dominant									
Decline — Average	1_C / 1_P	$1'_{CF}$							
Decline — Marginal									

Key: 1, 2 products   C = current   P = projected position
CF = expected position based on results of a conditional forecast analysis.

suming that only these two strategies are available, management should examine the trade-off between maintaining market share position but being below target on profits versus losing market share but achieving profit objectives.

Product 2, on the other hand, has a single "best" conditional forecast that moves the product from 2_C to 2_{CF}. This suggests that the marketing strategy behind this forecast is likely to result in an improved market share position (from average for 2_P to dominant for 2_{CF}).

Phase D To provide further guidelines for the firm's marketing strategies within the strategic product/market area, management may want to make additional diagnoses. Among the more useful diagnostic analyses are those that relate to the competitive structure and the effectiveness of the marketing efforts of the firm. Some of this information may be obtained as a by-product of the conditional forecast analyses, but some may require special studies.

Some of the more useful diagnostic tools are those that focus on the product's competitive position—product positioning [8] and brand-switching matrices—and on the effectiveness of the various marketing strategies, that is, promotion, distribution, and price. These diagnostic analyses can be undertaken using simple graphical analysis (e.g., plotting advertising expenditures or number of outlets against sales or market share or profitability), or they may take advantage of any one of a number of appropriate multivariate statistical techniques, such as multiple regression analysis. Such an analysis could establish the relative importance of each of the pertinent marketing variables for determining the firm's sales, market share, and profits. This, in turn, could result in three critical equations—one for sales, one for market share, and one for profits—that, in the simplified linear case, would be of the form:

$$Y = a + b_1 A - b_2 P + b_3 D$$

where:

$Y =$ Sales, market share, or profits
$A =$ The appropriate measures of advertising and promotion (e.g., dollars spent on advertising)
$P =$ The appropriate measure of price (e.g., actual price)
$D =$ The appropriate measure of distribution (e.g., percent of effective distribution obtained)
$b_1, b_2, b_3 =$ Parameter values, which are estimated separately for each equation

Phase E The analysis so far has not included an explicit consideration of competitive actions and changes in environmental conditions. To incorporate

---

[8] Yoram Wind and Patrick J. Robinson, "Product Positioning: An Application of Multidimensional Scaling," in *Attitude Research in Transition,* Russell I. Haley, ed. (Chicago: American Marketing Assn., 1972), pp. 155–175; and Yoram Wind, "A New Procedure for Concept Evaluation," *Journal of Marketing,* Vol. 37 (October 1973), pp. 2–11.

these factors into the analysis, a market simulation model is called for. Such a simulation can be developed for a given strategic product/market area and be based on four major phases, all of which should result in simulated information on sales, market share, and profit for each of a set of marketing alternatives. These four phases include analysis under the following conditions:

1. No competitive retaliation and no changes in any major environmental factors;
2. Competitive retaliation but no changes in environmental conditions;
3. Changes in environmental conditions but no competitive retaliation;
4. Competitive retaliation and changes in environmental conditions.

Operationally, such a simulation may be based on a large-scale consumer study coupled with managers' subjective judgments. The consumer study should be aimed at establishing the following input base:

1. Consumers' utilities for various components of any marketing strategy (benefits sought). These utilities can be derived from a conjoint measurement analysis.[9]
2. Evaluation of the products of the firm and its competitors on the relevant benefits.
3. Assessment of the possible impact of different environmental conditions on consumers' utilities for the various benefits and their evaluations of the available product/brand offerings.

A market simulation based on this, a similar,[10] or even a different, structure[11] can serve both as a useful planning tool and as a way of generating inputs for the product evaluation matrix. In the latter context, the simulation can result in estimated sales and market share for any given product under a variety of alternative marketing strategies, anticipated competitive action, and alternative environmental conditions. To provide inputs on the anticipated profitability, it might be useful to couple the market simulation with an appropriate subjective risk analysis or simulation.[12] Thus, information on all four dimensions— industry sales, company sales, market share, and profits—can be incorporated into the product evaluation matrix in the same way that the information from

---

[9] Paul E. Green and Yoram Wind, *Multiattribute Decisions in Marketing: A Measurement Approach* (Hinsdale, Ill.: The Dryden Press, 1973); and Paul E. Green and Yoram Wind, "New Way to Measure Consumers' Judgment," *Harvard Business Review,* Vol. 53 (July–August 1975), pp. 107–117.

[10] Yoram Wind, Steuart Joley, and Arthur O'Connor, "Concept Testing as Input to Strategic Marketing Simulations," in *Proceedings of the April 1975 AMA Conference,* Ed Mazze, ed. (Chicago: American Marketing Assn., forthcoming).

[11] Philip Kotler, "Competitive Strategies for New Product Marketing Over the Life Cycle," *Management Science,* Vol. 12 (December 1965), pp. 104–119.

[12] David Hergz, "Risk Analysis in Capital Investment," *Harvard Business Review,* Vol. 42 (January–February 1964), pp. 91–106; and Edgar A. Pessemier and H. Paul Root, "The Dimensions of New Product Planning," *Journal of Marketing,* Vol. 37 (January 1973), pp. 10–18.

the conditional forecast analysis was incorporated into the matrix, as illustrated in Figure 3.

CONCLUSIONS

A firm's major strategic product/market decision alternatives for its existing product line and the component products of that line in a given strategic product/market area are:

1. Do not change the product or its marketing strategy.
2. Do not change the product but do change its marketing strategy. This may involve a change in the type and level of advertising, distribution, and pricing strategies associated with a given positioning and given product attributes.
3. Change the product. This can involve product modifications either within the boundaries of the product's current market positioning or within a new positioning. Alternatively, it may involve no product modifications but rather a repositioning. In either case, a change in the associated marketing strategy is required.
4. Discontinue the product or the product line. This strategy may involve an interim product or product line "run out" (milking) strategy, pruning of the product line, or the immediate phasing-out of the product or the complete line.[13]
5. Introduce new product(s) into the line or add new product lines.

Traditional product life cycle analysis provides little guidance for making these decisions. It ignores the competitive setting of the product, the relevant profit considerations, and the fact that product sales are a function of the marketing effort of the firm and other environmental forces. The objective of this article was to propose a way of overcoming these shortcomings by taking these variables into account and hence providing management with the necessary product evaluation information for making the above decisions.

The results of experimentation with this approach in the International Harvester Company are encouraging, and the approach is now used on a regular basis in the preparation of all the firm's marketing plans. It is our belief that following the suggested approach (whether using the suggested criteria of sales, market share, and profitability, or others) may improve the strategic product/marketing decisions of industrial and consumer products companies.

The proposed approach requires five levels of analysis, each with an increasing specificity of guidance, for the firm's strategic marketing decisions. The first level is based on the evaluation of the product's current position with

---

[13] Walter J. Talley, Jr., "Profiting from the Declining Product," *Business Horizons*, Vol. 7 (Spring 1964), pp. 77–84; and Philip Kotler, "Phasing Out Weak Products," *Harvard Business Review*, Vol. 43 (March–April 1965), pp. 107–118.

Table 1 Levels of Analysis and Specificity of Guidance Provided by the Product Evaluation Matrix

Specificity of Guidance	Nature of Operation	Stage in the Analysis
Lowest	1. Current product position on industry sales, company sales, market share, and profitability	A and B
	2. Projected product position on sales, market share, and profitability, assuming no major changes in the firm's marketing activities, competitive action, and environmental conditions	C-1
	3. Projected product position on sales, market share, and profitability under alternative marketing strategies (conditional forecast), assuming no major changes in competitive action and environmental conditions	C-2
	4. The above plus diagnostic insights into the competitive structure and the effectiveness of the firm's marketing activities.	D
Highest	5. Projected product position on sales, market share, and profitability under alternative marketing strategies, anticipated competitive action, and alternative environmental conditions (based on computer simulation)	E

regard to industry and company sales, market share, and profitability, and it provides the vaguest and most limited guidance. The fifth level, on the other hand, provides detailed and specific guidance based on projected product position with regard to sales, market share, and profitability under alternative marketing strategies, anticipated competitive actions, and alternative environmental conditions. Table 1 summarizes these five levels of analysis.

Not every product/market situation requires the complete analysis at all five levels. Even in its simplest form (level 1) the product evaluation matrix goes well beyond traditional product life cycle analysis and offers valuable guidelines for product line management. Product performance information based on *hard data* on sales, market share, and profitability by strategic product/market units puts into context the commonly collected consumer-based positioning/segmentation information. The approach can also be applied to competitive products, thus providing management with an ongoing performance audit of its own and competitors' products.

Pricing Policies
for New Products

Joel Dean

How to price a new product is a top management puzzle that is too often solved by cost-theology and hunch. This article suggests a pricing policy geared to the dynamic nature of a new product's competitive status. Today's high rate of innovation makes the economic evolution of a new product a strategic guide to practical pricing.

New products have a protected distinctiveness which is doomed to progressive degeneration from competitive inroads. The invention of a new marketable specialty is usually followed by a period of patent protection when markets are still hesitant and unexplored and when product design is fluid.

Then comes a period of rapid expansion of sales as market acceptance is gained.

Next the product becomes a target for competitive encroachment. New competitors enter the field, and innovations narrow the gap of distinctiveness between the product and its substitutes. The seller's zone of pricing discretion narrows as his distinctive "specialty" fades into a pedestrian "commodity" which is so little differentiated from other products that the seller has limited independence in pricing, even if rivals are few.

Throughout the cycle, continual changes occur in promotional and price elasticity and in costs of production and distribution. These changes call for adjustments in price policy.

About the Author: Now president of Joel Dean Associates and professor of business economics at Columbia University, Mr. Dean was formerly on the faculty of the University of Chicago. During World War II, he was head of machinery price control and later of fuel rationing. Books he has written include *Managerial Economics* (Prentice-Hall, 1951), *Capital Budgeting* (Columbia University Press, 1951), and *Statistical Cost Estimation* (Indiana University Press, 1976).

Joel Dean, "Pricing Policies for New Products," *Harvard Business Review*, November–December 1976. Reprinted from E. C. Bursk and J. F. Chapman, eds., *Modern Marketing Strategies* (Cambridge, Mass.: Harvard University Press, 1964). Copyright © 1950, 1964 by the President and Fellows of Harvard College.

NOTE: For major assistance in preparing this article, I am indebted to Stephen Taylor of Joel Dean Associates. Professors James Bonbright and Carl Shoup and Mr. Samuel Richman of the Graduate School of Business, Columbia University, were kind enough to read the manuscript and make suggestions.

Appropriate pricing over the cycle depends on the development of three different aspects of maturity, which usually move in almost parallel time paths:

1. Technical maturity, indicated by declining rate of product development, increasing standardization among brands, and increasing stability of manufacturing processes and knowledge about them.
2. Market maturity, indicated by consumer acceptance of the basic service idea, by widespread belief that the products of most manufacturers will perform satisfactorily, and by enough familiarity and sophistication to permit consumers to compare brands competently.
3. Competitive maturity, indicated by increasing stability of market shares and price structures.

Of course, interaction among these components tends to make them move together. That is, intrusion by new competitors helps to develop the market, but entrance is most tempting when the new product appears to be establishing market acceptance.

The rate at which the cycle of degeneration progresses varies widely among products. What are the factors that set its pace? An overriding determinant is technical—the extent to which the economic environment must be reorganized to use the innovation effectively. The scale of plant investment and technical research called forth by the telephone, electric power, the automobile, or air transport makes for a long gestation period, as compared with even such major innovations as cellophane or frozen foods.

Development comes fastest when the new gadget fills a new vacuum made to order for it. Electric stoves, as one example, have risen to 50% market saturation in the fast-growing Pacific Northwest, where electric power has become the lowest cost energy.

Products still in early developmental stages also provide rich opportunities for product differentiation, which with heavy research costs holds off competitive degeneration.

But aside from technical factors, the rate of degeneration is controlled by economic forces that can be subsumed under rate of market acceptance and ease of competitive entry.

By *market acceptance* is meant the extent to which buyers consider the product a serious alternative to other ways of performing the same service. Market acceptance is a frictional factor. The effect of cultural lags may endure for some time after quality and costs make products technically useful. The slow catch-on of the "electric pig" (garbage-disposal unit) is an example.

On the other hand, the attitude of acceptance may exist long before any workable model can be developed; then the final appearance of the product will produce an explosive growth curve in sales. The antihistamine cold tablet, a spectacular example, reflects the national faith in chemistry's ability to vanquish the common cold. And, of course, low unit price may speed market acceptance of an innovation; ball-point pens and all-steel houses started at about the same time, but look at the difference in their sales curves.

Ease of competitive entry is a major determinant of the speed of degeneration of a specialty. An illustration is found in the washing machine business before the war, where with little basic patent protection the Maytag position was quickly eroded by small manufacturers who performed essentially an assembly operation. The ball-point pen cascaded from a $12 novelty to a 49-cent "price football," partly because entry barriers of patents and techniques were ineffective. Frozen orange juice, which started as a protected specialty of Minute Maid, is speeding through its competitive cycle, with competing brands now crowding into the market.

At the outset the innovator can control the rate of competitive deterioration to an important degree by nonprice as well as by price strategies. Through successful research in product improvement he can protect his specialty position both by extending the life of his basic patent and by keeping ahead of competitors in product development. The record of the International Business Machines punch-card equipment illustrates this potentiality. Ease of entry is also affected by a policy of stay-out pricing (so low as to make the prospects look uninviting), which under some circumstances may slow down the process of competitive encroachment.

STEPS IN PIONEER PRICING

Pricing problems start when a company finds a product that is a radical departure from existing ways of performing a service and that is temporarily protected from competition by patents, secrets of production, control at the point of a scarce resource, or by other barriers. The seller here has a wide range of pricing discretion resulting from extreme product differentiation.

A good example of pricing latitude conferred by protected superiority of product is provided by the McGraw Electric Company's "Toastmaster," which, both initially and over a period of years, was able to command a very substantial price premium over competitive toasters. Apparently this advantage resulted from (a) a good product that was distinctive and superior and (b) substantial and skillful sales promotion.

Similarly, Sunbeam priced its electric iron $2 above comparable models of major firms with considerable success. And Sunbeam courageously priced its new metal coffeemaker at $32, much above competitive makes of glass coffeemakers, but it was highly successful.

To get a picture of how a manufacturer should go about setting his price in the pioneer stage, let me describe the main steps of the process (of course the classification is arbitrary and the steps are interrelated): (a) estimate of demand, (b) decision on market targets, (c) design of promotional strategy, and (d) choice of distribution channels.

Estimate of Demand

The problem at the pioneer stage differs from that in a relatively stable monopoly because the product is beyond the experience of buyers and because

the perishability of its distinctiveness must be reckoned with. How can demand for new products be explored? How can we find out how much people will pay for a product that has never before been seen or used? There are several levels of refinement to this analysis.

The initial problem of estimating demand for a new product can be broken into a series of subproblems: (a) whether the product will go at all (assuming price is in a competitive range), (b) what range of price will make the product economically attractive to buyers, (c) what sales volumes can be expected at various points in this price range, and (d) what reaction will price produce in manufacturers and sellers of displaced substitutes.

The first step is an exploration of the *preferences and educability of consumers,* always, of course, in the light of the technical feasibility of the new product. How many potential buyers are there? Is the product a practical device for meeting their needs? How can it be improved to meet their needs better? What proportion of the potential buyers would prefer, or could be induced to prefer, this product to already existing products (prices being equal)?

Sometimes it is feasible to start with the assumption that all vulnerable substitutes will be fully displaced. For example, to get some idea of the maximum limits of demand for a new type of reflecting-sign material, a company started with estimates of the aggregate number and area of auto license plates, highway markers, railroad operational signs, and name signs for streets and homes. Next, the proportion of each category needing night-light reflection was guessed. For example, it was assumed that only rural and suburban homes could benefit by this kind of name sign, and the estimate of need in this category was made accordingly.

It is not uncommon and possibly not unrealistic for a manufacturer to make the blithe assumption at this stage that the product price will be "within a competitive range" without having much idea of what that range is. For example, in developing a new type of camera equipment, one of the electrical companies judged its acceptability to professional photographers by technical performance without making any inquiry into its economic value. When the equipment was later placed in an economic setting, the indications were that sales would be negligible.

The second step is marking out this *competitive range of price.* Vicarious pricing experience can be secured by interviewing selected distributors who have enough comparative knowledge of customers' alternatives and preferences to judge what price range would make the new product "a good value." Direct discussions with representative experienced industrial users have produced reliable estimates of the "practical" range of prices. Manufacturers of electrical equipment often explore the economic as well as the technical feasibility of a new product by sending engineers with blueprints and models to see customers, such as technical and operating executives.

In guessing the price range of a radically new consumers' product of small unit value, the concept of barter equivalent can be a useful research guide.

For example, a manufacturer of paper specialties tested a dramatic new product in the following fashion: A wide variety of consumer products totally

unlike the new product were purchased and spread out on a big table. Consumers selected the products they would swap for the new product. By finding out whether the product would trade even for a dish pan, a towel, or a hairpin, the executives got a rough idea of what range of prices might strike the typical consumer as reasonable in the light of the values she could get for her money in totally different kinds of expenditures.

But asking prospective consumers how much they think they would be willing to pay for a new product, even by such indirect or disguised methods, may often fail to give a reliable indication of the demand schedule. Most times people just do not know what they would pay. It depends partly on their income and on future alternatives. Early in the postwar period a manufacturer of television sets tried this method and got highly erratic and obviously unreliable results because the distortion of war shortages kept prospects from fully visualizing the multiple ways of spending their money.

Another deficiency, which may, however, be less serious than it appears, is that responses are biased by the consumer's confused notion that he is bargaining for a good price. Not until techniques of depth interviewing are more refined than they are now can this crude and direct method of exploring a new product's demand schedule hold much promise of being accurate.

One appliance manufacturer tried out new products on a sample of employes by selling to them at deep discounts, with the stipulation that they could if they wished return the products at the end of the experiment period and get a refund of their low purchase price. Demand for foreign orange juice was tested by placing it in several markets at three different prices, ranging around the price of fresh fruit; the result showed rather low price elasticity.

While inquiries of this sort are often much too short-run to give any real indication of consumer tastes, the relevant point here is that even such rough probing often yields broad impressions of price elasticity, particularly in relation to product variations such as styling, placing of controls, and use of automatic features. It may show, for example, that $5 of cost put into streamlining or chromium stripping can add $50 to the price.

The third step, a more definite inquiry into the *probable sales from several possible prices,* starts with an investigation of the prices of substitutes. Usually the buyer has a choice of existing ways of having the same service performed; an analysis of the costs of these choices serves as a guide in setting the price for a new way.

Comparisons are easy and significant for industrial customers who have a costing system to tell them the exact value, say, of a fork-lift truck in terms of warehouse labor saved. Indeed, chemical companies setting up a research project to displace an existing material often know from the start the top price that can be charged for the new substitute in terms of cost of the present material.

But in most cases the comparison is obfuscated by the presence of quality differences that may be important bases for price premiums. This is most true of household appliances, where the alternative is an unknown amount of labor of a mysterious value. In pricing a cargo parachute the choices are: (a) free fall in a padded box from a plane flown close to the ground, (b) landing the plane,

(c) back shipment by land from the next air terminal, or (d) land shipment all the way. These options differ widely in their service value and are not very useful pricing guides.

Thus it is particularly hard to know how much good will be done by making the new product cheaper than the old by various amounts, or how much the market will be restricted by making the new product more expensive. The answers usually come from experiment or research.

The fourth step in estimating demand is to consider the *possibility of retaliation by manufacturers of displaced substitutes* in the form of price cutting. This development may not occur at all if the new product displaces only a small market segment. If old industries do fight it out, however, their incremental costs provide a floor to the resulting price competition and should be brought into price plans.

For example, a manufacturer of black-and-white sensitized paper studied the possibility that lowering his price would displace blueprint paper substantially. Not only did he investigate the prices of blueprint paper, but he also felt it necessary to estimate the out-of-pocket cost of making blueprint paper because of the probability that manufacturers already in the market would fight back by reducing prices toward the level of their incremental costs.

Decision on Market Targets

When the company has developed some idea of the range of demand and the range of prices that are feasible for the new product, it is in a position to make some basic strategic decisions on market targets and promotional plans. To decide on market objectives requires answers to several questions: What ultimate market share is wanted for the new product? How does it fit into the present product line? What about production methods? What are the possible distribution channels?

These are questions of joint costs in production and distribution, of plant expansion outlays, and of potential competition. If entry is easy, the company may not be eager to disrupt its present production and selling operations to capture and hold a large slice of the new market. But if the prospective profits shape up to a substantial new income source, it will be worthwhile to make the capital expenditures on plant needed to reap the full harvest.

A basic factor in answering all these questions is the expected behavior of production and distribution costs. The relevant data here are all the production outlays that will be made after the decision day—the capital expenditures as well as the variable costs. A go-ahead decision will hardly be made without some assurance that these costs can be recovered before the product becomes a football in the market. Many different projections of costs will be made, depending on the alternative scales of output, rate of market expansion, threats of potential competition, and measures to meet that competition that are under consideration. But these factors and the decision that is made on promotional strategy are interdependent. The fact is that this is a circular problem that in theory can only be solved by simultaneous equations.

Fortunately, it is possible to make some approximations that can break the circle: scale economies become significantly different only with broad changes in the size of plant and the type of production methods. This narrows the range of cost projections to workable proportions. The effects of using different distribution channels can be guessed fairly well without meshing the choices in with all the production and selling possibilities. The most vulnerable point of the circle is probably the decision on promotional strategy. The choices here are broad and produce a variety of results. The next step in the pricing process is therefore a plan for promotion.

Design of Promotional Strategy

Initial promotion outlays are an investment in the product that cannot be recovered until some kind of market has been established. The innovator shoulders the burden of creating a market—educating consumers to the existence and uses of the product. Later imitators will never have to do this job; so, if the innovator does not want to be simply a benefactor to his future competitors, he must make pricing plans to recover his initial outlays before his pricing discretion evaporates.

His basic strategic problem is to find the right mixture of price and promotion to maximize his long-run profits. He can choose a relatively high price in pioneering stages, together with extravagant advertising and dealer discounts, and plan to get his promotion costs back early; or he can use low prices and lean margins from the very outset in order to discourage potential competition when the barriers of patents, distribution channels, or production techniques become inadequate. This question is discussed further shortly.

Choice of Distribution Channels

Estimation of the costs of moving the new product through the channels of distribution to the final consumer must enter into the pricing procedure since these costs govern the factory price that will result in a specified consumer price and since it is the consumer price that matters for volume. Distributive margins are partly pure promotional costs and partly physical distribution costs. Margins must at least cover the distributors' costs of warehousing, handling, and order taking. These costs are similar to factory production costs in being related to physical capacity and its utilization, i.e., fluctuations in production or sales volume.

Hence these set a floor to trade-channel discounts. But distributors usually also contribute promotional effort—in point-of-sale pushing, local advertising, and display—when it is made worth their while.

These pure promotional costs are more optional. Unlike physical handling costs they have no necessary functional relation to sales volume. An added layer of margin in trade discounts to produce this localized sales effort (with retail price fixed) is an optional way for the manufacturer to spend his prospecting money in putting over a new product.

In establishing promotional costs, the manufacturer must decide on the extent to which the selling effort will be delegated to members of the distribution chain. Indeed, some distribution channels, such as house-to-house selling and retail store selling supplemented by home demonstrators, represent a substantial delegation of the manufacturer's promotional job, and these usually involve much higher distribution-channel costs than do conventional methods.

Rich distributor margins are an appropriate use of promotion funds only when the producer thinks a high price plus promotion is a better expansion policy in the specialty than low price by itself. Thus there is an intimate interaction between the pricing of a new product and the costs and the problems of floating it down the distribution channels to the final consumer.

POLICIES FOR PIONEER PRICING

The strategic decision in pricing a new product is the choice between (a) a policy of high initial prices that skim the cream of demand and (b) a policy of low prices from the outset serving as an active agent for market penetration. Although the actual range of choice is much wider than this, a sharp dichotomy clarifies the issues for consideration.

Skimming Price

For products that represent a drastic departure from accepted ways of performing a service, a policy of relatively high prices coupled with heavy promotional expenditures in the early stages of market development (and lower prices at later stages) has proved successful for many products. There are several reasons for the success of this policy:

1. Demand is likely to be more inelastic with respect to price in the early stages than it is when the product is full grown. This is particularly true for consumers' goods. A novel product, such as the electric blanket or the electric pig, is not yet accepted as a part of the expenditure pattern. Consumers are still ignorant about its value compared with the value of conventional alternatives. Moreover, at least in the early stages, the product has so few close rivals that cross-elasticity of demand is low.

   Promotional elasticity is, on the other hand, quite high, particularly for products with high unit prices such as television sets. Since it is difficult for the customer to value the service of the product in a way to price it intelligently, he is by default principally interested in how well it will work.

2. Launching a new product with a high price is an efficient device for breaking the market up into segments that differ in price elasticity of demand. The initial high price serves to skim the cream of the market that is relatively insensitive to price. Subsequent price reductions tap successively more elastic sectors of the market. This pricing strategy is exemplified by the systematic succession of editions of a book, sometimes

starting with a $50 limited personal edition and ending up with a 25-cent pocket book.

3. This policy is safer, or at least appears so. Facing an unknown elasticity of demand, a high initial price serves as a "refusal" price during the stage of exploration. How much costs can be reduced as the market expands and as the design of the product is improved by increasing production efficiency with new techniques is difficult to predict. One of the electrical companies recently introduced a new lamp bulb at a comparatively high initial price, but they made the announcement that the price would be reduced as the company found ways of cutting its costs.

4. Many companies are not in a position to finance the product flotation out of distant future revenues. High cash outlays in the early stages result from heavy costs of production and distributor organizing, in addition to the promotional investment in the pioneer product. High prices are a reasonable financing technique for shouldering these burdens in the light of the many uncertainties about the future.

Penetration Price

The alternative policy is to use low prices as the principal instrument for penetrating mass markets early. This policy is the reverse of the skimming policy in which the price is lowered only as short-run competition forces it.

The passive skimming policy has the virtue of safeguarding some profits at every stage of market penetration. But it prevents quick sales to the many buyers who are at the lower end of the income scale or the lower end of the preference scale and who therefore are unwilling to pay any substantial premium for product or reputation superiority. The active approach in probing possibilities for market expansion by early penetration pricing requires research, forecasting, and courage.

A decision to price for market expansion can be reached at various stages in a product's life cycle: before birth, at birth, in childhood, in adulthood, or in senescence. The chances for large-volume sales should at least be explored in the early stages of product development research, even before the pilot stage, perhaps with a more definitive exploration when the product goes into production and the price and distribution plans are decided upon. And the question of pricing to expand the market, if not answered earlier, will probably arise once more after the product has established an elite market.

Quite a few products have been rescued from premature senescence by pricing them low enough to tap new markets. The reissues of important books in the 25-cent pocket book category illustrate this point particularly well. These have produced not only commercial but intellectual renascence as well to many authors. The patterns of sales growth of a product that had reached stability in a high-price market have undergone sharp changes when it was suddenly priced low enough to tap new markets.

A contrasting illustration of passive policy is the recent pricing experience of the airlines. Although safety considerations and differences in equipment and service cloud the picture, it is pretty clear that the bargain-rate coach fares of scheduled airlines were adopted in reaction to the cut rates of nonscheduled airlines. This competitive response has apparently established a new pattern of traffic growth for the scheduled airlines.

An example of penetration pricing at the initial stage of the product's market life, again from the book field, is Simon & Schuster's recently adopted policy of bringing out new titles in a $1, paper-bound edition simultaneously with the conventional higher priced, cloth-bound edition.

What conditions warrant aggressive pricing for market penetration? This question cannot be answered categorically, but it may be helpful to generalize that the following conditions indicate the desirability of an early low-price policy.

- A high price-elasticity of demand in the short run, i.e., a high degree of responsiveness of sales to reductions in price.
- Substantial savings in production costs as the result of greater volume—not a necessary condition, however, since if elasticity of demand is high enough, pricing for market expansion may be profitable without realizing production economies.
- Product characteristics such that it will not seem bizarre when it is first fitted into the consumers' expenditure pattern.
- A strong threat of potential competition.

This threat of potential competition is a highly persuasive reason for penetration pricing. One of the major objectives of most low-pricing policies in the pioneering stages of market development is to raise entry barriers to prospective competitors. This is appropriate when entrants must make large-scale investments to reach minimum costs and they cannot slip into an established market by selling at substantial discounts.

In many industries, however, the important potential competitor is a large, multiple-product firm operating as well in other fields than that represented by the product in question. For a firm, the most important consideration for entry is not existing margins but the prospect of large and growing volume of sales. Present margins over costs are not the dominant consideration because such firms are normally confident that they can get their costs down as low as competitors' costs if the volume of production is large.

Therefore, when total industry sales are not expected to amount to much, a high-margin policy can be followed because entry is improbable in view of the expectation of low volume and because it does not matter too much to potential competitors if the new product is introduced.

The fact remains that for products whose market potential appears big, a policy of stayout pricing from the outset makes much more sense. When a leading soap manufacturer developed an additive that whitened clothes and enhanced the brilliance of colors, the company chose to take its gains in a larger share of the market rather than in a temporary price premium. Such a decision was sound, since the company's competitors could be expected to match or better the product improvement fairly promptly. Under these circumstances, the price premium would have been short-lived, whereas the gains in market share were more likely to be retained.

Of course, any decision to start out with lower prices must take into account the fact that if the new product calls for capital recovery over a long period, the risk may be great that later entrants will be able to exploit new production techniques which can undercut the pioneer's original cost structure. In such cases, the low-price pattern should be adopted with a view to long-run rather than to short-run profits, with recognition that it usually takes time to attain the volume potentialities of the market.

It is sound to calculate profits in dollar terms rather than in percentage margins and to think in terms of percentage return on the investment required to produce and sell the expanded volume rather than in terms of percentage markup. Profit calculation should also recognize the contributions that market-development pricing can make to the sale of other products and to the long-run future of the company. Often a decision to use development pricing will turn on these considerations of long-term impacts upon the firm's total operation strategy rather than on the profits directly attributable to the individual product.

An example of market-expansion pricing is found in the experience of a producer of asbestos shingles, which have a limited sale in the high-price house market. The company wanted to broaden the market in order to compete effectively with other roofing products for the inexpensive home. It tried to find the price of asphalt shingles that would make the annual cost per unit of roof over a period of years as low as the cheaper roofing that currently commanded the mass market. Indications were that the price would have to be at least this low before volume sales would come.

Next, the company explored the relationship between production costs and volume, far beyond the range of its own volume experience. Variable costs and overhead costs were estimated separately, and the possibilities of a different organization of production were explored. Calculating in terms of anticipated dollars of profit rather than in terms of percentage margin, the company reduced the price of asbestos shingles and brought the annual cost down close to the cost of the cheapest asphalt roof. This reduction produced a greatly expanded volume and secured a substantial share of the mass market.

PRICING IN MATURITY

To determine what pricing policies are appropriate for later stages in the cycle of market and competitive maturity, the manufacturer must be able to tell when a product is approaching maturity. Some of the symptoms of degeneration of competitive status toward the commodity level are:

Weakening in Brand Preference This may be evidenced by a higher cross-elasticity of demand among leading products, the leading brand not being able to continue as much price premium as initially without losing position.

Narrowing Physical Variation among Products as the Best Designs Are Developed and Standardized This has been dramatically demonstrated in automobiles and is still in process in television receivers.

The Entry in Force of Private-Label Competitors This is exemplified by the mail-order houses' sale of own-label refrigerators and paint sprayers.

Market Saturation The ratio of replacement sales to new equipment sales serves as an indicator of the competitive degeneration of durable goods, but in general it must be kept in mind that both market size and degree of saturation are hard to define (e.g., saturation of the radio market, which was initially thought to be one radio per home and later had to be expanded to one radio per room).

The Stabilization of Production Methods A dramatic innovation that slashes costs (e.g., prefabricated houses) may disrupt what appears to be a well-stabilized oligopoly market.

The first step for the manufacturer whose specialty is about to slip into the commodity category is to reduce real prices promptly as soon as symptoms of deterioration appear. This step is essential if he is to forestall the entry of private-label competitors. Examples of failure to make such a reduction are abundant.

By and large, private-label competition has speeded up the inevitable evolution of high specialties into commodities and has tended to force margins down by making price reductions more open and more universal than they would otherwise be. From one standpoint, the rapid growth of the private-label share in the market is a symptom of unwise pricing on the part of the national-brand sector of the industry.

This does not mean that the manufacturer should declare open price war in the industry. When he moves into mature competitive stages, he enters oligopoly relationships where price slashing is peculiarly dangerous and unpopular. But, with active competition in prices precluded, competitive efforts may move in other directions, particularly toward product improvement and market segmentation.

Product improvement at this stage, where most of the important developments have been put into all brands, practically amounts to market segmentation. For it means adding refinements and quality extras that put the brand in the elite category, with an appeal only to the top-income brackets. This is a common tactic in food marketing, and in the tire industry it was the response of the General Tire Company to the competitive conditions of the 1930s.

As the product matures and as its distinctiveness narrows, a choice must sometimes be made by the company concerning the run of the competitive price ladder it should occupy—roughly, the choice between a low and a not-so-low relative price.

A price at the low end of the array of the industry's real prices is usually associated with a product mixture showing a lean element of services and reputation (the product being physically similar to competitive brands, however) and a company having a lower gross margin than the other industry members (although not necessarily a lower net margin). The choice of such a low-price policy may be dictated by technical or market inferiorities of the product, or it may be adopted because the company has faith in the long-run price elasticity of demand and the ability of low prices to penetrate an important segment of the market not tapped by higher prices. The classic example is Henry Ford's pricing decision in the 1920s.

IN SUMMARY

In pricing products of perishable distinctiveness, a company must study the cycle of competitive degeneration in order to determine its major causes, its probable speed, and the chances of slowing it down. Pricing in the pioneering stage of the cycle involves difficult problems of projecting potential demand and of guessing the relation of price to sales.

The first step in this process is to explore consumer preferences and to establish the feasibility of the product, in order to get a rough idea of whether demand will warrant further exploration. The second step is to mark out a range of prices that will make the product economically attractive to buyers. The third step is to estimate the probable sales that will result from alternative prices.

If these initial explorations are encouraging, the next move is to make decisions on promotional strategy and distribution channels. The policy of relatively high prices in the pioneering stage has much to commend it, particularly when sales seem to be comparatively unresponsive to price but quite responsive to educational promotion.

On the other hand, the policy of relatively low prices in the pioneering stage, in anticipation of the cost savings resulting from an expanding market, has been strikingly successful under the right conditions. Low prices look to long-run rather than short-run profits and discourage potential competitors.

Pricing in the mature stages of a product's life cycle requires a technique for recognizing when a product is approaching maturity. Pricing problems in this stage border closely on those of oligopoly.

ROLE OF COST

Cost should play a role in new product pricing quite different from that in traditional cost-plus pricing. To use cost wisely requires answers to some questions of theory: Whose cost? Which cost? What role?

As to whose cost, three persons are important: prospective buyers, existent and potential competitors, and the producer of the new product. For each of the three, cost should play a different role and the concept of cost should differ accordingly.

The role of prospective *buyers'* costs is to forecast their response to alterna-

Retrospective Commentary

Twenty-five years have brought important changes and have taught us much, but the basics of pricing pioneer products are the same, only clearer. New product pricing, if the product is truly novel, is in essence monopoly pricing—modified only because the monopoly power of the new product is (a) restricted because buyers have alternatives, (b) ephemeral because it is subject to inevitable erosion as competitors equal or better it, and (c) controllable because actions of the seller can affect the amount and the durability of the new product's market power.

In pricing, the buyers' viewpoint should be controlling. For example, buyer's-rate-of-return pricing of new capital equipment looks at your price through the eyes of the customer. It recognizes that the upper limit is the price that will produce the minimum acceptable rate of return on the investment of a sufficiently large number of prospects. This return has a broad range for two reasons. First, the added profits obtainable from the use of your equipment will differ among customers and among applications for the same customer. Second, prospective customers also differ in the minimum rate of return that will induce them to invest in your product.

This capital-budgeting approach opens a new kind of demand analysis, which involves inquiry into: (a) the costs of buyers from displaceable alternative ways of doing the job, (b) the cost-saving and profit-producing capability of your equipment, and (c) the capital management policies of your customers, particularly their cost of capital and cut-off criteria.

---

tive prices by determining what your product will do to the costs of your buyers. Rate-of-return pricing of capital goods illustrates this buyer's-cost approach, which is applicable in principle to all new products.

Cost is usually the crucial estimate in appraising *competitors'* capabilities. Two kinds of competitor costs need to be forecasted. The first is for products already in the marketplace. One purpose is to predict staying power; for this the cost concept is competitors' long-run incremental cost. Another purpose may be to guess the floor of retaliation pricing; for this we need competitors' short-run incremental cost.

The second kind is the cost of a competitive product that is unborn, but that could eventually displace yours. Time-spotted prediction of the performance characteristics, the costs, and the probable prices of future new products is both essential and possible. Such a prediction is essential because it determines the economic life expectancy of your product and the shape of its competitiveness cycle.

It is possible, first, because the pace of technical advance in product design is persistent and can usually be determined by statistical study of past progress. It is possible, second, because the rate at which competitors' cost will slide down the cost compression curve that results from cost-saving investments in manufacturing equipment, methods, and worker learning is usually a logarithmic function of cumulative output. Thus this rate can be ascertained and projected.

The *producer's* cost should play several different roles in pricing a new product, depending on the decision involved. The first decision concerns capital control. A new product must be priced before any significant investment is made in research and must be periodically repriced when more money is invested as its development progresses toward market. The concept of cost that is relevant for this decision is the predicted full cost, which should include imputed cost of capital on intangible investment over the whole life cycle of the new product. Its profitability and investment return are meaningless for any shorter period.

A second decision is "birth control." The commercialization decision calls for a similar concept of cost and discounted cash-flow investment analysis, but one that is confined to incremental investment beyond product birth.

Another role of cost is to establish a price floor that is also the threshold for selecting from candidate prices those that will maximize return on a new product investment at different stages of its life. The relevant concept here is future short-run incremental cost.

SEGMENTATION PRICING

Particularly for new products, an important tactic is differential pricing for separated market segments. To enhance profits, we split the market into sectors that differ in price sensitivity, charging higher prices to those who are impervious and lower prices to the more sensitive souls.

One requisite is the ability to identify and seal off groups of prospects who differ in sensitivity of sales to price and/or differ in the effectiveness of competition (cross-elasticity of demand). Another is that leakage from the low price segment must be small and costs of segregation low enough to make it worthwhile.

One device is time segmentation: a skimming price strategy at the outset followed by penetration pricing as the product matures. Another device is price-shaped modification of a basic product to enhance traits for which one group of customers will pay dearly (e.g., reliability for the military).

A similar device is product-configuration differentials (notably extras: the roof of the Stanley Steamer was an extra when it was a new product). Another is afterlife pricing (e.g., repair parts, expendable components, and auxiliary services). Also, trade channel discounts commonly achieve profitable price discrimination (e.g., original equipment discounts).

COST COMPRESSIVE CURVE

Cost forecasting for pricing new products should be based on the cost compression curve, which relates real manufacturing cost per unit of value added to the cumulative quantity produced. This cost function (sometimes labeled "learning curve" or "experience curve") is mainly the consequence of cost cutting investments (largely intangible) to discover and achieve internal substitutions, automation, worker learning, scale economies, and technological advances. Usually these move together as a logarithmic function of accumulated output.

Cost compression curve pricing of technically advanced products (for example, a microprocessor) epitomizes penetration pricing. It condenses the time span of the process of cutting prices *ahead* of forecasted cost savings in order to beat competitors to the bigger market and the resulting manufacturing economies that are opened up because of creative pricing.

This cost compression curve pricing strategy, which took two decades for the Model T's life span, is condensed into a few months for the integrated circuit. But though the speed and the sources of saving are different, the principle is the same: a steep cost compression curve suggests penetration pricing of a new product. Such pricing is most attractive when the product superiority over rivals is small and ephemeral and when entry and expansion by competitors is easy and probable.

IMPACTS OF INFLATION

Continuous high-speed inflation has important impacts on new product pricing. It changes the goal. It renders obsolete accounted earnings per share as the corporation's overriding goal—replacing it with maximization of the present worth (discounted at the corporation's cost of capital) of the future stream of real purchasing power dividends (including a terminal dividend or capital gain). Real earnings in terms of cash-flow buying power alone determine the power to pay real dividends.

Inflation raises the buyers' bench-mark costs of the new products' competitive alternatives. Thus it lifts the buyer benefits obtainable from the new products' protected distinctiveness (for example, it saves more wage dollars).

It raises the seller's required return on the investment to create and to launch the new product. Why? Because his cost of equity capital and of debt capital will be made higher to compensate for anticipated inflation. For the same reason, inflation raises the customer's cutoff point of minimum acceptable return. It also intensifies the rivalry for scarce investment dollars among the seller's new product candidates. Hence it probably tends to increase stillbirths, but may lower subsequent infant mortality. For these reasons, perennial inflation will make an economic attack on the problem of pricing new products even more compelling.

Pricing of new products remains an art. But the experienced judgment required to price and reprice the product over its life cycle to fit its changing competitive environment may be improved by considering seven pricing precepts suggested by this analysis.

1. Pricing a new product is an occasion for rethinking the overriding corporate goal. This goal should be to maximize the present worth, dis-

counted at the corporation's cost of capital, of the future stream of real (purchasing-power) dividends, including a terminal dividend or capital gain. The Wall Street traditional objective—maximizing the size or the growth of book earnings per share—is an inferior master goal that is made obsolete by inflation.

2. The unit for making decisions and for measuring return on investment is the entire economic life of the new product. Reported *annual* profits on a new product have little economic significance. The pricing implications of the new product's changing competitive status as it passes through its life cycle from birth to obsolescence are intricate but compelling.

3. Pricing of a new product should begin long before its birth, and repricing should continue over its life cycle. Prospective prices coupled with forecasted costs should control the decision to invest in its development, the determination to launch it commercially, and the decision to kill it.

4. Your new product should be viewed through the eyes of the buyer. Rate of return on customers' investment should be the main consideration in pricing a pioneering capital good: the buyers' savings (and added earnings), expressed as return on his investment in your new product, are the key to both estimating price sensitivity of demand and pricing profitably.

5. Costs can supply useful guidance in new product pricing, but not by the conventional wisdom of cost-plus pricing. Costs of three persons are pertinent: the buyer, your rival, and the producer himself. The role of cost differs among the three, as does the concept of cost that is pertinent to that role: different costs for different decisions.

6. A strategy of price skimming can be distinguished from a strategy of penetration pricing. Skimming is appropriate at the outset for some pioneering products, particularly when followed by penetration pricing (for example, the price cascade of a new book). In contrast, a policy of penetration pricing from the outset, in anticipation of the cost compression curve for manufacturing costs, is usually best when this curve falls steeply and projectably, and is buttressed by economies of scale and of advancing technology, and when demand is price sensitive and invasion is threatened.

7. Penetration and skimming pricing can be used at the same time in different sectors of the market. Creating opportunities to split the market into segments that differ in price sensitivity and in competitiveness, so as to simultaneously charge higher prices in insensitive segments and price low to elastic sectors, can produce extra profits and faster cost-compression for a new product. Devices are legion.

Price-Cost Planning

C. Davis Fogg and Kent H. Kohnken

Developing a financially healthy business for each distinct product line requires the formulation of a realistic price-cost plan. Specifically, such a plan should:

1. Establish *market share goals* appropriate to the firm's competitive strengths and the stage of the product line's life-cycle.
2. Define *profit goals* appropriate to the market share goals.
3. Structure a *pricing plan* to achieve the market share goals.
4. Establish *unit cost goals* which will achieve targeted profitability.
5. Develop a *manufacturing or cost reduction plan* that will result in targeted unit costs.

This article will focus on steps 1–4 and will describe a systematic process that has been successfully used to: (a) evaluate the competitiveness of an established price structure and make necessary short-term price changes, and (b) define a long-term price-cost plan for an established industrial product line in a highly competitive market.

First described are the roles of marketing and manufacturing in establishing a price-cost plan, and then each stage in the planning process—the information required to accomplish it and, where appropriate, a numerical example of the output.

Companies should consider using this process under the following key circumstances:

- A significant change in a competitor's price structure or product offering renders the company's price structure obsolete.
- Feedback from the marketplace indicates that the current price structure needs revision because significant volume is being lost on price, or quota-

About the Authors: C. Davis Fogg is Vice-President of Operations, Consumer Products Division, Bausch & Lomb, Inc., Rochester, New York; Kent H. Kohnken is Ceramic Product Manager, GTE Sylvania, Towanda, Pennsylvania.

Reprinted from *Journal of Marketing*, vol. 42 (April 1978), pp. 97–106, published by the American Marketing Association.

tions are frequently lower than that judged necessary to obtain desirable business.

- The firm is considering a significant change in profit strategy for the business which will result in substantial changes in market share goals and subsequent pricing policy.
- Manufacturing cost reductions have not been sufficient to maintain or attain the desired level of profitability.
- The firm is re-examining pricing policy at the time of the annual or periodic marketing plan development.

ROLES OF MARKETING AND MANUFACTURING

Marketing should be, and often is, the lead function in establishing a price-cost plan. The marketing function is normally responsible for defining product policy, marketing strategy, market share goals, and subsequently, development of pricing policy and product line profit targets. In highly competitive industrial markets, marketing has little leverage over the key profit determinants such as product mix and pricing, once basic marketing strategy and the pricing policy necessary to implement it are established.

Manufacturing has the responsibility for taking market-directed cost goals and establishing a long-term plan to meet them. The manufacturing function often has more leverage to control cost, and, consequently, profitability than does marketing. Manufacturing's ability to reduce cost is bound only by the resources available for cost reduction programs; the technologies available to effectively implement them; and manufacturing's ability to combine them to produce lower costs with an acceptable return on any capital investment involved.

If manufacturing, in fact, cannot meet marketing-directed cost goals, then the goals must be revised to those that can be realistically achieved; or the total market share—price-cost-profit plan—must be varied until a satisfactory option is found.

Time Frame

The price-cost plan often will cover a period of 1–3 or 1–5 years. Typically, modest cost reductions can take place in one year, while necessary major cost reduction programs take 2–5 years to implement, particularly if significant breakthroughs are required in process, equipment, or product design and construction technologies.

THE PRICE-COST PLANNING PROCESS

Exhibit 1 is a schematic overview of the process of developing a price-cost plan. The process assumes that the product line is already established in the marketplace, with well-defined price schedules that are consistent with the currently defined marketing strategy.

EXHIBIT 1

The Process of Developing a Price-Cost Plan

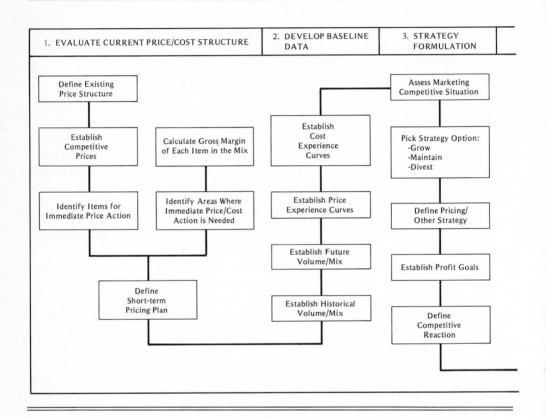

As shown in the exhibit, the process is divided into seven major stages, each of which will be described.

I. Evaluating the Current Price/Cost Structure

The purpose of evaluating the current product line price/cost structure is two-fold: *First,* to evaluate current pricing versus competition and to identify items where prices could be lowered to become competitive, or could be successfully raised to improve profitability. *Second,* to establish the profitability of each item in the product line—to identify items that are not sufficiently profitable and those items that require consideration of immediate cost reduction and/or price increases. The six steps in this stage are:

1. *Define the Current Price Structure* by obtaining unit prices for each product style and quantity break (line item) for *each* channel of distribu-

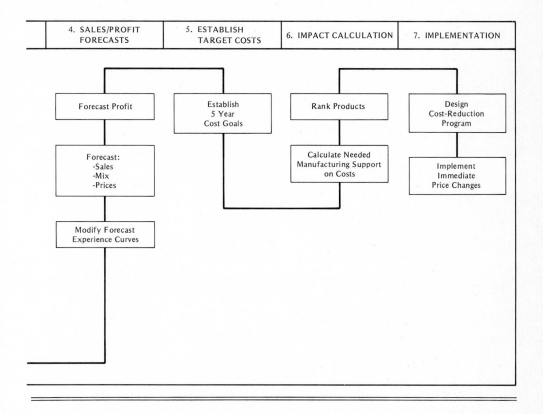

4. SALES/PROFIT FORECASTS	5. ESTABLISH TARGET COSTS	6. IMPACT CALCULATION	7. IMPLEMENTATION

tion such as direct sales, sales to distributors, readily available from published and internal price lists.

2. *Establish Competitive Prices* by line item where possible. A comprehensive list of competitive pricing information should be collected, recognizing that a large body of accurate information is extremely difficult to obtain.

   This information is normally obtained not only from published competitive price sheets from distributors or industrial buyers, but also through inputs from salesmen who collect such information as a matter of routine, i.e., during contract negotiations. Other sources for such information are lost business reports maintained by the sales or sales service organizations, or direct market research among customer purchasing personnel. Because of the difficulty of obtaining competitive pricing information, there will be many gaps in the data requiring intelligent interpolation.

EXHIBIT 2
Current Price Structure

	QUANTITY		
	1–10	100	1000+
Product A			
Our price	.90	.80	.70
Comp. price	.90 **(C)**	.80 **(C)**	.65 **(L)**
% difference	0%	0%	+7%
Product B			
Our price	.85	.75	.60
Comp. price	.85 **(C)**	.65 **(L)**	.60 **(C)**
% difference	0%	+15%	0%
Product C			
Our price	.70	.60	.45
Comp. price	.70 **(C)**	.60 **(C)**	.50 **(R)**
% difference	0%	0%	−10%

Strategy Implications:
(L) Consider lowering price–losing share.
(R) Opportunity to raise price without losing share.
(C) Competitive—hold price.

The output of this step is the simplified three-product matrix shown in Exhibit 2, comparing company prices with prices of key competitors.

3. *Identify Items Where Specific Price Increases or Decreases Should Be Considered* in light of the current or tentatively proposed marketing strategy. Items subject to change are identified in Exhibit 2.

4. *Calculate the Profitability of the Current Company Product Mix* by establishing current unit costs for each product and calculating the gross margin for the total product line and each item. Prices are obtained from Step 1 above. Costs from actual manufacturing cost records can only be used if they are available in sufficient detail. Detailed cost estimates for each major segment of the product line must often be specially developed to provide sufficient data for this analysis. The output of this stage, Exhibit 2, is a summary of current product line profitability. Note that this is a simple matrix with only 9 line items. An actual analysis may contain 50–300 line items.

5. *Identify Items of Unacceptable Profit* where immediate price increases or cost reductions should be considered, as indicated in Exhibit 3.

6. *Tentatively Define the Short-Term Pricing Structure.* Raising prices should

EXHIBIT 3
Current Product Profitability

| | QUANTITY | | | |
	1–10	100	1000+	TOTAL PRODUCT
Product A				
Price	.90	.80	.70	.75
Cost	.61	.56 **(X)**	.46	.51
G.M. %	32%	30%	34%	32%
Product B				
Price	.85	.75	.60	.75
Cost	.56	.51	.41	.51
G.M. %	32%	32%	32%	32%
Product C				
Price	.70	.60	.45	.60
Cost	.48	.43 **(X)**	.33 **(X)**	.43
G.M. %	32%	28%	26%	28%
Total				
Price	.82	.72	.58	.70
Cost	.55	.50	.40	.48
G.M. %	32%	31%	31%	31%

General Competitive Assessment: No significant product or nonproduct (service, quality, and so on) advantage over competition, but considered equal to top two competitors.

Strategy Implication:
(X) Consider price increase/cost reduction to immediately improve profitability, as below 31% current profitability average.

be considered where the current structure is below competition or profitability is unacceptable. Where the item is priced significantly above competition, another option may be lowering prices. All proposed changes in price and their magnitude must be considered in light of (a) their effect on current and future unit and profit volume, (b) any advantages over competition, in service, quality, and distribution (which might command a price premium), (c) the firm's tentative future plans for growth, maintenance, or divestiture of market share. If, at the end of this step, profitability, the revised price structure, and the market strategy are deemed adequate, the remainder of the analysis need not be completed. Exhibit 4 summarizes proposed actions if the firm chooses not to change market share.

If, however, changes in marketing and pricing strategy are contem-

EXHIBIT 4

Action Summary: Proposed Short-Term Action to Maintain Market Share

	QUANTITY		
	1–10	100	1000+
Product A			
Price	**(C)**	**(C)**	**(L)**
Profitability	OK	**(X)**	OK
Action	None	Price cannot be raised—cost must be lowered ASAP by 5% to get to acceptable profit.	Not losing share. No need to lower price.
Product B			
Price	**(C)**	**(L)**	**(C)**
Profitability	OK	OK	OK
Action	None	Losing share— need to lower prices 10% requir- ing additional 6¢ cost reduction to maintain accept- able profit.	None
Product C			
Price	**(C)**	**(C)**	**(R)**
Profitability	OK	**(X)**	**(X)**
Action	None	Cost must be re- duced by 3¢ to get acceptable profitability.	Price can be raised 10% to improve profitability.

plated, the short-term price plan is set aside, pending completion of the long-range analysis described below.

II. Developing Base Line Data

The purpose of this section is to develop the basic market and price forecasts needed to effectively evaluate proposed long-term alternate marketing strategies. The four steps in this process are:

1. *Establish Historical Unit Market Volume and Product Mix* for the company and the market, if it deviates significantly from the company's product mix. Overall market volume is readily available from published or

industry association data, from internal market research reports, or by estimation of company market share and "scaling up" company sales accordingly to estimated total market volume. Product mix, if not available from industry reports, can be estimated by adjusting the firm's actual product mix to account for observed deviations from the "typical" product mix.

2. *Forecast Market Volume and Mix* for a five-year period. Overall market volume forecasts are obtained from any of a number of suitable forecasting techniques—trend analysis, input/output analysis, modeling, Delphi studies, and market research among customers.

    Establishing the future product mix is more difficult, but it is normally accomplished by one or more of a number of methods: "eyeballing" the current mix and adjusting it for perceived changes; establishing trends in the company's historical mix into the future; input/output analysis or market research among customers to forecast expected changes in mix, and, particularly the need for new products which might radically alter future mix.

    Exhibit 5 shows the results of these steps—a five-year forecast of market volume and mix, and the cumulative volume produced to date. In

EXHIBIT 5
Current and Future Market Unit Volume and Mix by Product Style

			% UNIT SALES			
PRODUCT	CURRENT		YEAR			
STYLE	MIX	1	2	3	4	5
A	50	48	47	45	43	40
B	20	20	20	20	20	20
C	30	32	33	35	37	40

TOTAL MARKET (units)	TOTAL MARKET (cumulative units)
Current year—32 (M)	140
1—35	172
2—38	207
3—42	245
4—46	287
5—51	333

this example, the company mix and market mix are assumed to be the same.

3. *Establish Historical and Forecast Market Price Experience Curves* for the total product line and for any significant subsegments. An experience curve is constructed by plotting, on log-log coordinates, the cumulative unit volume produced by all producers at a number of historical points in time versus the constant dollar market price at each chosen point in time. Historical industry volume and market prices can usually be obtained from industry association production and pricing reports. Where such data are not available, they can be obtained through market research or extrapolation from the firm's price, volume, and market-share history.

The expected future market prices, assuming that competitive strategies and relative market shares remain constant, are obtained by extending the experience curve as shown in the simple example in Exhibit 6.

EXHIBIT 6
Market ASP Experience Curve

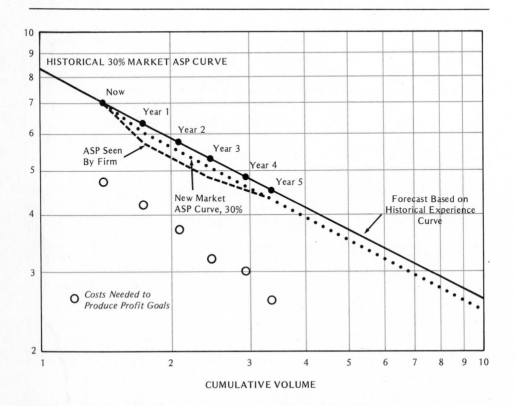

EXHIBIT 7

Cost Experience Curve

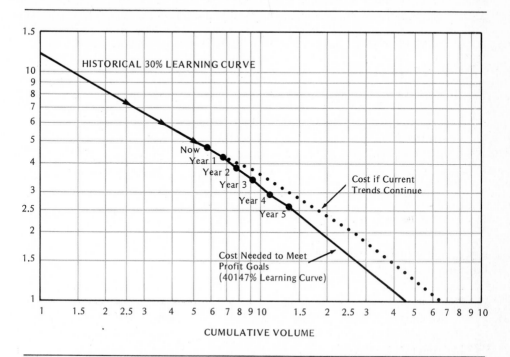

Extrapolation of experience curves is sometimes difficult, and the shape of the curve often depends upon the stage of market development, degree of competition, and competitive product and pricing strategies.[1]

4. *Establish the Cost Experience Curve* for the firm by plotting the firm's unit cost in constant dollars versus its cumulative unit volume at a number of points in time. Extend this experience curve to establish what the firm's costs will be if it continues to reduce costs at historical rates.

The firm's unit costs, past and forecast, can then be appropriately transferred to market price experience curves to establish historical and future profitability, if the price or cost curves or the firm's market share, or the volume continues to accumulate at the current annual rate, are all held constant. (See Exhibits 6 and 7.)

III. Strategy Formulation

The purpose of this stage is to examine or re-examine basic alternative long-term marketing strategies and their profit implications, establish or confirm a strat-

---

[1] See *Perspectives on Experience* (Boston: MA: Boston Consulting Group, 1969).

EXHIBIT 8
Basic Situation Analysis

DIMENSION	OUR SITUATION	COMMENTS
1. Market	High Growth	
2. Competitive Position	No. 2 by Narrow Margin	
3. Competitive Strengths	Equal to Top Two Competitors	
4. Current Profit	Low	Cost Reduction needed/possible
5. Forecast Profit	Low	
6. Pricing	Inconsistent	Easily Reconciled

egy and its pricing implications, and construct basic profit goals consistent with the chosen strategy. There are five steps:

1. *Situation Analysis.* The summary of the current business situation along key market and competitive dimensions is shown in Exhibit 8. Significant, but normally available knowledge about non-product competitive strengths—service, distribution, pricing, provision of customer assistance—is required to complete this analysis.

2. *Strategic Options.* A strategic option is chosen based on the current and future competitive situation and the basic goals established for the business by top management. Exhibit 9 summarizes basic strategic options, when they are used, and the pricing and financial implications of each option. Note that the option dictated by the market situation may be in conflict with legitimate management goals. For example, marketing strategy may dictate growth in share at the expense of current profitability, while management may want maximum profit now to invest in other projects or businesses. In the example presented here, it is assumed that the option selected is growth in share from 25% to 40%.

3. *Strategy Definition.* To accomplish selected goals, such as introduction of new products, correction of any service deficiencies, special promotions, etc., a strategy must be defined for pricing (and any other necessary strategic moves). In this example, it is assumed that share gain will be accomplished through price alone; that pricing 5% below competition for three years will accomplish that goal; that the price reductions will be implemented immediately; and that prices need not be reduced on the single item currently priced sufficiently below the competition to accomplish share goals.

EXHIBIT 9
Basic Strategic/Pricing Options

OPTION	WHEN TO USE IT	PRICING STRATEGY	FINANCIAL IMPLICATIONS
1. Significantly increase market share	• Growth market • Have or can get equal or superior competitive strength • No. 1 in market or good position to take it	Pricing at or below market, depending on competitive strength	• Low profit now • High profit later • Low cash flow now
2. Hold share	• No. 1 in market • Non-growth market • Very strong competition	Maintain or increase price	• Profits/cash flow now
3. Divest share	• Dying market • Inordinately high competitors' strength	High price premium	• Maximum profit/cash flow in near term

4. *Profit Goals.* A top-level management decision considering (a) the business's historical profitability, (b) the industry's profitability, (c) the pricing and market share strategy chosen for the business, and (d) management expectations—establishing profit goals for the business.

In this example, a target of 40% gross margin, consistent with achievement of leadership market share was selected for Year Five. Lower margins of 28%, 31%, 34%, 37% were targeted for the four earlier years, reflecting the need for cost reduction and the necessity of lowering prices to gain market share.

5. *Definition of Competitive Reactions.* Such a definition will result from the proposed strategy, in this case, a decrease in price. Effectively assessing a competitor's reaction to a firm's marketing strategy requires some basic information and assessment of the competitor's financial and technical strengths and weaknesses, nonproduct strengths and weaknesses in the marketplace, his marketing strategy, and his historical reaction to competitive moves.

This information is normally kept as part of any first-rate marketing effort and is obtained from analysis of public financial data, and other internal sources.

In this instance, it is assumed that the two competitors from which market share is to be taken will follow price cuts during the first two years of the company's, forcing an abnormal 3% reduction in each year and temporarily depressing the marketplace experience curve from its historical trend level. This will result in an overall 8% reduction experienced by the firm, which intends to keep prices 5% below competition.

IV. Forecasts

The sales price and profit forecasts will be used to establish long-range cost goals and are obtained through the following three steps:

1. *Price Forecast,* where the price experience curve is modified to account for the firm's pricing action and competitive reaction. Two curves are shown in Exhibit 6, presented earlier: (a) the competitive prices, 3% below normal trend; and (b) the price seen by the firm—8% below trend. It is assumed that the market stabilizes after three years, establishing a new starting point for the experience curve, while continuing to diminish at the pre-price reduction rate.
2. *Sales Forecast,* where a forecast of unit sales, overall price, sales mix, and mix price for each of five years is obtained by (a) applying market share figures to the market estimates (see Exhibit 5), (b) adjusting the company mix to reflect any planned mix changes, and (c) establishing the mix price by lowering current competitive prices by the percentage decrease dictated in each year by the price experience curve. The resulting five-year price-volume forecast for the firm is shown in Exhibit 10.
3. *Price Forecast,* where overall gross profits are obtained (assuming historical cost reduction trends continue) by multiplying the forecast sales volume by the difference between the forecast prices and the forecast experience curve as shown in Exhibit 6. In this instance, forecast profits do not meet established profit goals.

V. Establishing Target Costs

Target unit costs are calculated for the total product line and for each item in the product mix for each year by discounting the mix price structure by the margin desired in each year. These costs then become manufacturing cost goals (see Exhibit 10).

VI. Impact Calculation

There are two stages:

1. *Calculate the Cost Reduction Impact Required* in total and for each item in the mix by multiplying total volume for Years 1 through 5 by the difference between current costs and target costs in Year 5. This assumes that target costs will decrease steadily, which may not be the case if feasible cost reduction programs are expected to have the bulk of their impact in later years.

EXHIBIT 10
Overall Forecast for Price (in constant 1976 dollars)

PRODUCTS	PIECES	$	ASP	COST	G.M. %
Product A					
Now	4,000	$3000	.75	.51	32%
Year 1	4,536	2812	.62	.45	28%
Year 2	5,358	3054	.57	.39	31%
Year 3	6,237	3306	.53	.36	33%
Year 4	7,121	3703	.52	.33	36%
Year 5	8,160	3917	.48	.29	40%
Product B					
Now	1,600	$1200	.75	.51	32%
Year 1	1,890	1157	.61	.44	28%
Year 2	2,280	1295	.57	.39	31%
Year 3	2,772	1448	.52	.35	33%
Year 4	3,312	1734	.52	.33	36%
Year 5	4,080	1958	.48	.29	40%
Product C					
Now	2,400	$1400	.60	.43	28%
Year 1	3,024	1512	.50	.36	28%
Year 2	3,762	1693	.45	.31	31%
Year 3	4,851	2037	.42	.28	33%
Year 4	6,127	2512	.41	.26	36%
Year 5	8,160	3101	.38	.23	40%
Overall					
Now	8,000	$5640	.71	.48	32%
Year 1	9,450	5481	.58	.42	28%
Year 2	11,400	6042	.53	.37	31%
Year 3	13,860	6791	.49	.32	34%
Year 4	16,560	7949	.48	.30	37%
Year 5	20,400	8976	.44	.26	40%

	YEARS					
	NOW	1	2	3	4	5
Mkt. Pcs.	32	35	38	42	46	51
Mkt. Share	25%	27%	30%	33%	36%	40%

2. *Rank Priorities.* Each line item in the product line is then ranked in order of cost reduction impact required to single out items requiring the most immediate attention, as shown in Exhibit 11.

EXHIBIT 11
Cost Reduction/$ Saving

	A	B	C	D	E		
		COST			$\dfrac{A - B}{2}$		
PRODUCT	ACTUAL COST NOW	NEEDS YR. 5 FOR 40% G.M.	AVG. UNITS % MIX YRS. 1–5	AVG. UNITS SALES/YRS. 1–5	AVG. COST REDUCTION	YRS. 1–5 [1] AVERAGE SAVINGS	PRIORITY
A	.51	.29	44.6%	6282	.11	$ 691	1
B	.51	.29	20.0%	1518	.11	$ 167	3
C	.43	.23	35.4%	2171	.10	$ 217	2
Total			100.0%	9971	10.70	$1075	

[1] Average cost reduction necessary in constant $, assuming increased market share from 25% to 40%, and increasing G.M. % from 32% to 40%.

VII. Implementation

The final and critical stages in the process are designing and implementing the cost reduction program, a lengthy subject itself, and implementing the short-term price structure.

1. *Design the Cost Reduction Program,* normally a function of the manufacturing organization, in collaboration with the R&D function. During this phase, engineering and technical personnel examine the product construction and process for every conceivable means of reducing costs, frequently focusing on elimination of expensive material or construction techniques; improving the manufacturing process where there are sub-par selection rates or manufacturing rates, or mechanizing high labor content operations.

    Once the cost reduction programs are proposed, their impact calculated, and the cost and capital expenditure necessary to implement them estimated, then those with sufficient return on investment can be implemented.

    If the proposed pricing strategy coupled with the cost reduction program does not produce targeted profit margins, or if the return on incremental capital spent or cost reduction is not sufficient, then the proposed marketing and pricing strategy will have to be revised.

2. *Short-Term Price Structure.* The modified short-term structure proposed in Stage 1 is changed, if necessary, to be consistent with proposed strategy changes and the subsequent pricing strategy presented in Exhibit 9.

PRACTICAL CONSIDERATIONS

There are a number of practical considerations that should be taken into account in using and implementing this system:

- Computer programs are necessary to quickly do the complex calculations needed to complete the price-cost analysis presented earlier.
- Manufacturing and marketing must work together closely and frequently in both completing and implementing the analysis. They must philosophically be committed to *joint* management of the price-cost structure, a commitment that is often difficult to obtain in a company dominated by either the marketing or manufacturing function.
- Product line prices and costs must, obviously, be carefully tracked versus goals to insure that immediate action is taken to correct deviation from plan.
- There must be a commitment to spend sufficient money and resources on cost reduction over a long time period, and not on urgent or as needed basis, if cost goals are to be met.
- Cost-price analysis should be done on a regular basis, preferably annually, to insure that goals, price structure, and cost reduction programs are adequate and up-to-date.

S U M M A R Y

Manufacturing and marketing equally share the responsibility of producing acceptable profits by effectively managing the product line price-cost structure. Marketing is responsible for establishing the firm marketing and pricing strategy and establishing reasonable long-range cost goals. Manufacturing is responsible for achieving these goals. The most successful firms will aggressively manage the price-cost structure rather than let it evolve in response to competitive pressures or as a result of normal cost reduction or process improvement efforts. This article presents a systematic process for effectively establishing price-cost goals in the context of long-range marketing strategy, and the firm's relative competitive strengths.

Functional Spin-Off: A Key to Anticipating Change in Distribution Structure

Bruce Mallen

The purpose of this article is to suggest to anyone interested in understanding distribution channel change an approach whereby the channel designer may anticipate distribution change in his industry *before* such change has developed into an obvious trend. The channel designer would then be in a position to incorporate this information in planning his distribution strategy and in adapting to his distribution environment.

To successfully complete his task, the channel designer must closely analyze five factors: [1]

1. The selected target markets;
2. The rest of his marketing mix: price, product, promotion, physical distribution, etc.;
3. His company's resources;
4. Competition and other external forces;
5. Current and anticipated distribution structures in his industry.

Perhaps the most difficult of these factors to analyze is the future changes in distribution structure—those that have not yet developed into obvious trends. Typically, the channel designer must limit himself to reading futuristic type articles on distribution trends [2] and/or to surveying a cross-section of opinions in

About the Author: Bruce Mallen is chairman of Graduate Studies in the Faculty of Commerce and Administration, Sir George Williams University, Montreal, Canada.

Reprinted from *Journal of Marketing*, vol. 37 (July 1973), pp. 18–25, published by the American Marketing Association.

[1] For detailed description of the selection process, see Bruce Mallen, "Selecting Channels of Distribution for Consumer Products," in *Handbook of Modern Marketing*, Victor P. Buell, ed. (New York: McGraw-Hill, 1970), pp. 4-15 to 4-30.

[2] See, for example, William R. Davidson, "Changes in Distribution Institutions," *Journal of Marketing*, Vol. 34 (January 1970), pp. 7–10; and Philip B. Schary, "Changing Aspects of

his industry. The problem with the first information source is that such articles are usually too general to be of direct benefit to the reader and are extrapolations of current obvious trends rather than anticipations of changes which have not yet developed into trends. The problem with an opinion study is that the consensus may be completely wrong—nothing more than the reflection of a common pool of ignorance.

This article does not attempt to provide a comprehensive explanation of distribution structure based on empirical research. Rather it presents a sequence of relationships which can be used to aid in anticipating change.

THE CONCEPTUAL APPROACH

For approximately 60 years, economic and marketing scholars have recognized the concept of marketing functions and have related them in a more and more exact fashion to the determination of channel structure. Early contributions were made by Butler, Shaw, Weld, Cherington, Clark, Breyer, and Converse. More recently Stigler, Vaile, Grether, Cox, Alderson, and Bucklin have been major contributors to functionalism as it relates to channel structure.[3]

The basic message of all channel functionalists is as follows:

1. Marketing functions are the various types of job tasks which channel members undertake.
2. These functions can be allocated in different mixes to different channel members.
3. The functional mixes will be patterned in a way which provides the greatest profit either to the consumer (in the form of lower prices and/or more convenience) or the channel members with the most power (which depends on market structure).
4. Should one or more channel members (or potential members) see an opportunity to change the functional mix of the channel in order to increase his profits, he will attempt to do so.

Channel Structure in America," *British Journal of Marketing*, Vol. 4 (Autumn 1970), pp. 133–147.

[3] Ralph S. Butler, *Selling and Buying*, Part II, *Advertising, Selling and Credits of Modern Business*, Vol. IX (New York: Alexander Hamilton Institute, 1911), pp. 276–277; Ralph S. Butler, H. F. Debower, and J. G. Jones, *Modern Business*, Vol. III, *Marketing Methods and Salesmanship* (New York: Alexander Hamilton Institute, 1914), pp. 8–9; Arch W. Shaw, *Some Problems in Market Distribution* (Cambridge, Mass.: Harvard University Press, 1915), pp. 4–28; L. D. Weld, "Marketing Functions and Mercantile Organization," *American Economic Review*, Vol. 7 (June 1917), pp. 306–318; Paul T. Cherington, *Elements of Marketing* (New York: MacMillan, 1920), pp. 44, 56–59; Fred E. Clark, *Principles of Marketing* (New York: Macmillan, 1922); Ralph F. Breyer, *The Marketing Institution* (New York: McGraw-Hill, 1934); P. D. Converse, *Essentials of Distribution* (New York: Prentice-Hall, 1936); George J. Stigler, "The Division of Labor Is Limited by the Extent of the Market," *Journal of Political Economy*, Vol. 54 (June 1951), pp. 185–193; R. S. Vaile, E. T. Grether, and R. Cox, *Marketing in the American Economy* (New York: Ronald Press, 1952), pp. 121–133; Wroe Alderson, *Marketing Behavior and Executive Action* (Homewood, Ill.: Richard D. Irwin, 1957); Louis P. Bucklin, *A Theory of Distribution Channel Structure* (Berkeley, Calif.: Institute of Business and Economic Research, University of California, 1966).

5. Should the attempt be successful, and if the functional mix change is big enough, it will (by definition) change the institutional arrangement in the channel, i.e., the channel structure.

Thus, the channel functionalist attempts to answer two basic questions: What is the most efficient functional mix in a given situation, and how will this functional mix affect the channel structure?

There are four dimensions of distribution structure in which change can be anticipated:

1. The number of channel levels;
2. The number of channels or whether one, two (dual), or more (multi) channel types will be used;
3. The types of middlemen that will evolve;
4. The number of middlemen that will develop at each level.

Although the goal to attain market power and to manipulate demand is an important consideration in understanding structural change, the drive for efficiency is also of primary importance. The fundamental premise of this paper is that given a specific level of demand, firms will try to maximize profits by designing or selecting a channel which will generate the lowest total average costs for their organizations.

This drive for efficiency and its anticipated effects on the four dimensions of channel structure can be evaluated through the concept of "functional spin-off."

The Basic Concept of Functional Spin-Off

The basis for the functional spin-off concept is a 1951 article by Stigler.[4] In this article, Stigler provides a most important conceptual framework for measuring and anticipating channel structural arrangements. His approach to isolating the reasons why firms will "subcontract" some functions is to analyze or break down the average total cost curve of the firm by function rather than by the normal category of expense calculations such as salaries and interest. Included would be costs associated with functions such as ownership, promotion, information gathering, risk taking, negotiation, and so on. Each function will then have its own cost curve, and the sum of the cost curves for each function will be the total average cost curve of the firm.

These functional cost curves will have various shapes, and each may differ from the other to some degree. Average cost curves for some functions will increase with increasing volume whereas others will decrease with increasing volume. The average cost curves for some functions will assume a U-shaped design: they decrease with increasing volume and at some point start to increase with increasing volume. (Stigler assumes a U-shaped design for the total average cost curve.)

---

[4] Stigler, same reference as footnote 3.

Functional Spin-Off and the Number of Channel Levels It is economically beneficial to spin off to marketing specialists those distributive functions which have a decreasing curve as volume increases when the firm has a relatively small volume. When a firm enters or creates a new market, it typically produces a small volume in that market. Assuming the middleman specialist faces the same cost curve as the producer, the individual producer at this low volume will have a higher average cost for performing a function with a decreasing cost curve than the specialist who can combine the volumes of a number of producers and thus benefit from the economies that the performance of this particular function generates at higher volumes. If the middleman specialist passes on all or some of the lower costs, the producer's total average cost will decline as a result of this spin-off of the distributive function. In effect, the middleman has generated the basic *raison d'être* for his own existence by providing external economies to producer firms.

Although the falling functional cost curve is of most interest because it is probably the most common situation, the reverse curve also has implications for channel structure. With a rising functional cost curve, it would make sense economically to spin off certain functions to small specialists when the firm has achieved a high volume. These small specialists can perform the rising cost function at lower costs if they stay small and do not combine the volumes of too many producers. If they are competitive (a more likely event than in the falling cost functional curve situation) such savings will be passed on to the producer.

Some Qualifications At the beginning of the development of a new market, there may not be enough volume for a middleman to enter the market since there may not be enough producers from which the middleman can draw supplies to create the large volume required for a profitable operation. In this case, the producer will not have any middleman to whom he may spin off a high cost function. The situation may also occur during the declining stage of the product life cycle when industry volume has decreased to a point where insufficient total sales exist to justify a functional specialist. In the second case, vertical reintegration becomes necessary as middlemen leave the market.

As the market develops, more producers enter, industry volume increases, and it becomes viable for middlemen to operate. It is possible that with even greater volume, a given spin-off function will in turn be broken down into several subfunctions, some of which may be spun off by existing middlemen to even narrower specialists; for example, import distributors might spin off certain types of selling to domestic wholesalers. Thus several levels and other types of middlemen may be added to the structural arrangement.

It should be noted that even if the middleman is a monopolist, he cannot exploit his situation completely. A producer will distribute directly if a middleman attempts to charge more for his services than the producer would have to pay with direct distribution. In other words, the middleman faces an elastic demand curve for his services. At most, he can take all of the efficiencies that he provides in the form of his own profits, but no more. The middleman monopolist is more likely to be present at the beginning of a new market situation, where volume does not warrant the entry of competitive middlemen. Eventually, however, with increasing volume and no artificial barriers to entry, competitive middlemen will enter the market.

It should also be noted that functions are not independent but are interrelated. Therefore, the spin-off of one function could have repercussions, up or down, for the cost of one or more other functions. For example, coordination costs may fall with the spin-off of a function. That is, if a given function is not being performed in a company, there is no longer the need for internal company communication between the people that would have been performing the function and the rest of the company.

Extensions of the Functional Spin-Off Concept as Related to Channel Levels

U- or L-Shaped Average Cost Function   There are a number of important implications for industrial structure and, more specifically, channel structure on which Stigler did not elaborate. Perhaps the most important are the implications arising from a functional average cost curve which initially declines and then at some point starts to increase (really a U-shaped curve) or even flattens out.

If the cost curve does not continue to fall, at a high level of volume a point will be reached at which that producer can retake the function without losing economies. For example, in Figure 1 at volumes up to Q_1 it will pay the producer to spin off to middlemen the function shown by the cost curve. Between Q_1 and Q_2, performance by the producer or spinning it off will provide the same economies. After volume Q_2, however, it would be beneficial for the pro-

FIGURE 1   A U-Shaped Average Cost Curve for a Given Function Faced by an Individual Producer or Marketing Middleman

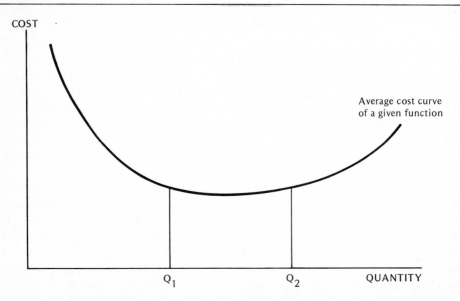

ducer to resume performance of the function (unless middlemen split them-selves up and form smaller firms or smaller middlemen are available in the market, so that a very large volume can be distributed among them). The re-sumption process can apply to any function. For example, the resumption of the ownership function removes the task from a merchant middleman and results in the producer selling direct to the market; self-performance of the advertising function means a producer will not use an advertising agency but relies com-pletely on his own personnel, and so on.

Functions with Continually Decreasing Average Cost Curves   Another ex-tension of the Stigler model is that if the functional cost curve continually falls, the middleman industry, and perhaps individual middleman firms which result from this situation, will become bigger and bigger.

Stigler's model can also be reconstructed into a dynamic rather than a static one. If the channel's costs fall, prices fall; so that given an elastic demand curve, volume will increase. In other words, the market situation propels itself further along the various functional cost curves, with the implications depend-ing on the shapes of these curves. For fall functional cost curves, another round of functional spin-offs, falling costs and prices, and increasing volume will take place. An implication of this last situation is that the middleman industry would become very large, perhaps creating extremely large firms. This process may have facilitated the rise of the mass merchandiser.

Extensions of the Functional Spin-Off Concept as Related to Other Structure Dimensions

Multi-Channel Structures   The concepts employed here can also be useful in explaining the rationale behind dual-channel or multi-channel distribution sys-tems. If the functional cost curves are analyzed by large retailer versus small re-tailer markets, it is possible for the same function to have different shapes in each market. For example, for the small retailer market the producer's functional cost curve at a given quantity may fall with increasing volume; whereas for the large retailer market the cost curve for that same function at the same given quantity may be flat or even increase with volume. This would occur if there were few economies associated with increasing volume in marketing to big re-tailers once any reasonable amount was sold to them; e.g., the selling effort and cost per unit which is required to sell X units to big retailers is the same as to sell 2X units.

If the above situation held true in a given case, it would be economically beneficial for the producer to spin off to a middleman the particular function in-volved in selling to the small retailer market and to sell directly to the large re-tailer market. Even if the shapes of the cost curves in each market were identi-cal, say declining and then leveling off, the spin-off in the small retailer market would be beneficial if the quantity being sold was still small enough to be on the declining portion of the curve. Of course, if the situation was reversed, i.e., sell-ing the small quantity to the large retailer market and large (flat portion of curve) quantity to the small retailer market, the spin-off would take place in

FIGURE 2   L-Shaped Average Cost Curves Faced by Individual Producers or Marketing Middlemen in Selling to a Large Retailer Market and a Small Retailer Market for the Same Given Marketing Function

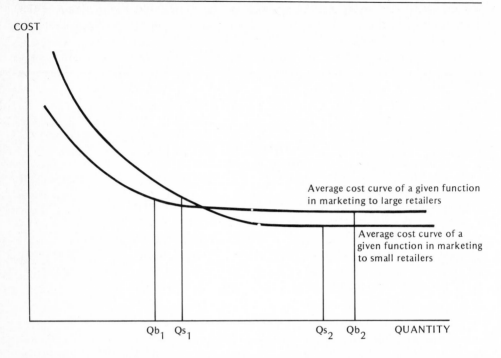

the large retailer market. This would lead to indirect distribution to large retailers and direct distribution to small retailers.

Figure 2 portrays the possible situations. Qs (1 or 2) is assumed to be the quantity sold to the small retailer market and Qb (1 or 2) is the quantity assumed to be sold to the large retailer market by a given producer. In the cost curves shown in this figure, the reason for selling directly to retailers (large or small) at high volumes is shown, i.e., leveling cost curves at Qs_2 or Qb_2; as well as the reason for selling indirectly, i.e., falling cost curves at Qs_1 or Qb_1.

Assume four possible volume situations:

1. Qs_1 and Qb_2;
2. Qs_2 and Qb_1;
3. Qs_2 and Qb_2;
4. Qs_1 and Qb_1.

In the first situation, if the producer is selling Qs_1 and Qb_2 it can be seen that lower average costs for a given marketing function to small retailers can be obtained at higher volumes (e.g., Qs_2). Hence, it makes economic sense for the producer to spin off the function of selling to small retailers to middlemen who, by combining the volume of two or more producers, can achieve these economies and, if competitive, pass them on to the producer. At Qb_2 it is obvious that no further economies (or diseconomies) are available at this and higher volumes to the firm. Therefore, it would not be reasonable to spin off the function to middlemen in marketing to larger retailers at that point.

In another situation, if a producer is selling Qb_1 and Qs_2 the reverse channel structure would result. The function would be spun off to middlemen in selling to large retailers and would be retained on a direct basis for small retailers.

Should the relevant volumes be Qb_2 and Qs_2, there would not be any multi-channels, i.e., there would be only direct distribution. Should the relevant quantities be Qb_1 and Qs_1, there would be spin-offs in both cases; and should the middlemen be the same firms in both cases, there would not be any multi-channel distribution, but simply indirect single-channel distribution. If, on the other hand, distribution to the large retailer market and the small retailer market required different types of middlemen, there would still be multi-channel distribution although of a different nature.

Middlemen Types The types of marketing intermediaries that are created will be directly determined by the mix of functions spun off to them, inasmuch as part of the definition of a middleman depends on the functions he performs. For example, if part of the ownership function is spun off, then merchants are created; if a negotiation function is spun off, then agents are created; if advertising only, then advertising agencies; if marketing research only, then marketing research agencies; and so on.

Horizontal Channel Structure Up to this point the discussion has dealt with only three of the four dimensions of structure listed earlier: the number of levels; the determination of the number of patterns of distribution—single-, dual-, or multi-channels; and their type (as defined by functions performed). Insight into the determination of one other channel dimension—horizontal structure, or the number of middlemen at each channel level—may also be provided by the functional spin-off concept. However, integration of certain concepts from the field of industrial organization with the spin-off concept is necessary.

The basic force which will determine the number of channel members at a given level appears to be the size of the market in relation to the optimum scale of the firm.[5] The greater the market size is in relation to the optimum scale size, the greater the number of channel members that will evolve, and vice versa. The optimum scale size will itself change from industry to industry and over time as technology changes.

In addition to this fundamental determining relationship, there are a number of other factors. Most of these factors are closely associated with scale and market size, which also help to determine how many members will exist at a channel level. The forces which tend to create more firms at a given channel level include: diseconomies of medium or large scale plants and firms, only

---

[5] For an excellent detailed discussion of this concept (though not interpreted in a channel context) see, Joe S. Bain, *Industrial Organization* (New York: John Wiley and Sons, Inc., 1968), Chapter 6.

small inefficiencies at smaller than optimum scale of operation, growth of market size, high profit potentials, inability to agree on merger terms, legal barriers on merger or monopolization, and buyers wishing the convenience of many outlets.

The forces which tend to create fewer firms at a given channel level include: no diseconomies of large scale operations or diseconomies commencing at only extremely high output of plants and firms; only small inefficiencies at a larger than optimum scale of operations; decline in market size; low profit potential; monopolization practices brought about through collusion, predatory behavior, or barriers to entry; and "outside" financial considerations in effecting mergers.

Although most theoretical discussions normally view diseconomies as starting almost immediately after the optimum scale is reached, in practice there appears to be a rather broad range of possible scales—from a minimum optimum scale to some maximum (which in some cases could accommodate a monopoly)—which could provide the same optimum efficiencies.

> We will seldom if ever find firms with a single unique optimal scale. Diseconomies of very large scale are typically encountered, if at all, only at scales substantially greater than the minimum optimal scale of a firm. This is in spite of the fact that a priori theories of pricing and market structure have usually represented the scale curves of firms as having a U shape. . . .[6]

> . . . the bulk of evidence is consistent with the hypothesis that the gigantic firms are in general neither more or less efficient than firms which are simply large.[7]

Hence, since diseconomies come slowly, if at all, a basic underlying trend could be toward fewer firms and, at the extreme, one (monopoly) channel member at a given level of a channel. In other words, it is conceivable that a channel level not only can be an oligopoly, duopoly, or even a monopoly and still operate, but *must* have that market structure in order to operate at an optimum scale.

This concept of a wide range of optimum scales when combined with the concept of functional spin-off has important implications for channel structure. It suggests the possibility of a structure which consists of all producers using direct channels, all using indirect channels, or some using direct and some using indirect. The first case is probable when all producers reach the minimum optimum point; the second is probable when none reach the minimum optimum point. The last case (of mixed structures) is most probable when some do and some do not reach this point; it is also optimally compatible when all reach the minimum optimum point, as in the first case.

Consider a hypothetical example of a market having a total volume of $10 million and a minimum optimum scale for distribution functions (whether undertaken by the producer or a middleman) of $1 million, with no diseconomies

---

[6] Same reference as footnote 5.
[7] Same reference as footnote 5.

up to the total market. If no producer reaches this minimum, then it is probable that all will distribute indirectly with a total of one to ten middlemen in the market. If one producer reaches 100% of the market, he can distribute directly with no middlemen in the market, he can distribute completely through one to ten middlemen, or he can distribute directly in part and indirectly in part through one to nine middlemen (nine, if he lets $9 million go indirectly). If only one producer reaches $1 million in output, he may distribute directly or indirectly. If he distributes indirectly, then the other producers, who will probably distribute indirectly in any case, will do so through one to nine middlemen. If there are ten producers, and eight producers each reach at least $1 million in sales for a total of $9 million, some of the eight may distribute directly and others indirectly, or all may distribute one way or the other. If all decide to distribute directly, then the remaining two producers will probably distribute indirectly through one middleman.

Thus the minimum optimum scale point only indicates the maximum number of channel members that are compatible with maximum efficiency, and so leaves room for a number of other forces (not discussed here) which will determine the actual point in the optimum range that will be utilized by the firms in the industry, i.e., the actual outcome in terms of number of channel members at different levels. Further, firms may not even choose to (or cannot) operate within the optimum range because of some of the factors listed earlier. These factors include: only small inefficiencies at nonoptimum scales, a decline in market size, a high profit potential even without optimum operation, monopolization practices, inability to merge, and a desire for outlet convenience. In spite of these possibilities, one cannot ignore what is a very key determinant of the number of channel members that will exist at each level—market size in relation to the optimum scale of firm and the spin-off ability.

HYPOTHESES

The key hypotheses generated by the functional spin-off and industrial organization concepts for distribution structure are as follows:

As Related to "Number of Levels" Dimension

1. A producer will spin off a marketing function to a marketing intermediary(s) if the latter can perform the function more efficiently than the former. This will logically be the case when economies can be effected for that function by a change in volume from that of the producer. The greater the economies, the greater will be the incentive to spin off. If the majority of producers in a given industry are in or will be in a similar position, then the use of marketing intermediaries will characterize, or come to characterize, that industry.
2. If there are continual economies to be obtained within a wide range of volume changes, the middleman portion of the industry (and perhaps individual middlemen) will become bigger and bigger.

3. A producer will keep or resume a marketing function from a marketing intermediary(s) if the former can perform the function at least as efficiently as the latter. This will logically be the case when no economies can be effected for that function by a change in volume from that of the producer. If the majority of producers in a given industry are in, or will be in, a similar position, then the nonuse of marketing intermediaries (direct distribution) will characterize, or come to characterize, that industry.

4. If in performing a marketing function a marketing intermediary finds that for a part of that function (i.e., a subfunction) another perhaps more specialized marketing intermediary can perform it more efficiently, then he will spin off that subfunction to the latter. This will occur for the same reasoning presented in hypothesis 1 above. Similarly, the first marketing intermediary will keep or resume a subfunction if there are no economies to be effected by a spin-off.

As Related to "Number of Channels" Dimension

5. If a producer finds that in marketing to one (or more) of his markets a middleman can perform a given marketing function more efficiently for the reasons noted in hypothesis 1 above and for another (or others) of his markets he can perform the same function at least as efficiently for the reasons noted in hypothesis 3 above, he will spin off that function in marketing to the first market(s) and keep or resume the function in marketing to the second. If the majority of producers in a given industry are in, or will be in, a similar position; then the use of dual- or multiple-channels will characterize, or come to characterize, that industry.

As Related to "Middlemen Types" Dimension

6. If marketing intermediaries characterize an industry, their nature will be determined by the mix of functions and subfunctions spun off. For example, if the ownership function is a prevalent spin-off function, then the merchant will be a prevalent type of marketing intermediary in the industry.

As Related to "Number of Middlemen" Dimension

7. The greater the market size is in relation to optimum scale size (at each channel level), the greater the number of channel members that will come into being. With the growth of market size, and especially if there exist diseconomies or only very small economies of larger scale, more firms may be expected to enter the channel. With a decline in market size, and especially if there exist economies of large scale, firms may be expected to leave the channel.

8. With a change in technology and the growth of optimum scale size, firms may be expected to leave the channel if there is no corresponding change in market size and vice versa.

IMPLICATIONS

Using the eight relationships hypothesized above, the channel planner is in a better position to anticipate trends in his industry by estimating relevant cost and market data. (It is beyond the scope of this article to describe a program of data collection or to suggest how to overcome the admittedly difficult, but not impossible, task of collecting competitive cost information.)

The channel planner must estimate the present and future total market volume, new technological changes which affect the optimum firm scale, and the volume and shape of the average cost curve for the key marketing functions of a representative sample of firms (producers and marketing intermediaries) in his industry. Fortunately, because his purpose is to gauge broad underlying trends, the data can be fairly rough without losing their usefulness. Trade associations often collect competitive cost data for use by their members. However, further estimates of different types of marketing costs by market being served would probably have to be made from such sources. He then can apply to his findings the structural results predicted by the eight hypotheses listed above.

For example, if he finds that producing firms in his industry in general have faced a declining average cost curve for the ownership function in the past but are now approaching a flat portion of the curve where no economies of scale are forthcoming, and further he predicts an increase in total market volume, he will anticipate in his channel strategy a general move by his industry to more direct ownership channels (see hypothesis 3 above). He will also anticipate more firms entering the market at the producer level (see hypothesis 7 above: note in this case that the market size may actually decline at the merchant middleman level because of the first conclusion). The exact change in number of channel members will depend on factors discussed earlier under the subtitle "horizontal channel structure." If, in the same example, the channel planner also finds that with the same volume increase the negotiation function cost curve declines sharply, he will also anticipate an increase in the number of agent middlemen.

The possible combination of cost and market size changes are numerous. The channel planner by collecting the data and applying the concepts discussed here should be able to anticipate distribution structure changes before they become obvious trends.

The functional spin-off concept is a powerful conceptual tool for the marketer in understanding many of the aspects of channel structure (which itself is one of the most and perhaps *the* most fundamental contribution of marketing as a discipline) [8] and in predicting structural outcomes in specific industries. It is also useful, in a micro or managerial sense, to the channel selector or designer who is seeking to conceptually organize and understand the framework of underlying economic forces within which he must operate and make his decisions and to which he must adapt.

---

[8] R. Ferber, D. Blankertz, and S. Hollander, *Marketing Research* (New York: Ronald Press Company, 1964), p. 471. See also, Michael Halbert, *The Meaning and Sources of Marketing Theory* (New York: McGraw-Hill, 1965), p. 10.

Reseller Strategies and the Financial Performance of the Firm

Bert C. McCammon, Jr., and Albert D. Bates

INTRODUCTION

The 1970s have been a sobering experience for many retailing and wholesaling executives. After a decade of relatively rapid expansion, distribution companies were suddenly confronted by double-digit inflation, wage and price controls, product shortages, rising energy costs, record interest rates, and a major economic recession. Since retailers and wholesalers operate on relatively slender margins, the cumulative effects of these developments were much more severe in distribution than in manufacturing.

In addition to coping with a roller coaster economy, retailers and wholesalers were also confronted by rising competitive pressures. In the 1970s, conventional retailers were seriously threatened by furniture warehouse showrooms, home improvement centers, super drugstores, and other innovative forms of competition. Though less publicized, the turmoil in wholesaling was equally severe.

Given this background, it is not surprising to observe that many companies are in the process of reviewing their strategic posture in the marketplace. During the first half of 1975, for example, Penney's, Federated, Oshawa, and Super Valu almost simultaneously announced that they were embarking on major long-run planning projects. Because of economic and market dislocations, strategic planning has emerged as a central corporate concern in the field of distribution.

The purpose of this paper is to explore the interrelationship between corporate strategy and financial performance. The findings of the paper are based on a careful analysis of all major publicly owned retailing and wholesaling corporations. Of the 391 companies analyzed, 269 are retailing concerns and the balance are wholesaling corporations.

The first section of the paper dramatizes the performance imperative in the

From Bert C. McCammon, Jr., and Albert D. Bates, "Reseller Strategies and the Financial Performance of the Firm," in *Strategy + Structure = Performance,* ed. Hans B. Thorelli (Bloomington: Indiana University Press), pp. 146–164.

field of distribution. Subsequent sections of the paper identify the mainstream strategies that have been most successful in retailing and wholesaling during the 1970–74 period.

THE PERFORMANCE IMPERATIVE

Analysts and executives agree that retailers and wholesalers are currently confronted by a major performance imperative: Distribution companies must improve their profitability, liquidity, and growth potential ratios over forthcoming budget periods.

Profitability Trends

The strategic profit model is a useful frame of reference for understanding the profitability challenge in distribution. As shown in Figure 1, the strategic profit model combines in a single profit-planning equation the principal elements of a company's operating statement and balance sheet. The model involves multiplying a company's profit margin by its rate of asset turnover and its leverage ratio to derive its rate of return on net worth.

The data in Figure 1 show that retailers and wholesalers experienced a sharp decline in profitability between 1968 and 1974. Obviously, much of this decline can be attributed to the 1974–75 recession. It should be emphasized,

FIGURE 1   Composite Strategic Profit Models for Retailing and Wholesaling Corporations,[1] 1968 and 1974

RETAILING CORPORATIONS

	$\dfrac{\text{Net profits (after taxes)}}{\text{Net sales}}$	$\times$	$\dfrac{\text{Net sales}}{\text{Total assets}}$	$=$	$\dfrac{\text{Net profits (after taxes)}}{\text{Total assets}}$	$\times$	$\dfrac{\text{Total assets}}{\text{Net worth}}$	$=$	$\dfrac{\text{Net profits (after taxes)}}{\text{Net worth}}$
1968:	1.4%		2.6		3.8%		2.3		8.8%
1974:	1.0%		2.6		2.6%		2.7		7.0%

WHOLESALING CORPORATIONS

	$\dfrac{\text{Net profits (after taxes)}}{\text{Net sales}}$	$\times$	$\dfrac{\text{Net sales}}{\text{Total assets}}$	$=$	$\dfrac{\text{Net profits (after taxes)}}{\text{Total assets}}$	$\times$	$\dfrac{\text{Total assets}}{\text{Net worth}}$	$=$	$\dfrac{\text{Net profits (after taxes)}}{\text{Net worth}}$
1968:	1.2%		2.9		3.6%		2.4		8.6%
1974:	1.1%		2.6		2.9%		2.6		7.5%

[1] The strategic profit model ratios may not multiply to the totals indicated because of rounding. Furthermore, the net profits to net sales ratios for 1974 have been recalculated to eliminate inventory profits and thereby minimize the effects of inflation.
Sources: Dun and Bradstreet, Inc., First National City Bank, Internal Revenue Service, and authors' calculations.

however, that rates of return on net worth in the field of distribution have declined steadily since the mid-1950s. Thus, recent developments can be interpreted as a continuation of long-term trends.

As shown in Figure 1, retailers and wholesalers are currently generating a composite rate of return on assets of less than 3.0 percent and a composite rate of return on net worth of less than 8.0 percent. By any criteria, these results are well below the levels of performance that will be required during the decade ahead.

Equally disquieting is the persistent increase in leverage ratios. As shown in Figure 1, retailers and wholesalers are currently operating on leverage ratios of more than 2.5 times; this suggests, particularly in an era of capital shortages and high interest rates, that many firms have reached their effective borrowing capacity.

To place these trends in perspective, it is useful to examine the performance criteria currently being emphasized by profit planners. Executives and analysts agree that retailers and wholesalers should program their operations to achieve a rate of return on assets of *at least* 8.0 to 10.0 percent and a rate of return on net worth of *at least* 15.0 to 20.0 percent. Furthermore, they contend that leverage ratios in the field of distribution should be maintained in the 2.0 to 2.5 range. By these standards, it is apparent that most distribution companies are currently confronted by a major profitability challenge.

Liquidity Trends

Retailers and wholesalers in recent years have also encountered liquidity problems, in part because of inflationary pressures and in part because of the collapse of capital markets. As indicated in Table 1, distribution companies currently have a composite current ratio of less than 2.0 times. Their cash to current liabilities ratio is also relatively low, at least by historical standards.

Table 1 Composite Liquidity Ratios for Retailing and Wholesaling Corporations, 1968 and 1974

	Retailing Corporations		Wholesaling Corporations	
Liquidity Ratios	1968	1974	1968	1974
Current assets to current liabilities (times)	1.8	1.7	1.7	1.5
Cash [1] to current liabilities (percent)	19.5	16.5	16.6	14.0
Net profits (before interest and taxes) to interest (times)	4.7	3.5	4.9	3.7

[1] Includes marketable securities.
Sources: Federal Trade Commission, First National City Bank, Internal Revenue Service, and authors' calculations.

More disquieting is the sharp decline in interest coverage ratios that has oc-curred since 1968. As shown in Table 1, the composite interest coverage ratio for retailers fell from 4.7 times in 1968 to only 3.5 times in 1974. During the same period, the interest coverage ratio for wholesalers decreased from 4.9 to 3.7 times. Thus, at the present time, retailers are finding it more difficult to cover their interest payments than are wholesalers.

At the macro-level, it is difficult to determine how severe the "liquidity crisis" is. Liquidity requirements vary widely by line of trade and by season. In addition, many firms can "afford" to maintain low cash balances because of the predictability of their receipts and disbursements, or because they have a strong working relationship with commercial banks, merchandise suppliers, and other creditors.

Despite these and other qualifications, most analysts agree that liquidity ratios must be improved in the field of distribution. Certainly, there is agree-ment that interest coverage ratios have declined to a dangerously low level given the current and projected volatility of the economy.

Growth Potential Trends

The ability of distribution companies to finance expansion is the final area of performance to be explored. Two growth potential ratios are particularly im-portant in this regard. The first ratio, net profits (after dividends) to net worth, roughly measures the rate at which a firm can expand without a disproportionate increase in outside financing. The second ratio, net profits (before interest and taxes) to total assets, roughly measures a firm's ability to leverage its earnings through the use of borrowed funds.

As indicated previously, retailers and wholesalers are currently generating a rate of return on net worth of less than 8.0 percent. After dividend payments, however, this rate of return declines to less than 6.0 percent (see Table 2). Ob-viously, this level of retained earnings can support only a modest rate of growth. Furthermore, the problem of internally financing expansion will become progres-sively severe as inflationary pressures persist.

Table 2   Composite Growth Potential for Retailing and Wholesaling Corporations, 1968 and 1974

Growth Potential Ratios	Retailing Corporations		Wholesaling Corporations	
	1968	1974	1968	1974
Net profits (after dividends) to net worth	6.7%	5.6%	6.3%	5.7%
Net profits (before interest and taxes) to total assets	8.2%	7.8%	7.9%	7.3%

Sources: Federal Trade Commission, First National City Bank, Internal Revenue Service, and authors' calculations.

To complicate matters further, retailers and wholesalers have also reached the limits of their borrowing capacity. As shown in Table 2, distribution companies generate a rate of return on assets (before interest and taxes) that is well below their effective borrowing cost. Thus, for many firms earnings can no longer be leveraged through the use of borrowed funds.

Management Implications

The above analysis suggests that retailers and wholesalers are indeed confronted by a major performance imperative. During the next decade, distribution companies must improve both their rates of return on investment and their liquidity positions. Furthermore, these improvements must be engineered without a significant increase in leverage ratios.

In short, retailers and wholesalers must *simultaneously* program their operations to generate higher yields while maintaining a quality balance sheet. To an increasing extent, this combination of high-yield performance and conservative financing will be required to maintain continuous access to capital markets and to satisfy fully stakeholder expectations.

THE CORRELATES OF PROFITABILITY

Of the performance gaps identified above, the profitability challenge is the most severe. In particular, rates of return on assets must be improved. Preliminary analysis suggests that four factors are critically important in determining the rate of return on assets achieved by distribution companies.

Space Productivity

The effective use of space is a critical determinant of corporate profitability in numerous lines of trade. While important at all levels of distribution, space productivity is a particularly significant variable at the retail level. Table 3 (data were derived from extensive regression analyses) shows the importance of increasing sales per square foot in two lines of retail trade.

Table 3 Space Productivity Requirements in Two Lines of Retail Trade, 1974

	Sales per Square Foot of Selling Area Required to Achieve the Following Rates of Return on Assets		
Line of Trade	5.0%	10.0%	Percent Increase
Supermarkets	$250	$325	30
Furniture stores	65	125	92

Source: Company annual reports and authors' calculations.

Supermarkets can significantly improve their rate of return on assets by increasing their sales per square foot, largely because supermarkets have a high level of fixed costs and, therefore, tend to be volume-sensitive operations. By comparison, furniture store profits are much less influenced by space productivity gains, in part because fixed costs are less significant in furniture retailing. In short, the relative importance of space productivity as a determinant of rate of return on assets varies widely by line of trade.

Inventory Productivity

Statistically, inventory productivity is a less important determinant of corporate profitability than is space productivity. The relationship between inventory productivity and rate of return on assets is still important, however, as Table 4 suggests.

The data in Table 4 show the importance of improving sales-to-stock ratios in the drug and variety store fields. Comparable increases in profitability can be achieved in other lines of retail trade through more aggressive inventory management programs. Furthermore, preliminary analysis suggests that improved inventory management has an even greater effect on profitability in wholesaling than in retailing.

Scale of Operations

Analysts have historically argued that economies of scale are required to achieve high levels of profitability in the field of distribution. On a preliminary basis, it appears that the size of individual firms does have an influence on profitability in some lines of trade.

In those lines of trade that are highly fragmented and in which the typical firm is relatively small, larger firms tend to generate higher levels of profitability than smaller ones. However, in those lines of trade in which most firms have crossed some minimal size threshold, the size of the firm plays little or no role in determining profitability. This appears to be true for both wholesalers and retailers.

Table 4 Inventory Productivity Requirements in Two Lines of Retail Trade, 1974

| Line of Trade | Sales to Inventory Ratios Required to Achieve the Following Rates of Return on Assets | | Percent Increase |
	5.0%	10.0%	
Drugstores	5.7	9.5	67
Variety stores	3.7	7.2	95

Source: Company annual reports and authors' calculations.

Marketing Strategies

Space productivity, inventory productivity, and economies of scale—all are related to the daily operation of the firm and they can have significant effects on profitability. A much more important determinant of profitability, however, is the firm's strategic posture in the marketplace.

For virtually all the companies analyzed, the *critical* factor associated with high levels of performance, and certainly with exceptional levels of performance, is the firm's ability to establish a unique or differentiated position in the marketplace. This does not imply that a unique strategy is a guarantee of success or that the lack of a differentiated strategy is an absolute barrier to success. However, the authors' analysis of publicly held retailers and wholesalers indicates that most of the firms producing exceptional results follow well-defined and relatively innovative strategies. On the other hand, companies producing less attractive results are typically committed to more conventional approaches to the marketplace.

The balance of this paper examines the strategies that have been most successful in retailing and wholesaling during recent years. The high-performance companies used to document this analysis are profiled in the appendixes to this chapter.

Before examining the strategies used by these companies, it may be useful to describe their performance. As indicated in Table 5, these "elite" firms achieved unusually high rates of growth between 1970 and 1974. Their sales increased at an annual rate of 21.3 percent a year, and their profits expanded even more rapidly. (The "elite" retailers increased their volume and profits even more rapidly than the wholesalers.)

The financial performance of these firms is even more compelling than their rates of growth. Table 6 shows that the "elite" companies in distribution are currently generating a median rate of return on assets of 10.1 percent and a median rate of return on net worth of 17.5 percent. Furthermore, they have achieved these results while maintaining a defensible liquidity position and a balanced capital structure. In short, the high performance of these companies underscores the importance of strategic planning in the field of distribution.

Table 5 Median Compound Annual Growth Rates for 42 Leading Retailers and Wholesalers, 1970–71/1974–75

Type and Number of Companies	Compound Annual Growth Rates [1] (1970–71/1974–75)	
	Net Sales	Net Profits
Retailing companies (19)	28.6%	31.6%
Wholesaling companies (23)	18.9	27.8
All companies (42)	21.3%	28.6%

[1] Adjusted for mergers and acquisitions.
Source: Company annual reports and authors' calculations.

Table 6   Median Financial Ratios for 42 Leading Retailers and Wholesalers, 1974–75

Financial Ratios	Type and Number of Companies		
	Retailing Companies (19)	Wholesaling Companies (23)	All Companies (42)
Strategic Profit Model Ratios [1]			
Net profits to net sales (percent)	4.0	4.8	4.2
Net sales to total assets (times)	2.6	2.2	2.3
Net profits to total assets (percent)	10.0	10.2	10.1
Total assets to net worth (times)	1.7	1.8	1.8
Net profits to net worth (percent)	18.1	17.5	17.5
Liquidity Ratios			
Current assets to current liabilities (times)	2.4	2.3	2.4
Cash [2] to current liabilities (percent)	40.4	7.5	21.6
Net profits (before interest and taxes) to interest (times)	16.7	15.4	15.4
Growth Potential Ratios			
Net profits (before interest and taxes) to total assets (percent)	20.9	21.0	21.0
Net profits (after dividends) to net worth (percent)	15.4	14.8	15.2

[1] The strategic profit model ratios will not multiply to the totals indicated because the ratios are medians rather than weighted averages.
[2] Includes marketable securities.
Sources: Company annual reports and authors' calculations.

HIGH PERFORMANCE STRATEGIES IN RETAILING

The history of retailing is the history of strategic innovation. In the early 1970s, retailers were continuously confronted by new and innovative forms of competition. Warehouse retailers, for example, emerged as an explosive competitive force; furniture warehouse showrooms, appliance and TV warehouse showrooms, and catalog showrooms expanded rapidly in most metropolitan markets. In addition, the most advanced form of warehouse retailing, the hypermarket, achieved a position of competitive saliency in Western Europe, and several units have recently been opened in North America. Thus, warehouse retailing has been a major source of competitive turbulence over the past five years.

As a group, however, warehouse retailers have yet to produce consistently attractive results. To phrase it charitably, their financial performance has been decidedly mixed. Thus, the warehouse retailing movement is ignored in this paper, even though both authors recognize its importance.

Also ignored are other strategic thrusts such as the fast-food service outlet in the restaurant field and the convenience food store in the grocery field. These latter developments are ignored because their impact has been for the most part confined to a single line of trade. In short, they are *specific* rather than *generic* strategies. In addition, the long-run potential of the convenience food store, given its low rate of return on assets and its high gross margin requirements, is yet to be demonstrated.

Our analysis concentrates on the *mainstream* strategies that have been most successful in retailing over the past five years. The taxonomy developed is neither exhaustive nor exclusive. It is, however, useful for understanding the importance of strategic planning in the field of retailing.

On the basis of line-of-trade and corporate data, it appears that seven mainstream strategies in retailing deserve particular emphasis. The strategies are discussed here.

Supermarket Retailing

The supermarket concept, though originally developed in the food field, is not limited to the sale of food products. It involves the use of five key factors to improve productivity and reduce the cost of distribution. These factors are: (1) self-service and self-selection displays; (2) centralization of customer services, usually at the checkout counter; (3) large-scale, low-cost physical facilities; (4) a strong price emphasis; and (5) a broad assortment and wide variety of merchandise to facilitate multiple item purchases.

During recent years, an increasing number of retailers, in multiple lines of trade, have adopted the supermarket concept. In the process they have strengthened their market position and improved their financial results. The extension of the supermarket concept to other lines of trade is unquestionably a major competitive development. This strategy has been particularly successful in the drug, home improvement, sporting goods, and toy fields.

Long's, for example, pioneered the super drugstore movement in the early 1960s. Since that time, the company has consistently achieved outstanding results. Long's currently operates 82 super drugstores in California and contiguous states. A typical Long's outlet contains 26,000 square feet of selling space, generates annual sales of more than $4.5 million, and operates on a gross margin of 25 percent. Thus, Long's relies on an aggressive pricing policy and economies of scale to generate an adequate rate of return on investment.

Standard Brands is pursuing a similar strategy in the home improvement field. At the present time, the company operates 55 paint and home decorating supermarkets, each of which contains more than 11,000 square feet of space. Standard Brands obtains 41 percent of its volume from self-manufactured products; this partially accounts for the company's high profit margin.

Oshman's, a Houston-based firm, has pioneered the supermarket concept in the sporting goods field. The company currently operates 44 sporting goods supermarkets, which generate an annual volume of more than $1.0 million each. Thus, the Oshman units have a substantial scalar advantage over conventional sporting goods dealers.

As these examples suggest, supermarket operators project a strong price image, which appeals to a major segment of the market. Given the importance of this segment, the supermarket approach is likely to remain successful for some time to come.

Store Positioning

As the consumer market becomes more fragmented, store positioning strategies become more important. A substantial number of retailers have already positioned (or are repositioning) themselves to capitalize on life style or demographic trends. Byerly's, Handy Andy, and Treasure Island, for example, have positioned themselves to appeal to the affluent grocery shopper. Crate and Barrel and Pottery Barn also concentrate on the affluent consumer, while Pier I focuses on the "under 35" market and Radio Shack on the electronics enthusiast. Positioning has emerged as a major strategic thrust. It can be particularly effective in the sale of "fashion" merchandise. In the apparel, home accessories, and home furnishings fields, for example, consumer preferences vary widely by social class and by life style. Thus there are numerous opportunities to focus on specific market segments.

Mervyn's and The Limited are retailers that have effectively positioned themselves in the apparel field. The Limited focuses on the 18 to 30-year-old "high fashion" shopper, while Mervyn's concentrates on the middle-income, middle-class, family market. Both companies have achieved enviable rates of growth, because they have developed a focused and competitively differentiated approach to the markets they serve.

In summary, store positioning offers numerous opportunities for creating a differential advantage. However, it is a difficult strategy to implement, because it requires a precise understanding of consumer buying behavior, as well as a sophisticated management team to capitalize on the opportunity.

Non-Store Retailing

Direct marketing is rapidly becoming a major force in the American economy. Established companies such as Sears and Ward's are continuing to expand their direct marketing programs. More important, however, is the entry of new and innovative firms, such as GRI, Mary Kay, and Unity Buying Service.

GRI sponsors the World of Beauty Club and other direct mail programs. Consumers belonging to the World of Beauty Club receive four to six cosmetics kits a year, each of which has a retail value of $15.00 or more. The membership price for these kits is approximately one-third the normal retail price. Thus, consumers can effect substantial savings by joining the World of Beauty Club. GRI has also developed direct marketing programs for flatware and vitamins. As a result, the company has emerged as a major competitor in the direct mail field.

Mary Kay has been equally successful in the cosmetics industry by using the party plan method of distribution. The company specializes in skin care products, which are marketed by 29,000 Sales Directors and Sales Consultants. As is the case with many direct marketing organizations, Mary Kay operates its own manufacturing facilities, thus increasing its profit margin.

Unity Buying Service is another high-performance company in the direct marketing field. The company sponsors the Unity Buying Club, which offers a wide variety of merchandise to consumers at "cost plus 8 percent." The Club's membership roll currently consists of 955,000 families. Furthermore, the membership renewal rate has increased steadily since the mid-1960s, which suggests that this program will continue to expand over the decade ahead.

Non-store retailing will become progressively more important in the 1970s as more and more consumers become disenchanted with the shopping process. In addition, of course, non-store retailing will continue to expand because of the innovative programs developed by GRI, Mary Kay, Unity Buying Service, and other leading firms.

Expansion into Secondary Markets

Retailers operating in secondary markets have consistently outperformed their metropolitan counterparts. Bi-Lo, Pamida, and Wal-Mart are companies that have achieved superior results by focusing on "fringe" markets. Bi-Lo operates discount supermarkets in small rural communities; Pamida locates its bantam discount stores in cities with populations of less than 10,000; and Wal-Mart operates discount department stores in county seat towns throughout the Southwest. By focusing on secondary markets, each of these organizations has been able to achieve a position of competitive dominance at a relatively low cost.

Obviously, secondary markets have several attractive characteristics, including a lower level of competition, a stable labor force, and a minimum number of zoning and environmental regulations. For these and other reasons, secondary market retailers are likely to outperform the "industry averages" over forthcoming budget periods.

Market Intensification

Companies adopting a market intensification strategy pursue a programmed and disciplined approach to corporate expansion. They restrict their expansion efforts to a limited number of "core" markets rather than expanding erratically into geographically distant markets. Almost without exception, market concentration retailers have performed better than their "national" counterparts. Caldor, Lowe's, and Weis are among the leading proponents of the market concentration philosophy.

Caldor, a discount department store chain, operates a compact group of stores in the urban corridor between New York and Boston; Lowe's, a home improvement center chain, operates primarily in six southeastern states; and Weis, an extraordinarily well-managed food chain, operates in only three states. By concentrating their efforts on a limited number of markets, these and companies like them have been able to generate unusually attractive results.

Some very important advantages accrue to firms operating in a contained expansion mode. These include advertising economies arising from multiple outlets in a single market, maximum utilization of a small number of distribution centers, high levels of customer awareness, and easy access to top management to prevent or resolve operating problems at the store level.

In short, market intensification results in both strategic and operating advantages that can dramatically affect profitability. Consequently, it is a strategic approach that should be given more attention than it presently receives.

Product Specialization

Analysts contend that "super" specialty stores could be the wave of the future. The explosive growth of Athlete's Foot, County Seat, The Gap, and Calculators, Inc. tends to confirm this hypothesis.

These and other specialty store operators have been conspicuously successful in rationalizing the distribution process. They have blended the advantages of product specialization with the economics of chain-store operation. As this trend develops, it will irretrievably alter the nature of competition in an increasing number of product categories.

Aaron Brothers, Child World, and Jerrico are among the leading proponents of the product specialization concept. Aaron Brothers specializes in artist's supplies, picture frames, and related lines of merchandise; Child World specializes in bicycles, toys, children's furniture, and leisure goods; and Jerrico is currently emphasizing its Long John Silver's Sea Food Shoppes. Each of these companies has achieved a distinctive niche in the marketplace by focusing on a limited number of product categories. Aaron Brothers and Child World achieve additional economies by operating on a supermarket basis.

Retail Diversification

The strategy of retail diversification produced mixed results between 1970 and 1974. Dayton Hudson, Supermarkets General, and Zale, for example, experienced operating difficulties as a result of their diversification programs. Other companies, however, coped successfully with the problems of managing multiple businesses. For these firms, diversification proved to be an effective growth vehicle. Currently, Edison Brothers and Melville Shoe are the most successful diversified retailers.

Edison Brothers operates 814 Edison Brothers shoe stores (under the Chandlers, Bakers, Leeds, Burts, the Wild Pair, and Joan Bari Boutiques names); 44 Handyman do-it-yourself hardware and building materials stores; 78 Size 5-7-9 shops featuring feminine clothing for sizes one through nine; 113 Jeans West stores offering jeans, tops, and outerwear for young adults; and 30 United sporting goods stores offering a complete line of sports equipment and apparel.

Melville Shoe operates 717 Meldisco shoe departments, all in K-Mart stores; three shoe chains (Thom McAn, Miles, and Vanguard); cvs, a chain of health and beauty aids stores; Foxmoor Casuals, a chain of fashion apparel stores directed at the 15 to 24-year-old, middle-income woman; Chess King, a fashion apparel chain targeted at young men; Clothes Bin, a chain of discount women's apparel stores; and 19 shoe and men's apparel manufacturing facilities.

As consumer markets become more segmented and as life styles become more diverse, an increasing number of retailers will probably diversify their operations, despite the managerial problems and risks involved.

HIGH PERFORMANCE STRATEGIES
IN WHOLESALING

Some wholesalers increased both their growth and their profits in the early 1970s. Seven kinds of strategic thrusts were particularly important.

Voluntary Group Programs

The voluntary group movement picked up momentum in the early 1970s as wholesalers either expanded existing programs or developed new programs for affiliated stores. In the grocery field, for example, Wetterau, Super Valu, and other voluntaries steadily increased their market share between 1970 and 1974. More important, however, is the rapid growth of voluntaries in other lines of trade. As shown in Table 7, voluntaries have become a major force in both the drug and hardware fields, with most of this expansion occurring in the early 1970s. Voluntaries are also expanding rapidly in the automotive, automatic vending, and variety store fields. In short, voluntary groups continue to be an important mechanism for rationalizing the distribution process.

Genuine Parts and The McLain Grocery Company illustrate the results that can be achieved by aggressive voluntary wholesalers. Genuine Parts, with annual sales of almost $600 million, is a charter member of NAPA, the largest voluntary group in the automotive field. The company provides a full range of services to affiliated jobbers, including a comprehensive inventory protection program.

McLain is a large IGA wholesaler operating in Ohio, Pennsylvania, and West Virginia. Like many other voluntary wholesalers, McLain has steadily diversified its inventories and expanded the scope of its services in recent years. As a result, the company is rapidly evolving into a total capability supplier, providing its

Table 7 Leading Voluntary Groups in the Drug and Hardware Fields, 1974

Voluntary Groups in the Drug Field	Number of Affiliated Stores	Voluntary Groups in the Hardware Field	Number of Affiliated Stores
Economost	5,000	Western Auto	4,230
Good Neighbor Pharmacies	1,400	Sentry	4,200
Associated Druggists	1,132	Pro	2,650
United Systems Stores	744	Ace	2,500
Family Service Drug Stores	350	Gamble-Skogmo	1,200
Triple A	300	Coast-To-Coast	1,040
Velocity	250	Trustworthy	800
Community Shield Pharmacies	200	Stratton & Terstegge	550
FIP	200	Farwell, Ozman, Kirk & Co.	495
Sell-Thru Guild	200	American Wholesale Hardware	175
Total	9,776	Total	17,840

Sources: Chain Store Age and Hardware Age.

customers with a high proportion of the merchandise and services they need to operate effectively in increasingly competitive markets.

Inventory Diversification

For many wholesalers, inventory diversification has proved to be an effective growth strategy. The logic of inventory diversification is fairly self-evident. By adding product lines, wholesalers can simultaneously increase their sales and strengthen their relationship with customers. Furthermore, wholesalers with highly diversified inventories have the option of positioning themselves as single-source suppliers, which partially insulates them from transactional competition.

Despite the complexities involved in inventory diversification programs, many wholesalers began to broaden their product lines in the early 1970s, particularly in the hardware, building materials, and grocery fields. Hughes and Rykoff are two high-performance companies that have increased their growth through inventory diversification programs.

Hughes, originally a plumbing supply wholesaler, began to diversify its inventories in the early 1970s. By 1974, the company had evolved into a *full-line* distributor of electrical, industrial, plumbing, and utility supplies. In the process, Hughes increased its rate of return on net worth from 5.2 percent in 1970 to 15.0 percent in 1974.

Rykoff has used a similar strategy. Originally an institutional food distributor, Rykoff has emerged as a full-line supplier in the food service field. The company currently distributes a broad range of nonfood products, including dinnerware, glassware, silverware, restaurant equipment, and supplies, which represent an increasing proportion of its sales.

Wholesale Diversification

Some wholesalers have gone beyond inventory diversification to establish separate profit centers in totally unrelated lines of trade. In wholesaling, as in retailing, however, the trend toward corporate diversification has tended to produce mixed results, largely because of the problems involved in managing multiple businesses. Some companies, however, have been conspicuously successful with their diversification programs. Bluefield Supply, Premier Industrial, and J. M. Tull are among the most successful of the diversified wholesalers.

Bluefield Supply is a highly diversified distributor with sales divided as follows: heavy construction and industrial equipment, 67.1 percent; hardware and industrial supplies, 17.8 percent; household appliances and home entertainment products, 10.5 percent; and hospital supplies, 4.6 percent. The company currently operates 28 distribution centers in six states and is rapidly expanding its operations for the future.

Premier Industrial is also highly diversified, as is J. M. Tull. The former, for example, operates separate profit centers in four unrelated fields: industrial maintenance, specialty chemicals, fire-fighting equipment, and electronic parts and supplies; while the latter operates nine metal service centers, an automotive parts distributorship, and an industrial supplies division. In short, these companies demonstrate that diversification programs can be used to generate unusually attractive returns.

Retail Diversification

In the early 1970s, numerous wholesalers began to operate retailing outlets. This trend was particularly apparent among grocery wholesalers.

Malone & Hyde, for example, currently operates 35 conventional supermarkets, 30 super drugstores, and 10 tonnage supermarkets. The company presently obtains 24.1 percent of its volume from its retail operations. Nash Finch, a Minneapolis-based grocery wholesaler, also operates a wide range of retail outlets, including 30 warehouse supermarkets and 25 family centers.

As profitability pressures intensify, more wholesalers will probably enter the retail field. Multi-level merchandisers like Malone & Hyde and Nash Finch will become increasingly common.

Product and Market Specialization

Specialized wholesalers have become a *major* competitive force in many product categories. As a group, specialists carry broader assortments of merchandise and maintain higher service levels than their general-line competitors. They maintain massive inventory investments and tend to offer more frequent deliveries and provide a higher level of technical support. As a result of these and other competitive advantages, specialists have steadily increased their market share over the past four years.

The range of specialization defies easy description. The following companies are among the leading specialists in their product lines: Bearings, Inc. (antifriction bearings and power transmission equipment and supplies); Farmer Bros. (coffee, condiments, and coffee brewing equipment); Kar Products (automotive and industrial maintenance supplies); Lawson Products (maintenance, repair, and operating supplies); and D. L. Saslow (dental equipment and supplies).

National Brand Programs

Wholesalers are becoming ever more involved in the total marketing process. Already, an increasing number of firms have the capability to design and develop complete marketing programs.

Ehrenreich Photo-Optical, for example, markets 19 brands of cameras on a national basis, including Nikon, Mamiya, and Bronica. S. Riekes is another national marketer of branded merchandise. The company designs and distributes a broad range of glassware products manufactured to its specifications. Heavy emphasis is placed on the firm's proprietary lines, including Riekes Crisa, Riekes Chalet, and The John Riekes Kristaluxus Collection.

Telecor and Waxman Industries are other wholesalers who provide complete marketing services. Telecor is the exclusive distributor of Panasonic products in California and 13 contiguous states. Waxman Industries markets its own lines of plumbing and electrical supplies, largely through home improvement centers. The company supports each of its lines with a comprehensive range of merchandising services.

All of these companies have enjoyed extraordinary success because of their ability to develop and execute complete marketing programs, a further indication that wholesalers have gone well beyond their traditional redistribution function.

Forward or Backward Integration into Manufacturing

Wholesalers steadily increased their manufacturing capability between 1970 and 1974, many of them evolving into self-supply organizations that also provide processing services to their customers.

Bristol Products and Superscope, for example, are totally committed to self-manufacturing programs. W. W. Grainger, Earle M. Jorgensen, and Pioneer Standard Electronics are other wholesalers who have made a major commitment to their manufacturing divisions.

The rise of manufacturing wholesalers dramatizes the shift in market power that has occurred in many product categories. Large wholesalers are becoming a dominant force in the marketplace.

CONCLUDING REMARKS

The "case studies" cited underscore the importance of developing high-performance strategies in the field of distribution. To an increasing extent, strategic rather than tactical decisions will determine corporate success in the 1970s. Distribution companies interested in improving their performance over the decade ahead should, therefore, make a major commitment to the strategic planning process.

An Attitudinal Framework for Advertising Strategy

Harper W. Boyd, Jr., Michael L. Ray,
and Edward C. Strong

Advertising and marketing researchers have developed a variety of new techniques for defining and measuring attitude and attitudinal change. These techniques have added much to the understanding of the communications process, but seldom have they been used in a comprehensive form to structure advertising strategies and tactics.[1] This article focuses on the nature of advertising objectives from an attitudinal perspective.

The proposed framework facilitates the formulation of a strategy of consumer attitudinal change and suggests that basically five advertising strategy alternatives are available to the decision maker. The nature of each of these strategy alternatives is discussed, but the framework also holds promise for meeting other marketing problems such as market segmentation and the development of product features and new products.

ATTITUDES AS ADVERTISING OBJECTIVES

The specification of advertising objectives is of critical significance for the formulation of advertising strategy. Therefore, it is important to select objec-

About the Authors: Harper W. Boyd, Jr. is Sebastian S. Kresge Professor of Marketing; director, International Center for the Advancement of Management Education; and director of Continuing Education, Graduate School of Business, Stanford University.

Michael L. Ray is associate professor of marketing at the Stanford University Graduate School of Business. He also holds a courtesy appointment in the Stanford Communication Department.

Edward C. Strong is assistant professor of marketing at INSEAD, Fontainebleau, France.

Reprinted from *Journal of Marketing,* vol. 36 (April 1972), pp. 27–33, published by the American Marketing Association.

[1] Lee Adler and Irving Crespi, eds., *Attitude Research at Sea* (Chicago: American Marketing Association, 1966) and *Attitude Research on the Rocks* (1968); Allan Greenberg, "Is Communication Research Really Worthwhile?" *Journal of Marketing,* Vol. 31 (January, 1967), pp. 48–50; and Charles K. Ramond, "Must Advertising Communicate to Sell?" *Harvard Business Review,* Vol. 43 (September–October, 1965), pp. 148–161.

tives that can be affected by advertising and that allow for efficient and continuous testing and evaluation.

The issue of objectives had been somewhat neglected in the advertising field until 1961 when the Association of National Advertisers published Colley's *Defining Advertising Goals for Measured Advertising Results*.[2] This book, and a subsequent monograph, suggested that the goals of advertising are most often goals of communication rather than those pertaining to sales.[3] These and similar publications essentially conceptualized the advertising process as a "hierarchy of effect."[4] Their view was that advertising's purpose was to affect some level of the hierarchy—such as awareness, comprehension, or conviction—and that this effect, combined with the effects of other variables in the marketing mix, would lead to the ultimate goals of sales and profits.

This "hierarchy" view was criticized on two fronts. First, quantitatively oriented researchers and managers argued that inasmuch as sales are the ultimate outcome of advertising efforts, sales should be measured.[5] Second, certain behavioral scientists contended that little evidence supported the hierarchy of effects itself; that is, learning does not necessarily lead to attitudinal change, nor does attitudinal change necessarily lead to behavioral change.[6] Thus, advertising goals formed on the basis of changes in intermediate variables—such as recall or comprehension—may be of questionable value.

Fortunately, this controversy about objectives created some insight and raised a number of significant issues. For example, one of the recent key developments in marketing research has been that of techniques for measuring attitude as a predispositional response—one that is indicative of future behavior.[7] Richard Reiser, executive director of the market research department of Grey Advertising, has commented:

---

[2] Russell Colley, *Defining Advertising Goals for Measured Advertising Results* (New York: Association of National Advertisers, 1961).

[3] Harry Deane Wolfe, James K. Brown, and G. Clark Thompson, *Measuring Advertising Results* (New York: National Industrial Conference Board, 1962).

[4] See for example, Rosser Reeves, *Reality in Advertising* (New York: Alfred A. Knopf, 1961); Darrell Blaine Lucas and Steuart Henderson Britt, *Measuring Advertising Effectiveness* (New York: McGraw-Hill, 1963); and Robert J. Lavidge and Gary A. Steiner, "A Model for Predictive Measurements of Advertising Effectiveness," *Journal of Marketing*, Vol. 25 (October, 1961), pp. 59–62.

[5] Kristian S. Palda, "The Hypothesis of Hierarchy of Effects: A Partial Evaluation," *Journal of Marketing Research*, Vol. 3 (February, 1966), pp. 13–24; Ramond, same reference as footnote 1; and Ambar G. Rao, *Quantitative Theories in Advertising* (New York: John Wiley & Sons, 1970).

[6] Leon Festinger, "Behavioral Support for Opinion Change," *Public Opinion Quarterly*, Vol. 28 (Fall, 1964), pp. 404–417; Jack B. Haskins, "Factual Recall as a Measure of Advertising Effectiveness," *Journal of Advertising Research*, Vol. 4 (March, 1964), pp. 2–8; and Herbert E. Krugman, "The Impact of Television Advertising: Learning without Involvement," *Public Opinion Quarterly*, Vol. 29 (Fall, 1965), pp. 349–356.

[7] Alvin A. Achenbaum, "An Answer to One of the Unanswered Questions about the Measurement of Advertising Effectiveness," in *Proceedings of the 12th Annual Meeting of the Advertising Research Foundation* (New York: Advertising Research Foundation, 1966), pp. 24–32; George S. Day, "Using Attitude Measures to Evaluate New Product Introductions," *Journal of Marketing Research*, Vol. 7 (November, 1970), pp. 474–482; and John C. Maloney, "Attitude Measurement and Formation," paper presented at the AMA Test Marketing Workshop (Chicago: American Marketing Association, 1966), mimeo.

Our reason for selecting attitudes as our basic way of looking at a market is based on more than the fact that one function of advertising is to affect attitudes. There is considerable evidence to show that the way a person thinks and feels about a brand—his attitudinal set—determines how he will behave. His reasons for wanting a product determine his selection: we have always found a close relationship between opinion towards a product and probability of purchase.[8]

Maloney also concluded that consumer attitudes do relate to sales. He offers considerable evidence that ". . . consumer data can become a focal point for defining marketing problems and determining marketing goals."[9]

Defining advertising goals in relation to attitudes and attitudinal change has considerable appeal. Attitudes have the operationally desirable quality of being measurable, albeit with difficulty and some lack of precision. Attitudes also have long been the object of investigation by behavioral scientists, and a considerable body of knowledge has resulted from their studies and models. Today's psychologists believe that attitude includes both perceptual and preferential components; i.e., attitude is an inferred construct. When one refers to an attitude he means that a person's past experiences predispose him to respond in certain ways on the basis of certain perceptions. Attitude, therefore, may be viewed as a variable which links psychological and behavioral components.[10]

Since attitudes reflect perceptions, they inevitably indicate predispositions. Thus, they permit advertising strategists to design advertising inputs which will affect perceptions and thereby change predispositions to respond or behave. This process is the foundation of the strategy suggestions contained in the following sections.

AN EMERGING FRAMEWORK

The possibility of linking perceptions and preferences in formulating advertising strategy has only recently occurred, because strategists and researchers have emphasized either perceptions or preferences to the exclusion of the other. Some have emphasized brand image with only vague regard to response; others have emphasized brand loyalty with little regard to the perception that led to that loyalty.[11]

Now, however, marketing has witnessed an active integration of research on the perceptual and the preference aspects of attitude. The Colley-DAGMAR and NICB books hinted at this integration.[12] Maloney suggested using both

---

[8] As quoted in *Advertising Age*, December 19, 1966, p. 1.

[9] Maloney, same reference as footnote 7.

[10] See Martin Fishbein, ed., *Readings in Attitude Theory and Measurement* (New York: John Wiley & Sons, 1967); Marie Jahoda and Neil Warren, eds., *Attitudes* (Baltimore: Penguin Books, 1966); and Gene F. Summers, ed., *Attitude Measurement* (Chicago: Rand-McNally, 1970).

[11] Summers, same reference as footnote 10, pp. 227–234 and pp. 149–158; and Jacob Jacoby, "A Model of Multi-Brand Loyalty," *Journal of Advertising Research*, Vol. 11 (June, 1971), pp. 25–31.

[12] Colley, same reference as footnote 2; and Wolfe et al., same reference as footnote 2.

perceptions and preferences with his CAPP (Continuous Advertising Planning Program) research.[13] Smith described General Motors' advertising evaluation program as including measurement of consumer perceptions of automobile characteristics and the relating of these characteristics to automobile preferences or likelihood of purchase.[14]

Even more recently, technical advances have been made in marketing that further allow managers to link perceptions and preferences in order to make advertising plans. These technical advances have come from two areas. One is the area of research for new product developments which is typified by the market structure studies pioneered by Stefflre and others.[15] The other area is that of consumer behavior models. These models typically examine the nature of the changes in the perceptions and preferences of consumers as they move toward a buying decision. Although a number of such models exist, they are typified by Amstutz's microsimulation model which posits that consumers move through four major stages in the purchase process: development of perceived need, decision to shop, purchase, and post-purchase. While moving through these stages, consumers can experience alterations in attitudinal structure.[16] His concept is the primary basis for the framework for advertising strategy suggested in this article.

Amstutz assumes that the consumer's attitudinal structure for any product class consists of a set of salient product class characteristics (choice criteria) and a set of brand perceptions regarding each of the salient product characteristics. That is, for a particular product class an individual considers a number of product characteristics to be salient. He also has a perception about what the ideal brand of this product would be like with respect to each of these characteristics or dimensions.

The consumer's choice criteria reflects his needs, values, prior product experience, and so on. In the case of mature products, the choice criteria are reasonably well defined. Such is not the case with many new products; therefore, the seller has the opportunity to play an important role in the building of attitudes toward the product class.

More specifically, the consumer is asked to indicate the extent to which each product characteristic is salient using a scale, say, of 0–10. The result is an attitudinal set which forms the consumer's choice criteria against which the individual brands belonging to the product class are evaluated. The consumer is

---

[13] Maloney, same reference as footnote 7.

[14] Gail Smith, "How G.M. Measures Ad Effectiveness," *Printer's Ink* (May 14, 1965), pp. 19–29.

[15] Volney Stefflre, "Market Structure Studies: New Products for Old Markets and New Markets (Foreign) for Old Products," in *Applications of the Sciences in Marketing Management* (New York: John Wiley & Sons, 1968), pp. 251–268; and Alvin J. Silk, "The Use of Preference and Perception Measures in New Product Development: An Exposition and Review," *Industrial Management Review*, Vol. 11 (Fall, 1969), pp. 21–37.

[16] Arnold E. Amstutz, *Computer Simulation of Competitive Market Response* (Cambridge, Massachusetts: M.I.T. Press, 1967). For other micro-type consumer behavior models see John A. Howard and Jagdish N. Sheth, *The Theory of Buyer Behavior* (New York: John Wiley & Sons, 1964); Francesco M. Nicosia, *Consumer Decision Processes* (Englewood Cliffs, N.J.: Prentice-Hall, 1966), pp. 155–191; and James F. Engel, David T. Kollat and Roger D. Blackwell, *Consumer Behavior* (New York: Holt, Rinehart & Winston, 1968).

Table 1 Hypothetical Example of Amstutz-Type Attitude Structure for Nutritional Ready-to-Eat Cereals

	Ratings		
Salient Product Characteristics	Product Category	Brand A	Brand B
Protein	8	9	5
Minerals	5	7	5
Vitamins	9	8	4
Absence of sugar	4	3	6

then asked to rate the same product characteristics for each relevant brand again on a scale of 0–10. Conceptually, the consumer chooses a particular brand by comparing his ratings toward each brand with his ratings of the ideal brand. The brand which compares most favorably with the "ideal" has the highest probability of being chosen. This is the link between perception and preference.

For example, a housewife who did not believe that nutrition was a highly salient product characteristic for a ready-to-eat cereal would, of course, be unlikely to buy such a cereal type. On the other hand, the following product characteristics might be salient to a housewife who *is* considering the purchase of such a cereal type: protein, minerals, vitamins, and the absence of sugar. Assume that a housewife is asked for her ideal saliency ratings on these four product characteristics using a scale of 0–10. Further assume that the same consumer is asked to rate brands A and B in the same fashion with the results shown in Table 1.

Based on such an attitudinal set the consumer would probably buy brand A over brand B. It should be stated that predictions of behavior based on such ratings are essentially probabilistic.

The above described perceptual structure holds considerable promise as a framework for advertising strategy formulation. Rather than assume that advertising's function is to affect sales directly or to have an effect on a level of the hierarchy, it would seem more functional to assume that advertising can maintain or shift attitudes with respect to salient product characteristics and their ratings. If such can be accomplished, it will lead to preference which affects sales and profits.

If advertising's overriding goal is to influence attitudinal structures such as those suggested in Table 1, then a manager can choose from among five broad strategy alternatives. He can seek to:

1. Affect those forces which influence strongly the choice criteria used for evaluating brands belonging to the product class;
2. Add characteristic(s) to those considered salient for the product class;
3. Increase/decrease the rating for a salient product class characteristic;

4. Change perception of the company's brand with regard to some particular salient product characteristic; or
5. Change perception of competitive brands with regard to some particular salient product characteristic.

The remainder of this article discusses these strategies.

STRATEGY ONE: AFFECT PRODUCT CLASS LINKAGES TO GOALS AND EVENTS

This strategy relates to the formulation of advertising which attempts to stimulate primary demand. Such a strategy would seek to enhance the saliency rating given one product class versus others with respect to obtaining certain goals. The framework is similar to that presented earlier in that the consumer has choice criteria which he uses to rate alternative product classes with respect to obtaining his goals.

If the advertiser knows (1) the goals of a given market segment with respect to (2) the choice criteria (salient product characteristics) used to evaluate the alternative product classes considered as ways of achieving the goals, and (3) the perceptions regarding each product class, he can better decide what action to take to stimulate demand for his product class. Inevitably he must link his product class to the relevant goals. But he must also seek to change the consumer's rating of his product class versus others with respect to the choice criteria involved.

The advertiser could seek to change the saliency of the consumer's goals and thus increase the demand for his product class. However, most of the change associated with goals comes about through environmental factors operating over long periods of time, although advertising can, no doubt, accelerate the trends.

Thus far no distinction has been made between "goals" and "needs." In the final analysis, products are judged on the basis of their function or role in helping the individual to attain some goal or in meeting a need. In the case of nutritional ready-to-eat cereal, the goal of many consumers is to maintain or improve health while not gaining (or losing) weight. Still other consumers might wish to achieve the goal of caring for their loved ones by ensuring that they receive their daily quota of minerals and vitamins. Many other goals could be outlined, but their importance lies, first, in that the goal(s) will partly determine what product class characteristics are salient (as well as how salient), and second, that the goal(s) will ultimately be reflected in the individual's attitudes toward alternative brands of the product. Thus, if goals are known—however imprecisely—they help to explain attitudinal ratings, or if salient product characteristics and ratings are known, goals may be deduced.

After the advertiser has differentiated individuals on the basis of goals and translated this differentiation into preference for one product class over another via saliency ratings, he now could try to alter these saliency ratings or product class choice criteria in the hope of attracting more consumers to *his* product class and ultimately to his brand. In the nutritional cereal example, at least one advertiser attempted to do this by making the appeal: "What's a mother to do . . . about vitamins . . . Serve . . . . the only leading cereal with a whole day's vitamin supply . . . Feel vitamin-safe all day." Another advertiser perceived another goal as instrumental and advertised: "Charge Up, Sleek Down . . . Feel Like a Healthy Animal." The first advertiser tied goals to product class choice criteria, while the latter simply stressed the goal to be obtained.

Other examples of attempting to change, influence, or create additional goals as they relate to the use of product classes or brands are safety in automobiles, health protection by eliminating oral bacteria and germs through the frequent use of a mouthwash, easing problems of mild insomnia by taking aspirin, reducing the financial burden of decentralized inventories through the regularized use of air freight, and the reduction in air pollution through the use of low-lead gasoline.

Once goals are set, the consumer will proceed to select products which will help him obtain his objectives. But there is an intervening consideration since most products are consumed as part of an "event"—that is, it is part of a situation which occurs at certain places at certain times and often involves the presence of more than one individual. The situation may be socially or work-oriented and often involves more than one product. The event is, of course, tied to the goal and is prescribed and constrained accordingly.

The possibility presented for strategy formulation at this level is the use of advertising to change the individual's attitude toward the use of a product class *within* a particular event. In other words, the salient product characteristics of alternative product classes will be judged according to how well they "fit" with the event to be pursued. The event itself is perceived by the individual as being associated with certain salient product class characteristics, and the decision process is similar to the notion of perception and brand choice. The advertiser seeks to change or modify the attitudes toward salient product class characteristics that the individual associates with the event, in order to increase the probability that the product class of interest will be chosen.

It is at the event level of demand that social or group influence on the individual's choice of brand becomes more apparent. This is only natural, because social encounter is viewed as an "event" by individuals, whether people gather for some jointly agreed purpose (specific goal-related activities) or merely meet "by chance." Frequently, a modification or influence of attitude sets at the event level entails changing attitudes of the group or at least changing the individual's perception of attitudes held by the group. A prominent example of such attempted influence involves the social acceptability of women smoking small cigars in public. Others include the serving of margarine to guests, the serving of wine at family meals to bring greater enjoyment to a commonplace affair, and the drinking of milk after strenuous exercise to reduce body temperature.

The first broad strategy alternative is a complex one, and this article can only hint at how the strategy can be implemented. Nevertheless, goals and events are important to consider since they affect the way each product class is perceived and thus help to explain consumer response to the product class. Further, they provide the most appropriate communication setting in which the appeals are embedded and thus enhance their acceptability.

THE TWO PRODUCT CLASS STRATEGIES

The strategist who observes that his brand does not "fit" the ideal product class characteristics is faced with the alternative of either changing consumer attitudes toward his brand or changing consumer attitudes concerning the "ideal." These two approaches are discussed below.

Adding a Salient Characteristic—Strategy Two

Through advertising, a firm can make consumers aware of an attribute of a product class which has previously not been considered salient or which may not even have existed. Examples of this strategy's application include the use of additives to gasoline, the adding of fluorides to toothpaste, the adding of minerals to cereals, and the incorporation of light meters into cameras.

This type of strategy is most often attempted when a product is at the mature stages in its life cycle since by this time consumer attitudes pertaining to choice criteria have been well established. The advertising change is frequently combined with a product modification, although this may not be necessary. Clearly, research must show that the new characteristic has the potential of becoming salient; further, the advertiser must believe that his brand can attain a high relative rating on the new characteristic. Ideally, he would like to appropriate it so that competitors who followed would reinforce the claims made for his brand while simultaneously building the saliency of the product characteristics.

Altering the Perception of Existing Product Characteristics—Strategy Three

Increasing Salience The advertiser who observes that his brand rates well on a product class characteristic which consumers do not consider too salient may wish to try to effect an increase in its salience. This strategy is an extension of the previous one and requires careful research to determine how the advertiser's brand and competitive brands are positioned by market segment. This kind of comparative examination is important since research has indicated that changing the importance of a product class characteristic will not affect preference for it unless one brand rates high and competitive brands are low with respect to that characteristic.[17] For example, an airline company which noted that "on schedule"

---

[17] For further discussion of this subject see Joel B. Cohen and Michael Houston, "The Structure of Consumer Attitudes: The Use of Attribute Possession and Importance Scores," Faculty Working Paper Number 2, University of Illinois at Urbana, 1971; Martin Fishbein, "A Behavior Theory Approach to the Relations between Beliefs about an Object and Attitude toward That Object," and "Attitudes and the Prediction of Behavior," in *Readings in Attitude Theory and Measurement,* Martin Fishbein, ed. (New York: John Wiley and Sons, 1967), pp.

was not given a high saliency rating might seek to increase the rating of this product class characteristic provided that it felt that its "on schedule" performance was better than that of its competitors.

Changing the Optimal Range   Underlying much of the above is an assumption of how advertising relates to brand and product perceptions and the way these relate to brand preference. Specifically, the purchase probability of any particular brand is the sum of the salient characteristics ratings multiplied by the brand ratings across all characteristics considered by a segment. In other words, the assumption is that the higher the brand is rated across all ideal characteristics, the more likely it is to be preferred and purchased.

This assumption probably holds true in only a few markets because, in order for it to be correct, consumers would have to desire an unlimited amount of any characteristic. More realistically, however, there may be optimal ratings below or beyond which preferences fall off. For instance, in the nutritional cereal example shown earlier, it is likely that for the characteristics "protein," "minerals," and "vitamins," the more a brand is perceived as having the characteristic, the more a consumer is likely to buy the brand. But, for the characteristic "absence of sugar," a point probably exists beyond which the consumer is not willing to go; that is, a cereal could have too little sugar. Possibly the relationships are also somewhat different on either side of the optimal point. In the case of the cereal example in Table 1, any deviation above the "4" ideal point on the characteristic "absence of sugar" may be enough to reject the brand. On the other hand, deviations below "4," however, may still be within the acceptable range.

These relationships can vary across the ideal characteristics within any given market. For instance, when price is considered as a variable, the ideal product rating usually represents a maximum level above which the consumer may not move and below which the consumer would happily go. For "quality," on the other hand, the ideal rating is usually a minimum level with higher rated brands acceptable and lower rated brands not acceptable. Moreover, interactions between characteristics often occur; e.g., consumers will accept infinite drops in price so long as no clearly perceptible quality decrease occurs. A price drop in some instances will affect the consumer's perception of the product's quality.[18]

Consequently, a manager must consider the optimal product rating not only with regard to its relation to brand perception and preference, but also with regard to (a) the distribution of that relationship around the ideal point, and (b) the relationships between distributions for all of the characteristics considered to be important by consumers. While this may appear to be extremely complex, the process is simplified by the fact that few product characteristics

---

382–389 and pp. 477–491; Jagdish N. Sheth and Wayne W. Talarzyk, "Relative Contribution of Perceived Instrumentality and Value Importance Components in Determining Attitudes," paper presented at the Fall Meetings of the American Marketing Association, Boston, 1970.

[18] See Alfred Oxenfeldt, David Miller, Abraham Schuchman and Charles Winick, *Insights into Pricing* (Belmont, California: Wadsworth Publishing Company, 1961), Chapter 4; and Joseph M. Kamen and Robert J. Toman "Psychographics of Pricing," *Journal of Marketing Research,* Vol. 7 (February, 1970), pp. 27–35.

seem to be utilized in any single product purchase decision.[19] Also, the characteristics by which products are identified and conceptualized are fairly stable over time. Further, managers have demonstrated their ability to understand and predict very well with the use of a few simple variables.[20]

Once the meaning of the saliency of product class characteristics is established, it is possible to consider the process which entails an attempt to change the nature of the acceptable distribution around the ideal point for a characteristic. If an advertiser is selling a higher-priced product than his competitors, for instance, he may not be able to change the ideal rating a segment would give for price. But he may be able to get consumers to consider a range of prices *above* the ideal rating by affecting the price-quality relationship which is perceived by many. He could point out the quality that is possible only with the higher-priced product.

Similar strategy examples could be cited for all the negative relationships discussed above. Thus, for example, one could attempt to deal with the potential negative relationship between the perception of sweetness and nutrition for cereals, initial cost and upkeep for machinery, horse power and safety for cars, taste and the effectiveness of mouthwashes, and so on. The goal of advertising is to change the nature of the range around the ideal point. Typically, this is done with advertising using two or more of the product characteristics.

A substantial amount of research has been conducted by psychologists on latitudes of acceptance and rejection in attitude.[21] This article does not discuss such research, but it will suffice to emphasize that the research indicates the significant value of considering strategies not only in terms of points but also in terms of the distribution around the points.

TWO BRAND-LEVEL STRATEGIES

Changing Perceptions of Advertiser's Brand—Strategy Four

Whereas strategies 2 and 3 were concerned with changing consumer perceptions of the ideal brand, the present strategy focuses on changing consumer perceptions of an advertiser's brand. In both cases, the strategy objective is to develop a better "fit" between the "ideal" brand and the advertiser's brand.

Little can be said about this strategy that has not been said already. Several significant suggestions, however, come from recent attitudinal research. An ob-

---

[19] Same reference as footnote 15. Also see David Klahr, "A Study of Consumers' Cognitive Structure for Cigarette Brands," paper presented at the meetings of the Institute of Management Sciences, May, 1968.

[20] David B. Montgomery, "Initial Distribution: A Gate Keeping Analysis of Supermarket Buyer Divisions," paper presented at the Institute of Management Sciences fall meetings, Detroit, 1971.

[21] Carolyn W. Sherif, Muzafer Sherif and Richard Nebergall, *Attitude and Attitude Change* (Philadelphia: W. B. Saunders, 1965); and George S. Day, "Theories of Attitude Structure and Change," in *Consumer Behavior: A Theoretical Source Book*, Scott Ward and Thomas Robertson, eds. (Englewood Cliffs, New Jersey: Prentice-Hall), forthcoming in 1973.

vious one is that advertisers should not attempt to change perceptions for their brand when the brand itself does not possess an adequate quantity of the characteristic in question. The basic assumption of the Stefflre product development system, for instance, is that the purpose of advertising is to communicate the characteristics which the brand actually has.[22]

The framework suggested here provides a clear and measurable set of criteria for selecting the particular brand perceptions to be emphasized. Analysis of the optimal points and ranges for the salient product characteristics can indicate those characteristics that are most crucial in their effect on preference—and can do so by segments. Indeed such a process would appear to be at the very core of any segmentation scheme. Within this set of characteristics, the advertiser should seek to emphasize those for which he has the most relative advantage. Ideally, these would be characteristics for which both he and his competitors have low brand perceptions. These characteristics provide an opportunity for a profitable change in brand perception. This is especially true for those characteristics that the brand possesses and which will be difficult for competition to copy.

These conditions—high salience of a characteristic and exclusive possession of it by one brand—occur so seldom in marketing that their presence constitutes good reason to believe that there is a substantial opportunity for product development. Much of the criticism that is leveled against advertising has to do with the use of trivial claims; i.e., those which the consumer cannot link to any salient product class characteristics.

Changing Perceptions of Competing Brands—Strategy Five

Under some conditions, success may be achieved by altering perceptions for a brand with regard to salient characteristics that are perceived as being possessed to a greater extent by a competitive brand. There are techniques which boost the advertiser's brand while pointing out the fallibility of competitive claims. Specifically, two-sided and refutational messages provide a vehicle for fairly presenting both sides of an issue while at the same time improving the perceptions of the brand being advertised.[23]

Examples are Avis and Hertz advertising dealing with the advantages of first or second position in the rental car industry; Volkswagen's refutation of the small and ugly car counterclaims; Bayer Aspirin's counterattacks against other forms of headache remedy; and, in the political arena, Mayor John Lindsay's

---

[22] Stefflre, same reference as footnote 15, p. 262.

[23] Carl I. Hovland, Irving Janis and Harold H. Kelley, *Communication and Persuasion* (New Haven, Connecticut: Yale University Press, 1953); William J. McGuire, "Inducing Resistance to Persuasion: Some Contemporary Approaches," *Advances in Experimental Social Psychology*, Vol. 1 (1964), pp. 192–231; Percy H. Tannenbaum, "The Congruity Principle Revisited: Studies in the Reduction, Induction, and Generalization of Persuasion," *Advances in Experimental Social Psychology*, Vol. 3 (1967), pp. 272–320; and Michael L. Ray, "Biases in Selection of Messages Designed to Induce Resistance to Persuasion," *Journal of Personality and Social Psychology*, Vol. 9 (August, 1968), pp. 335–339.

messages which refuted claims of his alleged mishandling of New York City's affairs. The strategy of dealing with competitive claims also occurs in industrial selling through the presentation of comparative cost data or competitive laboratory findings.

Once again, however, these techniques must be used carefully. Some evidence suggests that if they are not, the advertising can boomerang by giving support to competitive brands and claims.[24] Further evidence indicates that, unless the audience is relatively sophisticated and highly involved with the product, they are unlikely to comprehend two-sided messages fully. And if the audience is sophisticated and involved, their attitudes may be quite difficult to change with any kind of message.

CONCLUSION

For many years controversy has arisen concerning the determination of appropriateness of advertising effectiveness measures. No single measure suggested, however, has provided a basis for the formulation of advertising strategy, which has remained more art than science. Also, over the last several years, several theories of consumer behavior have made the marketing community sharply aware of the need to consider consumer behavior as a complete system. Few of these models specify the linkages between components of consumer behavior in sufficient detail to be managerially useful except for broad conceptual relationship. This article has taken a perspective of consumer brand choice from the model developed by Amstutz and extended it to various levels of demand. The resulting framework serves as a useful tool for advertising decision makers in developing comprehensive strategies of attitudinal change.

---

[24] Michael L. Ray, Alan G. Sawyer and Edward C. Strong, "Frequency Effects Revisited," *Journal of Advertising Research*, Vol. 11 (February, 1971), pp. 14–20; and Michael L. Ray and Alan G. Sawyer, "Behavioral Measurement for Marketing Models: Empirical Estimates of Advertising Repetition for Media Planning," *Management Science: Applications*, Vol. 17 (December, 1971), Part II, pp. 73–89.

Manage Your Sales Force as a System

Porter Henry

Sales managers, according to their critics, are not sufficiently "scientific" in their decision making. They pursue volume instead of profit, make piecemeal decisions instead of comprehensive plans, rely on instinct and hunch rather than on methodical decision-making processes.

Sales managers might well reply—and often do—that they are dealing with salesmen and customers who are capricious human beings, much more difficult to predict and control than a piece of production equipment.

It is true that the sales department is a complicated communications system, influenced by many variables that are difficult to quantify and that interact in unforeseen ways. For example, a sales training program designed to help salesmen sell more of a high-profit specialty product may fail because the company's compensation plan motivates salesmen to chase the volume dollars in easy-to-sell but low-profit items. Or an increase in the size of the sales force may result in a higher proportion of calls on marginal customers, creating an increase in the sales costs ratio and a decrease in profit per sales call instead of the intended higher profitability.

Because the function they are managing is so complex, sales managers can profitably use the basic principles, if not the mathematical trappings, of the most modern of all scientific methods. Known by such terms as "systems engineering," "systems analysis," "the total systems concept," and "the systems approach," this method has helped Americans produce energy from atoms and place men on the moon. It can also help increase the productivity of a sales department.

Essentially, a "system" consists of various inputs that go into a process or operation of some kind and result in a measurable output. The measurement is used to adjust the inputs or the process in order to produce desired results. To

About the Author: Porter Henry heads his own firm, Porter Henry & Co., Inc., located in New York City. Founded in 1946, the organization specializes in sales and marketing development for companies in a wide variety of industries.

describe this procedure of measurement and adjustment, systems engineers have borrowed a term from electronics: *feedback*. The methodology of systems analysis can be described in six steps:

1. Define the system to be investigated. For example, it may be an entire city, just the transportation network, or perhaps only the subway system.
2. Define what the system ought to accomplish as well as the means to measure this. For the subway system: What quality and quantity of service are desired?
3. Define the elements that make up the system and quantify their relationships. In the case of the subway system: What is the effect on passengers moved per hour of such variables as the pattern of passenger arrival frequencies at stations, length of platforms, length of trains, headway between trains, and number of doors on a car?
4. For each element, or for each major subassembly of elements, determine the measurable performance desired. To achieve the objectives of the subway system, what is required of the signals, motors, brakes, and crew?
5. Consider the cost effectiveness of alternative methods to improve the performance of the system. For each dollar spent to improve the performance of one element of the system, how many dollars' worth of improvement will be obtained in the performance of the total system?
6. Implement the most desirable decisions and measure the results.

Although it may not be possible to quantify all the interacting variables that constitute the sales department of a typical company, nevertheless, "systems engineering" can be used by the sales manager to increase the overall production of his department. Let us examine the steps he takes and their potential value to him.

DEFINING THE SYSTEM

The system of concern to the sales manager is, of course, the sales department. It is a subsystem of the corporation's marketing program, which is in turn a subsystem of the corporation (see Exhibit 1).

In the phraseology of systems engineering, the corporation's top management uses *feedback* from the marketplace and the results of previous marketing efforts to develop an *input* to the marketing system. This input includes the marketing objectives, the choice of products or services to be offered, the pricing strategy, and decisions about the resources to be committed to the attainment of marketing objectives.

Having developed products or services to meet identified customer needs, the corporation must then communicate their existence to potential customers. This communication is accomplished through two channels: (1) advertising and sales promotion, including every medium that reaches potential customers en

EXHIBIT 1

The Sales Force as Part of the Corporation's Marketing System

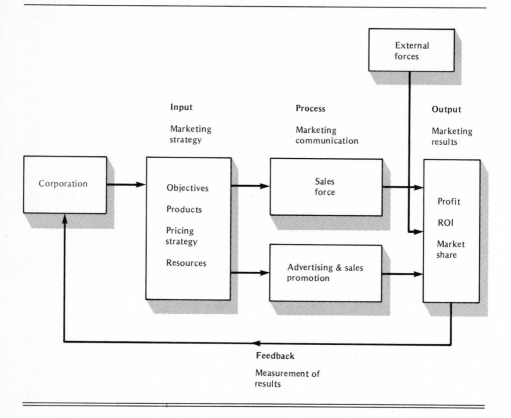

masse, and (2) the sales force, which communicates to prospects primarily on a one-to-one basis.

Essential to the systems approach is the measurement of output. The output of the corporation is usually measured in terms of return on investment and/or corporate growth. Market share, profits as a percentage of sales volume, and cash flow are other measures of performance that may be stressed.

MEASURING EFFICIENCY

But the sales force is a subsystem of a larger subsystem, and return on investment, profit ratio, and market share, while good measures for the whole company, are greatly influenced by factors not completely controlled by the sales force. If these measures improve, everybody claims credit for the improvement.

Is there some way to show whether a sales force is operating at 60%, or 83.7%, or perhaps even 100% efficiency? If sales managers could agree upon two or three standard indices of sales force productivity, they could compare the effectiveness of their systems with that of other sales forces in the same industry. The following is a list of five possible yardsticks:

1. *Contribution to Profit.* The company's products can be turned over to the sales force at cost, or at cost plus some markup representing the production department's contribution to profit. The sales force in turn sells the products at a markup. This margin, minus *all* costs of the selling operation—salesmen's salaries, sales management and supervision costs, travel and entertainment expenses, credit losses, interest on accounts receivable—represents the contribution of the sales department to corporate net profits.

2. *Return on Assets Managed.* The sales force requires certain capital investments—goods in warehouses, branch offices, salesmen's automobiles, money tied up in accounts receivable. If current sales expenses such as salaries, travel, and entertainment are subtracted from gross profit on sales volume, the balance represents the return on these investments.[1]

   If a company uses this yardstick, some costs that are now absorbed in the current budget are logically capitalized and depreciated. A sales training program useful for five years, for example, would more logically be written off over five years than in just one year.

3. *Sales Cost Ratio.* A frequently used index is the ratio of sales expenses divided by dollar sales volume. This ratio should be used in conjunction with other yardsticks, because a sales force selling $10 million at a 5% expense/volume ratio may not be as profitable as a sales force selling $20 million with a 7% cost ratio.

4. *Market Share.* This output is influenced by variables other than sales department productivity. If, however, product quality, pricing, advertising effectiveness, and competitors' activity remain relatively constant, an increased market share could be considered an indication of increased sales force productivity.

5. *Achievement of Company Marketing Goals.* In addition to, or instead of, indices for comparing companies in an industry, measurements of *desired* performance may be used. An example might be "to increase our market share from 15% to 25%, provided net profits as a percent of sales do not go below 10%."

Every engineer agrees that the efficiency of an engine is its energy output divided by its energy input. Sales managers are not universally agreed upon any corresponding measurement, or even upon which activities should be considered as input and which as output. However, this state of affairs does not mean management must throw up its hands. It can and should decide what measurements best meet the needs of its company. The measurements chosen may not be per-

---

[1] A more detailed description of this accounting method is contained in J. S. Schiff and Michael Schiff, "New Sales Management Tool: ROAM" (HBR July–August 1967), p. 59.

fect, but they can still be valuable, enabling management to apply the systems approach in a useful and productive way.

IMPROVING THE SYSTEM

Exhibit 2 is a flow chart of the sales force as a system. It employs four measurements of sales force output: contribution to profit, return on assets managed, sales costs ratio, and market share. If the sales manager discovers by these measurements or any others he chooses to adopt that sales force productivity is below its desired level, he then works his way *backward* through the flow chart, from right to left, to determine which control variables at the left need adjusting. As the chart indicates, no matter what improvement the sales manager seeks in output, there are only three ways in which the salesmen can achieve the change. These ways are labeled "Salesmen's output variables" because they are the result of every input salesmen can make. The output variables are:

- An increase in total sales volume, without any change in the product mix or sales cost ratio.
- A more profitable product mix, in which the products producing a higher profit represent a larger percentage of total sales volume.
- A reduction in the sales cost ratio, which can result from increasing sales without a corresponding increase in costs, or from decreasing sales costs. (This ratio refers to *all* sales costs, including such items as price concessions, service to the account, and adjustments of complaints.)

In most cases the desired profit goal will require some improvement in all three of the output variables. However, their relative importance is likely to vary from product to product and even from salesman to salesman. In using a systems approach, therefore, it is important to determine how much and what kind of emphasis should be placed on each variable.

Analyzing Sales Activity

If we now move one step to the left in the flow chart, we arrive at the "Salesmen's input variables." These are activities salesmen can change in order to alter the output variables. The arrows emerging from each input variable indicate which of the output variables is affected. Let us now consider the nature of the input variables.

1. The Number of Sales Calls Each salesman might be motivated to make more calls per week, or the company total could be increased by hiring more salesmen. An increased number of sales calls, Exhibit 2 indicates, will probably affect total sales volume and can affect the sales cost ratio—adversely, if additional sales calls are made on unprofitable prospects.

2. The Quality of the Sales Calls This input is measured by such yardsticks as calls per order, dollar sales or profits per call, or percentage of calls that achieve specific objectives. In this context, a sales call refers to a sales-man's conversation with one or more individuals. The "call" on a major plant might involve sales calls on many buying influences, but these calls should be considered separately in evaluating their quality and in establishing the frequency with which the buying influences should be contacted. As the flow chart indicates, call quality consists of these elements:

- The information content of the call. Is the salesman adequately informed about the customer's problems or plans, as well as about his own products and their applications?
- The effectiveness of the call as an act of communication. Does the sales-man deliver the message in an understandable and convincing manner? (This is where visual sales aids may be useful.) Is the salesman effective while on the receiving end of the conversation? That is, is he a good questioner and listener?
- The interpersonal aspects of the call. Does the salesman rub the customer the wrong way without being aware of it? When the customer's "inner child" speaks, does the salesman's "inner child" respond?

Most companies do a reasonably good job of giving the salesman informa-tion on customer needs and product applications, or at least make it possible for the salesman to absorb it. Many companies try to upgrade salesmen's skills in communication and interaction by using some kind of standardized training program. (Too often, though, the program tends to concentrate on one element while ignoring the other.) Few companies take the trouble to investigate the basic question: If our sales calls are not good enough, what is the nature of their weakness?

Improvement in call quality can increase any of the three output variables—total volume, product mix, and sales costs. The content of the training will de-termine which of the three is most affected. Occasionally, a sales manager may ask himself which of these outputs most needs changing, but many of us never see this happen. Instead, before launching a training program or procedural change, sales managers opt for training that is mostly motivational, without first identifying desired behavioral changes.

3. The Allocation of Sales Effort For each salesman and for the sales force as a whole, there is some optimum frequency of calls on large, medium, and small customers, and on large, medium, and small prospects, that will maximize the profit return per unit of sales effort expended. (Of course, customers may also be classified according to industry, geographical location, and other factors, but for the sake of simplicity let us assume here that volume and profit are the classifications used.)

Allocation of effort based on product profitability is related to allocation of calls by customer sizes or types: to sell more of the high-profit product, more time must be spent with customers who may buy it. If a salesman spends too much time with little customers, he will lose some of the additional potential

EXHIBIT 2
The Sales Force as a System

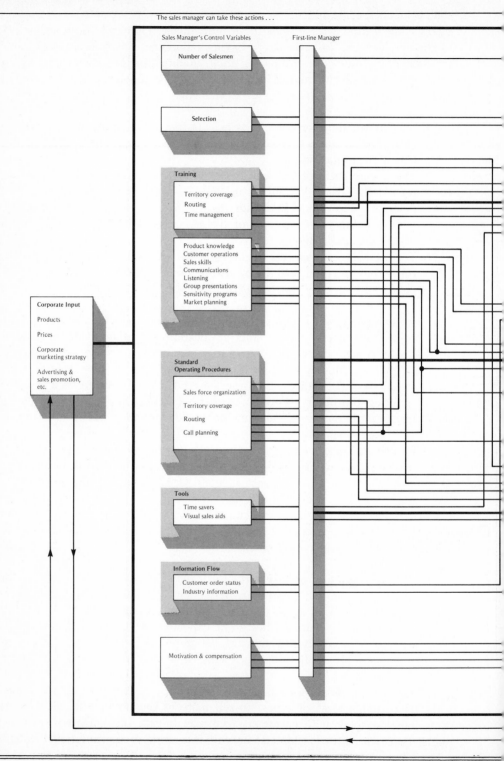

The sales manager can take these actions . . .

Sales Manager's Control Variables

First-line Manager

Number of Salesmen

Selection

Training

Territory coverage
Routing
Time management

Product knowledge
Customer operations
Sales skills
Communications
Listening
Group presentations
Sensitivity programs
Market planning

Corporate Input

Products

Prices

Corporate
marketing strategy

Advertising &
sales promotion,
etc.

Standard
Operating Procedures

Sales force organization

Territory coverage

Routing

Call planning

Tools

Time savers
Visual sales aids

Information Flow

Customer order status
Industry information

Motivation & compensation

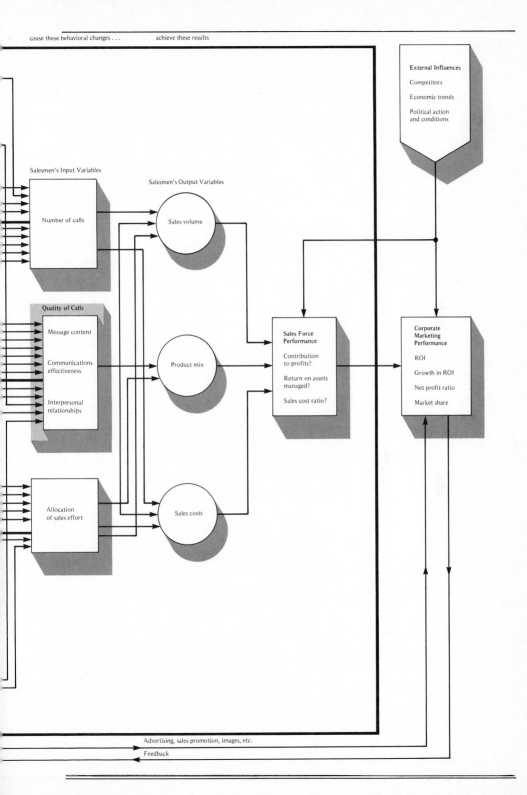

cause these behavioral changes . . .   achieve these results

External Influences

Competitors

Economic trends

Political action
and conditions

Salesmen's Input Variables

Salesmen's Output Variables

Number of calls

Sales volume

Quality of Calls

Message content

Communications
effectiveness

Interpersonal
relationships

Product mix

Sales Force
Performance

Contribution
to profits?

Return on assets
managed?

Sales cost ratio?

Corporate
Marketing
Performance

ROI

Growth in ROI

Net profit ratio

Market share

Allocation
of sales effort

Sales costs

Advertising, sales promotion, images, etc.

Feedback

volume from his key customers. On the other hand, if he calls too much on key customers, he will be trapped by the law of diminishing returns, for there comes a point at which additional calls could more profitably be made to smaller customers or prospective customers. If the salesman neglects prospect calls in favor of present customers, the inevitable attrition among those present customers will cost him future profits.

Except for those people following a rigid call schedule based on account classification and routing, most salesmen do not allocate their time for maximum returns. Selling is often a lonely and discouraging occupation, so it is only human to spend too much time with the friendly customers and easy buyers, while neglecting those psychologically chilling calls on hard-nosed buyers and non-buying prospects.

Many companies attempt to solve this problem by establishing a standard procedure for classifying accounts into groups, such as A, B, and C, and assigning a call frequency to each group. The procedure itself, however, is usually based on seat-of-the-pants judgment rather than on objective methods of optimizing the allocation of sales effort.

An improvement in this salesmen's input variable usually has a marked effect on product mix, for the sales efforts are more heavily concentrated on prospective users of the more profitable products. Total sales volume and the sales cost ratio may go either up or down, but net profitability will go up.

INTERMEDIATE MEASURES

Many sales managers set up budgets for salesmen's output variables—sales volume by product, and sales costs—but few attempt to establish quantified goals for all of the input variables—number of calls, quality of calls, and allocation of sales effort. Since it is fairly easy to set targets for the number of calls a salesman should make, this is likely to be the only input goal established. Such a practice is extremely frustrating to the conscientious salesman, who rightfully insists that the quality of his calls is at least as important as the sheer number of calls.

Measurements of call quality can be established. They can consist of such indices as the ratio of calls to orders or to long-range purchases, the average order size, the number of different items purchased by each customer ("across-the-board" selling), the ratio of proposals to sales, and many others. And it is relatively easy to set targets for the allocation of sales effort.

Such measurements of the intermediate functions in selling can be highly important in providing prompt feedback to salesmen involved in lengthy or highly technical selling, where the sale itself usually takes place so long after the initial contact that it neither motivates the salesman nor helps him correct his weaknesses on a week-to-week basis.

DECIDING ON CHANGES

Once the sales manager can compare his salesmen's present performance with the desired level of input variables, he can determine which of the "Sales manager's control variables" should be adjusted. There are 22 of these. Listed at the left of the flow chart in Exhibit 2, these control variables fall into seven categories:

1. The number of salesmen.
2. The selection of salesmen.
3. Training programs of various types.
4. Standard operating procedures.
5. Selling tools (visuals, demonstrators, films, and so on).
6. Information flow to and from salesmen.
7. Motivation, which also includes the practice of incentive compensation.

The arrows emerging from each control variable indicate which of the salesmen's input variables it primarily influences. For readers who do not like to trace arrows, Part A of Exhibit 3 lists the controls and the variables each affects; Part B works in reverse, showing for each desired behavior change the necessary control changes.

Standard operating procedures divide as follows:

- *Sales Force Organization.* This category concerns such questions as: Should all salesmen sell all products, or should they be specialists in markets or products? How many salesmen should report to each first-line manager? Should the manager have account responsibilities of his own?
- *Development of Routines.* If some part of the salesman's job can be reduced to a standard operating procedure, it is easier and more effective to hand him the procedure than to train him in the skill of designing his own procedure. This approach to productivity is often overlooked.

  If, for example, salesmen are required to develop an annual territory marketing plan, it is easier to provide them with a form to fill out than to give them a course in territory planning. Again, it is easier and more effective to establish a standard method of classifying accounts into sales call frequencies than to train salesmen in time allocation.

  This approach does not mean that the company is trying to make robots of its salesmen or is ignoring the potential for job enrichment. It does mean that if some aspect of the salesman's function can be routinized, it makes sense to provide the routine and free more of the salesman's time for the creative aspects of his job that cannot be condensed into a procedure.

Power of the First-Line Manager

The sales manager has one other control variable at his command. It is unique in that it can either weaken or amplify the effects of changes in the other control variables.

As the flow chart indicates, this multiplier variable is the first-line sales manager. In larger companies this is the district, divisional, or branch manager; in smaller companies it may be the sales manager himself, or even the owner.

Any actions taken to improve call quantity, call quality, or time allocation

EXHIBIT 3
Managerial Control and Salesmen's Action

A. EFFECT OF MANAGER'S CONTROL VARIABLES

THE MANAGER CAN MAKE THE FOLLOWING DECISIONS:	THESE ACTIONS OF THE SALESMAN ARE MOST AFFECTED:
Number of Salesmen	Number of calls
Selection of Salesmen	Call quality, primarily in communications effectiveness and interpersonal relationships
Training	
Territory coverage	Number of calls, allocation of sales effort
Routing	Number of calls
Time management	Number of calls, allocation of sales effort
Product knowledge	Call quality (message content)
Customer operations	Call quality (message content)
Sales skills, communications, listening, and group presentations	Call quality (communications effectiveness)
Sensitivity programs	Call quality (interpersonal relationships)
Market planning	Allocation of sales effort
Standard Operating Procedures	
Sales force organization	All three salesmen's input variables
Territory coverage	Number of calls, allocation of sales effort
Routing	Number of calls
Call planning	Call quality (message content and communications effectiveness)
Sales Tools	
Time savers (dictating equipment, calculators, etc.)	Number of sales calls
Visual sales aids	Call quality (communications effectiveness)
Information Flow	
Customer order status and industry conditions	Call quality (message content)
Motivation	
Incentive pay, contests, recognition, opportunities for personal growth and promotion, etc.	All three salesmen's input variables

B. SALESMEN'S INPUT VARIABLES AFFECTED BY CONTROL VARIABLES

THE SALESMAN CAN TAKE THE FOLLOWING ACTIONS:	THESE ACTIONS OF THE MANAGER INFLUENCE THE SALESMAN:
Number of Sales Calls	Number of salesmen
	Training in territory coverage, routing, and time management
	Standard operating procedures for sales force organization, territory coverage, and routing
	Tools for time-saving
	Motivation and compensation
Quality of Sales Calls	
a. Message content	Training in product knowledge and customer operations
	Information flow on customer status, industry trends, and call planning
b. Communications effectiveness	Salesmen selection
	Training in sales skills, communications, listening, and group presentations
	Standard operating procedures for sales force organization and call planning
	Visual sales aids
c. Interpersonal relationships	Salesmen selection
	Sensitivity training
	Motivation and compensation
Allocation of Sales Effort	Training in territory coverage, time management, and market planning
	Standard operating procedures for sales force organization and territory coverage
	Motivation and compensation

will not be fully effective unless the first-line manager follows through on them. There are times, in fact, when his operations are the only control variable the sales manager needs in order to fine-tune—when any desired changes in the salesmen's actions can be achieved through the training, supervision, and motivation provided by the first-line sales manager.

A sales manager can upgrade the performance of the field managers by employing any of the variables listed for salesmen; that is, he can provide more managers, he can do a better job of selecting, training, and motivating them, or he can provide them with better procedures, tools, or information.

With some notable exceptions, primarily in the pharmaceutical and packaged consumer goods industries, the importance of first-line sales management tends to be underestimated. Many companies do not give their field managers the necessary training in how to observe, evaluate, and develop the individual sales-man. Yet, second only to better sales time allocation, improved field supervision is usually the simplest and fastest way to improve sales force productivity.

APPROACHING MAJOR DECISIONS

In using the systems approach to increase sales force productivity, the sales manager works backward through the flow chart, first setting his improvement objectives and then tracing back through the salesmen's output and input variables to determine which control variables should be changed.

His analysis will usually suggest the desirability of improving several of the control variables. To determine how much time or money should be invested in improving each control, the manager can ask himself these questions:

- *How Important Is This Variable in Affecting the Salesmen's Input Variable I Am Trying to Improve?* If its influence is small, it can be omitted from the productivity improvement plan. A good way to assess the relative importance of the control variables is to assign to each one a weight from 1 to 10. This weight will vary greatly from company to company. Information about previous orders and shipments, for example, would be highly valuable to a salesman making repeat calls to industrial purchasers, but of no value to a one-call, door-to-door sales operation.
- *How Well Am I Handling This Control Variable Now?* Percentage ratings are useful for this answer. For example, is our performance half of what it should be, or 90%? The industrial company mentioned in the previous paragraph might rate its flow of information to the salesman at only 50%, although its weight might be 9 or 10.

    The weight is a judgment of the importance of this function in a particular company; the rating is a judgment of how well it is being performed. Although these numbers are not an accurate, objective measurement, they do make it easier to consider a complex array of variables. Whether he realizes it or not, a sales manager goes through a similar mental process in deciding how much of his available funds to spend on sales training, contests, or salary increases.
- *What Would It Cost to Improve the Performance of a Function?* Here the manager needs to be mindful of the S-shaped curve, which indicates that the better a function is now being handled, the more difficult it is to produce an improvement in it. While it takes a certain amount of effort to raise the rating of a function from 50% to 55%, it might take three times as much effort to raise it from 90% to 95%.
- *How Would Sales Force Productivity Be Affected by the Projected Improvement in This Variable?* This question calls for an estimate of the in-

crease in profit contribution, minus the immediate and continuing costs of the improvement in the control variable.

By using the systems engineer's approach, the sales manager can establish more useful long-term objectives. He can identify the most important changes that must be made to increase sales force productivity. And he can establish interim progress measurements for both himself and his salesmen.

A Strategic Framework for Marketing Control

James M. Hulbert and Norman E. Toy

The decade of the 1960's led many companies down the primrose path of uncontrolled growth. The turbulence of the 1970's has drawn renewed attention to the need to pursue growth selectively, and many companies have been forced to divest themselves of businesses which looked glamorous in the 1960's, but faded in the 1970's. Simultaneously with this re-appraisal has come a much more serious focus on problems of control—a concern with careful monitoring and appraisal to receive early warning on businesses or ventures that are suspect.

Yet, despite the extent to which control is stressed by authors,[1] there does not exist a generally agreed upon strategic framework for marketing control, and there has been little successful integration of concepts in marketing strategy and planning with those of managerial accounting. In particular, the work of the Boston Consulting Group,[2] the results of the PIMS study,[3] and a variety of other

About the Authors: James M. Hulbert is Associate Professor, Graduate School of Business, Columbia University, New York; Norman E. Toy is Dean, School of Public Health, Columbia University, New York.

Reprinted from *Journal of Marketing*, vol. 41 (April 1977), pp. 12–20, published by the American Marketing Association.

NOTE: The authors acknowledge the support of the Faculty Research Fund of the Columbia University Graduate School of Business, and the helpful comments of Professors Masai Nakanishi and Gordon Shillinglaw. Early drafts of this article were written while Prof. Hulbert was visiting at the Graduate School of Management, University of California, Los Angeles.

[1] See, for example, V. H. Kirpalani and Stanley S. Shapiro, "Financial Dimensions of Marketing Management," *Journal of Marketing*, Vol. 37 No. 3 (July 1973), pp. 40–47; David J. Luck and Arthur E. Prell, *Marketing Strategy* (Englewood Cliffs, N.J.: Prentice-Hall Inc., 1968); Philip Kotler, *Marketing Management: Analysis, Planning and Control* (Englewood Cliffs, N.J.: Prentice-Hall Inc., 1972).

[2] Boston Consulting Group, *Perspectives on Experience* (Boston: Boston Consulting Group, 1968); see also, Patrick Conley, "Experience Curves as a Planning Tool," in S. H. Britt and H. W. Boyd, eds., *Marketing Management and Administrative Action* (New York: McGraw-Hill, 1974), pp. 257–68; William E. Cox, "Product Portfolio Strategy: A Review of the Boston Consulting Group Approach to Marketing Strategy," in *Proceedings*, 1974 Marketing Educators' Conference (Chicago: American Marketing Association), pp. 465–70.

[3] Sidney Schoeffler, Robert D. Buzzell and Donald F. Heany, "Impact of Strategic Planning on Profit Performance," *Harvard Business Review*, Vol. 52 (March–April 1974), pp.

sources [4] have stressed the importance of market share objectives in marketing strategy, coincidentally emphasizing the need to know market size and growth rate and thus the importance of good forecasts. Typically, however, procedures for marketing control have not been related to these key parameters. (Incredibly, market size is sometimes even omitted from marketing plans, according to one knowledgeable author.) [5]

In this article we seek to remedy that state of affairs by outlining a strategic framework for marketing control. Using the key strategic concepts discussed above, we first present a framework for evaluating marketing performance versus plan, thus providing a means for more formally incorporating the marketing plan in the managerial control process.

The plan, however, may well provide inappropriate criteria for performance evaluation, especially if there have been a number of unanticipated events during the planning period. A second stage of this article, therefore, is to provide a means of taking these kinds of planning variances into account, so as to provide a more appropriate set of criteria for performance evaluation. Two conceptual developments are shown as Part 1 and Part 2 of the Appendix.

PERFORMANCE VS. PLAN

In Exhibit 1 we show the results of operations for a sample product, *Product Alpha*, during the preceding period. In the analysis which follows, we shall focus on analysis of variances in profit contribution. As we discussed elsewhere,[6] an analysis of revenue performance is sometimes required; the procedure here is analogous. Organizationally, one of the results we would like to achieve is to be able to assign responsibility, and give credit, where due.

A variety of organizational units were involved in the planning and execution summarized in Exhibit 1, and an important component of control activity is to evaluate their performance according to the standards or goals provided by the marketing plan. We should also note, however, that the type of analysis we shall discuss has limited potential for *diagnosing* the causes of problems. Rather, its major benefit is in the *identification* of areas where problems may exist. Determining the factors which have actually caused favorable or unfavorable variances requires the skill and expertise of the manager.

The unfavorable variance in contribution of $100,000, for *Product Alpha* could arise from two main sources: [7]

137–45; Robert D. Buzzell, Bradley T. Gale and Ralph G. M. Sultan, "Market Share—A Key to Profitability," *Harvard Business Review*, Vol. 53 (January–February 1975), pp. 97–106.

[4] See Bernard Catry and Michel Chevalier, "Market Share Strategy and the Product Life Cycle," *Journal of Marketing*, Vol. 38 No. 4 (October 1974), pp. 29–34; C. Davis Fogg, "Planning Gains in Market Share," *Journal of Marketing*, Vol. 38 No. 3 (July 1974), pp. 30–38.

[5] F. Beaven Ennis, *Effective Marketing Management* (New York: Association of National Advertisers, 1973), pg. 11.

[6] James M. Hulbert and Norman E. Toy, "Control and the Marketing Plan," paper presented to the 1975 Marketing Educators' Conference of the American Marketing Association.

[7] To simplify this example, no variances in either variable costs or marketing program costs are included.

EXHIBIT 1
Operating Results for Product Alpha

ITEM	PLANNED	ACTUAL	VARIANCE
Revenues			
Sales (lbs.)	20,000,000	22,000,000	2,000,000
Price per lb. ($)	0.50	.4773	0.227
Revenues	10,000,000	10,500,000	500,000
Total market (lbs.)	40,000,000	50,000,000	10,000,000
Share of market	50%	44%	(6%)
Costs			
Variable cost per lb. ($)	.30	.30	—
Contribution			
Per lb. ($)	.20	.1773	.0227
Total ($)	4,000,000	3,900,000	(100,000)

1. Differences between planned and actual quantities (volumes).
2. Differences between planned and actual contribution per unit.

Differences between planned and actual quantities, however, may arise from differences between actual and planned total market size and actual and planned market share (penetration) of that total market. The potential sources of variation between planned and actual contribution, then, are:

1. Total market size.
2. Market share (penetration).
3. Price/cost per unit.

This format for variance decomposition permits assignment into categories which correspond to key strategy variables in market planning.[8] The analysis proceeds as follows.

Price-Quantity Decomposition

In order to measure volume variance with the standard yardstick of planned contribution per unit, actual quantity is used to calculate the price/cost variance. (This procedure is standard accounting practice.) To be more concise, we utilize the following symbols:

S—share of total market
M—total market in units

---

[8] For algebraic exposition, see Appendix, Part 1.

Q—quantity sold in units

C—contribution margin per unit.

We use the subscript "a" to denote *actual* values, and "p" to denote *planned* values. The subscript "v" denotes *variance*. Thus the price/cost variance is given by

$$(C_a - C_p) \times Q_a = (.1773 - .20) \times 22{,}000{,}000$$
$$= -\$500{,}000;$$

and the volume variance is given by

$$(Q_a - Q_p) \times C_p = (22{,}000{,}000 - 20{,}000{,}000) \times .20$$
$$= \$400{,}000. [9]$$

The sum of these contribution variances therefore yields the overall unfavorable contribution variance of $-\$100{,}000$ shown in Exhibit 1.

Penetration—Market Size Decomposition

The second stage of the analysis is the further decomposition of the volume variance in contribution into the components due to penetration and total market size. Exhibit 2 is helpful in the exposition of the analysis.

As a first step, we should like to explain differences in quantities sold $(Q_a - Q_p)$, where actual and planned quantities are the product of the market size times share $(Q_a = S_a \times M_a$, and $Q_p = S_p \times M_p)$. From Exhibit 2, rectangles I and II are clearly assignable to share and market size, respectively. Rectangle III, however, is conceptually more complex.

We argue that discrepancies in forecasting market size should be evaluated using the standard yardstick of planned share, just as the dollar value of the quantity variance is measured using the standard of planned contribution. Thus, actual market size is used to calculate share variance, while both share and forecast components (which together comprise the quantity variance) are measured using planned contribution. This procedure is also consistent with recommended accounting practice.[10]

Then the variance in contribution due to share is given by

$$(S_a - S_p) \times M_a \times C_p = (.44 - .50) \times 50{,}000{,}000 \times .2$$
$$= -\$600{,}000;$$

---

[9] Algebraically, we have:

$$(C_a - C_p)Q_a + (Q_a - Q_p)C_p = C_aQ_a - C_pQ_a + C_pQ_a - C_pQ_p$$
$$= C_aQ_a - C_pQ_p$$

[10] "Report of the Committee on Cost and Profitability Analyses for Marketing," *Accounting Review*, Supplement to Vol. XLVII (1972), pp. 575–615.

EXHIBIT 2

Variance of Total Market Size vs. Share

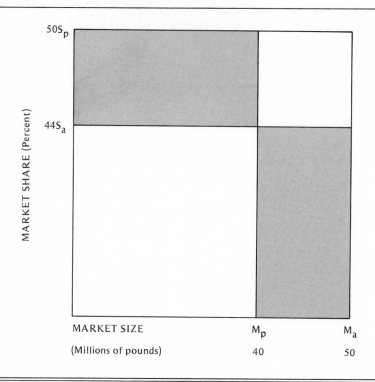

and the market size variance is given by

$$(M_a - M_p) \times S_p \times C_p = (50,000,000 - 40,000,000) \times .5 \times .2$$
$$= \$1,000,000.$$

The sum of the market size and share variances yields the overall favorable volume variance in contribution of $400,000 derived in the previous section.

We may now summarize the variances which in total constitute the overall variance as follows (see Exhibit 3):

Planned profit contribution		$4,000,000
Volume variance		
Share variance	(600,000)	
Market size variance	1,000,000	
		400,000
Price/cost variance		(500,000)
Actual profit contribution		$3,900,000

Interpretation

Conceptually, variances may occur because of problems in forecasting, execution, or both. In using the results of the analysis for performance evaluation, however, responsibility will have to be assigned. Generally, variances in total market size, for example, will be viewed as the responsibility of the market forecasting group.

Share or penetration variances present a more difficult case. They may arise due to incorrect forecasts of what "expected performance" should be, or due to poor performance itself. Apportioning responsibility in this case clearly necessitates managerial judgment. However, where marketing and sales personnel participate in the development of market share objectives, or where share declines relative to previous performance, the burden of proof is more likely to fall on the operating unit rather than on a separate planning or forecasting group.

Responsibility for price variances may also be difficult to assign. For example, prices may be seriously affected by changes in market or general economic conditions beyond the control of the operating group but which should have been foreseen by forecasters or planners. On the other hand, prices are an integral part of the marketing mix, and variances may well indicate problems in marketing or selling tactics.

With these considerations in mind, we may now review the results of the variance analysis:

First, *the favorable volume variance of $400,000 was in fact caused by two larger variances cancelling each other out. And while one of these variances was positive, the other negative, both are undesirable! By not achieving planned share of market, we lost $600,000 in profit contribution.*

The loss of market share may be due to poor planning, poor execution, or both . . . and managerial judgment is the key factor in diagnosing the causes of this discrepancy.

This unfavorable share variance was more than compensated for—or so it appears—by the $1,000,000 positive contribution variance due to the fact that the market turned out to be much larger than was forecast. This variance is unequivocally the responsibility of the forecasting group, though whether or not they should have been able to foresee the expansion is an issue which the manager must decide.

However, this nominally favorable variance is, in fact, a danger signal. *We seriously underestimated the size of the market, which was 25% greater, at 50 million pounds, than the forecast (40 million pounds).* As the dominant competitor, we have lost market share in what is apparently a fast-growing market, the kind of error which can soon lead to loss of competitive position.[11]

In this instance, then, the share/size decomposition of the volume variance serves to emphasize the importance of good planning—and good information for planning—in terms directly related to two crucial variables in strategy design. This form of decomposition, we submit, generates considerably more useful

---

[11] Boston Consulting Group, *Perspectives on Experience*, same as reference 2 above.

EXHIBIT 3
Ex post Performance Evaluation: Analysis of Contribution

ITEM	COMPOSITION	TYPE OF VARIANCE			
		PLANNING VARIANCE	PERFORMANCE VARIANCE	VARIANCE TOTALS	RECONCILIATION
Planned Contribution					$4,000,000
Quantity Variance					
Share					
Planning variance	$(S_r - S_p) \cdot M_r \cdot C_p = (.49 - .50)$ $\times 49,000,000 \times .20$	(98,000)			
Performance variance	$(S_a - S_r) \cdot M_a \cdot C_r = (.44 - .49)$ $\times 50,000,000 \times .18$		(450,000)		
Total				(548,000)	

Market Size				
Planning variance	$(M_r - M_p) \cdot S_p \cdot C_p$ $= (49{,}000{,}000 - 40{,}000{,}000)$ $\times .5 \times .20$	900,000		
Performance variance	$(M_a - M_r) \cdot S_r \cdot C_r$ $= (50{,}000{,}000 - 49{,}000{,}000)$ $\times .49 \times .18$		88,200	
Total			988,200	
Total Quantity Variance				440,200
Price Variance				
Planning variance	$(C_r - C_p) \cdot Q_r = (.18 - .2)$ $\times 24{,}010{,}000$	(480,200)		
Performance variance	$(C_a - C_r) \cdot Q_a = (.1773 - .18)$ $\times 22{,}000{,}000$		(60,000)	
Total			(540,200)	
Total Price Variance				(540,200)
Total Planning Variance		321,800		
Total Performance Variance			(421,800)	
Total Variance			(100,000)	
Actual Contribution				$3,900,000

insight into issues of marketing control *than isolation of only the volume variance, which is much less clearly interpretable.*

The final variance component is the unfavorable price variance of $500,000. Again, interpretation is the job of the manager. However, we should note that the accounting procedures used here (and generally) treat price and volume variances as if they were separable. *Yet, for the vast majority of products and services, demand is price-elastic to some degree so that variances in total revenue are the combined result of the interaction, via the demand function, of unit prices and quantities.*

In this example, for instance, the lower levels of prices may well have been an important factor in expanding industry and company demand. Nonetheless, the fact remains that failure to attain planned price levels led to a $500,000 decrease in actual versus planned profit contribution. The reasons for this variance may lie with performance (e.g., poor tactics) or planning (e.g., inaccurate forecasts).

Diagnosis and responsibility assignment procedures will be explored in more detail in the following section.

MONDAY MORNING QUARTERBACKING

A crucial issue, which we have thus far skirted, is the appropriate criterion for performance evaluation. This is a basic yet nagging problem underlying the whole area of strategic control. In the foregoing analysis, for example, we assumed that the marketing plan provides an appropriate set of criteria. The objectives therein are usually derived after considerable participation, discussion, and negotiation between interested parties,[12] and may well represent the most appropriate set of criteria that are available, at least at the beginning of the planning period.

In many companies, however, performance during the previous planning period serves as an additional set of evaluation criteria. In fact, the search for more "objective" criteria for performance evaluation led to the origins, at General Electric, of the PIMS project and the subsequent "par" criterion.[13]

The facts are, of course, that the marketing plan—which we used as our criterion—is generally based upon the best information which is available on an *ex ante* basis. The conditions which are manifest during the planning period, however, may be vastly different from those envisaged at the time of plan development. In some company planning systems, some of these changes may be encompassed by contingency planning, while in others the plan is updated when major environmental changes occur.[14] In many other instances the plan is not updated—at least in any formal way.[15]

---

[12] John A. Howard, James M. Hulbert and John U. Farley, "Organizational Analysis and Information System Design: A Decision Process Perspective," *Journal of Business Research,* Vol. 3.

[13] Schoeffler, Buzzell and Heany, same as reference 3 above.

[14] Ennis, same as reference 5 above, pg. 57.

[15] Noel Capon and James M. Hulbert, "Decision Systems Analysis in Industrial Marketing," *Industrial Marketing Management,* Vol. 4, 1975, pp. 143–60.

Nonetheless, irrespective of the comprehensiveness of systems to provide flexibility in plans, when the time arrives to review performance, most marketing managers use some *ex post* information. In other words, the criteria of evaluation—implicitly or explicitly—are generally "what performance should have been" under the circumstances which actually transpired. Nor is this "Monday morning quarterbacking" undesirable, for it is eminently more sensible than blind adherence to a plan which is clearly outdated by violation of planning assumptions.[16]

For example, supply may be affected unexpectedly; a major competitor may drop out of the market—or an aggressive new competitor may enter; or demand may have an unexpected change—e.g., because of weather. Either of these would likely change the appropriate par market share for the company. The purpose of this second stage of the analysis, therefore, is to provide a variance decomposition which permits comparison of performance versus the criterion of "what should have happened under the circumstances."

Naturally, there are inherent dangers in such a process. Re-opening the issue of what constitutes an appropriate criterion for performance evaluation may mean opening a Pandora's Box. Equally clearly, however, there are frequently occasions when unforeseen events can significantly affect what target performance should be. In such instances, it is surely preferable that any adjustment process be systematic and orderly, explicit and visible.

Using "Expert" Information

Continuing with our previous operating results, then, let us construct the scenario which occurred during the planning period, using the *ex post* information which would be available to the marketing manager at the time of performance review:

1. A new competitor—Consolidated Company—entered the market early in the year. The competitor was a large, well-financed conglomerate, which used an aggressive promotional campaign and a lower price to induce trial purchase.
2. A fire in the plant of a European manufacturer led to totally unforeseeable foreign demand for one million pounds of *Product Alpha*.

With a small amount of additional work by the manager, we may now develop an appropriate *ex post* performance analysis. For example, the fact that the new competitor was quite prepared to subsidize his entry into our market out of his other operations was an important cause of the price deterioration, and also guaranteed that he would "buy" a share of market sufficient for him to run his new plant at close to standard capacity. At the same time, this aggressive entry and the price competition which ensued was an important factor in further expanding total industry demand.

In quantitative terms Consolidated's effective mean selling price for the year was $0.465 per lb. We had forecast an industry mean of $0.495 and a price

---

[16] Joel S. Demski, "An Accounting System Structured on a Linear Programming Model," *The Accounting Review*, Vol. 42 (October 1967), pp. 701–12.

for our own product of $0.475, and we realized $0.4773 per lb. Competitive intelligence informed us that Consolidated's new plant had a capacity of only 1.33 million pounds so that its inability to supply more set a lower limit for market prices, above that of Consolidated's introductory price.

We now reconstruct the discrepancy between conditions forecast at the time of planning and the conditions which subsequently prevailed.

Market Share

As noted, our intelligence estimates indicated that Consolidated's capacity would be 1.33 million pounds. Our historical market share had hovered around 50% for some time, so that *everything being equal,* we might expect that 50% of Consolidated's sales would be at our expense. However, knowing that we were (a) the dominant competitor and (b) the premium-price competitor, we also know that we were the most vulnerable to a price-oriented competitive entry. Consequently, we used as a planning assumption the supposition that 60% of Consolidated's sales would be at our expense. That is, we assumed that $.6 \times 1.33$ million pounds, or 800 thousand pounds of sales volume which we would otherwise have obtained, would be lost to Consolidated. Thus, we had the following two conditions:

If no entry: forecast market share equal to $20.8 \div 40 = 52\%$.

With entry: forecast market share equal to $20 \div 40 = 50\%$.

Since we were certain that Consolidated would enter early in the year, we used the latter assumption. However, while our intelligence estimates on the size of Consolidated's plant were excellent, we did not glean the information that they would use 3-shift operation rather than two shifts which have been standard practice for the industry. As a result Consolidated's effective standard capacity was raised from 1.33 to 2.0 million pounds. Under these conditions, then, assuming the 60% loss rate holds, we should have expected to lose $.6 \times 2.0$ or 1.2 million pounds to Consolidated, rather than 800,000 lbs. Thus with perfect foresight we *should have* forecasted a market share of $19.6 \div 40$, or 49%.

Price

We had forecast an industry mean price of $0.495 per pound, and planned for a net price to us of $0.50 per pound. This $.005 per pound premium had been traditional for us because of our leadership position in the industry, with slightly higher quality product and excellent levels of distribution and service.

The actual industry mean price was $0.475 per pound, and our net mean price was $0.4773, so that we only received a premium of $0.0023 per pound.[17] Here, then, we have some basis for separating the planning variance from the performance variance.

---

[17] Some judgment is evidently involved here. Percentage differentials might well be used instead of absolute differentials.

Although the basis for this distinction again involves managerial judgment, for present purposes we assume that the planning group should have foreseen that Consolidated's entry would be based on a low price strategy which would lead to an overall deterioration in market prices. On the other hand, our selling and marketing tactics were responsible for the deterioration in our price premium.

Market Size

Finally, there was no possibility that our planning group could have foreseen the European fire, and it would be demonstrably unfair to hold them responsible for this component of the variance.

On the other hand, the remainder of the market expansion should have been foreseen, and the responsibility should be assigned to them. Their failure in this regard was no doubt related to the oversight in the pricing area, for it seems entirely plausible that demand was more price elastic than we had realized, and the price decrease brought a whole new set of potential customers into the market.

Variance Decomposition

The full *ex post* decomposition using this information is displayed in Exhibit 2.[18] To simplify the exposition, we employ a third subscript, "r," which indicates the standard which "should have been"—in other words, the plan as *revised* by *ex post* information. A number of useful insights are generated by the tableau.

The first issue is the nature of planning variances, which is somewhat counter-intuitive. Consider, for example, the planning variance in market share— a negative $98,000. What this is really telling us is that, considering only this factor in isolation, our planned market share was set unrealistically high, and that adjusting for this factor alone would have implied planning for a total contribution of $4,000,000 less the $98,000, or $3,902,000. Conversely, however, positive (or favorable) planning variances are in fact undesirable and represent, potentially, opportunity losses.

For example, the $900,000 favorable planning variance in market size, which is responsible for the fact that overall variance is favorable, represents lost profit contribution due to the fact that we had not correctly anticipated the market growth rate (given, of course, that there were no short-run capacity constraints). The $88,200 performance variance in market size is viewed as unassignable in this instance. We have decided that the planners could not have foreseen the foreign demand, and that we don't feel it should be assigned to sales.

Similar issues arise with the price variance. The planning group's failure to correctly predict market prices is responsible for the bulk of the price variance. However, there is no way that this component might have been recovered; it simply indicated the fact that our plan was subsequently shown by events to be unrealistic in its price expectations. In contrast, the failure of the marketing

---

[18] For algebraic exposition, see Appendix, Part 1.

department to maintain our traditional price premium is reflected in the unfavorable performance variance in price of $60,000.

Again, however, we should point out that the most important element of the analysis is the market size/market growth rate issue. Picture the poor salesmen as they operate during the planning period. They know they are feeling some price pressure, to which, as we have seen, marketing responded. However, they also know that their quantity of sales is up—22 million pounds of product versus a planned amount of 20 million pounds.

Thus, it is entirely feasible that our salesmen were not pushing that hard, since they appeared to be having a banner year, handsomely exceeding their monthly volume quotas and prior periods' performance. In fact, during this period we were frittering away our market position through our ignorance of the rate at which the market had expanded.

However, accurate and timely industry sales statistics, in combination with a flexible planning system which could readily incorporate these data in a revised plan and set of sales quotas, would preempt a problem which, by the time we recognized it, had developed into a fair-sized disaster. While market information is always important, it truly takes on new meaning for the company competing in a high-growth market.

Finally, we should note that the aggregate variances for quantity (including share and market size) and price/cost shown in Exhibit 3 do not agree with those developed in the first part of the article. The reason is, of course, that there are now two possible criteria or yardsticks against which to compare actual results: the original plan (subscripted "p") and the revised plan (subscripted "r").

Following the conceptual development of Part 2 of the Appendix, therefore, we have used what we believe to be the soundest analysis. Alternative decompositions, which permit the retention of identical aggregate variances to the preliminary "versus plan" comparison are possible, but their conceptual framework is less defensible.

SUMMARY

To be useful to the marketing manager, a framework for control should be related to strategic objectives and variables and, whenever possible, should permit assignment of responsibility for differences between planned and actual performance. The procedures described in this article utilize the key strategic variables of price, market share, and market size as a framework for marketing control.

The framework was first used to analyze marketing performance vs. plan, decomposing quantity variance into components due to under- or over-achievement of planned market share and over- or under-forecasting of market size. Then, recognizing that the plan may well not constitute an adequate criterion for evaluation, we extended the example to illustrate how *ex post* information might be utilized to develop more appropriate evaluative criteria, which permitted isolation of the planning and performance components of the variance.

While there is evidently a considerable amount of managerial judgment involved in the decomposition procedure, marketing planning and control has never been exactly bereft of managerial judgment. There is nothing radical about the procedure, which simply recognizes that it is not always possible to update and modify plans to reflect changing conditions, but that such changes may nonetheless be taken into account in appraisal and evaluation via *ex post* revision of the plan.

The example we worked with also indicates the dangers of not continuously

---

APPENDIX
Part 1: Variance Decomposition—Comparison with Plan

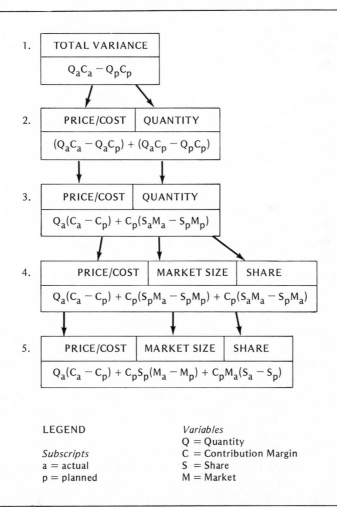

1. | TOTAL VARIANCE |
$$Q_a C_a - Q_p C_p$$

2. | PRICE/COST | QUANTITY |
$$(Q_a C_a - Q_a C_p) + (Q_a C_p - Q_p C_p)$$

3. | PRICE/COST | QUANTITY |
$$Q_a(C_a - C_p) + C_p(S_a M_a - S_p M_p)$$

4. | PRICE/COST | MARKET SIZE | SHARE |
$$Q_a(C_a - C_p) + C_p(S_p M_a - S_p M_p) + C_p(S_a M_a - S_p M_a)$$

5. | PRICE/COST | MARKET SIZE | SHARE |
$$Q_a(C_a - C_p) + C_p S_p(M_a - M_p) + C_p M_a(S_a - S_p)$$

LEGEND

Subscripts
a = actual
p = planned

Variables
Q = Quantity
C = Contribution Margin
S = Share
M = Market

APPENDIX
Part 2: Variance Decomposition—Use of Ex Post Information

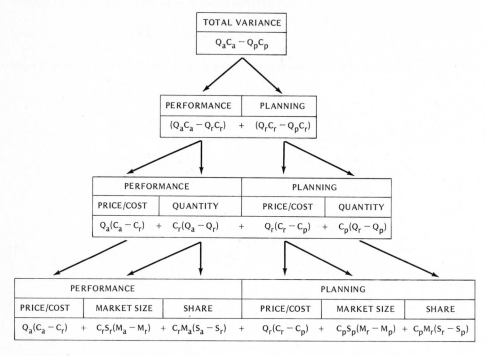

TOTAL VARIANCE

$$Q_a C_a - Q_p C_p$$

PERFORMANCE	PLANNING
$(Q_a C_a - Q_r C_r)$ +	$(Q_r C_r - Q_p C_r)$

PERFORMANCE		PLANNING	
PRICE/COST	QUANTITY	PRICE/COST	QUANTITY
$Q_a(C_a - C_r)$ +	$C_r(Q_a - Q_r)$ +	$Q_r(C_r - C_p)$ +	$C_p(Q_r - Q_p)$

PERFORMANCE			PLANNING		
PRICE/COST	MARKET SIZE	SHARE	PRICE/COST	MARKET SIZE	SHARE
$Q_a(C_a - C_r)$ +	$C_r S_r(M_a - M_r)$ +	$C_r M_a(S_a - S_r)$ +	$Q_r(C_r - C_p)$ +	$C_p S_p(M_r - M_p)$ +	$C_p M_r(S_r - S_p)$

LEGEND

Subscripts	Variables
a = actual	Q = Quantity
p = planned	C = Contribution margins
r = revised	S = Share
	M = Market

monitoring markets and revising plans and objectives, particularly when market conditions are fluid. In such markets, good tracking procedures [19] and responsive tactics are essential for any company seeking to maintain or increase its market position. The importance of marketing control—so long a stepchild—will surely increase in the years ahead. The markets of the late 1970's will differ considerably from those of the 1960's, and pressures of costs and competition will force companies to be more effective in performance appraisal and evaluation.

[19] John U. Farley and Melvin J. Hinich, "Tracking Marketing Parameters in Random Noise," in *Proceedings, 1966 Marketing Educators' Conference.*

Marketing Cost Analysis: A Modularized Contribution Approach

Patrick M. Dunne and Harry I. Wolk

In recent years, an increasing use of accounting information for planning, controlling, and evaluating the firm's marketing performance has been advocated in the literature.[1] Some of this published material is very sophisticated, and indeed there is almost no limit to how far one can go in analyzing the effectiveness of marketing operations by accounting techniques. At the same time, it is truly astounding that many marketing managers do not use even some of the more elementary accounting tools that are available.

The authors know of one company where Product X was generating an annual profit of $800,000, and Product Y was losing money at the rate of $600,000

About the Authors: Patrick M. Dunne is Associate Professor of Marketing, Texas Tech University, Lubbock; Harry I. Wolk is a Professor of Accounting, Drake University, Des Moines.

Reprinted from *Journal of Marketing*, vol. 41 (July 1977), pp. 83–94, published by the American Marketing Association.

[1] For example, "Report of the Committee on Cost and Profitability Analyses for Marketing," *The Accounting Review Supplement* (1972), pp. 575–615; W. J. E. Crissy, Paul Fischer and Frank H. Mossman, "Segmental Analysis: Key to Marketing Profitability," *Business Topics* (Spring 1973), pp. 42–49; V. H. Kirpalani and Stanley J. Shapiro, "Financial Dimensions of Marketing Management," *Journal of Marketing*, Vol. 37 No. 3 (July 1973), pp. 40–47; Leland L. Beik and Stephen L. Buzby, "Profitability Analysis by Market Segments," *Journal of Marketing*, Vol. 37 No. 3 (July 1973), pp. 48–53; Frank H. Mossman, Paul Fischer and W. J. E. Crissy, "New Approaches to Analyzing Marketing Profitability," *Journal of Marketing*, Vol. 38 No. 2 (April 1974), pp. 43–48; Merritt J. Davoust, "Analyzing a Client's Customer Profitability Picture," *Management Adviser*, May–June 1974, pp. 15–19; Harry I. Wolk and Patrick M. Dunne, "Modularized Contribution Margin Income Statements for Marketing and Physical Distribution Analysis," *Research Issues in Logistics*, James F. Robeson and John Grabner, eds. (Columbus: The Ohio State University, 1975), pp. 199–210; Stephen L. Buzby and Lester E. Heitger, "Profit Oriented Reporting for Marketing Decision Makers," *Business Topics*, Summer 1976, pp. 60–68; Richard L. Lewis and Leo G. Erickson, "Distribution System Costing: An Overview," *Distribution System Costing: Concepts and Procedures*, John R. Grabner and William S. Sargent, eds. (Columbus: The Ohio State University, 1972), pp. 1–30.

per year—and management was totally unaware of the situation, just pleasantly happy to be making $200,000! They were simply astounded when a little accounting by product line revealed Product Y to be such a drain.

Not quite that elementary, but still well within the group of non-accounting trained managers, is the *modular contribution margin income statement.* This technique spotlights the behavior of controllable costs and indicates each segment's contribution to profit and indirect fixed costs. It is a very useful tool for marketing managers who are concerned not only with the efficiency of the operation for which they are responsible, but also with the profitability of the product, various territories, channels, types and sizes of customer, etc.

In order to generate accounting information for specific marketing segments, a detailed data base is a necessity. All transactions entering the system must be classified and coded so that costs can be matched with revenues at desired aggregation levels for different combinations of relevant factors. But the payoff is usually worth the effort. The modular contribution margin approach to marketing analysis enables management (a) to judge the profitability of a specific marketing mix in a specific area and (b) to decide whether or not to take action to change it.

CASE EXAMPLE

Consider the D-W Appliance Company, a small appliance manufacturer that produces blenders and mixers on separate production lines. The firm's marketing division is organized along territorial lines (East and West), and the products are sold by sales representatives through two marketing channels: (1) to wholesalers, who, in turn, distribute to small retailers, and (2) directly to large retailers. Order size is also important: channel costs are lower for orders of 100 units or more of either product.

If the Marketing Division Manager wanted to assess the profitability of his functional area, he might request an income statement. Under the full-cost approach to financial statements, costs would be separated according to function: cost of goods sold and operating expenses. A portion of the general expense of the company cost centers (accounting, corporate headquarters, etc.) would arbitrarily be allocated to the operating expense of the Marketing Division. (See Exhibit 1.)

This type of statement is, however, better suited to external reporting than to internal managerial planning and control, since it contains costs which do not directly affect decisions in the marketing area and which are not controllable by the Marketing Division Manager. Furthermore, in order to apply variance analysis to this kind of statement, comparing budgeted results with actual results for control purposes, the costs would first have to be separated by activity before the analysis could distinguish between cost changes in the level of an activity and those due to other causes.

The main advantage of the modular contribution margin approach as a

---

EXHIBIT 1
Income Statement Models

FULL-COST APPROACH

Revenue
　Less: Cost of goods sold.
Gross Margin
　Less: Operating expenses (including the division's allocated share of company administrative and general expenses).

Net Income

CONTRIBUTION MARGIN APPROACH

Revenue
　Less: Variable manufacturing costs. Other variable costs directly traceable to the segment.
Contribution Margin
　Less: Fixed costs directly traceable to products. Fixed costs directly traceable to the market segment.

Segment Net Income

===

managerial tool for planning and control is that it separates costs, by behavior, into variable and fixed costs.[2]

Variable costs are those costs which vary predictably with some measure of activity during a given time period. For example, commissions on sales for D-W are set at 10% of sales revenue. Total commission expense varies as sales vary.

Fixed costs, on the other hand, are costs which do not change in the short run, e.g., the Marketing Division Manager's salary.

COST BEHAVIOR AND CONTROLLABILITY

The modular contribution margin model, which allows separation of costs by behavior, can be expanded to include separation of costs by controllability.

---

[2] Sophisticated methods for separating fixed and variable costs are shown in William J. Baumol and Charles H. Sevin, "Marketing Costs and Mathematical Programming," *New Decision-Making Tools for Managers,* Edward C. Bursk and John F. Chapman, eds. (New York: New American Library, Inc., 1963), pp. 247–65; and R. S. Gynther, "Improving Separation of Fixed and Variable Expenses," *Management Accounting,* June 1963, pp. 29–38.

Controllable costs are those costs which originate in the particular organizational unit under consideration. Whether a cost is classified as controllable or uncontrollable obviously depends on the organizational segment under consideration. Territorial expenses in the statement for East Territory would be controllable costs for that territory and for the Marketing Division, but not for the West Territory.

As just suggested, controllability relates to the degree of influence over a cost by the relevant division manager. Labor costs that exceed standard costs for actual production in a particular department are a classic example of a cost for which the appropriate manager would be held accountable. However, even for this classification, a great deal of care must be exercised. Actual controllable labor costs may exceed standard because of many reasons beyond the manager's scope or control. For example, delivery time for shipments may be delayed by severe weather. Furthermore, controllability may be constrained by economic externalities. Selling costs would be a controllable variable cost of the Marketing Division, while the manager probably has little, if any, influence over a price decline precipitated by a competitor's action.

Controllable fixed costs are rarely controllable in the very short run. Once a fixed asset is acquired, there is virtually no control over the annual depreciation charges. One may select the depreciation method, but no differences will arise between actual and budgeted costs except in those situations where depreciation can be calculated on usage. There are, however, some intermediate-term fixed costs (often called discretionary or programmed costs because they are determined annually on a budgetary basis) which may be highly controllable; i.e., actual costs may exceed budgeted costs. Advertising and R&D costs fall into this category.

Controllable Variable Costs	Controllable Fixed Costs
Uncontrollable Variable costs	Uncontrollable Fixed costs

Uncontrollable variable costs are variable costs which are not incurred in the segment under consideration. Therefore, the costs should be expressed as standard costs so that a manager will not be held responsible for the inefficiencies of another department. Variable manufacturing costs of blenders and mixers would be indirect variable costs for the Marketing Division, and should be expressed in the budget at standard costs.

Uncontrollable fixed costs are not included in segmental income statements since any basis of allocation to the segment would necessarily be arbitrary. Uncontrollable costs are often called common costs and for the Marketing Division would include a portion of those costs of the corporate headquarters and those manufacturing costs which couldn't be directly allocated to blenders and mixers, such as the plant manager's salary.

SEGMENTAL ANALYSIS

Contribution margin income statements by department are useful for budgeting, performance analysis, short-run decision-making, pricing, and decisions between alternatives—e.g., whether to close down a warehouse or relocate it; whether to lease a fleet of trucks or own them. Market segment income statements are also useful for such marketing decisions as whether to drop a product line and whether to alter the physical distribution system; and they aid in the redirection of effort to the company's more profitable markets. The usual market segmentation is by product line, territory, channel, order size, and customer, but any of the segmentation bases of the marketing matrix of the firm's target markets could be used.

A modular data base also facilitates statements focusing on functional areas, depending on management's judgment about what information is relevant for decision-making and control. For example, if transportation is judged to be a crucial function in the case of blenders, then the expense for shipping blenders would be coded by that function and by the relevant variables (territory, channel, product, order size, customer, date). Revenue, in turn, would be coded at the time of each transaction.

Unless the company's information system is somewhat sophisticated, there is usually some initial difficulty in constructing accounting statements of functional/departmental areas.[3] Costs for a specific department must be broken out of the natural accounts via estimation techniques. (Since costs are usually accumulated in natural accounts, such as salary expense, the salary expense for the Marketing Division would have to be calculated.)

Under the modular contribution margin approach not all costs are allocated to segments. Rather, only those costs are considered which would disappear if the company were to drop that department or segment. Note that this is acceptable only for purposes of internal decision-making, and *not* for differential cost justification under the Robinson-Patman Act (as demonstrated in the Borden case) or for general financial reporting purposes (audited reports to stockholders, IRS returns, and SEC reports).

ALLOCATION OF COSTS

Other refinements can be added to the modular contribution margin model. The charge for the specific assets used by the department (depreciation) could be based on the decline in the market value of the resources during the period. Or an interest charge on the working capital used by the department (based on the firm's actual cost of capital) could be included to give a clear picture of the department's operations and actual contribution.

Allocation, however, cannot be made arbitrarily on the basis of sales volume since that focus might overlook other relevant information. For example, how do

---

[3] Mossman, same as reference 1, pg. 44.

you attach distribution expense to blenders and mixers for a mixed shipment of both products, when blenders are bulkier, heavier, and require more handling? Or if mixers are easy to sell to large retailers, while blenders require extensive sales effort, the entry of salesmen's expenses to blenders and mixers should reflect this difference.

If costs are based on a factor such as weight or space occupied, this may allow an equitable basis of cost assignment. This does not always happen, though, and so assigning costs to departments on the basis of weight can be highly misleading for analytical purposes. Suffice it to say that wherever variable costs are predictable and vary with a given base, standard costs should be used in budgeting for the Marketing Division.

The value of a modular contribution margin statement is the ability to match costs with revenues for the smallest market segments desired and then to aggregate these modules into statements for larger segments. Essentially, the modular data base provides management with the capability of transforming accounting information into two systems: one based on departments within the firm, the other based on market segments.

USEFUL INFORMATION

The flexibility and responsiveness of the modular contribution margin approach for market segments can be shown by applying it to the D-W Appliance Company. The first step is for management to decide on the relevant factors for examination. In this example, *product line* was chosen as the basic unit of interest, and the market was further segmented by territory, channel, and order size. (The modular data base could just as easily have provided for primary segmentation by territory or channel, or whatever.) The exhibits which follow show the posisible modular income statements that can be constructed.

Exhibit 2 shows the hierarchy and linkages among the segmental contribution margin income statements illustrated here.

Basic data for the illustration are shown in Exhibit 3, the Master Cost Data Sheet. Unit sales and channel of distribution costs are broken down by territory, product, and channel in Exhibit 4.

Income for the entire firm is shown in Exhibit 5. It is the only statement containing $430,000 of costs (territory costs, joint manufacturing costs, and corporate headquarters costs) which are joint to the product oriented segmental income statements shown in Exhibits 6–19.

CLUES FOR ACTION

The loss at the corporate level (as shown in Exhibit 5), indicates that the firm should either strengthen, if possible, those segments which are weakest and/or reallocate more of its resources to those segments which are strongest.

In Exhibits 6 and 13, Total Income Statements for blenders and mixers, blenders are stronger than mixers in terms of Contribution Margin (32.7% versus 21.6%) although slightly less profitable after taking into account direct fixed costs (13.1% versus 14.8%). This may indicate that not enough programmed advertising costs are being budgeted to blenders. More advertising effort may be needed to effectively exploit higher Contribution Margin of blenders.

At the same time, the further breakdowns indicate that the Segment Income of the West Territory is lagging behind the East Territory for both blenders and mixers (see Exhibits 7, 10, 14, and 17). The biggest reason for this poor performance is the very low Segment Income of the Wholesaler Channels in the West Territory (Exhibits 11 and 18).

Action to improve the situation is especially called for in the Wholesaler Channel for blenders in the West Territory. Not only is the Segment Income percentage (6.5%) the lowest for any segment in the whole analysis, but the corresponding Contribution Margin is relatively strong (27.9%). The problem is one of spreading heavy fixed costs of manufacturing over more sales. The solution, again, would be to take advantage of the good Contribution Margin percentage through increased advertising effort or, perhaps in this case, by expanding the sales force.

As another indication of the revealing capability of this kind of analysis, consider the profitability of the two channels. If they had simply been compared in total (as a form of primary segmentation), the figures would have been:

Channel	Contribution Margin (%)	Segment (%)	Income ($)
Wholesaler	26.3%	12.9%	$212,588
Large retailer	27.8%	14.3%	$208,807

The two channels would have appeared to be very even in profitability. Yet recombining in various ways brings out still more information. Exhibit 20 shows that if the Wholesaler Channel in the West could be improved to match the Wholesaler Channel in the East, the total Wholesaler Channel would have outperformed the Large Retailer Channel.

Within the Large Retailer Channel, blenders and mixers in the East are relatively more profitable in terms of both Contribution Margin and Segment Income percentages than their counterparts in the West. However, Segment Income in total dollars for blenders and mixers in the East ($74,209) is barely half of that for the corresponding products in the West for the Large Retailer Channel ($134,598). Maybe the East Territory for Large Retailers needs a greater dosage of advertising dollars to exploit its relative advantage. Perhaps the whole Large Retailer Channel needs some kind of revamping—a need that otherwise would never have been revealed except through segmental analysis.

EXHIBIT 2

Segmental Contribution Income Statements: D-W Appliance Company

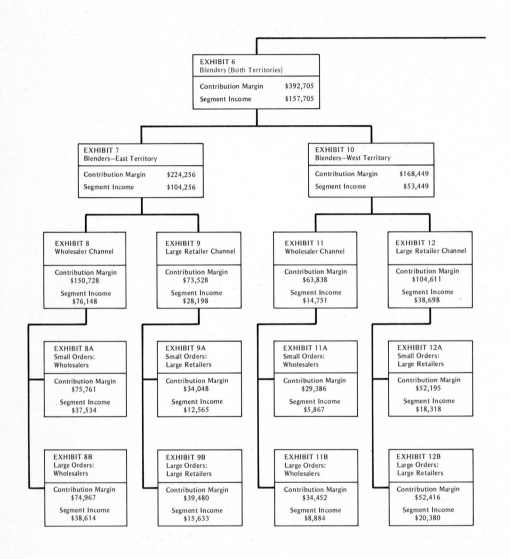

EXHIBIT 6	
Blenders (Both Territories)	
Contribution Margin	$392,705
Segment Income	$157,705

EXHIBIT 7	
Blenders—East Territory	
Contribution Margin	$224,256
Segment Income	$104,256

EXHIBIT 10	
Blenders—West Territory	
Contribution Margin	$168,449
Segment Income	$53,449

EXHIBIT 8	EXHIBIT 9	EXHIBIT 11	EXHIBIT 12
Wholesaler Channel	Large Retailer Channel	Wholesaler Channel	Large Retailer Channel
Contribution Margin $150,728	Contribution Margin $73,528	Contribution Margin $63,838	Contribution Margin $104,611
Segment Income $76,148	Segment Income $28,198	Segment Income $14,751	Segment Income $38,698

EXHIBIT 8A	EXHIBIT 9A	EXHIBIT 11A	EXHIBIT 12A
Small Orders: Wholesalers	Small Orders: Large Retailers	Small Orders: Wholesalers	Small Orders: Large Retailers
Contribution Margin $75,761	Contribution Margin $34,048	Contribution Margin $29,386	Contribution Margin $52,195
Segment Income $37,534	Segment Income $12,565	Segment Income $5,867	Segment Income $18,318

EXHIBIT 8B	EXHIBIT 9B	EXHIBIT 11B	EXHIBIT 12B
Large Orders: Wholesalers	Large Orders: Large Retailers	Large Orders: Wholesalers	Large Orders: Large Retailers
Contribution Margin $74,967	Contribution Margin $39,480	Contribution Margin $34,452	Contribution Margin $52,416
Segment Income $38,614	Segment Income $15,633	Segment Income $8,884	Segment Income $20,380

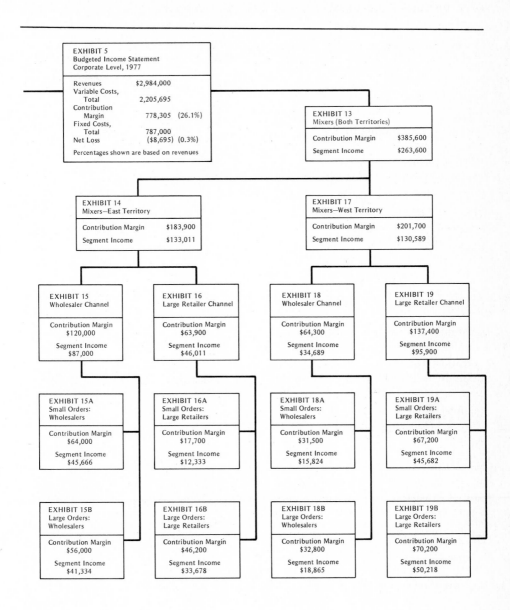

EXHIBIT 5
Budgeted Income Statement
Corporate Level, 1977

Revenues	$2,984,000	
Variable Costs, Total	2,205,695	
Contribution Margin	778,305	(26.1%)
Fixed Costs, Total	787,000	
Net Loss	($8,695)	(0.3%)

Percentages shown are based on revenues

EXHIBIT 13
Mixers (Both Territories)

Contribution Margin	$385,600
Segment Income	$263,600

EXHIBIT 14
Mixers—East Territory

Contribution Margin	$183,900
Segment Income	$133,011

EXHIBIT 17
Mixers—West Territory

Contribution Margin	$201,700
Segment Income	$130,589

EXHIBIT 15
Wholesaler Channel

Contribution Margin	$120,000
Segment Income	$87,000

EXHIBIT 16
Large Retailer Channel

Contribution Margin	$63,900
Segment Income	$46,011

EXHIBIT 18
Wholesaler Channel

Contribution Margin	$64,300
Segment Income	$34,689

EXHIBIT 19
Large Retailer Channel

Contribution Margin	$137,400
Segment Income	$95,900

EXHIBIT 15A
Small Orders:
Wholesalers

Contribution Margin	$64,000
Segment Income	$45,666

EXHIBIT 16A
Small Orders:
Large Retailers

Contribution Margin	$17,700
Segment Income	$12,333

EXHIBIT 18A
Small Orders:
Wholesalers

Contribution Margin	$31,500
Segment Income	$15,824

EXHIBIT 19A
Small Orders:
Large Retailers

Contribution Margin	$67,200
Segment Income	$45,682

EXHIBIT 15B
Large Orders:
Wholesalers

Contribution Margin	$56,000
Segment Income	$41,334

EXHIBIT 16B
Large Orders:
Large Retailers

Contribution Margin	$46,200
Segment Income	$33,678

EXHIBIT 18B
Large Orders:
Wholesalers

Contribution Margin	$32,800
Segment Income	$18,865

EXHIBIT 19B
Large Orders:
Large Retailers

Contribution Margin	$70,200
Segment Income	$50,218

EXHIBIT 3

D-W Appliance Company Master Cost Data Sheet for 1977

	EAST		WEST	
	BLENDERS	MIXERS	BLENDERS	MIXERS
Revenue (per unit)	$ 42.00	$ 26.00	$ 38.00	$ 24.00
Variable manufacturing costs	$ 20.00	$ 15.00	$ 20.00	$ 15.00
Variable selling costs (10% of revenue)	4.20	2.60	3.80	2.40
Total	$ 24.20	$ 17.60	$ 23.80	$ 17.40
Contribution margin per unit before channel costs	$ 17.80	$ 8.40	$ 14.20	$ 6.60
Programmed advertising costs [1]	$20,000	$12,000	$15,000	$10,000
Budgeted sales (units)	15,000	28,000	15,000	44,000

	BLENDERS	MIXERS	EAST	WEST	UNALLOCATED
Controllable direct manufacturing costs	$200,000	$100,000			
Territorial fixed costs (joint to products)			$50,000	$30,000	
Joint fixed manufacturing costs					$100,000
Corporate headquarters costs					$250,000

[1] Programmed advertising costs are fixed costs that are reviewed each year through the budget process. (Therefore, they are not in a direct relationship with sales revenue or units sold. This could result from having a particular ad aimed at only one channel member or group of channel members. An example would be a trade magazine ad in a conference program for a wholesalers convention. Such an ad would not reach the retailer.)

Another aspect of the problem lies in order size. Exhibit 21 reveals that this is most evident within the Large Retailer Channel in the West. Within that territory and channel, distribution costs for small order sizes of mixers are 50% greater per dollar of revenue than for large orders. Similarly, small orders of blenders in the West in the Large Retailer Channel are out of line relative to large orders (31% excess). Small order costs are also out of line relative to large orders for mixers in the East in both channels (39.1% and 42.6% for Large Retailers and Wholesalers). Efforts must be made to increase the size of Large

EXHIBIT 4
Budgeted Channel of Distribution Costs

	WHOLESALER SMALL ORDER	CHANNEL LARGE ORDER	LARGE RETAILER SMALL ORDER	CHANNEL LARGE ORDER
EAST:				
Blenders:				
Budgeted sales (units)	5,119	4,868	2,381	2,632
Cost per unit	$ 3.00	$ 2.40	$ 3.50	$ 2.80
Total	$15,357	$11,683	$ 8,334	$ 7,370
Mixers:				
Budgeted sales (units)	10,000	8,000	3,000	7,000
Cost per unit	$ 2.00	$ 1.40	$ 2.50	$ 1.80
Total	$20,000	$11,200	$ 7,500	$12,600
WEST:				
Blenders:				
Budgeted sales (units)	2,881	3,132	4,619	4,368
Cost per unit	$ 4.00	$ 3.20	$ 2.90	$ 2.20
Total	$11,524	$10,022	$13,395	$ 9,610
Mixers:				
Budgeted sales (units)	9,000	8,000	14,000	13,000
Cost per unit	$ 3.10	$ 2.50	$ 1.80	$ 1.20
Total	$27,900	$20,000	$25,200	$15,600

Retailers' small orders, or the retailers responsible for these orders must be converted to buying from wholesalers.

BENEFITS OF SEGMENTATION

These are just a few of the possible areas where the use of the modular contribution margin income statement could improve management control and planning, for the sake of greater profitability. In addition, actual results can be compared against the projected budget for each segment to analyze management's performance or the effect of uncontrollable factors on that performance.

If segmental analysis had not been done at all, or if the segmentation had been conducted just by product (or just by territory, just by channel, or just by order size) many ideas for corrective action or expanded effort might not have been generated.

While the benefits of segmental statements must exceed costs of preparation, the power of the computer should lessen costs enough to make segmental analysis beneficial to an increasing number of companies.

EXHIBITS 5 and 6–12
Total Income Statements

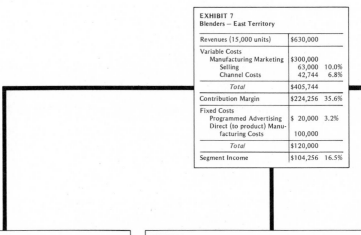

EXHIBIT 7
Blenders — East Territory

Revenues (15,000 units)	$630,000
Variable Costs	
Manufacturing Marketing	$300,000
Selling	63,000 10.0%
Channel Costs	42,744 6.8%
Total	$405,744
Contribution Margin	$224,256 35.6%
Fixed Costs	
Programmed Advertising	$ 20,000 3.2%
Direct (to product) Manufacturing Costs	100,000
Total	$120,000
Segment Income	$104,256 16.5%

EXHIBIT 8
Wholesaler Channel

	Small Order (5119 units)		Large Order (4868 units)		Total	
Revenues	$214,998		$204,456		$419,454	
Variable Costs						
Manufacturing						
Marketing	$102,380		$ 97,360		$199,740	
Selling	21,500	10.0%	20,446	10.0%	41,946	10.0%
Channel Costs	15,357	7.1%	11,683	5.7%	27,040	6.4%
Total	$139,237		$129,489		$268,726	
Contribution Margin	$ 75,761	35.2%	$ 74,967	36.7%	$150,728	35.9%
Fixed Costs						
Programmed Advertising[1]	$ 4,100	1.9%	$ 3,900	1.9%	$ 8,000	1.9%
Direct (to product) Manufacturing Costs[2]	34,127		32,453		66,580	
Total	$ 38,227		$ 36,353		$ 74,580	
Segment Income	$ 37,534	17.5%	$ 38,614	18.9%	$ 76,148	18.2%

EXHIBIT 9
Large Retailer Channel

	Small Order (2381 units)		Large Order (2632 units)		Total	
Revenues	$100,002		$110,544		$210,546	
Variable Costs						
Manufacturing						
Marketing	$ 47,620		$ 52,640		$100,260	
Selling	10,000	10.0%	11,054	10.0%	21,054	10.0%
Channel Costs	8,334	8.3%	7,370	6.7%	15,704	7.5%
Total	$ 65,954		$ 71,064		$137,018	
Contribution Margin	$ 34,048	34.0%	$ 39,480	35.7%	$ 73,528	34.9%
Fixed Costs						
Programmed Advertising[1]	$ 5,700	5.7%	$ 6,300	5.7%	$ 12,000	5.7%
Direct (to product) Manufacturing Costs[2]	15,783		17,547		33,330	
Total	$ 21,483		$ 23,847		$ 45,330	
Segment Income	$ 12,565	12.6%	$ 15,633	14.1%	$ 28,198	13.4%

[1] Direct to the Large Retailer Channel and allocated in accordance with revenues. The same procedure is used for channel analysis in later exhibits.

[2] Allocated in proportion of number of units sold in each order size for the channel to total sales. The same procedure is used in later exhibits.

EXHIBIT 5
Corporate Level, 1977

Revenues	$2,984,000	
Variable Costs		
Manufacturing Marketing	$1,680,000	
Selling	298,400	10.0%[1]
Channel Costs	227,295	7.6%
Total	$2,205,695	
Contribution Margin	$ 778,305	26.1%
Fixed Costs		
Programmed Advertising	$ 57,000	1.9%
Direct (to product) Manufacturing Costs	300,000	
Territory Costs	80,000	
Joint Manufacturing Costs	100,000	
Corporate Headquarters Costs	250,000	
Total	$ 787,000	
Net Loss	($8,695)	(.3%)

[1] Percentages shown are based upon revenues.

EXHIBIT 6
Blenders (Both Territories)

Revenues (30,000 units)	$1,200,000	
Variable Costs		
Manufacturing Marketing	$ 600,000	
Selling	120,000	10.0%
Channel Costs	87,295	7.3%
Total	$ 807,295	
Contribution Margin	$ 392,705	32.7%
Fixed Costs		
Programmed Advertising	$ 35,000	2.9%
Direct (to product) Manufacturing Costs	200,000	
Total	$ 235,000	
Segment Income	$ 157,705	13.1%

EXHIBIT 10
Blenders — West Territory

Revenues (15,000 units)	$570,000	
Variable Costs		
Manufacturing Marketing	$300,000	
Selling	57,000	10.0%
Channel Costs	44,551	7.8%
Total	$401,551	
Contribution Margin	$168,449	29.6%
Fixed Costs		
Programmed Advertising	$ 15,000	2.6%
Direct (to product) Manufacturing Costs	100,000	
Total	$115,000	
Segment Income	$ 53,449	9.4%

EXHIBIT 11
Wholesaler Channel

	Small Order (2881 units)		Large Order (3132 units)		Total	
Revenues	$109,478		$119,016		$228,494	
Variable Costs						
Manufacturing						
Marketing	$ 57,620		$ 62,640		$120,260	
Selling	10,948	10.0%	11,902	10.0%	22,850	10.0%
Channel Costs	11,524	10.5%	10,022	8.4%	21,546	9.4%
Total	$ 80,092		$ 84,564		$164,656	
Contribution Margin	$ 29,386	26.8%	$ 34,452	28.9%	$ 63,838	27.9%
Fixed Costs						
Programmed Advertising	$ 4,312	3.9%	$ 4,688	3.9%	$ 9,000	3.9%
Direct (to product) Manufacturing Costs	19,207		20,880		40,087	
Total	$ 23,519		$ 25,568		$ 49,087	
Segment Income	$ 5,867	5.4%	$ 8,884	7.5%	$ 14,751	6.5%

EXHIBIT 12
Large Retailer Channel

	Small Order (4619 units)		Large Order (4368 units)		Total	
Revenues	$175,522		$165,984		$341,506	
Variable Costs						
Manufacturing						
Marketing	$ 92,380		$ 87,360		$179,740	
Selling	17,552	10.0%	16,598	10.0%	34,150	10.0%
Channel Costs	13,395	7.6%	9,610	5.8%	23,005	6.7%
Total	$123,327		$113,568		$236,895	
Contribution Margin	$ 52,195	29.7%	$ 52,416	31.6%	$104,611	30.6%
Fixed Costs						
Programmed Advertising	$ 3,084	1.8%	$ 2,916	1.8%	$ 6,000	1.8%
Direct (to product) Manufacturing Costs	30,793		29,120		59,913	
Total	$ 33,877		$ 32,036		$ 65,913	
Segment Income	$ 18,318	10.4%	$ 20,380	12.3%	$ 38,698	11.3%

EXHIBITS 5 and 13–19
Total Income Statements

EXHIBIT 5
Corporate Level, 1977

Revenues	$2,984,000	
Variable Costs		
Manufacturing Marketing	$1,680,000	
Selling	298,400	10.0%
Channel Costs	227,295	7.6%
Total	$2,205,695	
Contribution Margin	$ 778,305	26.1%
Fixed Costs		
Programmed Advertising	$ 57,000	1.9%
Direct (to product) Manufacturing Costs	300,000	
Territory Costs	80,000	
Joint Manufacturing Costs	100,000	
Corporate Headquarters Costs	250,000	
Total	$ 787,000	
Net Loss	($8,695)	(.3%)

EXHIBIT 14
Mixers — East Territory

Revenues (28,000 units)	$728,000	
Variable Costs		
Manufacturing Marketing	$420,000	
Selling	72,800	10.0%
Channel Costs	51,300	7.0%
Total	$544,100	
Contribution Margin	$183,900	25.3%
Fixed Costs		
Programmed Advertising	$ 12,000	1.6%
Direct (to product) Manufacturing Costs	38,889	
Total	$ 50,889	
Segment Income	$133,011	18.3%

EXHIBIT 13
Mixers (Both Territories)

Revenues (72,000 units)	$1,784,000	
Variable Costs		
Manufacturing Marketing	$1,080,000	
Selling	178,400	10.0%
Channel Costs	140,000	7.8%
Total	$1,398,400	
Contribution Margin	$ 385,600	21.6%
Fixed Costs		
Programmed Advertising	$ 22,000	1.2%
Direct (to product) Manufacturing Costs	100,000	
Total	$ 122,000	
Segment Income	$ 263,600	14.8%

EXHIBIT 15
Wholesaler Channel

	Small Order (10,000 units)		Large Order (8,000 units)		Total	
Revenues	$260,000		$208,000		$468,000	
Variable Costs						
Manufacturing						
Marketing	$150,000		$120,000		$270,000	
Selling	26,000	10.0%	20,800	10.0%	46,800	10.0%
Channel Costs	20,000	7.7%	11,200	5.4%	31,200	6.7%
Total	$196,000		$152,000		$348,000	
Contribution Margin	$ 64,000	24.6%	$ 56,000	26.9%	$120,000	25.6%
Fixed Costs						
Programmed Advertising	$ 4,445	1.7%	$ 3,555	1.7%	$ 8,000	1.7%
Direct (to product) Manufacturing Costs	13,889		11,111		25,000	
Total	$ 18,334		$ 14,666		$ 33,000	
Segment Income	$ 45,666	17.6%	$ 41,334	19.8%	$ 87,000	18.6%

EXHIBIT 16
Large Retailer Channel

	Small Order (3,000 units)		Large Order (7,000 units)		Total	
Revenues	$78,000		$182,000		$260,000	
Variable Costs						
Manufacturing						
Marketing	$45,000		$105,000		$150,000	
Selling	7,800	10.0%	18,200	10.0%	26,100	10.0%
Channel Costs	7,500	9.6%	12,600	6.9%	20,100	7.7%
Total	$60,300		$135,800		$196,100	
Contribution Margin	$17,700	22.7%	$ 46,200	25.4%	$ 63,900	24.6%
Fixed Costs						
Programmed Advertising	$ 1,200	1.5%	$ 2,800	1.5%	$ 4,000	1.5%
Direct (to product) Manufacturing Costs	4,167		9,722		13,889	
Total	$ 5,367		$ 12,522		$ 17,889	
Segment Income	$12,333	15.8%	$ 33,678	18.5%	$ 46,011	17.7%

EXHIBIT 17
Mixers — West Territory

Revenues	$1,056,000	
Variable Costs		
Manufacturing Marketing	$ 660,000	
Selling	105,600	10.0%
Channel Costs	88,700	8.4%
Total	$ 854,300	
Contribution Margin	$ 201,700	19.1%
Fixed Costs		
Programmed Advertising	$ 10,000	.9%
Direct (to product) Manu-		
facturing Costs	61,111	
Total	$ 71,111	
Segment Income	$ 130,589	12.4%

EXHIBIT 18
Wholesale Channel

	Small Order (9000 units)		Large Order (8000 units)		Total	
Revenues	$216,000		$192,000		$408,000	
Variable Costs						
Manufacturing						
Marketing	$135,000		$120,000		$255,000	
Selling	21,600	10.0%	29,200	10.0%	40,800	10.0%
Channel Costs	27,900	12.9%	20,000	10.4%	47,900	11.7%
Total	$184,500		$159,200		$343,700	
Contribution Margin	$ 31,500	14.6%	$ 32,800	17.1%	$ 64,300	15.8%
Fixed Costs						
Programmed						
Advertising	$ 3,176	1.5%	$ 2,824	1.5%	$ 6,000	1.5%
Direct (to prod-						
uct) Manufac-						
turing Costs	12,500		11,111		23,611	
Total	$ 15,676		$ 13,935		$ 29,611	
Segment Income	$ 15,824	7.3%	$ 18,865	9.8%	$ 34,689	8.5%

EXHIBIT 19
Large Retailer Channel

	Small Order (14,000 units)		Large Order (13,000 units)		Total	
Revenues	$336,000		$312,000		$648,000	
Variable Costs						
Manufacturing						
Marketing	$210,000		$195,000		$405,000	
Selling	33,600	10.0%	31,200	10.0%	64,800	10.0%
Channel Costs	25,200	7.5%	15,600	5.0%	40,800	6.3%
Total	$268,800		$241,800		$510,600	
Contribution Margin	$ 67,200	20.0%	$ 70,200	22.5%	$137,400	21.2%
Fixed Costs						
Programmed						
Advertising	$ 2,074	.6%	$ 1,926	.6%	$ 4,000	.6%
Direct (to prod-						
uct) Manufac-						
turing Costs	19,444		18,056		37,500	
Total	$ 21,518		$ 19,982		$ 41,500	
Segment Income	$ 45,682	13.6%	$ 50,218	16.1%	$ 95,900	14.8%

EXHIBIT 20

Aggregate Comparison of Wholesaler Channel and Large Retailer Channel

CHANNEL	CONTRIBUTION MARGIN (%)	SEGMENT (%)	INCOME ($)	TOTAL
WHOLESALERS [1]	[26.3%] [3]	[12.9%] [3]		[$212,588] [3]
West				
Blenders	27.9%	6.5%	$14,751	
Mixers	15.8%	8.5%	$34,689	
Subtotal				*$ 49,440*
East				
Blenders	35.9%	18.2%	$76,148	
Mixers	25.6%	18.6%	$87,000	
Subtotal				*$163,148*
LARGE RETAILERS [2]	[27.8%] [3]	[14.3%] [3]		[$208,807] [3]
West				
Blenders	30.6%	11.3%	$38,698	
Mixers	21.2%	14.8%	$95,900	
Subtotal				*$134,598*
East				
Blenders	34.9%	13.4%	$28,198	
Mixers	24.6%	17.7%	$46,011	
Subtotal				*$ 74,209*

[1] Exhibits 8, 11, 15, and 18.
[2] Exhibits 9, 12, 16, and 19.
[3] Aggregate totals.

EXHIBIT 21
Relative Distribution Costs by Order Size

TERRITORY	PRODUCT	LARGE ORDER [1]	SMALL ORDER [1]	RELATIVE COST EXCESS [2]
Large Retailers				
West	Blenders	5.8%	7.6%	31.0%
West	Mixers	5.0%	7.5%	50.0%
East	Blenders	6.7%	8.3%	23.9%
East	Mixers	6.9%	9.6%	39.1%

TERRITORY	PRODUCT	LARGE ORDER [2]	SMALL ORDER [3]	RELATIVE COST EXCESS [2]
Wholesalers				
West	Blenders	8.4%	10.5%	25.0%
West	Mixers	10.4%	12.9%	24.0%
East	Blenders	5.7%	7.1%	24.6%
East	Mixers	5.4%	7.7%	42.6%

[1] Channel costs as a percentage of revenues from Exhibits 9, 12, 16, 19.
[2] Percentage is based on large order size; for example, 7.6% — 5.8% = 1.8% and 1.8%/5.8% = 31%.
[3] Channel costs as a percentage of revenues from Exhibits 8, 11, 15, 18.

5

Strategic Response
to Change

Perhaps at no other time in the recent history of our social, political, and economic history has the business enterprise faced such unstable environments. Accordingly, plans that provide a strategic response to change are needed. A cursory review of the first reading in this text documents this point. So different are the present environments, that new terms have been coined to describe them. In recent years, such terms as *stagflation, product recall, shortages,* and *future shock* have become commonplace.

Three articles in this section describe reformulation and recovery marketing strategies to confront inflation, shortages, slowed economic growth, and product recall contingencies. Each of these four threats will have become a fact of corporate life in the 1980s. In the first article in this section, "Strategic Remarketing: The Preferred Response to Shortages and Inflation," Kotler and Balachandran recommend a variety of actions that management could adopt to minimize the effects of inflation and shortages. Specifically, they show how an organization's customer mix, product mix, and resource mix can be adjusted to satisfy customers and also preserve the well-being of the organization. "Marketing When the Growth Slows" provides an overview of actions taken by organizations under conditions of slowed economic growth. The article by Kerin and Harvey, entitled "Contingency Planning for Product Recall," shows how a firm can establish a strategic readiness to recall products if the need arises.

In the fourth reading in this section, "Strategic Windows," Abell highlights the need for constant vigilance in strategic marketing management. He notes that market evolution, market redefinition, and changes in marketing channels represent either problems or opportunities depending upon the fit between market success requirements and an organization's distinctive competence.

The last reading in this section departs from the main theme of the section by reiterating the inherent conflict between operating and strategic management in changing environments. "Cure for Strategic Malnutrition," by Gluck, Foster, and Forbis, is a case study of a firm facing this dilemma and how they overcame it. This article serves as a summary statement on this text which, in effect, comes full circle to a reconsideration of the thirty articles preceding it.

SELECTED ADDITIONAL READINGS

Clifford, Donald K., Jr., "Thriving in a Recession," *Harvard Business Review* (July–August 1977), pp. 57–65.

Cooper, Arnold C. and Dan Schendel, "Strategic Response to Technological Threats," *Business Horizons* (February 1976).

Lazer, William, "The 1980s and Beyond: A Perspective," *MSU Business Topics* (Spring 1977), pp. 21–36.

Lodge, George Cabot, "Business and the Changing Society," *Harvard Business Review* (March–April 1974), pp. 59–72.

Meitz, A. A. and Breaux B. Castleman, "How to Cope with Supply Shortages," *Harvard Business Review* (January–February 1975), pp. 91–96.

Strategic Remarketing:
The Preferred Response to
Shortages and Inflation

Philip Kotler and V. Balachandran

INTRODUCTION

This study focuses on the particular problem of companies adapting to a business environment characterized by shortages and inflationary pressure. It is intended as an addition to the much needed literature on coping with shortages that began to appear in the early 1970s.[1] It offers a conceptualization of the key decision options facing executives during a period of shortages.

Some businessmen feel that shortages is a past problem and therefore in less need of modeling than the problem of surviving in a recessionary economy marked by continuous cost-induced inflation. This view, however, is in error for the following reasons.

1. Some industries continue to experience shortages of raw material or productive capacity in spite of the return of the general economy to a surplus position. For example, natural gas is in short supply and most experts predict that the situation will worsen.[2]

2. Certain industries pass through a shortage-surplus cycle every few years. For example, the paper industry is not investing in new plant capacity because current prices and costs yield a poor return on further investment. As a result, a paper shortage is inevitable in the future as demand continues to grow while capacity stands still.

From *Sloan Management Review*, vol. 17, no. 1 (Fall 1975), pp. 1–17. Reprinted by permission. This paper was prepared for presentation at XXII TIMS International Meeting. The Institute of Management Sciences, Kyoto, Japan, July 23–25, 1975.

[1] See, for example, Cravens [1], Dominquez [2], Kotler [6], and "How to . . . Economy" [4].

[2] See "Natural Gas . . . Future" [10].

3. Certain industries are deliberately underproducing and keeping their customers on allocation in order to extract higher prices. For example, chemical companies, in the face of declining demand, have decided to reduce production and raise prices rather than produce at capacity and cut prices. Through "controlled production" they maintain artificial shortages of their products.[3]

4. Various raw material exporting countries, individually and collectively, are forcing up prices and terms for their raw materials. They are also requiring more home processing of their raw materials, thus reducing supplies abroad. They can, at will, cut off exports and plunge the world into a new round of shortages.

5. Some analysts forecast mass and continuous shortages of key resources for the rest of this century resulting not from political maneuvering, but from the sheer increase in demand as a result of population growth and industrialization. The book *The Limits to Growth* caused a sensation by presenting computer scenarios of increasing shortages of food and materials, as a result of exponential growth of demand against stable levels of supply.[4] Shortages, rather than being a temporary and localized condition facing certain firms or industries, may become a generalized state for the economies of the world for a considerable number of years into the future, at least until technological or social solutions are found.

The importance of these developments is that business, or some business firms, will have to learn the theory and art of managing their resources in periods of shortages. During the last shortage period, many firms reacted either by doing nothing or by raising their prices drastically and injuring long-run customer goodwill. During the next shortage period, companies will want to be better prepared to act with a more measured response that harmonizes their interests, their customers' interests, and society's interests.

DECISION OPTIONS FACING MANAGEMENT DURING PERIODS OF SHORTAGES AND INFLATION

When a company suddenly finds itself lacking a key resource, either a raw material, fixed plant, working capital, or labor, it must undertake some adjustments, the very least of which is to put customers on allocation for the available supplies or stretch out the promised delivery dates. A whole series of intermediate and ultimate adjustments are possible. The choice among them depends on the perceived *severity* and *duration* of the shortage period, and the long- and short-range objectives of the particular company. The main adjustments occur in the *resource mix, product mix,* and *customer mix.* Ten different decision options are identified in Figure 1 and they are highly interdependent.

---

[3] See "The Smart . . . Makers" [12].
[4] See Meadows, et al. [9].

FIGURE 1   Management Decision Options in a Period of Shortages

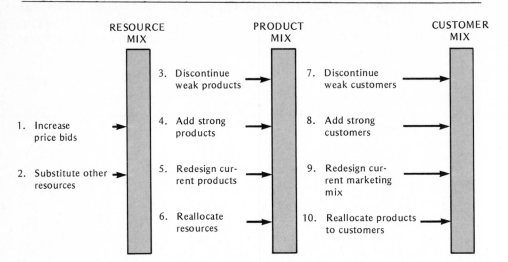

Any and all of these adjustments can be undertaken, making the number of possible strategies combinatorially large. There is great interdependence in the moves that might be made. Suppose the company decides to pay premium prices to the suppliers of the scarce resource to attract a larger supply. This means that it does not have to crack down so hard on marginally profitable products and customers nor impose as much tight allocation. It can continue its investments in new product development and new customer attraction. Its major need will be to raise its prices (redesign its marketing mix) to pass on the higher purchasing costs.

Ultimately, a model is needed that incorporates all of these decision alternatives so that their mutual effects can be explored. However, one must first consider each decision option and the issues that it raises. These issues will convey the complexity facing the builder of a total model for shortage management and marketing.

We shall begin by examining the adjustment mechanisms in reverse order of their presentation in Figure 1. A market-oriented view of the business mission is to start with the customer mix, then work backward to the product mix, and finally end with the needed resource mix.

CUSTOMER MIX

When a company cannot supply all of its current customers and must proceed cautiously in the recruitment of new customers, it is time for the company to pause and reexamine its customer objectives. This means nothing short of examining the basic businesses it is in. A business relies upon the choice of a set of customers whose needs the company believes it can serve at a satisfactory profit.

During good times the company carries, in addition to clearly profitable customers, a number of other customers of marginal profitability. Some of these customers will grow into strong customers over time; others will continue as marginally profitable customers; and still others will fall by the wayside. Many firms do not, during good times, pay strong attention to customer profitability, but during stressful times they begin to get interested in control and the question of customer profitability. The core question is: which customers should be retained and how much allocation should they get? We will look at customer mix issues in terms of the four decision options available to the firm.

Discontinue Weak Customers

One response to the overdemand situation is for the firm to terminate its supplier relation to certain customers whose profit contribution to the firm has been marginal. As a rule, a small percentage of a company's customers account for a large percentage of its sales and profits (the so-called "20–80" rule). Some of the firm's smaller customers have been maintained (1) out of a hope that they would eventually grow into larger customers, (2) out of a desire for sales volume as such, (3) to prevent competitors from picking them up, or (4) out of a feeling that some firm has to agree to serve them. Some of the firm's larger customers may not be highly profitable because they bicker over prices too much, they cancel or postpone orders too freely, they require too much sales or service time, or they are unreliable or troublesome in other ways. Facing an overdemand situation, the firm is in a position to reconsider the value of these dubious customers.

The firm should be guided by a calculation of the long-run expected profitability of each customer. Most companies classify their customers into A-B-C-D type accounts based either on sales volume, sales growth, profit margin, and/or expenses of serving the account. Management will want to develop a more comprehensive framework for assessing long-run customer profitability. Long-run customer profitability may be viewed as the *present value of the future profit stream expected over a given time horizon of transacting with the customer.*

Management must examine all the relevant factors contributing to long-run account profitability. Using present value, the company can establish boundaries between key accounts (A), good accounts (B), fair accounts (C), and poor accounts (D). Key accounts are those which provide the company with an above-average rate of return. Good accounts are those which yield the company's target rate of return. Fair accounts are those which yield less than the target rate of return but which are desirable to retain for other reasons. Poor accounts are those on which the company loses money or earns a very low rate of return. The money released by abandoning these poor accounts could be invested in attracting profitable new accounts.

It is important to emphasize that the classification of customers into account types is based not on *past buying history and profitability* but on *future expected profitability.* The firm should prepare a list of the poorer customers, preferably a ranked list. It might discover that if all the dubious customers were terminated, the firm would face an underdemand rather than overdemand situation. This would allow it to go after profitable new customers. We will examine this possibility in the next section. The main point is that the firm must determine a cutoff point for weak customers because this has implications for the scarce resource pressure it will face and its new customer development potential.

A company may decide, for other reasons, not to drop in a wholesale fashion all of its weak customers.

1. It has the alternative of retaining these customers but changing the marketing mix in a way that makes these less profitable customers more profitable. The company can raise its prices or cut its services or costs to these customers. To avoid the charge of price discrimination, extra charges may be put on small orders. The firm can reduce its sales calls to smaller firms, stretch its delivery time, and in other ways reduce its costs. Some customers will not find the new terms acceptable and will drop out on their own accord. Those who remain will become more profitable to the supplier.

2. The supplier does not want to lose too much of the sales volume which a great number of small buyers buy in total. If the firm's average cost curve falls with volume, the effect of dropping too many small customers, even when they are individually of marginal profitability, may be to raise the firm's costs and cut into profits. The interaction between the firm's production cost curve and its customer size distribution is described and modeled elsewhere by one of the authors.[5]

3. The supplier must avoid creating concern and demoralization among his better customers. Arbitrary behavior by the firm may decrease their goodwill and confidence and accelerate their search for alternative sources of supply.

This leads to the question of how the firm should proceed to terminate or discourage its poorer customers. Three approaches are available that differ in their directness.

1. Send termination notices to the poorer customers stating the reasons for discontinuing the supply relationship and the effective date.

2. Raise prices and cut services to customers on the "unwanted list" without directly talking about terminating the supplier relationship.

3. Talk to these customers individually about the problems, objectives, and profit needs of the firm. Leave the door open to continue the relationship on a more profitable basis or agree to a phase-out plan that does not place the customer in an impossible supply position.

The whole problem of terminating relations with customers is loaded with social, psychological, competitive, and legal implications that must be handled in the most thoughtful way.

---

[5] See Kotler [5], pp. 207–212.

Add Strong Customers

The firm is subject to opposite forces when it comes to determining its policy on new customer acquisition during a period of shortages. One force comes from existing customers who get angry when they see the company agreeing to supply new customers. Every new customer means less allocation of the scarce product to the existing customers. If they could have their way, they would want the supplier to put a moratorium on adding new customers.

The other force comes from the great opportunities created by the shortages to win new customers who were not penetrable in normal times. Many buyers are reluctantly put on allocation by their current suppliers and in response are ripe prospects. Suddenly the firm supplying the scarce product finds itself on the receiving end of numerous phone calls from companies that refused to see them in the past. To take the hard-line and refuse their business is to cancel any chance of attracting their business when demand returns to normal. There is no question that the firm should welcome, even solicit, certain accounts during this period. It is a golden opportunity. In doing this, however, there are three questions to be considered.

1. How much new sales volume can the firm take on without diluting the interests of its current customers to the point of turning their goodwill into bad will? Much depends on how many weak customers the firm plans to terminate, what marketing mix adjustments the firm plans to make, how much it plans to pay for scarce resources to attract additional supply, what allocations it plans to make to current customers, and so on. Given these other policy determinations, it is possible to calculate the amount of additional sales volume the company can safely offer as bait to new customers.

2. Would the company be better off attracting a few large new accounts or several small but profitable new accounts? From the viewpoint of visibility of the move to existing customers, both would be noticed. From the viewpoint of profitability, it may be more profitable to wedge into a few large important accounts. Little can be said *a priori*.

3. Which specific prospects would be the best to add to the company's customer mix? After assessing existing customers, the company will want to evaluate prospects. At the same time, additional considerations arise which have to do with achieving balance in the customer mix so that the company does not become too dependent on particular companies or industries. During a shortage period, suppliers who are attracted only by immediate profitability may concentrate on the customers in a particular industry because they are the most profitable to serve under the given price-cost relations. But this concentration may backfire because that industry starts to run short of other key resources. For example, a nylon manufacturer who has limited his customers to those in the tire industry because of its high profits may suddenly find his demand fall off because this industry starts experiencing a shortage of rubber. The supplier may find that after the shortage period the economics of this particular industry

change in an unfavorable way from the viewpoint of the supplier. Suppliers must try to maintain a well-balanced portfolio of different industries so they can ride out the storms affecting particular industries at particular times.

Redesign Current Marketing Mix

The supplier must also consider adjustments in his marketing mix as a means of protecting or increasing his customer profitability during a shortage period. There are three contrasting types of marketing program responses of suppliers during periods of shortages.

1. *Status Quo Marketing.* Suppliers decide that the shortage will not be very deep or long lasting and they should ride it out doing things as they have done them in the past. They put customers on some allocation but do not change substantially prices, advertising, sales-force activity, services, product quality, marketing research or other marketing activities. They fear alienating the good-will of loyal customers by seeming to exploit the situation. They will introduce small price increases and reduce a few services but avoid taking more drastic steps that might anger customers. They will generally hold to the current marketing mix, product mix, and customer mix.

2. *Aggressive Demarketing* (or profit building). The supplier decides to take aggressive advantage of the situation and build up current profits. His steps include:

    a. Reducing product quality or features,
    b. Reducing advertising expenditures to a bare minimum,
    c. Reducing sales force costs,
    d. Reducing customer services,
    e. Reducing marketing research, and
    f. Increasing prices substantially.

These steps succeed in boosting current profits because prices are higher and marketing costs are lower, without loss of major customers or demand. On the other hand, this strategy may take a toll on long-term company growth and profitability. Many customers may be alienated by the reduced services and higher prices. Their feelings will show up when the shortage vanishes.

3. *Strategic Remarketing.* Strategic remarketing does not start with an answer but rather with a set of tasks in which management must engage. The supplier must first reexamine market needs and opportunities in the short run and the long run. Then he must redetermine the best markets to be in, customers to serve, and competitors to compete with, in terms of long-run profitability. Finally, he must develop and implement plans for a transition to the future market position he wants to occupy. Strategic remarketing does not spell out what he should specifically do with his prices, advertising, services, and so on. Rather, it calls for a set of earlier steps which once determined will suggest the needed adjustments in the marketing mix in the current period.

Reallocate Products to Customers

The result of all the previous steps—determining how many customers to discontinue, how many new customers to add, and what new marketing mix to use—is the creation of a certain expected demand level for the scarce product. The firm knows its potential supply level. The ratio of supply to demand is the overall *allocation percentage* the company has available for customers. Suppose the supplier finds that he can supply 70 percent of total customer requirements on the basis of the other policies he is adopting.

There are two alternative allocation rules available to him. The first or *straight allocation rule* is to supply all customers with 70 percent of their demand level, where demand is interpreted as their buying level in the last period before the shortage or some smoothed historical demand level to take into account that some customers bought an unusually low or high amount of the product in the last preshortage period. There are at least three reasons why this rule may be adopted by the supplier.

1. Straight allocation may be required by government policy to protect intermediate and final customers against arbitrary supplier action. For example, U.S. oil companies were required during the shortage period to supply their customers with a common percentage of their normal order level. Had the oil companies been given latitude to favor certain customers over others, they might have squeezed out the independent gasoline marketers and seriously undersupplied low profitability segments, such as the home fuel market.
2. Straight allocation may be adopted because it minimizes customer complaints of unfair treatment. The company puts every customer on a 70 percent allocation and avoids the charge of favoritism, especially where favoritism can boost the profits and competitive positions of certain competitors over others.
3. This allocation rule may be adopted by the firm as the easiest to administer, at least initially. The company sends out single announcements to its customers. It need not analyze different levels of customer profitability in the search for variable allocation levels that would build up current profits. It need not train its sales force in customer profitability analysis and allocation analysis.

The contrasting rule, that of *variable allocation*, calls upon the supplier to vary the allocation percentage according to customer profitability. An example of such a rule would be:

Supply 100 percent of the requirements of Class A accounts as long as their requirements are not substantially greater than preshortage order levels; 80 percent of the preshortage order levels of Class B accounts; 50 percent of the preshortage order levels of Class C accounts; and 20 percent of the preshortage order levels of Class D accounts.

FIGURE 2   Behavior of Two Types of Customers in Response to Allocation Levels

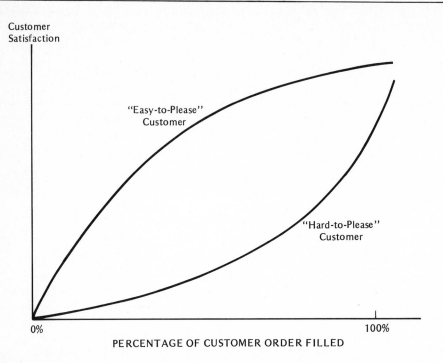

This approach to customer allocation is likely to be more profitable to the company. It concentrates marketing effort and market satisfaction on the customers who are more profitable. The more profitable customers are rewarded and this reinforces their loyalty. The task, of course, is to correctly identify the more profitable customers.

Companies normally shy away from any rigid rating and allocation scheme because a great number of other factors about the account are known and relevant to the decision. Decisions are made in committees concerning how much to allocate to each account on the basis of its past loyalty, potential growth, current profitability, geographical location, industry, influence on other customers, and likely reaction to different allocation levels.

One of the more illusive factors is how the customer will react to his allocation! The higher the customer's allocation percentage, the higher will be his satisfaction and future loyalty. But the relationship is not typically linear. Figure 2 distinguishes between two extreme types of customers. The "easy-to-please" customer, depicted in the upper curve, appreciates whatever he receives; his satisfaction increases at a decreasing rate the more he receives of his order. The "hard-to-please" customer, depicted in the lower curve, gets very little satisfaction unless he receives most of his requirements; his satisfaction increases at an increasing rate. If he receives much less than he requires, he will switch suppliers when supply becomes abundant. He does not easily forgive or forget.

If the supplier can correctly classify his customers into these two classes, he could maximize loyalty by supplying high allocations to the "hard-to-please" customers and low allocations to the "easy-to-please" customers. It is not, however, easy to classify customers. Furthermore, if the "easy-to-please" customers caught on to this practice, they would put on a facade of unforgivingness in order to get high allocations.

Some of the normal disappointments or anger of customers in receiving less than their requirements can be minimized by training salesmen in the art of saying "no" without alienating the customer. The customer's reaction depends on (1) how he learns of his allocation, (2) the explanation he is given, and (3) what he sees happening to other customers. Suppliers must give almost as much thought to the presentation of the allocation level as to determining the level to allocate.

PRODUCT MIX

The previous discussion on customer mix decisions assumed a single product. However, most firms are multiproduct firms. Furthermore, several of their products may be hit simultaneously by the same scarce resources. For example, zinc is a basic product in the production of steel. If zinc is in short supply, the steel manufacturer must decide how to allocate the existing zinc among several steel products. Sometimes, a more generalized resource becomes scarce, such as fuel or electricity. The manufacturer is forced to cut back his operations and figure out what amounts of each product to produce. Thus, product mix becomes an adjustment mechanism for responding to overdemand. Four decision options are available in the product mix (see Figure 1).

Discontinue Weak Products

The first step the company can take is to review its product mix in the search for those product lines, individual products, or product items that are of such marginal profitability that they can be temporarily or permanently withdrawn from production. They may be products that were of little worth before the shortage but were retained out of inertia, full product line requirements, lack of alternative opportunities, or straightforward sentimentality. They may be products that suddenly become questionable because of the new price and cost relations caused by the shortage.

It is clear that shortages lead many companies into product line pruning actions. *Sales Management* polled ninety-three industrial companies about product pruning intentions; 63 percent of these companies said they intended to eliminate slow-moving items, and 23 percent said they would reduce the number of sizes and colors.[6] These words have been followed by pruning actions in a number of companies:

In its pursuit of higher profits, General Electric Co. has dropped blenders, fans, heaters, humidifiers, and vacuum cleaners. Shell Chemical Co. is ending produc-

---

[6] See *Sales Management,* January 21, 1974, p. 27.

tion of styrene butadiene rubber, isoprene rubber, and fertilizer (ammonia, urea, and ammonium sulfate). Philco-Ford Corp. has eliminated 50 percent of its color-TV screen sizes and 40 percent of its refrigerator models. Crown Zeller-bach Corp. and other papermakers have cut their lines by as much as 60 percent.[7]

What is less clear is whether these companies are applying sound standards in identifying their "weaker" products. The weak product identification problem can be handled in a number of ways.[8]

There are essentially two useful dimensions for judging the long-run profit-ability of a company product. The first is the product's *rate of return on invest-ment* (ROI). This may be measured by taking a weighted average of the most recent annual ROIs. The annual ROI can be measured as the *cash flow gen-erated per dollar of asset* tied up in the product. It reflects the capacity of the product to produce current profit in relation to the value of assets employed in its production and marketing. To derive this figure, it is necessary to be able to determine the amount of assets that are supporting the production, distribution, and marketing of each product in the line. While it is relatively easy to map the income statement items into each product, it is admittedly more difficult to map balance sheet items to product lines and items without getting involved in highly arbitrary allocations. Each company must do its best, however, to allocate as much overhead to each product as can be carefully reasoned.

The second dimension is *sales growth*. This is the recent weighted annualized rate of sales growth. A "good" product is one that has good actual or potential sales growth. New products that have a high sales growth are considered suc-cessful even if they initially generate negative profit.

The two dimensions are combined in Figure 3 in a product profitability grid. The company's task is to locate each of its products in this grid. Product A, for example, shows a 15 percent sales growth and a 10 percent ROI. Product B shows a 10 percent growth rate and a 5 percent ROI. Product C shows a 5 percent sales growth and a 0 percent ROI.

The grid is further divided into three parts reflecting management's view of strong products, satisfactory products, and weak products. The best products are those strong in both sales growth and current ROI. But management also con-siders products strong if they have an exceptional sales growth rate or ROI. The dividing line between strong products and satisfactory products, and between satisfactory products and weak products, reflects the tradeoff between these two criteria in management's mind.

Any products that show up as weak can be checked further for their be-havior over time. The typical product shows a *life cycle trajectory* similar to that shown in Figure 4. It starts off as a product with a weak ROI but good sales growth (introduction stage). Its growth continues strong but at a diminishing rate while its ROI improves substantially (growth stage). Later, it becomes a mature product with relatively little sales growth but a stable cash flow (ma-

---

[7] See "The Squeeze . . . Mix" [13].
[8] See Kotler [7], and Hamelman and Mazze [3].

FIGURE 3   Product Profitability Grid

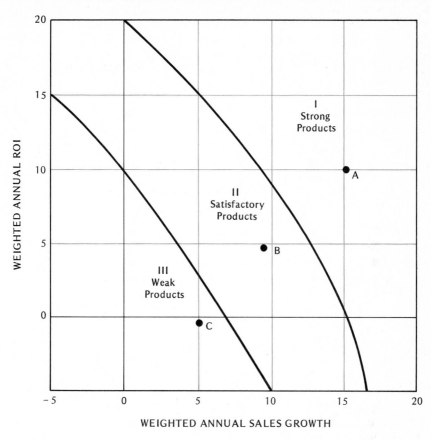

Source: Kotler [6]

ture stage). At this stage, it is equivalent to an intermediate-term annuity. Finally, the product starts to decline in sales and in ROI (declining stage). At this point, the product must be identified as a candidate for pruning. Thus, the product's present position in the "weak product" part of the grid, plus the characteristics of a concave trajectory, will indicate its readiness for elimination. Of course, before making any final decision on the fate of the weak product, the company will want to consider: (1) whether the trajectory can be refreshed in a positive direction through relaunching or remarketing, (2) the contribution of the product to generating sales of other products in the line, and (3) the contribution of the product to covering fixed costs.

Add Strong Products

During a period of shortages, a company will be tempted to defer or delay its new product development program, especially that part of it which would bring forth those new products that would put additional strain on scarce resources.

FIGURE 4   Trajectory of a Typical Product over Its Life Cycle

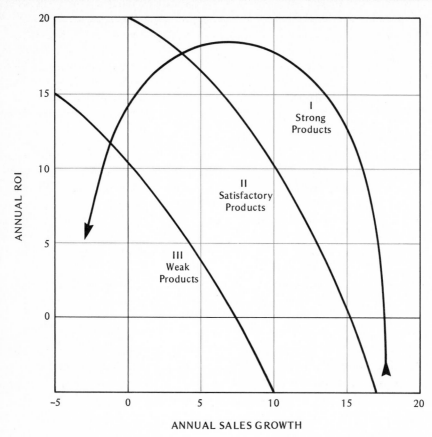

ANNUAL SALES GROWTH

Source: Kotler [6]

During 1973 many packaged goods companies found it difficult to obtain sufficient paper or plastic for their packaging and had to delay new product introductions. New products that do not compete for scarce resources, of course, can be continued under development. In fact, a shortage period is a time to increase investment in new product research and development to find long-term replacements or substitutes for the products that are showing reduced availability.

A company is justified in adding new products that put a strain on existing resources if substantial profitability is expected. The profitability of these new products must allow for the lessened profitability of products that will have to be dropped or reduced in production because of the shift of resources away from them.

Redesign Current Products

Redesigning existing products is another avenue for adjustment to shortages. It may be possible to do with less material or to find satisfactory substitutes. The key question is the impact of the redesign on *perceived product quality.* Where redesign or reformulation will not hurt perceived product quality, the firm is well-advised to go ahead. The problem arises when the resource reduction or substitution reduces perceived product quality. The firm is tampering with customer preference for its products. Is the saving worth the cost in customer preference? The company must take the utmost pains to explain to its customers the change in product formulation necessitated by the shortage, how to use the redesigned product satisfactorily, and how long the change will be in force.

Reallocate Resources

The adjustments hitherto made or contemplated by the firm in its customer and product mix become the basis for estimating supply of the scarce resource(s) that will be available for allocation to the various retained company products. This supply will probably be less than the total demand. The company may find that it has 80 percent of the scarce resource supply it needs to meet all demand.

Again, the company can proceed according to one of two principles. It can cut the planned production of all products by 20 percent. Or it can use a variable allocation rule, cutting more into those products of lower profitability. A variable allocation rule makes more sense since products differ greatly in profitability.

A mathematical programming approach may be tried because the problem can be expressed as one of allocating scarce resources to competing products differing in profitability and demand levels.[9] But it must be stressed that this overlooks the subtle interaction of the various decision options shown earlier in Figure 1.

RESOURCE MIX

The resource mix provides the third major adjustment element in trying to respond to sudden shortages. Companies that are heavily dependent on one or two major resources in scarce supply must give thorough consideration to their future mix. They must increase the rate of search for substitute resources. They must consider substitutions of capital for labor, or vice versa, if this will conserve on the scarce resource. They may reformulate the products to use less of the scarce resource. They may decide to enter whole new businesses which are not dependent on the scarce resource.

In the short run, the company has two options.

Increase Price Bids

Shortages pose a major challenge to purchasing management. The marketing problem shifts from its location in the marketing department to its location in

---

[9] See Kotler [5], Chapter 7.

the purchasing department.[10] The purchasing executives must "market" their company's needs to their suppliers. They must convince suppliers that they absolutely need all of their requirements and that their loyalty and future buying potential should count for a great deal. When this does not work fully, they should show a willingness to increase their price offer for the scarce material and thus outbid their competitors. When this does not fully work, they might bring power to bear where they hold reciprocal resources needed by the suppliers.

Substitute Other Resources

Resource substitution takes more time than offering to pay price increases to attract more scarce resources. The company will nevertheless want to increase its rate of search for substitutes. In the short run, it can reduce usage levels of the scarce material through simple product reformulation, although at some risk to perceived product quality. In the long run, it can find basic resources for producing the product. The extent to which a deep and expensive search for new alternatives should be financed depends on the expected severity and duration of the shortage.

S U M M A R Y

Although the intensity of shortages has diminished for the time being, they can be expected to emerge again and afflict particular companies and industries. Some forecasters expect the last quarter of the twentieth century to be one of increasing scarcity of basic resources.

Management can respond to shortages by adjusting its customer mix, product mix, and resource mix. We have treated the major adjustment variables to shortages in relative isolation to illustrate the complexities of the optimization problem even where only single elements are involved. We also indicated, however, that the different decision elements interact. Thus, a policy of terminating weak customers increases the allocations available to the better customers and reduces the pressure on eliminating certain products, and so on. The optimization problem is further complicated by (1) the difficulty of adjusting all the elements in the short run and (2) the variable timing of the lagged effects of adjusted elements.

This might well suggest that the problem of an optimal adjustment path over time in the face of shortages is an insoluble one, at least analytically. More might be gained by a simulation model on which alternative strategies are tested for their effects on current profitability, customer satisfaction and loyalty, market growth, and market share. We have not, unfortunately, been able to develop a simulated model of a broad enough scope to be used by any industry. We are of the opinion that a generalized model might be of less value than

---

[10] See Kotler and Levy [8] and "Purchasing . . . Operation" [11].

specific models built for specific industries that feature the key adjustment variables and decision options available in those industries.

REFERENCES

1. Cravens, D. W. "Marketing Management in an Era of Shortages." *Business Horizons,* February 1974, pp. 79–85.
2. Dominquez, G. S. *Marketing in a Shortage Economy.* New York: AMA COM, American Management Association, 1974.
3. Hamelman, P. W., and Mazze, E. M. "Improving Product Abandonment Decisions." *Journal of Marketing,* April 1972, pp. 20–26.
4. "How to Keep a Sales Force Running in a Crunch Economy." *Sales Management,* January 21, 1974.
5. Kotler, P. *Marketing Decision Making: A Model Building Approach.* New York: Holt, Rinehart & Winston, 1971.
6. Kotler, P. "Marketing during Periods of Shortage." *Journal of Marketing,* July 1974, pp. 20–29.
7. Kotler, P. "Phasing Out Weak Products." *Harvard Business Review,* March–April 1965, pp. 107–118.
8. Kotler, P., and Levy, S. J. "Buying Is Marketing Too!" *Journal of Marketing,* January 1973, pp. 54–59.
9. Meadows, D. H., et al. *The Limits to Growth.* New York: Signet Book, 1972.
10. "Natural Gas Shortage Worsens, and Doubts Grow over the Future." *Wall Street Journal,* June 27, 1975, p. 1.
11. "Purchasing Becomes a 'Selling' Operation." *Industry Week,* December 10, 1973, pp. 46–47.
12. "The Smart Game Plan for Chemical Makers." *BusinessWeek,* July 7, 1975, pp. 42ff.
13. "The Squeeze on Product Mix." *BusinessWeek,* January 5, 1974, pp. 50–55.

Marketing When the Growth Slows

BusinessWeek

Burt F. Raynes, chairman of Rohr Industries, Inc., keeps a complete file of charts in his desk that plot population curves and the life of the world's known mineral deposits. Such charts, of course, make dismal reading for most growth-minded companies. They show a steadily declining birthrate for the United States. They also show rapidly shrinking reserves of manganese, chromium, aluminum, tin, nickel, cobalt, tungsten, silver, copper, bauxite, and other basic raw materials. Then there is the biggest growth inhibitor of all: the soaring cost of energy.

While world economists and scholars may argue the validity of long-term resource forecasting—and the doomsday prophecies that it inevitably gives rise to—even the mere prospect of permanent scarcity carries major and unmistakable implications for economic growth. Impressed by what it sees ahead, Rohr is transforming its entire approach to doing business. Where it previously drew 100 percent of its sales from aerospace, Rohr is now shifting its marketing emphasis toward mass transit and other energy-conserving transportation systems.

"This was not a matter of image," Raynes says. "It was a matter of economics. We foresaw the day when it would no longer be economic to put 4,000 pounds of irreplaceable resources into an automobile and then pump 5,000 gallons of gasoline through the car to run it."

Rohr is among a burgeoning group of companies that is confronting what promises to become one of the premier marketing challenges of the 1970s: how to grow in a low-growth or no-growth economy. While the current recession will be temporary, many economic forecasters warn that low growth rates are here to stay—at least, into the 1980s and possibly beyond. Over the last quarter-century, the U.S. gross national product averaged 3.9 percent a year in real growth. From 1973 through 1988, according to revised forecasts by the Economics Department of McGraw-Hill's Publications Division, the growth rate will run only 3.2 percent a year—sharply under the 3.9 percent that McGraw-Hill projected a few years ago for the 1970–85 period.

Reprinted from *BusinessWeek*, April 14, 1975, pp. 44–50.

Sales of some major industries will continue to boom through 1988. Starting from 1973, McGraw-Hill projects that chemicals and allied products will go up 172.2 percent in real or constant dollars; rubber and plastic products, 166.7 percent; electric utilities, 150.3 percent; instruments, 136.7 percent; electrical machinery, 125.3 percent, and nonferrous metal products, 94.7 percent.

However, other key industries—accounting for nearly 20 percent of the gross national product—are heading into a period of markedly reduced growth. Confronted by stagnant or declining markets and dwindling sales, they will act as a drag on the total economy, tempering the growth of more prosperous companies that might otherwise expand at a far faster clip.

The "slow-growth" group, as projected by McGraw-Hill, includes metal, stone, and earth minerals (69.4 percent), coal, oil, and gas (69.4 percent), food products (68 percent), petroleum products (65.9 percent), textile mill products (63.3 percent), motor vehicles and parts (57.9 percent), printing and publishing (57 percent), fabricated metal products (55.3 percent), and clay, glass, and stone products (52.9 percent). Then there are the leading "low-growth" and "no-growth" industries: lumber and related products (41.6 percent), iron and steel (35.4 percent), apparel (33.7 percent), tobacco (26.8 percent), ordnance (7.7 percent), and leather and related products (a decline of 16.2 percent).

RECESSION'S DEAD WEIGHT

Obviously, the biggest immediate deterrent to growth is the recession. But once that passes, there are also the energy crunch, shrinking resources, and the leveling-off of population growth. Since 1970, the rate of U.S. population expansion has been less than 1 percent a year. By 1988, population projections put the total increase at only 13.6 percent, or one third slower than the 20.3 percent gain of 1958–73. This limits both the size of the market for goods and services and the size of the labor pool for producing those goods and services.

Along the way, the economic shift from high-productivity manufacturing industries toward low-productivity service industries will also weigh heavily. Output per man-hour, in 1973 dollars, is projected at $11 in 1988, compared with less than $8 in 1973. That represents a 2.3 percent annual increase, or a 12 percent drop from the 1948–73 rate.

The biggest puzzle of all, however, promises to be the American consumer. The so-called conspicuous consumer of the 1950s and 1960s is suddenly less conspicuous, more conservation-minded, and far more difficult to reach—recession or no recession. He is wearing his clothes longer, driving his car more years, and buying fewer fads and fashions. He is also warier of the products he buys and the companies he deals with. As Harvard sociologist David Riesman puts it: "People are not as easily sold or satisfied, and they are more prone to litigation." Riesman points to the explosive rise in the proportion of doctors hit by malpractice suits—more than double that of five years ago—and "the more than 100,000 people in law school, one quarter of our current legal population." To Riesman, this suggests far more litigation and consumer resistance to come. "It seems to me," he warns, "that the problems of marketing are grave indeed."

FIGURE 1   Leaders and Laggards in Industrial Growth: 1973–1988

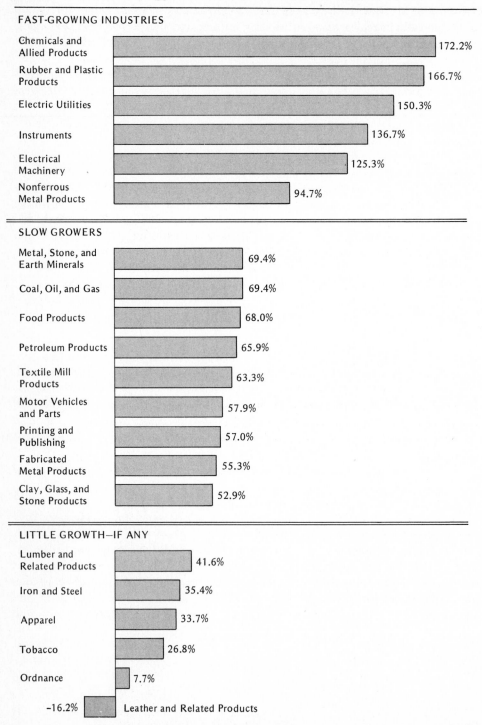

FAST-GROWING INDUSTRIES

Chemicals and Allied Products	172.2%
Rubber and Plastic Products	166.7%
Electric Utilities	150.3%
Instruments	136.7%
Electrical Machinery	125.3%
Nonferrous Metal Products	94.7%

SLOW GROWERS

Metal, Stone, and Earth Minerals	69.4%
Coal, Oil, and Gas	69.4%
Food Products	68.0%
Petroleum Products	65.9%
Textile Mill Products	63.3%
Motor Vehicles and Parts	57.9%
Printing and Publishing	57.0%
Fabricated Metal Products	55.3%
Clay, Glass, and Stone Products	52.9%

LITTLE GROWTH—IF ANY

Lumber and Related Products	41.6%
Iron and Steel	35.4%
Apparel	33.7%
Tobacco	26.8%
Ordnance	7.7%
–16.2%	Leather and Related Products

Source: McGraw-Hill Publications Economics Department.

So far, most companies have been slow on the uptake. Richard Hansen, chairman of the marketing department at Southern Methodist University, cites the auto industry. Last year, after a 3 percent drop in per capita disposable personal income and a 11 percent spurt in consumer prices, "what do auto manufacturers do but raise prices?" He adds: "A lot of people think that the current slowdown is a temporary phenomenon, and that we are going to get back on course in a year or so, and things will go merrily ever after. I really don't think there is an awareness that we are in for some real significant changes in the way of doing business."

Among the biggest changes:

1. A hefty chunk of any one company's sales growth will increasingly come out of another company's market share, rather than from any automatic expansion of the total market. "This means that products will have to be 'positioned' far more precisely in terms of the competition," says Philip Kotler, marketing professor at Northwestern University. "There will be less emphasis on imitative, 'me-too' products and more on products that are really new and preemptive in technology, packaging, and promotion." To sop up a larger market share, low-growth strategy also calls for more models and line extensions—but only where there is a profitable customer segment and where the line extension does more than simply duplicate what is already on the market.

2. With the greater shift to a share-of-market emphasis, there will be far more attention paid to distribution—up to now, the "economy's dark continent," as management pundit Peter F. Drucker describes it. The cost of moving products from the factory to the marketplace accounts for almost 20 percent of the gross national product and in some industries has nearly doubled during the last eight years—often without any notable increase in efficiency. "In the past," says market researcher Joseph G. Smith, president of Oxtoby-Smith, Inc., "you could have sloppy distribution and still move a lot of product. But in a smaller market, you've got to get maximum market share, and you can only do that with maximum distribution."

3. Product strategies will veer away from the concept of planned obsolescence that produced throwaway appliances not worth repairing, automobiles that are redesigned every 2 or 3 years, packaging that can be used only once, and buildings that last only 10 or 20 years. With economic pressures and the prospect—or reality—of material shortages, the new emphasis will be on product value, reusability, and longer life.

4. Companies may have to lower their financial sights. "We have had a financial ethic that says it's really not a good investment unless the return is 7 percent to 10 percent," says consultant Harold S. Becker, vice president of the Futures Group. "We may have to move into an era where an acceptable return on investment will be 2 percent or 3 percent"—meaning, of course, a massive rethinking and reorganization of capital structures and values. "We may have to reinstitutionalize ourselves and change all our targets," Becker notes.

THE PRODUCT FLOOD

The challenge in a low-growth economy goes beyond simply building sales—though that is part of it. The far more fundamental challenge will be in overcoming the traditional marketing tendency toward trying to satisfy all needs in a given market and being all things to all customers.

Since the 1920s, when modern marketing principles first began taking hold, the push has been on demand stimulation: finding more ways to get more people to consume more goods and services. On through the 1950s, this meant introducing products that served the broadest possible needs of what became an increasingly affluent and acquisition-hungry mass market. Then in the 1960s, the mass market began giving way to the "class market." Companies started pigeonholing their customers into smaller groups or segments and tailoring products for each segment—by size, flavor, smell, and even psychological appeal or life-style.

The tactic was to create new markets on a smaller scale—and many companies succeeded: Procter & Gamble, General Foods, General Electric, Coca-Cola, Bristol-Myers, IBM, Philip Morris, and Campbell Soup among them. In several instances, however, some of these same companies—plus many others—went too far. With a big number of their products, they only fragmented existing markets and contributed to a rising product flood that confused and frustrated the average customer. Campbell Soup ran into this problem with both its dehydrated and frozen soups, Bristol-Myers with its aerosol Ipana toothpaste, and General Foods with its Post cereals with freeze-dried fruits.

Over all, from 1960 to 1970, the number of breakfast cereals jumped 125 percent, cigarette brands 130 percent, car models 54 percent, general-purpose computers 285 percent, electric toasters 250 percent, and refrigerators 52 percent. Along with a doubling of disposable income, this burst of products helped trigger a buying binge that raised personal consumption expenditures a staggering 86 percent during the same period. Yet as competition multiplied, product life cycles slipped as much as 60 percent to 70 percent, new-product failure rates zoomed as high as 80 percent, and brand loyalty went out the window.

Now there is the recession. As sales level off or drop, marketing strategists are finally beginning to balance demand stimulation with "demand management." They are spending more time analyzing product-line profitability, pruning out the losers, and refining market segments. As the realization of long-term low growth begins sinking in, says Northwestern's Kotler, the first impulse of marketers—rightly or wrongly—will be to seek out new markets and ways to transfer their "customer franchise" or following into new fields.

All through the 1960s, of course, farm-equipment makers, chemical companies, food processors, tobacco companies, the railroads, and countless other growth-hungry businesses tried to do the same thing. In their frantic drive to diversify, however, they often added volume for the sheer sake of volume—with sometimes disastrous results. Now more and more of these companies are just as frantically undiversifying many of the lines they added.

Yet this is not deterring today's low-growth companies from trying to diversify the same way. With sales vulnerable in their main lines, Gerber Products Co. (babyfoods) is going into ketchup and other adult foods, Avon Products, Inc. (door-to-door cosmetics) is adding plastic housewares and mail-order apparel, and Armstrong Cork Co. (ceiling and floor tiles) is mounting a major offensive into the furniture and carpeting markets. Few low-growth industries, however, can match the diversification ardor of gasoline retailing, one of the businesses hit the hardest by sluggish growth. Under the onslaught of soaring fuel prices, rising station costs, and less driving, the number of service stations tumbled from 220,000 five years ago to 200,000 last year. By 1980, according to some forecasts, there will only be 125,000 stations.

INTERRELATED TECHNOLOGY

James S. Morrison, vice president for marketing at Atlantic Richfield Co., notes that ten years ago, the oil companies looked at gasoline retailing as one big market. He says: "When you expanded, you just cranked out another station. From now on, we're interested in identifying targets or segments for different stations. Retailers have got to generate more revenue than is conceivable even from 50¢-per-gallon gasoline."

Within their stations, the major oil companies are now testing or fully operating more than a score of new retailing sidelines. They range from drive-in banks and dry cleaners to convenience stores, film-processing services, drug stores, garden centers, restaurants, boating outlets, and bike shops. Because the marketplace is already loaded with such services, the trick will be to build up a brand following or franchise in these new businesses—especially now that brand loyalty has gone the way of 36.9¢ gasoline. "Many consumers," says Arco's Morrison, "have decided that brand loyalty is a waste of time and that they'll buy only where they get value."

In their pursuit of growth, technology companies obviously have an edge— if they can keep new concepts rolling out of their development labs. Yet even among these companies, customer loyalty is faltering. As William F. Ballhaus, president of Beckman Instruments, Inc., puts it: "Salesmen used to say, 'Give me any instrument with the Beckman name on it, and I'll sell it.' It's not that way anymore. Name is still important, but no one buys for the intangible benefit of owning a Beckman."

Even the $2.6 billion U.S. market for scientific instruments, which happens to be a high-growth industry, is no longer the cornucopia it was a few years ago, Ballhaus concedes. Yet he adds determinedly: "There are still new markets and growth to be had. It's simply a matter of busting your bottom to get them." For Beckman, that means widening its customer franchise with labor-saving instruments that pay for themselves and—where possible—combine several functions.

Today's most frequent medical tests, for instance, are glucose analysis and blood urea analysis. Traditionally, instrument makers sold separate products for each test. These are semiautomatic and analyze only one sample at a time. So last August Beckman introduced an analyzer that runs both tests, handles 30 to

40 samples at a time, and is automatic. While the instrument sells for more than twice the amount of two old-type individual analyzers, Beckman claims that the cost per test runs only 10.8¢ with its new product, compared with 12¢ to 14¢ the old way.

Gould, Inc., the Chicago manufacturer of electrical and electronic systems, is consolidating technologies in a different way. For a high-technology company, says Delbert O. Fuller, Gould's vice president for marketing, the way to defy a low-growth economy and broaden a customer following is to interrelate technologies and create families of products that draw on common technologies. "In our case," Fuller says of Gould, "the technologies are electronics, electrochemistry, electromechanics, and metallurgy. But the principle would apply just as well to any multitechnology company."

In the battery field, for instance, Fuller notes that Gould's lead acid battery "led us to industrial batteries, then submarine batteries. Now our developmental work on a much more efficient nickel/zinc battery has helped us win the largest contract ever awarded for electric vehicle power systems"—an estimated $1 million contract for a highly compact, simplified power system that will be installed in 350 U.S. Postal Service vehicles.

Theodore A. Andersen, professor of economics at UCLA and a director of 12 companies, claims that the low-growth buzzwords—implicit in Gould's research into battery-powered electrical systems—are product miniaturization and simplification. Andersen notes that as the public becomes more mindful of cost and conservation ("Look at the last election—almost without exception, growth people lost"), industrial and consumer preferences alike are turning increasingly to "smaller, lighter, simpler products that consume less." Like Gould's new battery system for the Postal Service, this trend shows up in the shift to everything from compact, high-density housing, small cars, and portable TVs to combination kitchen appliances, multifunction machine tools, and, as Andersen phrases it, "pocket calculators, pocket cameras, pocket tape recorders, and pocket this-and-that."

This way, the customer benefits by having a simpler product that is presumably easier to repair and thus longer-lived. Yet he also ends up with a stripped-down, bare bones product that will lose in features whatever it may gain in value or functionalism. "That is the marketing message of the future," Andersen says of low-growth product design. "From now on, everyone works harder to get less"—including the customer who buys the product and the company that sells it.

. . . After the financial flop of auto rebates, General Motors Corp. has stripped down nine of its small-car models, eliminating steel-belted tires, four-speed transmissions, and other features from its list of standard equipment. By making such items optional, GM managed to chop prices as much as 8 percent. At troubled Chrysler Corp., a scaled-down car could also emerge from a sweeping production overhaul ordered by Chairman Lynn Townsend. Preparing for the worst, Townsend wants Chrysler manufacturing geared to a new set of long-range production economies that will enable the company to turn a profit even if annual sales of U.S.-built cars level off at only 6 million units per year. That would be one third less than the record sales of 1973.

NO-FRILLS HOUSING

Miami-based Deltona Corp., caught in the worst housing slump in 40 years, is downgrading its entire product line. Up to last December, Deltona offered homes in the $30,000 to $46,000 range. Then, with an eye on declining birthrates and family formations, economists began forecasting an annual industry growth rate of only 1.8 million to 2.2 million new housing starts into the late 1980s. That compares with the industry peak of 2.4 million in 1972 and this year's depressed rate of 977,000 starts, based on February figures.

Forewarned—and already suffering a severe slump in its sales—Deltona switched to smaller, less lavish homes selling for $17,800 to $30,000. "There's no question that the buyer would like to get more home, but we think he'll be willing to settle for less frills," says Ernest D. Balint, Deltona's senior vice president for marketing.

Along with trimming product features, many companies are also trimming their number of new-product introductions—still a dizzying 10,000 a year, according to some estimates. "Yet this does not mean companies will necessarily spend less on overall product development," stresses Barry Marcus, president of Dunham & Marcus, Inc., venture marketing consultants. "Many will still maintain their previous development budgets. They will simply be more selective and give more support to a smaller number of products." This happens in almost every recession, Marcus notes, "but we will see more of it in a long-range, low-growth situation."

In the food-products business, where real growth is projected at only 68 percent from 1973 to 1988, Del Monte Corp. is maintaining its product development budget but is reducing actual introductions by 30 percent. "We are putting more emphasis on how we can make our present products better," says Fernando R. Gumucio, marketing vice president for U.S. grocery products. Right now, Del Monte has two new products on the market, three in home tests, and three more in development.

In line with declining birthrates and the sluggish housing business, Schlage Lock Co., a subsidiary of Ingersoll-Rand Co., is also battening down on long-term, new-product development. "New designs and new lock finishes are just not as exciting to dealers as they used to be," says corporate economist Clyde Hartz. Where Schlage previously brought out two or three new designs at once and kept the old ones, it now introduces only one or two new designs and drops a similar number.

Persistent material shortages—or rising prices that force material substitutions—could further compromise product variety. To minimize the impact, corporate purchasing is beginning to move out of the backroom of manufacturing "and becoming one of the most influential adjuncts of marketing," says market researcher Solomon Dutka, president of Audits & Surveys Co. "You can't sell it if you can't produce it—however big or small the market."

Anticipating long-range material scarcities that could crimp their growth, more and more companies have recently elevated purchasing executives into key vice presidencies: Gillette, Champion Intrnational, Union Camp, Pfizer, Kaiser Aluminum, A-T-O, McGraw-Edison, Celanese, Sperry Univac, and Du Pont—to name only a few. "Feedstock economics has become a major factor determining which businesses grow and which ones die," says David K. Barnes, vice president and general manager of Du Pont's new Energy & Materials Department. Heading into a low-growth future with materials uncertainty, says Barnes, more companies are coming to realize that tighter control of raw materials "might be required for survival—not just as an option to reduce costs."

At Xerox Corp., where materials now account for 75 percent of the manufactured cost of a product, a new computerized commodity code is being tested that would permit worldwide buyers to get an instant rundown on thousands of materials and substitutes. "With this system, we can also ask suppliers for a price on a family of items, instead of buying similar items at random from five different suppliers," says Gaylord Powell, director of material. With worldwide use of the code, expected later this year, Xerox hopes to cut its total procurement list from 90,000 individual items to as few as 10,000 "product families."

Low growth is forcing a similar reassessment of distribution—possibly at the expense of the consumer. Management consultant Robert W. Eichinger, a vice president of Lifson, Wilson, Ferguson & Winick, Inc., foresees "a shift away from what the consumer wants and more critical emphasis on establishing a relationship with the jobber, wholesaler, and retailer."

This would be part of a larger shift away from building market demand and toward market share. "We may have to do studies of retail purchasing people to find out what a manufacturer must do to put more of his product into retail distribution," says Eichinger. "Instead of asking what kind of toothbrushes the consumer wants, one must go to Kresge, Sears, and the drug stores and find out from purchasing sources what kind of packaging, display cases, delivery, pay terms, and buying incentives they need."

DIRECT TO THE PUBLIC

Many manufacturers are going even further. They are beginning to duck around the middleman altogether and sell directly to some of their customers, boosting both margins and volume. Among the biggest and latest to go retail are Edmos (yarns and knits), Pepperidge Farms (baked goods), Eaton (auto parts), Dannon (yogurt), Texas Instruments and Hewlett-Packard (calculators), GAF (duplicating supplies and services), Sherwin-Williams (paints and home-decorating centers), plus hundreds of manufacturers who are quietly opening retail warehouse outlets. One of them is Keller Industries, Inc., of Miami, which makes carpeting, tubular furniture, and aluminum doors, windows, and other products for residential construction. Norman S. Edelcup, vice chairman and senior vice president, sums up the thinking behind the trend when he says: "This is a good way to increase volume and also let the public know about all the other products we offer."

Right now, the broader chores of distribution—order processing, storage, and transportation—tend to be scattered through the corporation and handled piecemeal by manufacturing, marketing, and finance. Consultant John R. Dowdle, vice president of Booz, Allen & Hamilton, Inc., suggests that low growth will magnify pressures for integrating and coordinating distribution—often by centralizing it within the marketing function.

In an analysis for the Conference Board, Dowdle cites the recent example of a grocery products manufacturer. With $300 million in sales in three major lines, the manufacturer used a combination of 60 public warehouses and company-owned facilities for shipping 450 million pounds of goods a year. The company had separate sales organizations for each line, and its distribution costs ran about $20 million.

The alternative strategy was to combine sales for all products in a single direct-sales force. This cut the number of orders 25 percent to 50 percent, lowered processing and freight costs, and eliminated a split-shipment restriction. While costs of carrying inventory rose an estimated $250,000, the company came up with savings of $500,000 to $1 million in order processing, warehousing, and freight. In the low-growth years ahead, says Dowdle, "the trend toward simplified distribution systems will mean there will be fewer distribution points in the network, with a corresponding opportunity for more centralization of distribution control."

WAREHOUSE ON WHEELS

Spotting this trend, Ryder System, Inc., launched a program last year that cuts out several intermediate warehousing operations for its truck-leasing customers. In the same way that conservation-minded consumers want more life out of the products they buy, William O. Cullom, Ryder's vice president for marketing, says: "We've got to prove to our customer that by doing more with the equipment he has, we can improve his cash flow."

As one answer to low-growth pressures, which Cullom bames on "our new deconsumption society," Ryder has begun offering the truck as a rolling warehouse. Cullom notes that newly manufactured goods usually go first into the manufacturer's warehouse, next are shipped to a retailer's warehouse, and then are shipped once again either to the store or to the retail customer. "There's a minimum of six loadings and unloadings into warehouses before the goods get to their final destination [the retail customer]," says Cullom. "We want to eliminate many of those steps and keep more goods in the trucks, cutting down on storage space and cost." By minimizing loadings and unloadings and speeding up the shipment cycle, Ryder claims it can whittle the customer's trucking needs by 20 percent.

Before introducing its new service, Ryder approached its markets like most other companies that took growth for granted. Cullom says: "The customer came in or we went to him and we made a deal, not really looking down the road. We wanted his business, sure, but if we lost it, we knew there was plenty more where that came from." Now Ryder—like many other companies—takes nothing for granted. Especially growth.

Contingency Planning
for Product Recall

Roger A. Kerin and Michael Harvey

Product recall is fast becoming a fact of business life among consumer goods manufacturers. Approximately 25 percent of all consumer goods firms listed in *Fortune's* 500 were involved in recall campaigns in 1974 and *The Conference Board* estimates that more than 25 million product units will be recalled every year.[1]

While removing products from the market is not a new phenomenon, the pervasiveness and extent of product recovery *is*. It would seem that no consumer goods manufacturer is immune. In 1975, for example:

- Matsushita Electric Corporation of America recalled 300,000 color television sets because of radiation emission difficulties.
- General Motors recalled 234,000 1975 Cadillacs after a faulty hood latch was discovered.[2]

When one considers the mushroom scare of 1973 and the Bon Vivant botulism threat in 1971, the need to at least *anticipate* that a product recall may occur becomes apparent.

In spite of the frequency and importance of the task involved in recovering products, little published commentary has focused on developing a contingency plan or mechanism for product recall in the event that a recall is required. Accordingly, firms facing this risk presumably have a number of questions relating to a contingency plan for product recall.

About the Authors: Roger A. Kerin and Michael Harvey are faculty members in marketing at Southern Methodist University.

Roger A. Kerin and Michael Harvey, "Contingency Planning for Product Recall," pp. 5–12, *MSU Business Topics*, Summer 1975. Reprinted by permission of the publisher, Division of Research, Graduate School of Business Administration, Michigan State University.

[1] E. P. McGuire, "Product Recall and the Facts of Business Life," *The Conference Board Record*, February 1975, pp. 13–15.

[2] "A Flood of Shoddy Products—What's Being Done to Stem It." *U.S. News and World Report*, 24 February 1975, pp. 39–40.

Four multifaceted questions pertaining to organization, information and record-keeping, recall strategy, and financing seem relevant to the development of a contingency product recall plan.

1. What type of internal organizational structure is best suited for performing a product recall? Who should be responsible for the recall and what authority should be assigned to this individual or group?
2. What kinds of information are necessary to implement an effective product recall? Who should provide this information and who should receive it?
3. Is a product recall campaign simply a marketing program in reverse or do subtleties of the process require modified approaches?
4. How does a firm finance a product recall? Is this risk insurable?

A notable attempt to wrestle with different aspects of each question was initiated by *The Conference Board* in 1974.[3] This article will expand and integrate the ideas introduced at their conference.

At the outset it is recognized that a manufacturer's orientation is directed toward efficient and effective distribution of products to specified target markets. However, organizational structure as defined by responsibility and authority linkages is not necessarily equipped for recovering products from the market. The process of product recall is unique in that it is a transitory set of activities of an extraordinary nature, requiring efficiency and effectiveness in planning and implementation due to the urgency and importance of the task involved.

RECALL ORGANIZATION

Given the nature of the problem, what type of organizational structure is best suited for the recall task? The approach recommended is that of a task force comprised of individuals representing functional areas directly involved in the production and distribution of products and ancillary personnel necessary to facilitate implementation. The concept of a task force is best described by A. K. Wickesberg and T. Cronin:

> The task force approach is essentially a team effort. A task force . . . is created to accomplish some specific objective or mission. Its members are drawn mainly from *within* the organization . . . and are selected because of their potential contribution to successful attainment of the mission. Once the objective has been reached and the . . . specific assignment finished, the members of the task force are returned to their original organizational unit.[4]

---

[3] E. P. McGuire, ed., *Managing Product Recalls* (New York: The Conference Board, 1974).

[4] A. K. Wickesberg and T. Cronin, "Management by Task Force," *Harvard Business Review*, November–December 1962, pp. 107–14.

Certain benefits accrue to organizations that adopt this approach. For example, the task force model has the benefit of continuity over time associated with a committee. Yet it marshalls the time and resources of its members on a full-time basis when the need arises for pre-planning recall contingency measures and later implements the measures should a recall become necessary. The task force model draws from the project management approach in that it places identifiable responsibility and authority on a select group of individuals—and specifically, a task force leader—to accomplish the product recall task. Yet, it does not create an extra-organizational unit with potential long-term accompanying difficulties such as coordination, personnel displacement, and intra-organizational conflict. Finally, the task force approach instills a sense of urgency and importance in the organization for considering recall measures.

The size and composition of the task force may vary between organizations. Six functional areas appear to require representation because of their potential contribution in terms understanding the production and distribution of products and technical expertise. They are: engineering/quality control executives; customer service/sales executives; production/inventory control executives; distribution executives; public relations executives; and corporate counsel.[5]

LEADER, RESPONSIBILITY, AND AUTHORITY

Who should be selected as the task force leader and what responsibility and authority should be assigned to this group? Typically, the task force manager is appointed from the middle management ranks and is given the direct responsibility for the detailed planning, coordination, and ultimate outcome of the recall. It would seem appropriate to select that group member most familiar with the movement of products to the market. Therefore, the individual most likely to assume this position is the customer service or distribution executive depending upon the position description and functional responsibilities in each organization.

The recall task force should have complete responsibility and the necessary authority for policy development and implementing measures related to product recall. Three reasons are offered in support of this contention. First, the recall should proceed without the unnecessary strain on other line and staff executives outside of their specific tasks related to recall. Second, because recalls are often instituted after a safety defect has been identified, rapid action is a prerequisite to effective implementation before consumer injury occurs. Therefore, predefined authority to implement the recall plan should be delegated to the task force. In addition, by designing a well-defined resource control system, the organization allows for stewardship of assets, that is, conservation of human resources, maintenance of consumer goodwill, presentation of capital, and ensuring the regulations of diverse intra- and inter-organizational activities.[6]

---

[5] J. Locke, "Organizational Considerations of a Company Recall," in *Managing Product Recalls*, pp. 27–30.

[6] W. Newman, *Constructive Control: Design and Use of Control Systems* (Englewood Cliffs, N.J.: Prentice-Hall, Inc., 1975), p. 72.

One specific responsibility assignable to the task force concerns the notification of the Consumer Product Safety Commission (CPSC) once a product defect has been identified or a product recall begun. This requirement is stated formally in Section 15(b) of the Consumer Product Safety Act.[7] Should a firm fail to inform the CPSC or other safety agencies, the firm's chief operating officer is held responsible. Designating an individual before the fact is therefore essential since fixed time limits exist for reporting safety defects (typically twenty-four hours). Experience to date indicates that a corporate or divisional vice-president is assigned this responsibility.[8]

INFORMATION SYSTEMS

A second question concerns the nature and flow of information necessary to implement a recall campaign. Figure 1 presents a summary of the sources, type,

FIGURE 1 Source, Type, and Flow of Information Necessary for Product Recall

SOURCE	TYPE	FLOW
Quality control/ engineering	1. Nature of defect 2. Production/facility/materials/ design causing defect → 3. Remedial action	Production/inventory control
Production/ inventory control	1. Product/codes/names/batches 2. Amount manufactured 3. Work-in-process, in-plant finished goods inventories	↓ Distribution
Distribution	1. Quantity of product shipped 2. Location/name of resellers 3. Product-in-transit 4. Reseller inventory quantity 5. Off-plant warehouse inventory quality	↓ Customer service
Customer service	1. Invoice data (price, discounts, and so forth) 2. Instructions for recall procedure 3. Names of customers if available 4. Summary of data collected from quality control, production/ inventory control, distribution	↓ Public relations
Public relations	1. Formal notification of recall publics containing information collected above	↓ Regional district sales and services managers, government agencies, resellers, customers

---

[7] Public Law 92, 1972.

[8] E. P. McGuire, "Delegating Executive Responsibility for Notification," in *Managing Product Recalls*, p. 39.

and flow of information to effectively implement a recall campaign. The structure outlined is designed to illustrate the "building effect" of different types of information, identify responsibility areas in the information and record-keeping system, and to order the information flow to communicate with groups and diverse publics which require data to act in the most expeditious fashion.

It is no coincidence that the information flow among functional areas corresponds to the membership in the recall task force. Task force membership is predicated on each functionary's potential contribution to the recall mission both in terms of generating and managing the orderly flow of information. In this respect, the task force acts as the nervous system of a recall campaign.

CRITERIA AND APPLICATIONS

The information system described here, and indeed all automated or manual multipurpose identification-record keeping systems, should meet a number of basic criteria. First, the system should mirror the entire manufacturing and distribution system employed by the firm. Special emphasis should be placed on critical processes including ingredients mixing, assembly activities, and physical flow and handling of finished goods. Second, the system should be accessible, current, and able to cross-reference data to identify products by location and by customer or intermediary. Third, the system should be understood not only by the principal user (for example, production or engineering, but also by secondary users (for example, customer service or distribution). Finally, the information system should be integrated into the firm's existing production, accounting, and marketing information system in disaggregative files to facilitate access.

Elaborate information systems have been developed by both durable and non-durable goods manufacturers. Two systems, in particular, illustrate potential applications. The Pillsbury Company has developed the Product Control and Identification System (PCIS), an automated information system which identifies critical processes in manufacturing, assembling, and packaging of products in addition to locating products in shipment or in retail inventories.[9] The capability of PCIS is illustrated by its ability to trace and achieve product control of 98 percent of its products within twenty-four hours and virtually 100 percent traceability within days.[10] A second example of a comprehensive and automated information system is that used by the Ford Motor Company and referred to as the North American Vehicle Information System (NAVIS).[11] Like Pillsbury's system, NAVIS serves both as a quality control and recall tracking system. In addition to the automobile's serial number, NAVIS provides identification of a vehicle's 15,000-odd parts on either an individual basis or "batch" numbers for approximately 4,000,000 units sold annually.

---

[9] J. Haaland, "Product Recall Problems and Options—Nondurable Products," in *Managing Product Recalls*, pp. 57–65.

[10] "Managing the Product Recall," *BusinessWeek*, 26 January 1975, pp. 46–48.

[11] G. Robertson, "Identification of Products for Potential Recall," in *Managing Product Recalls*, pp. 66–71.

PHYSICAL RECALL OF PRODUCTS

Organizing for recall and developing production and distribution information systems represents internal, company managed and operated aspects of product recall campaigns. The physical removal of products, however, extends into the marketplace including distributors, intermediate users, and ultimate customers.

The removal of products from the market can be viewed as *reverse* promotion and distribution activities. In a product recall campaign a manufacturer must identify those individuals or firms having purchased the product in question and develop information and distribution systems for communicating with and collecting and transporting products from customers. The physical recall task is not without its intricacies, particularly when the ultimate customer is far removed from the manufacturer in terms of distribution intermediaries.

IDENTIFYING CUSTOMERS

Identifying customers becomes increasingly difficult as the length and variety of marketing channels increases. The least complex channel arrangement for identifying final users is the direct channel. Unfortunately, this channel arrangement is an atypical method of distribution or only one of several channel structures used by firms. Examples of more complex channel arrangements are found for automobile and electrical parts and convenience products with multiple primary distributors, intermediate resellers, and retail organizations comprising hundreds of autonomous units. Moreover, since transactions at the consumer level occur at the cash register, it is virtually impossible to accurately identify each consumer of a defective product.

Two identification methods appear to offer partial remedies for customer and product location. Warranty cards provide a means for identifying durable goods customers. However, industrial experience indicates that customers do not necessarily return these cards thus minimizing their use as a foolproof tracing device.[12] Accordingly, manufacturers should attempt to improve return rates by stressing their importance to distributors or asking distributors to develop their own product registration procedures for durable goods.

Geographical isolation of defective products represents a means for the aggregate identification of non-durable goods purchasers. In other words, since firms with multiple manufacturing facilities often serve selected geographical areas and selected product batch lots often reach specific areas, each may assist in identifying major cities, SMSAs, or regions receiving defective items. Although this approach offers only a gross approximation of product location, it serves to focus the reverse distribution strategy employed by the firm.

STRATEGIES FOR RECOVERING PRODUCTS

A reverse distribution strategy should be developed once product purchasers have been identified both at the customer and distributor level. The strategy

---

[12] E. P. McGuire, "Tracing via Warranty Cards," in *Managing Product Recalls*, p. 68.

involves two steps: informing distributors and customers, and physically removing products. The information strategy is designed to inform distributors to "freeze" inventories of questionable products and communicate remedial programs, and also to inform possible or actual customers who may have purchased the defective product. The firm can employ both "push" and "pull" information strategies simultaneously to reach distributors and customers, respectively.

The *push* strategy requires personal contact by the firm's sales/distribution group in the field (that is, regional and district sales organizations) to inform distributors of a recall and coordinate inventory, warehousing, credit, collection, and transportion of defective products held by distributors. The *pull* strategy is designed to alert customers to the existence of a defective product and the suggested procedure for returning the item. The CPSC has issued suggested guidelines for news releases for customers who have not or cannot be reached directly by the manufacturer. The news release should identify the product and the hazard, provide a means for identifying the product (model or serial number), inform purchasers of how to gain restitution for the defective item, state the name of the producing firm and distributors in local areas, and give a source to which purchasers can contact for further information about the product.[13]

The product recovery campaign itself involves managing a reverse or backward channel of distribution. Two options seem viable to the manufacturer. Product recall can proceed using either traditional middlemen or direct recovery from the consumer by the manufacturer through returning products to the plant or company-owned distribution centers.

The reverse distribution strategy should consider the same factors as those examined for typical channel decisions; namely, customer characteristics, product characteristics, middlemen characteristics, and company characteristics.[14] Recognition of the problems and costs to middlemen and company-owned distribution centers is necessary and must be acknowledged in the strategy planning of product recall. Anticipation of potential conflict in distribution channels is important for the development of remedial measures.

Possible criteria for evaluating the alternative reverse distribution strategies include the nature of the defect, market (geographical) coverage, product type, recall type, middlemen quality, remedial program required, existing distribution system, and financial capacity of the firm. This listing is not meant to be exhaustive, but suggestive. A manager may add factors unique to his firm's situation, or delete some that are not applicable. Furthermore, the strategy of reverse distribution may not be a clear choice between the two options. This situation would most likely occur when a firm employs many channel designs for reaching different target markets.

Finally, a testing of the firm's total recall program should be considered. A mock recall should be enacted to determine how quickly a firm can marshall its managerial resources, identify defective products and customers, convey recall information to appropriate recipients, and implement the physical recall of

---

[13] "CPSC Guidelines for News Releases" (Washington, D.C.: Office of Public Affairs, Consumer Product Safety Commission).

[14] P. Kotler, *Marketing Management: Analysis, Planning and Control*, 2d ed. (Englewood Cliffs, N.J.: Prentice-Hall, Inc., 1972), pp. 564–69.

products. A simulated recall should identify possible gaps, problem areas, and should determine the speed of implementation.

FINANCING THE PRODUCT RECALL

The last question raised concerns the issue of financing the recall campaign. Even though there is little published information on the cost of recalling products, General Motors recently spent $3.5 million in postal expense alone when a problem with motor mounts was detected in 6.5 million cars.[15] Matsushita Electric Corporation expects its cost of location and repair of defective television sets to approach $11 million.[16] Moreover, the bankruptcy of Bon Vivant after the detection of botulism was partially attributed to product withdrawal. These examples suggest a need to consider measures for financing recall campaigns.

ALTERNATIVE STRATEGIES

Two extreme alternatives which exist for the firm are internal financing or product recall insurance. The decision to select either alternative depends on the severity of recall cost to the firm and the availability and expense of product recall insurance. Severity of cost is relative to the firm potentially involved in a recall campaign. For example, an expected recall expense of $100,000 may not be considered severe to a large, well-capitalized firm, but may bankrupt a less financially sound firm. The financial estimate itself is contingent upon the careful costing of the recall strategy developed by the recall task force and the number and type of units recalled.

An objective appraisal of potential costs includes costs of contacting intermediaries and customers, that is, telephone and telegraph, newspaper, radio and television announcements, and postal expense including stationery; costs of hiring additional personnel and overtime for regular employees; and expenses incurred for the storage and transportation of defective products.

Internal financing of the recall is basically an out-of-pocket cost. A firm may either finance a recall from working capital or from a budgeted contingency fund specifically designed for recall. However approached, internal financing represents a means for handling the recall risk of current operating capital.

Alternatively, an organization may choose to purchase product recall insurance. This coverage must be secured in addition to a firm's comprehensive general liability policy which expressly excludes product withdrawal coverage. The costs covered with recall insurance are essentially those already described.

A detailed application is required for obtaining recall insurance. Special consideration of product type, manufacturing and quality control, and record-keeping provisions is necessary. Furthermore, a detailed statement of recall pro-

---

[15] "Managing the Product Recall," *BusinessWeek*.
[16] "Once Is Not Enough," *Time*, 12 May 1975, p. 70.

grams or strategies is strongly recommended. The premium payment is determined by the firm's loss exposure, potential, and previous loss experience. The typical insurance policy contains a flat deductible of about $5,000 for each occurrence in addition to a loss participation feature requiring the insured to cover between 10 to 20 percent of the loss exceeding the deductible expense.[17]

DECISION ANALYSIS

The decision to apply either strategy for financing recall campaigns can be structured within the context of decision analysis.[18] For example, assume a firm is considering both strategies and identifies two possible outcomes in a given year—a product recall or no product recall. A description of the dollar expense for either outcome given each strategy is shown in Figure 2A. Figure 2B pro-

FIGURE 2 Decision Analysis for Financing Approach to Product Recall

A.

Potential Occurrence in One Year

FINANCING STRATEGIES	Product recall (S_1)	No product recall (S_2)
Internal financing	Full cost of recall	No dollar outlay
Recall insurance	Premium cost + deductible + participation percent of recall expense $P(S_1) = P$	Cost of premium $P(S_2) = 1 - P$

B.

Assume:	Cost of recall	= $500,000
	Premium cost	= $ 30,000
	Insurance deductible	= $ 5,000
	Participation percent =	20%

Potential Occurrence in One Year

FINANCING STRATEGIES	Product recall (S_1)	No product recall (S_2)
Internal financing	$500,000	$ 0
Recall insurance	$135,000	$30,000
	$P(S_1) = P$	$P(S_2) + 1 - P$

$$P(500,000) + 1 - P(O) = P(135,000) + 1 - P(30,000)$$
$$500,000(P) = 105,000(P) + 30,000$$
$$P = .08$$

Decision: If the probability of a product recall is greater than .08, then one would select a recall insurance strategy to minimize the expected monetary value of the loss.

[17] J. O'Neal, "Products Recall Insurance," *CPCU Annals*, March 1974, pp. 40–43.

[18] B. Morgan, *An Introduction to Bayesian Statistical Decision Processes* (Englewood Cliffs, N.J.: Prentice-Hall, Inc., 1968).

vides an illustration for a hypothetical situation given a specified recall cost, insurance premium cost, insurance deductible and loss participation rate within a decision matrix. Because the expected costs (loss) attributed to each strategy differ by the potential of a recall, the probability of a recall during the year should be subjectively estimated. A number of subjective methods are available for obtaining these probability estimates.[19] A useful approach for "ranging" the probability estimate is shown in Figure 2B. By setting the strategy outcomes equal to each other, the probability of a recall (given these cost estimates) that will change the strategy selected is computed as eight chances out of 100. Stated in the form of a decision rule: *If the probability of a product recall is greater than .08, then one should select a recall insurance strategy to minimize the expected monetary value of the loss.* An important question to pose to the recall task force is therefore whether the probability of a recall is greater than eight chances out of 100.

The analysis just discussed should flow from the creation of a recall task force, the development of product record and information systems, and the delineation of recall campaign strategies. Only by objectively appraising each can the dollar cost of recall programs be estimated. Moreover, without the product withdrawal considerations cited earlier, the availability of recall insurance is diminished and the potential for higher costs of recall implementation is increased.

This article addressed a number of questions related to recalling products from the market. Figure 3 summarizes the objectives and tasks involved in pre-

---

FIGURE 3   Objectives and Tasks for Planning a Product Recall

---

Objective 1: Identify Recall Task Force.
   Tasks: • Define membership.
         • Define responsibility and authority.
         • Select a task leader.
Objective 2: Develop a Recall Information System.
   Tasks: • Identify sources of product/market information.
         • Identify necessary types of product/market information.
         • Determine appropriate flow of product/market information.
Objective 3: Develop Recall Strategy.
   Tasks: • Determine method(s) for identifying distributors and customers.
         • Determine information strategy for contacting distributors and customers.
         • Determine reverse distribution strategy to remove products from distributors and customers.
         • Simulate recall strategy to identify problem areas.
Objective 4: Identify Recall Financing Approach.
   Tasks: • Estimate potential costs of recall.
         • Evaluate alternative financing strategies within the context of potential recall.

---

[19] P. Kotler, "A Guide to Gathering Expert Estimates: The Treatment of Unscientific Data," *Business Horizons*, October 1970, pp. 74–87.

planning the product recall. In light of government legislation and consumerist pressures for product safety, firms must anticipate and develop contingency mechanisms in the event that a recall may occur. Without anticipating and planning contingency recall measures, an organization will suffer unexpected, unnecessary and substantial loss.

Strategic Windows

Derek F. Abell

Strategic market planning involves the management of any business unit in the dual tasks of *anticipating* and *responding* to changes which affect the marketplace for their products. This article discusses both of these tasks. Anticipation of change and its impact can be substantially improved if an organizing framework can be used to identify sources and directions of change in a systematic fashion. Appropriate responses to change require a clear understanding of the alternative strategic options available to management as a market evolves and change takes place.

DYNAMIC ANALYSIS

When changes in the market are only incremental, firms may successfully adapt themselves to the new situation by modifying current marketing or other functional programs. Frequently, however, market changes are so far reaching that the competence of the firm to continue to compete effectively is called into question. And it is in such situations that the concept of "strategic windows" is applicable.

The term "strategic window" is used here to focus attention on the fact that there are only limited periods during which the "fit" between the key requirements of a market and the particular competencies of a firm competing in that market is at an optimum. Investment in a product line or market area should be timed to coincide with periods in which such a strategic window is open. Conversely, disinvestment should be contemplated if what was once a good fit has been eroded—i.e., if changes in market requirements outstrip the firm's capability to adapt itself to them.

Among the most frequent questions which management has to deal with in this respect are:

- Should funds be committed to a proposed new market entry? Now? Later? Or not at all? If a commitment is to be made, how large should it be?
- Should expenditure of funds of plant and equipment or marketing to sup-

About the Author: Derek F. Abell is Associate Professor of Business Administration, Harvard University, Graduate School of Business Administration, Cambridge, MA.

Reprinted from Derek F. Abell, "Strategic Windows," *Journal of Marketing* (July 1978), pp. 21–25, published by the American Marketing Association.

port existing product lines be expanded, continued at historical levels, or diminished?

- When should a decision be made to quit and throw in the towel for an unprofitable product line or business area?

Resource allocation decisions of this nature all require a careful assessment of the future evolution of the market involved and an accurate appraisal of the firm's capability to successfully meet key market requirements. The strategic window concept encourages the analysis of these questions in a dynamic rather than a static framework, and forces marketing planners to be as specific as they can about these future patterns of market evolution and the firm's capability to adapt to them.

It is unfortunate that the heightened interest in product portfolio analysis evident in the last decade has failed to adequately encompass these issues. Many managers routinely classify their various activities as "cows," "dogs," "stars," or "question marks" based on a *static* analysis of the *current* position of the firm and its market environment.

Of key interest, however, is the question not only of where the firm is today, but of how well equipped it is to deal with *tomorrow*. Such a *dynamic* analysis may foretell non-incremental changes in the market which work to disqualify market leaders, provide opportunities for currently low share competitors, and sometimes even usher in a completely new cast of competitors into the market-place. Familiar contemporary examples of this latter phenomenon include such products as digital watches, women's pantyhose, calculators, charter air travel, office copiers, and scientific instrumentation.

In all these cases existing competitors have been displaced by new contenders as these markets have evolved. In each case changing market requirements have resulted in a *closing* strategic window for incumbent competitors and an *opening* window for new entrants.

MARKET EVOLUTION

The evolution of a market usually embodies more far reaching changes than the relatively systematic changes in customer behavior and marketing mix due to individual product life cycles. Four major categories of change stand out:

1. The development of new primary demand opportunities whose marketing requirements differ radically from those of existing market segments.
2. The advent of new competing technologies which cannibalize the existing ones.
3. Market redefinition caused by changes in the definition of the product itself and/or changes in the product market strategies of competing firms.
4. Channel changes.

There may be other categories of change or variants in particular industries. That doesn't matter; understanding of how such changes may qualify or disqualify different types of competitors can still be derived from a closer look at examples within each of the four categories above.

New Primary Demand

In a primary demand growth phase, decisions have to be reached by existing competitors about whether to spend the majority of the resources fighting to protect and fortify market positions that have already been established, or whether to seek new development opportunities.

In some cases, it is an original entrant who ploughs new territory—adjusting his approach to the emergent needs of the marketplace; in other cases it is a new entrant who, maybe basing his entry on expertise developed elsewhere, sees a "strategic window" and leapfrogs over the original market leader to take advantage of the new growth opportunity. Paradoxically, pioneering competitors who narrowly focus their activities in the early stages of growth may have the most difficulty in making the transition to new primary demand growth opportunities later. Emery Air Freight provides an example of a company that did face up to a challenge in such a situation.

Emery Air Freight This pioneer in the air freight forwarding business developed many of the early applications of air freight in the United States. In particular, Emery's efforts were focused on servicing the "emergency" segment of the market, which initially accounted for a substantial portion of all air freight business. Emery served this market via an extensive organization of regional and district offices. Among Emery's major assets in this market was a unique nationwide, and later worldwide, communications network; and the special competence of personnel located in the district offices in using scheduled carriers in the most efficient possible way to expedite deliveries.

As the market evolved, however, many new applications for air freight emerged. These included regular planned shipments of high value-low weight merchandise, shipments of perishables; "off-line" service to hard-to-reach locations, and what became known as the TCC (Total Cost Concept) market. Each of these new applications required a somewhat different approach than that demanded by the original emergency business.

TCC applications, for example, required detailed logistics planning to assess the savings and benefits to be obtained via lower inventories, quicker deliveries and fewer lost sales through the use of air freight. Customer decisions about whether or not to use air freight required substantially more analysis than had been the case for "emergency" use; furthermore, decisions which had originally been made by traffic managers now involved marketing personnel and often top management.

A decision to seek this kind of business thus implied a radical change in Emery's organization—the addition of capability to analyze complex logistics systems and to deal with upper echelons of management.

New Competing Technologies

When a fundamental change takes place in the basic technology of an industry, it again raises questions of the adaptability to new circumstances of existing firms using obsolete technology.

In many cases established competitors in an industry are challenged, not by another member of the same industry, but by a company which bases its approach on a technology developed outside that industry. Sometimes this results from forward integration of a firm that is eager to develop applications for a new component or raw material. Texas Instrument's entry into a wide variety of consumer electronic products from a base of semi-conductor manufacture is a case in point. Sometimes it results from the application by firms of a technology developed in one market to opportunities in another. Or sometimes a breakthrough in either product or process technology may remove traditional barriers to entry in an industry and attract a completely new set of competitors. Consider the following examples:

- Watchmakers have recently found that a new class of competitor is challenging their industry leadership—namely electronic firms who are seeking end market applications for their semi-conductors, as well as a new breed of assemblers manufacturing digital watches.
- Manufacturers of mechanical adjustable speed drive equipment found their markets eroded by electrical speed drives in the early 1900's. Electrical drives were based on rotating motor-generator sets and electronic controls. In the late 1950's, the advent of solid state electronics, in turn, virtually obsoleted rotating equipment. New independent competitors, basing their approach on the assembly of electronic components, joined the large electrical equipment manufacturers in the speed drive market. Today, yet another change is taking place, namely the advent of large computer controlled drive systems. This is ushering yet another class of competitors into the market—namely, companies whose basic competence is in computers.

In each of these cases, recurrent waves of new technology fundamentally changed the nature of the market and usually ushered in an entirely new class of competitors. Many firms in most markets have a limited capability to master all the technologies which might ultimately cannibalize their business. The nature of technological innovation and diffusion is such that most *major* innovations will originate outside a particular industry and not within it.

In many cases, the upheaval is not only technological; indeed the nature of competition may also change dramatically as technology changes. The advent of solid state electronics in the speed drive industry, for example, ushered in a number of small, low overhead, independent assemblers who based their approach primarily on low price. Prior to that, the market had been dominated by the large electrical equipment manufacturers basing their approach largely on applications engineering coupled with high prices and high margins.

The "strategic window" concept does not preclude adaption when it appears feasible, but rather suggests that certain firms may be better suited to compete in certain technological waves than in others. Often the cost and the difficulty of acquiring the new technology, as well as the sunk-cost commitment to the old, argue against adaption.

MARKET REDEFINITION

Frequently, as markets evolve, the fundamental definition of the market changes in ways which increasingly disqualify some competitors while providing opportunities for others. The trend towards marketing "systems" of products as opposed to individual pieces of equipment provides many examples of this phenomenon. The situation of Docutel illustrates this point.

Docutel   This manufacturer of automatic teller machines (ATM's) supplied virtually all the ATM's in use up to late 1974. In early 1975, Docutel found itself losing market share to large computer companies such as Burroughs, Honeywell, and IBM as these manufacturers began to look at the banks' total EFTS (Electronic Funds Transfer System) needs. They offered the bank a package of equipment representing a complete system of which the ATM was only one component. In essence their success may be attributed to the fact that they redefined the market in a way which increasingly appeared to disqualify Docutel as a potential supplier.

Market redefinition is not limited to the banking industry; similar trends are underway in scientific instrumentation, process control equipment, the machine tool industry, office equipment, and electric control gear, to name but a few. In each case, manufacturers basing their approach on the marketing of individual hardware items are seeing their "strategic window" closing as computer systems producers move in to take advantage of emerging opportunities.

CHANNEL CHANGES

Changes in the channels of distribution for both consumer and industrial goods can have far reaching consequences for existing competitors and would-be entrants.

Changes take place in part because of product life cycle phenomena—the shift as the market matures to more intensive distribution, increasing convenience, and often lower levels of channel service. Changes also frequently take place as a result of new institutional development in the channels themselves. Few sectors of American industry have changed as fast as retail and wholesale distribution, with the result that completely new types of outlets may be employed by suppliers seeking to develop competitive advantage.

Whatever the origin of the change, the effect may be to provide an opportunity for a new entrant and to raise questions about the viability of existing competitors. Gillette's contemplated entry into the blank cassette tape market is a case in point.

Gillette   As the market for cassettes evolved due to increased penetration and new uses of equipment for automotive, study, business, letter writing, and home entertainment, so did distribution channels broaden into an increasing number of drug chains, variety stores, and large discount stores.

Presumably it was recognition of a possible "strategic window" for Gillette that encouraged executives in the Safety Razor Division to look carefully at ways in which Gillette might exploit the cassette market at this particular stage in its evolution. The question was whether Gillette's skill in marketing low-priced, frequently purchased package goods, along with its distribution channel resources, could be applied to marketing blank cassettes. Was there a place for a competitor in this market to offer a quality, branded product, broadly distributed and supported by heavy media advertising in much the same way that Gillette marketed razor blades?

Actually, Gillette decided against entry, apparently not because a "strategic window" did not exist, but because profit prospects were not favorable. They did, however, enter the cigarette lighter business based on similar analysis and reportedly have had considerable success with their *Cricket* brand.

PROBLEMS AND OPPORTUNITIES

What do all these examples indicate? *First,* they suggest that the "resource requirements" for success in a business—whether these be financial requirements, marketing requirements, engineering requirements, or whatever—may change radically with market evolution. *Second,* they appear to suggest that, by contrast, the firm's resources and key competencies often cannot be so easily adjusted. The result is a *predictable* change in the fit of the firm to its market—leading to defined periods during which a "strategic window" exists and can be exploited.

The "strategic window" concept can be useful to incumbent competitors as well as to would-be entrants into a market. For the former, it provides a way of relating future strategic moves to market evolution and of assessing how resources should be allocated to existing activities. For the latter, it provides a framework for diversification and growth.

Existing Businesses

Confronted with changes in the marketplace which potentially disqualify the firm from continued successful participation, several strategic options are available:

1. An attempt can be made to assemble the resources needed to close the gap between the new critical marketing requirements and the firm's competences.
2. The firm may shift its efforts to selected segments where the "fit" between requirements and resources is still acceptable.
3. The firm may shift to a "low profile" approach—cutting back severely on all further allocation of capital and deliberately "milking" the business for short-run profit.
4. A decision may be taken to exit from that particular market either through liquidation or through sale.

All too frequently, however, because the "strategic window" phenomenon is not clearly recognized, these strategic choices are not clearly articulated. Instead, "old" approaches are continued long after the market has changed with the result that market position is lost and financial losses pile up. Or, often only half-hearted attempts are made to assemble the new resources required to compete effectively; or management is simply deluded into believing that it can adapt itself to the new situation even where this is actually out of the question.

The four basic strategic choices outlined above may be viewed hierarchically in terms of *resource commitment*, with No. 1 representing the highest level of commitment. Only the company itself can decide which position on the hierarchy it should adopt in particular situations, but the following guideline questions may be helpful:

- To what extent do the changes call for skills and resources completely outside the traditional competence of the firm? A careful analysis has to be made of the gap which may emerge between the evolving requirements of the market and the firm's profile.
- To what extent can changes be anticipated? Often it is easier to adapt through a series of minor adjustments—a stepping stone approach to change—than it is to be confronted with a major and unexpected discontinuity in approach.
- How rapid are the changes which are taking place? Is there enough time to adjust without forfeiting a major share of the market which later may be difficult to regain?
- How long will realignment of the functional activities of the firm take? Is the need limited to only some functions, or are all the basic resources of of the firm affected—e.g., technology, engineering, manufacturing, marketing, sales, and organization policies?
- What existing commitments—e.g., technical skills, distribution channels, manufacturing approaches, etc.—constrain adaption?
- Can the new resources and new approaches be developed internally or must they be acquired?
- Will the changes completely obsolete existing ways of doing business or will there be a chance for coexistence? In the case of new technologies intruding from outside industry, the decision often has to be made to "join-em rather than fight-em." Not to do so is to risk complete obsolescence. In other cases, coexistence may be posssible.
- Are there segments of the market where the firm's existing resources can be effectively concentrated?
- How large is the firm's stake in the business? To the extent that the business represents a major source of revenues and profit, a greater commitment will probably need to be made to adapt to the changing circumstances.
- Will corporate management, in the event that this is a business unit within a multi-business corporation, be willing to accept different goals for the business in the future than it has in the past? A decision not to adapt to

changes may result in high short-run returns from that particular business. Looking at the problem from the position of corporate planners interested in the welfare of the total corporation, a periodic market-by-market analysis in the terms described above would appear to be imperative prior to setting goals, agreeing on strategies, and allocating resources.

New Entrants

The "strategic window" concept has been used implicitly by many new entrants to judge the direction, timing, and scale of new entry activities. Gillette's entry into cigarette lighters, major computer manufacturers entry into ATM's, and Procter & Gamble's entry into many consumer markets *after* pioneers have laid the groundwork for a large scale, mass market approach to the specific product areas, all are familiar examples.

Such approaches to strategic market planning require two distinctly different types of analysis:

1. Careful assessment has to be made of the firm's strengths and weaknesses. This should include audits of all the key resources of the company as well as its various existing programs of activity.
2. Attention should be directed away from the narrow focus of familiar products and markets to a search for opportunities to put unique competencies to work. This requires a broader appreciation of overall environmental, technical and market forces, and knowledge of many more markets, than is encountered in many firms today. It puts a particular burden on marketing managers, general managers, and business planners used to thinking in terms of existing activities.

   Analysis of patterns of market evolution and diagnosis of critical market requirements in the future can also be of use to incumbent competitors as a forewarning of potential new entry. In such cases, adjustments in strategy can sometimes be made in advance, which will ultimately deter would-be new competitors. Even where this is not the case, resource commitments may be adjusted to reflect the future changes in structure of industrial supply.

CONCLUSION

The "strategic window" concept suggests that fundamental changes are needed in marketing management practice, and in particular in strategic market planning activities. At the heart of these changes is the need to base marketing planning around predictions of future patterns of market evolution and to make assessments of the firm's capabilities to deal with change. Such analyses require considerably greater strategic orientation than the sales forecasting activities which underpin much marketing planning today. Users of product portfolio chart analysis, in particular, should consider the dynamic as opposed to the static implications in designating a particular business.

Entry and exit from markets is likely to occur with greater rapidity than is often the case today, as firms search for opportunities where their resources can be deployed with maximum effectiveness. Short of entry and exit, the allocation of funds to markets should be timed to coincide with the period when the fit between the firm and the market is at its optimum. Entering a market in its early stages and evolving with it until maturity may, on closer analysis, turn out to be a serious management error.

It has been said that while the life of the product is limited, a market has greater longevity and as such can provide a business with a steady and growing stream of revenue and profit if management can avoid being myopic about change. This article suggests that as far as any one firm is concerned, a market also is a temporary vehicle for growth, a vehicle which should be used and abandoned as circumstances dictate—the reason being that the firm is often slower to evolve and change than is the market in which it competes.

Cure for Strategic Malnutrition

Frederick W. Gluck, Richard N. Foster and John L. Forbis

Casper Wallingham, new CEO of Farflung Industries, a large, diversified, technology-based company, senses problems in his product line. He digs in and finds that his corporate control systems have evolved so as to provide him with tight financial control over divisional operations but little visibility of the soundness of their business and technological strategies. Moreover, he becomes convinced that the division heads, following the corporate lead, are managing for short-term operating results. By examining the management of his own and several similar companies, Casper gains insights that should be valuable for all top managers. "Look, Don, I know you guys have been pretty successful. In one way or another, you've been telling me that for months now. And maybe I haven't quite got my arms around this outfit yet, but I'm not exactly a stranger to the business, either. And there are some things around here that are beginning to bother me a lot."

Casper Wallingham, president and CEO of Farflung Industries, Inc., swung out of his chair and began to pace the floor of his office. A tall, heavyset Texan whose country-boy manner had survived 20 years in the East, he struck most people as an odd successor to Lowell Keyes, the methodical Bostonian who had presided over Farflung's most spectacular decade of growth.

However, a year ago, when Keyes had unexpectedly succumbed to a stroke on a business trip, it had taken the board just two meetings to settle on Casper Wallingham for the new CEO. As president of Diamond Steel, one of Farflung's key suppliers, Wallingham had won a reputation as one of the toughest and most talented top executives in the business, and Lowell Keyes had been one of his warmest admirers.

About the Authors: Frederick W. Gluck is a director and Richard N. Foster and John L. Forbis are associates in the New York office of McKinsey & Company. The authors have special interests in the areas of strategy and technology-based companies.

So, for that matter, had been Don Blair, then a division manager, now vice president for corporate development. But Blair's enthusiasm had cooled in the ten months since Casper took office. It wasn't that he respected Casper less as a manager. The man's intelligence and integrity were beyond doubt. But in Blair's eyes, and he was not alone, Casper hadn't yet really grown into the job or developed the qualities it demanded—the lighter touch, the willingness to delegate, the concern for orchestrating people's contributions instead of trying to second-guess their decisions. In a lot of ways, he was still a rough diamond—a heavy-handed, take-charge line manager. And on this particular afternoon, after an hour of none-too-harmonious discussion, Blair was beginning to feel decidedly tense and irritated.

"Casper, I hate to sound like a broken record but—managing a billion-dollar company with 6 major groups and 25 divisions—"

"Yeah, I know," Casper interrupted, "it's a different ball game from running a one-product-line outfit like Diamond. But it's not so different that I'm going to sit back and relax when I see our profits bumping along at $90 million or so for the past three years. We ought to be doing twice that and you know it. And so does Wall Street."

Don sighed. "Look, Casper, we've been through all this before. I've told you we're still getting squeezed on price. I'm satisfied that we're still the lowest-cost producer on three-quarters of our lines. Close to it, anyway."

"Close to it? Look, Don, I know we've got the latest thing in standard cost systems, but that doesn't mean our costs are where they should be. I keep probing our facts and coming up against untested assumptions. And that bugs me. By the way, what did you find out about those lost orders?"

"Pretty much of a false alarm," Don said. "Six or seven divisions involved. Just an isolated case here and there. I called some of the customers to find out why. Incidentally, that got the division managers' backs up the way I told you it would. Anyway, I'm sure the customers leveled with me. Different stories, of course, but no particular pattern, except that in each case they'd gone for a competitive product or a proposal that happened to be a little more responsive to their needs. Actually all but one went out of his way to assure me that we could continue to expect most of their business."

"That must have been reassuring," Casper said sarcastically. "Don, I know the signs. Somewhere out there we've got problems with our product lines. That's why I want to take a hard look at our whole R&D effort."

"Okay, Casper, but you'd better realize we're getting into deeper water with the line people every day. I was once in that same situation, you know, and believe me I needed help from corporate like I needed a hole in the head. If you really think the product lines are in trouble, then you ought to go after the division managers."

"But Don, how can I go after them when I really don't know what, if anything, is wrong? What I need from you is an appraisal of our R&D management in four areas—budgeting and control, corporate allocation of resources, financing, and performance measurement, plus any changes you want to recommend. Will four weeks be enough?"

CASPER UNDAUNTED

A month later, meeting with Don to review his report, Casper began on a genial note.

"Don, that report of yours is an impressive piece of staff work. I spent half the weekend on it, and I learned a lot. I don't think it's really going to solve the problem, though. Let's go over the four issues and I'll try to explain.

"On budgeting and control, you looked at 20 comparable companies and found that we were spending half as much on R&D as the average. So you concluded we ought to raise our sights. You recommend setting R&D spending targets for each division and for the company as a whole and segregating R&D expenditures, for control purposes, into four categories: cost reduction, new products, product maintenance, and exploratory research.

"Think about it, Don. Even if we really knew we weren't spending enough by some standard, what should we do? Tell the divisions to spend 40% more? That doesn't make sense unless each division manager has really thought through what he's going to be spending for. But I see that's what you're recommending."

"Fair enough, but we had to start somewhere. What about the classification system? Does that strike you as a useful control, at least?"

"Interesting, yes. Useful? Only in a very limited way. Suppose we know what percentage of each division's R&D effort is going into each category? How do we know it's the right balance? How do the numbers help us?"

"The numbers can highlight gaps in our programs," replied Don. "You know, if you don't have the ingots in inventory, you can't make the forging. Well, if you're not spending on new products, you can't expect to get them."

"So you set objectives by categories, and what happens? Easy—people do what they must to make the numbers look right. And we're still no nearer to controlling R&D. Maybe we're further behind because now we have to get through that smoke screen."

"Okay, Casper, so what should we use instead?"

"Good question. I just don't have an answer right now. Let's go on and look at resource allocation.

"Your people found we weren't concentrating our R&D spending on our high-growth businesses; in fact, we're spending it pretty evenly across the divisions. So you think we should start allocating R&D by division, according to rate of growth. I agree that our growth businesses should get the R&D and other resources they need. But just because one business is growing at a rate of 20% a year doesn't mean it needs twice the R&D funding of another that's perking along at 10%. Maybe it doesn't need as much. You can't figure out what it does need unless you look at a lot of other factors—competitive position, management talent, market size, market share—you get my point. So what good is your formula?"

"Look, Casper, I know there's no magic in those R&D-to-sales comparisons. But setting our priorities among our businesses is basic. If growth alone isn't good enough as a criterion, maybe we can build a profitability factor. But we can't do it without some formulas. As Lowell Keyes used to say, simple measures, or formulas, are the only way to control a corporation as large and diversified as this one. With all respect, I don't think you're sufficiently aware of the risk of too much detail."

"Maybe not," Casper said dryly. "But, again, let's move on. In your report you say we should continue to charge R&D to the divisions. Basically, I guess I agree with you. But some of those managers are going to try to jack up their short-term performance no matter what it costs us in the long run. How are we going to spot that kind of stuff in time?"

"Casper, I honestly don't see how we can have it both ways. Either we give the division managers responsibility for their businesses, or we don't. When I had that job, I felt it was up to me to look out for the company's long-term interests. If I'd felt I was being second-guessed by corporate, I'd have cared a lot less—to put it mildly."

"Look, I'm not questioning anyone's intentions, only the way we do things. We can't assume that the division managers are going to make our longer-range technical decisions in the company's best long-term interests. They don't always have the perspective, even if they do have the motivation—and, given the general thrust of our bonus plan, I wouldn't rest too easy on that score. Granted that the divisions should be picking up the tab for their R&D and should have a big say in how the money is spent, we still need to find much better ways of satisfying ourselves at the group and corporate level that our major R&D decisions are sound from an overall corporate point of view."

Casper paused, then continued, "That brings us to your last area, performance measurement. That was a shocker. Our average project is overruning by 40% in time and 60% in cost."

"That's 64%," Don corrected him.

"Right. That really shook me. But then I began to wonder what those figures tell me. What do I really care if an R&D project overruns by X%? Maybe everybody's do. What I want to know is, did we come up with something that really strengthens our competitive position?"

"No matter what it cost? Come on, Casper, you know you can't close your eyes to overruns."

"Sure, you need project control. But cost and time alone don't measure *performance*. It's so easy to get hypnotized by these numbers that you could still be in the dark about everything that really counts.

"Anyway, Don, I'm still uncomfortable, but I've got an idea. I was chatting a couple of days ago with one of our outside board members, Dick Fredericks. You know, he's the former chairman of Data Handling. We got on to R&D, and I kind of let my hair down. Dick's a good listener. Anyway, when I'd finished, he just said, 'Why don't you let me take a look at the situation as a special one-man committee of the board? Management of technology-based companies has always been my special interest.' "

"I told him I'd like to think a little bit about it, and I have. Dick had a fine track record before he stepped down early at Data Handling; and all of it was with big, diversified companies. I would suggest that we get an okay from the board and ask him to take a look."

"It sounds a little unusual, Casper, but we are sort of at an impasse and maybe a fresh point of view would be helpful."

MANAGING STRATEGICALLY

Six weeks later, Dick Fredericks was ready to give his reading of the situation. He had been briefed by Casper and Don; he had reviewed Don's report, talked with a number of other executives, and probed more deeply into the areas where he suspected problems.

"Well, Dick," said Casper after the exchange of greetings, "our people tell me you wasted no time in getting around to see them."

"And they didn't mince any words in telling me what they thought was wrong with Farflung."

"Good. Let's get started. Do we have a problem, or not? What did you think of the staff report?"

"Casper, I think you're suffering from strategic malnutrition, and the report won't do much to enrich your diet."

"Strategic malnutrition? What the hell is that?"

"I'll get to that, Casper. First just let me say that I see why you've been uncomfortable. It's a good report—well written and carefully reasoned. *But it starts from the assumption that better procedures are the way to get better control of R&D.* In fact, winning or holding a strong long-range competitive position is a strategic problem. If those strategic decisions aren't being made right, no amount of procedure polishing is going to help. Resource allocation, for example. That's a strategic decision, all right, but the report treats it only procedurally. It takes the correctness of the strategic decisions for granted."

"Now what do you mean by that?" Don was visibly exasperated. "The only thing we take for granted is that each of our division managers knows what resources he needs."

"Exactly."

"But I don't see how we can avoid that assumption. That's what those guys get paid for. Corporate management, or staff, for that matter, can't run around second-guessing division managers on *those* decisions."

"No, but it's possible we could help them. And we could equip ourselves at the same time to make better resource-allocation decisions at the corporate level."

"Don and I are all ears," Casper broke in.

"Okay, then, let me start by laying out a few ideas about how you gain control of R&D and do a good job of strategic planning—in a complex, diversified, multidivisional, technology-based company like Farflung."

"Makes sense to me," said Casper. "Go ahead."

"Right. Well, I'd argue that R&D goals are part of the broader business goal of controlling your competitive position. So, to make sound decisions on R&D spending, you've got to know your technological opportunities plus your strategic objectives for the businesses or product lines.

"Obviously, these two factors interrelate, so you've got to make sure at the division, or profit-center, level that your strategic objectives reflect the technological opportunities and that the opportunities you pursue are those best suited to take the business where you want it to go. Let's call that developing product-line strategies.

"Higher up, at the group and corporate levels, you've got to do three things. First, size up your divisional strategies in the light of overall corporate capability and objectives. Second, make sure those strategies take account of the main risks and opportunities. Third, allocate resources among divisions where necessary, and work out cross-divisional strategies when these are called for. Do you follow me?"

"Well, I get the general picture. But you know we're already doing a lot of that stuff. We've used a corporate screen to sort our businesses into strategic categories—you know, invest or grow, maintain or manage for income, and harvest or low-growth."

"Yes, I know you use the portfolio approach, Casper. It helps in getting a grasp of the problem if you've got total confidence in your data and you know the choices developed are sound. But that's a pretty big 'if.' And, in any case, it doesn't tell your division managers how to allocate their R&D resources—or any other resources, for that matter.

"Look at your Medical Products Division, which you consider an invest-grow business. Its main strategic objective, as I understand it, is to introduce three new laboratory products a year. So it's got half a dozen R&D programs at various stages. But I was completely stymied when I tried to get Joe Tibbets to tell me how those products would affect your overall competitive position or even his own division economics. It's apparent he's just not thinking in those terms.

"Or take Toby Cook in Plastics—a business you're trying to harvest. One of his paper objectives is to keep R&D expenses at least level and to decrease them where possible. At the same time his plans call for holding maintenance cost increases down to 4% a year. In fact, they've been going up at roughly 15% per year since 1972, and no wonder. The plant has been running for 18 years now, and the last major capital improvements are at least 5 years old. There's not a single technical project aimed at controlling maintenance costs. So margins are slipping, you could be forced to increase prices, and before you know it you'll be losing market share. He seems to be taking the fact that he's running a so-called harvest business too literally and is skimping on R&D dollars without fully understanding what it's doing to his competitive product position. He simply hasn't put the effort into carefully thinking through his product line strategy."

"I see what you're driving at, Dick," Casper said a shade impatiently, "but I still don't know what you think constitutes good objectives or how you'd go about developing them."

"Fair enough, Casper. The trouble is, the only really good way to show that to anyone is to involve him in doing it. But perhaps the next best way is to show him how someone else did it. Let me see . . . suppose I tell you about an experience I had at Data Handling with minicomputers."

Number One: Minicomputers

Microminicomputer, leader in its field, had achieved a dominant market share with a single standard product. High volumes had permitted rapid cost reduction and enabled the company to maintain price leadership. At one point, however, competitors offering still lower-priced equipment had begun to chip away at certain segments of the market. Anxious to protect its share across the board, top management had decided to reduce prices to retain market share, thus meeting the competitive threat in the short run, and invest heavily to develop, within four years, a new-generation standard product that would once again serve all markets and maintain economies of scale.

Analyses of Micromini's situation raised the following issues: First, were the competitors accepting lower margins (as Micromini's management thought) or had they actually achieved cost leadership? Second, given the tremendous growth in the market, did a strategy based on a single standard product still make sense? Finally, given the vigor of competition, could Micromini safely wait four years to introduce its new-generation product?

Engineers took apart competitors' products to build up manufacturing cost estimates. Examining components, circuits, and system architecture, plus reliability information, they found that by sacrificing some incremental computation speed of no use to certain types of customers, the competitors had gained a real cost advantage. In doing so, however, they had also reduced their machines' flexibility. This meant that while first costs were lower in many applications, total operating costs, especially costs of reprogramming, tended to be higher over the useful life of the equipment.

Next, it appeared that by resegmenting its market into customers requiring low-, medium-, and high-computation speeds, Micromini could gain flexibility in design while maintaining most of the advantages of volume production. Finally, it was determined that price cuts—besides being outlandishly expensive given Micromini's dominant market share—could not forestall serious share erosion over the next four years. A three-model strategy, however, would enable Micromini to introduce a low-cost, low-speed design within 18 months followed by the medium-speed design a year later and the high-speed design as originally planned.

With these new insights, the basic business strategy was redirected, as shown in Exhibit 1, toward the gradual development of three standard products. Meanwhile, prices were maintained and the sales message was changed to focus on life-cost, rather than first-cost, selling.

An animated 30-minute presentation followed, the substance of which appears in boxed insert No. 1 above (see also Exhibit 1).

After the presentation of Micromini's strategy, Casper took up the discussion again, pointing out that the approach might be applicable in a few of Far-flung's divisions with fairly complex product lines, but he questioned whether it made sense for simpler product lines.

EXHIBIT 1
Summary of Case Examples

	ORIGINAL STRATEGY	REVISED STRATEGY	IMPACT
Microminicomputer	Reduce prices to maintain market share. Develop new standard product within 4 years.	Hold prices and retrain sales force to focus on life-cost, rather than first-cost, selling. Phase introduction of new products, beginning within 1.5 years.	Share erosion forestalled. R&D program refocused with no increase in costs. Overall: profits doubled.
Jiffy Fasteners	Price low to gain market share. Target sales effort on lost accounts. Invest heavily in R&D to regain product leadership.	Hold prices and focus sales effort on new applications for loyal customers. Shift R&D focus from product differentiation to cost reduction.	Doubled size of sales force and tripled productivity. Reduced R&D by 80%. Overall: improved profitability from −24% ROI to +24% ROI.
Multichem	Build share in commodity markets as rapidly as possible. Phase out intermediate line. Hold off development of proprietary line until demand materializes.	Phase out commodity. Build market share for intermediate line. Reduce cost for present proprietary line and develop new line.	Cut R&D to only those projects with an early payout. Increased R&D focus on cost reduction opportunities. Redirected program to focus on improvement of physical properties of importance to OEMs. Overall: improved profitability from −2% ROI to +15% ROI.

Number Two: Industrial Fasteners

Jiffy Fastener had been a leader in its markets for many years until an obscure competitor introduced a new higher-priced product that cut user labor costs substantially. After losing 30% of its sales to the competitor, Jiffy had brought out an almost identical product and engaged in a battle for market share based on a strategy of pricing low to gain market share, concentrating sales efforts on lost accounts to regain market share, and investing heavily in R&D to regain product leadership. A year later, with Jiffy still very much the underdog, management began asking some serious questions. First, how significant was price in the buying decision? Would a low price woo back lost customers? Second, could the company realistically aim to be a price leader, given its cost structure? Finally, did the opportunities for product differentiation justify the heavy R&D spending?

When detailed reverse engineering was undertaken to establish what it would cost Jiffy to manufacture and sell the competing product, it appeared that Jiffy was, in fact, very much a cost follower and would probably remain so. Moreover, detailed assessment of the R&D program revealed little potential for establishing any significant product differentiation.

Customer interviews indicated that past service performance, not price, was the key to the purchase decision. Few would switch from a familiar supplier with a proven record just for a marginal price break.

On the other hand, these interviews also showed that most customers had so many unexploited applications for the product that Jiffy's sales force could be more productively employed by concentrating on the customers they already had rather than by chasing after the strays.

With these new insights, the basic business strategy was reformulated as shown in Exhibit 1. By abandoning the futile product differentiation effort and instituting a cost reduction program, management was able to reduce the R&D budget by 80%.

Dick answered by describing his experience with a simple product line: an industrial fastener business (see boxed insert No. 2 above).

Casper conceded that Dick had made his point for product businesses but wondered if the approach would work in his plastics business, which is more process oriented. Dick then explained his experience with a process-oriented business that had used the same approach. He illustrated this example (see boxed insert No. 3 on page 484).

"The point is, you see," said Dick, as he finished the Multichem story, "that, no matter what kind of business they are running, division managers can easily fall into the trap of developing strategies without really analyzing their economic and competitive situations or testing their current strategic assumptions. So their long-range plans tend to be extrapolated from the present situation, and they concentrate on operating like crazy to meet them. That's why so many five-year plans are thin on strategic content."

Number Three: Chemicals

Multichem was a medium-sized division of a large, diversified company. Its industrial chemicals unit had profit-center responsibility for three product lines, all produced in two plants. The basic product, from which the other two were made, was a commodity sold to several markets, in each of which Multichem had only a small share. But the total market had been growing rapidly, and Multichem's standard cost system showed that the commodity line was profitable. Accordingly, the company's strategy was built around increasing market share as fast as possible in this segment.

Multichem's second product line, an intermediate, appeared to be only marginally profitable, and the strategy was to phase it out gradually.

In the third line, coating materials, Multichem had a proprietary position. Despite considerable market potential, the line was losing money. The strategy thus was to defer development until demand materialized, while continuing to build a market.

However, top management challenged three assumptions: Was an aggressive strategy in the commodity segment feasible? Did the standard cost system fairly reflect production economies? Was demand dormant in the specialty business or was the marketing strategy off?

Investigation showed that the commodity product line had no competitive advantages, market growth would diminish in the future, and an effort to build market share, backed by a small and unaggressive sales force, was likely to prove a costly failure. Moreover, the standard cost system had, for historical reasons, unduly favored the commodity product by assigning all production losses to the intermediate line, which, thanks to its greater production rate, was really the most profitable of the three lines.

Finally it appeared that demand for the specialty line had been slow only because sales and customer development had been wrongly targeted at custom coaters rather than original equipment manufacturers who specified coating characteristics. And the older plant, which required much more maintenance than the other, turned out to be far less profitable than had been thought.

These findings persuaded management to progressively transfer all production from the commodity business to the new plant and divert production into the intermediate and specialty business (Exhibit 1). Further market penetration would be sought for the very profitable intermediate, and expected profits would be channeled into R&D. The R&D program would refocus on reducing costs of the present specialty line by eliminating several additives from the specialty coatings materials and developing a new line tailored to the needs of end users. Further R&D efforts would be directed at cutting manufacturing costs for the commodity product and reducing maintenance costs to a minimum at the older plant while it was being phased out.

"All right, Dick, I see what you mean by setting specific objectives for technology. But how do you get to them? That's the $64,000 question."

Fredericks grinned. "I was just coming to that. Well, using product line strategies to guide R&D is simple in concept but challenging to carry out, as you know. On the other hand, for a business where the competitive standing of the product line is crucial, it can have an enormous payoff—a long-lasting one, too—because once you understand the product line situation, it's a lot easier to keep up with new developments. Also, you need a sound product line strategy to guide your key functions—R&D, sales, manufacturing, and what have you.

"Incidentally, when I talk about product line strategies, I mean strategies for groups of products that can be thought of as a business. In industrial goods companies, you want to maintain a superior product-market position for years, not just succeed with a particular new product. So your strategic focus has to be on businesses rather than on individual products or projects. Of course, getting your product line or business definitions right can be quite a job in itself, because the right definition doesn't always coincide with existing organizational lines."

"That makes good sense," Casper said. "I've always been suspicious of these project-by-project evaluations. You could work yourself into a corner if you focused on return-on-investment justifications instead of listening to your customers and figuring out whether they'll buy what some joker thinks you ought to make."

"That's exactly right. It takes a longer range perspective and a harder look at all the parts of the picture."

"Now wait a minute, Dick!" said Don, sitting forward. "That's precisely what our division managers do. They all prepare long-range plans, and my corporate development group reviews them."

"Reviews them for what, Don? Have you ever turned down a plan or bounced one back for any substantial modifications?"

"Turned one down, no. Bounced one back, sure. Any time they weren't complete or the numbers didn't hang together."

"I see," said Dick. "Look, why don't we just take a minute to consider what it takes to develop a sound, analytically based product line strategy? As we go along, we can ask whether your division managers' five-year plans are doing the trick, Don. This chart lays out the way we approach the problem of developing product line strategies at Data Handling—situation analysis, strategy synthesis, strategy refinement, and implementation planning." (Dick's chart is shown in Exhibit 2.)

"That looks straightforward."

"It's a lot more difficult and iterative than you'd think to look at it, Casper. Let me explain. The first step is situation analysis. It's aimed at raising the main issues facing the product line, taking a detailed look at a lot of factors, some relatively standard, a few peculiar to our business. We start out, as a rule, with a careful analysis of the competitive position of the product line and how it's been changing. Then we look at competitive prices and cost structures and compare them to our own. We try to determine the true economic value of each product

EXHIBIT 2

Strategy Development Process, Showing Progression from General to Specific Objectives

STAGE AND   OUTPUT
TYPICAL ANALYSES

Situation analysis

Market analysis and forecast	Industry attractiveness
Competitive position analysis	Competitive position
Economic value to the customer	Technological opportunities
Product line economics and financial performance	Implicit strategy
	Key issues for further analysis

Issue resolution/strategy synthesis

Issue resolution through:	Basic business strategy
In-depth competitive studies	Specific objectives for each part of the strategy
Assessment of technological choices	Posing of strategic problems
Creative resegmentation of market	
Basic strategy synthesis	

Strategy refinement

Definition and evaluation of alternative programs	Definition of strategic programs
Evaluation of commitment vs. risk	Evaluation of programs
Consistency testing	Redefinition of objectives
	Identification of major risks
	Identification of major contingencies

Implementation

Definition of specific programs	Time-phased plan of actions, decisions, and expected results
Definition of performance measures	Team committed to plan
Adjustment of organization and of management processes	

to the customer, looking for ways in which it might be enhanced and examining the requirements or opportunities for technical innovation.

"We also look for early warning signals, especially in high-growth or developing markets, like relative position in key technologies. With all these analyses in hand, we then assess the overall attractiveness of the product line to the company.

"Next, we examine the actions that are currently being taken in each major function and try to spell out the strategy they imply. At the same time, we try to articulate the technical objectives, strategies, and programs for each business and lay out the current technical programs against them, so that we can characterize the implicit technical strategy as well. To wind up the situation analysis, we pull all our data together and try to pinpoint the main issues that need to be resolved. Or, to say it in a slightly different way, we identify the assumptions—on cost, market segmentation, pricing, product differentiation, and so on—that need to be tested to confirm that the current implicit strategy is sound or point to needed changes.

"Once these issues have been identified—usually there are no more than four or five—we deal with them in depth. This might involve a detailed study of the relative cost structures or a comprehensive analysis of the strategies of major competitors or a comprehensive survey of all available technological approaches to a given problem.

"After the issues are resolved, we're ready to revise our business strategy, set new technological objectives, and develop detailed implementation plans, including timing, future decision points, and contingency actions. And that's it in a nutshell. The key is making sure that your technical effort is sharply focused on solving important, specific business problems rather than on achieving general objectives."

"Fair-sized nutshell, I'd say," Casper commented dryly. "But it does make good sense. And it doesn't sound like all that big a deal—at least not if you're as staff-heavy as we are."

"It takes time, Casper, and it's not just a question of bodies," Dick said quickly. "Your results are going to depend almost completely on the quality of your team. Also, it's far from an exact science: two good teams might well come up with different strategies. On the other hand, at Data Handling, and other companies I've managed, it's proved to be an effective discipline. Once you get talented people doing this, you're almost sure to end up with better business or product line strategies—*and* with a management team that's committed to carrying them out."

"Going back for a minute," Casper put in, "I'd like to get this time-and-effort aspect straight. What do you figure it would take, say, in a company like ours?"

"An initial cut at a product line strategy might take six months' work for a team of four to eight managers. Usually this includes a couple of our corporate guys who've been through it a few times."

"Well, Dick," said Don, "any way we do it, that's three to four man-years of effort for each business, and we've got 25 businesses. Is it worth it?"

"As I said, it's not easy. But you don't have to do every business every year.

Really sound business strategies that are modified as conditions change shouldn't need to be completely overhauled more often than once every three or four years.

"As for whether it's worth the effort, isn't it pretty vital to know what you're trying to accomplish, and why? A while ago, I had one of our economists at Data Handling take a sample of projects and analyze how much money was actually committed at the time a decision was made to invest in an R&D project. He discovered that for every dollar in the original authorization for R&D funds, another 6 to 10 dollars eventually had to be spent for R&D overruns, manufacturing facilities, merchandising costs, and so on, before a single revenue dollar was generated. I call that pretty convincing proof that the leverage is up front."

"Hm, 6 to 10 bucks? Don, do you have any idea if that'd be right for us or not?"

"We've never looked at it that way, Casper. It sounds high to me. What intrigues me, Dick, is that you seem to think our R&D people don't know what they're trying to accomplish. Do you honestly believe that?"

"Not exactly, Don. I think they've got pretty clear objectives for their technology. I'm saying that those objectives aren't properly related to overall business strategy. It's not the R&D guys' fault. The trouble is that they aren't getting sufficient direction. Suppose I asked you what was the main thrust of your R&D in your major product lines. Would you be able to tell me?"

"Well, not very specifically. But should I be able to?"

"It depends on how important you and Casper think your future product position is to the corporation."

"Come on, Dick," said Casper. "You know it's critical. Our customers are a hard-nosed bunch. The dilemma is that we pay our division managers to maintain product position, and I'm not sure how involved I should be in that—or for that matter, even what our group executives' responsibilities should be."

"Finding the right balance is a problem, Casper, but you have to assure yourself that the divisions and groups are approaching strategic decisions in a way that leads to well-thought-through product line strategies. If you wait for the answer to show up in profitability or market share—well, bluntly, you've abdicated your strategic responsibility and become a spectator."

"Hold on a minute, Dick. I understand your point, but I could get a lot more excited about it if I wasn't already convinced that our division general managers had pretty tight control over their R&D programs."

"Do they, Don? When I talked to them, I heard a lot of ROI-by-project stuff, but the support analysis was pretty much a numbers exercise to justify an engineering point of view. Not one of them had really stopped to figure out those projects in terms of competitive product position or market share. As I said before, those division managers of yours develop their five-year plans on the basis of extrapolation and operate like mad to make them come true. Mind you, this isn't only a problem in Farflung. It's been a problem in every technology-based company I've ever seen, and I've seen quite a few."

"And to manage R&D the way we should, Dick, you think we need to revamp our entire management approach starting from the divisions and going right to the top?"

"I wouldn't want to be presumptuous, Don, but if you and your group executives don't understand your R&D programs and how they relate to your divisional shortages, you're at the mercy of the division general managers, who may or may not really know where they're going."

"All right, Dick," said Casper. "I understand now what you meant by strategic malnutrition. But I'm still not clear on what to do. What you're saying sounds like common sense, but the idea that there's no answer short of revamping our entire management approach from top to bottom—do you understand the disruption that can cause? There's got to be some way of getting at these problems without opening Pandora's box. What do you say, Don?"

"Well, Casper, it's been a fascinating session, but I just can't accept that our problems are serious enough to warrant such vast changes. Before we go off half-cocked, let's see whether a lot of this isn't already being done in the divisions, at least in essence. And I think we ought to sound out the group VPs, too."

"What do you think, Dick?"

"I think it would be a good idea for Don to do a little homework in the divisions. And in the meantime, maybe you could begin sounding out the group VPs."

"Okay, Don, you're on. I'd like to get a report from you as quickly as possible. Say two weeks from today."

"I'll do my best, Casper."

PROOF OF THE PUDDING

Two weeks later, Don Blair sent the following memorandum to Casper:

Having been through three divisions in depth with Dick Fredericks's guidance and talked to another dozen division managers, I am now satisfied that Dick's analysis was essentially correct:

- Some of our basic tools for the control of R&D (strategic categorization, ratio of R&D to sales, project evaluations, etc.) are, at best, ineffectual.
- Sharper *strategic* objectives for technology—by product line—are needed to guide our development efforts. Also, more systematic identification of crucial strategic gaps in our underlying technological capability is needed to better focus our exploratory development.
- We probably do need to reexamine our whole approach to setting objectives and measuring performance in R&D, including a reassessment of the corporate R&D program and the role of the Corporate VP for Technology.
- Our principal problem is the lack of thoughtful, analytically based divisional product line strategies. Unfortunately, once you get by the controllers with their budget orientation, the present divisions are extremely weak on analytical capability.

This fact-finding exercise has, I believe, proved well worth the effort. As Dick Fredericks pointed out, without sound divisional strategies we lack the basic building blocks for corporate strategy.

I would like to go on record as acknowledging that your original concerns were well founded. The problem is there, and I am convinced that Dick's ideas for solving it are correct in all essentials. You can count on my enthusiastic support in the major building job that lies ahead.

My detailed findings are set forth in the attached report.

A CHANGE IN DIET

Within a few weeks Casper and Don, with some assistance from Dick, had agreed on the general outlines of a five-year program for Farflung. Casper captured its essence in the closing address that he gave to the company conference where the program was laid out:

"The steps we have to take are clear. To begin with, we need to undertake a long-term effort to build analytical capability in the divisions and groups. This will be a monumental task. But, if we go at it carefully and deliberately, I know we can do it. We're going to start in one of the weaker divisions, going through the strategy development process that Don described yesterday and using some handpicked people from our organization and whatever other help we need. This pilot project will enable us to develop an approach that makes sense for Farflung. As we progress, other division managers will be kept up to date, and over a number of years we will modify the approach and expand it appropriately to each division.

"Beyond that, we are going to change our fundamental management approach at the group and corporate levels. Heretofore, from an operating point of view, we have been tightly controlled from the top, but from a strategic point of view, we've been more like a holding company. That just doesn't make sense. I'm going to become personally much more involved in strategy development—all of us are, in fact. We can't afford to lose operating control as we change, so we are going to evolve slowly, but we will evolve. Here are the broad outlines of what we are going to do.

"First, group-level executives are going to be equipped with the capability to identify and test the strategic assumptions underlying our divisional plans. Look at this slide (Exhibit 3). Don and his staff prepared this analysis of the Medical Products five-year plan. They took the division's long-range forecast of revenues, earnings, cash flows, and capital investments and, by testing the assumptions underlying them, evaluated the implicit division strategy. As you can see, there are some problems in Medical Products.

"Now I'm not showing this to put the heat on Medical Products—it's gotten plenty of that already. And in this particular area, it hasn't been doing any worse a job than any other division, as far as I can tell. But I want you all to recognize that this is the wave of the future. No more automatic budget reviews. Division autonomy is going to have to be earned.

"Now as we begin to take strategic planning seriously, a major job at the group and corporate level will be to see that the divisions do a good job of developing basic product line strategies, that the assumptions and risks in these strategies are clearly identified and discussed with higher management in the

EXHIBIT 3

Strategy Evaluation: Medical Products Division's Five-Year Plan

ITEM	FORECAST CHANGE (1976–1981)	KEY ASSUMPTIONS	IMPLICIT STRATEGY	CREDIBILITY OF FORECAST	REVISED FORECAST	IMPACT
Revenue	Up 73%	New product line will account for 80% growth by penetrating new market segment.	Keep development costs low by being "second to market."	Low—required market penetration unlikely in view of "second to market" approach.	Up 50%	**Projected profitability decreased from +25% to +17%.**
Earnings	Up 85%	Present product costs can be reduced by 30% by increasing plant labor productivity.	Extend life of present manufacturing facilities as long as feasible to reduce capital investment requirements.	Low—labor productivity likely to decrease as plants age.	Up 44%	
Capital investment	Up 50%	Asset turnover can be improved by 28% through further plant automation.	Go for full plant automation.	Low—plants already fully automated and few significant technical advances foreseen.	Up 70%	

initial stages of strategy development, and that the strategies themselves are supported by sound long-range forecasts. Testing these forecasts in the light of the division strategies will also become a chief responsibility of the group vice presidents. Their objective will be to reach agreement with their divisions on sound, clearly articulated division strategies and accompanying forecasts that truly reflect our competitive position, our strengths and weaknesses, and our strategic opportunities.

"I'm also going to ask the group vice presidents to take on another set of responsibilities relating to minimization of risks and maximization of future opportunity. Beyond making sure that the basic division strategy is sound and has a reasonable chance of coming out on target, it will be their job to determine the risks that are being taken and the opportunities that are being foregone by the division and to see that additional resources are made available, if this is in the best long-range or strategic interest of the group.

"In other words, I want the group executives to work with the division managers to anticipate and prepare for future problems and opportunities, not second-guess their basic strategies once they've been developed. All that usually leads to is unproductive argument and delays in implementation. This will involve a lot of judgment and a lot of negotiation, but I want the issues of risk and opportunity to be carefully aired in the initial stages of strategy development, not as part of an after-the-fact review process. Quite possibly the group or corporate level will have to incur some R&D expense, either in the divisions or at the corporate labs, but we must make certain that we are covering our strategic technical bases.

"I'll be asking group-level executives to assume one additional responsibility—that of developing cross-divisional product and market strategies. Let me explain. As we grow, some of our divisions are beginning to compete for the same business or serve the same markets in different ways. In these cases, we intend to head off trouble by developing cross-divisional strategies at the group level, much as individual product line strategies are developed at the divisional level. It's going to be tougher than developing individual product line strategies, but we think it's going to be absolutely essential. Also, it will be a good preparation for moving into future reorganization if that should ever be required.

"Now this has been a quick preview of what will be a fairly complex and difficult-to-manage process of evolution at the group level. It's aimed at strengthening the strategic roles and responsibilities of our group executives and providing them with the information and analytical capability they will need to do this bigger job. At the same time, it will highlight the corporate issues and clarify the dimensions of the job facing us at the corporate level. I recognize that all these moves will probably cause some dislocations, and they'll certainly jar us from the complacency that has been bred by our past successes. But I'm convinced that if we all rise to the challenge, this company's future can be even brighter than its past."

Casper drew to a close with the standard appeals for cooperation and commitment. He could sense from the questions that his speech had been well received, that he had captured the imagination of his executive group. As he stepped down from the podium, he felt that he had made a start at getting key executives out of the tangle of overdependence on processes and abstract schemes for allocating resources and back to realities. He said to himself, *I'll bet we're not too far off from the way Lowell Keyes ran things when he started, when the company was small enough so that he could do situation analysis and issue resolution almost by gut feel.*

He reasoned that, as the company grew and the entrepreneurs were replaced by professional managers, the systems and procedures developed for managing the business were too abstract and sterile to replace the experience and know-how of the entrepreneurs. He said to himself, *At any rate, we're on the way to solving the problem of strategic malnutrition. Next I'll probably have to deal with strategic overeating. I sure hope there's a simpler cure for that.*